NEW TESTAMENT

EXPANDED PARAPHRASE IN EVERYDAY ENGLISH

Timothy R. Jennings, M.D.

Published by Lennox® Publishing
PO Box 28266 Chattanooga, TN 37424, U.S.A.

in conjunction with

No portion of this book may be reproduced, stored in a retrieval system, or transmitted in any form or by any means—electronic, mechanical, photocopy, recording, scanning, or other—except for brief quotations in critical reviews or articles, without the prior written permission of the publisher.

This title may be purchased in bulk for educational, business, fund-raising, or sales promotional use.

For information, please e-mail requests@comeandreason.com

Cover Design: Dean A. Scott, mfa
Editing and Layout: Mirra Huber

Printed in U.S.A.
2016

11 10 09 08 07   5 4 3 2 1

Library of Congress Cataloging-in-Publication Data

Jennings, Timothy R., 1961–

ISBN: 978-0-9858502-6-5

1. Bible, New Testament

Table of Contents

a 501(c)(3) not-profit Christian ministry

at **Come And Reason**...

we focus

on making God's methods and principles practical,
understandable and applicable to human living here and now;

we are dedicated

to helping people to learn
how to think for themselves and to hone and refine their
reasoning powers
in order to increase their ability
to discern right from wrong and healthy from unhealthy;

we work

to bring truth, love, and healing to everyone;

we recognize

that rightly understood, Scripture and Science
always agree with each other.

to that end we use

the Integrative Evidence-based Approach
which harmonizes Scripture, Science and Experience
in understanding reality.

Our free resources are available at
comeandreason.com

Preface to The Remedy

With so many Bible translations and paraphrases already available, some will invariably ask, Why another paraphrase?

I ask your indulgence for just a few pages in order to lay out why this paraphrase is not only unique but worthy of your consideration.

As all Bible students know, Scripture tells us that God is Love (1John 4:8). But what many have not considered, and what this volume acknowledges, is that when God built His universe, He built it to operate in harmony with His own nature of love. The construction protocol on which God built His universe is known as God's Law. And this law is the Law of Love—an expression of His nature and character. Thus the Bible writers expressed it like this:

- ○ Love does no harm to its neighbor. Therefore love is the fulfillment of the law. (Romans 13:10)
- ○ The entire law is summed up in a single command: "Love your neighbor as yourself." (Galatians 5:14)
- ○ If you really keep the royal law found in Scripture, "Love your neighbor as yourself..." (James 2:8)

Functionally, Paul describes this law as "love seeks not its own," or "love is not self-seeking" (1Corinthians 13:5). This means that love is selfless rather than selfish. Love is giving rather than taking. And life is actually built, by God, to operate on this principle of giving.

A simple example of this law in action is respiration. With every breath we breathe we *give* away carbon dioxide (CO_2) to the plants, and the plants *give* back oxygen to us (the law of respiration). This is God's design for life—an expression of God's character of love, a perpetual circle of free giving—and life is built to operate on it. If you break this law (this circle of giving) by, for example, tying a plastic bag over your head and selfishly hoarding your body's CO_2, you break the design protocol for life, and the result is death: "The wages [result] of sin is death" (Romans 6:23). This circle of giving is the law that God constructed life to operate on.

After Christ's ascension, the church taught a theology that focused on the principles of love, and therefore taught that Christ's mission was to reveal truth (John 14:6), defeat Satan (Hebrews 2:14), destroy death (2Timothy 1:10), and restore the law of love into humankind (1John 3:8). This is known as the *recapitulation theory* of atonement.

PREFACE

Justin Martyr (A.D. 103–165) taught that Christ came to do three things: (1) to overthrow death, (2) to destroy Satan, and (3) to restore humanity back to God's design, thus providing eternal life to fallen humanity:

> [Christ] having been made flesh submitted to be born of the Virgin, in order that through this dispensation (1) the Serpent, who at the first had done evil, and the angels assimilated to him might be put down and (2) death might be despised.[1]

Robert Franks describes Justin's theology:

> In fact, we find in Justin clear indications of the presence to his mind of the recapitulation theory, afterwards more fully developed by Irenaeus, according to which (3) Christ becomes a new head of humanity, undoes the sin of Adam by reversing the acts and circumstances of his disobedience, and finally communicates to men immortal life.[2]

Franks also describes the theology of Irenaeus (2nd century A.D.– c. A.D. 202):

> We come here to the famous Irenaean doctrine of Recapitulation. The conception is that of Christ as the Second Adam, or second head of humanity, who not only undoes the consequences of Adam's fall, but also takes up the development of humanity broken off in him, and carries it to completion, i.e. to union with God and consequent immortality.
>
> "It was God recapitulating the ancient creation of man in Himself, that He might slay sin, and annul death, and give life to man. ... The Son of God, when He was incarnate and was made man, recapitulated in Himself the long line of men, giving us salvation compendiously (in compendio), so that what we had lost in Adam, viz. that we should be after in the image and similitude of God, this we should receive in Jesus Christ."[3]

Amazingly, the early church understood that Christ's mission was to rebuild humanity back into God's original design. They realized that God's law of love was the template on which He built His universe, and rightly realized that—in order to save humankind—the law on which life is constructed to operate had to be restored into humanity. Christ's mission was to restore humankind back into harmony with God!

But this truth was lost, and another concept of law replaced it: Romanism. Imperial Rome's concept of government and law infected Christian thought after the emperor Constantine converted to Christianity. Prior to Constantine's

---

[1] Robert S. Franks, A History of the *Doctrine of the Work of Christ in Its Ecclesiastical Development*, vol. 1 (London: Hodder and Stoughton, 1918), p. 21

[2] Ibid., p. 22

[3] Ibid., pp. 37–38

conversion, Christianity understood God's law as the law of love: "Therefore *love is the fulfillment of the law*" (Romans 13:10, emphasis mine; see also Psalm 19:7; Proverbs 12:28; 21:21; Matthew 12:37–40; Galatians 5:14; James 2:8).

After Constantine's conversion, the Christian church accepted Rome's redefinition of God's Law, and what was that change? That God's Law is an imposed law—with no inherent consequence, thus requiring the lawgiver to police breaches in the law and inflict punishment—rather than the truth that God's Law is the natural law of love, the design protocol on which God created life to operate.

Eusebius (A.D. 263–339), the first church historian, documented clearly how Christianity exchanged God's law of love for an imposed Roman construct:

> There are no reserves in the stilted encomium [praise] with which Eusebius closes his history, no wistful regret for the blessings of persecution, no prophetic fear of imperial control of the Church. His heart is full of gratitude to God and Constantine. And it is not only his feelings that are stirred. He is ready, with a theory, indeed a theology, of the Christian Emperor. He finds a correspondence between religion and politics. ... With the Roman Empire monarchy had come on earth as the image of the monarchy in heaven.[4]

Thomas Lindsay, in his book *A History of the Reformation,* describes this infection of Christian thought this way:

> The great men who built up the Western Church were almost all trained Roman lawyers. Tertullian, Cyprian, Augustine, Gregory the Great (whose writings form the bridge between the Latin Fathers and the Schoolmen) were all men whose early training had been that of a Roman lawyer,—a training which moulded and shaped all their thinking, whether theological or ecclesiastical. They instinctively regarded all questions as a great Roman lawyer would. They had the lawyer's craving for exact definitions. They had the lawyer's idea that the primary duty laid upon them was to enforce obedience to authority, whether that authority expressed itself in external institutions or in the precise definitions of the correct ways of thinking about spiritual truths. No Branch of western Christendom has been able to free itself from the spell cast upon it by these Roman lawyers of the early centuries of the Christian church.[5]

Christians lost sight of God's law of love, and instead accepted an imposed law system modeled after human governments. After all, if they still believed that God's law was the design law of love, like the law of respiration, would they ever

---

[4] S. L. Greenslade, *Church and State from Constantine to Theodosius* (London: SCM Press, 1954); emphasis mine.

[5] Thomas Lindsay, *A History of the Reformation* (Bibliolife, 2009), p. 168; emphasis mine.

have thought a church committee could vote to change such a law (something the church did vote in committee to do)? But they could only vote to change God's law after they first accepted the concept that His law is imposed, not natural.[6]

This idea of an imposed law altered the view of God held by Christians, and changed the way Christianity functioned. Thus Christians went from a body of believers who lived communally, shared their possessions to help each other, and died as martyrs, to an organization of Crusades, burning dissenters at the stake, Inquisition, and active participation in genocide (e.g. Nazis in Germany and Christians in Rwanda).

Sadly, by the time the Bible was eventually translated into the language of the people, the imposed law construct was deeply engrained orthodoxy accepted as fact by believers. Essentially, all Bible translations have been done by people operating through the lens of imposed law. This means that Bible translations artificially introduce imposed law with fear-inducing ideas about God.

This Bible paraphrase offers an alternative. My bias is that God is the Creator, Builder and Designer, and when He constructed His universe, He built it to operate in harmony with His own nature of love. Thus God's law is not a set of imposed rules, but the design parameters on which He built life to exist.

The Remedy is an expanded New Testament Bible paraphrase in which interpretation is filtered through the lens of God's design law of love—the template on which life is built. This paraphrase is intentional in its focus to re-orient the Christian mind to God's character of love and His mission to heal and restore humankind, as taught by the early church.

I hope you find this paraphrase an aid in developing your trust-relationship with God, culminating in becoming a partaker of God's eternal Remedy!

The Author

---

[6] Compare the Catholic versus the Protestant Ten Commandments. The Catholic version removes number two (graven images), splits number ten into two commandments, changes the language of the Sabbath commandment (number four in Protestant versions; due to eliminating number two, the Sabbath commandment is number three in the Catholic version). They also, in their catechism, claim to have changed the holiness of Sabbath from Saturday to Sunday. I do not argue any of these points. I only use this to illustrate the acceptance of a change in God's Law from a natural law to an imposed law. If theologians viewed God's Law as a principle on which life is built, like the law of gravity, thermodynamics and respiration, they would not have voted in committee to make changes to it. The fact that they have changed it reveals the acceptance of imperial Rome's concept of law.

Matthew

1 Jesus Christ was a descendant of Abraham and of David. Here is his family line:

Mt 1:2 Abraham had Isaac, who had Jacob.

Mt 1:3 Jacob had Judah and his brothers, and Judah had Perez and Zerah by Tamar. Perez had Hezron, who had Ram, and

Mt 1:4 Ram had Amminadab, who had Nahshon, and Nahshon had Salmon.

Mt 1:5 Salmon had Boaz by Rahab, and Boaz had Obed by Ruth, and Obed had Jesse, 6 who was the father of King David. David had Solomon by the former wife of Uriah.

Mt 1:7 Solomon had Rehoboam, who had Abijah, and Abijah had Asa.

Mt 1:8 Asa had Jehoshaphat, who had Jehoram, who had Uzziah.

Mt 1:9 Uzziah had Jotham, who had Ahaz, who had Hezekiah.

Mt 1:10 Hezekiah had Manasseh, who had Amon, who had Josiah.

Mt 1:11 Josiah had Jeconiah and his brothers at the time of the Babylonian exile.

Mt 1:12 After returning from the Babylonian exile, Jeconiah had Shealtiel, who had Zerubbabel.

Mt 1:13 Zerubbabel had Abiud, who had Eliakim, who had Azor.

Mt 1:14 Azor had Zadok, who had Akim, who had Eliud.

Mt 1:15 Eliud had Eleazar, who had Matthan, who had Jacob.

Mt 1:16 And Jacob was the father of Joseph, the husband of Mary, of whom Jesus, who is the Messiah, was born.

Mt 1:17 So there were fourteen generations from Abraham to David and fourteen generations from David to the exile to Babylon, and fourteen generations from the exile to the Messiah.

Mt 1:18 The birth of Jesus Christ happened like this: Mary, his mother, was engaged to Joseph, but before they had physical intimacy, she was already pregnant by the Holy Spirit. 19 Because Joseph wanted to do what was right for Mary, and he didn't want to disgrace or humiliate her publicly, he planned to end his engagement quietly.

Mt 1:20 But before he could do this, an angel from God appeared to him in a dream and said: "Joseph son of David, don't be afraid to marry Mary; she is pregnant by the Holy Spirit, not by any man. 21 She will have a son, and you are to name him Jesus—God heals—because he will heal and restore humanity from selfishness and sin."

Mt 1:22 All of this happened just as the Lord foretold through his spokesperson: 23 "The virgin will become pregnant and give birth to a son, and they will call him Immanuel" (which means "God with us").

Mt 1:24 When Joseph awoke, he did just what the Lord's angel had instructed him to do. He married Mary and brought her home as his wife. 25 But they didn't have sex until after she gave birth to a son whom they named Jesus.

2 Jesus was born in a small Judean town called Bethlehem, during the rule of King Herod. At that time, scholars and scientists from the East came to Jerusalem searching for Jesus. 2 They inquired, "We saw a new star in the sky — the star of the newborn king of the Jews. Where is he, that we may worship him?"

Mt 2:3 This news stirred up excitement in Jerusalem, but King Herod was extremely agitated when the report reached him. 4 He called together the nation's religious leaders, theologians and lawyers, and asked them to tell him where the Messiah was to be born. 5 They told him, "In a little town called Bethlehem, in Judea. For God's spokesperson wrote:

Mt 2:6 'Bethlehem, in Judah,
you are certainly not the least important city in Judah,
because from you
will come the prince
who will restore my people.'"

Mt 2:7 Herod called a secret meeting with the scientists and scholars from the East and discovered the exact time the star had appeared. 8 Then he sent them to Bethlehem, telling them, "Make a thorough search, and when you find the child, tell me right away so I can also come and worship him."

Mt 2:9 After talking with the king, they were excited to complete their journey, so they followed the star they had seen in the east until it stopped over the place where Jesus was. 10 And they were so happy to see that star! 11 When they arrived at the house, they saw Jesus in the arms of his mother Mary, and they fell down in adoration, worshipping him. They gave him expensive gifts of gold, frankincense, and myrrh. 12 God had warned them in a dream not to tell Herod where Jesus was, so they returned to their homeland by a different route.

Mt 2:13 After the scholars had gone, an angel from God came to Joseph in a dream and said: "Wake up! Herod is plotting to kill baby Jesus. He will soon send soldiers looking for him, so take the child and his mother and escape to Egypt. Wait there until I tell you it is safe to return."

Mt 2:14 Joseph got up immediately, quickly packed what he could, took baby Jesus and Mary, and fled that night for Egypt. 15 They stayed in Egypt until Herod died, and thus God's prophecy

"I called my son back from Egypt"
was fulfilled.

Mt 2:16 When Herod realized that the professors from the East had not been duped by his scheme, he was furious and ordered all the boys in Bethlehem and its vicinity, under two years of age, to be killed (he determined the age based on the scholar's report of when the star appeared). 17 Thus Jeremiah's prophecy was fulfilled:

Mt 2:18 "An outcry was heard in Ramah—
the sound of heart-breaking weeping—
Rachel sobbing for her children and unable to be comforted because they are dead."

Mt 2:19 After Herod died, an angel from God appeared in a dream to Joseph, who was in Egypt, and said, 20 "It's time to go home. Take the child and his mother back to Israel, as those who sought to kill the child are dead."

Mt 2:21 As instructed, he took the child and his mother home to Israel. 22 After learning that Herod's son Archelaus was reigning in Judea, and after receiving a warning in a dream, Joseph was afraid to go back to Judea, so instead went to Galilee 23 and lived in a town called Nazareth. Thus it was fulfilled what was prophesied through God's spokespersons,

"He will be called a Nazarene."

3 When Jesus was still living in Nazareth, John the Baptist began preaching in the desert of Judea. 2 He called out to the people: "Turn away from fear and selfishness, and surrender your hearts to God, for the kingdom of heavenly love is upon us!" 3 John is the one who God's spokesman Isaiah foretold,

"A voice calling in a dark and desolate land:
'Prepare your minds, untwist your hearts,

2

and make ready for the Lord to come with his healing Remedy.'"

Mt 3:4 John wore clothing made of camel's hair and tied with a leather belt. He ate locusts and honey found in the wild. 5 From Jerusalem and all Judea, large crowds went out to hear him speak. 6 Those who immersed their hearts in the truth and acknowledged their selfishness, he dipped in the Jordan River.

Mt 3:7 But when he saw the lawyers and theologians of the Pharisee and Sadducee schools arrive where he was dipping people in the Jordan, he said to them: "You poisonous snakes! What are you doing here? Do you think you can get right with God by washing in the Jordan? 8 Your hearts must be cleansed and characters renewed, so that your lives bring forth actions in harmony with God's character of love. 9 And don't try claiming that you're right with God just because you're genetic descendants of Abraham. Biological descent is irrelevant. The descendants of Abraham are as numerous as the stones lying on the shore. 10 The axe of selfishness is already cutting through the roots of Israel, and every person who refuses to be renewed in love and bring forth character of righteousness will be cut off and destroyed.

Mt 3:11 "I immerse people in water, which symbolizes their repentance. But One is coming after me whose sandals I am not even fit to hold. He will immerse you in the Holy Spirit and in the cleansing fire of God's love and truth. 12 He sifts the wheat from the chaff, purifying his people by consuming all defects with unstoppable fire."

Mt 3:13 Jesus came from Galilee to the Jordan to be immersed in water by John. 14 But John recoiled, saying, "I am the one whose mind and heart need to be immersed in your perfection, and you want me to symbolically wash you with water?" 15 Jesus gently said, "It must be this way in order for me to complete my mission of restoring

humanity to righteousness." So John agreed. 16 After Jesus was immersed, he walked out of the river. Immediately the sky parted, and he saw the Spirit of God come down out of heaven in the form of a dove and gently rest upon him. 17 Then a voice from heaven said: "This is my Son whom I love dearly; with him I am totally pleased."

4 Then the Spirit led Jesus into the desert to confront and overcome the temptations of the devil. 2 Jesus fasted for forty days and nights, and was very hungry 3 when the tempter came to him and said, "You don't look like God's Son—you're starving! If you really are God's Son, turn these stones into bread—use your power to provide food for yourself."

Mt 4:4 But Jesus replied, "The Scripture says: 'Life doesn't operate upon the principle of self-preservation, but by abiding in harmony with every word proceeding from the mouth of God.'"

Mt 4:5 Satan then took Jesus to Jerusalem and placed him upon the highest point of the temple. 6 The evil one tried to trick Jesus by quoting Scripture out of context: "If you truly are God's Son, jump off! For the Scripture says:
'He will command his angels to
    guard and protect you,
and they will catch you in their
    hands so that you won't be
    crushed on the rocks.'"

Mt 4:7 Jesus immediately answered, "The Scripture also says: 'Don't test God to provide miracles when he has already provided overwhelming evidence upon which to base one's beliefs and know one's duty.'"

Mt 4:8 Then the devil took Jesus to a high mountain and displayed to him all the splendor, riches, and kingdoms of the world. 9 The evil one said, "I am the rightful ruler of this world, and I will give it all to you—without you having to experience any suffering or pain—if you will simply bow down and worship me."

Mt 4:10 Jesus immediately replied, "Get away from me, Satan! For the Scripture says: 'Worship the Lord your God and serve only him—with your entire heart.'"

Mt 4:11 Upon hearing these words, the devil fled, and angels of God came and helped Jesus.

Mt 4:12 When Jesus heard that John was in prison, he went back to Galilee. 13 He went from Nazareth to Capernaum near the lake in the region of Zebulun and Naphtali, 14 just as God's spokesman Isaiah foretold:

15 "The land of Zebulun and Naphtali,
along the Jordan, toward the sea,
Galilee of the Gentiles—
16 the people whose minds have been
clouded by lies
have seen the great light of
heavenly truth;
upon those living in the land
darkened by death
the source of eternal life shines."

Mt 4:17 And from then on, Jesus preached: "Turn away from selfishness, for the kingdom of heavenly love has arrived."

Mt 4:18 Jesus was walking beside the Sea of Galilee when he saw two brothers, Simon (also known as Peter) and Andrew. They were fishermen, and were throwing their net into the lake. 19 Jesus looked at them and said, "Follow me, and I will make you fishers of people." 20 Immediately they both left their nets and followed Jesus.

Mt 4:21 A short distance from there, he saw two other brothers, James and John, sons of Zebedee. They were in a boat with their father, preparing to cast their nets, when Jesus called them to follow him. 22 Immediately they left the boat and their father, and followed him.

Mt 4:23 Jesus traveled throughout Galilee, teaching the truth about God's kingdom of love, distributing the Remedy for selfishness and sin, and demonstrating God's ultimate healing plan by curing every physical disease and alleviating every malady among the people. 24 The news about him spread like wildfire all over Syria, and the crowds flocked to him, bringing to him all who were sick with disease—those with chronic pain, the mentally ill, the demon-possessed, those with seizures, and the paralyzed—and he healed them all. 25 Huge crowds from Galilee, Decapolis, Jerusalem, Judea, and the region across the Jordan followed him.

5 When Jesus saw the crowds, he went up the mountainside to a flat place and sat down. His disciples gathered around him, 2 and he began to teach, saying:

Mt 5:3 "Blessed are those who know their spiritual need, for they will receive the Remedy from heaven.

Mt 5:4 "Blessed are those with tender hearts—those who feel the pain that selfishness causes—for they will be comforted.

Mt 5:5 "Blessed are those with humble hearts—who surrender self in order to help others—for they are living in harmony with the kingdom of heaven.

Mt 5:6 "Blessed are those who hunger to be renewed in righteousness—to overflow with truth and love—for they will be filled.

Mt 5:7 "Blessed are the merciful—those who are compassionate to others—for they will experience mercy.

Mt 5:8 "Blessed are those whose hearts have been purified in other-centered love, for it is they who will see God.

Mt 5:9 "Blessed are those who seek peace, who seek to reconcile all people—of all nations, races, and cultures—to God for all time, for they will be known as the children of God.

Mt 5:10 "Blessed are those who are persecuted for doing what's right and loving others more than self, for theirs is the kingdom of heaven.

Mt 5:11 "Blessed are you when people turn against you, misrepresent you, say all kinds of evil things about you, and persecute you because you accurately reveal me and my kingdom of love.

¹²Rejoice, knowing that you are being treated just as God's spokespersons who lived before you, and be glad because you have a great reward in heaven.

Mt 5:13 "You are like salt to humanity: preserving the knowledge of God, providing the flavor of heaven, and increasing the thirst for God. But if salt loses its saltiness, unless it becomes salty again, it is useless and will be thrown out and trampled upon.

Mt 5:14 "You are beacons of light in a world of darkness. A shining city on a hill cannot be hidden, ¹⁵and people don't light a lantern and hide it under a bucket. No, they display it prominently, so everyone receives its light. ¹⁶Be like that! Let your lives radiate the light of heavenly love and truth by the way you treat others so that they may give thanks to your Father in heaven.

Mt 5:17 "And don't think that I have come to destroy what the Old Testament—Torah and Prophets—taught about God and his methods; I have not come to destroy but to fulfill them. ¹⁸Here is the simple truth: Heaven and earth would disappear if even the slightest change were made to God's design protocol for life—what you call his 'Law.' I am not here to destroy the Law, but accomplish everything it requires. ¹⁹Anyone who violates God's design (law) and teaches others to do so is out of harmony with heaven; but anyone who practices God's methods (law) and teaches others to do so is in harmony with the kingdom of heaven. ²⁰I tell you plainly, if your characters are not renewed with righteousness surpassing that of the Pharisees and lawyers, it simply won't be possible for you to enter the heavenly kingdom of love.

Mt 5:21 "You know what our forefathers said: 'Do not murder, for anyone who murders is subject to trial.' ²²But I am here to tell you a deeper reality: Anyone who is angry with another person damages their own character and is in danger of being diagnosed incurable. And anyone who demeans another's ability, calling them 'stupid,' needs counseling. But anyone who presumes to judge another's motives, calling them 'evil' or 'scoundrel,' hardens their own heart and is in danger of eternal destruction.

Mt 5:23 "Therefore, if you come to God with a gift and remember that you have not set right an offense against another, ²⁴put your gift aside and first make things right and be reconciled with them, and only then bring your gift to God.

Mt 5:25 "If someone holds a grudge against you and sues you, do all you can to settle the dispute quickly. If it goes to court, you may end up in jail ²⁶or have to pay a steep fine.

Mt 5:27 "You know that the Scripture says 'Do not commit adultery.' ²⁸But I am here to tell you a deeper reality: God is concerned with character; and anyone who looks on another lustfully commits adultery and corrupts their heart. ²⁹If you are vulnerable to visual temptation, then throw away the media and don't look at sensual material. You should be so resolutely committed to doing what is right that you would rather lose part of your body than lose eternal life. ³⁰And if you are tempted by what you touch, then touch only that which is good. You should be so resolutely committed to doing what is right that you would rather lose part of your body than lose eternal life.

Mt 5:31 "It has been said, 'Anyone who divorces his wife must do it legally, giving her a divorce certificate to protect her rights.' ³²I'm here to tell you a deeper reality: Divorce happens when love breaks down and selfishness wins. No one wants to lose a limb, but we sever a gangrenous limb to save the person; to sever a healthy limb is damaging and wrong. Likewise, anyone who divorces their spouse, except for the gangrenous situation of marital betrayal, inflicts unfaithfulness upon their

The Remedy

spouse and whomever the divorced spouse should later marry.[1]

Mt 5:33 "You have heard another saying from long ago, 'If you swear to do something, then keep your oaths, especially if you swore by the Lord.' [34] But I am here to tell you a deeper reality: Be so consistently honest in all you do that there is never a need to swear or take an oath. Don't claim heaven as your witness while you perjure, for it is God's throne and won't support a liar. [35] Don't use the earth to prove you are honest while practicing deception, for it is God's lesson book, and you will be exposed. Don't swear by Jerusalem to infer you can be trusted, for it is God's city, not yours. [36] Don't even say 'on my own head,' for you cannot make even one hair grow— so how does the fact that your head grows hair prove that what you say is true? [37] Simply, be honest in all you do. Let your 'Yes' be 'Yes,' and your 'No' be 'No;' anything more is used by the evil one to obscure and confuse.

Mt 5:38 "Remember that it was said long ago, 'An eye for an eye, and tooth for a tooth.' [39] But I am here to tell you a deeper reality: Love others! Do not fight against the evil person. If someone strikes your cheek, turn to him the other cheek also. [40] And if someone sues you to take your coat, let him have your suit as well. [41] If someone forces you to carry their burden for a mile, carry it two miles. [42] God built the universe to operate upon love—free giving—so give freely to the one who asks you, and don't be selfish and turn away from someone who wants to borrow something from you.

Mt 5:43 "You have heard it said, 'Love your neighbor and hate your enemy.' [44] But I am here to tell you a deeper reality: Life is constructed only to operate upon the law of love. So if you want to live, love your enemies and pray for those who mistreat you, [45] that you may live as sons and daughters of your Father in heaven. He is constantly giving of himself for the good of all, causing the sun to rise on the evil and the good, and sends the rain on the righteous and unrighteous. [46] If you love only those who love you, what difference will that make? — for selfishness still lives in your heart. Don't those who you consider 'evil' do that much? [47] And if you show hospitality only to your family, how is your love greater than others? Don't even pagans do that? [48] Live in harmony with God's design for life: Be perfect in love, just as your Father in heaven is perfect.

6 "Be sure not to live your life for show—acting righteous in order to impress others. Such behavior is based on selfishness and prevents the benefit that results from living in harmony with your Father in heaven.

Mt 6:2 "So when helping someone in need, don't make a show or create an advertisement in order to get more people to adore you, as the politicians—both in and out of the church— do. I tell you plainly, they have received the reward for which their selfish hearts crave. [3] When you help others, do it discretely— [4] not seeking to make yourself the center of attention, but because you are motivated by love; then the secret intent of your heart will be in tune with your Father, and you will receive the reward that comes from being in unity with him.

Mt 6:5 "And when you pray, don't be like those pretentiously pious spiritual fakers who love to pray in public to get attention for themselves. I tell you plainly, they have received the reward

---

[1] Adultery is a heart issue, as Jesus said in the verses before. Divorcing a spouse whose heart is not unfaithful, but because of selfishness in one's own heart, forces the divorced spouse into a situation in which their heart still longs for their first spouse. If they remarry, their heart longs for the one they have lost, thus the new marriage is built on divided loyalties and longings, creating an adulterous situation.

their selfish hearts crave. ⁶ But when you talk with God, go to a private place where you can be genuinely intimate with your Father and be open with him—then you will experience the reward that comes from sharing the secrets of your heart with him.

⁷ Remember that prayer is conversation with God, as talking to your closest friend. So don't pray like pagans, who recite mantras, repeat memorized prayers over and over, or simply do all the talking, thinking that if they talk long enough, they will get what they want. ⁸ Don't be fooled by such gimmicks. Remember that you are talking with your Father, and he knows what you need and longs to do everything for your eternal good—even before you ask him.

Mt 6:9 "This is an example of how to talk with God:
Our Father in heaven,
your character is beautiful and holy;
reveal more of yourself to us.
¹⁰ Let your kingdom of love come
and your perfect will be done on earth
just like it is in heaven.
¹¹ Provide for us our daily needs,
¹² and forgive us our wrongs,
as we forgive those who have wronged us.
¹³ Lead us away from temptation,
and deliver us from evil.
For yours is the kingdom of love,
and the power of love,
and the glory of love,
forever and ever.
So let it always be!

Mt 6:14 "For it is when you forgive others their wrongs that your heart is open to receive the forgiving and healing power your heavenly Father extends to you. ¹⁵ But if you harden your heart and refuse to forgive others their sins, your heart is closed and unable to receive the forgiveness your heavenly Father extends to you.

Mt 6:16 "When you fast, don't publicize it like the spiritual charlatans do: they moan, groan, and use make-up to appear gaunt and to make it obvious to people that they are fasting. I tell you plainly, they have received the reward their selfish hearts desire. ¹⁷ Therefore, when you fast, shower and clean yourself up ¹⁸ so that no one can tell that you are fasting; but your Father in heaven knows the secrets of your heart, and you will experience the reward of his involvement in your life.

Mt 6:19 "Don't spend your energy trying to get earthly wealth which thieves can steal, or which decays by rust, or which merely loses value over time. ²⁰ Instead, use your energy to build a heavenly treasure of love and goodness, which cannot be stolen and will not decay. ²¹ For whatever you treasure the most is what holds the devotion of your heart, and it is where you will want to be.

Mt 6:22 "Your eyes are windows into your mind. If your eyes are open wide and you are honest with the evidence, your mind will be filled with light and truth. ²³ But if you view things through jaded eyes, tainted with selfishness, then you will distort the evidence and your mind will be darkened; and then, even the light that enters will be warped into greater self-deception, and the darkness will be great!

Mt 6:24 "No one can be loyal and true to two antagonistic principles: If you embrace selfishness, you will hate selflessness; and if you love beneficence, you will hate greed. You cannot serve both the God of love and the god of money.

Mt 6:25 "Therefore I tell you, do not worry about how the future will turn out or where your next meal will come from, or about what you will wear. Life is not built to operate on survival-of-the-fittest principle—constantly seeking to get food for yourself, or the latest clothes. ²⁶ Look at the birds: they don't worry about planting, or harvest time, or storing food in barns, because your heavenly Father is constantly giving of himself to provide for them. Are you not much more valuable than the birds? 27 Who of you, by worrying, has improved their life or added even a single hour to it?

Mt 6:28 "Why waste energy worrying about your clothes? Look at the lilies of the field: they don't sew or weave, 29 yet I tell you that Solomon in his most magnificent robes was not dressed as one of these. 30 If that is how God clothes the grass in the field, which is here today and gone tomorrow, will he not do much more for you? Oh, how you trust him so little! 31 Stop worrying all the time saying, 'Oh, where will we get groceries? What is there to drink? What will we wear?' 32 The pagans, who don't know God, are constantly preoccupied with getting for self, seeking to survive at all costs. But your heavenly Father knows all your needs and longs to provide them. He wants you to embrace his kingdom of giving, 33 so seek first to live in harmony with God's kingdom of giving and all its righteousness, and all your needs will be met as well. 34 Stop worrying about how the future will turn out, don't weigh yourselves down with imaginary future problems that haven't even happened yet, and trust God with your future.

7 "Do not be a fault finder, condemning and judgmental toward others, or you will discover that you are only exposing your own defects of character. 2 For the way you treat others reveals the attributes of your own character, and the reality of your own condition is what determines your destiny.

Mt 7:3 "Why do you try to find the smallest defect in someone else's character, but ignore the malignant pathology in your own? 4 How can you possibly think you can help another remove defects in their character when all the while your character is corrupt with selfishness? 5 You charlatans! Healthy interventions require healthy minds:

first address the defects in your own character, and then you will have the clarity and ability to help others remove defects in theirs.

Mt 7:6 "Don't give your resources for spreading the Remedy to those who will waste them, and don't try to nurture with truth those who are gorging on lies lest they become enraged and attempt to destroy you.

Mt 7:7 "Ask for the Remedy, and it will be given to you; seek, and you will find; knock, and the recovery door will be opened to you. 8 For everyone who asks, receives; those who seek spiritual healing, find it; and to those who knock, the door of restoration will be opened.

Mt 7:9 "Who among you, if your child is hungry and asks for bread, will give them dirt? 10 Or if your child is hungry and asks for a fish, will you give them a snake? 11 If you, who are selfish, know how to give good gifts to your children, how much more will your Father in heaven give good gifts to those who ask him! 12 So in all things, do what is in the eternal best interest of others—just as you would have them do for you. Such love is the central truth upon which the Scripture rests.

Mt 7:13 "The way to heaven is through the gate built precisely upon God's law of love—God's design protocol for life. There are many theories, philosophies and teachings that are less precise and suggest a broader, less exacting road, but all such paths are incompatible with life, and they result in destruction—and far too many prefer them. 14 Uncompromising is the gate and exact is the way that leads to life, and only a few find it.

Mt 7:15 "So be on guard against false teachers: They come to you pretending to be sheep from my flock and claiming to have my Remedy, but beneath their pretense they are destructive wolves pawning off the infection as a cure. 16 Their methods will bear fruit, and from their fruit you will recognize them: grapes don't come from thorn-bushes, or figs from thistles. 17 Just as a good tree brings forth good fruit, and a bad tree — bad fruit, those who take my Remedy will have a mature character and will bear fruit of love. But those who take the false remedy will remain selfish, their characters will wither, and they will bear fruit of selfishness. 18 The tree of love cannot produce evil, and the tree of selfishness cannot produce good. 19 Every tree cut off from love cannot produce good, and therefore will be relinquished to the fire. 20 Thus, by the fruits of their character you will recognize them.

Mt 7:21 "Not everyone who professes me as Lord will enter the heavenly kingdom of love, but only those who have partaken of the Remedy, have been healed in heart, and live in harmony with my Father who is in heaven. 22 There will be many who will cry out to me that day, 'Lord, Lord, don't you remember that we preached many sermons, saying "Jesus saves," we performed exorcisms, saying "Jesus cast you out," and performed many miracles, saying "in Jesus' name, be healed"?' 23 Then I will tell them the reality of their situation: 'You never trusted me, and we were never united in heart. Depart, because you are hardened in selfishness!'

Mt 7:24 "So understand this: Those who hear the truth I speak, and apply it to their lives, are like the wise person who built their house upon a solid rock foundation. 25 Then when it rained, and flood waters rose, and winds beat against that house, it did not fall, because it stood upon solid rock. 26 But everyone who hears the truth I speak and does not apply it to their lives is like the foolish person who built their house upon sand. 27 Then when it rained, and flood waters rose, and the winds beat against that house, it collapsed with a loud crash."

Mt 7:28 The crowds were stunned and in awe after listening to Jesus speak,

29 because he taught clear truths that made sense—like a person who understood the reality of the universe—and not the confusing ideas taught by the religious leaders and lawyers.

8 So when he came down from the mountainside, masses of people followed him. 2 An outcast suffering with leprosy came and humbled himself before Jesus and said, "Lord, I know you can make me clean if you are willing."

Mt 8:3 Jesus gently reached out and touched the man whom no one else would touch, and said, "I am very willing. Be clean!" Immediately he was cured, the leprosy disappeared, and his skin became healthy and normal again. 4 Then Jesus cautioned him, "Don't tell anyone that it was I who healed you, until you first go to the priests, with the offering Moses instructed, and get their official verdict of clean health."

Mt 8:5 Shortly after Jesus arrived at Capernaum, a Roman centurion came to him asking for help. 6 He said, "Lord, my servant is at home paralyzed and suffering terribly."

Mt 8:7 Jesus replied, "Don't worry, I will go and heal him."

Mt 8:8 But the centurion answered: "Lord, I am not worthy of you coming to my home. I know you don't actually need to be there in person; just say the word and my servant will be healed. 9 I myself am a man under authority, and I have soldiers under me. When I give orders, my soldiers obey, so I know that when you give the word, my servant will be healed."

Mt 8:10 When Jesus heard such confidence and understanding, he was deeply moved and said to those with him: "I tell you plainly, I haven't found one person in all Israel with such unshakable confidence. 11 Understand this clearly: There will be many who come from other cultures around the world who will feast together in heaven with Abraham, Isaac, and Jacob. 12 But many others, who—because of ancestry or up-bringing—considered themselves members of God's family, will be abandoned into eternal darkness, with great weeping and heartache."

Mt 8:13 Then Jesus turned to the centurion and said, "Go home; it is done just as you believed it would be." And his servant was healed at that very moment.

Mt 8:14 When Jesus arrived at Peter's home, he saw Peter's mother-in-law lying in bed sick with fever. 15 He gently touched her hand, giving of himself to dispatch the sickness, and she was immediately healed. She got up and began to give of herself to minister to him.

Mt 8:16 That evening, many whose minds were dominated by demons were brought to him, and he not only freed them from demons, but also healed all who were physically sick. 17 This was in fulfillment of what Isaiah prophesied: "He took our infirmities from us and carried away our diseases."

Mt 8:18 When Jesus saw the crowd pressing in, he told his disciples to take him to the other side of the lake. 19 A lawyer came to him and said, "Teacher, take me with you; I want to be one of your students and go wherever you go."

Mt 8:20 Jesus made it clear for him what to expect, saying, "I don't even have the comforts of a fox's den or a bird's nest. If you come with me, it will be rough, often sleeping on the bare ground."

Mt 8:21 A different disciple said to him, "As soon as I bury my father and settle his estate, I will be back to follow you and learn what you have to teach me."

Mt 8:22 But Jesus told him, "Now is the time for you to follow me and pursue life; let the dead take care of the dead."

Mt 8:23 Then Jesus got into the boat, and his disciples joined him. 24 As soon as they were away from shore, a vicious storm came up and the waves washed over the boat, threatening to capsize it. But Jesus slept through the storm. 25 The disciples, though many were seasoned fisherman and familiar with the sea, were terrified and woke Jesus, calling, "Lord, do something! We're going to drown! Save us!"

Mt 8:26 He calmly replied, "Why do you trust so little? What is there to fear?" Then he stood up and said, "Be still!" Immediately the winds ceased, the rains stopped, the waves calmed, and it was peaceful again.

Mt 8:27 The disciples were awed and said to each other, "This is incredible! Who is this man? Even the wind and waves obey him!"

Mt 8:28 When they arrived on the other side of the lake, in a region known as Gadarenes, two men possessed by demons came out of the tombs to confront them. These men were so violent that people no longer traveled past the area. 29 When they saw Jesus, they shouted: "What do you want with us, Son of the Most High God? Have you come here so we will suffer before the appointed time?"

Mt 8:30 There was a large herd of pigs feeding a short distance away. 31 The demons, eager to flee the presence of Jesus, begged him, "If you make us leave, let us go into the herd of pigs."

Mt 8:32 Jesus said to them, "Go now!" So they left and went into the pigs, and the entire herd ran over a cliff into a lake and drowned. 33 Those tending the pigs ran into town and told the owners all that happened. 34 Then the townspeople came out, and being more interested in their investments than in people, they asked Jesus to leave their region.

9 Jesus got into the boat and crossed back over the lake to Capernaum, where he lived. 2 Some men brought to him a paralyzed man lying on a mat. When Jesus saw their trust, he said to the paralyzed man, "Son, cheer up! Your sin is forgiven."

Mt 9:3 When some of the lawyers heard

this, they began murmuring amongst themselves, "This guy is blaspheming!"

Mt 9:4 But Jesus knew what they were thinking, so he said: "Why do you allow such evil thoughts to overwhelm your hearts? 5 What do you think is easier to do: forgive sin or heal paralysis? 6 But I will make it simple for you to understand: My mission is to heal humanity from all the damage of sin—mental, physical, and spiritual. And just so there will be no doubt that I have authority to forgive sin..."—turning to the paralyzed man, Jesus continued—"stand up, take your mat, and walk home." 7 And the man stood up, picked up his mat, and walked home. 8 The crowd was stunned with awe, and they praised God for sending Jesus to do his healing work.

Mt 9:9 Shortly thereafter, Jesus saw Matthew the tax collector sitting at his collection booth. Jesus looked directly at him and said, "Follow me." Matthew immediately left his booth and followed Jesus.

Mt 9:10 Jesus then went to Matthew's house for dinner, and many tax collectors and those deemed "sinners" by the religious leaders ate with him and his disciples. 11 When the Pharisees saw Jesus socializing with such people, they asked his disciples, "Why does your teacher socialize with tax collectors and sinners?"

Mt 9:12 Jesus heard their question and answered: "Those who think they are healthy don't recognize their need for a doctor, but those who know they are sick do recognize their need. 13 Rather than critiquing others, your time would be better spent exploring what the Scripture means when it says, 'I want mercy, not ritual sacrifice.' For I haven't come to call those who are right and healthy in heart and mind, but those who are sick and in need of restoration to God's original ideal."

Mt 9:14 John's disciples came to Jesus and asked, "We and the Pharisees fast regularly; why is it that your disciples don't fast?"

Mt 9:15 Jesus answered, "How can the friends of the bridegroom mourn at the wedding while he is with them? But the time will come when the bridegroom is taken from them; then they will grieve and fast.

Mt 9:16 "No one uses cloth that has not been shrunk to patch an old garment, because the new cloth will tear away from the old material, making a bigger hole. 17 And people don't put new wine in old wineskins, because the skin will burst and the wine will be lost. As new wine is poured into new wineskins—preserving both—so too new truth must be poured into renewed hearts."

Mt 9:18 As Jesus was speaking, a Jewish leader, ignoring everything around him, walked right up to Jesus, knelt before him, and said, "My daughter has just died, but I know that if you touch her she will live. Please, won't you come and raise her from the dead?" 19 Jesus stood up and went with him, and his disciples followed.

Mt 9:20 But the crowd was large, and as they moved through it, a woman who had been bleeding for twelve years reached out and gently touched his robe. 21 She thought to herself, "If only I can touch his robe, I will be healed."

Mt 9:22 But Jesus knew her plight, and turning to her, said, "Be happy! You trusted me, so now you are well." And the woman was healed at that very moment.

Mt 9:23 When Jesus entered the Jewish leader's house, he saw the mourners wailing, playing flutes, and making noise. 24 He said: "Please leave. The girl is not dead but asleep." The crowd laughed at him, for they knew she was dead. 25 But after the crowd had been escorted out, he went to the girl, took her hand, and she got up. 26 News about this spread through the entire region.

Mt 9:27 When Jesus left the leader's house, two blind men followed him, shouting out: "Jesus, Son of David,

The Remedy

please have mercy on us and heal us!"

Mt 9:28 After he went indoors, the blind men came to Jesus, and he asked them, "Do you believe I am able to heal you?"

"Yes, Lord," they replied.

Mt 9:29 Jesus reached out, touched their eyes, and said, "It will be done because you have trusted me," 30 and their sight was instantly restored. In order to avoid prejudice of the religious leaders, Jesus warned the two men not to tell anyone, 31 but they were so overwhelmed with gratitude and joy that they couldn't keep quiet; and they spread the news about Jesus, and what he had done, throughout the entire region.

Mt 9:32 When the men healed from blindness were leaving, another man, who was afflicted by the work of devils and couldn't speak, was brought to Jesus. 33 And when Jesus overruled the work of the devils and healed the mute man, the man spoke. The crowd was stunned with awe and said, "Nothing like this has ever been seen in all Israel."

Mt 9:34 But the Pharisees, more concerned with their own selfish ambitions than the healing of people, sought to cast doubt on Jesus and said, "It is by the prince of devils that he overrules the work of devils."

Mt 9:35 Jesus visited all the towns and villages in the region. He taught in their synagogues and preached the good news of his kingdom of love and of the Remedy he brought, demonstrating his mission by healing every disease and sickness. 36 When he looked into the crowds, his heart ached with compassion because they were hurting, suffering, and helpless to heal themselves. They were like injured sheep without a shepherd to tend their wounds. 37 He turned to his disciples and said, "Abundant are those who are ready to be brought into the kingdom of love, but those working to do so are few. 38 Ask the Lord to send workers to spread the Remedy."

10 Jesus called over his twelve devoted apostles-in-training and empowered them to heal every disease and sickness, and drive out evil forces.

Mt 10:2 These are the names of twelve apostle interns who were trained by Jesus: Simon (also called Peter) and his brother Andrew, James and John (the sons of Zebedee), 3 Philip, Bartholomew, Thomas, Matthew the tax collector, James (the son of Alphaeus), Thaddaeus, 4 Simon the Zealot, and Judas Iscariot who later failed his training and betrayed Jesus.

Mt 10:5 Jesus sent these twelve out with the following instructions: "On this mission, don't go to the Gentiles or to any of the Samaritan towns. 6 Focus your attention on healing and mobilizing the suffering children of Israel. 7 Tell them, 'The Remedy from heaven is here' 8 and then demonstrate my purpose to heal humanity from sin by healing the sick, raising the dead, cleansing the lepers, and freeing minds from the influence of demons. But don't accept payment. You have received the Remedy freely, so freely give it away, 9 and you will receive more in return. Therefore don't wait until you fill your wallets with money, 10 and don't slow yourselves down with luggage and extra clothes. Those whom you heal will provide for your needs.

Mt 10:11 "When you enter a town, stay with someone whose heart is open to the truth. 12 When you enter their house, let them know that you come in peace, as a friend. 13 If they greet you with friendship, then stay; but if they are hostile or oppositional, then depart. 14 If a town or family is hostile and will not welcome you, don't waste time fighting to be heard, but simply shake the dust off your feet to let them know that they are responsible for chasing you away, and then quietly go. 15 The sad reality is that on diagnosis day—the day they face the truth about their terminal condition—they will be more sorrowful than Sodom and

Gomorrah. [16] I am sending you out amongst those who want to destroy you—like sheep amongst wolves—so be innocent as doves and don't antagonize; and remain alert and shrewd like serpents, quietly withdrawing when obvious danger presents itself.

Mt 10:17 "Have your mental defenses ready when dealing with people: those who oppose this message will betray you, report you to authorities, seek to have you imprisoned, and lash out against you—both with tongue and whip—right in church. [18] Because you are my representatives, you will be brought before governors, judges and kings, but you will testify to them and to the Gentiles of the Remedy I bring. [19] But when arrested, don't worry about what to say, or think you need a speechwriter. At that time, your minds will be enlightened with what to say, [20] for you won't be speaking your own ideas, but the Spirit of your Father in heaven will be speaking through you.

Mt 10:21 "People will be so selfish that siblings will turn over their own brothers and sisters to be put to death, and children will renounce their own parents and have them executed. [22] Everyone who refuses the Remedy will hate you because of me, but all those who persevere until the end will be eternally healed. [23] When in a place where the people persecute you and seek to kill you—and hatred is so intense that minds are closed to the Remedy—don't stay and let them kill you, but get away and spread the Remedy somewhere else. I tell you the simple truth, you will not run out of people with whom to share the Remedy before the Son of Man comes.

Mt 10:24 "A medical student doesn't receive more respect and better treatment than his instructor who not only taught him but developed the cure, nor does a servant receive greater reward than his master. [25] So don't be discouraged when you, my students, are called every vile and evil name possible, as they have already called me 'god of the dung-eating maggots.'

Mt 10:26 "Don't be intimidated by them. Speak the truth; for one day, everything will be seen as it really is. All their dirty secrets will be exposed, and the truth of your love will be plainly seen. [27] What I am teaching you in private, I want you to proclaim to the world. [28] Don't be afraid of those who can destroy the body: they cannot touch your psyche, your mind, your individuality. Rather, be afraid of unremedied sin, which destroys both body and mind and results in eternal destruction. [29] Think of a sparrow: one is sold for less than a penny—considered by men as almost worthless—yet not one sparrow falls to the ground without touching the heart of your Father in heaven. [30] You are so much more precious to him! He even knows the number of hairs on your head. [31] So don't live in fear, for you are worth infinitely more than a sparrow.

Mt 10:32 "Those who unite themselves with me before humanity on earth will be united with me before my Father in heaven. [33] But those who sever themselves from me before humanity on earth will be severed from me before my Father in heaven.

Mt 10:34 "Don't think that I have come to make peace with a selfish world. I have not come to bring peace with selfishness, but a sword to cut selfishness out of the hearts of people. [35] I have come to cut dysfunctional family ties: to free a son from selfish loyalty to his father's ambitions and feuds, to sever a daughter from the control of an oppressive and manipulative mother, to cut through the fear and hostility a daughter-in-law has toward her mother-in-law. [36] A person's worst enemies are often members of their own family.

Mt 10:37 "Those who love parental approval more than they love me are untrustworthy of me and the Remedy I bring; and those who love the approval of their children more than me are untrustworthy of me and the Remedy I bring. 38 Anyone who refuses to die to selfishness and follow me—loving others more than self—cannot be trusted by me to distribute the Remedy I bring. 39 Whoever seeks to save self remains infected with selfishness and will die of their unhealed condition, but whoever surrenders self in love to me will experience healing of heart, and find eternal life.

Mt 10:40 "Whoever welcomes you welcomes me, and whoever welcomes me welcomes my Father who sent me. 41 Anyone who helps one of God's ambassadors shares in the joy of representing God and spreading the Remedy. And anyone who helps someone who is doing right because it is right will share in the joy of rightly representing God and spreading the Remedy. 42 And anyone who helps spread the Remedy, even by giving a cup of water to a thirsty student of mine, will share in the joy that comes from living in harmony with God's methods of love."

11 When Jesus finished giving these instructions to his twelve disciples, they went to the towns of Galilee to preach and teach the people.

Mt 11:2 When John the Baptist, who was in prison, heard what Jesus was doing, he sent his students 3 to ask Jesus, "Are you the promised Messiah we have been waiting for, or should we look for someone else?"

Mt 11:4 Jesus replied: "Stay with me today and watch what happens, and then go and tell John what you see: 5 The blind receive their sight, the paralyzed can walk, those with leprosy are healed, the deaf can hear, the dead are brought back to life, and the Remedy is given freely to the poor. 6 Happy and healthy is the one who doesn't reject me."

Mt 11:7 John's disciples turned to leave, and Jesus began speaking to the crowd about John: "Why did you go out into the desert? Did you go to see a stand-up comic blowing around from one thought to the next? 8 Or did you go to see a fashion show? No, those who are preoccupied with the latest fashions are found living in palaces. 9 Then what did you go out to the desert to see? A spokesman of God? Certainly, but I tell you plainly, he wasn't just any spokesman of God. 10 This is the spokesman of whom God foretold in the Scripture: 'I will send my messenger ahead of you to prepare the hearts and minds of the people for your arrival.'

Mt 11:11 "Let me tell you what all this means: No one born on earth prior to John has had a more important role in God's plan to save humanity than John the Baptist. Yet, even those with the least role on earth, but who are in the kingdom of heaven, will be greater than he is here. 12 From the time John started preaching in the desert until this very moment, the kingdom of love and truth has been forcefully advancing against lies and selfishness; and those who earnestly embrace love and truth take hold of it. 13 The entire Old Testament Scripture proclaimed God's kingdom of love and truth—right up until John came. 14 If you are a lover of truth, you will understand that John was the Elijah who the Old Testament foretold would come to open the way for the kingdom of God. 15 Those whose ears are open to hear the truth, let them hear.

Mt 11:16 "How can I describe what the people living today are like? They are like children who sit around and find fault with one another. 17 If one child plays a happy song, the others make fun and refuse to join in harmony. If the child plays a sad song, the others call them weak and refuse to mourn.

Mt 11:18 "Likewise, John lived very strictly —he fasted and drank no wine—and the religious leaders mocked him, calling him a fanatic. 19 And when the Son of Man came—spending time with people, socializing, eating and celebrating—the religious leaders say that he is a glutton, a drunk, and a friend of apostates and addicts. But God's wisdom is proved to be right by its own results."

Mt 11:20 Because the people in the cities where Jesus performed most of his miracles refused to turn away from selfishness and accept the Remedy, he pronounced the unavoidable result: 21 "Korazin, your suffering will be great, and Bethsaida, your agony will be horrible! If the evidence and miracles that were presented to you would have been done in Tyre and Sidon, they would have humbled themselves, rejected selfishness, accepted the Remedy, and been restored to love. 22 On the day each person faces ultimate truth, Tyre and Sidon will have less guilt and agony to bear than you. 23 And you, people of Capernaum, will you soar into heaven? Oh no, you will shrivel up and decay into the depths. If the miracles performed in you were done in Sodom, that city would still be here today. 24 On the day each person faces ultimate truth, Sodom will have less guilt and agony to bear than you."

Mt 11:25 Then Jesus turned his face toward heaven and said: "Father, Lord of heaven and earth, I thank you that your ways of love are so straightforward and easy to understand that the honest-hearted know your methods while the conniving and sophisticated do not comprehend. 26 Truly, Father, you are pleased to keep the truth plain and easy to understand.

Mt 11:27 "Everything necessary to rid the universe from sin and restore mankind to perfection, the Father has entrusted to me. The Father and Son are intimately united in heart and mind, and no one knows the Son like the Father, nor does anyone know the Father like the Son and those who learn of the Father from the Son.

Mt 11:28 "So come to me, all who are tired, worn down and exhausted from fear, selfishness, and fighting to survive on your own, and I will give you rest. 29 Join up with me and learn my methods—the principles upon which life is built to operate—for I am gentle and humble in heart, and you will find healing and rest for your souls. 30 For joining up with me and living in harmony with the way life is designed to operate is what makes life easy and lightens life's burdens."

12 One Sabbath, Jesus and his disciples were walking through a grain field. His disciples were hungry, so they picked some heads of grain and began to eat. 2 When the church leaders saw it, they said to Jesus: "Look! Your disciples are breaking the Sabbath law—they are harvesting crops on the Sabbath."

Mt 12:3 Jesus smiled patiently and said: "Have you never read what David and his men did when they were hungry? 4 They entered God's temple and ate the consecrated bread—which violates ceremonial law, as that bread is only for the priests. 5 Or have you never read in the books of Moses that the priests in the temple work on the Sabbath, breaking the Sabbath rules, yet have done nothing wrong? 6 I tell you plainly, what is happening now is much more important than the temple. 7 If you understood the principles taught in Scripture, such as 'I desire sacrificial service to help others, and not ritual offerings,' you would care more about the welfare of people, and wouldn't condemn those who may have broken your rules but harmed no one. 8 For the Son of Man is Lord of the Sabbath."

Mt 12:9 Jesus and his disciples went to the local synagogue 10 where they encountered a man with a deformed and withered hand. The theologians, trying to find a reason to accuse Jesus before the people as one who breaks the law, asked him: "Do you believe it is lawful to heal on the Sabbath?"

Mt 12:11 Jesus replied, "What do you do when, on the Sabbath, one of your sheep falls into a ditch? Don't you lift it out? 12 How much more valuable is a human being, made in God's image, than a sheep! So of course it is lawful to do good on the Sabbath—to deliver people from suffering, to restore people toward God's design!"

Mt 12:13 He turned to the man with a withered hand and said, "Use your arm normally," and he did, and his arm was completely restored to normal. 14 But the church leaders and theologians went out and plotted how they could kill Jesus.

Mt 12:15 Knowing what the religious leaders were plotting against him, Jesus left that place. Many of the people followed him, and he healed all their sick, 16 instructing them not to make a big deal out of the fact that he was healing on the Sabbath. 17 He healed them just as Isaiah foretold the Messiah would do:

Mt 12:18 "Here is my ambassador whom
    I have chosen to represent me:
He is the One I love,
    and he pleases me completely.
I will fill him with my Spirit,
    and he will reveal to the world
    what justice in my kingdom is like.
Mt 12:19 "He will not argue to promote
    himself,
    nor cry out about life not being
    fair.
No one will hear him complaining
    or accusing others of wrong.
Mt 12:20 "He will not discard anyone
    who is bruised like a reed,
    nor condemn anyone who is
    smoldering, like a wick, in sin.
No, he will be victorious in doing
    what is right.
Mt 12:21 "In him the world will put
    their hope."

Mt 12:22 Then some people brought to Jesus a man who was afflicted by demons and was blind and unable to speak. Jesus healed the man, and he could immediately see and talk. 23 The crowd was stunned with awe and murmured, "Could this be the Messiah, the Son of David?"

Mt 12:24 The Pharisees heard the crowd's growing confidence in Jesus and sought to undermine him, saying: "This is evil sorcery. It is by power from Beelzebub—lord of devils and flies—that he drives out demons."

Mt 12:25 Jesus knew their selfish motives and said to them: "Every kingdom that wars against itself destroys itself, and every town or home that fights against itself will collapse. 26 If Satan drives out Satan, then he wars against himself. How can his kingdom survive? 27 And if I free minds from the domination of demons by the power of Beelzebub, then by whose power do your people drive out demons? Your own practices reveal that you know better than to accuse me of using evil powers. 28 No! We all know it is not by Satan's power that I drive off demons; it is by the power of God's Spirit—which is evidence that God's kingdom of love has arrived.

Mt 12:29 "Or think of it this way: How can a person enter the house of a strong man and carry away his possessions unless they first neutralize the strong man? Only then can they take what is his.

Mt 12:30 "Whoever is not united with me—working on my team to unite humanity together in love—is against me, causing division and disunity. 31 So let me tell you plainly: Every sin—every deviation from God's design—can be healed, except the rejection of the Spirit, for the Spirit administers the Remedy which renews the heart in love. 32 Anyone who speaks against the Son can still be healed, but speaking against the Holy Spirit cannot be healed, either now or in the future, for it is the Spirit that works in the heart to administer the Remedy, and the Spirit works only in a willing heart. 33 Make a tree good and it will bring forth good fruit; make a tree bad and it will bring forth bad fruit—for a tree is recognized by its fruit. 34 You slither and plot like a pit of vipers. Do you really think that you, who are evil in heart, can say anything good? For the true character of one's heart is revealed by what a person says and does. 35 The good person speaks and does good out of the wellspring of good stored within them, and the evil person speaks and does evil out of the wellspring of evil stored within them. So, speaking against the Holy Spirit reveals that one's heart is closed to the working of the Spirit. 36 I tell you plainly, every word spoken will be accounted for—an accurate symptom will be tied directly to the correct diagnosis of each person's heart. 37 The words you speak reveal the true condition of your heart, either 'healed' or 'terminal.'"

Mt 12:38 Then some of the theologians, lawyers and pastors said to him, "Teacher, stop talking and prove yourself with a miracle."

Mt 12:39 He said to them: "It is a rebellious generation—one that has given their hearts to false gods—that asks for miraculous signs! But none will be given it except the sign of God's spokesman Jonah. 40 Just as Jonah spent three days and nights in the belly of a large fish, so too the Son of Man will spend three days and nights in the heart of the earth. 41 The people of Nineveh will hold you to blame for your terminal state on the day your true condition is made public, for they turned away from their destructive ways and accepted the Remedy at the preaching of Jonah — and One far greater than Jonah is here speaking to you. 42 On the day your diagnosis is made public, the Queen of Sheba will stand up and hold you to blame for rejecting the Remedy and its healing, for she came from far away to listen to Solomon's wisdom—but One far greater than Solomon is here speaking to you.

Mt 12:43 "When the mind of a person is freed from an evil spirit, the spirit seeks another to harass. But if the spirit finds no other, 44 it says, 'I will return to the one I left.' If, when it arrives, it finds the mind not filled with God's Spirit but instead empty and uncommitted, 45 it gets seven other spirits more wicked than itself and infiltrates the mind with lies, temptations, and distorted thinking. And the condition of that person is worse than before, because truth no longer has any impact on them. That is how it will be with this wicked generation."

Mt 12:46 While Jesus was speaking to the people, his mother and brothers waited outside, wanting to speak with him. 47 Someone told Jesus, "Your mother and brothers are outside and want to speak with you."

Mt 12:48 He replied, "Who is united with me as a mother or brother?" 49 Pointing to his disciples, he said, "Here are those who are devoted to me like a mother and brothers. 50 Anyone who lives in harmony with my Father in heaven, practicing his methods and following his will, is united with me like my brother and sister and mother."

13 Later that same day, Jesus went out and sat down by the lake. 2 Soon, a large crowd of people gathered. The crowd was so large that Jesus got into a boat, sat in it, and moved a little way off shore, while the people gathered along the shore.
3 Then he taught them many truths, using parables. He said: "A farmer went out to plant seed. 4 As he spread the seed, some fell along the road, and birds quickly ate it up. 5 Some fell amongst the rocks, where there wasn't much soil, and it sprouted quickly because the soil was shallow; 6 but when the sun came up, the plants withered and died because they had no roots. 7 Other seed fell among the weeds and thorns which grew and choked the good plants. 8 Still other seed fell on good soil, where it took root and produced a bountiful crop — a hundred, sixty, or thirty times what was sown. 9 Those whose minds are open to truth,

let them understand."

Mt 13:10 Jesus' disciples came to him and asked, "Why do you use parables, metaphors and illustrations when speaking to the crowds?"

Mt 13:11 He told them: "The understanding of the secrets of God's kingdom of love is taught to you because your hearts are open to receive it, but their minds are not ready to accept the truth, so parables must be used.

12 Whoever embraces the truth and applies it to their lives will experience expansion of their understanding and will comprehend more truth. But whoever closes their mind to truth, refusing to embrace and apply it, will lose even the little understanding they have. 13 So, why do I speak to them in parables? Because though they see with their eyes, their minds do not comprehend; and though they hear with their ears, they do not understand the meaning.

Mt 13:14 "God's spokesman Isaiah was talking about these people, and others just like them, when he said:

'You hear but you don't understand;
you see but you don't comprehend.
15 For this reason,
    people's hearts have hardened
    and are insensitive to truth;
they close their ears to ideas
    that challenge their traditions
    and close their eyes to truths
    that would require a change of
    their habits.
If they didn't, they would see the
    truth of their condition
    and hear the promise
    of the healing Remedy,
and understand with their hearts
    their need of me.
They would turn to me in trust,
    and I would heal them.'

Mt 13:16 "But you are blessed, because your eyes are open and your minds understand what you see; and your ears are open and you comprehend what you hear. 17 I tell you the plain truth, many of God's spokespersons—and others whose hearts were healed—longed to be where you are, see what you see, and hear what you hear, but they could not.

Mt 13:18 "So pay attention as I explain what the parable of the farmer means: 19 The seed represents the truth about God's kingdom of love. Whenever someone hears the truth about God's kingdom of love but doesn't understand it, Satan distracts them, filling their minds with worldly things so that the truth is quickly forgotten—this is the seed that fell on the road. 20 The seed that fell amongst the rocks represents the person who hears the truth and immediately accepts it with joy, 21 but the truth was only accepted as an idea—it did not take root in the heart, get applied to life, or get incorporated into the character. Such a person doesn't last long when living out the truth results in trials or persecutions, and they quickly abandon it. 22 The seed falling amongst the weeds and thorns represents those who hear the truth, but allow worries, fears, insecurities about temporal matters, and the false security in wealth to strangle it; and their life remains selfish and fails to bear the fruit of a loving character. 23 But the seed falling on good soil represents those who hear, comprehend and apply the truth to their lives. They experience a transformation of character, and love others more than self, yielding a harvest of a hundred, sixty, or thirty times what was sown."

Mt 13:24 Jesus used another parable to teach them: "God's creation is like a man who planted only good seed in his field; 25 but while everyone was sleeping, an enemy slipped in, planted weeds among the wheat, and then snuck away. 26 When the wheat sprouted and produced heads, the weeds grew up with the wheat. 27 The owner's laborers came to him and asked, 'What happened? Didn't you sow good seed in your field? Where did all the weeds come from?' 28 He told them,

'An enemy has done this.' So the workers asked, 'Do you want us to go and pull up the weeds?' 29'No!' he answered; 'While pulling up the weeds, you may uproot the wheat with them. 30Let both grow together until harvest time. At that time, the harvesters will separate the weeds from the wheat: the weeds will be burned, and the wheat will be brought into my barn.'"

Mt 13:31 Jesus told them another parable: "Consider how the kingdom of heaven is similar to a mustard seed which someone planted in their field. 32Though the mustard seed is the smallest seed they sow, when it grows, it becomes the largest plant in the garden, growing into a tree that provides shade and comfort for the birds. Consider how the smallest act of love is like that seed."

Mt 13:33 He told them yet another parable: "God's kingdom of love is like yeast mixed into a large amount of flour until it permeates the entire dough."

Mt 13:34 Jesus never spoke to the people without using parables, 35so he fulfilled what God's spokespersons foretold:

"I will teach in parables,
revealing truths obscured
since the creation of the world."

Mt 13:36 After Jesus left the crowd and went into the house, his disciples came to him and said, "Please explain to us the meaning of the parable of the weeds in the field."

Mt 13:37 He said: "The Son of Man is the One who planted the good seed. 38The field represents the world, and the good seed represents those who have accepted the Remedy and have loving characters, and are therefore children of the kingdom of love. The weeds are those who have rejected the Remedy and have selfish characters, and are therefore children of the evil selfish one; 39and the enemy is the devil. The harvest is the end of time, and the harvesters are the angels.

Mt 13:40 "Just as the weeds are pulled and consumed in the fire, so too, at the end of time, the wicked will be consumed. 41The Son of Man will send out his angels who will weed out all the terminally ill—those who refused healing—and every source of the infection of evil. 42They will be thrown into the eternal fire of God's love and truth, where all sin and selfishness is consumed, causing overwhelming agony of mind and torment of soul. 43But the righteous will shine brighter than the sun in the eternal kingdom of their Father. Those with minds open to hear and comprehend will understand.

Mt 13:44 "God's kingdom of heavenly love is like a hidden treasure discovered in a field. It is so valuable that the person who finds it becomes so overwhelmed with awe that they sell everything they own in order to possess that field.

Mt 13:45 "Or, the kingdom of heavenly love is like a jeweler looking for the finest pearls. 46When they find a perfect one of immense value, they sell everything they own in order to possess it.

Mt 13:47 "Or, God's kingdom of heavenly love is like a dragnet let down into the sea, which caught every kind of fish. 48When it was full, the fisherman pulled it in and collected the healthy fish, but threw away the diseased ones. 49This is how it will be at the end of time: The angels will come and separate the healed from those who remain terminal in sin and selfishness.

50The terminal—those who refused healing—will be thrown into the eternal fire of God's love and truth, where all sin and selfishness is consumed, causing overwhelming agony of mind and torment of soul.

Mt 13:51 "Have you understood the meaning of these parables?" Jesus asked.

"Yes," they replied.

Mt 13:52 So he told them, "Then remember that every effective intern—one who teaches the healing power of

The Remedy

God's methods and principles—is like a homeowner who knows the worth and use of both old and new treasures, and brings out the most appropriate valuable at the right time."

Mt 13:53 After Jesus finished telling these parables, he left the area. 54 When he came to his hometown, he went to the synagogue and began teaching the people. They were stunned by what he taught. "Where did he learn such wisdom and get such miraculous abilities?" they asked. 55 "Didn't he grow up here as the son of the carpenter? Isn't he Mary's son? Aren't his brothers James, Joseph, Simon, and Judas? 56 Doesn't he have sisters who live here? So where did he learn all of this and get these abilities?" 57 They were incensed that he would presume to teach them, so Jesus said to them, "Only at home—in his hometown—is a spokesman of God devalued and discounted."

Mt 13:58 He was unable to do many miracles because they were so distrustful and suspicious.

14 When Herod, the ruler of Galilee, heard the report about Jesus, 2 he said, "He must be John the Baptist risen from the dead! That is why he is able to work miracles."

Mt 14:3 Herod had arrested and imprisoned John because of Herodias, his brother Philip's wife. 4 John had confronted Herod, telling him, "It is not lawful for you to have your brother's wife." 5 This enraged Herod, and he wanted to kill John, but he feared what the people would do, because they considered John a spokesman of God.

Mt 14:6 But on Herod's birthday, Herodias' daughter danced for the guests, and Herod was extremely pleased—so much so 7 that he promised her, under oath, whatever she wanted. 8 Urged by her mother, she said, "I want the head of John the Baptist on a platter." 9 Herod was conflicted, but because he had given an oath in front of his guests, he granted her request, 10 and John was beheaded in prison. 11 His head was brought to the girl on a platter, and she gave it to her mother. 12 John's disciples took his body and buried it, and then went and told Jesus.

Mt 14:13 When Jesus heard what had happened to John, he went by boat to a place where he could be by himself. But the crowds from the nearby towns heard where he'd gone and followed him on foot. 14 When Jesus came near the shore and saw the large crowds seeking him, his heart was moved with compassion for them, and he healed their sick.

Mt 14:15 As the day faded away, his disciples were hungry and said, "We are in the middle of nowhere, and it's getting late. Send the people back to town so they can buy something to eat."

Mt 14:16 Jesus replied, "There is no reason for them to leave. You give them something to eat."

Mt 14:17 The disciples were startled and said, "But we only have five loaves of bread and two fish between us all."

Mt 14:18 Jesus replied, "Bring them to me." 19 Then he gave instructions to the people to sit down on the grass. He took the five loaves and two fish, and looking toward heaven, thanked his Father, and then broke the loaves into pieces and gave them to the disciples, and the disciples distributed them to the people. 20 Everyone ate as much as they wanted, and the disciples picked up twelve basketfuls of leftovers. 21 Approximately five thousand men, plus women and children, were fed.

Mt 14:22 Immediately after feeding the crowd, Jesus directed the disciples to leave in the boat without him and go to the other side of the lake, while he stayed to dismiss the crowd. 23 After the crowd departed, Jesus climbed a hillside by himself to talk with his Father. When the sun set, he was there by himself. 24 The boat was already well away from land, and was battered by the waves as the wind blew against it.

Mt 14:25 Around four o'clock in the morning, Jesus walked on the surface of the lake out to where the boat was. 26 When the disciples saw him walking on the water, they were petrified with fear and shouted, "It's a ghost!"

Mt 14:27 But Jesus gently called out to them, "Calm down! It's me! Don't be afraid."

Mt 14:28 Peter immediately called back, "Lord, if it's really you, command me to come to you walking on the water!"

Mt 14:29 "Well, come on!" Jesus said. So Peter stepped out of the boat and walked on the water toward Jesus, 30 but when he took his eyes off Jesus and looked at the wind and waves, he was overcome with fear and began to sink. He cried out, "Lord, save me!"

Mt 14:31 Instantly Jesus reached out his hand and lifted him up. "Your trust is so small. Why did you doubt me?" he asked.

Mt 14:32 As soon as they were in the boat, the wind calmed down. 33 The disciples knelt down in awe, worshipping him, and said, "You really are the Son of God."

Mt 14:34 They landed on the other side of the lake in a place called Gennesaret. 35 When the people there recognized Jesus, they sent runners throughout the countryside, telling everyone. And the people brought to him all those who were sick, infirmed, or disabled, 36 begging him to just let them touch the edge of his clothing; and all who touched him were healed.

15 Then some of the lawyers and theologians from church headquarters in Jerusalem came to challenge Jesus. They asked, 2 "Why don't your disciples follow the rules the elders established and undergo ceremonial cleansing before they eat?"

Mt 15:3 Jesus, not being intimidated, replied: "Why do you break God's own design and law for the sake of your own man-made traditions? 4 For God designed us to love, and said, 'Honor your father and mother,' and 'Anyone who curses their parents must be put to death.' 5 Yet you teach people to tell their parents, 'Whatever resources I have are dedicated to the church, and therefore won't be available to help you.' 6 They are instructed by you not to honor their parents with their resources, thus you nullify God's word and replace his design of love with your own selfish tradition. 7 You are hypocrites! It is you who Isaiah was describing when he said:

Mt 15:8 "'These people
proclaim their love for me
with their mouths,
but their hearts are as far away
from love for me and my methods
as they can get.
9 Their worship is useless,
and their teachings are nothing
but man-made rules.'"

Mt 15:10 Jesus turned to the crowd, called them to himself, and said: "Listen and understand what really matters: 11 What goes in a person's mouth doesn't change their character, so it cannot make them 'unclean,' but what comes out of their mouth is an expression of their character and is what makes them 'unclean.'"

Mt 15:12 His disciples came to him later and said, "Don't you realize that you are upsetting the church leaders by saying such things?"

Mt 15:13 Jesus replied, "Understand this clearly: Every tree that was not planted by my Father will be pulled up by the roots. 14 Don't worry about them. They are blind to the reality of my Father's kingdom, yet they try to guide others to it. But you know that when a blind person leads another blind person, they both fall into the same pit."

Mt 15:15 Peter said, "Will you explain this parable to us?"

Mt 15:16 Looking at them, Jesus answered: "Are you really so steeped in tradition that you don't understand? 17 Don't you realize that what enters the body through the mouth goes into the stomach, passes through and then leaves the body? 18 But what comes out of the mouth is an expression of what is in the heart—an expression of the character; and what is evil in the character makes a person 'unclean.' 19 For evil thoughts, murder, adultery, sexual perversity, dishonesty, theft, deceit, gossip—they all come out of the heart. 20 It is selfishness in the heart, manifested in words and deeds, that makes a person 'unclean;' but eating with hands not ceremonially washed doesn't have any impact on character and thus doesn't make one 'unclean.'"

Mt 15:21 Jesus left that place and went to the vicinity of Tyre and Sidon. 22 Suddenly, a Canaanite woman began crying out to him, calling: "Lord, Heir of David, have compassion on me! My daughter is being tormented by a demon!"

Mt 15:23 Jesus wanted to see how his disciples would respond, so he remained silent. His disciples said to him, "Send her away; she's being such a nuisance, crying out after us wherever we go."

Mt 15:24 Jesus looked at her and said, "I was sent to the lost sheep of Israel."

Mt 15:25 But she didn't lose heart; instead, she pressed forward, fell at his feet, and said, "Lord, please help me!"

Mt 15:26 He gently said, "It isn't proper to take the food off the table before the children have eaten and give it to their puppies."

Mt 15:27 "You're right, Lord," she pressed, "but even the puppies eat the crumbs that fall from their master's table before his children are fed properly."

Mt 15:28 Jesus smiled and said, "Young lady, your trust and determination are amazing. What you desire, you now have." And her daughter was healed at that very moment.

Mt 15:29 From there, Jesus went along the coast of the Sea of Galilee, then walked up a hillside and sat down. 30 Large multitudes flocked to him, bringing their sick, paralyzed, blind, crippled, deaf, mute, and anyone else who was disabled, and presented them before Jesus. He healed every one of them. 31 The people were overwhelmed with awe when they saw mutes speak, the paralyzed stand and walk, the blind see, and the sick made well. They shouted praises to the God of Israel.

Mt 15:32 Looking upon the crowds, Jesus called his disciples and said, "I am concerned for the people. They have been here three days and haven't eaten. It's a long journey home, and I don't want to send them away hungry; they might collapse from exhaustion."

Mt 15:33 His disciples, apparently forgetting to whom they were talking, said, "Where could we possibly get enough bread to feed this crowd? We're in the middle of nowhere!"

Mt 15:34 Jesus smiled and asked, "How many loaves do you have?"

"We only have seven, and a few small fish," they replied.

Mt 15:35 Jesus directed the crowd to sit down on the ground, 36 then took the seven loves and few fish, and after thanking his Father, broke them and gave the pieces to the disciples who passed them on to the people.
37 Everyone ate until they were full. Afterward, the disciples picked up seven basketfuls of leftovers. 38 Four thousand men, plus women and children, were fed. 39 After they finished eating, Jesus dispersed the crowd, got into a boat, and went to the region of Magadan.

16 The lawyers and theologians from church headquarters came to challenge Jesus, questioning his legitimacy as a Bible teacher, and demanded that he show them a sign from heaven.

Mt 16:2 But Jesus said: "You have a saying, 'Red sky at night, sailors' delight; 3 red sky at morning, sailors take warning.' How is it that you can read the signs for the weather but don't recognize the signs of the times? 4 Only a generation lost in selfishness, who rejects God's methods, looks for miraculous signs while ignoring the evidence all around them. But no sign will be given except the sign of Jonah." Then Jesus turned and left.

Mt 16:5 They crossed the lake, but once on the other side, the disciples realized that they hadn't brought anything to eat. 6 Jesus said to them, "Keep sharp, stay vigilant, and watch closely to keep the yeast of the lawyers and theologians out of church headquarters."

Mt 16:7 The disciples were too concrete in their thinking and said, "Is it because we didn't bring any bread with us that he mentioned yeast?"

Mt 16:8 Overhearing their conversation, Jesus said: "Do you have such little confidence in me? Is your perspective so small that you think only about food for the body? 9 Don't you realize what is happening? Remember when we fed over five thousand people with five loaves? How many baskets of leftovers did you gather? 10 Or when we fed over four thousand with seven loaves—how many baskets of leftovers did you gather then? 11 Do you really think I am mainly concerned about food for the body? So keep sharp and stay vigilant, and watch closely to keep out the yeast of the lawyers and theologians from church headquarters." 12 Then they understood that he was not talking about the yeast used in food for the body, but against the doctrines, theologies, traditions, and teachings of the lawyers and theologians from church headquarters.

Mt 16:13 When Jesus arrived in Caesarea Philippi, he asked his disciples, "Who do the people say the Son of Man is?"

Mt 16:14 They answered, "Some people believe you are John the Baptist, others think you are Elijah, and still others believe you must be Jeremiah or one of the other of God's spokesmen."

Mt 16:15 "What about you? Who do you tell people I am?"

Mt 16:16 Simon Peter answered instantly, "You are the Messiah, the Son of the living God!"

Mt 16:17 Jesus smiled and said: "Well done, Simon, son of Jonah. You did not gain this truth from humans, but from my Father in heaven. 18 And though you are Peter—your name meaning small stone—it is on the solid Rock of the Son of Man that I will build my church, and hell's barricade of selfishness and lies will not stop it. 19 I will give you the Spirit empowering you with truth and love, which are the keys to the kingdom of heaven. Whatever you bind to truth and love on earth will be bound to truth and love in heaven, and whatever you loose from fear and selfishness on earth will be loosed from fear and selfishness in heaven." 20 Then Jesus instructed his disciples not to tell people that he was the Messiah, because it was not yet time.

Mt 16:21 From then on, Jesus began explaining to his disciples that he must face the church leaders in Jerusalem, suffer many abuses at the hands of the church elders, pastors, priests, church administrators and lawyers, and that they would kill him, but on the third day after his death he would arise to life.

Mt 16:22 Peter was shocked. He pulled Jesus into a corner and tried to dissuade him from this course, saying, "No way, Lord! Never will this happen to you!"

Mt 16:23 Jesus looked at Peter and said, "Get Satan's ideas of selfishness away from me! You are not encouraging me but trying to trip me up; you are not thinking through the lens of God's methods of love but allowing human fear and selfishness to dominate your thinking."

Mt 16:24 Then Jesus said to all the disciples: "If anyone wants to follow me into unity with my Father, they must surrender their life, willingly choose to die to selfishness, and follow me in love. 25 For anyone who follows the survival-of-the-fittest instinct and seeks to save their life, will lose it because the infection of selfishness will not be eliminated; but anyone who loses their life in love for me will find eternal life, for they will have been restored back to God's design for life—selfless, other-centered love. 26 What good does it do to selfishly hoard all the treasures of the world only to die eternally, consumed by selfishness? Or how much is a person's soul—their eternal existence — worth to them?

27 For the Son of Man is going to return in the fullness of his Father's glory, with his angels, and then each person will receive the reward they have chosen. 28 I tell you the plain truth, some of you right here will not sleep in the grave before you see the Son of Man glorified in his kingdom of love."

17 Six days later, Jesus took with him Peter and the two brothers—James and John—and led them up a high mountain where they could be alone. 2 There, the veil was pulled back and his divine glory shone through the cloak of his humanity. His face shone bright like the sun, and his clothes radiated intense white light. 3 And in his fiery presence stood Moses and Elijah, talking with Jesus.

Mt 17:4 "Lord," Peter exclaimed, "this is awesome, and we are glad to be here to see it! If you want, I will put up three shelters—one for you, one for Moses, and one for Elijah."

Mt 17:5 But while Peter was still speaking, a brilliant cloud settled over them and a voice from within the cloud said, "This is my Son. I love him and am absolutely pleased with him, so listen to him!"

Mt 17:6 When the disciples heard the voice, they were frightened, and fell face down on the ground. 7 But Jesus came and touched them, saying, "Get up; there is no reason to be afraid." 8 When they lifted their heads and looked up, they saw only Jesus.

Mt 17:9 On their way down the mountain, Jesus told them, "Be sure you don't tell anyone about what you saw until after the Son of Man rises from the dead."

Mt 17:10 His disciples asked him, "Why do the Bible teachers always say that Elijah must come first?"

Mt 17:11 Jesus replied, "Absolutely. Elijah comes to prepare the way. 12 But let me tell you straight, the Elijah messenger has already come; but the church leaders did not recognize him, and they led the people to reject and mistreat him. The Son of Man will suffer in the same way at their hands." 13 Then they realized that he was talking about John the Baptist.

Mt 17:14 As they came to a crowd, a man knelt down before Jesus 15 and said, "Lord, please take pity on my son and heal him. He has seizures that cause terrible suffering. He often gets injured, sometimes falling into the fire or water. 16 I brought him to your disciples, but they couldn't heal him."

Mt 17:17 With disappointment, Jesus said, "How sad. What a confused and superstitious people you are. How long will I need to be with you before you understand? How long must I endure your suffering? Bring the boy to me." 18 Jesus commanded the evil spirit to leave the boy, and the child was instantly healed.

Mt 17:19 The disciples waited until they were alone with Jesus, then asked, "Why couldn't we heal the boy?"

Mt 17:20 Jesus, looking toward the Temple Mount, replied: "You failed because your confidence in God is so weak, and you are still blinded by misunderstanding. I tell you plainly, if your trust in God was even as much as a mustard seed, you could let go of your attachment to the Temple Mount and say to the mount 'Away with you,' and the symbolic rituals would no longer hold you back; you could do anything you want! 21 But this type of evil is only overcome by talking with my Father."

Mt 17:22 When they arrived in Galilee, Jesus said to them, "The Son of Man will be betrayed and turned over to human authorities. 23 They will kill him, but on the third day he will destroy death and arise to life." The disciples were deeply distraught.

Mt 17:24 When Jesus and the disciples were in Capernaum, local tax collectors confronted Peter about the tax, which was worth two days' wages, asking: "Doesn't your teacher support the temple and pay the temple tax?"

Mt 17:25 Peter impulsively replied, "Of course he does." Then, when Peter went into the house, Jesus asked him, "Simon, tell me what you think. From whom do the kings of the earth collect taxes: from their own children, or from others?"

Mt 17:26 "From others, of course," Peter replied.

Jesus looked at him and said, "Then the king's children are exempt; 27 but to avoid unnecessary conflict on a side-issue, go to the lake and throw out your fishing line. Take the first fish you catch, open its mouth, and you will find a large coin. Use it to pay for my tax and yours."

18 The disciples then asked Jesus, "In heaven's system, what constitutes true greatness?"

Mt 18:2 Jesus called over a small child 3 and said, "Let me make it as clear as I can: Unless you become lovers of truth, teachable like a child, you will never leave the errors of this world and become part of heaven's kingdom of truth and love. 4 Therefore it is those who humble themselves and become teachable and responsive to love and truth who will be transformed and great in heaven's kingdom.

Mt 18:5 "And anyone who welcomes those who have childlike trust in my character, protecting, nurturing and leading them in truth, receives me into their heart. 6 But it is better to drown in the sea with a heavy stone tied around one's neck than to lead a person with childlike trust to deviate from God's design for life.

Mt 18:7 "Horrible suffering is upon the world because of that which leads people to deviate from God's design for life! Such deviations will happen, but sorrow and pain will be the portion for those who promote it. 8 If you use your hands or feet to participate in activities that destroy your mind, sear your conscience and warp your character, then discard the hand or foot. It is better to have a sound mind with Christlike character and enter life as an amputee than to have both hands and two feet—but a seared conscience and a warped character—and enter into eternal fire. 9 And if your eye looks at things that destroy your mind, sear your conscience and warp your character, then lose the eye. It is better to have a sound mind with Christlike character and enter life with one eye than to have both eyes—but a seared conscience and a warped character—and be consumed with overwhelming guilt and shame in the fiery lake of unveiled truth and love.

Mt 18:10 "Be certain you don't disregard or belittle one of these small children. I am telling you straight, their guardian angels always meet face to face with my Father in heaven. 11 The Son of Man came to find and heal that which is deviant from God's design for life."

Mt 18:12 "Think of it this way: If a man owns a hundred sheep and one of them gets lost, won't he leave the ninety-nine that are safe, and go to look for the one that is lost? 13 And if he finds the one lost sheep—I tell you the simple truth—he rejoices more over that one sheep than over the ninety-nine that were never lost. 14 This is how it is with our Father in heaven: He doesn't want to lose even one of these little ones.

Mt 18:15 "If someone who has partaken of the Remedy deviates from God's design and wrongs you, causing a fracture in the unity of your relationship, go to them—one on one—and privately show them their fault. If they comprehend, you have won a friend. 16 But if they refuse to listen, then take one or two others—who have partaken of the Remedy—to reach out to your friend so that your concern for that person can be validated by two or three others. [17] If your friend refuses to listen to them, bring your concern to the church; and if they refuse the loving direction of the church, then they have hardened their heart to you and are no more your friend than a pagan or tax collector.

Mt 18:18 "I tell you the plain reality of God's kingdom: Whatever you tie your heart to on earth, you will be tied to in eternity; and whatever you let go of on earth, you will be free from in eternity.

Mt 18:19 "So understand that if two of you here on earth come into agreement on something and ask for the blessing of my Father in heaven, he will honor your choice. [20] For wherever two or three with hearts renewed with my character of love unite together, I am there with them."

Mt 18:21 Peter then spoke up and asked Jesus, "Master, how many times must I forgive my friend who wrongs me? Is seven times sufficient?"

Mt 18:22 Jesus smiled and said, "I tell you the reality of God's kingdom: Forgive not just seven times, but perpetual sevens of never-ending perfection of forgiveness.

Mt 18:23 "Let me put it in terms you can understand: Consider God's kingdom to be like a king who wanted to settle all his servants' accounts. [24] As he started, a man who owed one million dollars was brought before the king. [25] The man was not able to pay, so the king ordered the man and his entire family to be sold into slavery to pay the debt. [26] But the man fell on his knees before the king and begged for more time to repay the debt. [27] The king had compassion on him, cancelled the entire debt, and let him go.

Mt 18:28 "But when the servant left the king, he found another servant, who owed him ten dollars. He pinned him against the wall and began choking him, demanding the ten dollars back.

[29] The man fell on his knees and begged him for more time to repay the debt; [30] but he refused and called the authorities, and had the man locked in prison until the debt was paid. [31] When others heard what had happened, they were very upset and told the king all about.

Mt 18:32 "Then the king called the ungrateful man in and said, 'You hard-hearted servant! I cancelled your debt of one million dollars because you asked me to be merciful. [33] Should you not have internalized this grace into your heart and shown mercy to your fellow servant for the pittance he owed you?' [34] Angry that his mercy didn't transform his servant's heart, the king gave him over to the isolation and torment that a hard heart causes, until his debt of mercy was fully paid.

Mt 18:35 Likewise, my Father in heaven is angry when your hearts are not transformed despite his mercy; for if you refuse to forgive each other from your heart, you demonstrate that you have not been healed. My Father will respect your choice and give you up to the agony of mind and torment of soul that unremedied sin brings."

19 After Jesus finished teaching them these things, he left Galilee and went to Judea on the other side of the Jordan. [2] Huge crowds of people followed him, and he healed them there.

Mt 19:3 Some of the religious leaders and lawyers came to Jesus, trying to trick him. They asked, "Is it legal for a man to divorce his wife for any reason he so chooses?"

Mt 19:4 Jesus gently replied, "Haven't you studied God's design as recorded in Scripture? It says that in the beginning, the Creator 'made them male and female; [5] and because of this, a man will leave his parents and be united to his wife, and — though they are two — they will become one flesh.' [6] So they are no longer two but one. Therefore what God has joined into unity, let no person tear apart."

Mt 19:7 But they didn't like his answer, so they asked, "Why then did Moses instruct that a man should give his wife a certificate of divorce and send her away?"

Mt 19:8 Jesus answered: "Divorce happens when love breaks down and selfishness wins. No one wants to lose a limb, but we sever a gangrenous limb to save the person. To sever a healthy limb is damaging and wrong. Moses' instructions—to sever toxic relationships and save individuals—were given because of the hardness of your hearts. 9 But anyone who divorces their spouse except for the gangrenous situation of marital betrayal commits adultery and inflicts injury."

Mt 19:10 The disciples were troubled, and concluded, "If marriage is like this, maybe it is better not to marry."

Mt 19:11 Jesus replied: "Healthy relationships require healthy people, and not everyone is suited for a healthy marriage relationship. 12 Some people are born without any interest in marriage, others have been so traumatized that they prefer to live as single people, and still others choose not to marry because they devote themselves to God's work. But those who are capable of marriage as God designed—should get married."

Mt 19:13 Then some small children were brought to Jesus to lay hands upon and pray for, but the disciples scolded the parents who brought them.

Mt 19:14 Jesus said, "Let the children come to me; don't put any barriers up to make it difficult for them, for God's kingdom of love is for ones just like these." 15 After he put his hands on them, he left that place.

Mt 19:16 A short while later, a man came up to Jesus and asked, "Teacher, what good act must I do to obtain eternal life?"

Mt 19:17 Jesus replied, "Why do you seek me to find what is good? There is only One who is the source of good. If you want to be healed and enter eternal life, then follow God's instructions."

Mt 19:18 "Which of God's instructions?" the man sincerely asked.

Jesus answered, "Those that describe God's design protocol of love—how to love your neighbor as yourself. If you love, then you do not murder, do not commit adultery, do not steal, do not give false testimony, 19 and you do honor your mother and father."

Mt 19:20 "All of these I have done," the young man said, "yet I still don't have peace. What am I missing?"

Mt 19:21 Jesus looked him in the eye and said, "If you want to be perfectly healed and have a right character, go and sell all your possessions which you hold as evidence of your good standing before God, and then, in love, give all you have to bless the poor, and you will have a rich reward in heaven's kingdom of love. Then come and join me, and live as I do."

Mt 19:22 When the young man heard this, he left with a heavy heart, because he had great wealth from which he derived security.

Mt 19:23 Jesus turned to his disciples and said: "I tell you the simple truth: It is hard for those who are rich—who derive a sense of security from their possessions—to surrender all and enter into heaven's kingdom of love and trust. 24 It is easier for a camel to kneel down, remove its load, and crawl through the small gate known as the 'eye of the needle' than for a rich person to humble themself, surrender their wealth, and enter God's kingdom of love and trust."

Mt 19:25 When the disciples heard this, it shocked them, because they were biased by their culture to believe that wealth was a sign of being right with God. So they asked, "If not the rich, then who can possibly be saved?"

Mt 19:26 Jesus looked directly at them and said, "Humans have no chance to cure their own terminal condition. The only possibility for eternal life is to trust God and partake of the Remedy."

Mt 19:27 Peter said to him, "We've left everything we have to follow you! What's in store for us?"

Mt 19:28 Jesus replied: "I tell you truly, when all things are restored to perfection, when the Son of Man sits on his throne of glory, you who have partaken of the Remedy and followed me will also sit on twelve thrones, providing your good judgment to the twelve tribes of Israel. 29 And every person who has left behind their property, brothers, sisters, parents, children, stocks, or any valuable in order to be united with me will receive more than one hundred times as much as they gave up, and will also receive eternal life. 30 But those who think they deserve to be first will actually find themselves last, while those who are humble and consider themselves last will find themselves first in God's kingdom.

20 "For God's kingdom of love is like this: One day, a wealthy estate owner went out to the marketplace at six o'clock in the morning to hire people to work in his vineyard. 2 After he agreed to pay them one day's wage each for the entire day, he sent them into his fields.

Mt 20:3 "About nine o'clock he went out and found others standing in the market-square, doing nothing. 4 He told them, 'Go and work in my vineyard, and I will pay you what is right.' 5 So they went. He went out again at noon, and at three in the afternoon, and did the same thing. 6 Then at five o'clock, with only one hour left in the workday, he went out and found still others standing around. He asked them, 'Why have you been doing nothing all day?'

Mt 20:7 "They answered, 'Because no one has hired us.' He said to them, 'Then go and work in my vineyard.'

Mt 20:8 "At six in the evening, when the workday was over, the owner instructed his foreman: 'Call the workers and pay them their wages. Start with those who came to the field last, and go back, finishing with those who came to the field first.'

Mt 20:9 "The workers who were hired at five o'clock came first, and each received one day's wage. 10 When those who were hired first and started at six in the morning came to get paid, they expected to receive more, but each one was given the same amount. 11 When they received their pay, they began to complain that the estate owner was unfair. 12 They grumbled, 'These people hired at five only worked an hour and have been paid the same as us who have labored all day in the heat!'

Mt 20:13 "But the owner answered them gently, 'Friends, I have done you no wrong. Didn't you agree to work for one day's wage? 14 Take your pay and go home happy. I want to give the people who came last the same as I gave you. 15 Don't I have the right to do what I want with my resources? Why can't you rejoice for your fellow workers? Are you jealous because of my generosity?'

Mt 20:16 "So those who consider themselves last will find themselves first in God's kingdom, while those who think they deserve to be first will actually find themselves last."

Mt 20:17 As Jesus was traveling to Jerusalem, he took his twelve disciples aside to prepare them. He said: 18 "We are going to Jerusalem; and when we get there, the Son of Man will be betrayed into the hands of the church leaders, theologians and lawyers. They will sentence him to death 19 and will turn him over to the Gentile authorities to be beaten, abused, mocked, and crucified. But on the third day he will arise to life!"

Mt 20:20 Then the mother of Zebedee's sons brought her boys and knelt before Jesus in order to ask him a favor.

Mt 20:21 Jesus inquired, "What is it that

you want of me?"

She said, "I ask that you allow my sons to sit beside you in your kingdom—one on the left and the other on your right."

Mt 20:22 Jesus said with warning in his voice, "You have no idea what you are asking." Then he looked at them and said, "Do you think you can drink of the same cup as I am going to drink?"

"Yes, we can," they replied.

Mt 20:23 Jesus said somberly, "Yes, you will drink from my cup; but it is not up to me who will sit on my right or left. These places will go to those for whom my Father has prepared them."

Mt 20:24 When the other ten disciples heard about this request, they became resentful and angry with the two brothers. 25 Jesus called all twelve together and said: "You know how the rulers of the Gentiles—those who have not partaken of the Remedy—abuse power and lord over others, using their high office to dictate and control those beneath them. 26 It should not be like this with you. Instead, those who want to be great among you must use their energies to serve, uplift, and bless the others. 27 Whoever wants the first position in God's kingdom must be a slave to the welfare of others, 28 just as the Son of Man did not come to be served but to serve the needs of humanity, and to give his life as the healing Remedy to set many free from their terminal state."

Mt 20:29 As Jesus and his disciples were leaving Jericho, they were followed by a large crowd. 30 Beside the road sat two blind men. When they heard that Jesus was passing by, they began shouting, "Son of David, have mercy on us!"

Mt 20:31 The crowd, rather than helping, scolded the blind men, telling them to be quiet. But they shouted all the louder, "Son of David, have mercy on us!"

Mt 20:32 Jesus stopped and called out to them, "What would you have me do for you?"

Mt 20:33 They answered eagerly, "Lord, we want to see!"

Mt 20:34 Jesus was merciful to them and touched their eyes. Immediately they were cured and could see, and they followed him.

21 When they neared Jerusalem, they came to Bethphage on the Mount of Olives, and Jesus sent two disciples ahead, 2 telling them, "Go to the village up ahead. You will find a donkey tied there with her colt. Untie them and bring them to me. 3 If anyone asks what you are doing, tell them that the Lord needs them, and they will send them immediately."

Mt 21:4 This was in fulfillment of what God's spokesman Zechariah had written:
5 "Get ready, children of Zion.
   Look, your king and deliverer is
      coming,
   riding gently on a donkey's colt."

Mt 21:6 The disciples followed Jesus' instruction and 7 brought the donkey and her colt. They placed their coats on them, and Jesus got on. 8 A huge crowd had gathered and spread their clothes on the road in front of Jesus, while others cut palm branches and spread them on the road. 9 The crowds running ahead and those all around him shouted, "Salvation through David's Son! Blessed is he who comes with the character of God! Salvation to the highest!"

Mt 21:10 When Jesus entered Jerusalem, the entire city was excited, and everyone was asking, "Who is this?"

Mt 21:11 Those with Jesus answered, "This is Jesus from Nazareth in Galilee, the messenger of God."

Mt 21:12 Jesus entered the temple stage and drove out all who were misrepresenting God—those who by buying and selling animals for sacrifice were failing to follow the healing script. He turned over the moneychangers' tables and the stands of those selling doves. 13 He said to them, "It is written: 'My house will be a place of prayer for everyone,' but you corrupt it and make it a house of extortion!" With all of this, he was announcing his mission to cleanse the true Temple—the Spirit Temple—from selfishness and greed.

Mt 21:14 The blind, sick, infirmed and crippled were not afraid and came to him at the temple, and he displayed God's plan by healing them all. 15 But when the theologians and church leaders saw the wonderful things he did, and heard the children shouting in the temple: "Salvation from David's Son!" they were outraged.

Mt 21:16 They confronted Jesus: "Do you hear what these children are saying? They are saying that you are the source of salvation!"

Jesus smiled and replied, "Have you never read the psalm, 'From the lips of children and babes comes truthful praise'?"

Mt 21:17 And he walked away and went out of Jerusalem to Bethany, where he spent the night.

Mt 21:18 Early the next morning, as Jesus was on his way back to Jerusalem, he was hungry. 19 He saw a fig tree along the road, and knowing that the fruit appears before the leaves, he went up to it to get some figs, but found nothing but leaves. Then he said, "This tree will never bear fruit!" and immediately the tree withered.

Mt 21:20 The disciples were stunned when they saw this and asked, "How did the fig tree wither so quickly?"

Mt 21:21 Jesus replied: "I tell you the plain truth: If you have genuine trust in God and don't doubt him or his methods, not only will a pretentious tree that has no fruit wither in your presence, but you won't need the Temple Mount to anchor your faith. You will be able to say to the mount, 'Go, off to the sea,' and it will happen. 22 If you ask God for help, and trust him to provide it, you will receive the answer to your prayers."

Mt 21:23 Jesus went up to the temple and was teaching in the court when the church leadership team, lawyers, and General Conference committee came to him. "Who has authorized you to carry out your ministry? On whose authority do you preach what you do?" they demanded.

Mt 21:24 Jesus calmly replied, "I'll ask you a question, and if you answer me, then I will tell you by what authority I carry out my ministry: 25 John's baptism — was it ordained of heaven, or was it merely of human origin?" The leaders huddled quickly to discuss their answer. They said among themselves, "If we admit his baptism is ordained of heaven, then he will ask us: 'Why don't you believe John's testimony of me?' 26 But if we say John's baptism is human in origin, the people will turn on us because they believe John was a representative and speaker from God."

Mt 21:27 So they evaded the answer by saying, "We don't know." Then Jesus said to them, "Neither will I tell you by what authority I conduct my ministry.

Mt 21:28 "Tell me what you think of this: A man with two sons told his first son, 'Go and work in the vineyard today.' 29 The son answered, 'No,' but after dad left, he changed his mind and went and worked in the vineyard. 30 Then the father went to his other son and told him to go and work in the vineyard. The second son said, 'Yes sir!' but did not go. 31 Which of the two sons actually did what the father wanted?"

"The first," they said.

Jesus looked straight at them and said: "I tell you the simple truth, it is just like this in God's kingdom: Tax collectors, prostitutes and other sinners —who start their lives by first saying 'No' to God, but then change their minds—will go into God's kingdom ahead of you who proclaim your willingness to do God's will but never actually live in harmony with God's design. 32 For John came to show you what 'right' is and what God's kingdom looks like, but you did not believe him, yet the tax collectors and prostitutes did. Even after you saw the healing power upon the lives of the tax collectors and prostitutes, you refused to change your ways, humble yourselves, and believe what John taught.

Mt 21:33 "Consider another parable: A developer planted a vineyard on his property. He put a security fence around it, built a watchtower, and constructed a winepress. Then he leased the vineyard to some farmers and went away on a trip. 34 When the harvest was due, he sent a servant to collect his portion of the fruit. 35 The farmers attacked the servants: they beat one, murdered another, and stoned a third. 36 The owner sent more servants, but they were all abused and despised in the same way. 37 Finally, he sent his only son, thinking, 'They will honor my son.' 38 But when the farmers saw the son, they greedily said to each other, 'This is the heir to this property. Come on, let's kill him and claim the inheritance for ourselves!' 39 So they grabbed the son, dragged him out of the vineyard, abused, and then killed him. 40 Now, what do you think the owner will do to these farmers when he comes to his vineyard?"

Mt 21:41 They answered, "He'll destroy those scoundrels and lease the vineyard to others, who will give him his portion of the harvest."

Mt 21:42 Jesus looked straight at them and said, "Exactly! But somehow, you fail to understand what you read in the Scripture where it says,

'The stone rejected by those in
    charge of building
    has become the foundation stone;
God has made sure
    it would be this way
    and it is incredible to us.'

Mt 21:43 "So let me make this plain to you: God's kingdom of love and truth will be taken away from you who cling to lies and selfishness, and given to those who will bring forth fruit of righteousness. 44 Whoever falls down on this stone will be broken in pieces of humility, but the weight of truth from this stone will crush whomever it falls upon."

Mt 21:45 When the church leaders, lawyers and theologians heard Jesus' parables, they understood very clearly that he was talking about them. 46 They schemed for ways to arrest him, but were afraid to take action because the crowds were huge, and the majority of people thought Jesus was a spokesman of God.

22 Jesus told them another parable: 2 "God's kingdom of love is like a king who prepared a wedding feast for his son. 3 When those who had received an invitation failed to come, he sent messengers asking them to come, but they refused.

Mt 22:4 "So he sent more messengers, instructing them, 'Tell those I invited that I have prepared a great banquet; the meats have been roasted and the tables set—the meal is ready. Come to the wedding feast.'

Mt 22:5 "But they ignored the messengers and went about their own interests: one went to supervise their fields, another to their business. 6 The rest of them attacked, beat, and killed his messengers. 7 The king was outraged and sent his soldiers to eliminate those murderers and burn their city.

Mt 22:8 "Then he instructed his messengers, 'The wedding feast is ready, but the ones I invited rejected the privilege and demonstrated themselves unfit. 9 Go out to the general public— anyone you can find—and bring them in.' 10 So the messengers fanned out across town and brought everyone they could find—whether sick or healthy— and the banquet hall was filled with guests.

Mt 22:11 "But when the king came in to visit with the guests, he noticed a guest who was not wearing the wedding garments the king had freely provided.

The Remedy

12 'Friend,' the king asked, 'how is it that you are here without wearing the wedding attire?' The guest had nothing to say.

Mt 22:13 "Then the king instructed his servants, 'Bind him over to his choice, put him out of the light into eternal darkness, where there will be terrible remorse and anguish of mind. 14 For many are invited, but few choose to accept.'"

Mt 22:15 Then the lawyers, theologians and religious leaders plotted to trap Jesus in his own words. 16 They sent to him their theology students, along with representatives of Herod's political party. Pretending to be deferential, they said, "Teacher, we know you are wise and always do what is right, constantly teaching the truth in harmony with God's methods and principles. You don't let the opinions of others influence you, because you stand for truth and not for what's popular at the moment. 17 Tell us then: In your opinion, is it right to pay taxes to Caesar or not?"

Mt 22:18 But Jesus wasn't fooled. He knew the evil in their hearts and that they plotted against him, so he said, "You connivers, do you think you're clever, trying to trap me? 19 Show me a coin used to pay taxes." So they brought him a Roman coin. 20 He asked them, "Whose picture is on this coin? And whose name is on it?"

Mt 22:21 "Caesar's," they said.

Jesus looked straight at them and said, "Then give to Caesar what belongs to Caesar and to God what belongs to God."

Mt 22:22 When they heard this, they were stunned and didn't know what else to say, so they left him and went away.

Mt 22:23 Later that day, the lawyers and theology professors from the school of the Sadducee—those who teach that there is no resurrection—came to question Jesus. 24 They asked:

"Wise Teacher, Moses instructed us that if a man dies without having children, then his brother is to marry the widow and have children for him. 25 Well, we recently had a situation involving seven brothers: The oldest married and died without having children, so his brother married the widow. 26 But he also died without having children, as did the third brother who married her, and the rest of them—right down to the seventh. 27 Eventually, the woman herself died. 28 Can you tell us, when the dead awaken to live again, whose wife will she be since she was married to all seven?"

Mt 22:29 Jesus answered without hesitation, "Your entire question is flawed, because you don't understand neither what Scripture teaches nor God's power and methods. 30 When those who sleep in the grave arise to life, it will be into God's heavenly kingdom, and they will be like the angels in heaven, who neither marry nor are given in marriage. 31 Regarding your speculation about the resurrection, you would have better conclusions if you remembered what God has said to you. 32 God says: 'I am'—not 'I was'—the God of Abraham, the God of Isaac, and the God of Jacob.' He is not the God of the dead—those who no longer exist—but the God of the living."

33 The crowds were absolutely astonished when they heard his teaching.

Mt 22:34 When the professors from the school of the Pharisees heard how Jesus had shut down the Sadducees, they put their heads together to come up with their own scheme to trap Jesus. 35 One of their Supreme Court lawyers attempted to trick him with a question about the law: 36 "Teacher, which is the greatest of all the commandments of God's Law?"

Mt 22:37 Jesus confidently said, "'Love the Lord your God with your entire being, heart, soul, and mind.' 38 This is the foundation upon which life exists and is therefore the first and greatest commandment. 39 And the second is the natural product of the first: 'Love others as yourself.' ⁴⁰ All God's laws—design protocols—and the teachings of God's spokespersons are built upon these two commandments."

Mt 22:41 When the lawyers and theology professors from the school of the Pharisees were gathered together, Jesus asked them, ⁴² "What do you think about the Messiah? Whose son is he?"

They answered instantly, "The son of David."

Mt 22:43 Jesus looked at them and asked, "Then how is it that David, inspired by the Spirit of God, calls him 'Lord'? For David says,

⁴⁴ 'The Lord said to my Lord:
"Sit on my right hand
until I place your enemies
under your feet."'

Mt 22:45 "So think about it: If David calls the Messiah 'Lord,' how can he be nothing more than his son born of natural descent?" ⁴⁶ Not one of those supposed experts on Scripture had a word to say, so from then on they didn't dare ask him any more of their trick questions.

23 Then Jesus said to the people and to his disciples: ² "The theology professors, church lawyers and pastors sit in the instructor's seat, like Moses, and know the history, ³ so listen carefully to all they teach. But think for yourselves and don't follow their example, for they don't understand the true meaning of what they teach, as evidenced by their failure to live in harmony with it. ⁴ They create man-made rules that discourage, exhaust, and weigh people down with religious rituals, fear, and guilt. They control people this way and refuse to relieve these false burdens.

Mt 23:5 "All their actions are designed for effect—to be seen—and they yearn to create a sense of admiration and respect for themselves: They make prayer beads and carry them for display, and wear special clothing meant to mark them as distinct; ⁶ they love to be recognized and honored wherever they

go, and especially they seek the highest exaltation in church. ⁷ They also love any attention they can get when people stop them in the shops or restaurants and call them Professor, Doctor, or Pastor.

Mt 23:8 "But don't let people idolize you, for you are all equals—learning the truth from the same Teacher. ⁹ And be sure you don't surrender your thinking to religious leaders—like young children do to their fathers—for you have one Father in heaven and you must surrender yourselves only to him. ¹⁰ Nor are you to claim to be the final authority on truth—determining what is right and wrong—like teachers are to their students, for you have the One true Teacher, the Messiah. ¹¹ So those who are truly the greatest will give the most of themselves in helping others. ¹² For whoever promotes self will destroy self, but whoever humbles self will experience healing and exaltation.

Mt 23:13 "Misery is yours, you who teach a legal religion, you penal theologians, you counterfeits! Your false teachings obstruct people from being healed and entering God's kingdom of love. You certainly are not healed and do not enter into salvation, but worse still, you actively work to prevent others, who want to be saved, from being healed. ¹⁴ Misery is yours, you who teach a legal religion, you penal theologians, you counterfeits! You con widows from their homes, yet you make public displays of praying long prayers. Unhealed you choose to remain! Your suffering will be most severe.

Mt 23:15 "Misery is yours, you who teach a legal religion, you penal theologians, you counterfeits! You go around the world trying to convert one person, and when you do, you indoctrinate them so deeply into your false penal system that they become twice the child of lies and selfishness as you are.

Mt 23:16 "Misery is yours, you irrational and unthinking teachers! Unbelievably, you say: 'If anyone swears by the temple, it doesn't count; but if anyone swears by the gold of the temple, then they are bound by the oath.' 17 You make no sense at all! Think about it: Which is truly most important — the gold, or the temple that makes the gold holy? 18 Another of your sayings is: 'If anyone swears by the altar, it doesn't count; but if anyone swears by the gift on the altar then they are bound by the oath.' 19 You don't understand the simplest truths! Think about it: Which is truly most important—the gift, or the altar that makes the gift holy? 20 Don't you get it? The one who swears by the altar swears by it and everything on it. 21 And whoever swears by the temple, swears by it and by the One whose dwelling place it is. 22 And oaths sworn before heaven are promises made before God's throne; and the One who sits on it knows the true intent of the heart.

Mt 23:23 "Misery is yours, you who teach a legal religion, you penal theologians, you counterfeits! You keep rules, such as proudly paying a pre-tax tithe and even giving a tenth of the herbs in your garden, but you fail to do what actually matters—to live in harmony with God's Law which is his design for life. You fail to 'do what is right because it is right.' You are not merciful but judgmental and critical, and you cannot be trusted to protect those struggling with sin. You should have lived lives of love for others, without neglecting the simple instructions of God. 24 You are truly irrational and unthinking teachers! You are so focused on keeping the rules—such as dietary laws—that you fail to understand that their purpose is to promote health. You're so confused that you actually think it would be a virtue to die of starvation rather than eat something not on the 'approved' list.

Mt 23:25 "Misery is yours, you who teach a legal religion, you penal theologians, you counterfeits! You work so hard to make yourselves look good on the outside, but the inside—the heart—is full of selfishness, arrogance, and greed. 26 You truly don't understand anything about God's kingdom! The mind, the character, the heart—they all must be cleansed first, and then the outside will also be clean.

Mt 23:27 "Misery is yours, you who teach a legal religion, you penal theologians, you counterfeits! You are like highly polished burial vaults: they look beautiful on the outside but inside are nothing but the bones of the dead, and everything that defiles. 28 You are just like that. On the outside you appear to people as good and righteous, but on the inside you are full of lies, selfishness, and evil. You are great counterfeits!

Mt 23:29 "Misery is yours, you who teach a legal religion, you penal theologians, you counterfeits! You go to great lengths to give praise and honor to God's spokespersons and church leaders of the past. 30 You say, 'If we would have lived back then, we would never have rejected God's spokespersons or joined those who killed them.' 31 By such claims you condemn yourselves, because you acknowledge such actions as wrong, yet by your actions today you reveal you are the true descendants of those who murdered God's spokespersons. You're just like them, 32 and your sins pile on top of the sins of your forefathers!

Mt 23:33 "You slippery serpents! You brood of venomous vipers! You think you can cure yourselves with your own snake oil? 34 It's because of your false remedy—your penal legal trickery—that I am sending my spokespersons, instructors and Bible scholars, some of whom you will attack, kill, and crucify; others you will beat—some physically, some verbally—right in church, running them out of town with beatings and the most vicious gossip. 35 The pure and holy lives that have been sacrificed through history—from Abel all the way through to Zechariah the son of Berekiah, who was murdered right in church, at the altar—testify the truth to you. 36 But the sad truth is that this generation will reject all this evidence.

Mt 23:37 "O Jerusalem, Jerusalem, you sick and hard-hearted people who have rejected the Remedy, killed God's spokespersons, and stoned those sent to you with the cure! How my heart has longed to pull you to safety, like a hen gathers her chicks under her wings, but you would not let me. 38 Look around: I leave your house to you abandoned without Remedy, and infected without cure. 39 For I tell you plainly, when you see me next, you will say: 'He is the One sent by God to reveal God's true character and provide the Remedy.'"

24 As Jesus was walking away from the temple, his disciples caught up to him and pointed with great admiration toward the beauty and majesty of the temple. 2 Jesus said to them, "Do you see this entire temple complex? I tell you now, not one stone will remain upon another. The entire complex will be turned to rubble."

Mt 24:3 Later, when Jesus was sitting on the Mount of Olives alone, the disciples came to him and asked, "Tell us, when will the temple be destroyed and what will be the warning signs of your return and of the end of this age?"

Mt 24:4 Jesus answered: "Be careful to think for yourselves so that no one fools you, 5 for over the years, there will be many people who arise claiming they come from me, or represent me, or even claiming they are 'the Messiah, Christ returned.' And many who don't think for themselves will be taken in by their charisma. 6 Before the end, there will be wars and murmurings of war, but don't be afraid: such things will happen; but the end comes later.

7 Nation will rise against nation, and kingdom will war against kingdom. Nature will suffer as famines, earthquakes, and other natural disasters occur around the world; 8 but just as a woman in labor experiences birth pains

that increase in intensity and frequency right up until delivery, so too these events are just the beginning of the labor pains.

Mt 24:9 "You will be abused, rejected, tortured and executed, and you will be hated throughout the world because of me. 10 During the time of persecution, many will lose heart and reject me and my methods, and even betray and hate each other and their family and friends. 11 Many false teachers and fraudulent spokespersons of God will appear and deceive vast numbers of people. 12 Because selfishness and wickedness will increase, the love of most people will grow cold, 13 but all those who stay faithful, practicing my methods of truth and love until the end, will be saved. 14 And the good news of the kingdom of love will be preached throughout the entire world — to all peoples — to provide evidence of God's true character and methods; and then the end will come.

Mt 24:15 "So when you see 'the abomination that causes desolation'—spoken of by Daniel—occupying the holy place, understand this: 16 Those who are in Judea should flee to the mountains. 17 Don't waste time trying to gather your things, but leave immediately. 18 If you're outside, flee; don't even go inside for a coat. 19 It will be a horrible time, especially for pregnant women and nursing mothers! 20 Pray that you will not have to flee in the winter or on the Sabbath, 21 for that time of trouble will be the worst the world has ever seen, or will ever see. 22 If God didn't intervene to stop it, no one would live through it; but for the sake of those who have partaken of the Remedy, God will shorten those troubled times.

23 At that time in history, if anyone proclaims, 'Look, the Messiah or Savior is here!' or 'There is the Savior!'—don't believe it, 24 for false messiahs and false apostles will appear around the world —some even performing miraculous signs in order to deceive those who

don't think for themselves. Their counterfeit will be so close to the true that it will almost dupe those who have partaken of the Remedy. 25 So remember that I have warned you before it happens: Be prepared! 26 If anyone tells you, 'The Messiah is in wilderness near Palestine,' don't go there; or 'The Savior can be found in secret meetings,' or 'His coming is a secret event' — don't believe it. 27 For the coming of the Son of Man will be visible to the entire world, just like sunlight dawns in the east and shines to the west, covering the entire planet. 28 You can be certain that you will not find the Son of Man where people seek to speak with the dead. Think of vultures eating corpses, for that is what's happening there.

Mt 24:29 "As soon as those days of trouble are over, 'light from the sun and moon will no longer be seen as evidence of God's creatorship, but their light will be darkened by evolutionism. The stars in heaven will be disregarded as evidence of the Creator, and the power of heaven will be shaken out of the land and out of the hearts of people.'[2]

Mt 24:30 "At that time, the Son of Man will appear in the sky: Everyone will see him, and all the nations of this selfish world will be grief-stricken. They will see the Son of Man arriving amongst the clouds of the sky, with the unveiled power and splendor of infinite love

and truth. 31 And with the loud blast of a trumpet, he will direct his angels to gather all those who have partaken of the Remedy, from the entire world— from one end of the globe to the other.

Mt 24:32 "So apply what you know about the fig tree: When the buds form and leaves sprout, you know that summer is near. 33 Likewise, when all of these things transpire, realize that the end is very near — the Son of Man is right at the door. 34 I tell you the truth, this sinful race will not pass away until all these things happen. 35 This atmosphere and the earth's surface will pass away, but what I have said will not be passed by.

Mt 24:36 "No one knows the day or hour when the end will occur: not the angels in heaven, not even the Son; only the Father knows. 37 When the Son of Man returns, the condition on earth will be similar to that at the time of Noah. 38 When the world was about to be destroyed by flood, people ignored all the warning signs: they were caught up in their routines—working to put food and drink on the table, marrying and planning for their families' future— right up until Noah entered the ark and the door was shut. 39 They were so focused on themselves and their routines that they were unaware of what was about to happen, until the flood came and swept them all away. That is how people will be when the Son of Man returns. 40 There will be two men working at their job: one will have taken the Remedy and be ready to go to heaven, the other—won't. 41 Likewise, there will be women who work together: some will have taken the Remedy and be ready to go to heaven, while others will not.

Mt 24:42 "Therefore stay vigilant. Don't become complacent, because you do not know the day your Lord will return. 43 You do understand that if a homeowner knew when a thief was going to break into his home, he would be ready and not caught unaware. 44 So, you too must keep alert, stay aware and be

---

[2] This rendering is clearly interpretive, intended to cause the reader to think. Which sign would be more helpful to God's people on earth: a single day in which—in one small section of the globe—the sun and moon darken, and some years later there is a meteor shower (as some Christian groups suggest), or a global change in the minds of people, in which God's celestial beacons marking His Creatorship are cast aside? But for those preferring a more traditional reading, this is alternative rendering: "As soon as those events are over, 'the sun and moon will no longer give their normal light, stars will fall from the sky, and the power of heaven will be shaken.'"

ready, because the Son of Man will return at a time when he is least expected.

Mt 24:45 "Who then is qualified to share the Remedy and nurture the master's staff? Whom will the master trust with this duty? An aide who understands the situation, loves the master, and faithfully carries out their responsibilities. 46 It will be the most awesome experience for that aide when the master returns to find them reliably doing so. 47 Truly, that aide will be trusted with all of their master's possessions. 48 But what if one of the master's aides is self-centered and says to themself: 'The master has been gone a long time; who knows when he will return?' 49 and rather than nurturing the staff, they berate, abuse and mislead them, and then go and use the master's resources to party with gluttons and drunkards? 50 That aide will be totally surprised—caught completely unaware—on the day their master returns. 51 The master will let that wicked aide go: their relationship shredded, that aide will be outcast with all the other counterfeits and frauds who have peddled false remedies. For them, there is only pain, suffering. and death.

25 "At that time in earth's history, God's people on earth will be like ten undefiled bridesmaids who took their lamps and went out into the dark world to meet the bridegroom. 2 While all ten were sincere students of the Word, only five were wise; the other five were foolish. 3 The five foolish went out into the dark world with their lamps of God's Word, but they didn't fill themselves with the oil of the Holy Spirit. 4 The wise, however, not only carried their lamps of God's Word but also filled the jars of their hearts with the Holy Spirit. 5 The bridegroom took much longer in coming than they expected, and all ten bridesmaids became drowsy and fell asleep.

Mt 25:6 "In the middle of the night, a loud cry was heard: 'The bridegroom is here! Come and meet him!'

Mt 25:7 "All ten bridesmaids awoke and started to prepare their lamps to shine brightly, 8 but the foolish ones realized they could not prepare without the oil of the Holy Spirit. They looked to the five wise ones and said, 'Give us some of your oil; our light is going out.'

Mt 25:9 "But the five wise said, 'We can't! The oil of the Spirit that enables us to shine brightly is only provided in a sufficient quantity for each lamp. You must go to the source yourselves and get your own supply.'

Mt 25:10 "While the foolish ones were out searching for oil, the bridegroom arrived. The five bridesmaids who were prepared went in to the reception with him, and the door was closed tightly.

Mt 25:11 "Later, the foolish ones came banging on the door, shouting, 'Master, let us in!'

Mt 25:12 "But he replied, 'The truth is, you're not my friends; I don't know you.'

Mt 25:13 "So stay alert and be vigilant, because you don't know when the Lord will return.

Mt 25:14 "Similarly, it will be like a man who takes a trip; but before he leaves, he turns over his property to his assistants to maintain, invest and develop for him. 15 He gives five thousand dollars to one, two thousand to another, and one thousand to a third, entrusting each with the amount appropriate to their experience and ability. Then he leaves on his trip. 16 The assistant who received five thousand dollars immediately invested the funds and gained five thousand more. 17 Likewise, the one who received two thousand dollars gained two thousand more. 18 But the assistant who had received one thousand dollars did not use what they received but neglected it, burying it in the ground.

Mt 25:19 "After being gone a long time, the master finally returned and assessed how well the assistants had done with the resources entrusted to them. 20 The one who had received five thousand dollars brought the other five thousand and said, 'Master, you entrusted me with five thousand dollars, and I am happy to report that I have gained another five thousand.'

Mt 25:21 "The master smiled and said, 'Excellent! You have done very well and are a trustworthy and reliable assistant! You have handled well the few things I entrusted to you; I will trust you with much more. Come and enjoy partnership with me!'

Mt 25:22 "The assistant who had received two thousand dollars came and said, "Master, you entrusted me with two thousand dollars, and I have gained two thousand more.'

Mt 25:23 "The master smiled and said, 'Excellent! You have done very well and are a trustworthy and reliable assistant! You have handled well the few things I entrusted to you; I will trust you with much more. Come and enjoy partnership with me!'

Mt 25:24 "Then the assistant who had received one thousand dollars came and said, "Master, from what I know about you, you are a harsh man, taking from people what is not yours, and expecting payments to appease your anger. 25 I was afraid of you, and terrified to disappoint you and lose your money, so I hid it in a hole in the ground. See, here is your one thousand dollars that has never been used.'

Mt 25:26 "The master was saddened and said, 'Your mind is filled with wicked lies about me, and you were too lazy to discover the truth. But if you thought that I was harsh and take from people what is not mine, and that I expect payment to assuage my wrath, 27 then why did you not at least put my money in a bank so that you could give it back to me with interest?'

Mt 25:28 "'Take the one thousand dollars from this wicked assistant and give it to the one who has ten thousand, 29 for everyone who uses what they have will develop more. But whoever doesn't use what they have will lose it, for if you don't use it you lose it. 30 Send that useless assistant out into the darkness, where there is no remedy but only pain, suffering and death.'

Mt 25:31 "When the Son of Man comes again in his unveiled fiery glory, all his angels will be with him, and he will sit upon his throne in heavenly splendor. 32 All humanity will come before him, and he will separate the healed—those who have partaken of the Remedy—from the unhealed as easily as a shepherd separates sheep from goats. 33 He will put the healed on his right and the unhealed on his left.

Mt 25:34 "Then the King will gladly say to those on his right, 'Come home, you who have been healed by my Father; receive your inheritance—the kingdom of love—designed for you at the creation of the world. 35 For you lived in harmony with my kingdom of love: I was hungry and you fed me; I was thirsty and you gave me drink; I was a stranger and you invited me home; 36 I didn't have clothing and you clothed me; I was sick and you took care of me; I was in prison and you visited me.'

Mt 25:37 "Then the healed, whose hearts are right with God's kingdom of love, will answer the King, 'Lord, what are you talking about? When did we see you hungry and feed you, or thirsty and give you drink? 38 When were you a stranger to us, or without clothes, that we needed to clothe you? 39 When did we ever nurse you when sick or visit you in prison?'

Mt 25:40 "The King will smile and say, 'The truth of my kingdom of love is this: Whatever love you gave to the least of my family on earth, you gave it to me.'

Mt 25:41 "Then the King will say to the unhealed—those on his left, whose hearts remain embittered with fear and selfishness: 'You have what you've chosen: Depart from me, you who are terminal, doomed by your own condition; your end is eternal fire prepared to consume evil. 42 For I was hungry and you let me starve; I was thirsty and you let me thirst; 43 I was a stranger and you left me on the street; I needed clothes and you gave me none; I was sick and you let me suffer; I was in prison and you let me be abused.'

Mt 24:44 "They will be shocked and protest, 'Lord, it isn't so! We never mistreated you. When did we fail to feed you, or give you drink, or invite you home, or provide you clothing, or nurse you when sick, or help you in prison?'

Mt 25:45 "The King will reply, 'The truth of my kingdom of love is this: Whatever you did not do for one of the least of my earthly family, you did not do for me.'

Mt 25:46 "Then they will pass away for all eternity, but the healed—those whose hearts are in harmony with God's kingdom of love—will receive eternal life."

26 After Jesus finished explaining these things to the disciples, he looked at them and said, 2 "Know that in two days, during the Passover, the Son of Man will be turned over to be crucified."

Mt 26:3 The theologians, senior pastors, priests and local politicians met at the offices of Caiaphas the high priest. 4 Together they plotted how they could arrest and kill Jesus without the people finding out. 5 They said, "We can't do it during the Passover or the people might riot against us."

Mt 26:6 When Jesus was in Bethany, he attended a feast at the home of Simon the Leper. 7 During the feast, a woman approached him with an extremely expensive bottle of perfume and anointed his head while he was lounging at the table.

Mt 26:8 Immediately the smell permeated the room and drew the disciples' attention. When they realized what she had done, they expressed outrage: "What a waste of resources! 9 This woman is an opportunist, trying to make herself look good with such an extravagant gift;

if she cared about others, she would have sold the perfume and donated the money to our 'homeless' fund!"

Mt 26:10 Jesus intervened: "Why do you criticize this woman? She has beautifully expressed her love for me. 11 When I am gone, the poor will still be here for you to help, but I will not be here much longer. 12 She knows this, and has poured this perfume on me to prepare my body for burial.

13 The truth is, wherever the Remedy is taken throughout the world, what she has done will be told in honor of her love for me."

Mt 26:14 Then Judas Iscariot, one of the Twelve, snuck off to the church leaders — those plotting against Jesus — 15 and asked, "What will you pay me if I betray him to you?" They eagerly paid him thirty silver coins. 16 From that moment on, Judas looked for the best opportunity to hand Jesus over to them.

Mt 26:17 It was the first day of the Feast of Unleavened Bread when the disciples asked Jesus where he wanted them to prepare to eat the Passover.

Mt 26:18 He instructed them to go into the city, find a specific man, and say to him: "The Teacher says, 'The time appointed for me to complete my mission is here. I am going to celebrate the Passover with my disciples at your house.'" 19 The disciples did as Jesus instructed, and made ready for the Passover.

Mt 26:20 That evening, while reclining at the Passover table with the Twelve, 21 Jesus said, "The sad truth is, one of you will betray me and turn me over to the church leaders who plan to kill me."

Mt 26:22 The disciples were stunned and very sad, and began to ask him, one after the other, "It isn't me, is it, Lord?"

Mt 26:23 Jesus said, "It is the one who puts his hand into the bowl when I do. He will betray me. 24 The Son of Man will go quietly, just as the Scriptures foretold, but horrible will it be for the one of you who betrays the Son of Man! It really would have been better for

The Remedy

39

him had he never been born."

Mt 26:25 Then Judas, the one who already accepted money to betray him, asked, "Surely, it isn't me, Master?"

Jesus looked him in the eye and said, "Yes, Judas, it is you."

Mt 26:26 While they were eating the meal, Jesus took some of the unleavened bread and thanked his Father, then broke it and gave it to his disciples, telling them, "Eat this, for it is symbolic of my body."

Mt 26:27 Then Jesus took the cup of unfermented wine and thanked his Father, then passed it to them, telling them, "Drink from it, all of you. 28 This is symbolic of the Remedy of which you must partake: my perfect life which is poured out for many, so that sin—fear and selfishness—in the character of human beings might remit. 29 And know this: I will not drink this wine again until the day we all drink it together in my Father's kingdom."

Mt 26:30 Then, after they sang a hymn, they went out to the Mount of Olives.

Mt 26:31 Trying to prepare them for the coming ordeal, Jesus said, "Tonight, every one of you will be ashamed of me and run away, for the Scripture says: 'Attack the shepherd, and the flock will scatter.'

Mt 26:32 "But after I have risen from the dead, I will go to Galilee before you."

Mt 26:33 Peter protested, "Master, rest assured that even if all the others run and hide, pretending they don't know you, I never will!"

Mt 26:34 With a sad smile, Jesus answered, "Peter, the sad truth is that tonight, before sunrise, before the rooster crows, you will deny knowing me—three times."

Mt 26:35 But Peter persisted, "No way! I would rather die than deny knowing you!" And then the other disciples mumbled their agreement.

Mt 26:36 Jesus led his disciples to a place called Gethsemane, and told them, "Stay here while I go over there and talk with my Father." 37 He took with him Peter and the two sons of Zebedee, James and John. His heart became overwhelmed with sadness and pain. 38 He told them, "I'm dying. The pain is overwhelming. I have never hurt so badly. My heart is breaking. Please, stay close by and watch with me."

Mt 26:39 Then Jesus went a little farther into the garden and fell down with his face on the ground, and cried out, "Papa, it hurts. Please, Papa, if there is any other way, take this cup from me. Yet, Father, not as my feelings desire, but let your will be done. Your will is what I choose."

Mt 26:40 When he returned to his disciples, he found them all asleep. Looking at Peter, he said, "Were you not able to stay alert and watch with me for one hour? 41 Please, stay alert and guard your mind with prayer, so you won't fall when tempted. Your heart desires to do right, but your body is frail and weak."

Mt 26:42 Then Jesus went to pray a second time: "Papa, if there is no other way to achieve the Remedy except I drink this bitter cup, I accept. Your perfect will be done."

Mt 26:43 When he came back to his disciples, he again found them asleep, for they were very tired. 44 He let them sleep and returned to talk with his Father a third time, and again committed himself to achieve the Remedy.

Mt 26:45 When he returned to his disciples, he found them still asleep, and said to them, "Are you still napping? Wake up, it is time: The Son of Man is betrayed into the hands of the selfish.

Mt 26:46 "Get up, let's get going! Here comes my betrayer!"

Mt 26:47 Before Jesus finished what he was saying, Judas—one of the Twelve—walked up. A large crowd sent by the church leaders and local politicians was with him, and they were armed with clubs and swords. 48 The betrayer had arranged a signal for the mob: "The person I kiss is the one; arrest him." 49 Judas went to Jesus and said, "Teacher, how good to see you!" and kissed him on a cheek.

Mt 26:50 With compassion, Jesus said, "Friend, do what you came to do."

Then they grabbed Jesus and arrested him. [51] But one of Jesus' disciples pulled his sword and attacked, cutting off the ear of the servant of the high priest.

Mt 26:52 But Jesus quickly intervened, saying, "Stop! Put your sword away. Everyone who uses weapons on others will be destroyed by the use of weapons. [53] Think about it: Don't you realize that I could call upon my Father and have more than twelve divisions of angels here to fight on my behalf? [54] But if I did that, then how would the Scripture—which foretells that all of this must happen in order to achieve the Remedy—be fulfilled?"

Mt 26:55 Jesus looked to the mob and said, "Do you think I am some terrorist trying to evade the authorities that you come here at night with clubs and swords to capture me? Day after day I sat openly in the temple courts teaching, and you didn't arrest me. [56] But this is happening exactly as the writings of God's spokespersons foretold." Then all his disciples ran away.

Mt 26:57 After they arrested Jesus, they took him to Caiaphas the high priest, where the lawyers, local politicians, theologians and church leaders had gathered. [58] Peter stayed back, following discretely at a safe distance, but eased right up to the courtyard of the high priest. He quietly snuck in and sat down near the guards to watch what was happening.

Mt 26:59 The senior pastors, church board and religious lawyers were scrambling to fabricate false evidence against Jesus in order to justify executing him. [60] But they couldn't find anything against him, even though many paid informants and false witnesses were interviewed. Finally, two witnesses came forward [61] and proclaimed, "This man said, 'I can destroy the temple of God and rebuild it in three days.'"

Mt 26:62 Frustrated, Caiaphas stood up and confronted Jesus, saying, "Aren't you going to say anything? Don't you have an answer to the testimony these men have brought against you?" [63] But Jesus didn't say a word. The high priest, not knowing what else to do, said to Jesus, "I place you under an oath by the living God: Tell us plainly, are you the Messiah, the Son of God?"

Mt 26:64 Jesus, with calm nobility, said clearly, "Yes, it is exactly as you have said. But I tell all of you now that in the future you will see the Son of Man sitting on the right hand of the Almighty God and coming in the clouds of heaven."

Mt 26:65 Instantly, in a feigned display of horror, the high priest tore his clothes and said, "He has spoken sacrilege and profaned the name of God! What need is there for any more witnesses when you have heard blasphemy from his own mouth? [66] What is your verdict?"

"He deserves to die!" they shouted.

Mt 26:67 Then they pounced upon him: they spat on him, punched him, slapped him and abused him. [68] They mocked him, saying, "Tell us, O Messiah, who hit you?"

Mt 26:69 As Peter was sitting in the courtyard watching, a servant girl saw him and said, "I recognize you. You're one of the followers of Jesus of Galilee."

Mt 26:70 But he turned to them all and instantly denied it: "I don't know what you're talking about."

Mt 26:71 He quickly moved away to the gate, but another girl saw him and said to the crowd, "This man was with Jesus of Nazareth. He's one of his followers."

Mt 26:72 This time Peter gave an oath in his denial: "I swear I don't know the man!"

Mt 26:73 A short while later, the people standing nearby went up to Peter and said, "Don't fool with us; you are one of his followers. You speak just like he does."

Mt 26:74 Then Peter began to speak street slang with vulgar curses, and swore again: "I don't know the man!" At that very moment, a rooster crowed. 75 Peter remembered what Jesus had said: "Before the rooster crows, you will deny me three times." Horrified by what he had done, he ran away and cried so hard he wanted to die.

27 In the early hours of the morning, before dawn, the senior pastors, theologians and local politicians who gathered to condemn Jesus came to a unanimous decision to put him to death. 2 So they tied his hands and took him to Pilate, the Roman governor.

Mt 27:3 Judas, who betrayed him, had been watching; and when he saw that Jesus didn't deliver himself but surrendered and was sentenced to death, he regretted that his scheme to force Jesus to take the throne didn't work. He gave the thirty silver coins back to the senior pastors and local politicians, telling them, 4 "I was wrong! I betrayed an innocent man!"

But they looked at him with contempt and said, "Who cares!? That's your problem!"

Mt 27:5 So Judas threw the money into the temple and fled. He then went and hanged himself.

Mt 27:6 The senior pastors collected the coins and said to each other, "We follow the law, and our law won't allow blood money to go into the temple treasury." 7 So they used the money to buy a potter's field to use as a cemetery for foreigners. 8 That is why, even to this day, it is called "Blood Field." 9 It was in fulfillment of what Jeremiah foretold: "They used thirty silver coins to buy the honor of him who could be bought with a price by some of Israel's descendants, 10 and bought a potter's field, just as the Lord foretold."

Mt 27:11 When Jesus arrived before the Roman governor, the governor asked him, "Are you the king of the Jews?"

Jesus answered directly, "Your words, not mine."

Mt 27:12 The senior pastors, theologians and local politicians shouted various accusations at Jesus, but he didn't respond to anything they said. 13 So Pilate looked at him and asked, "Do you hear what they are saying about you, and the charges they are making against you?" 14 But Jesus remained silent, not answering even one charge against him. The governor was stunned by his calm and dignified demeanor.

Mt 27:15 During Passover, it was the custom of the Roman governor to release one prisoner chosen by the people. 16 At that time, they had a serial killer in prison, named Barabbas. 17 Pilate had both Barabbas and Jesus brought before the mob that had gathered, and asked, "Which one do you want me to release: the serial killer Barabbas, or Jesus who is called Messiah?" 18 Pilate did this because he knew that it was out of jealousy and petty envy that they'd brought Jesus to him, seeking his execution.

Mt 27:19 While Pilate was still deliberating his judgment, he received a message from his wife, saying: "Don't be tricked into judging this innocent man, for all night I have been distraught over a dream I had about him."

Mt 27:20 But the senior pastors, theologians and local leaders persuaded the mob to shout for Barabbas and demand that Jesus be executed.

Mt 27:21 "Which of these two men do you want released?" Pilate asked.

"Barabbas!" they shouted.

Mt 27:22 "Then what would you have done with Jesus who is called Messiah?" the governor asked.

They screamed, "Crucify him!"

Mt 27:23 "Why? What has he done wrong?" Pilate asked.

But they screamed over and over again, "Crucify him!"

Mt 27:24 When Pilate saw that the mob was not listening, that their agitation was escalating, and that things were getting out of control, he took water and washed his hands in front of the crowd, saying: "I wash my hands of responsibility for the death of this man. Let his death be on you. It is your responsibility!"

Mt 27:25 All the people shouted, "Let the blame fall on us and on our children after us!"

Mt 27:26 So Pilate released Barabbas to the mob, and had Jesus flogged and handed over to be crucified.

Mt 27:27 The Roman soldiers shoved Jesus into the courtyard of the government building, and the entire garrison surrounded him. 28 They stripped off his clothes and put a red-colored robe on him, 29 and then made a crown out of thorns and crammed it onto his head. They put a rod in his right hand and then mocked him by kneeling down in front of him, saying, "Hail, O King of the Jews!" 30 They spat in his face and beat him with the staff, striking him on the head repeatedly. 31 After they made fun of him and derided him, they pulled off the robe, put his own clothes back on him and took him to be crucified.

Mt 27:32 When they were leaving the government house, they came across Simon from Cyrene, and the soldiers forced him to carry the cross. 33 They arrived at Golgotha (which means 'the hill that looks like a skull'). 34 They offered Jesus an anesthetic made of wine and gall, but after tasting it, he refused to drink it, as he didn't want anything to dull his mind. 35 After they had nailed him to the cross, the soldiers threw dice to see who got his clothing, 36 and then sat down to guard the area. 37 On the cross, above his head, they placed a sign citing the charge against him:

THIS IS JESUS, THE KING OF THE JEWS

38 Two thieves were crucified with him, one on each side. 39 The people who passed by cursed him, called him names and ridiculed him, 40 saying, "You thought you were going to destroy the temple and rebuild it in three days. Look at yourself: You can't even save your own life! Save yourself if you are so great! Come on, come down off the cross and show us how great you are. You are the Son of God, aren't you?"

Mt 27:41 The senior pastors, theologians, lawyers and local politicians mocked him in the same way: 42 "He saved others, but look, he isn't anything special—he can't even save himself! If he's going to be Israel's king, then let him come down from the cross and we will believe him. Save yourself and we will believe you! 43 He claims he trusts God; well then, let God rescue him now if God thinks he is innocent. Remember, this fellow had the audacity to say, 'I am the Son of God.'" 44 And the thieves also verbally accosted him, cursed him and mocked him, tempting him to save himself.

Mt 27:45 From noon until three o'clock in the afternoon, a thick darkness fell over the countryside around the cross. 46 Around three in the afternoon, Jesus cried out in a loud voice, *"Eloi, Eloi, lama sabachthani?"* (which means, "My God, my God, why have you let go of me and given me up?")

Mt 27:47 But some of those standing around the cross misunderstood what Jesus had said. They commented, "He's calling for God's spokesman Elijah."

Mt 27:48 One of the bystanders quickly soaked a sponge in the wine vinegar anesthetic and offered it to Jesus to drink. 49 But the rest were more cruel and said, "Leave him alone! He called for Elijah; let's see if Elijah saves him."

Mt 27:50 But Jesus cried out one last time and gave up his life.

Mt 27:51 At that very moment, the inner curtain of the temple was ripped open from the top to the bottom. There was a great earthquake, and rocks broke apart. 52 Graves ruptured open and the bodies of many people who trusted God were raised to life. 53 They came out of the graves, alive, and after Jesus' resurrection, they went into Jerusalem and witnessed to many people.

Mt 27:54 When the captain of the Roman

soldiers and those guarding Jesus saw the earthquake and all that happened, they were scared nearly to death. Trembling all over, they said, "He really was the Son of God!"

Mt 27:55 Some distance away, there was a group of women who had followed Jesus from Galilee in order to care for him. 56 Among these were Mary Magdalene, Mary the mother of James and Joseph, and the mother of Zebedee's sons.

Mt 27:57 As sunset was approaching, Joseph of Arimathea—a rich man who had partaken of the Remedy and trusted Jesus—came to the cross. 58 He went to Pilate and asked for the body of Jesus, and Pilate ordered that it be given to him. 59 Joseph reverently wrapped the body in clean white linen, 60 and laid it in his own, brand new tomb he had carved in the rock. Then he rolled a large stone over the entrance and left. 61 Mary Magdalene and the other Mary stayed by, sitting across from the tomb.

Mt 27:62 On Sabbath—the day after Preparation Day—the senior pastors and church lawyers went to Pilate. 63 "Your honor," they said, "we just remembered that this conman said: 'I will arise from the dead on the third day.' 64 We suspect his disciples will try to steal his body and claim to the people that he has risen from the dead, creating an even greater deception than his claim to be king. So, we request that you order a guard to secure the tomb until three days are past."

Mt 27:65 Pilate, disgusted with their political intrigue, said, "Fine! Take a guard and make the grave as secure as you know how."

Mt 27:66 So they posted a guard at the tomb and put a seal on the stone.

28

When the Sabbath was over, early on Sunday, as dawn approached, Mary Magdalene and the other Mary went to visit the tomb. Mt 28:2 Suddenly, there was a powerful earthquake, for an angel of God came down from heaven, went to the tomb, rolled back the stone blocking the entrance, and then sat on the stone. 3 The angel radiated light like lightening, and his clothing was an intense white—whiter than snow. 4 The guards were so terrified that their hands and knees shook; and then they passed out.

Mt 28:5 The angel turned to the women and said, "Don't be frightened. I know you are here looking for Jesus who was murdered on a cross. 6 You'll be happy to know that he is no longer here, for—just as he told you—he has arisen from the dead. Come and see for yourselves: the tomb where he was placed is empty. 7 Go as quickly as you can and tell his disciples: 'Jesus is alive. He has risen from the dead and is going ahead of you into Galilee. Go there and you will see him for yourselves.' Now I have told you what you need to know."

Mt 28:8 The women ran away from the tomb as fast as they could. They were excited and trembling with joy as they rushed to find the disciples.

9 Unexpectedly, Jesus appeared to them and said, "Good morning!" They fell down before him, grabbed hold of his feet and worshipped him. 10 Jesus smiled and said, "Don't be frightened. Go and tell my friends — those tied to me by the bonds of brotherly love — to go to Galilee, and I will meet them there."

Mt 28:11 While the women were on their way to tell the disciples, some of the guards recovered and then went into the city and reported to the senior pastors and church lawyers all that had happened at the tomb. 12 When the church leadership met with the local politicians, they scrambled to figure a way out for themselves. They decided to bribe the soldiers with large sums of money. 13 They proposed, "Here is what we want you to do: Tell the people, 'We fell asleep, and while we were sleeping, his disciples came and stole the body.' 14 Don't worry. If the governor hears about this, we will speak to him and you won't get into trouble." [15] So the soldiers took the bribe and told the lie the church leaders gave them. And this false account has spread widely among the Jews and is still told today.

Mt 28:16 The eleven disciples went to the mountain in Galilee, where Jesus had instructed them to go. [17] When they saw him, they poured their hearts out in worship and adoration to him; but some had doubts that this was really Jesus. [18] Then Jesus walked up to them and said, "All authority in heaven and on earth has been given to me. [19] So go and spread the Remedy to the entire world: Teach the people of every nation, immersing their hearts and minds into the character and methods of the Father and of the Son and the Holy Spirit, [20] and teach them to live in harmony with the law of love—the design protocols upon which life is built—exactly as I have instructed you. And you can be sure that I am always with you—all the way, right through to the very end of time."

Mark

1 The Remedy originated with Jesus Christ, God's Son.

Mk 1:2 God's spokesman Isaiah wrote:

"I will send my herald before you,
who will prepare the people for
your arrival.

3 A voice calling in a dark and
desolate land:

'Prepare your minds, untwist your
hearts, and make ready for the Lord
to come with his healing Remedy.'"

Mk 1:4 And so John arrived, immersing people in water in a desolate region, and preaching, "Immerse your minds into truth and love, and turn away from lies and selfishness so that your sinful hearts can be healed." 5 Huge crowds of people from all over Judea and Jerusalem flocked to John, and confessing their sinfulness, they were immersed by him in water in the Jordan River. 6 John was dressed in a camel hair cloak tied with a leather belt, and he ate locust and honey found in the wild. 7 He proclaimed, "The One coming after me is so awesome that I am not even worthy to tie his shoes. 8 I only immerse you in water, but he will immerse your minds and characters in the Holy Spirit."

Mk 1:9 Then Jesus, having come from Nazareth in Galilee, walked up, and John immersed him in the Jordan. 10 As Jesus was stepping out of the river, he saw the fabric of reality torn open, and the Holy Spirit come through, settled down upon him in the form of a dove, 11 and a voice from heaven was heard: "You are my Son, and I love you. You please me in every way."

Mk 1:12 Immediately the Spirit directed him into the desert 13 to do battle with Satan and overcome his temptations. The battle lasted forty days, and he was alone in the wild with the animals, but angels watched over him.

Mk 1:14 After John was imprisoned, Jesus went to Galilee and began preaching the good news about God's kingdom of love: 15 "Now is the time the prophets foretold, for God's kingdom of love is being established on earth. Turn away from the selfishness of the world and believe the good news about God's kingdom of love!"

Mk 1:16 When Jesus was walking on the shore of the Sea of Galilee, he saw two brothers—Simon and Andrew, who were fishermen—casting their net in the lake. 17 Jesus called to them, "Come and follow me, and I will teach you how to fish people out of the sea of sorrow and sin and pull them into the kingdom of God!" 18 Without hesitation, they dropped their nets and followed Jesus.

Mk 1:19 After walking a little farther down the coast, he saw two more fishermen brothers in a boat, James and John, the sons of Zebedee, getting their nets ready to cast. 20 Jesus called them to follow him, and they left their father Zebedee in the boat along with some employees, and followed Jesus.

Mk 1:21 Together they walked to Capernaum. On the Sabbath, Jesus went to church and began teaching. 22 What he taught thrilled their hearts and brought joy to their minds, because what he taught made sense, and had the authority of evidence and truth. He didn't teach like the theologians and church lawyers who talked in complicated theories and jargon, and often said things that didn't make sense. 23 As he was speaking, a man in attendance, whose mind was controlled by evil forces, shouted out in a terrified voice: [24] "What do you want with us? Are you here to use your power to kill us? Don't try and pretend with me; I know who you are! You're the Holy Promised One sent here by God!"

Mk 1:25 "Silence!" Jesus commanded; "Leave his mind now!" [26] The evil intelligence, in a last act of spite, caused the man to jerk violently and scream, but then left him.

Mk 1:27 The people were stunned. With amazement, they began to whisper: "What's going on? Is this a new procedure, or a new method in dealing with evil forces that actually has power to work? He commands, and his words have such authority that even the evil intelligences obey him!" [28] Very quickly after that, the news about Jesus spread over the entire region of Galilee.

Mk 1:29 When they left church, the group, including James and John, went to the home of Simon and Andrew. [30] When they arrived, they discovered that Simon's mother-in-law was in bed with a high fever, so they told Jesus about her. [31] He went to her, and when he touched her, the fever went away. She got up and began to wait on them.

Mk 1:32 That evening after sunset, when the Sabbath was over, the people brought to Jesus all their sick and those who had surrendered their minds to the control of evil intelligences—fallen angels called "demons." [33] The entire town crowded around the house, [34] and Jesus healed all their physical diseases. He also cleansed the minds of those controlled by demons, sending the evil angels away, but he would not allow the demons to speak, because they knew who he was.

Mk 1:35 Before dawn, Jesus left the house and went to a quiet place to be alone and talk with his Father in heaven. [36] Simon and his friends searched for him, [37] and when they found him, they reported, "The entire town is out looking for you!"

Mk 1:38 Jesus said, "It's time we move on to another town so that I can tell them the good news as well; that is why I am here." [39] So he went from town to town, all through Galilee, preaching and teaching in their churches, and driving out evil forces.

Mk 1:40 A desperate man, riddled with leprosy, fell down before Jesus begging, "Please, I know that if you're willing, you can heal me and make me clean."

Mk 1:41 Jesus, with his heart filled with tenderness and mercy, reached out and touched what others considered untouchable. As he touched the man, he said, "I am willing. Be clean!" [42] Instantly the leprosy disappeared and the man was completely cured.

Mk 1:43 As Jesus sent him away, he gave him explicit instructions: [44] "Keep what I have done for you in confidence. But be sure you present yourself to the priests and offer the appropriate sacrifices for cleansing—as Moses instructed—so that you may be restored to full fellowship." [45] But he was so excited and overjoyed that rather than following Jesus' instruction, he went out and told everyone whom he met on his way what Jesus did for him. As a result, Jesus couldn't enter a town without being mobbed. So Jesus stayed outside the cities, in the unpopulated places, but the people all over the region still found him.

2 Several days later, Jesus returned to his home base in Capernaum, and word quickly spread that he was back. [2] Huge crowds packed the place, so there was not even standing room left outside in the courtyard as Jesus taught them the truth. [3] Four men carried a paralyzed man, attempting to bring him to Jesus. [4] But when they couldn't get through the crowd to reach Jesus, they climbed up on the roof, opened a hole in the roof and lowered the stretcher with the paralyzed man on it down in front of Jesus. [5] When Jesus saw their confidence and

trust in him, he looked at the paralytic and said, "Son, your sin is abolished and removed."

Mk 2:6 When the church leaders who promoted a legal theology heard this, they thought to themselves, 7 "Who does he think he is? What does he think he is doing? It's easy to say 'your sin is removed,' but only God can remove sin. He's blaspheming!"

Mk 2:8 Jesus knew that their hearts were afraid and that they were confused in their thinking because of their legal theology, so he said to them: "Why are you thinking such judgmental thoughts? 9 Which is easier to say to the paralyzed man: 'Your sin is abolished and removed,' or 'Stand up, pick up your stretcher and walk'? 10 Just so you will know for certain that the Son of Man has authority on earth to abolish and remove sin..." Jesus paused, looked at the paralyzed man, and continued, 11 "Do as I say: stand up, pick up your stretcher and walk home." 12 Instantly, the man was healed. He stood up, picked up his stretcher and walked out in front of the entire crowd. Everyone was absolutely awed and they shouted praises to God, proclaiming, "We have never seen such clear revelations of God's healing love!"

Mk 2:13 Later on, Jesus went back to the lakeshore. As was becoming the norm, a large crowd gathered around him. He began teaching them the truth of God's kingdom of love. 14 As he walked along, he came to Levi, the son of Alphaeus, manning the tax collector's station. Jesus looked at him and said, "Come and join me, and be one of my disciples." Levi jumped up and instantly followed him.

Mk 2:15 Later on, Jesus and his disciples were dining at Levi's home together with many tax collectors and others, whom the religious leaders considered to be "sinners." (There were quite a few of these "sinners" who followed him.) 16 When the theologians, who taught a legal religion, and the Pharisees, who focused on external behavior, saw with whom Jesus was eating, they asked his disciples: "Why does he eat with tax collectors and sinners?"

Mk 2:17 Jesus heard what they said and replied, "Those who believe they are healthy don't go to the doctor; only the sick do. I cannot help those who believe they are already right with God, but only those who know they are sick with sin."

Mk 2:18 The disciples of John and the Pharisees were fasting. When they noticed that Jesus' disciples were not fasting, they came to Jesus and asked, "Why is it that John's disciples and the theology professors and students from the school of the Pharisees fast, but your disciples do not?"

Mk 2:19 Jesus smiled and said, "People at a wedding reception don't fast. As long as the bride and groom are together, they feast. 20 But when the groom is separated from his bride, then they will fast."

Mk 2:21 "An old system, filled with inconsistencies, is like an old, worn-out garment full of holes. One cannot fix the old garment with new cloth: if one does, the new piece will tear the old apart. Likewise, the truth of God's kingdom I bring cannot be merged into the inconsistent legal system you have created: trying to do so will tear the old system apart. 22 It is also like pouring new, unfermented wine into old, dried out wineskins: if one does, the new wine will burst the old skin. Likewise, trying to squeeze the truth I bring into the rigid legal theology you practice will fail. You must have new wineskins for the new wine, and a new heart for the truth I bring."

Mk 2:23 Jesus and his disciples were walking through a field of grain one Sabbath, when the disciples began to pull some of the heads of grain to eat. 24 The Pharisees—those theology professors who teach a legal religion—protested to Jesus: "Look at what your disciples are doing! Why are they breaking the law and working on the Sabbath?"

Mk 2:25 Jesus answered, "Don't you know the truth of God's kingdom and methods as taught in Scripture? Remember what David and his companions did when they were hungry and without food? 26 When Abiathar was high priest, David entered the sanctuary and ate the holy bread, which only the priests could lawfully eat. And he gave some to his companions as well."

Mk 2:27 After giving them a moment to think, he said, "The Sabbath was created as a gift for humanity—to be a blessing for human beings. Human beings were not created as a gift for the Sabbath. 28 Understand this clearly: The Son of Man doesn't serve the Sabbath; the Sabbath serves him."

3 On another day, Jesus went into the house of worship, and a man with a contractured and withered hand was there. 2 Some of the church leaders and theology professors—who taught a legal religion and thus focused on rules rather than healing human beings—were trying to find a reason to make allegations against Jesus, so they watched closely to see if he would heal the man on the Sabbath. 3 Jesus asked the man with the deformed hand to stand up front, where everyone could see him.

Mk 3:4 Then Jesus turned to the religious leaders and said, "According to your own rules, which is lawful to do on the Sabbath: good or evil? To save life or to kill?" But they didn't say a word, revealing that they were more interested in their rules than in helping others.

Mk 3:5 Jesus looked at them, angry at the depth of selfishness infecting their hearts, and distressed at their lack of compassion. He turned to the man and said, "Extend your hand and be well." The man immediately lifted his hand and used it normally, as it was completely healed. 6 Then those religious leaders and theology professors who taught a legal religion went out and found some local politicians of the Herodian party and plotted with them how they might kill Jesus.

Mk 3:7 Jesus and his disciples left the city and went out to the lake, and large crowds from Galilee followed him. 8 When the word about him and his ministry spread, people flocked to him from Judea, Jerusalem, Idumea, the land across the Jordan, and the area near Tyre and Sidon. 9 The crowd was growing very large, so Jesus told his disciples to have a boat ready if needed. 10 He had healed many people, and this caused those with sickness to press to the front of the crowd and try to get near enough to touch him. 11 Whenever someone whose mind was controlled by an evil angel saw him, they would fall down before him and cry out, "You are God's Son!" 12 But Jesus ordered them to keep silent.

Mk 3:13 Jesus climbed up on a mountainside and selected those he wanted to join him, and they came to him. 14 Twelve of those who followed him, he appointed to be his Ambassadors, that they might spend time with him and then go out and preach the truth of his kingdom 15 and have the authority to drive out evil forces. 16 The Twelve he appointed as his Ambassadors were Simon (whom Jesus affectionately called Peter, or Pebble), 17 James and John the sons of Zebedee (because they were so passionate and intense, he affectionately nicknamed them Boanerges, which means "Thunder Boys"), 18 Andrew, Philip, Bartholomew, Matthew, Thomas, James the son of Alphaeus, Thaddaeus, Simon the Patriot, 19 and Judas Iscariot, who later betrayed him.

Mk 3:20 Once Jesus returned home, a crowd gathered so quickly that neither he nor his disciples had time to eat. 21 When those who considered themselves "close to Jesus" heard how the crowds were constantly pressing him, they thought, "He's not thinking clearly enough to handle all the fame," so they sought to manage Jesus' time and schedule.

Mk 3:22 And the theology professors, who taught a legal religion, came over from Jerusalem and said, "He wants to be a celebrity, and just like the devil, he tries to make himself the center of attention. He uses Satan's power to drive out evil forces."

Mk 3:23 So Jesus confronted them publicly with parables: "How can Satan enter into a person, and by coming, get rid of Satan? Think about it: It would be like using water to get rid of wetness. 24 If a kingdom fights against itself, it collapses. 25 If a family turns against each other, its cohesion is destroyed. 26 If Satan opposes himself, he neutralizes his own efforts, his work collapses, and his effectiveness is ended. 27 It is not possible to enter the domain of a strong man and take away his possessions unless one first neutralizes the strong man. Only when the strong man is restrained can one take his possessions. 28 So here is the simple truth: Every sin—every deviation from God's design—can be healed. 29 But anyone who speaks against the Holy Spirit cannot be healed, either now or in the future, for it is the Spirit who works in the heart to administer the Remedy, and the Spirit only works in a willing heart. Closing the heart to the Spirit prevents healing and results in eternal sinfulness." 30 He told them this because they were closing their hearts by saying, "He is working through an evil spirit."

Mk 3:31 Jesus' mother and brothers arrived, but couldn't get in through the crowd. They passed a message to him to come out. 32 The crowd told him, "Your mother and brothers are outside, waiting for you."

Mk 3:33 "Who is bonded in love with me like a mother or brother?" he asked.

Mk 3:34 Then looking over those gathered around him, he said, "Here are those whose hearts are bonded in love to me like a mother and brothers. 35 Those who partake of the Remedy and experience renewal of hearts such that they live in harmony with God's will and design are my true family."

4 On another day, when Jesus was teaching at the lakeshore, the crowd grew so large that he got into a boat, pushed back from shore and spoke to the people who gathered at the water's edge. 2 He used a variety of parables to teach them. He said, 3 "Consider the meaning of this: A farmer went out to plant seed. 4 He scattered his seed broadly. Some fell on the road and the birds gobbled up the seed immediately. 5 Some of the seed fell in gravel without much soil. Though it sprouted quickly, because the soil was shallow, it didn't penetrate deeply into the soil, 6 so when the sun came up, the young sprouts couldn't take the heat and withered because they had no root. 7 Other seed fell among thorns and weeds which grew up and choked the good plants before they could mature and bear fruit. 8 But some of the seed reached good soil, where it took root, grew up, and produced an abundant harvest, multiplying up to a hundred times what was planted."

Mk 4:9 Jesus looked at them and said, "Those whose minds are open to truth, let them understand the meaning."

Mk 4:10 Later, when he was alone, the Twelve Ambassadors and others devoted to his cause asked him about his parables. 11 He told them, "The truth about God's kingdom of love, which to many seems mysterious, has been revealed to you because your hearts are open to the truth. But to those whose hearts are not open to truth, I speak in parables, so even

12 'Though they see with their eyes,
    their minds do not comprehend;
and though they hear with their ears,
    they do not understand the
    meaning.

If they did understand, they would
turn to me in trust,
and I would heal them!'"

Mk 4:13 So Jesus said to them: "Don't you understand that this illustration demonstrates that God's kingdom operates upon natural law—design protocols for life? If you don't understand this, you will misunderstand all my illustrations. 14 The farmer plants the words of truth into the hearts of people. 15 Some people have hearts that are hard and callous, like a road, and they don't respond to the truth when it is presented. They hear the truth, but they don't consider it seriously: Satan distracts them with some temptation or problem, and the truth is forgotten. 16 Other people have hearts like gravel —shifting and unstable: they respond with excitement to every new idea, but nothing takes root. 17 And since the truth doesn't take root in their hearts, they only stay involved briefly. As soon as the truth requires some sacrifice or actual work on their part, they quit and move on to their next emotional fix. 18 There are other people, who have minds like soil filled with weeds and thorns. They hear the truth, 19 but the thorns of worry and fear, or the weeds of seeking healing of heart in fame, fortune, or other earthly desires choke out truth and love, and make their hearts desolate. 20 But there are those whose hearts are like fertile soil. They hear the truth, comprehend it, love it, embrace it, nurture it, choose it, and build on it; and it heals, transforms and renews them, causing them to produce fruits of righteousness even more than a hundred times what was planted in them."

Mk 4:21 Then Jesus asked them, "Do you bring in a lantern only to cover it with a bucket or put it under a bed so its light won't be seen? Or do you instead hang it from the ceiling, or put it on a stand, so that its light will penetrate widely? 22 What has been hidden by Satan's lies is meant to be revealed, and whatever is concealed by misunderstanding, confusion or ignorance is intended to be brought out into the open for all to see and understand. 23 Those whose minds are open to truth, let them understand the meaning. 24 Pay attention and understand the way God's kingdom works: Behavior has consequences. The standard you use to judge others reveals the actual condition of your own heart, thus your condemnation of others is really condemnation of yourself. 25 Whoever accepts and holds God's love and truth in their heart will receive more; but whoever refuses God's love and truth, whatever had been poured out upon them will be eventually taken back."

Mk 4:26 He continued with another example: "God's kingdom of love operates upon natural law — law built right into nature — and therefore it is like this: A person spreads seed on the ground. 27 Once the seed is spread, regardless of what the person does— watches it or sleeps — the seed sprouts and grows, even though the person cannot explain how. 28 Without help from any human, the soil produces grain, and it develops naturally in a predictable course: first a stalk, then a head, and then full kernels in the head. 29 And when the grain is ripe, then it is cut, for harvest time has come."

Mk 4:30 Jesus told them another example: "What is God's kingdom of love like? What illustration should I use to help you understand it? 31 It starts out small, like a mustard seed, planted in the soil of the heart. 32 But when it takes root and grows, it becomes the largest of all the plants in the garden of the heart, with such big branches of love that everyone, like birds of the air, can perch in its shade and find sanctuary and rest."

Mk 4:33 Jesus taught them with many illustrations, stories, metaphors and parables, endeavoring to help them understand the true nature of God's kingdom of love. 34 He didn't speak to the general public without using illustrations and parables. But when he was in private, with his disciples, he explained everything to them.

Mk 4:35 Later that day, shortly after sunset, Jesus said to his disciples, "Let's cross the lake." 36 So they left the crowds, climbed in a boat, and headed across the lake; and other boats followed them. 37 A fierce storm blew up, and the waves were so high they crashed into the boat nearly sinking it. 38 Jesus was asleep on a cushion in the stern. The disciples—some of whom were fishermen and were quite experienced with boating—were terrified and woke Jesus, crying out to him: "Master, we're drowning! Don't you care what happens to us?"

Mk 4:39 Jesus calmly stood up and instructed the wind and the waves to calm down: "Stop blowing and be still!" And the wind immediately stopped blowing and it was completely calm, and the water was tranquil.

Mk 4:40 He spoke gently to his disciples and asked, "Why are you so frightened? Do you still have difficulty trusting me?"

Mk 4:41 They were stunned with awe and asked each other, "Who is he? He has power over the wind and sea!"

5 They completed the crossing of the lake and arrived in the land of the Gerasenes. 2 As Jesus got out of the boat, a man whose mind was controlled by an evil angel came out of the burial grounds to confront him. 3 This man lived amongst the dead and no one had been able to restrain him—not even with chains. 4 Even though he had been shackled with chains—both hands and feet—on numerous occasions, he had broken the chains repeatedly. No one had the means to restore his self-control. 5 He would constantly, day and night, wander the burial grounds and hills about, crying out and cutting himself with sharp objects.

Mk 5:6 But when he saw Jesus, he ran to him and fell down on his knees before him. 7 In a loud voice, he shouted, "Why have you come here? What is it that you want with me, Jesus, Son of the Most High God? I'm afraid you are going to torture me! Swear to God that you won't!" 8 Jesus had already commanded him, "Let go of his mind and leave him alone, you evil angel!"

Mk 5:9 Then Jesus asked him, "What do you call yourself?"

"I go by Legion," the evil angel replied, "for there are many of us." 10 And he begged Jesus again and again not to send him away.

Mk 5:11 There was a large herd of pigs feeding nearby. 12 The demonic angels begged Jesus, "Let us go among the pigs and take control of them." 13 Jesus permitted them the freedom to do as they asked, and the evil angels let go of their hold on the man's mind and took control of the pigs. There were about two thousand pigs in the herd, and they immediately went berserk, stampeded down a steep bank, plunged into the lake, and drowned.

Mk 5:14 The men watching the pigs ran away and told everyone in the town and throughout the country side what happened. The people who heard it went to see for themselves. 15 When they found Jesus, they saw the man, whose mind had been controlled by the legion of evil angels, sitting calm and composed, neatly groomed, and in full control of all his faculties. They were struck with awe. 16 The people who had actually seen what had transpired told the new arrivals how the demon-controlled man had been restored to himself, and what happened to the pigs. 17 Then the locals insisted that Jesus leave their region.

Mk 5:18 As Jesus was climbing into the boat, the man whose mind had been controlled by demonic angels begged to go with him. 19 But Jesus gently told him, "You need to go home. Your family needs to know how much the Lord has done for you, and to see the mercy of God manifest through you."

20 So the man went throughout Deca-polis, telling everyone whom he met about all that Jesus had done for him. And all those who heard were amazed by what he said.

Mk 5:21 By the time Jesus crossed back over the lake, a large crowd had formed on that side of the lake and gathered around him on the shore. 22 One of the local church leaders, named Jairus, came to him there. He bowed down at Jesus' feet 23 and pas-sionately begged Jesus, "My little girl is dying. Please come and just touch her. I know that if you just touch her she will be healed and live. Please, come and touch her." 24 So Jesus went to his home, and the large crowd followed.

Mk 5:25 There was a woman in the crowd who had chronic bleeding ongo-ing for twelve years. 26 She had spent her entire fortune on many doctors, endur-ing their supposed treatments which caused great pain and suffering; but instead of getting well, she only wors-ened. 27 She had heard about Jesus, so she came up behind him in the crowd, and when close enough—reached out and touched his clothes. 28 She did this because she thought, "Just touching the clothes of Jesus will be enough to heal me." 29 And instantly her bleeding stopped and her body was invigorated with energy, and her pain was gone.

Mk 5:30 Jesus realized instantly that healing energy had gone out from him. He stopped, and turning to the crowd, asked, "Who touched my robe?"

Mk 5:31 The disciples were confused and asked, "You're being jostled by this huge crowd on all sides, and you ask, 'Who touched me?'"

Mk 5:32 But Jesus scanned the faces of the crowd, looking for the person who had touched him. 33 Finally, the woman, knowing he was looking for her, stepped forward and knelt down be-fore him, frightened and insecure. She told him what she had done and how she was healed. 34 He smiled at her and said, "Child, your trust is what allowed you to be healed. Live healthy and happy, free from your suffering."

Mk 5:35 While Jesus was still speaking with the woman, messengers from Jairus' house arrived and said, "Your daughter is dead. There's no need to bring Jesus any more."

Mk 5:36 But Jesus ignored them and looked at the church leader with com-passion in his eyes and said, "Trust me! Don't panic, it will be alright."

Mk 5:37 But for this mission, he would not let anyone come along except Peter, James and his brother John. 38 When they came to Jairus' house, there was near chaos: some were wailing and crying, while others were speculating on why this happened. 39 Jesus walked in and said with a clear voice: "What is all the crying and fuss about? The child is not dead; she is only asleep." 40 But they mocked and ridiculed him, so he had them all leave; and then, after they were out of the house, he took the child's parents and his disciples who came with him, and went to where the child lay. 41 He took her hand in his and said to her, *"Talitha koum!"* (which means, "Little girl, get up!"). 42 Immediately she opened her eyes, took a deep breath, then stood up and walked around. She was twelve years old. The parents and dis-ciples were overwhelmed with awe; they were all just speechless. 43 Jesus commanded them not to tell people what he had done, and to give the girl something to eat.

6 Jesus and his disciples returned to his home in Nazareth. 2 On Sab-bath, he went to the local worship cen-ter and began to teach. Those who heard him were astounded. "How does he know all this?" they asked. "What he says makes sense and has power to actually change lives!" 3 But some ob-jected, "Wait a minute! He's just the son of a carpenter. You remember him, don't you? He's Mary's boy, the brother of James, Joseph, Judas, and Simon.

His sisters still live here, don't they?" So they discounted the truth he taught.

Mk 6:4 Jesus told them, "Sadly, the people who grow up with God's spokespersons—their neighbors and family—are the ones who refuse to listen or embrace the wisdom they bring."

5 He could not do much to help them; only a few of the sick let him lay hands on and heal them. 6 He was astounded at their refusal to trust him, so he moved on, teaching from one town to the next. 7 He sent the Twelve out in pairs and gave them the ability to overcome evil agencies.

Mk 6:8 He told them: "Don't pack anything for this trip, except a walking stick. Don't take food, luggage, or money in your wallets. 9 Wear comfortable walking shoes, but don't take extra clothes. 10 If you accept someone's hospitality, then stay at that home until you leave town. 11 But if any place opposes you or refuses to listen, don't waste time fighting to be heard; just shake off the rejection like dust off your feet, and your grace in the face of rejection will be a witness to them."

Mk 6:12 So they went out and proclaimed the Remedy, admonishing people to turn away from their terminal condition. 13 They drove away many evil forces, tended to the sick, applied oil, and healed them.

Mk 6:14 All of these events were reported to King Herod, because Jesus was becoming famous and everyone was talking about him. Some people were even suggesting, "He is John the Baptist resurrected from the dead, so that would explain his power to work miracles."

Mk 6:15 But others argued, "No way! He is Elijah!" Still others said, "No, he is one of God's spokesmen, like those in the past."

Mk 6:16 But Herod, when he heard about Jesus, said, "It is John, the innocent man I beheaded. He's come back to life!"

Mk 6:17 Herod was guilt ridden, because he had personally ordered for John to be arrested, and had him shackled and imprisoned. He arrested John because Herodias, to whom he was married, was his brother Philip's wife, and 18 John had exposed his wrongdoing. He had told Herod, "To take your brother's wife as your own violates God's law of love." 19 This outraged Herodias who resented John and plotted to kill him; but she couldn't, 20 because Herod knew that John was a righteous man—a messenger from God—and was afraid to harm him. Herod, living in sin as he did, was confused by what John taught, but still liked to listen to him, so he protected John.

Mk 6:21 But Herodias finally got her chance: Herod threw a huge party on his birthday, inviting powerful politicians, military commanders and business leaders from Galilee. 22 Herodias' daughter amazed them with her dancing. She was so incredible that Herod said to her, "Ask me for anything—anything at all—and I will give it to you." 23 He made a promise in front of all his guests, with an oath, "I will give you whatever you choose, even if it is half of my kingdom."

Mk 6:24 She ran to her mother, "Mom, what should I request?"

Herodias answered immediately, "The head of John the Baptist."

Mk 6:25 The girl rushed back to the king and said, "I want you to bring me right now the head of John the Baptist on a platter."

Mk 6:26 Herod was sick, torn, and angry, but because he gave a public oath in front of his guests, he didn't want to tell her "No." 27 So he sent the headman with orders to bring back John's head. The man went to the prison and severed John's head 28 and brought it back on a platter and gave it to the girl, who gave it to her mother. 29 When John's disciples heard he had been executed, they retrieved his body and buried it in a tomb.

Mk 6:30 The Twelve Ambassadors met

with Jesus and gave an account of all they had taught and done. ³¹ But it was so busy with the traffic of people that they didn't even have time to eat, so Jesus said to them, "Let's go someplace quiet where we can relax and unwind together."

Mk 6:32 So they took a boat and headed to an isolated place. ³³ But many of the people who saw them leave recognized where they were headed and spread the word; and people from all the towns nearby ran and got there ahead of them. ³⁴ When Jesus arrived at shore and saw the large crowd already waiting there, his heart stirred with longing for their healing, for they were wandering in confusion about God, like sheep wandering without a shepherd to guide them. So he presented them with many truths about God's kingdom of love.

Mk 6:35 It was approaching dinner time, so his disciples came to him and said, "It's getting late and we're in the middle of nowhere. ³⁶ End the meeting so people can go to nearby towns and find something to eat."

Mk 6:37 But Jesus told his disciples, with all seriousness, "No need to do that; you give them something to eat." Startled, they replied, "Are you serious? That much food would cost almost an entire year's pay! Do you really want us to spend that much on bread to give away?"

Mk 6:38 So Jesus asked them, "How much food do you have with you?" They checked and replied, "Five loaves of bread and two fish."

Mk 6:39 Jesus instructed them to have the crowd break into smaller groups and sit down on the green grass, ⁴⁰ so the people sat down in groups of fifties or hundreds. ⁴¹ Then Jesus looked to heaven, gave thanks, and broke the loaves, handing the pieces to the disciples, who gave them to the people. He did the same with the fish. ⁴² The entire crowd ate until they were full, ⁴³ and the disciples collected twelve basketfuls of leftover fish and bread. ⁴⁴ The number of men who ate (not even counting women and children) was five thousand.

Mk 6:45 As soon as the meal was concluded, Jesus instructed his disciples to sail ahead of him to Bethsaida, while he dismissed the crowd. ⁴⁶ When he was alone, he climbed the mountainside and talked with his Father in heaven.

Mk 6:47 That night, Jesus was alone on shore, while the boat was out in the middle of the lake. ⁴⁸ The disciples were heading into a strong wind, and Jesus could see that they were rowing hard but making little headway. Around four o'clock in the morning, Jesus approached them, walking on the surface of the water. It appeared as if he was about to walk right past them, ⁴⁹ and when they saw him walking on the water, they freaked out thinking he was some ghost. ⁵⁰ They screamed in terror when they saw him, but he immediately reassured them, "Don't be frightened. It's me! Everything will be okay now." ⁵¹ And as he stepped into the boat, the wind stopped and it was calm. They were stunned and confused, ⁵² as they were still trying to comprehend the significance of feeding thousands of people with five loaves and two fish. Their minds couldn't grasp all that was happening.

Mk 6:53 After they crossed the lake, they anchored at Gennesaret. ⁵⁴ And as soon as they made it to shore, people recognized Jesus. ⁵⁵ Quickly word about Jesus spread through the region, and crowds gathered, bringing their sick (some they carried on mats) to wherever they thought Jesus would be. ⁵⁶ No matter where he went—small hamlets, towns, cities, or out in the countryside—the people brought their sick. They begged to touch him—even just the edge of his coat—and everyone who did, was healed.

7 The theology professors from the school of the Pharisees, along with

some of the church lawyers—all of whom cherished a legal theology—came from Jerusalem to monitor what Jesus was doing. [2] They saw some of his disciples eating with hands that had not been washed in the proscribed ritualistic way. [3] (The Pharisees, promoting the tradition of church elders who taught a legal religion, influenced the Jews so much that none would eat unless they first performed a ritualistic washing with an insignificant amount of water. [4] When they return from shopping, they won't eat unless they perform the ritualistic hand washing. And they observe many other rituals—such as washing of cups, pots, and pans—thinking that doing so provides moral purity, but in reality, it doesn't.)

Mk 7:5 So these legal religion theologians asked Jesus, "Why don't your disciples live by the standards of church tradition and respect the church elders, instead of ignoring our tradition by eating with hands that have not been ritually cleansed?"

Mk 7:6 Jesus didn't hesitate in his reply: "Isaiah got it right when he described charlatans like you—those who pretend to partake of the Remedy, but instead promote spiritual poison. Just as he wrote,

'These people proclaim their love for me with their mouths,
but their hearts are as far away from love for me and my methods as they can get.
[7] Their worship is useless,
and their teachings are nothing but man-made rules.'

Mk 7:8 "You have thrown away God's healing prescription and are promoting a counterfeit cocktail of dos and don'ts thought up by men."

Mk 7:9 He continued, "You have perfected the art of throwing away God's healing prescription and replacing it with your own worthless traditions! [10] For Moses taught God's Remedy, 'Love your father and your mother,' and 'Anyone who fails to love his father or mother will certainly die.' [11] But you come along with your own rules—which are the poison of selfishness—and throw out God's prescription of love when you say that if a person says to their father or mother: 'Whatever help I might otherwise give to you it is now Corban (that is, the resources are designated for the Temple), [12] then you excuse their responsibility to love and provide for their parents. [13] This is just one example of how you make God's healing Remedy useless by replacing it with your worthless traditions handed down through the generations. You do many things just like that."

Mk 7:14 Jesus turned to the crowd, called them to himself, and said: "Everyone, listen to me and understand what really matters: [15] There is nothing outside a person that by being ingested can change the person's character, therefore it cannot make them impure. But what comes out of their mouth is an expression of their character, and that is what makes them impure. [16] Let those whose minds are open to truth understand."

Mk 7:17 After they left the crowd and returned home, the disciples asked Jesus to explain what he had meant by this example. [18] Looking at them, Jesus asked: "Are your minds so dulled by tradition that you don't understand? Don't you realize that nothing that enters the body from the outside can contaminate or defile? [19] Why not? Because it doesn't enter the mind—it doesn't become part of the character—but simply goes into the stomach and then out of the body." (Jesus was making it clear that no food could make a person morally impure.)

Mk 7:20 He explained further: "What comes out of the mouth is an expression of what is in the heart—an expression of the character—and evil in the character is what makes a person impure. [21] For evil originates from the infection of selfishness in the heart, such as evil thoughts, sexual perversity, murder, dishonesty, theft, betrayal of trust, ²² greed, cruelty, deception, vulgarity, envy, evil-speaking, gossip, pride, and foolishness. ²³ All these destructive deviations from God's design come from inside, and this is what makes a person impure."

Mk 7:24 Jesus moved on to the region of Tyre. When he arrived, he went into a house, hoping to remain unnoticed, but he couldn't keep his presence a secret. ²⁵ No sooner did he arrive than a woman came and fell at his feet. She had a little daughter whose mind was not working as God designed. ²⁶ The woman was not Jewish but Canaanite, born in Syria, near Phoenicia. She begged Jesus to heal her daughter—to remove any defect or evil from her.

Mk 7:27 Jesus gently said, "The children must first eat their fill. It isn't appropriate to take the bread baked for the children and throw it to their pets."

Mk 7:28 Instantly the woman replied, "So true Lord, but even the pets are fed the scraps left over from the children's meal."

Mk 7:29 Jesus smiled and said, "Your answer is true. Go home; the evil afflicting your daughter is gone."

Mk 7:30 She returned home and found her child resting in bed, with her mind at peace.

Mk 7:31 After healing the Canaanite woman's daughter, Jesus left Tyre, walked through Sidon, down by the Sea of Galilee and into the district of Decapolis. ³² When he arrived, some people brought to him a deaf man who could only mumble, and they begged Jesus to put his hands on the man.

Mk 7:33 Jesus took the man aside, and meeting the man's expectation for healing, put his fingers in the man's ears. Then he spat on his finger and touched the man's tongue. ³⁴ He looked heavenward, groaning at how far from God's design this man was, and said to him, "Ephphatha!" (which means "Be opened!"). ³⁵ Immediately the man could hear and speak, and began talking normally.

Mk 7:36 Jesus instructed them not to tell anyone, but the more he told them to be discrete, the more they kept talking about it. ³⁷ The people were thrilled with joy and amazed with all he did. They said, "Everything he does, he does perfectly. He even gives hearing to the deaf and enables the mute to speak."

8 A short time later, another large crowd assembled, and they also didn't have any food to eat. Jesus took note of their situation, called his disciples, and said, ² "I care about these people; they have spent three days with me and now have nothing to eat. ³ If I send them home on an empty stomach, some may faint from exhaustion, because many of them have come from far away."

Mk 8:4 His disciples replied with uncertainty, "But we're in the middle of nowhere! From where are we to get enough bread to feed them?"

Mk 8:5 So Jesus asked them, "How many loaves do you have?"

"Seven," they replied.

Mk 8:6 So Jesus instructed the crowd to sit down on the ground. After giving thanks for the seven loaves, he broke them and gave them to his disciples who gave them to the people. ⁷ They also had a few small fish, which Jesus took, gave thanks for them, then passed the fish to the disciples to give to the people. ⁸ The crowd ate all they desired, and when everyone was full, the disciples collected seven basketfuls of leftovers. ⁹ There were about four thousand men present (plus women and children). Once the meal was over, Jesus sent them home, ¹⁰ then got into a boat with his disciples and sailed to the district of Dalmanutha.

Mk 8:11 The theologians from the school of the Pharisees, who prefer a legal theology, came and began to challenge Jesus. They demanded a sign from heaven to prove his right to teach what he did. ¹² He groaned at how closed their minds were to evidence and truth, and said, "Indeed, the people of today prefer miraculous signs, but I am here to tell you the truth: No miraculous sign will be given to them."

13 Then he left them standing there, got back in the boat, and crossed back to the other side.

Mk 8:14 Once on the boat, the disciples realized they hadn't brought any food, except for one loaf of bread. 15 Jesus said to them, "Keep sharp, stay vigilant, and watch closely to keep out the yeast of legal theologies—like those taught by the Pharisees, and imposed law constructs used by human governments like Herod's—from the church."

Mk 8:16 The disciples were too concrete in their thinking and wondered, "Is it because we didn't bring any bread with us that he mentioned yeast?"

Mk 8:17 Aware of their conversation, Jesus said, "Why are you focusing on bread? Is your perspective so small that you think only about food for the body? Don't you realize what is happening? Are your minds too steeped in tradition to figure it out? 18 You have eyes, but fail to comprehend, and you have ears, but fail to understand! Don't you learn from experience? 19 Remember when I, with just five loaves, fed over five thousand people? How many baskets of leftovers did you gather?"

"Twelve," they replied.

Mk 8:20 "Or what about when I fed over four thousand with seven loaves; how many baskets of leftovers did you gather then?"

"Seven," they mumbled.

Mk 8:21 He gently urged, "Think about it. Don't you understand yet?"

Mk 8:22 When they came to Bethsaida, some people brought a blind man to Jesus and begged Jesus to touch him. 23 He led the blind man by the hand outside the village. Then, to avoid introducing doubt, Jesus met the man's expectations for how healing was done and put saliva on the man's eyes, and then placed his hands on him. Then Jesus asked, "What do you see?"

Mk 8:24 The man looked up and said, "I see people; but it's kind of blurry; they look like trees moving about."

Mk 8:25 So Jesus touched the man's eyes once more, wiping them clean. Then the man could see everything clearly. 26 Jesus sent him home, instructing him, "Don't go back to the village."

Mk 8:27 Jesus and his disciples continued on to the towns around Caesarea Philippi. While they were walking, Jesus asked them, "Who do people say I am?"

Mk 8:28 So they told him, "Some say you are John who immersed people in water; others say you are Elijah; and still others say you are one of the other of God's spokesmen from the past."

Mk 8:29 "Well," Jesus said, "what about you? Who do you say I am?"

Peter answered without hesitation, "You are the Messiah, our Savior."

Mk 8:30 Jesus warned them that it was not the time to tell people about this.

Mk 8:31 Then Jesus began to explain to them the full extent of his mission: "The Son of Man, in order to provide the Remedy to sin, must suffer the weight of many things, including rejection by the church leaders, and condemnation by the theologians, senior priests, pastors, and church lawyers. He must be killed, and on the third day rise to life again." 32 He didn't hide the truth, but told them plainly what was going to happen. Peter didn't like what he was hearing, so he took Jesus aside and tried to direct him down a different path.

Mk 8:33 Jesus saw all the disciples watching, and turned to Peter and said, "Get Satan's methods of selfishness away from me! You do not have God's methods of love in mind, but are promoting the survival-of-the-fittest ways of fallen humanity."

Mk 8:34 Then he summoned the crowd to join him and his disciples and said: "If anyone wants to follow me into unity with my Father, they must surrender their life, willingly choose to die to selfishness, and follow me in love.

35 For whoever follows the survival-of-the-fittest principle and seeks to save their life will lose it, because the infection of selfishness will not be eliminated; but whoever loses their life in love for me will find eternal life, for they will have been restored back to God's design for life—selfless, other-centered love. 36 What good does it do to selfishly hoard all the treasures of the world only to die eternally? 37 Or how much is one's individuality—their eternal existence—worth to them? 38 If anyone is ashamed of me and my methods of truth and love and chooses unity with this disloyal and selfish generation, the Son of Man will be unable to unite such selfish people into his 'family' when he comes in the fullness of his Father's glory with his holy angels."

9 And he told them, "I tell you truly, some of you standing right here will not sleep in the grave before you see God's kingdom of love arrive with power."

Mk 9:2 Six days later, Jesus took Peter, James and John, and went up a high mountain where they were alone. There, the veil separating heaven and earth was pulled back, and Christ's divine glory shone through his humanity. 3 His clothing became brilliant—near blinding white, more intensely white than any bleach could ever make them. 4 And standing right there with Jesus were Elijah and Moses, and they were talking with him.

Mk 9:5 Peter said to Jesus, "Master, this is incredible, and it is great that we can be here to see it. If you want, we can set up three shelters: one for you, one for Moses, and one for Elijah." 6 (Peter was just rambling nonsense, not knowing what to say, because he was so overwhelmed.)

Mk 9:7 Then a cloud surrounded them, and a voice thundered from the cloud: "This is my precious Son. I love him, so listen to him!"

Mk 9:8 In an instant—or so it seemed—they looked around and saw no one else there, except Jesus.

Mk 9:9 On their way down the mountain, Jesus gave them strict orders to keep what they had seen to themselves until the Son of Man had risen from the dead. 10 They did keep this confidential, only discussing amongst themselves what Jesus meant by "rising from the dead."

Mk 9:11 They asked Jesus, "Why do theology professors say that Elijah must come first?"

Mk 9:12 Jesus answered them, "Because Elijah does come first, in order to prepare the hearts and minds of people for the coming of the Son of Man. But if he came to prepare their hearts, why is it written that the Son of Man must suffer so much and be rejected? 13 Let me tell you, Elijah has come, but they didn't respect him and instead treated him with contempt, just as it was written about him."

Mk 9:14 When they arrived where the other disciples waited, a large crowd had surrounded them, and theologians who taught a legal theology were arguing with them. 15 As soon as the people saw Jesus, they were startled with amazement and wonder from the lingering traces of radiance upon him, and they ran to welcome him.

Mk 9:16 Jesus asked them, "What is this commotion about?"

Mk 9:17 A man in the crowd answered, "Oh Teacher, I brought my son to you because some evil overtakes him and prevents him from speaking. 18 It comes episodically, and when the evil seizes him, he will fall to the ground, foam at the mouth, grind his teeth, and become stiff. I begged your disciples to drive the evil from him, but they couldn't do it."

Mk 9:19 With sadness for them, Jesus said, "What a confused and superstitious people you are. How long will I need to be with you before you understand? How long must I endure your suffering? Bring the boy to me."

Mk 9:20 So they brought the boy to Jesus.

When the evil angel saw Jesus, it caused the boy to have a seizure. He fell to the ground, writhing and foaming at the mouth.

Mk 9:21 "How long has he suffered like this?" Jesus asked the boy's father.

"Ever since he was a small child," he answered. 22 "It has even tried to kill him by throwing him into fire or water. So, if you can do anything to help, please have mercy on us and help the boy."

Mk 9:23 "'If?' you say?" Jesus prodded. "Those who believe know that all things are possible."

Mk 9:24 Instantly the boy's father cried out, "I do believe; please help me overcome my doubts!"

Mk 9:25 When Jesus saw a crowd forming around the writhing boy, he commanded the evil force to leave. "You deaf and dumb deviation from God's design," Jesus said, "I command you, get out of him and stay out!"

Mk 9:26 The boy seized violently, and with a scream the evil left him. The boy collapsed and was so unresponsive that some said, "He's dead." 27 But Jesus grasped his hand and the boy stood up.

Mk 9:28 After Jesus had gone inside, his disciples came to him and asked, "Why wouldn't the evil leave when we told it to?"

Mk 9:29 He answered, "This type of evil is only overcome by talking with my Father."

Mk 9:30 They left that place and journeyed through Galilee. Jesus didn't want people to find them, 31 because he wanted time alone with his disciples to teach them. He said, "The Son of Man is going to be betrayed and turned over to human authority. They will kill him, but after three days he will arise from the dead." 32 But they didn't understand what he was talking about and were too insecure to ask him to explain it further.

Mk 9:33 They went on to Capernaum. Once indoors, he asked them, "Now, what were you quarrelling about on the walk here?" 34 They squirmed, but didn't answer because they had been arguing over which of them would be the greatest.

Mk 9:35 Jesus sat down, called the Twelve to him, and said, "If anyone desires to be first in God's kingdom, he must not promote self, but put self last in order to promote the eternal welfare of others—serving the eternal interests of all."

Mk 9:36 Jesus took a small child in his arms and said to the Twelve, 37 "Anyone who opens their heart and receives those with childlike trust in the way I would—with love and affection, practicing my methods—also opens their heart to receive me; and whoever opens their heart to receive me, not only receives me, but also the One who sent me."

Mk 9:38 "Master," John said, "when we came upon a man driving out evil angels by using your name, we told him to stop, because you hadn't specifically called him to be one of us."

Mk 9:39 Jesus gently answered, "Don't stop him. A person who claims me as the source of their strength and power will not in the next moment ridicule and reject me. 40 Anyone who is not warring against us is helping us. 41 The truth is, any person who simply gives you a cup of water because you are a Christian is helping to spread the Remedy, and thus honors me and shares in the reward such love brings.

Mk 9:42 "But it is better to drown in the sea with a heavy stone tied around one's neck than to lead one of these little ones who trust me to deviate from God's design for life. 43 If you have habits of using your hand to sear your conscience and warp your character, then cut them out. It is better to have a healed mind and enter into eternal life as an amputee than have two hands with a warped character and therefore be tormented when the eternal fires of love and truth burn free. 44 There, 'their worm of selfishness does not die, and the fire of truth and love will burn eternally.'[1] [45] And if you have habits of using your foot to sear your conscience and warp your character, then sever them. It is better to have a healed mind and enter into eternal life lame than have two feet with a warped character and be tormented in the consuming fire of God's life-giving glory. [46] There, 'their worm of selfishness does not die, and the fire of truth and love will burn eternally.'[2] [47] And if you have the habit of using your eye to look at material that warps your character and sears your conscience, then cut it out. It is better to have a healed mind and enter into eternal life with one eye than have both eyes and a warped character and be cast into torment, [48] where 'their worm of selfishness does not die, and the fire of truth and love will burn eternally.'[3]

Mk 9:49 "Everyone will be purified by the eternal fire of love and truth emanating from the presence of the Father—just as salt purifies a sacrifice. [50] Salt—like love and truth—purifies, but if salt loses its saltiness, how can it be made salty again? Likewise, how can a person who loses all desire for love and truth be purified? Have the salt of love and truth in your hearts, and be real friends with each other."

10 Jesus left Capernaum and went to Judea, and then crossed the Jordan. Quickly, crowds began to follow him, and—as was his practice—he taught them the truth of God's kingdom of love.

Mk 10:2 Some of the theology professors from the School of the Pharisees came to Jesus, trying to trick him, and asked, "Is it legal for a man to divorce his wife?"

---

[1] [2] [3] "Their worm of selfishness does not die" is intended to say, "where they do not die to self," or "where selfishness is not removed from their character." Thus, they do not survive when all sin and selfishness is consumed by the life-giving glory of God's fiery presence.

Mk 10:3 Jesus asked them in return, "What did Moses instruct you?"

Mk 10:4 They said, "Moses allowed a man to provide his wife with a divorce certificate and then send her away."

Mk 10:5 Jesus answered, "It was because your hearts were gangrenous with selfishness, hardened, and did not love that Moses gave you this rule on how to sever a destructive marriage most mercifully. [6] But in the beginning, God constructed life to operate in other-centered love—'he made them male and female.' [7] 'Because of this design, a man will leave his parents and be united in love with his wife, [8] and the two will become one flesh.' They are no longer merely two individuals but one, united by bonds of love. [9] Therefore what God has joined together in the unity of love, no person is to allow selfishness to tear it apart."

Mk 10:10 Later, when the disciples were back indoors and alone with Jesus, they asked him about this. [11] He answered, "Any man who divorces his faithful wife and marries another betrays his first wife. [12] And any woman who divorces her loyal husband and marries another betrays her first husband."

Mk 10:13 Parents were bringing their children to Jesus to have him touch them, but the disciples tried to stop them. [14] When Jesus saw this, he was not happy with what they were doing. He instructed them, "Let the children come to me without any barriers or hindrances, for God's kingdom of love belongs to people just like these. [15] Truly, people who will not receive God's kingdom of love as openly and freely as a child, will never enter it." [16] Then he picked up the children, hugged them, sat them on his lap, and blessed them.

Mk 10:17 As Jesus was leaving, a man ran up to him and fell down on his knees in front of him: "Good teacher, tell me what I must do to receive everlasting life?"

Mk 10:18 "Why do you address me as

'good'?" Jesus asked. "No human is good; only God is good. [19] You know God's prescription—his instruction on life being constructed to operate upon love—so if you love, you 'do not murder, do not commit marital betrayal, do not steal, do not speak falsely about others, do not cheat, and you honor your mother and father.'"

Mk 10:20 "Teacher, I have done all of these since childhood," he proclaimed.

Mk 10:21 Jesus looked kindly on him, and with compassion said: "Only one thing remains for you to do. Go and sell all your possessions which you cling to as evidence of your good standing before God. In love, give it all to the poor and you will have the treasure of heaven. Then come, join me, and live as I do."

Mk 10:22 When the young man heard this, his face saddened, and he left with a heavy heart because he had great wealth and derived security from his possessions.

Mk 10:23 Jesus turned around and said to his disciples, "I tell you the simple truth, it is hard for those who are rich—who derive a sense of security from their possessions—to surrender all and enter into heaven's kingdom of love and trust."

Mk 10:24 This stunned the disciples because they were biased by culture to think that wealth was evidence of God's blessing. But Jesus continued his instruction, "My children, understand it clearly: It is hard for the rich—who derive security from their possessions—to surrender their wealth and enter heaven's kingdom of love and trust. [25] It is easier for a camel to kneel down, remove its load, and crawl through the small gate known as the 'eye of the needle' than for a rich person to humble themself, surrender their wealth, and enter God's kingdom of love and trust."

Mk 10:26 The disciples were shocked, because they always thought wealth meant blessings of God. They asked each other, "Who can be saved if the rich have such a hard time?"

Mk 10:27 Jesus looked them in the eye and said, "It is impossible for human beings to cure their own terminal condition, but not for God: healing is possible only by uniting with God, trusting him, and partaking of the Remedy."

Mk 10:28 Peter reminded Jesus, "But we have already left everything we have to follow you."

Mk 10:29 Jesus replied, "I tell you truly, no person who has left behind property, brothers, sisters, parents, children, stocks or any valuable in order to be united with me and help distribute the Remedy [30] will fail to receive here, in this time, a hundred times the reward they could ever experience from homes, brothers, sisters, parents, children, stocks or any valuable—even if persecuted; and in the age to come, they will receive eternal life. [31] But those who think they deserve to be first will actually find themselves last, while those who are humble and consider themselves last will find themselves first in God's kingdom."

Mk 10:32 Jesus was leading as they walked on their way to Jerusalem, and the disciples were still stunned by what he had taught them. The others, who followed further behind, were afraid. He took the Twelve aside to prepare them for what was to happen to him. [33] "We are on the way to Jerusalem," he told them, "and when we arrive, the Son of Man will be betrayed to the church leaders and the theologians who teach a legal theology. They will sentence him to death and hand him over to the Romans, [34] who will mock him, spit on him, whip him, and execute him. Three days later he will rise from the dead."

Mk 10:35 Then Zebedee's sons, James and John, came to him and said, "Master, we want you to promise to do what we ask of you."

Mk 10:36 "What is it you want me to do for you?" he asked.

Mk 10:37 They answered, "Permit one of

us to have the seat of honor on your right, and the other—the seat of honor on your left when your glory is revealed."

Mk 10:38 Jesus answered them somberly, "You have no idea what you are asking. Do you think you can drink from the cup of suffering I will have to endure, or—like me—surrender yourself totally, being immersed in selfless love so completely that you won't shrink from death?"

Mk 10:39 "We can," they answered. Then Jesus told them, "You will drink from the cup of suffering from which I drink and be immersed in selfless love as I am, 40 but who sits on my right and left is not my decision to make. It will be as God has prepared."

Mk 10:41 When the other ten disciples heard what James and John had requested, they became angry. 42 So Jesus called them all together and said, "You know that the rulers of the Gentiles—those who have not partaken of the Remedy—abuse power and lord over others, using their high office to dictate and control those beneath them. 43 It is not like this with you. Instead, those who want to be great among you must use their energies to serve, uplift, and bless the others. 44 Whoever wants the first position in God's kingdom must be a slave to your welfare, 45 just as the Son of Man did not come to be served, but to serve the needs of humanity and to give his life as the healing Remedy to set many free from their terminal state."

Mk 10:46 Soon they arrived at Jericho. When Jesus was leaving the city, accompanied by his disciples and a very large crowd, a blind man named Bartimaeus (which means Son of Timaeus) was begging beside the road. 47 When he heard that it was Jesus of Nazareth who was approaching, he began shouting loudly, "Jesus, Son of David, please have mercy on me!"

Mk 10:48 Many people in the crowd told Bartimaeus to be quiet, but he only shouted louder: "Son of David, have mercy on me!"

Mk 10:49 Jesus stopped and said, "Bring him here."

They said to Bartimaeus, "Quiet down now, and cheer up. Get up; it's your day! He's calling for you to come to him." 50 Tossing his coat aside, he jumped up and came to Jesus.

Mk 10:51 Jesus asked him, "What do you want me to do for you?"

The blind man said, "Teacher, I want to see."

Mk 10:52 Jesus smiled and said, "Go! Your trust has enabled your healing." Immediately he could see and followed Jesus down the road.

11 As they came to Bethphage and Bethany, near the Mount of Olives, Jesus sent two of his disciples ahead, 2 instructing them, "Go to the next village; and as you enter, you will find a colt tied there, which has never been ridden. Bring it to me. 3 If anyone questions what you are doing, tell them, 'The Lord needs to borrow it and will have it returned shortly.'"

Mk 11:4 They went to the next village and found a colt in the street, tied to a doorway. As they were untying it, 5 a group of people nearby asked, "What are you doing with that colt?" 6 They gave the answer Jesus provided, and the people let them go. 7 Then they brought the colt to Jesus, put their coats on it, and he sat upon it. 8 As he rode upon the colt, many people laid their coats on the road before him, while others spread branches they had cut in the fields. 9 The people all around them shouted, "Salvation has come! Praise him who comes with the character of God! 10 Praise the coming kingdom of David! Salvation in the fullest!"

Mk 11:11 Jesus entered Jerusalem, went to the temple, looked around, and took a careful note of everything. But it was late, so he went out to Bethany with the Twelve.

Mk 11:12 The next day, they were leaving

Bethany and Jesus was hungry. [13] In the distance, he spotted a fig tree in leaf, and since figs typically appear when the tree is in full leaf, he went out to get some fruit. But when he got to the tree, there was nothing on it but leaves. It was not quite the season for figs, yet the tree had leaves, suggesting it was fruitful. [14] So he said to the tree, "No one will ever eat fruit from you again;" and his disciples heard him say this.

Mk 11:15 When he arrived at Jerusalem, Jesus entered the temple and began driving out all those who were buying and selling and thus misrepresenting God and his healing plan. He turned over the tables of the currency exchangers and the stands of those selling doves, [16] and he would not allow merchandise to be moved through the temple courts. [17] He directed their minds to the truth, saying, "Don't the Scriptures say: 'My house will be called a place of prayer for every nation'? But you have turned it into a 'house of extortion, a highway of robbery.'"

Mk 11:18 The senior church leaders and the theologians who taught a legal religion heard what Jesus was doing, and began plotting how they could kill him. They were afraid of his growing popularity and influence with the people, because the whole crowd was amazed with the truths he taught.

Mk 11:19 Near sunset, Jesus and his disciples left the city.

Mk 11:20 The next morning, as they were traveling, they spotted the fig tree dried up and dead. [21] Peter, remembering what Jesus had said, looked to Jesus and proclaimed, "Look Master! The fig tree you cursed has died!"

Mk 11:22 Jesus said: "Trust in God. [23] And the simple truth is, you won't need the Temple Mount to anchor your faith, as you will be able to say to the Mount 'Go and fall into the sea!' and if you don't doubt in your heart but genuinely trust God, then it will be so. [24] Understand clearly what I am telling you: If you ask God for help, and trust him to provide it, you will receive answers to your requests. [25] And when you are talking with God, if you hold resentment, bitterness, or anything against anyone, don't harden your heart but forgive them, so you may experience the forgiveness of your sin from your Father in heaven. [26] For if you refuse to forgive, you close your heart to the forgiveness of your Father in heaven."

Mk 11:27 Again they entered Jerusalem, and while Jesus was walking through the temple grounds, the senior church pastors, elders, and the theology professors who teach a legal theology came to challenge him. [28] "What gives you the right to what you are doing? By whose authority do you do this?" they demanded.

Mk 11:29 Jesus calmly answered, "I will ask you one simple question. If you answer my question, then I will tell you by what authority I do these things. [30] You remember John. Tell me: was his baptism ordained of heaven, or merely from men?"

Mk 11:31 They huddled together to strategize, saying to each other, "If we admit John's baptism was ordained of heaven, he will ask, 'Then why don't you believe him and support me?' [32] But if we say it is from men, the people will reject us because they believe John was really a spokesman from God."

Mk 11:33 So they answered Jesus noncommittally, "We don't know." Jesus replied, "Since you won't answer my question, then I will not tell you by what authority I am doing these things."

12

Then he began teaching them in parables: "A developer planted a vineyard. He built a watchtower and constructed a winepress, and then he leased the vineyard to some farmers and went away on a trip. [2] When the harvest was due, he sent a servant to collect his portion of the fruit. [3] But they attacked and beat the servant and sent him away with nothing. [4] The owner sent another servant, but they hit him on the head and abused him. [5] The owner sent another servant, but they killed that one. He sent many more: some were beaten, some killed. [6] The only person left to send was his son whom he loved very much. He sent him last, saying, 'They will recognize and honor my son.' [7] But when the farmers saw the son, they greedily said to each other, 'This is the heir to this property. Let's kill him and claim the inheritance for ourselves!' [8] So they grabbed the son, killed him, and tossed his body out of the vineyard.

Mk 12:9 "Now, what do you think the owner will do to these farmers when he comes to his vineyard?" Jesus asked. "I tell you, he will come and destroy those scoundrels and give the vineyard to others."

Mk 12:10 Jesus, looking straight at them, said: "Haven't you read in the Scripture where it says:

'The stone rejected by those in
   charge of building
   has become the foundation stone.
[11] God has made sure it would be this
   way and it is incredible to us'?"

Mk 12:12 They searched for any pretext upon which they could arrest him, because they knew this parable was about them. But they feared the crowd, so they let him be and went away.

Mk 12:13 Sometime later, some of the theologians from the school of the Pharisees and politicians from Herod's party were sent to Jesus to try to entrap him in his words. [14] Pretending to be deferential, they said, "Teacher, we know you are wise and always do what is right, constantly teaching the truth in harmony with God's methods and principles. You don't let the opinions of others influence you, because you stand for truth, and not what's popular at the moment. So please tell us: In your judgment, is it right to pay taxes to Caesar or not? [15] Should we pay the tax or not?"

But Jesus wasn't fooled, as he knew the evil in their hearts, and that they plotted against him; so he asked, "Why are you trying to trap me? Bring me a coin used to pay taxes." [16] So they brought him a Roman coin, and he asked them, "Whose picture is on this coin? And whose name is inscribed on it?"

Mk 12:17 "Caesar's," they said.

Jesus looked straight at them and said, "Then give to Caesar what belongs to Caesar and to God what belongs to God."

And everyone was amazed by his answer.

Mk 12:18 Next, the theology professors from the school of the Sadducees—those who teach there is no resurrection—came to question Jesus. [19] They asked: "Wise Teacher, Moses instructed us that if a man dies without having children, then his brother is to marry the widow and have children for him. [20] Well, we recently had a situation involving seven brothers: The oldest married and died without having children. [21] The second brother married the widow, but also died without having children, and so did the third brother. [22] In fact, all seven married her and died without children, and then she died, too. [23] Can you tell us, when the dead awaken to live again, whose wife will she be since she was married to all seven?"

Mk 12:24 Jesus answered without hesitation, "Your entire question is flawed because you neither understand what Scripture teaches nor God's power and methods. [25] When those who sleep in the grave arise to life, it will be into God's heavenly kingdom, and they will be like the angels in heaven, who neither marry nor are given in marriage. [26] And now, about your speculation regarding the resurrection of the dead: Don't you read the Bible? What did God say to Moses at the bush? He said, 'I am'—not 'I was'—the God of Abraham, the God of Isaac, and the God of Jacob.' [27] He is not the God of the dead—those who no longer exist—but the God of the living. You are completely wrong!"

Mk 12:28 One of the professors of theology, who focused on the law, heard them debating. Impressed with Jesus' answer, he asked him, "Which of all God's commandments is the most important?"

Mk 12:29 Jesus answered, "The most important is this: 'Understand, O Israel: The Lord our God is One Lord. 30 Love the Lord your God with your entire being—heart, soul, mind, and strength.' 31 And the second is this: 'Love others as yourself.' There is no commandment superior to these."

Mk 12:32 The professor smiled and said, "Well said, teacher. Well said, indeed. You are absolutely right that God is One; and there is no other God but him. 33 And to love him with all one's heart, mind and strength, and others as self, is more important than all the rituals, ceremonies, sacraments and offerings combined."

Mk 12:34 When Jesus heard how wisely the man answered, he said to him, "You are very close to God's kingdom of love." And from that point on, no one dared to attempt to trap him with more questions.

Mk 12:35 Later, when Jesus was teaching in temple grounds, he asked those gathered there, "Why do the theology professors—those who teach a legal religion—say that the Messiah is the son of David? 36 Yet David himself, under the inspiration of the Holy Spirit, declared:

"'The Lord has said to my Lord:
   Sit beside me, at my right hand,
   until I subdue your enemies
   beneath your feet.'

Mk 12:37 "So, if David himself calls the Messiah 'Lord,' how can he be his son?"

The large crowd was thrilled with the truth they heard from Jesus.

Mk 12:38 As Jesus taught, he warned them: "Be careful of following the theologians who teach legal theologies. They act for effect, seeking to garner attention, admiration, and respect. They wear distinctive clothing, seeking recognition in the shopping districts. 39 They desire their opinions to be most revered in church, and seek the places of honor at social events. 40 They play on people's fears, conning widows and the vulnerable out of their homes, yet make public displays of praying long prayers. Such persons will suffer most severely."

Mk 12:41 Jesus sat down across from the offering chest and watched the people as they put their money into the church coffers. Many of the rich made quite a display as they noisily threw in large amounts. 42 But one poor widow quietly slipped in two very small coins, worth less than a penny.

Mk 12:43 Jesus called his disciples to him and said, "Truly, this poor widow gave more than anyone else. 44 They gave a portion of their savings; but she, out of her poverty, gave everything she had—every cent she had left to live on."

13 When Jesus was leaving the temple, one of his disciples said to him, "Master, look at the Temple. Isn't it magnificent? Look at the size of the stones and the incredible stonework!"

Mk 13:2 Jesus paused, then said, "Yes, look at all these great buildings. But I want you to understand that they will all be torn down. Not even one stone will be left upon another."

Mk 13:3 Peter, James, John and Andrew came privately to Jesus as he was sitting on the Mount of Olives, and asked, 4 "When is all this destruction going to happen? And how will we know it is about to happen? What signs will let us know?"

Mk 13:5 Jesus answered: "Keep your minds sharp so that no one deceives you. 6 There will be many who will come using my name or claiming to be from me, or even claiming to be 'the One;' and vast numbers of people who haven't kept their minds sharp and who don't think for themselves will be duped. [7] Don't think it is the end when you hear of wars and the talk of warmongers. These symptoms of selfishness will happen before the end, but the end itself comes later. [8] Nations and kingdoms will oppose each other vying for domination, power, and control. The biosphere will be affected, and there will be earthquakes and climate change with famines all over the world. But all of this is only the beginning of the labor pains—just the start of the pain before delivery.

Mk 13:9 "You must keep your minds sharp, for you will be turned over to the authority of local church and state leaders, who will beat you right at their worship centers. Because you embrace me and take my Remedy to the world, you will witness the truth before governors, kings, presidents, and prime ministers. [10] Before the end, the Remedy must be presented to all the peoples of the world. [11] And when you are arrested and put on trial, don't stress over what you will say. Just speak honestly, from your heart, for the Holy Spirit will enlighten your minds and give you the words to speak.

Mk 13:12 "Siblings will betray each other, parents will sell out their children, and children will turn on their parents and have them executed. [13] Everyone who hasn't taken the Remedy will hate you because you represent me, but whoever stands firm until the end will be saved.

Mk 13:14 "When you see 'the abomination that causes desolation' set up where it is never supposed to be, then the reader should know it is the time for those who are in Judea to leave the city and flee to the mountains. [15] Don't get caught by trying to take your possessions. If you're on the roof, don't go inside to pack your belongings, but leave immediately. [16] If you're already out in the country, don't go back home to get clothes. [17] Those days will be horrible, especially for pregnant women and nursing mothers. [18] Pray that it won't happen in the winter, [19] because

this time of trouble will be the most horrible time in the history of earth—from creation until now—and never will there be such a terrible time again. [20] It will be so bad that if God had not intervened to shorten this troubled period, no one would survive. But for the sake of God's chosen people—those who have elected to partake of the Remedy—he has shortened those days. [21] At that time in history, if you hear reports 'Join us, come here, the Messiah is here!' or, 'Look there! The Messiah, the Savior is there!'—don't believe it. [22] For false Messiahs and frauds claiming to speak for God will appear, some of whom will perform various signs or miracles that deceive all those who have not elected to take the Remedy and think for themselves. [23] So keep your minds sharp; I have told you all of this before it actually happens, so that you can be prepared.

Mk 13:24 "But in the days following all that distress, 'light from the sun and moon will no longer be seen as evidence of God's creatorship, but their light will be darkened by evolutionism. [25] The stars in heaven will be disregarded as evidence of the Creator, and the power of heaven will be shaken out of the land and out of the hearts of people.'[4]

Mk 13:26 "Then, at that time in earth's history, the Son of Man will appear in the clouds, with great power and glory,

---

[4] This rendering is clearly interpretive, intended to cause the reader to think. Which sign would be more helpful to God's people on earth: a single day in which—in one small section of the globe—he sun and moon darken, and some years later there is a meteor shower (as some Christian groups suggest), or a global change in the minds of people, in which God's celestial beacons marking His Creatorship are cast aside? But for those preferring a more traditional reading, this is alternative rendering: "As soon as those events are over, 'the sun and moon will not give their normal light, stars will fall from the sky, and the power of heaven will be shaken.'"

and every person on earth will see him for themselves. 27 He will send his angels to gather from all over the entire earth, sky and seas those who have elected to partake of the Remedy.

Mk 13:28 "Learn from what a fig tree can teach you: When it buds, and leaves appear, you know by this sign that summer is near. 29 Likewise, when you see the events I have described take place, know that the end is near, right at the door. 30 Truly, this sinful race will not pass away before all these things have happened. 31 Earth and its atmosphere will one day pass away, but my words will never fail to happen.

Mk 13:32 "I can't tell you the specific date and time when the end comes, because no one knows the date and hour; angels in heaven don't know it, nor does the Son—only the Father knows. 33 So keep your minds sharp! Stay on guard, for you don't know the exact time when the end will come. 34 Think of it like this: A man leaves his estate and puts some servants in charge, each with their assigned duties, and tells the one at the gate to keep watch for his return.

Mk 13:35 "So be vigilant as you watch for the master, because you don't know when he will return. Will it be in the afternoon, at midnight, or dawn? 36 If he arrives suddenly, don't let him find you asleep. 37 I am telling you what I tell everyone, 'Keep Watch!'"

14 The Passover and the Feast of Unleavened Bread were just two days away, and the senior church leaders and theology professors who taught a legal theology were looking for some underhanded way to arrest Jesus and have him executed. 2 "But," they insisted, "we best not do it during the feast lest the people riot against us."

Mk 14:3 While Jesus was in Bethany, he was eating a special dinner hosted by Simon who was known for having had leprosy. While they were dining, a woman came in with a jar of very expensive perfume made of pure nard. She broke the jar and poured the perfume on Jesus' head.

Mk 14:4 Some of the people eating with Jesus became hostile toward the woman and what she had done. They began murmuring to each other, "Why has she wasted this perfume? 5 It could have been sold for more than an entire year's salary, and the money given to us to manage for the poor." So they verbally rebuked her, alleging her wasteful and not caring for the poor.

Mk 14:6 But Jesus would have none of their ugliness, and he said: "Leave her alone. Why are you so unkind to her? Don't you realize what a beautiful thing she has done to me? 7 You will always have the poor with you, and you can minister to them at any time. But I will not be with you much longer. 8 She did what she could for me: she poured this perfume upon me to prepare my body for burial. 9 Truly, wherever in the world the Remedy is taken and my kingdom presented, what she has done will also be told in memory of her."

Mk 14:10 It was then that Judas Iscariot, one of the Twelve, turned and went to the senior church leaders and agreed to betray Jesus to them. 11 They were so thrilled when they heard Judas' offer that they promised him money. So he kept watch for the best moment to hand him over.

Mk 14:12 On the first day of the Feast of Unleavened Bread, when the Passover lamb was customarily sacrificed, Jesus' disciples asked him, "Where would you like to celebrate Passover? Tell us, and we will get everything ready."

Mk 14:13 He sent two disciples, instructing them, "Go into the city. You will find a man carrying a jar of water. Follow him home. 14 Find the owner of the house and say to him, 'The Teacher asks: What room do you have for me to celebrate the Passover with my disciples?' 15 He will show you a great room on the second floor, already set up and ready. Make our preparations there."

Mk 14:16 The disciples went into the city and found things exactly as Jesus told them, so they got everything ready for the Passover.

Mk 14:17 That evening, Jesus arrived at that house with the Twelve. 18 They were eating together around the table when Jesus said, "Listen carefully: The truth is, one of you will turn against me and betray me—one who is eating this meal with me."

Mk 14:19 They were heartsick, and, one at a time, they said to him, "It isn't me, is it?"

Mk 14:20 Jesus answered, "It is one of my closest—one of the Twelve; one so close that he dips his bread into the bowl with me. 21 The Son of Man will fulfill all that the Scriptures say he will. But misery will be the portion of the one who betrays the Son of Man! Better never to be born than to do this."

Mk 14:22 During their meal, Jesus paused, took some bread, thanked his Father in heaven, then broke the bread and gave the pieces to his disciples, telling them, "Eat it; this is symbolic of my body."

Mk 14:23 Then he took the cup, thanked his Father in heaven, and passed it around. After they had all taken a drink from it, 24 he said, "This is symbolic of my perfect character—the life-blood of the Remedy, which is poured out for many. 25 I tell you the plain truth: I will not again drink the juice of grapes until the day when I drink it fresh in God's kingdom."

Mk 14:26 They sang a hymn, then went out to the Mount of Olives.

Mk 14:27 Jesus told them, "All of you will run away and leave me, for it is written: 'Strike the shepherd and the sheep will scatter.' 28 But after I rise from the dead, I will go into Galilee ahead of you."

Mk 14:29 But Peter protested, "No way Lord! All the others may run and hide, but I will not."

Mk 14:30 Jesus calmly told him, "Yes, Peter, you will. The truth is, tonight, before the rooster crows twice, you will deny me three times."

Mk 14:31 But Peter refused to believe it and said, "Absolutely not! I will stay by you even if I have to die. I will never abandon you." And all the others made similar promises.

Mk 14:32 When they arrived at Geth-semane, Jesus said to his disciples, "Sit here while I pray." 33 But he took Peter, James and John with him. Soon he was in deep anguish and emotional distress. 34 He told them, "My heart is breaking with overwhelming sadness. I feel like I am dying inside. Please, stay here and stay alert."

Mk 14:35 Going a short distance farther, Jesus fell to the ground and asked that, if possible, this burden might be taken from him. 36 He cried out, "Papa, Daddy, it hurts so bad! Please... I know you can do anything... Please take this cup from me; but Daddy, not as my feelings desire—do only what is in harmony with your will."

Mk 14:37 Then he went back to his disciples and found them sleeping. He said to Peter, "Simon, you're not sleeping, are you? Could you not stay awake for one hour? 38 Keep your minds alert and talk with God so that you will not succumb to temptation. Your heart desires to do right, but your body is weak."

Mk 14:39 Jesus again went a short distance away and prayed the same prayer as before. 40 When he returned to his disciples, he found them sleeping again (as they were exhausted); but they didn't make any excuses.

Mk 14:41 He came back to them a third time and said, "Are you still asleep?" Well, that will have to be enough, for the time has come: It's time for the Son of Man to be betrayed into the hands of the selfish. 42 Get up! Let's go! Here comes my betrayer."

Mk 14:43 Just as he finished saying this, Judas—one of the Twelve—walked up. He brought with him a mob armed with clubs and swords, sent from the senior clergy, theologians who teach a legal religion, and the church leadership team.

Mk 14:44 The traitor had arranged a signal with the mob: "The person I kiss is the one; arrest him and take him away under guard." 45 Without wasting time, Judas walked right up to Jesus and said, "Master!" and kissed him on a cheek. 46 Men grabbed hold of Jesus and arrested him. 47 One of his followers standing close by drew his sword and attacked, striking the servant of the high priest and cutting off his ear.

Mk 14:48 Jesus spoke to the mob: "Why have you come out in the night, with clubs and swords, to capture me? Do you think I am some terrorist leading a rebellion? 49 I am not in hiding. Daily I came to you, teaching openly in the temple courts, but you did not arrest me. But these events will take place just as the Scripture foretold." 50 Then all his followers abandoned him and fled, trying to save themselves.

Mk 14:51 One young man was there covered only in a bed sheet. When they tried to grab him, 52 he let go of the sheet and ran away naked.

Mk 14:53 The mob took Jesus to the high priest, and all the senior church leadership, pastors, and theology professors who promote a legal religion were there. 54 Peter, following from a safe distance, walked right into the courtyard of the high priest. He sat down with the guards to get warm by the fire.

Mk 14:55 The senior pastors and the entire high court were searching for any evidence they could use against Jesus so that they could execute him, but they could not find any. 56 Many people gave false testimony against him, but their accounts contradicted each other.

Mk 14:57 Finally, some came forward with this false testimony against him: 58 "We heard him say, 'I will destroy this temple made by men and in three days replace it with one not built by men.'" 59 But even their testimonies did not agree.

Mk 14:60 Exasperated, the high priest confronted Jesus and asked, "Aren't you going to say anything? What do you have to say for yourself? What answer to these allegations do you give?" 61 But Jesus stood silent and gave no answer. So the high priest asked him directly, "Are you the Messiah, the promised Son of the Blessed God?"

Mk 14:62 Jesus said, "I am! You will see with your own eyes the Son of Man sitting at the right hand of the Almighty returning on the clouds of heaven."

Mk 14:63 Immediately the high priest tore his clothes. "Do we need any more witnesses?" he asked. 64 "You have heard his blasphemy for yourselves. What do you think?" So they condemned him as deserving to die.

65 Then some of the church leaders began to spit on him; they put a blindfold on him and punched him, saying, "Prophesy!" And the guards took him and beat him some more.

Mk 14:66 While Peter was out in the yard, one of the housemaids of the high priest walked by. 67 When she saw Peter warming himself, she paused and took a good look at him. Then she said, "You are one of the followers of Jesus, the Nazarene."

Mk 14:68 But Peter denied it. "I don't know what you're talking about," he said, and walked toward the entryway.

Mk 14:69 When the housemaid saw him there, she repeated her concern to those standing around: "This man is one of Jesus' followers." 70 Again Peter denied it. But a little while later, some of the people standing by said to Peter, "You must be one of his followers, for you're from Galilee."

Mk 14:71 So he began cursing, and said, "I swear, I don't know this man you are talking about."

Mk 14:72 Immediately the rooster crowed the second time and Peter remembered Jesus' words "Before the rooster crows twice you will deny me three times."

And Peter broke down and cried bitterly.

15 It was very early in the morning when the senior pastors, church leadership team, lawyers and theology professors reached their decision. They had Jesus bound and taken to Pilate. ^Mk 15:2^ Pilate asked Jesus, "Are you the king of the Jews?"

"You said it, not me," Jesus replied. ^Mk 15:3^ The senior priests were making all sorts of allegations against Jesus, 4 so Pilate asked him several times, "Aren't you going to defend yourself? Is there nothing you want to say in your own behalf? Don't you hear all they are accusing you of?" ^Mk 15:5^ But Jesus stood there, at peace with himself, and said nothing. Pilate was amazed.

^Mk 15:6^ It was customary during the Passover Feast to release one prisoner requested by the people. 7 A murderer and revolutionary named Barabbas was currently in prison. 8 The crowd came to Pilate and asked him to release a prisoner, according to custom.

^Mk 15:9^ "Do you want me to release the king of the Jews to you?" Pilate asked, 10 because he knew that the senior priests were jealous of Jesus and that's why they were seeking his execution. 11 But the senior priests had incited the crowd to request Barabbas.

^Mk 15:12^ Pilate asked them, "What would you have me do with the One you call King of the Jews?"

^Mk 15:13^ "Crucify him!" they shouted.

^Mk 15:14^ Pilate tried to reason with them, asking, "Why? What crime has he committed?" But the crowd shouted even louder, "Crucify him!"

^Mk 15:15^ In order to appease the crowd, Pilate relented and released Barabbas and had Jesus beaten and turned over to be crucified.

^Mk 15:16^ The soldiers dragged Jesus away to the government building (that is, the Praetorium), and surrounded him with an entire company of soldiers. 17 They dressed him in a purple robe and made a crown out of thorns and crammed it onto his head. 18 Then they began mocking him, shouting, "Hail the King of the Jews!" 19 They hit him again and again on the head with a rod and spat on him. Then they feigned worship, falling on their knees before him. 20 When they finished making fun of him, they took off the purple robe and put his own clothes back on him. Then they led him out to crucify him.

^Mk 15:21^ Simon, a man from Cyrene, the father of Alexander and Rufus, was walking by on his way in from the countryside when the soldiers grabbed him and forced him to carry the cross. 22 They marched Jesus to the place called Golgotha (which means "the place that looks like a skull"). 23 They offered him an anesthetic made from wine mixed with myrrh, but he would not drink it. 24 Then they crucified him, and they cast lots to divide his clothes between them.

^Mk 15:25^ It was nine o'clock in the morning when they nailed him to the cross. 26 The charges written against him read:

THE KING OF THE JEWS.

27 Two robbers were crucified with him, one on the right, the other on the left, 28 so the Scripture came true that said, 'He shared the fate of lawbreakers.'

29 People who passed by shouted insults at him. Shaking their heads, they said, "So! You're so great, are you? Are you going to destroy the temple now, and rebuild it in three days? 30 Come down off the cross and save yourself, and we will believe you!"

^Mk 15:31^ The senior pastors and theologians who teach a legal religion mocked him in the same way. "He saved others," they said, "but—so sad—he just can't save himself! 32 Let this latest Messiah, this pretender to the throne, this so-called 'King of Israel,' come down now from the cross, so we may see it for ourselves and believe." The thieves crucified with him also shouted insults upon him.

Mk 15:33 At noon, a thick darkness overshadowed the entire region, and it lasted until three o'clock in the afternoon. 34 At three o'clock, Jesus cried out in a loud voice, *"Eloi, Eloi, lama sabachthani?"* (which means, "My God, my God, why have you given me up and let me go?").

Mk 15:35 Some of those standing nearby heard this and said, "He's calling for Elijah."

Mk 15:36 One man soaked a sponge in vinegar, put it on a stick, and was extending it toward Jesus to drink; then he changed his mind and said, "Wait! Let's see if Elijah will come and take him off the cross."

Mk 15:37 With a loud cry, Jesus expired his last breath and died.

Mk 15:38 The inner curtain of the temple was torn in two from the top to the bottom. 39 When the centurion standing guard in front of Jesus heard his cry and saw how he died, he said, "This really was God's Son!"

Mk 15:40 In the distance stood some women who were watching, including Mary Magdalene, Mary the mother of James the younger and Joseph, and Salome. 41 These women had followed him during his ministry in Galilee, and provided for his needs. Many other women, who had followed him to Jerusalem, were also there.

Mk 15:42 It was Friday, the day of preparation for the Sabbath. So as sunset approached, 43 Joseph of Arimathea, a leader of the Jewish high court, who longed for God's kingdom of love, went courageously to Pilate and asked for Jesus' body. 44 When Pilate heard that Jesus was already dead, he was surprised, so he summoned the centurion to inquire if Jesus had, in fact, died. 45 When it was confirmed by the centurion, Pilot gave the body to Joseph. 46 Joseph brought linen cloth, took down the body, wrapped it in the cloth and placed it in a tomb hewn in the rock. Then he rolled a stone over the entrance to the tomb. 47 Mary Magdalene and Mary the mother of Joses saw where Jesus was laid.

16

After Sabbath was over, Mary Magdalene, Mary the mother of James, and Salome took spices to the tomb to anoint the body of Jesus. 2 Very early on Sunday—the first day of the week—just after sunrise, as they were walking to the tomb, 3 they asked each other, "Who will we get to roll the stone away from the entrance of the tomb?"

Mk 16:4 But when they arrived, they saw that the massive stone had already been rolled away. 5 They entered the tomb and saw a young man dressed in white robes sitting on the right side of the tomb, and were startled.

Mk 16:6 "Don't be afraid," he said. "You're here looking for Jesus of Nazareth, who was crucified. He is no longer dead, but has risen and is not here. Look, the place where they laid him is empty. 7 Go and tell his disciples (and make sure you tell Peter!), 'He is going ahead of you into Galilee. You will see him there, just as he told you.'"

Mk 16:8 Trembling with joy and excitement, they ran as fast as they could from the tomb, saying nothing, because they were stunned.

Mk 16:9 Jesus, after arising from the dead early on Sunday, appeared first to Mary Magdalene—the woman from whom he had driven seven demons. 10 She went and told the others who had been with him, but who were now crying and grieving. 11 But they did not believe her when she told them that Jesus was alive and she had seen him.

Mk 16:12 Later, Jesus presented himself with a different appearance to two of them who were walking in the country. 13 These two returned and told the rest; but they didn't believe them either.

Mk 16:14 At a later time, the Eleven were eating together, and Jesus appeared to them. He rebuked them for not trusting him to do what he said he would do, and for their stubborn refusal to believe those who had already seen him since he had risen.

Mk 16:15 Then he instructed them: "Go throughout the entire world and take the Remedy to all creation. [16] Those who believe and immerse themselves into the Remedy will be healed, but those who don't believe and reject the Remedy remain terminal. [17] And these will be the evidences of those who believe: In my character of truth and love, they will drive back evil angels; they will speak new languages; [18] if they are bitten by poisonous snakes, or ingest some toxin, it will not harm them. They will minister to the sick and lay hands on them, and the sick will get well."

Mk 16:19 When the Lord Jesus finished speaking to them, he ascended into heaven and sat down at the right hand of God. [20] Then the disciples went out and began spreading the Remedy everywhere, and the Lord worked with them, providing evidence that their message was true.

Luke

1 Many people have attempted to write a history of the events that have been fulfilled— ²like the Old Testament Scriptures which were written down and then handed down to us by those who were eyewitnesses to the events—and served to preserve the truth. ³Therefore, since I have personally thoroughly investigated all these things from when they started, I thought it was a good idea to write an accurate account for you, most honorable Theophilus, ⁴so that you can be confident knowing that what you have been taught is true and accurate.

^{Lk 1:5} During the reign of King Herod of Judea, there was a priest named Zechariah. He was a member of the priestly division of Abijah, and his wife was also a descendant of Aaron. ⁶Both he and his wife trusted God, had renewed hearts, and lived in harmony with God's methods and principles. ⁷But they were childless, as Elizabeth was barren, and both were old and past the normal age for childbearing.

^{Lk 1:8} One day, when Zechariah was serving as priest (because his division was on duty), ⁹he was selected by lot— as was the custom for priests—to go into the temple of the Lord and burn incense. ¹⁰When it was time to burn the incense, the worshippers assembled and prayed outside.

^{Lk 1:11} It was then that an angel from God appeared to him. The angel stood on the right side of the golden altar. ¹²Zechariah startled, and was afraid when he saw the angel. ¹³But the angel said to him: "Don't be afraid, Zechariah. I'm here in answer to your prayer. Your wife Elizabeth will bear you a son, and you are to name him John. ¹⁴He will fill your lives with joy and delight, and many people will rejoice because of his birth, ¹⁵for he will do a great work for God. He is never to drink wine or any other fermented drink. He will be filled with the Holy Spirit from birth, ¹⁶and he will turn the hearts of many people in Israel back to the Lord their God. ¹⁷He will go before the Lord with the spirit and power that Elijah had. He will proclaim the truth about God's character of love in order to turn the hearts of the fathers to their children, and those living outside God's design parameters of love he will bring back to the wisdom of the righteous— to prepare people to meet the Lord."

^{Lk 1:18} Zechariah, wanting further assurance, asked the angel, "How can I believe this? I am an old man, and my wife is past childbearing age."

^{Lk 1:19} The angel answered, "I am Gabriel. I stand in God's very presence, and God sent me to speak to you and tell you this great good news. ²⁰Because you did not believe what I have told you, which will come true when the time is right, you will be mute—not speaking a word until the day this happens."

^{Lk 1:21} Outside, the people were concerned, wondering why Zechariah was taking so long in the temple. ²²When he came out, he was unable to speak to them. They realized he had seen a vision in the temple because he used hand gestures; but he remained unable to speak.

^{Lk 1:23} When his time of service was complete, he returned home. ²⁴Afterward, his wife Elizabeth became pregnant and remained secluded for five months. ²⁵She said joyfully, "The

Lord has blessed me! He has taken away my shame and shown me his favor."

$^{Lk\,1:26}$ It was the sixth month when God sent the angel Gabriel to the Galilean town of Nazareth, ^{27} to a virgin engaged to a man named Joseph who was a descendant of David. The virgin was called Mary. ^{28} The angel went to her and said, "Good morning, dear one! You are very special to God, and he is with you."

$^{Lk\,1:29}$ Mary was quite unsettled by the angel's words and was trying to figure out what the greeting might mean, ^{30} when the angel said to her, "It's okay, you don't have anything to fear. God has chosen you for a great blessing. ^{32} You will become pregnant and give birth to a son, and you must name him Jesus. ^{32} He will be great and will be called the Son of the Most High. The Lord God will give him the throne of his ancestor David, ^{33} and he will be the sovereign over the house of Jacob forever; his kingdom of love will never end."

$^{Lk\,1:34}$ Mary was baffled and asked the angel, "But how can this be, since I am a virgin?"

$^{Lk\,1:35}$ The angel smiled and said, "The Holy Spirit will come upon you and the power of the Most High will surround you. So understand that the child born to you will be the holy Son of God. ^{36} Even your cousin Elizabeth, who is old and barren, is barren no longer. She is six months pregnant and is going to have a son. ^{37} Nothing is impossible with God."

$^{Lk\,1:38}$ Mary humbly replied, "I am the Lord's and will serve as he desires. Let it be as you have said." Then the angel departed.

$^{Lk\,1:39}$ After the visit from the angel, Mary didn't wait around but packed some things and went to a town in the hills of Judea. ^{40} She went straight to Zechariah's home to see Elizabeth. ^{41} When Elizabeth heard Mary greet her, the baby in her womb leaped for joy,

and Elizabeth was filled with the Holy Spirit. ^{42} She proclaimed in a loud voice: "You are blessed among all women of the earth, and the child you bear is also blessed! ^{43} But who am I that the mother of my Lord should visit me? ^{44} The moment I heard the sound of your greeting, the baby in my womb leaped for joy. ^{45} Happiness is yours, because you believe that what the Lord has said will come true."

$^{Lk\,1:46}$ Then Mary said:

"My heart praises the Lord
^{47} and my mind overflows
  with happiness in God my Savior,
^{48} for he thought of me for this
  mission, lowly as I am.
  Because of this, all generations
  will recognize how privileged I am.
^{49} The Mighty One, whose character is
  holy,
  has done a great thing for me.
^{50} His kindness flows out
  to those who revere him,
  from one generation to the next.
^{51} His arm is powerful
  to accomplish great things;
  he confounds the arrogant,
  those who believe they are
  great in their own minds.
^{52} He has removed despots from their
  thrones,
  but has exalted those
  who humbly trust in him.
^{53} Those who hunger for good
  he fills,
  but those who believe they are rich
  and in need of nothing
  go away empty.
^{54} He has remembered his child
  Israel,
^{55} mercifully sending help to
  Abraham and all his descendants,
  just as he promised to our
  ancestors he would."

$^{Lk\,1:56}$ Mary stayed with Elizabeth for three months, and then returned home.

$^{Lk\,1:57}$ When the time came for Elizabeth to have her baby, she gave birth to a son. ^{58} Her neighbors and relatives had heard how God had blessed her, and they celebrated with her. ⁵⁹ It was the eighth day after the child's birth— the day they came to circumcise him— and the officials were going to name the child Zechariah, after his father. ⁶⁰ But Elizabeth objected and said, "No! He is to be named John."

Lk 1:61 They inquired, "But why? No one in your family has the name John."

Lk 1:62 So they made gestures, asking the father what he wanted to name the child. ⁶³ He asked for a writing tablet and shocked everyone when he wrote, "His name is John." ⁶⁴ Instantly, his mouth was opened and he began to speak praises to God. ⁶⁵ Everyone there was filled with awe, and word spread throughout Judea about all these events. ⁶⁶ Everyone who heard the story began asking, "What will this child grow up to do?" For God had a special purpose for him.

Lk 1:67 Then his father Zechariah was filled with the Holy Spirit and prophesied:

Lk 1:68 "Thanksgiving and adoration to
the Creator, the God of Israel,
because he has come and rescued
his people.
⁶⁹ The Remedy to heal us he has
raised in the family of David,
⁷⁰ just as he foretold through his
spokespersons of old.
⁷¹ He promised freedom from fear
and selfishness,
freedom from the power of all
who hate us,
⁷² to give mercy to our forebears,
and fulfill his holy vow to us.
⁷³ He swore the promise to our
ancestor Abraham
⁷⁴ to deliver us from our terminal
condition
and enable us to live for him—
no longer controlled by fear
⁷⁵ but in purity, selflessness and love,
for his glory, all of our days.
Lk 1:76 "And you, my son, will be a
spokesperson of the Most High God;
for you will go before the Lord
to prepare the minds of the people

to receive him,
⁷⁷ to teach the people God's plan
to heal humanity
by taking away their sinfulness
and remitting them
back to his perfect ideal.
⁷⁸ Our God is so kind, gentle and
merciful
that he brings the Remedy from
heaven,
gentle like a sunrise,
yet growing ever brighter
⁷⁹ to shine into the minds and hearts
of those lost in darkness,
stumbling in the shadow of death,
and to lead us to safety
and eternal peace."

Lk 1:80 And the child grew and became physically healthy, with a sharp mind and discerning spirit. He lived in the desert until he began his public ministry in Israel.

2 It was during the time when Caesar Augustus ordered that a census be taken of the entire Roman empire. ² This was the first census, when Quirinius was governor of Syria. ³ Everyone was required to go to their hometown to register.

Lk 2:4 So Joseph, being a descendant of David, left Nazareth in Galilee and went to Bethlehem, the city of David, in Judea. ⁵ He went there to register with his fiancée Mary, who was pregnant. ⁶ While in Bethlehem, Mary went into labor, ⁷ and gave birth to her first child, a son. She wrapped him in fragments of cloth and laid him in a feeding trough because there was no room for them in the inn.

Lk 2:8 Nearby shepherds lived out in the fields, watching over their flocks at night. ⁹ One of God's angels appeared to them, and the fiery brilliance of heavenly light shone all around them; and they trembled in fear. ¹⁰ But the angel said gently to them, "Don't be afraid. I've come to share with you the best news of incredible joy that is for all humanity. ¹¹ Today, in Bethlehem, the city of David, the promised Savior was born: he is Christ the Lord. [12] You will recognize him by this: You will find the baby wrapped in fragments of cloth lying in a feeding trough."

Lk 2:13 Then a great number of heavenly beings appeared with the angel and they all began singing praises to God. [14] They sang,

"Glory to God in the highest,
    and on earth peace
    to every person who partakes of
        his goodness."

Lk 2:15 After the angels had returned to heaven, the shepherds said to each other, "Let's go to Bethlehem right now and see what God has revealed to us."

Lk 2:16 So they rushed to Bethlehem and found Mary, Joseph, and the baby who was lying in the feeding trough. [17] Once they had seen him, they began telling everyone what they had been told about the child, [18] and those who heard their account were astounded. [19] But Mary held these things close to her heart and contemplated their meaning. [20] The shepherds returned to their flocks with hearts overflowing with praise and thanksgiving to God for all they had seen and heard, which was exactly as the angel said it would be.

Lk 2:21 Eight days later, on the day of his circumcision, he was named Jesus—the name the angel gave Mary before the baby was conceived.

Lk 2:22 When their time of purification—according to the script given through Moses—was complete, Joseph and Mary took Jesus to Jerusalem to present him to the Lord. [23] The Lord's little theater had a script which directed, "Every firstborn male is to be dedicated to the Lord," [24] and to present a sacrificial offering as the Lord's script directed: "A pair of doves or two young pigeons."

Lk 2:25 In Jerusalem, there was a faithful and pure-hearted man named Simeon. He was waiting to see the Deliverer, promised to come through Israel; and his mind was enlightened by the Holy Spirit. [26] The Holy Spirit had revealed to him that he would not die before he had seen God's Remedy. [27] Impressed and directed by the Holy Spirit, he went to the temple courts. When Mary and Joseph brought baby Jesus to fulfill the rituals required by the script, [28] Simeon held him in his arms and praised God. He said:

Lk 2:29 "Sovereign God,
    you have kept your promise to me
    and now I can retire in peace.
[30] For with my own eyes
    I have seen your Remedy
[31] whom you have sent
    for all the people to behold—
[32] a beacon of truth
    to enlighten the world—
    and for the complete restoration
    and glorification
    of your triumphant people."

Lk 2:33 The boy's father and mother were deeply moved by what this man said about Jesus. [34] Then Simeon gave them his blessing and said to Mary, the boy's mother: "This child's purpose and mission is to cause the downfall of selfishness and the rising up of love in those who overcome through God's power, and to be the supreme evidence of God's character of love; but many will oppose him. [35] As a result, the true thoughts and motives of many hearts will be revealed, and a sword will pierce your soul."

Lk 2:36 Anna, the daughter of Phanuel of the tribe of Asher, was one of God's spokespersons. She was quite old at eighty-four; her husband had died after seven years of marriage, [37] and she had never remarried. She stayed at the temple and worshipped constantly, day and night, fasting and praying. [38] She approached them right then, gave thanks to God, and began speaking about the child to everyone looking for the healing and restoration of Jerusalem.

Lk 2:39 When Joseph and Mary had completed all that the Lord's script had required, they went home to Nazareth in Galilee. ⁴⁰ And the child grew physically strong and mentally wise, for he was the grace of God.

^{Lk 2:41} Each year, Jesus' parents traveled to Jerusalem for the Passover Feast. ⁴² When he was twelve years old, they went to the Feast, as was their custom. ⁴³ After the Feast ended, his parents left for home, but unbeknownst to them, the boy Jesus stayed behind in Jerusalem. ⁴⁴ Thinking that he was with them, they traveled on for the entire day, and then they began to search for him amongst their friends and relatives. ⁴⁵ When they could not find him, they returned to Jerusalem to look for him. ⁴⁶ After three days of searching, they found him in the temple courts, sitting among the professors, listening and asking questions. ⁴⁷ All those who heard him were astonished at his level of understanding and the depth of his answers. ⁴⁸ His parents were amazed when they saw him. His mother asked him, "Son, why did you do this to us? Your father and I have been frantically looking for you."

^{Lk 2:49} Jesus replied, "Why did you search all over for me? Didn't you know I would be in my Father's house?" ⁵⁰ But they didn't comprehend what he meant. ⁵¹ So he left with them and went back to Nazareth and was an obedient son. His mother cherished all of these experiences in her heart, ⁵² and Jesus developed a perfect human character in harmony with God—full of strength and wisdom.

3 It was the fifteenth year of the reign of Caesar Tiberius. Pontius Pilate was governor of Judea; Herod Antipas—a son of Herod the Great—was ruler (tetrarch) in Galilee, and his brother Philip ruled in Iturea and Traconitis; Lysanias ruled in Abilene; ² and Annas was the former high priest and the father-in-law of Caiaphas, the current official high priest. It was during this time that John, the son of Zechariah, was in the desert and received a message and mission from God. ³ He went throughout the country all over the Jordan valley, preaching a message of immersion in truth, a turning away from distortions about God, and a cleansing of hearts from fear and selfishness— ⁴ as God's spokesman Isaiah wrote:

"A voice calling in a desolate land,
  'Prepare your minds,
  untwist your hearts,
  and make ready for the Lord
  to come with his healing Remedy.
⁵ To those who partake of the
  Remedy,
  every gutter of sin will be filled,
  every mountain of pride will be
  made low,
the crooked thoughts and mental
  paths will be made straight,
  and rough character will be
  smoothed.
⁶ And all humanity will see
  God's healing Remedy.'"

^{Lk 3:7} It had become quite popular to be immersed in water by John, so John challenged the crowds: "You children of that poisonous snake! Who told you that you would be safe from destruction by running here? ⁸ Rituals change nothing! You must experience a new heart motivated by love, and produce fruits consistent with a heart of love. And don't begin claiming false security by saying, 'We are genetic descendants of Abraham.' God could take these stones and create biological children of Abraham. ⁹ The ax is about to fall; the time to choose is now. Every person who does not—like a green tree—produce good fruit, will—like a dead tree—be cut down and thrown into the fire."

^{Lk 3:10} "What do we need to do?" the crowd begged.

^{Lk 3:11} John told them, "Live in harmony with God's design of love—Live to Give. The person with two coats should give one to a person who has none, and those who have food should share with those who are hungry."

Lk 3:12 When tax collectors came to be immersed in water, they asked John, "Teacher, what should we do?"

Lk 3:13 John told them, "Be honest in all your dealings. Don't collect one cent more than is required."

Lk 3:14 Then some soldiers asked, "What are we supposed to do?"

John instructed them, "You are in a position of trust and responsibility, so carry out your duties honorably. Don't use your power to exploit, extort, abuse, or accuse people falsely; be honest in all your dealings and be content with your wages."

Lk 3:15 The people were anticipating the Messiah and were wondering in their hearts if John might be him. 16 John didn't let that idea take root. He said to them all, "I immerse you in water, but One more powerful than I is coming. I am not even worthy to untie his shoes. He will immerse your minds and hearts with the Holy Spirit and fill you with the fires of truth and love. 17 In his hand is the power to dissect evil and selfishness from hearts and minds, remove all defects, and purify the character with the unquenchable fire of truth and love." 18 John spoke many more words of encouragement and instruction, and taught them about the Remedy.

Lk 3:19 But John, motivated by love and a desire to see Herod the tetrarch partake of the Remedy, rebuked him, making it clear that his selfish actions—including the taking of Herodias, his brother's wife—were deadly, destroying his mind and warping his character. 20 But Herod chose to add another act of selfishness to his long list of evil—he locked John in prison.

Lk 3:21 When the crowds were being immersed in water by John, Jesus also was immersed. And while he was talking with his Father, heaven opened up 22 and the Holy Spirit came down and rested upon him in the physical form of a dove. And a voice was heard from heaven, saying: "You are my Son.

I love you, and in you is my complete pleasure."

Lk 3:23 Jesus was about thirty years old when he began his ministry.
He was commonly believed to be the
son of Joseph, who was
son of Heli,
24 son of Matthat, son of Levi,
son of Melki, son of Jannai,
son of Joseph,
25 son of Mattathias, son of Amos,
son of Nahum, son of Esli,
son of Naggai,
26 son of Maath, son of Mattathias,
son of Semein, son of Josech,
son of Joda,
27 son of Joanan, son of Rhesa,
son of Zerubbabel,
son of Shealtiel, son of Neri,
28 son of Melki, son of Addi,
son of Cosam, son of Elmadam,
son of Er,
29 son of Joshua, son of Eliezer,
son of Jorim, son of Matthat,
son of Levi,
30 son of Simeon, son of Judah,
son of Joseph, son of Jonam,
son of Eliakim,
31 son of Melea, son of Menna,
son of Mattatha, son of Nathan,
son of David,
32 son of Jesse, son of Obed,
son of Boaz, son of Salmon,
son of Nahshon,
33 son of Amminadab, son of Ram,
son of Hezron, son of Perez,
son of Judah,
34 son of Jacob, son of Isaac,
son of Abraham, son of Terah,
son of Nahor,
35 son of Serug, son of Reu,
son of Peleg, son of Eber,
son of Shelah,
36 son of Cainan, son of Arphaxad,
son of Shem, son of Noah,
son of Lamech,
37 son of Methuselah, son of Enoch,
son of Jared, son of Mahalalel,
son of Kenan,
38 son of Enosh, son of Seth,
son of Adam, the son of God.

4 Jesus, with his human mind filled with the Holy Spirit, returned from the Jordan and was led by the Spirit into the desert, ²where, for forty days, he battled the devil and overcame his temptations. He ate nothing during those days, and by the end of them was very hungry.

Lk 4:3 The devil came to him and said, "God's Son shouldn't starve to death; if you are him, command these stones to become bread—save yourself!"

Lk 4:4 But Jesus answered, "The Scriptures teach that life doesn't come from eating bread alone, separated from God, but from partaking of all truth originating in God."

Lk 4:5 Satan led Jesus to a high mountain and flashed before him a panorama of all the kingdoms of the world, ⁶and then said to him, "All this has been given to me, and I can give it to anyone I choose. I will give you all their power and glory; ⁷just kiss my hand and recognize me as your one true lord, and it will all be yours."

Lk 4:8 Jesus said, "The Scriptures teach, 'God alone is Lord, worship and serve only him.'"

Lk 4:9 Then Satan took him to the top of the temple in Jerusalem and said, "If you are God's Son, then jump off from here. ¹⁰For the Scriptures clearly state, 'God will direct his angels to watch over you, to protect and guard you, and keep you safe;' ¹¹and, 'They will hold you in their hands so you won't even hurt your foot stumbling on a stone.'"

Lk 4:12 Jesus calmly replied, "It also says, 'Don't take actions designed to put God in the box of your predetermined ideas, testing to see if he will do what you believe is right in any given situation.'"

Lk 4:13 When the devil ended that round of temptations, he left Jesus, but watched for another opportunity to tempt him again.

Lk 4:14 With his humanity empowered by the Spirit, Jesus returned to Galilee where news about him quickly spread throughout the entire region. ¹⁵He taught in their worship centers, and everyone praised him.

Lk 4:16 He went to his home town of Nazareth, and as he always did on the Sabbath day, he went to the worship service. He stood up and read ¹⁷from the book of God's spokesman Isaiah, which was handed to him. He unrolled the scroll and read from the place where it is written:

Lk 4:18 "God's Spirit is on me
    because I am his anointed One to
    bring the Remedy to the afflicted.
He has sent me to bring freedom
    to those held in the bondage
    of fear and selfishness,
    and a clear understanding
    to those blinded by Satan's lies,
to exterminate oppression,
    to remove human brokenness,
¹⁹and to make God's pleasure known
    this year."

Lk 4:20 He then rolled up the scroll, handed it back to the minister, and sat down. Everyone in the sanctuary watched him closely, ²¹and he told them plainly, "Today, right here, within the sound of my voice, this Scripture is fulfilled."

Lk 4:22 Those who heard him recounted how well he spoke, and were impressed with his wisdom, but they also asked, "But isn't this the son of Joseph the carpenter?"

Lk 4:23 Jesus said to them, "Are you now going to quote this proverb to me: 'Physician, heal your own sickness,' or 'Do some miracles here like we heard you did in Capernaum?'

Lk 4:24 "The truth is," Jesus continued, "no spokesperson of God is listened to in their hometown. ²⁵In Elijah's day, when it didn't rain for three and a half years and there was severe famine throughout the land, there were many widows in Israel, ²⁶but Elijah was not sent to live with any of them. No; he was sent to a widow in Zarephath in Sidon. ²⁷And when Elisha was God's spokesman, there were many in Israel with leprosy, yet not one of them was healed—just Naaman the Syrian. Stop waiting for miracles and embrace the truth already revealed."

Lk 4:28 When the worshippers heard this, they became enraged. 29 The mob rose up and drove him out of the town to the edge of the cliff on which the town was built, so they could throw him off. 30 But he walked right through the riotous crowd and continued on his way.

Lk 4:31 Then he went to the town of Capernaum, in Galilee, and on the Sabbath began teaching the people. 32 They were overwhelmed with awe at his message because it resonated with the authority of truth.

Lk 4:33 In the worship center was a man whose mind was controlled by a demon—a fallen angel. He screamed as loud as he could, 34 "You! What are you going to do to us, Jesus of Nazareth? Are you here to kill us? I know you are the Holy God!"

Lk 4:35 "Silence!" Jesus said, and commanded, "Leave him!" Then the demon caused the man to fall down, and left without harming him.

Lk 4:36 The people were dumbfounded and wondered to each other, "What kind of a decree is this? He orders demons and has the authority and power to make them leave!" 37 And his fame spread throughout the surrounding countryside.

Lk 4:38 Jesus then left the worship center and went to Simon's house. Simon's mother-in-law was sick with a high fever, and they asked Jesus to help her. 39 So he leaned over her and ordered her body to be well, and the fever went away. She immediately got up and began serving them.

Lk 4:40 At sunset, the people brought to Jesus those suffering with a variety of illnesses and disabilities. He laid hands on them and healed them all. 41 Not only that, but from many, he commanded demons to leave, and they left, shouting, "You are God the Son!" But

he gave them firm instructions to be silent, and would not grant them permission to speak, because they knew he was the Messiah.

Lk 4:42 At dawn, Jesus went to a remote location. The people searched for him and when they found him, they tried to keep him with them. 43 But he said, "I must take the Remedy from God's kingdom of love to other towns as well; that is why I was sent." 44 And he continued spreading the truth about God's Remedy at worship centers throughout Judea.

5 One time, Jesus was beside Lake Gennesaret, and the people were pressing closer and closer, seeking to better understand the truth of God's kingdom. 2 At the shore, Jesus spotted two boats left by fishermen who were beside them washing their nets. 3 He climbed into Simon's boat and asked him to put out a few yards from shore. Sitting in the boat, he taught the people on shore.

Lk 5:4 When he finished teaching, he told Simon, "Go out to deeper water and cast your nets."

Lk 5:5 Simon-the-fisherman thought to teach Jesus-the-carpenter and said, "Master, we've fished all night during prime fishing time and didn't catch anything. But because you said to do it, I will put out the nets."

Lk 5:6 As soon as the nets were in the water, they were overflowing with fish to the point of nearly tearing apart. 7 So the fishermen called their partners in the other boat to come and help them, and when they came, both boats were so full of fish that they were near sinking.

Lk 5:8 When Simon Peter saw the catch, he fell down on his knees at Jesus' feet and cried out, "Leave me, Lord, for I am a selfish man and unworthy to be in your presence!" 9 When this catch of fish was pulled in, Simon was overwhelmed with awe and admiration, as were his companions 10 and his fishing partners, James and John, Zebedee's sons.

But Jesus didn't leave. Instead, he said to Simon, "Don't be frightened; from this point forward, you will catch men for my kingdom of love." [11] So they hauled their boats ashore and left everything behind and followed Jesus.

Lk 5:12 When Jesus was in one of the towns, a man approached him, who had a very advanced case of leprosy, with his body covered in lesions. As soon as he saw Jesus, he bowed, and with face to the ground, begged him: "Lord, if you are willing, you can make me clean."

Lk 5:13 Jesus didn't hesitate but touched the man and said, "I am glad to. Be clean!" And instantly the leprosy was gone.

Lk 5:14 But Jesus, knowing the bigotry of the religious leaders, instructed him: "Before telling anyone, go straight to the priests, get inspected, offer the sacrifices indicated in the script from Moses—so the symbolic enactment will testify to God's healing plan—and have the priests certify you 'clean to return to the community.'"

Lk 5:15 The news about Jesus spread like wildfire, and the crowds flocked to him, seeking to be healed from their sicknesses. [16] But Jesus would take frequent breaks in solitary locations for rest and communion with his Father.

Lk 5:17 Once, Jesus was teaching, and the Pharisees and theology professors who teach a legal religion had come from all over Galilee, Judea and Jerusalem, and sat around him, watching closely. The power of God was there, and he healed the sick. [18] Some men approached, carrying a paralyzed man on a stretcher and trying to get him into the house to see Jesus. [19] The crowd was so dense that they couldn't get through, so they climbed up on the roof, moved the tiles, and lowered the man down on his mat into the crowd, right in front of Jesus.

Lk 5:20 When Jesus saw their trust in him, he said, "Brother, your sin is abolished and removed."

Lk 5:21 The Pharisees and theology professors who taught a legal religion began thinking to themselves, "Who does this guy think he is to say such blasphemy? Who can release from sin except God alone?"

Lk 5:22 But Jesus knew what they were thinking, so trying to help them understand God's plan to heal the heart from sin, he said, "Why are you thinking such things in your hearts? [23] Which is easier: to say 'Your sin is abolished and removed,' or to say 'Stand up and walk'? [24] So that there can be no confusion and that you may know without a doubt that the Son of Man has the authority to abolish and remove sin..."— turning to the paralyzed man, he continued—"follow my instructions: Stand up, pick up your mat, and walk home." [25] Instantly he was healed and jumped up in front of them, picked up the mat he had been lying upon, and went home praising God. [26] Everyone was in awe, stunned with amazement, and gave praise to God. They said, "What we have seen today is simply incredible."

Lk 5:27 After this, Jesus went outside and saw a tax collector named Levi sitting at his booth. Jesus said to him, "Come with me," [28] and Levi got up immediately, left everything behind, and followed him.

Lk 5:29 Levi was so appreciative of being called that he held an extravagant banquet for Jesus at his house. Feasting with them was a large crowd of tax collectors and other persons of questionable reputation. [30] When the self-righteous Pharisees and the theologians who taught a legal religion saw this, they complained to Jesus' interns: "What are you doing eating and drinking with tax collectors and 'sinners?'"

Lk 5:31 Jesus intervened, "Only those who acknowledge they are sick go to the doctor—not those who think they are healthy. [32] I cannot help those who already believe they are right with God—only those who know they are sick with sin."

Lk 5:33 They challenged him, "John's interns know the value of fasting and prayer, and do it often—as do the students of the Pharisees—but your interns go on eating and drinking."

Lk 5:34 Jesus answered, "People don't fast at a wedding reception; they feast! 35 But when the time comes that the groom is separated from his bride, then they will fast."

Lk 5:36 He told them this parable: "An old system, filled with inconsistencies, is like an old, worn-out garment full of holes. One cannot fix the old garment with a patch of new cloth. If one does, the new piece will tear the old apart. Likewise, the truth of God's kingdom I bring cannot be merged into the inconsistent legal system you have created. Trying to do so will tear the old system apart. 37 No one pours unfermented wine into old, dried-out wineskins. If one does, the new wine will burst the old skin. Likewise, trying to squeeze the truth I bring into the rigid legal theology you practice will fail. 38 You must have new wineskins for the new wine, and a new heart for the truth I bring. 39 But those habituated to the old wine don't want the new, for they say 'the old is better.'"

6 Jesus and his interns were walking through a field of grain one Sabbath, when his interns began picking heads of grain, rubbing them in their hands, and eating the kernels. 2 Some of the Pharisees immediately protested: "What are you doing? Why are you breaking the Sabbath and God's Law?"

Lk 6:3 Jesus tried to enlighten them: "Don't you understand the reality of God's kingdom of love? What did David do when he and his friends were hungry? 4 He understood that the symbolic script doesn't overrule the reality of the laws of health, and entered God's little theater (sanctuary) and ate bread that the script (law) said was only for the priests; and he gave some to his friends as well." 5 Then Jesus told them directly, "The Son of Man doesn't serve the Sabbath; he created and rules it."

Lk 6:6 On a different Sabbath, he went to the worship center and was teaching, when he saw a man whose right hand was withered and useless. 7 The Pharisees and theologians who taught a legal religion were watching him closely, trying to find some point on which to accuse Jesus. They watched to see if he would heal this man on the Sabbath. 8 But Jesus knew their thoughts and motives, and directed the man with the withered hand to stand up in front of everyone. So the man got up and stood in front.

Lk 6:9 Then Jesus turned to the religious leaders and said, "Let me ask you this: Is it right and in harmony with God's Law to do good on the Sabbath, or to do evil? Should we save life or destroy it on the Sabbath?"

Lk 6:10 He looked around the room, meeting each one's gaze, but they said nothing. So Jesus said to the man, "Use your hand." And he did so and his hand was completely restored to normal. 11 But the religious leaders were enraged and began plotting how they could get rid of Jesus.

Lk 6:12 One day, Jesus went to a mountainside and spent the entire night talking with his Father. 13 The next morning, he called his followers and chose these twelve to be his ambassadors: 14 Simon (also called Peter) and his brother Andrew, James, John, Philip, Bartholomew, 15 Matthew, Thomas, James (Alphaeus' son), Simon the Zealot, 16 Judas (son of James), and Judas Iscariot, who betrayed him.

Lk 6:17 He led them down to a level place. Many of his interns were there, as well as a large crowd of people from across Judea, Jerusalem, and the coast of Tyre and Sidon. 18 They had come eager to listen to him and to be healed from all disease and defect. Those whose spirits were disturbed by evil had their minds set free. 19 And everyone tried to touch him because life-giving energy was radiating from him and healing them all.

Lk 6:20 Looking toward his interns, he said so all could hear:

"Blessed are you who know
the poverty of your condition,
for God's kingdom is for you.

Lk 6:21 "Blessed are you
when you hunger for more
than this world can give,
for you will be filled.

Blessed are you whose tender hearts
cry from the pain
selfishness causes,
for you will be the ones
who rejoice in the end.

Lk 6:22 "Blessed are you when people
despise you, are prejudiced
against you, speak lies about you,
slander you and reject you, calling
you evil—all because you promote
the Remedy I bring.

23 Rejoice when this happens, for your great reward is in heaven; and realize that in this world, evil always attacks good—just as their ancestors attacked God's spokespersons in the past.

Lk 6:24 "But misery and suffering is
yours, you who rest secure in riches;
for having rejected the Remedy,
you have all you will ever receive.

Lk 6:25 "Misery is yours, you who are
satisfied with this world;
for disconnected from me—the
only source of life—you will starve.

Misery is yours, you who laugh at the
pain and suffering in the world;
the only outcome for you
is suffering and grief.

Lk 6:26 "Misery is yours,
you who are praised by the selfish;
for you will be duped into
complacency with your terminal
condition—
and that is how their ancestors
adored frauds, liars
and those with false remedies.

Lk 6:27 "But I am here to tell you the deep reality of how God constructed life to operate, so hear me: Life is built upon the principle of giving. If you want to live, you must love your enemies, do good to those who can't stand you, 28 be a blessing to those who spit upon you, and ask God to heal those who abuse you. 29 If an enemy strikes you on one side of your face, offer him the other side as well. If someone steals your coat, offer him your shirt as well. 30 Give what is beneficial to everyone who asks, and if someone steals from you, don't fight to get it back. 31 Treat others as you would like to be treated yourself.

Lk 6:32 "If you only love those who love you, what's the point? Selfishness still lives in your heart. Even the unhealed love those who love them. 33 And if you do good only to those who do good to you, what's the point? Selfishness still lives in your heart. Even the unhealed know how to do that. 34 And if you lend only to those with good credit scores, whom you know will pay you back in full, what good is that? Selfishness still lives in your heart. Even the unhealed lend to the unhealed with good credit scores, expecting full repayment. 35 But you are to live in harmony with God's design for life, so love your enemies, do good to them, and lend without expecting to get anything back. Then you will get the greatest reward: a character like the Most High God's and you will be his true sons and daughters, for he is kind to the unhealed—those still consumed with selfishness. 36 So, be gentle and kind just as your Father in heaven is gentle and kind.

Lk 6:37 "Do not form a judgmental character, and you will not be diagnosed as unhealable. Do not condemn others, and you will not be diagnosed as terminal. Forgive, and you will experience God's forgiveness. 38 Life is constructed to operate upon giving, so give; and the more you give, the more will be given to you: a great abundance of love—concentrated, intense, overwhelming and all-consuming—will be poured into your being. For the way you treat others reveals the condition of your own character, and your own condition determines your destiny."

Lk 6:39 He told them this illustration as well: "What happens when a blind person leads another blind person? Don't they both get lost? 40 Students don't instruct their teacher. No; students become like their teacher, so be careful who you accept as your teacher.

Lk 6:41 "Why do you try to find the smallest defect in someone else's character, but ignore the malignant pathology in your own? 42 How can you possibly think you can help another remove defects in their character when all the while your character is corrupt with selfishness? You charlatans! Healthy interventions require healthy minds: first address the defects in your own character, and then you will have the clarity and ability to help another remove defects in theirs.

Lk 6:43 "Healthy trees don't produce diseased fruit, nor do diseased trees produce healthy fruit. 44 The health of the tree is recognized by its fruit. People don't get figs from thornbushes, or grapes from thistles. 45 Likewise, the healthy person who has taken my Remedy will bring forth love and goodness out of the love and goodness accumulated in their heart, but the selfish person who rejects my Remedy will bring evil and selfishness out of the evil and selfishness accumulated in their heart. For a person's actions reveal what flows in their heart.

Lk 6:46 "Why do you call me Master, Doctor,[1] or Lord, yet ignore what I say?

---

[1] The term "doctor" traces its roots back to the early church, when the term referred to the Apostles, church fathers, and other Christian authorities who taught the Bible. Only later did it come to refer to physicians. Thus, in the book of Luke—understanding that the plan of salvation is the plan to heal sinners, and written by a physician— I wanted to merge the idea of "teacher and healer" and thus used the term "doctor" rather than "teacher." (Verger, J. (1999), "Doctor doctoratus", *Lexikon des Mittelalters* 3, Stuttgart: J.B. Metzler, cols 1155-1156)

47 Let me tell you what the person who not only hears my instructions but understands them and puts them into practice is like: 48 Such a person, who builds on the solid rock of the truth of my teaching, is like a builder who digs down to bedrock and establishes the foundation of their house on solid rock. When a flood came, the rushing water struck the house but couldn't shake it because it was built on a solid foundation. 49 But those who hear my words of truth and do not embrace and apply them are like the builder who built a house on dirt, with no solid foundation. The moment swirling waters struck that house, it collapsed and was completely destroyed."

7 When Jesus had finished teaching the people, he entered Capernaum. 2 A Roman centurion had a servant he valued highly, who was very sick and about to die. 3 The centurion had heard of Jesus and sent some Jewish leaders to ask Jesus to heal his servant. 4 They came to Jesus and made an earnest appeal, "Please heal his servant; he is truly worthy, and besides, we owe him, 5 for he has shown great love to our people and even built our worship center." 6 So Jesus went with them. But as they neared the house, the centurion sent friends to tell him, "Sir, I did not mean to inconvenience you so, and I don't deserve the honor of having you visit my home. 7 I didn't even consider myself worthy to come to you myself. I know that all you need to do is simply say so, and my servant will be healed. 8 I am a man who understands authority: I obey my orders, and my soldiers obey me. I tell this one, 'Go' and he goes; and another, 'Come,' and he comes. When I tell my servant, 'Do this,' he does it."

Lk 7:9 When Jesus heard the confidence in him, he was deeply moved, and turning to the crowd, said, "I tell you plainly, I haven't found another person in Israel whose confidence in me is as great as his." ¹⁰ Then the men who had been sent went back to the house and found the servant completely well.

Lk 7:11 Shortly thereafter, Jesus went to the town of Nain, followed by his interns and a very large crowd. ¹² As he neared the town gate, a funeral procession was leaving the town; the corpse was the only son of his mother who was already a widow. A large crowd from the city was with her. ¹³ When Jesus saw her, his heart was filled with compassion, and he said gently, "Don't cry."

Lk 7:14 Then Jesus walked over and put his hand on the coffin, and those carrying it stopped. He said, "Young man, I tell you, get up!" ¹⁵ The dead man sat straight up and began to talk, and Jesus returned him to his mother.

Lk 7:16 The crowd was overwhelmed with awe and praised God. "A mighty spokesman of God has come to us," they said; "God has come to heal his people." ¹⁷ After this, news about Jesus spread like wildfire throughout Judea and the surrounding country.

Lk 7:18 John's students told him everything Jesus was doing. He called two of them ¹⁹ and sent them to Jesus to ask, "Are you the One who God promised to send, or should we look for another?"

Lk 7:20 When the students came to Jesus, they said to him, "John the Baptist sent us to ask you, 'Are you the One who God promised to send, or should we look for another?'"

Lk 7:21 As they stood watching, Jesus demonstrated God's methods: he cured many people of disease, infections and mental oppression, and to those who were blind, he gave sight. ²² Then he turned to John's students and said, "Go back and tell John what you have witnessed here: The blind see, the paralyzed walk, those with leprosy are cured, the deaf hear, the dead are raised to life, and the Remedy is given freely to the poor. ²³ Happy and healthy is the person who doesn't reject me."

Lk 7:24 After John's students left, Jesus turned to the crowd and spoke about John: "What did you go to the desert to see? A standup comic blowing around from one idea to the next? ²⁵ No? Then what did you go to see? A fashion show? No; fashion is indulged by those living in luxury and in palaces. ²⁶ Then what did you go out to see? One of God's spokesmen? Absolutely, and I tell you plainly, he was even more. ²⁷ This is the one of whom it was foretold,

'I will send my spokesperson
ahead of you
to prepare the hearts and minds of
the people for your arrival.'

Lk 7:28 "I tell you plainly, no person born on earth prior to John has had a more important role in God's plan to save humanity than John the Baptist. Yet, even those with the least role on earth who are in the kingdom of heaven will be greater than he is here."

Lk 7:29 All the people, including the tax collectors, whose minds had been immersed in the truth brought by John—and thus were immersed by him in water—and who heard Jesus' words, praised God's way as right. ³⁰ But the Pharisees and those theologians who taught a legal religion rejected God's design and plan for their healing, for they had refused to immerse their minds in the truth John brought.

Lk 7:31 "How can I describe what the people living today are doing? To what can I compare them? ³² They are like children who sit around picking on each other, trying to promote themselves by finding fault in another: If one child plays a happy song, the others refuse to celebrate with them; if another child plays a sad song, the others laugh and refuse to mourn with them.

Lk 7:33 "You are like these children—bent on finding fault. John lived very strictly: he fasted and drank no wine, and you mocked him calling him 'evil' and 'demon-possessed.' ³⁴ And when the Son of Man came, spending time with people, socializing, eating and celebrating, you say, 'He's a glutton, a drunk, and a friend of apostates and addicts.' ³⁵ But God's wisdom is shown to be true by the transformed lives of those who embrace it."

^{Lk 7:36} One of the Pharisees invited Jesus to his home for dinner, so he went to the Pharisee's house and reclined at the table. ³⁷ A local woman who had been living an immoral life learned that Jesus was at the Pharisee's home and she brought an alabaster jar of perfume. ³⁸ She stood by Jesus' feet weeping, and began washing his feet with tears. Then she dried his feet with her hair, kissed them, and poured the perfume on them.

^{Lk 7:39} When the Pharisee in whose home they were dining saw this, he thought to himself, "If this man was really from God, he would know what a vile and sinful woman was touching him."

^{Lk 7:40} Jesus, knowing his thoughts, turned to him and said, "Simon, I want to tell you something."

"Please, Doctor, tell me," he replied.

^{Lk 7:41} "There were two people, and both owed a banker money. One owed him five thousand dollars, the other only fifty; ⁴² but neither had any money to pay him back, so the banker canceled both debts and absorbed the loss. Which of the two do you think will love him more?"

^{Lk 7:43} Hesitantly, Simon replied, "I would think the one who had the larger debt canceled."

"You are absolutely right," Jesus confirmed.

^{Lk 7:44} Then Jesus looked toward the woman, but spoke to Simon: "Do you see this woman? Even though I am in your house, you did not provide water to wash my feet; but she has washed my feet with her tears and dried them with her hair. ⁴⁵ You did not welcome me with a kiss, but this woman, from the moment I arrived, hasn't stopped kissing my feet. ⁴⁶ You did not anoint

my head with inexpensive olive oil, but she has anointed my feet with the most expensive ointment. ⁴⁷ Understand how reality works: She has been forgiven much, and having received this forgiveness, she loves much. But he who accepts only a little forgiveness, loves only a little."

^{Lk 7:48} Then Jesus reassured her, "You are forgiven; your sinfulness has been removed."

^{Lk 7:49} The other guests began to mumble, "Who does he think he is to claim to forgive and remove sin?"

^{Lk 7:50} Smiling, Jesus said to the woman, "Your trust in me has healed you; go with a mind restored to peace."

8 After this, Jesus traveled from town to town, proclaiming the good news of God's Remedy and the kingdom of love. The Twelve went with him, ² along with some of the women whose minds had been cleansed of evil and bodies healed of diseases: Mary Magdalene whom he had freed from demonic harassment seven times, ³ Joanna the wife of Chuza who was the chief of staff to Herod, Susanna, and many others. These women used their own resources to support Jesus and his interns.

^{Lk 8:4} A large crowd had gathered, as people from many towns were coming to Jesus. He told them this parable:

⁵ "A farmer went to plant seed in his field. As he spread the seed, some fell on the path where it was either trampled or the birds came and ate it. ⁶ Some fell on the rocks and sprouted, but quickly withered and died because it had no water. ⁷ Other seed fell among the thorns which grew and choked out the good plants. ⁸ Still other seed fell on good soil. This seed sprouted and brought forth an abundant crop—a hundred times that which was planted." Then he said, "Those whose minds are open to truth, let them understand."

^{Lk 8:9} When his interns asked him what this parable meant, ¹⁰ he explained: "The understanding of the secrets of

God's kingdom of love is taught to you because your hearts are open to receive it, but their minds are not ready to accept the truth, so parables must be used because

'though they see with their eyes,
    their minds do not comprehend;
and though they hear with their ears,
    they do not understand the
    meaning.'

Lk 8:11 "This is what the parable means: The seed represents the truth about God's kingdom of love. 12 The seeds on the path are the ones who hear the truth about God's kingdom of love but don't embrace it, so Satan infects their hearts with a lie, and thus they do not trust and are not healed. 13 The seeds on the rocks are people who hear the truth and immediately accept it with joy, but the truth is only accepted as an idea—it does not take root in the heart, get applied to life, or get incorporated into the character, so when trials or persecution come, they quickly abandon it. 14 The seeds that fell amongst the thorns are those who hear the truth but allow worries, pleasure and wealth to strangle it; they remain selfish and fail to bear the fruit of a loving character. 15 But the seed that fell on good soil represents those who hear, comprehend and embrace the truth of God's kingdom, and by applying it to their lives, experience the fruit of a transformed character.

Lk 8:16 "No one lights a lantern and puts it under a bucket, or covers it with blankets. No; a person puts it on a stand, so everyone sees its light.

17 Reality will one day be revealed for what it is; there is no secret that will not one day be exposed. 18 Therefore be thoughtful and deliberate in how you deal with what you hear. Those who develop their talents will expand their abilities; those who don't use and develop their abilities will lose what they have."

Lk 8:19 Jesus' mother and brothers came to see him, but the crowd was so large that they couldn't get to him. 20 Someone told Jesus, "Your mother and brothers are waiting for you outside."

Lk 8:21 He told them, "Anyone who lives in harmony with my Father in heaven, practicing his methods and following his will, is united with me like my mother and brothers."

Lk 8:22 Once, Jesus told his interns, "Let's cross the lake to the other shore," so they got in a boat and set sail. 23 As they sailed, Jesus fell asleep. A vicious storm came up and the waves washed over the boat, threatening to capsize it. The danger was very great.

Lk 8:24 The interns woke Jesus, crying, "Master, the boat is swamped, we're going to drown!"

Jesus stood up and told the wind to slow and the waves to calm, and the storm immediately dissipated, and everything was still. 25 Then he looked at his interns and asked, "Don't you have any confidence in me?"

In awe and uncertainty, they asked each other, "Who is he? He has power to control the wind and waves."

Lk 8:26 They sailed on to the region of Gerasenes, across the lake from Galilee. 27 When Jesus went ashore, a man from the town, whose mind was controlled by evil angels, confronted him. The man had not worn clothes or lived in a house for a long time; he lived in the graveyard. 28 When he saw Jesus, he fell down at his feet and began shouting as loud as he could, "What do you want with me, Jesus, Son of the Most High God? Please don't torture me!" 29 Jesus commanded the evil intelligence to leave the man's mind. Many times through the years it had taken control of his mind, and though he was chained hand and foot and guarded, it had broken the chains and driven the man into desolate places.

Lk 8:30 Jesus asked him, "What is your name?"

"Legion," he replied, because many evil intelligences had taken control of his mind. 31 They begged Jesus repeatedly not to order them into isolation from living beings.

Lk 8:32 There was a large herd of pigs feeding on the hill nearby. The evil angels begged Jesus for permission to take control of the pigs, and he granted it. 33 The fallen angels left the mind of the man and went into the minds of the pigs: the herd went berserk and stampeded down a steep bank into the lake and drowned.

Lk 8:34 When those tending the pigs saw what had happened, they ran into town and told everyone, 35 and the people came out to see it for themselves. When they came to Jesus, they found the man whose mind had been freed from demons, sitting at Jesus' feet, dressed, calm and coherent; and this frightened them. 36 Those who had seen all that transpired told the new arrivals how the man had been freed from the evil agencies. 37 Then all the people from the region of Gerasenes were so terrified that they asked Jesus to leave, so he got in the boat and left.

Lk 8:38 The man whose mind had been freed from demons begged to go with Jesus, but Jesus had another mission for him. He told him, 39 "Go home and tell everyone how much God has done for you." So the man went away and told everyone he encountered how much Jesus had done for him.

Lk 8:40 When Jesus returned from the region of Gerasenes, a large crowd welcomed him back, for they had been watching for him. 41 A man named Jairus, a church official, came and fell down at Jesus' feet, begging him to come to his house 42 because his only daughter, a girl of about twelve, was dying. As Jesus made his way, the crowds were so large that they almost crushed him.

Lk 8:43 There was a woman in the crowd who had suffered with bleeding for twelve years, and no doctor had been able to heal her. 44 She snuck up behind Jesus and touched the edge of his robe, and instantly her bleeding ceased.

Lk 8:45 Jesus stopped and asked, "Who touched me?"

When no one came forward, Peter said, "Master, the crowd is immense; everyone is pushing against you."

Lk 8:46 But Jesus clarified, "Someone touched me: I felt power go out from me."

Lk 8:47 Then the woman, realizing she could not escape unnoticed, came forward trembling and fell down at his feet. In front of the crowd, she explained why she had touched him and how she had been instantly healed. 48 He smiled and said, "Daughter, your trust in me has healed you. Live in peace."

Lk 8:49 While Jesus was speaking to the woman, a messenger came from the home of Jairus, the church leader. "Your daughter is dead," he told him. "It's too late, don't bother the Doctor any more."

Lk 8:50 Hearing this, Jesus said to Jairus, "Don't let fear control you. Trust in me and she will be healed."

Lk 8:51 When they arrived at Jairus' home, Jesus didn't let anyone go in with him except Peter, James and John, along with the child's father and mother. 52 All the people were crying, wailing, and mourning for her. Jesus said to them, "Stop crying. The child is not dead but asleep."

Lk 8:53 They all laughed at him because from a human perspective she was dead. 54 But Jesus took her hand and said, "My child, wake up!" 55 Her life returned to her and she stood up at once. Then Jesus instructed them to give her something to eat. 56 Her parents were stunned with joy, but he ordered them not to tell anyone what had happened.

9 Jesus called the Twelve together and empowered them to cure diseases, and gave them the authority to drive out all evil forces. 2 He sent them out to reveal God's kingdom of love, demonstrating how it works by healing

the sick. [3] He told them, "Don't pack anything for this trip except a walking stick. Don't take food, extra clothes, or money. [4] Whatever home accepts you, stay there until you leave town. [5] If you are opposed, or people won't listen, don't waste time getting upset or fighting to be heard; just shake the rejection like dust off your feet when you leave their town, and your gracious behavior will be a witness to them." [6] So they went from town to town, spread the good news of God's Remedy and demonstrated God's plan by healing people everywhere.

Lk 9:7 When Herod the tetrarch heard about all that Jesus was doing, he became very distraught because some people murmured that John had been raised from the dead, [8] while others said that Elijah had come, and still others thought one of God's old-time spokesmen had risen from the dead. [9] But Herod said, "It can't be John. I beheaded him, so who is this fellow I hear so much about?" And he tried to see Jesus.

Lk 9:10 When the twelve interns returned from their mission trip, they reported to Jesus their experiences. Then he and the Twelve went on a private retreat in the town of Bethsaida, [11] but it didn't stay private for long. Soon the crowds found out where he was and flocked to him. He was gracious and made them welcome. He spoke to them about God's kingdom of love, and he demonstrated this kingdom by healing all who needed it.

Lk 9:12 In late afternoon, the Twelve came to him and said, "You need to disperse the crowd so they have time to make it to the nearby towns and find food and lodging before everything closes, for we're in the middle of nowhere out here."

Lk 9:13 Jesus smiled and said, "Don't send them away hungry; you feed them."

Somewhat shocked, they said, "Are you serious? We only have five loaves of bread and two fish—we'd have to go and buy a lot more food to feed this crowd." [14] (About five thousand men plus women and children were there.)

But Jesus reassured them and said, "Don't worry. Have them sit down in groups of about fifty each." [15] So the disciples did as Jesus instructed, and everyone sat down. [16] Jesus took the five loaves and two fish, and looking up toward heaven, he thanked his Father and broke them, then he gave the pieces to his interns to pass out to the people. [17] The entire crowd ate until all had their fill, and the interns collected twelve basketfuls of leftovers.

Lk 9:18 When Jesus was again alone with his interns, he asked them, "Who do the people say that I am?"

Lk 9:19 "Some say you are John the Baptist," they told him, "others say you are Elijah who went to heaven in a chariot of fire. Still others say you are one of God's old-time spokesmen who has risen from the dead."

Lk 9:20 "What do you think? Who do you say I am?" Jesus asked them.

Peter immediately blurted out, "The Messiah—the Savior of all humanity—sent from God."

Lk 9:21 Jesus gave them strict warning not to tell this to anyone else at this time. [22] Then he told them what would transpire: "The Son of Man must bear the hostility, abuse, mistreatment and rejection of the church leaders, elders, chief priests and theologians who teach a legal religion, and then be killed; and on the third day—arise back to life."

Lk 9:23 Then Jesus said to them all: "If anyone wants to follow me into unity with my Father, they must surrender their life, willingly choose to die to selfishness, and follow me in love. [24] Whoever follows the survival-of-the-fittest instinct and seeks to save their life will lose it because the infection of selfishness will not be eliminated; but whoever loses their life in love for me will find eternal life, for they will have been restored back to God's design for life—to selfless, other-centered love.

25 What good does it do to selfishly hoard all the treasures of the world only to die eternally, consumed by selfishness? 26 If anyone is ashamed of me and my methods of truth and love, the Son of Man will feel a shame—a real shame—that they are not healed and able to live in his presence when he comes with his holy angels, in his unveiled splendor and in the fullness of his Father's glory. 27 I tell you the plain truth, some of you right here will not sleep in death before you see the Son of Man glorified in his kingdom of love."

Lk 9:28 Eight days later, Jesus took Peter, James and John, and went up on a mountain to talk with his heavenly Father. 29 As he was talking with his Father, his face began radiating light, and his clothes became brighter, shining like lightening. 30 Out of nowhere, Moses and Elijah 31 appeared with him physically, also in brilliant fiery light, like the sun, and they talked with Jesus. They spoke about the completion of his mission to procure the Remedy, which he was about to accomplish in Jerusalem. 32 Peter, James and John were very sleepy, but when fully alert, they saw the splendor, the brilliant light, and the two men standing with Jesus. 33 As Moses and Elijah were leaving, Peter said to Jesus, "Master, this is awesome, and we are so thankful to be here. If you like, we can put up three shrines: one for you, one for Moses, and one for Elijah." (He was rambling nonsense because he was so overwhelmed that he didn't know what else to say.)

Lk 9:34 While Peter was still talking, a brilliant cloud appeared and settled over them, and they were awed as the cloud covered them. 35 A voice came from the cloud that said, "This is my Son; I have chosen Him to fulfill my purpose, so listen to him." 36 After the voice had spoken, they found themselves alone with Jesus. Peter, James and John didn't talk about this, and didn't tell anyone at that time what they had seen.

Lk 9:37 The next morning, when they came down from the mountain, a large crowd was waiting for Jesus. 38 A man in the crowed shouted, "Doctor, please have mercy, I beg you! Please look at my son. He is my only child. 39 Some evil force seizes him and he will scream, fall down convulsing, and foam at the mouth. It comes on him almost constantly and is killing him. 40 I begged your interns to heal him, but they couldn't."

Lk 9:41 With disappointment, Jesus said, "What a confused and superstitious people you are. How long will I need to be with you before you understand? Bring your son to me."

Lk 9:42 As the boy approached Jesus, the evil agency caused the boy to have a seizure and he convulsed on the ground, but Jesus ordered the evil force to leave, healed the boy, and restored him back to his father. 43 And everyone was in awe of the magnificence and greatness of God. As the crowd was in wonder over all that Jesus did, he pulled his disciples aside and said, 44 "Listen closely, as this is important: I, the Son of Man, am going to be betrayed into the hands of human beings." 45 But they didn't understand what he was trying to tell them. Their expectations prevented them from realizing what he meant, and they feared the answer if they asked him, so they didn't ask.

Lk 9:46 Then the interns started arguing over which of them would be the greatest.

Lk 9:47 Jesus knew they were struggling with the infection of selfishness and were arguing over who would be the greatest, so he had a small child stand next to him. 48 Then he looked at his interns and said, "Any person who opens their heart and receives those with childlike trust as I would—with love and affection — practicing my methods, also opens their heart to receive me; and whoever opens their heart to receive me, not only receives me but also the One who sent me. It is the one who has the least amount of selfishness who is the greatest."

Lk 9:49 John tried to change the subject: "Master, we saw a man driving out evil beings using your name, and we told him to stop, because he isn't one of us."

Lk 9:50 Jesus corrected him, "No, don't stop him, for there are only two sides: love and selfishness; and anyone who is not selfishly against you is on your side of love."

Lk 9:51 As the time drew near for Jesus to return to heaven, he, with resolve, set out for Jerusalem. 52 He sent envoys into a Samaritan town to prepare for him, 53 but the people there were not happy about it because he was on his way to Jerusalem. 54 When his interns James and John saw that the people grumbled, they asked, "Lord, do you want us to call fire down from heaven and destroy them?" 55 But Jesus corrected their misunderstanding of his methods and said, "You don't yet realize the depth of the infection of fear and selfishness in your hearts: 56 The Son of Man did not come to destroy human beings, but he came to heal and save them." And they moved on to another village.

Lk 9:57 As they were traveling down the road, a man said to Jesus, "I want to be one of your interns, to learn from you and go wherever you go."

Lk 9:58 Jesus told him, "I don't have the comforts of a fox's den or a bird's nest. If you come with me, it will be rough. We often sleep on the ground, and I don't even have a pillow for my head."

Lk 9:59 Jesus invited another man, "Join me."

But the man replied, "Lord, I must first go and bury my father."

Lk 9:60 Jesus told him, "Now is the time to spread God's Remedy; let the dead bury the dead."

Lk 9:61 Still another person said, "Lord, I will join you as soon I get back from saying good-bye to my family."

Lk 9:62 Jesus said, "No one who puts their hand to sowing seeds of truth—yet has their heart longing for the world—is capable of sharing the Remedy from the kingdom of God."

10 After this, the Lord selected seventy-two other interns and sent them ahead in pairs to every town and village he planned to visit. 2 He said to them: "Those ready to be brought into the kingdom of love are plentiful, but those willing to work to spread the Remedy are few. Ask the Lord of life to send workers out who will spread the Remedy. 3 Go now. I am sending you out—like gentle lambs into a brutally savage world—to reveal love. 4 This isn't a shopping trip, so don't take a lot of money; it isn't a vacation, so don't take luggage or other belongings, as you will only be burdened by watching after them; and don't get distracted from your mission by stopping on the road to pay homage and give long, protracted displays of appreciation to those you meet.

Lk 10:5 "When you enter a house, extend your hand in peace. 6 If the host takes your hand in peace, then you will both relax in peace; if not, your peace will be your own. 7 Accept the hospitality of your host and eat what they prepare, for this is how the law of love works: You give your time, wisdom and energy, and they give you support. And show how stable you are by staying in one place.

Lk 10:8 "When you enter a town and are warmly received, demonstrate the law of love by accepting their hospitality graciously, 9 and then give to them by healing the sick among them, and telling them that this is how God's kingdom operates. 10 But when you enter a town and are rejected, publicly declare, 11 'Because you don't want us here, we are leaving. But understand this: We brought you the Remedy from God's kingdom of love, but you have rejected it. So we shake the dust off our feet to let you know that we are not responsible for your decision.' 12 The truth is, Sodom will have less guilt to bear than that town.

Lk 10:13 "Korazin, your suffering will be great! Misery will be yours, Bethsaida! If the miracles and evidence that were presented to you would have been done in Tyre and Sidon, they would have humbled themselves, rejected selfishness, accepted the Remedy, and been restored to love. 14 On the day each person faces ultimate truth, Tyre and Sidon will have less guilt and agony to bear than you. 15 And people of Capernaum, will you soar into heaven? Oh no; having rejected the Remedy, you will shrivel up and decay into the depths.

Lk 10:16 "Those who embrace the truth you bring are embracing me; those who reject the truth you bring are rejecting me; and those who reject me are rejecting my Father who sent me."

Lk 10:17 When the seventy-two returned, they were jubilant, saying, "Lord, even evil angels obeyed our commands issued in your name."

Lk 10:18 He replied, "Like lightening falling from the sky, I see Satan exposed (for all to see) and falling from the affections of the heavenly intelligences. 19 All Satan's forces are like snakes and scorpions—ready to strike you—but I have given you power over them and they cannot harm you. 20 But take no joy in the fact that evil forces flee before you; rather, rejoice in the knowledge that you have partaken of the Remedy and are registered as 'healed' in the books of heaven."

Lk 10:21 Hearing this, Jesus rejoiced, and inspired by the Holy Spirit, said: "Thank you, Father, Sovereign of heaven and earth, because you have revealed the truth of your kingdom of love to those whose minds are like little children's, open and eager to learn; but from those who have closed their minds—thinking they already have all the answers—the truth is hidden. Yes, Father, this is exactly what pleases you—to present the truth in love, and leave your intelligent beings free to embrace or reject it.

Lk 10:22 "Everything necessary to rid the universe from sin and restore creation to perfection the Father has entrusted to me. The Father and Son are intimately united in heart and mind, and no one knows the Son except the Father, nor the Father—except the Son and those who learn of the Father from the Son."

Lk 10:23 Then, turning to his interns and speaking privately, he said: "Happy are those who see and embrace what you have seen and embraced. 24 Many of God's spokespersons and kings longed to stand here and see what you are seeing, but they didn't have the opportunity; they longed to hear the truths you have heard, but they didn't have the chance."

Lk 10:25 On one occasion, one of the nation's top lawyers stood up to test Jesus: "Doctor, what is required for me to do in order to receive eternal life?"

Lk 10:26 Jesus smiled and asked him, "What is written in the Law, and how do you understand it?"

Lk 10:27 He answered, "Love the Lord your God with your entire being, heart, soul and mind, and love your neighbor as yourself."

Lk 10:28 "That's right," Jesus replied, "live in harmony with God's design for life—the law of love—and you will have eternal life."

Lk 10:29 But the lawyer wanted a loophole to justify his bigotry, so he asked Jesus, "But who is my neighbor?"

Lk 10:30 Jesus gave this answer: "A man was traveling from Jerusalem to Jericho when he was attacked by thieves. They beat him, took all he had, and left him naked and bleeding, and nearly dead, on the road. 31 When a pastor came down the road and saw the man lying there, he crossed to the other side and walked on by. ³²Likewise, a member of the church leadership team came by and saw him, then crossed to the other side and walked on by. ³³But then came a Samaritan, a member of a race hated by the Jews. When he saw the man lying there, he had compassion for him. ³⁴He went over to him, cleaned his wounds, and applied salve and bandages. Then he lifted him onto his donkey, took him to an inn, and tended him. ³⁵The next day he paid the innkeeper and said, 'Take care of him for me. I will compensate you for any additional costs when I return.'

Lk 10:36 "In your judgment, which of these three was a neighbor to the man who was mugged by the thieves?"

Lk 10:37 The lawyer begrudgingly replied, "The one who was merciful to him."

"Go and live just like that," Jesus instructed him.

Lk 10:38 As Jesus and his interns were traveling, they came to a small town where a woman named Martha invited them to stay. ³⁹She had a sister, Mary, who loved to sit at Jesus' feet and listen to all he had to say. ⁴⁰But Martha, who was preparing for guests, was too preoccupied to listen. Frustrated, she interrupted and said: "Lord, doesn't it matter to you that my sister has abandoned me to do all the work? Tell her to help me!"

Lk 10:41 Jesus answered gently, "Dear Martha, you fret over so many things, ⁴²but only one thing is essential—partaking of the Remedy. Mary has chosen it, and it won't be taken away from her."

11 One day, when Jesus finished talking with his Father, one of his interns said to him, "Master, please teach us to talk to God, like John taught his disciples."

Lk 11:2 Jesus said to them, "When you talk to God, say this:

'Father, your character is beautiful and holy;
let your kingdom of love come.
³Provide us with what we need each day.
⁴Forgive us our wrongs as we also forgive all those who wrong us.
And lead us away from temptation.'"

Lk 11:5 Then he told them: "Consider going to one of your friends in the middle of the night and saying, 'My friend, please lend me some food; ⁶another friend arrived at my place unexpectedly and I don't have anything to feed him.'

Lk 11:7 "But the one inside answers, 'I'm asleep! The door is locked, alarm is on, and the kids are in bed—I can't get up right now. Come back tomorrow.' ⁸The truth is, although a human friend may not get up just for friendship's sake, they will get up because you keep banging at the door; and they will give you what you need.

Lk 11:9 "But I tell you, God is not like this! Just ask, and what you need will be given you; seek, and you will find; knock, and the door will open to you. ¹⁰For everyone who asks, receives; those who seek, find; and to the one who knocks—doors open.

Lk 11:11 "Parents, which of you, if your child asks for a fish, will give them a snake? ¹²Or if they ask for an egg, will give them a scorpion? ¹³If you then, even though you are infected with selfishness, know how to give good gifts to your children, how much more will your Father in heaven give the Holy Spirit to those who ask him!"

Lk 11:14 Jesus healed a man who had been unable to speak because of a demon. When the demon was gone, the man who had been mute spoke, and the crowd was astonished. ¹⁵But some critics said, "This is sorcery! It is by the evil powers of Beelzebub—the god of flies and demons—that he is driving out demons." ¹⁶Others asked him to give a sign from heaven to prove himself.

Lk 11:17 Jesus knew their selfish motives,

so he said to them: "Every kingdom that wars against itself destroys itself, and will collapse. ¹⁸ If Satan fights against himself, how can his kingdom survive? I ask you this because you claim I drive out demons by the power of Beelzebub. ¹⁹ But if I free minds from the domination of demons by the power of Beelzebub, then by whose power do your people drive out demons? Your own practices reveal that you know better than to accuse me of using evil powers. ²⁰ I drive off demons by the power of God, and this is evidence that God's kingdom of love has arrived.

Lk 11:21 "Or think about it like this: When a strong, well-armed thief guards their hideout, their loot is secure. ²² But when a stronger person with better weapons overpowers them, they can only do so by neutralizing the weapons and armor in which the thief trusted, and then recover what was taken.

Lk 11:23 "We are at war. Those not on my team—not working with me to unite humanity in love—are against me, inciting division and discord.

Lk 11:24 "When the mind of a person is freed from the control of an evil angel, the evil angel seeks someone else to harass. But if the angel finds no other, it says, 'I will return to the one I left.' ²⁵ If, when it arrives, it finds the mind not filled with God's Spirit, but instead empty and uncommitted, ²⁶ then it gets seven other angels more wicked than itself and infiltrates the mind with lies, temptation, and distorted thinking. And the condition of the person is worse than before, because truth no longer has any impact on their mind."

Lk 11:27 As Jesus said this, a woman in the crowd shouted, "Blessed is the mother who bore you and nursed you!"

Lk 11:28 But Jesus replied, "More blessed are those who hear of God's Remedy, partake of it, and follow God's treatment plan."

Lk 11:29 As the crowds increased in size, Jesus said to them: "It is a rebellious generation—one that has given their hearts to false gods—that asks for miraculous signs! But none will be given except the sign of God's spokesman Jonah. ³⁰ Just as Jonah—delivered to them after spending three days in the belly of a fish—was a sign to the Ninevites, the Son of Man will be a sign to this generation. ³¹ The Queen of the South will stand up on the day your diagnosis is revealed and hold you to blame for not accepting the Remedy and being healed, for she came from far away to listen to Solomon's wisdom; but One far greater than Solomon is here speaking to you. ³² The people of Nineveh will hold you to blame for your terminal state on the day your true condition is made public, for they turned away from their destructive ways and accepted the Remedy at the preaching of Jonah; and One far greater than Jonah is here speaking to you.

Lk 11:33 "No one turns on a lamp and then puts it under a cover—where it will be hidden—or under a bucket. No; they put it on a stand so its light illuminates all who come in. ³⁴ Your mind's eye is the lamp of your being. When your mind's eye is discerning and open to learning truth, your entire being is invigorated by the light. But when your mind's eye is clouded and no longer advances in truth, then your entire being is full of darkness. ³⁵ So be certain to advance in truth so that the light in you doesn't turn to darkness. ³⁶ Understand then that if your entire being is full of light—and no darkness remains—it will radiate that light fully, as when the light of a lamp shines upon you."

Lk 11:37 When Jesus had finished speaking, a legal theologian of the Pharisee sect invited him home to eat; so Jesus went and reclined at the table. ³⁸ But because Jesus didn't first do a ceremonial washing of his hands before the meal, the Pharisee was shocked.

Lk 11:39 So the Master tried to enlighten

him and said, "You, legal and behaviorally focused Pharisees, work so hard to make yourselves look good on the outside, but the inside—the heart—is full of selfishness, arrogance, and greed. [40] You really don't understand God's kingdom of love! Did not God, who crafted your outside in his image, also design your inside—your heart and character—to be like him? [41] So give from your inside—from your heart—to help the less fortunate, and then everything about you will be clean.

[Lk 11:42] "Misery is yours, you who teach a legal religion, you Pharisees! You proudly pay a pre-tax tithe and even give a tenth of the herbs in your garden, but you fail to do what actually matters: to do what is right because it is right, and to live in harmony with God's law of love—his design for life. Rather, you should have lived lives of love for others, without neglecting the simple instructions of God.

[Lk 11:43] "Misery is yours, you legal theologians, you Pharisees, because you love to put yourselves at the center; you seek the most important places, and—whether at church or the marketplace—crave admiration.

[Lk 11:44] "Misery is yours, you legal theologians, Pharisees! You're like unmarked graves: appearing inviting like a lawn, but beneath the surface are full of death and decay."

[Lk 11:45] One of the Supreme Court lawyers challenged him: "But Doctor, don't you realize that what you're saying is rude and offensive? You insult us."

[Lk 11:46] Jesus answered him, "And misery is yours, you lawyers, because you create a false legal religious system with so many imposed rules that burden people needlessly with guilt and fear, and you won't even make any effort to help them.

[Lk 11:47] "Misery is yours, you who teach a legal religion! You build tombs and memorials to God's spokespersons, but it was your ancestors who killed them. [48] Thus the memorials you build are a witness against you, for your hearts are no different than the hearts of those who killed them. [49] Because of your false remedy and penal legal trickery, God in his wisdom said, 'I will send them my spokespersons, instructors and Bible scholars: some they will execute, others they will persecute.' [50] Understand then that this generation is responsible for rejecting the witness of every one of God's spokespersons who have been killed since the creation of the world, [51] from the murder of Abel to that of Zechariah, who was killed in church right at the altar. I tell you truly, this generation is responsible for rejecting all the evidence those righteous witnesses gave.

[Lk 11:52] "Misery is yours, you lawyers and legal theologians! You have the Scriptures—the keys to the knowledge of God's kingdom of love—but you have refused to understand them, and have created a false legal interpretation that prevents others from understanding them."

[Lk 11:53] When Jesus left that place, the legal theologians of the Pharisee sect, and the lawyers, aggressively opposed him and followed him berating him with questions, [54] and trying to trick him into saying something they could use against him.

12 As a crowd of many thousands gathered, and people were pressing in so tightly that they were stepping on each other, Jesus began speaking to his interns. He said: "Be vigilant. Guard your minds from being infected with the yeast of the legal theologians and Pharisees who teach loyalty to God's kingdom of love while practicing Satan's methods of selfishness. [2] One's true character always comes out: there is no secret sin that won't be revealed, or hidden defect of character that won't be exposed. [3] What you have said in darkness will be heard in the light, and the secrets whispered in soundproof rooms will be broadcast for all to hear.

Lk 12:4 "Oh, my friends, I tell you plainly, don't let fear of those who can kill the body stop you from sharing the Remedy. That's all they can do, for they can't damage your psyche, your soul, your individuality. 5 But I will tell you what you should fear: Fear unremedied sin, which not only damages your body, but sears your conscience, warps your character, and has the power to throw you into a miserable hell. Yes, this you should fear.

6 Consider the sparrows: are not five sold for less than a couple of pennies, regarded by men as almost worthless? Yet not even one sparrow is lost without touching the heart of God. 7 He even knows the number of hairs on your head; so don't live in fear, for you are worth infinitely more than a sparrow.

Lk 12:8 "I tell you the truth: Whoever unites themself with me before humanity, will be united with the Son of Man before the angels of God. 9 But whoever severs themself from me before humanity on earth, will be severed from me before the angels of God. 10 Anyone who speaks against the Son of Man can still be healed, but one calling the Spirit of God 'the spirit of Satan' cannot be healed, for such a belief closes the heart to the Spirit who works in the heart to administer the Remedy.

Lk 12:11 "When you are summoned to appear before church boards, political authorities and national rulers, don't worry about what to say, or think that you need a speechwriter, 12 for the Holy Spirit enlightens your minds and gives you the words to speak."

Lk 12:13 A man in the crowd called out to Jesus, "Doctor, command my brother to divide his inheritance with me!"

Lk 12:14 Jesus answered, "Man, it is not my mission to act as arbiter between you and your brother." 15 Then he said to the crowd, "Stay alert! Be on guard against selfishness and greed, for the value of a person's life is not determined by how much wealth they possess."

Lk 12:16 Then he told them this parable: "The farm of a rich landowner produced an abundant crop. 17 He thought to himself, 'This is more than I can store; what should I do?' 18 So he decided, 'I know, I will tear down my barns and build bigger ones to store up all this wealth. 19 And then I'll say to myself, "You have wealth—plenty of reserves for years to come. Relax and enjoy the good life."'

Lk 12:20 "But God enlightened him to reality: 'Oh, you foolish man! Don't you realize that tonight you will die? Then who will get all your wealth?'

Lk 12:21 "This is what happens to those who—motivated by fear and selfishness—store up wealth for themselves but don't become rich in God's love."

Lk 12:22 Then, turning to his interns, Jesus said: "Therefore I tell you, do not worry about how the future will turn out, or about where your next meal will come from, or with what to clothe your body. 23 Life is not built to operate on the survival-of-the-fittest principle— constantly seeking to get food for yourself, or wear the latest fashion. 24 Look at the ravens: they don't worry about planting or harvesting, or storing food in barns or silos, because your heavenly Father is constantly giving of himself to feed them. You are infinitely more valuable than the birds! 25 Who of you by worrying has added even a single hour to your life? 26 If your worry can't do this simple thing, then why worry about the rest?

Lk 12:27 "Look at the lilies of the field: they don't sew or weave, yet I tell you that Solomon in his most magnificent robes was not dressed as one of these. 28 If that is how God clothes the grass in the field, which is here today and gone tomorrow, will he not do much more for you? Oh, how you trust him so little. 29 Stop worrying all the time, saying, 'Oh, where will we get groceries? What is there to drink?' 30 The pagans, who don't know God, are constantly preoccupied with getting for self and seeking to survive at all costs. But your heavenly Father knows all your needs and longs to provide them, ³¹ so seek first to live in harmony with God's kingdom of giving, and all your needs will be met as well.

Lk 12:32 "Don't live in fear, for fear is part of the infection of sin and turns your mind to self. It is your heavenly Father's pleasure to give you his kingdom of love. ³³ So live to give: sell what you don't need, and give to bless the less fortunate. Let your hearts cherish and hold to love, and therefore be like a purse that won't decay, filled with an eternal treasure that will never run out, and which no thief can steal. ³⁴ For what you treasure most is where your heart is.

Lk 12:35 "Be dressed and prepared to serve; keep your minds alert and your hearts burning with the desire to help, ³⁶ like people eagerly anticipating their lord's return from a wedding reception, and who, when he knocks, instantly open the door for him. ³⁷ It will be a joyful day for those servants who are prepared and watching for their lord to return. The truth is, he will have them sit at the banquet table, and he will serve them. ³⁸ It will be a joyful day for those servants who are prepared and ready when their master arrives, even if he arrives in the middle of the night. ³⁹ Understand the importance of being ready: If a homeowner knew the exact time a thief was coming, he would not have been unaware, and his house would not have been burglarized. ⁴⁰ You must live in a state of readiness because the Son of Man will return at a time you don't expect."

Lk 12:41 Peter asked, "Lord, did you tell this parable for us, or for everyone?"

Lk 12:42 Jesus gave this answer: "Who then is an intelligent and wise manager—one qualified to share the Remedy effectively in order to nurture the master's staff? ⁴³ It will be the most awesome experience for that aide when the master returns to find them reliably doing so. ⁴⁴ Truly, that aide will be trusted with all of the master's possessions. ⁴⁵ But what if the master's aide is self-centered and says to themself, 'The master has been gone a long time, and who knows when he will return?' and rather than nurturing the staff, they berate, abuse and mislead them, and then go and use the master's resources to party with gluttons and drunkards? ⁴⁶ That aide will be totally surprised and caught completely unaware on the day their master returns. The master will let that wicked servant go, cutting their relationship and casting them out with all the other counterfeits and frauds who have peddled false remedies.

Lk 12:47 "The aide who understands the Master—his design, the problem being addressed, and how to apply the Remedy—and either doesn't heed his instructions or applies a false remedy will suffer many blows: a guilty conscience, warped character, damaged reason, broken relationships, and ultimately, a destroyed soul. ⁴⁸ But the one who doesn't know about the Remedy, or how to apply it, and therefore doesn't share it, or applies a false remedy, will suffer few blows—regret, disappointment, and grief. The more you are given, the more you possess to share with others; the greater your abilities, the more gifts you have to give away.

Lk 12:49 "I have come to ignite the fire of truth and love upon the earth, and oh, how I wish it were already an inferno! ⁵⁰ But I have a mission to complete, and the pressure on me to complete it is overwhelming. ⁵¹ Do you think I have come to make peace with this selfish world? Absolutely not! I have not come to make peace with selfishness, but to cut selfishness out of the hearts of people. ⁵² From now on, those who choose the Remedy will cut dysfunctional family ties, and a family of five will be divided—two against three, and three against two. ⁵³ Love will free a son from selfish loyalty to his father's ambitions and feuds, and a father from the selfish exploits of his son; love will sever a daughter from the control of an oppressive and manipulative mother, and a mother from the selfish demands of her daughter; love will cut through the fear and hostility a daughter-in-law has toward her mother-in-law, and mother-in-law toward daughter-in-law."

Lk 12:54 Jesus turned to the crowd and said: "When you see storm clouds rising, you instantly say, 'It's going to rain,' and it does. 55 And when the wind comes from the south, you say, 'It's going to be another hot day,' and it is. 56 Imposters! If you can interpret the signs of earth and sky, then how is it that you don't understand what is happening right now in earth's history?

Lk 12:57 "Why can't you decide for yourselves what is right? 58 If an adversary has sued you, do all you can to settle the dispute before you get to court, or the judge may find against you and turn you over to law enforcement who will throw you in prison. 59 If that happens, you won't get out until you have paid back every cent you owe."

13 Some people in the crowd, thinking themselves favored of God because of their good fortune, and having morbid satisfaction at the misfortune of others, told Jesus about some Galileans who were massacred by Pilate while offering sacrifices thus having their blood mixed with the blood of the sacrifice.

2 Jesus cut right to the point: "Do you think these Galileans were worse sinners than you and all others because they died in this way? 3 Let me make this absolutely clear: No, they were not! But unless you experience a change in your hearts from selfishness to love, you will all die. 4 Do you think those eighteen who died when the tower at Siloam fell on them were more evil and more guilty of sin than you or all others living in Jerusalem? 5 Let me make this absolutely clear: No, they were not! But unless you experience a change in your hearts from selfishness to love, you will all die."

Lk 13:6 Then he told them this parable: "A man had a fig tree in his garden, but when he went to look for fruit, there was none. 7 So he said to the gardener, 'I've come looking for fruit on this tree for three years and have never found any. Cut it down! Why should it draw nutrients from the soil only for them to be wasted?' 8 But the gardener replied, 'Sir, give it one more year. I'll invest more into it, dig around it, and fertilize it. 9 If next year it bears fruit—awesome! but if not, then cut it down.'"

Lk 13:10 One Sabbath, when Jesus was teaching in one of the worship centers, 11 a woman was there whose mind had been oppressed by an evil spirit for eighteen years. She looked oppressed and was severely bent over and unable to stand up straight, no matter how hard she tried. 12 Jesus, when he saw her, said to her, "Dear lady, you are set free." 13 Then he put his hands upon her, and she immediately stood straight up, smiling and praising God.

Lk 13:14 The worship center leader was outraged that Jesus had healed this poor woman on the Sabbath, and said to the people in attendance, "God has given six days in each week to do work, so come and be healed on one of those days. Don't break the Sabbath by coming to be healed on it."

Lk 13:15 The Lord defended God's character: "You fraud! You misrepresent God and the Sabbath. Doesn't each one of you, on the Sabbath, take your donkey or ox out of the stall and give it water? 16 Then should not this poor lady—a daughter of Abraham, one of God's children—who has been bound by Satan for eighteen miserable years, be set free of what bound her, on the Sabbath day?"

Lk 13:17 The truth of what he said stung the pride of his enemies, but the rest of the people were thrilled with his wisdom and all the amazing things he was doing.

Lk 13:18 Jesus asked them, "How do I explain to you what God's kingdom of love is like? What example should I use? 19 It is like a mustard seed—so small, yet when planted in the good soil of the garden, it grows and becomes a tree whose branches provide shade and comfort to the birds. Consider how the smallest act of love is like that seed."

Lk 13:20 Again he asked, "How do I explain God's kingdom of love to you? What example can I use? 21 God's kingdom of love is like yeast mixed into a large amount of flour until it permeates the entire dough."

Lk 13:22 Jesus traveled toward Jerusalem, going through towns and villages and teaching as he went. 23 Someone along the way asked him, "Lord, will only a few people be saved?"

He told them, 24 "Be determined to be reconciled to God and choose his methods of love, because many will try other theories, philosophies and teachings but will not be able to enter. 25 And once the owner of the house has closed the door, you will bang and plead, 'Sir, please open the door for us!' But he will answer, 'We were never friends; your hearts are not united in love with me, and you don't practice my methods.'

Lk 13:26 "Then you will say, 'Of course we do; we ate and drank with you, and you taught in our cities.'

Lk 13:27 "But he will reply, 'We were never friends. Your hearts are not united in love with me, and you don't practice my methods. Depart, because your hearts are hardened in selfishness.'

Lk 13:28 "Oh, there will be terrible torment of mind and agony of heart when you see Abraham, Isaac and Jacob, and all God's spokespersons in God's kingdom of love, but you will be outcasts. 29 People from every corner of the earth—those who have partaken the Remedy—will be seated at God's great celebration banquet. 30 Those who think they deserve to be first will find themselves last, while those who are humble and consider themselves last will find themselves first in God's kingdom of love."

Lk 13:31 As he finished saying this, some legal theologians from the Pharisee sect came to Jesus and said, "You better leave here, and do it quickly! Herod wants to kill you."

Lk 13:32 Jesus instructed them, "Go and tell that fox that I will continue my mission of advancing the kingdom of love: I will drive out demons and heal people for two more days, and on the third day I will reach my goal. 33 Regardless, I must keep advancing for the next three days—for surely no spokesperson of God can die outside Jerusalem!

Lk 13:34 "O Jerusalem, Jerusalem, you sick and hard-hearted people who have rejected the Remedy, killed God's spokespersons and stoned those sent to you with the cure! How my heart has longed to pull you to safety, like a hen gathers her chicks under her wings, but you would not let me. 35 Look around! I leave your house to you abandoned and without Remedy, infected and without cure. I tell you plainly, you won't see me again until you say, 'He is the One sent by God to reveal God's true character and provide the Remedy.'"

14 One Sabbath, Jesus went to lunch at the home of a leader of the Pharisee sect, and the Pharisees were watching closely for some way to accuse him. 2 Right in front of him was a man suffering from heart failure, with very swollen legs. 3 Jesus asked the Pharisees and lawyers, both of whom promoted a legal religion, "What is your opinion: is it lawful to heal on the Sabbath, or let people suffer and die?" 4 But they refused to answer, so Jesus put his hands on the man, healed him, and sent him home.

Lk 14:5 Then, trying to help them realize the truth of God's law of love, he asked them, "If your child or pet fell into a well on the Sabbath day, would you not immediately pull them out?" 6 But they still refused to answer.

Lk 14:7 When he noticed how the guests were vying for the best seats, he told them this parable: 8 "When you are invited to a social event, don't take the best seats, presuming they are for you, for a more important person than you may have been invited. 9 And if that is the case, then you will be humiliated when the host comes to you and asks you to move. 10 Instead, when you arrive, take the least important seat; then, if the best seats are yours, you will be honored in front of all the other guests when the host moves you to the better seats. 11 For those who promote self will destroy themselves, but whoever humbles self will experience healing and exaltation."

Lk 14:12 Turning to his host, Jesus said: "When you hold a dinner event, don't limit your invitations to friends and family, or prominent neighbors—those who in all likelihood will return the favor. 13 Instead, live in harmony with the law of love and include to your banquet the poor, sick, infirmed and underprivileged, 14 and you will be blessed. Although they cannot repay you in kind, you will receive an eternal reward at the resurrection of the healed."

Lk 14:15 When one of the guests overheard this, he said to Jesus, "The person who eats at the feast in God's kingdom is the one who is truly blessed."

Lk 14:16 Jesus replied, "A wealthy man prepared a great celebration and invited many guests. 17 When everything was prepared, he sent messengers to tell the invited guests, 'The food is prepared; it is time to come.'

Lk 14:18 "But being concerned with their own interests, they all began making excuses. The first said, 'I have fields that I must tend. I'll take a rain check, please.'

Lk 14:19 "Another said, 'I have just bought a new car, and I'm heading out on a test drive. Sorry, but I can't make it.'

Lk 14:20 "Yet another said, 'I just got married; my spouse needs my attention so I won't be able to come.'

Lk 14:21 "The messengers returned and told this to their employer. The owner of the estate was angry, knowing what those he loved would miss out on. He turned to the messengers and said, 'Go quickly out into the streets, alleys and underpasses, and bring all the poor, sick, crippled, blind and diseased you can find.'

Lk 14:22 "'Sir,' the messenger said, 'we have done this and there is still room for more.'

Lk 14:23 "Then the master told his messengers, 'Go out into the country, canvas every lane, byway, trail and farm road and bring in everyone you find, so that my house will be full. 24 The sad truth is that not one of those people who rejected my invitation will taste of the bounty I have prepared.'"

Lk 14:25 Very large crowds followed Jesus. He turned to them and said: 26 "Any person who loves their mother, father, wife, children, brothers or sisters—and yes, even their own life—more than me, keeps selfishness supreme in their heart and cannot be on my spiritual health-care team. 27 Anyone who refuses to die to selfishness and follow me in loving others more than self cannot be trusted by me to distribute the Remedy that I bring.

Lk 14:28 "If you want to build a tower, would you not, before you start, consider the cost and be sure you have enough resources to complete it? 29 If you lay the foundation, but then don't complete it, all who see it will think you are foolish 30 and say, 'That person doesn't complete what they start.'

Lk 14:31 "Or what kind of king would go to war without first considering whether his ten thousand soldiers could win against the twenty thousand of his enemy? 32 If winning is unlikely, would he not send a peace delegation, long before the battle begins, to seek a peaceful solution? 33 In the same way, anyone who does not die to selfishness —giving up heart attachment to all they possess—cannot be trusted by me to distribute the Remedy that I bring.

Lk 14:34 "Salt is good, but if no longer salty, can it be made salty again? 35 It is just waste at that point—no good for planting in, nor good as manure for fertilizing—so it is thrown away. Those with minds open to truth will understand."

15 The tax collectors and others, considered the worst "sinners" by the religious leaders, were crowding around to hear Jesus. 2 But the legal theologians of the Pharisee sect, and the lawyers, grumbled, "This fellow befriends sinners and socializes with them."

Lk 15:3 So Jesus told them this parable: 4 "Suppose one of you owns a hundred sheep, and one of them gets lost. Will he not leave the ninety-nine that are safe and go after the one lost sheep until he finds it? 5 And when he finds it, he happily puts the sheep on his shoulders 6 and carries it back home. Then he calls all his friends and neighbors and says, 'Let's celebrate, I have found my lost sheep!' 7 The truth of God's kingdom is just like this: Not wanting any to be lost, the heavenly beings rejoice more over one sinner who turns away from selfishness and partakes of the Remedy than over the ninety-nine who are already right with God.

Lk 15:8 "Or consider a woman who has ten gold coins and loses one. Will she not turn on the lights, look under the furniture and search diligently until she finds it? 9 And when she finds it, she celebrates with family and friends, saying, 'Be happy and rejoice with me for I have found my lost coin!' 10 The truth of God's kingdom is just like this: Not wanting any to be lost, the angels rejoice in the presence of God over one

sinner who turns away from selfishness and partakes of the Remedy."

Lk 15:11 Jesus continued to teach them the truth of God's kingdom of love: "There was a wealthy man who had two sons. 12 The younger son went to his father and said, 'Father, give me my share of the estate.' So he divided the property between the two sons.

Lk 15:13 "Shortly thereafter, the younger brother converted all his property to cash and left home to see the world, where he squandered his wealth on pleasures and wild living. 14 When he was penniless, there was a severe famine in the country where he was living, and he began to starve. 15 So he found a job working for a citizen of that country—feeding the man's pigs. 16 No one gave him any food, and he was so hungry that he ate the slop given to the pigs.

Lk 15:17 "In this desperate state, he remembered his father and said, 'My father's servants have food to spare; why am I staying here and starving to death? 18 I will go home to my father and tell him: Father, I've been a fool and sinned against heaven and you. 19 I don't deserve to be your son; please take me back as one of your servants.' 20 So he left the pigs and went home to his father.

"But the father, who had been watching every day for his lost son, saw him coming while he was still far away. His heart was filled with compassion for him and he ran to meet his son, and threw his arms around him and kissed him.

Lk 15:21 "The son began to protest, 'Father, I have wronged you and sinned against heaven. I don't deserve to be your son.'

Lk 15:22 "But the father, overjoyed, called to his servants, 'Quickly, bring the finest suit of clothing and put it on him. Put the ring with the estate seal and authority upon his finger, and the best shoes on his feet. 23 Tell the cooks to prepare the finest meal we have ever had. Let's have a party! It's time to celebrate! 24 For this son of mine was dead but lives again; he was lost but now is found.' So the celebration began.

Lk 15:25 "But while all of this was going on, the older brother was working in the field. When he neared the house, he heard the music and saw the dancing. 26 So he called one of the servants and asked what was happening. 27 'It's your brother!' he told him excitedly, 'He has come home and your father has prepared the best party we've ever seen, because he has your brother back home safe and sound!'

Lk 15:28 "The older brother was furious and refused to go in and welcome his brother or rejoice with his father, so his father went out and pleaded with him. 29 But he told his father what he thought: 'I can't believe it! I have been slaving away all these years for you and never once broke one of your rules, yet you never had even a small party for my friends and me. 30 But when this rebellious son of yours, who has thrown away your wealth on prostitutes, comes crawling back in shame, you throw the biggest party we've ever had!'

Lk 15:31 "'My dear son,' the father tenderly said, 'you have had the pleasure of being with me this entire time, and all I have is yours. 32 But our gladness couldn't be contained; we had to celebrate because your brother was dead and is alive again—he was lost but now is found!'"

16 Jesus told his disciples: "You may have heard of a certain wealthy estate owner whose chief steward was exposed as negligent and fraudulent with the owner's property. 2 So he called his steward and said, 'I have heard what you have been doing. Bring in the ledgers and sum up the accounts, because I am terminating you as my chief steward.'

Lk 16:3 "The steward thought to himself, 'What am I to do? I am being fired. I don't have the strength for manual labor, and it is too humiliating to stand on the corner with a sign: Will Work for Food. 4 I know what I need to do so that others will help me when I need it.'

Lk 16:5 "So he contacted each person who was indebted to his master He asked the first, 'How much do you owe my master?'

Lk 16:6 "'Eight hundred gallons of olive oil,' he told him. The steward offered a discount (that was not for him to give) and said, 'I'll reduce your bill to four hundred gallons.'

Lk 16:7 "Then he asked the second debtor, 'How much do you owe?'

"'A thousand bushels (twenty-five tons) of wheat,' he replied.

"The steward again offered to give what was not his to give, and said, 'I'll change your bill to eight hundred bushels (twenty tons).'

Lk 16:8 "When the master found out what the dishonest steward had done, he commended him for so shrewdly preparing for his future. Those driven by the survival-of-the-fittest instinct of this world are shrewder in taking advantage for themselves than people who live in the light of truth and love. 9 So use up this world's wealth trying to get ahead, and when it fails, take the Remedy and be welcomed into eternal life.

Lk 16:10 "Those who are honest and careful in small matters can be trusted with much, but those who are dishonest and negligent in small matters cannot be trusted at all. 11 So if you have been dishonest and negligent in handling worldly wealth, how can you be trusted with the Remedy? 12 And if you haven't protected and cared for the property of others, who would give you property of your own?

Lk 16:13 "No one can be loyal and true to two antagonistic principles: If you embrace selfishness, you will hate selflessness, and if you love beneficence, you will hate greed. You cannot serve both the God of love and the god of money."

Lk 16:14 The theologians of the legalistic Pharisee sect loved money, and began snickering at Jesus when they heard this. 15 He said to them, "You work to promote yourselves and make yourselves look good to people, but God knows the true condition of your hearts. The selfishness and greed that humans value, and think so highly of, is detestable to God.

Lk 16:16 "The symbols and metaphors of the Old Testament were proclaimed until John. Since that time, the good news of what it all means—the reality of the true Remedy from God's kingdom of love—is being made known, and it is compelling all who understand it to partake of it and enter God's kingdom. 17 It is easier to erase heaven and earth and start again than to change—even in the slightest—God's design-protocol for life, what you call 'God's Law.'

Lk 16:18 "Anyone who divorces a faithful wife in order to marry another woman commits adultery; and the man who encourages the divorce in order to marry her—also commits adultery.

Lk 16:19 "You know the circulating story of a wealthy man who dressed in fine clothes and lived in luxury every day. 20 At the entrance to his estate was a beggar named Lazarus, who was sick and covered in sores. 21 He would have been happy with the scraps from the rich man's table. He was so badly off that the dogs licked his sores.

Lk 16:22 "As the story goes, when the beggar died, angels transported him to heaven and sat him next to Abraham, but when the rich man died, he was buried in the ground. 23 The rich man looked up while being tormented in hell, spotted Abraham millions of light years away, and noted Lazarus beside him. 24 So he cried out, his voice carrying over the expanse of the universe: 'Oh, Father Abraham! Take pity on me and send Lazarus to dip his finger in water and cool my tongue because I am in agony in this fire.'

Lk 16:25 "But, as the story goes, Abraham replied, 'Son, don't you remember all the wealth and health you had during your lifetime while Lazarus suffered in poverty and sickness? He now is rejoicing here, while you are in agony. 26 Besides, the kingdom of love and the kingdom of selfishness are separated by such a chasm that those fixed in one cannot cross over to the other.'

Lk 16:27 "He answered, 'Then please, Father, send Lazarus to my family, 28 for I have five brothers who need to know. Have him warn them, so that they won't end up fixed in selfishness and suffer in torment.'

Lk 16:29 "Abraham replied, 'They have the Scriptures—it contains all they need to know.'

Lk 16:30 "'No, Father Abraham,' he pleaded, 'they need more than the Scriptures. If someone from the dead goes to them, they would turn away from selfishness, partake of the Remedy, and be renewed in love.'

Lk 16:31 "Abraham said to him, 'If they don't value the Scriptures and won't listen to the instructions God has provided therein, they will not be convinced even if someone returns from the dead.'"

17 Jesus told his interns: "Things that lead people to deviate from God's design for life will occur in this world, but sorrow and pain will be the portion of those through whom the deviations come. 2 It is better to drown in the sea with a heavy stone tied around one's neck than to lead a person with childlike trust to deviate from God's design for life. 3 So stay alert.

"If someone you love—like your own family member—deviates from God's design, then go to them and explain it, seeking to bring them back into harmony with God's design for life. If they are sorrowful and turn back, then be reconciled to them and forgive them. 4 If they act selfishly toward you seven times in a day, and seven times come back to you and say, 'I was wrong. It's selfishness in my heart. I hate being this way. I'm sorry. Please forgive me!'—then forgive them."

Lk 17:5 The interns said to the Lord, "Increase our confidence and trust in you!"

Lk 17:6 He replied, "If you had the confidence in your purpose for me that a mustard seed has in its purpose, then—when it is in harmony with my purpose—you could say to the mulberry tree, 'Pull yourself up and go and grow in the sea,' and it would happen.

Lk 17:7 "Suppose one of you had a servant whose purpose was to serve you. When he comes in after working all day plowing your field or tending your sheep, do you deny him the privilege of serving you by waiting on him? 8 Would you not rather grant him the joy of service and say, 'Prepare supper, change clothes, and serve dinner; and when that is done, then you may eat and drink'? 9 Would you praise the servant for fulfilling his purpose and doing as instructed? 10 So it is with you: When you have fulfilled your purpose and followed your instructions, say, 'It has been a privilege to serve; we have fulfilled our purpose.'"

Lk 17:11 Heading toward Jerusalem, Jesus traveled along the border between Samaria and Galilee. 12 As he was entering one village, ten lepers came to him. They stayed a respectable distance away 13 and shouted, "Lord Jesus, have mercy on us!"

Lk 17:14 When he saw them, he smiled and said, "Go to the priests and let them examine you." And as they went, they were healed.

Lk 17:15 One of the ten, after he was healed, came back shouting praises to God. 16 He fell down at Jesus' feet and thanked him profusely; and he was a Samaritan.

Lk 17:17 Jesus said, "Weren't ten lepers cured? What happened to the other nine? 18 Did no one return to give thanks to God except this foreigner—the only one not raised in church?"

19 Then he told him, "Get up and go; you trusted me, and that is why you are healed."

Lk 17:20 Once, one of the theologians of the Pharisee sect asked Jesus when God's kingdom would come, and Jesus said, "God's kingdom of love does not come by calculating prophetic dates or careful observance of rules, 21 nor will it be found in any specific geographic location, because God's kingdom of love is the principle upon which life exists, and is written upon your hearts and minds."

Lk 17:22 Jesus turned to his interns and said: "The time will soon be here when you will long for these days we have spent together, but they will be gone. 23 If people tell you, 'Jesus is here!' or 'He's over there!' don't believe it and don't follow them. 24 For my return will be impossible to miss; it won't be some secret thing, but will be like lightening blazing across the entire sky. 25 But first, I must complete my mission here; I must suffer many things and be rejected by this generation.

Lk 17:26 "The conditions on earth when I return in glory will be like it was in the time of Noah: 27 People were caught up in their routines, focused on themselves, working to put food and drink on the table, marrying and planning for their family's future—right up until Noah entered the ark. Then the flood came and put them all in the grave.

Lk 17:28 "It was the same in Lot's day: People were consumed with self-gratification, partying, making money, and building estates. 29 But on the day Lot left Sodom, fire came out of heaven and destroyed them all.

Lk 17:30 "Sadly, the condition of people on earth will be like this—absorbed with self—on the day the Son of Man is revealed. 31 On that day, don't let anything tie your hearts to this world of sin and selfishness. Be ready to let it all go: no matter where you are, don't turn back for your favorite possessions. 32 Remember Lot's wife: her body

The Remedy

was leaving the city, but her heart did not. 33 Whoever holds to the survival-of-the-fittest principle and seeks to save their life, hasn't been healed, and will lose it. But whoever, having taken the Remedy, dies to self, will be healed and live eternally. 34 The truth is, on that night two people will be in one bed: one will have taken the Remedy and be ready to go to heaven, and the other, having rejected the Remedy—won't. 35 Two women will be working at the mill: one will have taken the Remedy and be ready to go to heaven, and the other, having rejected the Remedy—won't. 36 Two men will be working in the field: one will have taken the Remedy and be ready to go to heaven, and the other, having rejected the Remedy—won't."

Lk 17:37 "Where will we find you, Lord?" they asked.

He said, "You can be certain you will not find the Son of Man where people seek to speak with the dead. Think of vultures eating corpses, for that is what's happening there."

18 Then Jesus told a parable to his interns to help them understand the importance of regular conversations with God and not quit talking with him. 2 He said: "There was a judge who didn't believe in God or care about the welfare of people. 3 And a widow, who had been exploited, kept petitioning the judge to do what was right and restore what her adversary had taken.

Lk 18:4 "The judge refused for a long time, but he finally said to himself, 'Even though I don't believe in God or care about people, 5 I am tired of this woman bothering me, so I will do what is right and she will finally leave me alone!'"

Lk 18:6 Then the Lord explained: "Take a lesson from this unjust and godless judge: 7 If he—not caring about anyone but himself—finally did the right thing, won't God set all things right for his children who cry out to him con-

stantly? Will he ignore them? 8 I tell you truly, he will set all things right, and quickly. But when the Son of Man comes, will he find any on earth who trust him to set things right?"

Lk 18:9 Some of the people were self-righteous and so confident in themselves that they looked down on everyone else, so Jesus told them this parable: 10 "Two men went to church to pray: one was a Pharisee, known for obeying all the rules of the church, the other—a tax collector. 11 The Pharisee stood up so people would see him, and began praying about how good he was: 'God, thank you so much. I am better than others and not like the lowly robbers, rapists, addicts—or even like this tax collector. 12 I eat only the right foods and pay a pre-tax tithe.'

Lk 18:13 "But the tax collector, avoiding the attention of others, found a quiet place, bowed his head low, and not even looking toward heaven, beat his breast in grief and begged, 'God, have mercy on me, a sinner.'

Lk 18:14 "I tell you the truth, it was this humble man—and not the other—that went home with a heart set right with God. For anyone who promotes self will destroy themself, but whoever surrenders self to God in love will be fully healed and exalted."

Lk 18:15 Parents brought their babies to Jesus for him to touch and bless them. When the interns saw this, they began telling the parents not to bother Jesus. 16 But Jesus called the children to him and said, "Let the children come to me, and don't put any barriers up to make it difficult for them, for God's kingdom of love is for ones just like these. 17 The truth is, anyone who will not receive God's kingdom of love like these children, with open and receptive heart, will never be part of it."

Lk 18:18 A wealthy leader asked Jesus, "Good Doctor, what act must I do to obtain eternal life?"

Lk 18:19 Jesus, seeking to open his mind to the truth of who Jesus really was, asked, "Why do you call me 'good'? There is only One who is the source of good, and it is God. 20 You know God's directives for living in harmony with his design of love: 'Do not commit adultery, do not murder, do not steal, do not give false testimony, and honor your father and mother.'"

Lk 18:21 "I have done every one of these since childhood," the man said, "yet I still don't have peace. What am I missing?"

Lk 18:22 Jesus heard his answer and said, "One thing you still need to do: If you want to be perfectly healed and have a right character, you must let go of your earthly possessions which you cling to as evidence of your good standing with God. Instead, sell your possessions, and in love, give all you have to bless the poor, and you will have a rich reward in heaven's kingdom of love. Then come and join me, and live as I do."

Lk 18:23 When the young man heard this, it grieved him deeply because he had great wealth, and his heart was tied to his possessions. 24 Jesus looked at him and said, "It is hard for those who are rich—who derive a sense of security from their possessions—to surrender all and enter into heaven's kingdom of love and trust. 25 In truth, it is easier for a camel to kneel down, remove its load, and crawl through the small gate known as the 'eye of the needle' than for a rich man to humble himself, surrender his wealth, and enter God's kingdom of love and trust."

Lk 18:26 The interns who heard this were dumbfounded because they were biased by their culture to believe that wealth was a sign of being right with God. So they asked, "If not the rich, then who can possibly be saved?"

Lk 18:27 Jesus looked directly at them and said, "Humans have no chance of curing their own terminal condition. The only possibility for eternal life is to trust God and partake of the Remedy."

Lk 18:28 Peter said to him, "We've left everything we have to follow you!"

Lk 18:29 Jesus replied, "I tell you truly, no person who has left home or spouse or siblings or parents or children to partake of the Remedy and be part of God's kingdom of love 30 will fail to receive much more here and now, and eternal life when all is made new."

Lk 18:31 Jesus had a private meeting with the Twelve and told them, "We are now going to Jerusalem where all the prophecies written about the Son of Man will be fulfilled. 32 His own people will reject him and turn him over to the Romans. They will mock him, curse him, call him names, spit on him, beat him, and then kill him. 33 But on the third day, he will arise from the dead."

Lk 18:34 The Twelve didn't understand what he meant: biased by so much tradition, they couldn't comprehend the meaning of Jesus' words.

Lk 18:35 As Jesus approached Jericho, he encountered a blind man begging beside the road. 36 When the blind man heard the crowd passing by, he asked, "What's going on?" 37 They told him, "Jesus of Nazareth is coming through."

Lk 18:38 He immediately began shouting, "Son of David, have mercy on me!"

Lk 18:39 The people leading the procession told him to be quiet and not to bother Jesus, but he shouted even louder, "Son of David, have mercy on me!"

Lk 18:40 Jesus stopped and told them to bring the man to him. When he was before Jesus, Jesus asked him, 41 "What would you have me do for you?"

"Lord, I want to see!" the man cried.

Lk 18:42 Jesus smiled and said, "Then see! Your trust in me has healed you." 43 Immediately, his sight was restored, and he followed Jesus, shouting praises to God. When the crowd saw it, they also praised God.

19 Jesus entered Jericho and was passing through. 2 There was a wealthy man named Zacchaeus there who was chief tax collector. 3 He longed

to see Jesus but was too short to see over the crowds, 4 so he ran ahead and found a sycamore tree with branches hanging over the road. He climbed up and waited for Jesus to pass.

Lk 19:5 When Jesus reached the spot under the tree, he looked up and said to him, "Zacchaeus, hurry down, because today I am to be a guest in your house." 6 Zacchaeus jumped down immediately and welcomed him with great joy.

Lk 19:7 But the people in the crowd began grumbling, "It's not right! What's wrong with him? He's entering the house of a 'sinner!'"

Lk 19:8 But Zacchaeus was so moved by Jesus' graciousness toward him that he stood up and said, "Lord! Right here and now I give half of all my wealth to the poor, and from the remainder, if I have cheated anyone out of anything, I will repay them four times what I took."

Lk 19:9 Jesus smiled and said to him, "Today, healing and restoration of God's methods of love have come to this home, for this man is also a true son of Abraham. 10 The Son of Man has come for this very purpose—to find and heal that which is deviant from God's design for life."

Lk 19:11 While Jesus had their attention, he went on to tell them a parable, because—as he approached Jerusalem—the people thought that the time had come for God's kingdom to appear on earth. 12 So he said: "A prince went to a distant land to have himself anointed king and then to return home. 13 So he called ten of those who volunteered to serve him, and gave them each a gold coin. He told them, 'Put this money to good use until I get back.'

Lk 19:14 "People from his kingdom hated him and sent a delegation to him, saying, 'We don't want you to be our king.'

Lk 19:15 "He was made king anyway, and returned home. He sent for the servants, to whom he had entrusted money, in order to find out how well they had invested it.

Lk 19:16 "The first one reported, 'Sir, with your gold coin I earned ten more.'

Lk 19:17 "'You have done well and are a good servant!' the king replied. 'Because you have been trustworthy in this small matter, I am placing you in charge of ten cities.'

Lk 19:18 "The second one said, 'Sir, with your gold coin I earned five more.'

Lk 19:19 "The king answered, 'Well done, I am placing you in charge of five cities.'

Lk 19:20 "Then another servant came and said, 'Sir, here is your gold coin: I have kept it safe for you, hidden in a cloth. 21 I believe you are a hard man, and I fear you too much to risk losing what you gave me. I believe you take what is not yours and reap when you have not sown.'

Lk 19:22 "The king replied, 'It is by your own words and beliefs—not by my true character—that you will be diagnosed, for your words reveal the wickedness of your heart. If you believed that I am a hard man, taking what is not mine and reaping where I did not sow, 23 then why didn't you at least put my money in the bank to earn interest?'

Lk 19:24 "Then he said to his attendants, 'Take the gold coin away from this negligent servant and give it to the one who earned ten.'

Lk 19:25 "But the servant protested, 'Sir, they already have ten. It's not fair!'

Lk 19:26 "The king replied, 'I tell you the truth of God's kingdom: Everyone who uses what they have will receive more, but if you don't use it, you will lose it. 27 But as for those enemies of mine and my kingdom of love—those who value selfishness and don't want me for their king—bring them to me; and in my presence they will die.'"

Lk 19:28 After Jesus told them this, he continued on his mission, going up to Jerusalem. 29 Approaching Bethphage and Bethany, near the Mount of Olives, he sent two interns ahead, telling them, 30 "Go to the next village, and as you enter, you will find a colt tied there which has never been ridden. Untie it and bring it to me. ³¹ If anyone asks what you are doing, tell them, 'The Lord needs it.'"

Lk 19:32 The two who were sent ahead found the colt, just as Jesus told them they would. ³³ As they were untying it, its owners said, "That's our colt, what are you doing untying it?"

Lk 19:34 They answered, "The Lord needs it."

Lk 19:35 So they brought it to Jesus, put their coats on its back, and then put Jesus on it. ³⁶ As he rode along, the people began spreading their coats on the road in front of him.

Lk 19:37 When they came to the split in the road heading down the Mount of Olives, all those following began rejoicing and praising God in loud voices for all the miracles they had seen:

Lk 19:38 "Worthy of all praise is he who comes with the perfect character of God!"

"Peace in heaven and glory in the highest!"

Lk 19:39 Some of the theologians of the Pharisee sect were irritated by this and told Jesus, "Doctor, silence your followers!"

Lk 19:40 Jesus replied, "The truth is, if they don't shout the truth, the rocks will shout it."

Lk 19:41 As he approached Jerusalem and saw the city, he wept, ⁴² and said, "O Jerusalem, if you only knew what peace you could have had; but you have closed your eyes to me and to the truth I bring. ⁴³ It won't be long before your enemies will surround you and build barricades on all sides, sealing you in. ⁴⁴ They will throw you to the ground, and your children will die within your walls. Not one stone will be left on another, because you failed to realize when God's kingdom of love came to you."

Lk 19:45 He then entered the temple stage and drove out the conmen in priests' robes — the loan-sharks in Levitical garb who misrepresented God's character of love. ⁴⁶ He said, "It is written, 'My house will be a place of prayer,' but you corrupt it and make it a 'house of extortion.'"

Lk 19:47 Daily he taught in the temple. The senior pastors, priests, theologians who taught a legal religion, and community leaders were plotting to kill him, ⁴⁸ but they couldn't figure out how, because the people were so interested in hearing him.

20

One day, while Jesus was teaching in the temple and presenting the truth about the Remedy, the senior pastors, priests, and theologians who taught a penal and legal religion, together with the elders, confronted him in a show of their authority: ² "We demand that you tell us by what right and authority you are doing these things. Who gave you this authority?"

Lk 20:3 Jesus calmly replied, "I'll ask you a question first. Tell me: ⁴ John's baptism—was it ordained of heaven, or was it merely of human origin?"

Lk 20:5 The leaders stepped back to discuss their answer. They said to themselves, "If we admit that his baptism is ordained of heaven, then he will ask us, 'Why don't you believe John's testimony of me?' ⁶ But if we say 'John's baptism is human in origin,' the people will stone us because they believe John was a representative and speaker from God."

Lk 20:7 So they evaded the answer by saying, "We don't know where it was from."

Lk 20:8 Jesus said to them, "Then neither will I tell you by what authority I do these things."

Lk 20:9 He told them this parable: "A developer planted a vineyard, then leased it to some farmers and went away on a long trip. ¹⁰ When the harvest was due, he sent a servant to collect his portion of the fruit. But the tenants beat the servant and sent him away with nothing. ¹¹ The owner sent another servant, but they abused him and treated him awfully, and sent him away with nothing. [12] Still, he sent a third servant, and they stabbed him and left him in an alley.

Lk 20:13 "Then the owner of the vineyard said, 'What more can I do? I will send my son whom I love; surely they will respect him.'

Lk 20:14 But when the tenants saw the son, they greedily said to each other, 'This is the heir to this property. Let's kill him and claim the inheritance for ourselves!' [15] So they grabbed the son, dragged him out of the vineyard and killed him. Now, what do you think the owner will do to them? [16] He will come and do away with those people and give the vineyard to others."

When the people heard this, they remembered that Israel was called God's vineyard, and said, "No, this can never happen!"

Lk 20:17 Jesus looked directly at them and asked, "Then what is the meaning of the Scripture

'The stone rejected by the builders
    has become the foundation stone
    of life'?

Lk 20:18 "Everyone who falls on that stone will have all deviations from God's design broken into pieces and removed, but the one on whom it falls will be crushed."

Lk 20:19 The teachers of the penal theology and the senior pastors and priests searched for a way to arrest Jesus right then, because they understood that the parable was about them. But they were afraid of what the people would do if they tried.

Lk 20:20 They kept him under surveillance and had spies, pretending to be sincere, who tried to trap him into saying something they could use to get him into legal trouble with the Roman governor. [21] So the spies asked him, "Doctor, we know you are wise and always do what is right, constantly teaching the truth in harmony with God's methods and principles. You don't let the opinions of others influ-

ence you, because you stand for truth and not for what's popular at the moment. [22] So tell us: Is it right to pay taxes to Caesar or not?"

Lk 20:23 But Jesus saw through their tricks and said, [24] "Show me a coin used to pay taxes. Whose picture is on this coin?"

Lk 20:25 "Caesar's," they said.

Jesus looked straight at them and said, "Then give to Caesar what belongs to Caesar, and give to God what belongs to God."

Lk 20:26 Unable to trap him in what he said, they sat there so stunned by his answer that they didn't say another word.

Lk 20:27 Next, some of the theology professors from the school of the Sadducees—those who teach that there is no resurrection—came to question Jesus. [28] They said, "Wise Doctor, Moses instructed us that if a man dies without having children, then his brother is to marry the widow and have children for him. [29] Well, a man who had six brothers married a woman but died without having any children. [30] One brother married her, [31] then another, and eventually all seven married her, but none had children with her before they all died. [32] Eventually, the woman herself died. [33] Can you tell us: In the resurrection, when the dead awaken to life, whose wife will she be since she was married to all seven?"

Lk 20:34 Jesus answered, "Your entire question is flawed. You think that because people marry here on this earth, it will be that way in heaven. [35] But those who partake of the Remedy and are restored to unity with God, and who arise in the resurrection from the dead, will neither marry or be given in marriage. [36] They can no longer die, and will be in a unity of love, like the angels. They are the children of the immortal God, since they have arisen from the dead. [37] But even Moses at the burning bush showed that the dead arise, for he called the Lord 'the God of

Abraham, and the God of Isaac, and the God of Jacob.' ³⁸ He is not the God of the dead—those who no longer exist—but the living, because all still exist and thus all are alive to God."

Lk 20:39 Some of the lawyers were moved and said, "Well said, bravo Doctor!" ¹⁰ And no one else dared to question him.

Lk 20:41 Then Jesus asked them, "How is it that it is taught that the Messiah is the Son of David? ⁴² David himself in the Psalms says:

'The Lord said to my Lord:
    Sit on my right hand
⁴³ until I place your enemies
    under your feet.'

Lk 20:44 "So think about it: If David calls the Messiah 'Lord,' how can he be nothing more than his son born of natural descent?"

Lk 20:45 While all the people were listening intently, Jesus told his interns: ⁴⁶ "Be wary of those who teach a legal theology. Having rejected the Remedy that renews the heart, they rely on external trappings and rituals. They like to go around in clerical garb, to be greeted in stores, have reserved seating in churches, and sit at the head table at banquets. ⁴⁷ But they exploit the weak and powerless, and turn prayer into a ritual or show. Such people, having never been cured, will suffer most severely."

21 Jesus looked up and saw the wealthy putting their large donations into the collection basket, and ² then he noticed a poor widow putting in two tiny coins. ³ "The truth is," he said, "this poor widow has given more than all the others. ⁴ Everyone here gave donations from reserves they'll never use, but this woman gave what she couldn't afford; she gave all she had to live on."

Lk 21:5 Some of the interns were proudly talking about the beauty of the temple, its costly stones, and gifts dedicated to God. But Jesus said, ⁶ "The time is coming when everything you see here in this temple complex will be destroyed. Not one stone will be left on another—it will all be rubble."

Lk 21:7 With great urgency, they asked, "Please, Doctor, tell us, when will this happen? And what signs will warn us when it is about to occur?"

Lk 21:8 He replied: "Keep your minds alert, and think for yourselves, so you are not fooled. For many will come using my name, some even claiming to be me. Others will warn, 'It's the end,' but don't follow them. ⁹ There will be wars and revolutions before the end, but don't be frightened—the end is still to come."

Lk 21:10 He continued, "One nation will attack another, and kingdoms will war against each other. ¹¹ Earthquakes will be more severe and frequent, famines and diseases will occur in different parts of the world, and storms and cataclysms will be so horrible that it will seem like the sky is falling.

Lk 21:12 "But before nature starts unraveling, religious leaders will persecute and beat you. They will take you before religious tribunals, condemn and imprison you, drag you before kings and governors—all because you value my character and distribute my Remedy. ¹³ This will give you an opportunity to reveal the truth to them. ¹⁴ Don't make pre-planned speeches, or worry what you will say in defense of yourselves, ¹⁵ for I will enlighten your minds with wisdom and give you the words to speak so that none of your adversaries will be able to contradict you. ¹⁶ Your own parents, siblings, relatives and friends will betray you, and some of you will be killed. ¹⁷ Everyone who loves the survival-of-the-fittest principles of this world will hate you because you reveal me. ¹⁸ But don't fear! No part of you—not even a hair from your head—will be eternally lost. ¹⁹ By standing firm in love, you gain eternal life.

Lk 21:20 "When you see armies surround Jerusalem, know with certainty that its desolation is at hand. [21] That will be the time for those in Judea to flee to the country and hide in the mountains. Anyone in the city needs to get out, and those in the country need to stay away. [22] For this is the time when Jerusalem is abandoned to reap what it has chosen, and will be decimated in fulfillment of all that has been written. [23] It will be awful for pregnant women and nursing mothers! The pain and suffering of the people and the violence against them will be terrible. [24] They will be killed by sword, imprisoned, and scattered throughout the nations of the world. Jerusalem will be governed by those who reject the Remedy, until the time of those who reject the Remedy is complete.

Lk 21:25 "The sun, moon and stars will give evidence of the nearness of the end. The planet earth will begin to destabilize, the governments of the world will become worried and struggle to find ways to save the planet, but the oceans will become unstable and the storms increase. [26] Humanity will become frantic and frightened, terrified by what is happening to the world, for it will seem as if the laws of nature are unraveling. [27] At that time, the Son of Man will be seen in the sky, powerful and glorified. [28] So when you see these events happening, don't get discouraged; instead, stand tall and look to heaven with confidence, because final delivery is very near."

Lk 21:29 He gave them this example: "Remember the lesson of the fig and other trees: [30] You know that when the buds form and leaves sprout, summer is near. [31] Likewise, when all of these things transpire, realize that the end is very near. [32] The truth is, this sinful race will not pass away until all these things happen. [33] This atmosphere and the earth's surface will pass away, but my word is eternal.

Lk 21:34 "Guard yourselves: Be careful what you become attached to lest your hearts become so tied to amusement, sports, soap operas, movies, alcohol, drugs, investments, properties and careers that you become trapped, and the opportunity to sever ties to this selfish world passes you by. [35] The time of decision will come to every person who lives on the face of the earth, [36] so stay aware of what is actually happening, and ask God for the wisdom, strength and renewal of heart to make it safely through all that is going to happen, and to enable you to stand before the Son of Man."

Lk 21:37 Every day he taught in the temple, and each evening he went out to the Mount of Olives; [38] and the crowds came out early each morning to hear him at the temple.

22 It was nearing the time for the feast of bread without yeast—also called the Passover— [2] and the penal-view-preferring theologians, senior pastors, church leaders and lawyers were plotting together, trying to figure out a way to get rid of Jesus, but they were afraid of what the people would do. [3] Then Judas, called Iscariot, one of the Twelve, embraced Satan's plan and was filled with satanic desire. [4] He went to the church leaders and officers of the guard, and together they formed a plan for him to betray Jesus.

[5] The church leaders were very happy with the plot and agreed to give Judas money for betraying Jesus. [6] Judas accepted the payment, and then began watching for an opportunity to turn Jesus over to them when he was isolated from the crowds.

Lk 22:7 The day came when the Passover lamb had to be sacrificed. [8] Jesus instructed Peter and John to prepare a place where they could share the Passover meal together.

Lk 22:9 "Where would you like it to be?" they asked.

Lk 22:10 He replied, "As you enter the city, you will be met by a man carrying a jar of water. Follow him to the house he enters, [11] then say to the owner of the house, 'The Doctor asks for a guestroom where he may eat the Passover with his interns.' 12 He will then show you a large room on the second floor, completely furnished. Prepare our meal there."

Lk 22:13 They went and found the room all furnished, just as Jesus told them, so they made ready for the Passover.

Lk 22:14 When the time came, they reclined around the table. 15 Jesus said to them, "I have really looked forward to eating this Passover with you before my ordeal. 16 Know that I will not eat this meal again until all that it symbolizes becomes reality and we eat together again in God's kingdom of love."

Lk 22:17 He picked up the cup of pure wine untainted by fermentation, and said, "Each of you partake of this. 18 I will not drink grape juice again until we drink together in God's kingdom of love."

Lk 22:19 He picked up the bread, gave thanks to his Father, broke it, and handed it to his interns, saying, "This is symbolic of my body which is given for your healing and restoration: when you break bread, remember me."

Lk 22:20 Likewise, after the meal, he took the cup and said, "This cup symbolizes the Remedy—my perfect life poured out to heal you. 21 But the one who is going to betray me is sharing this meal with me. 22 The Son of Man will go quietly, just as the Scriptures foretold, but horrible will it be for the one who betrays him." 23 They began asking each other who could it be that would do this.

Lk 22:24 Then they began debating which of them was the best intern and who should be their chief resident. 25 Jesus spoke patiently to them: "In this world of selfishness, those in power who have not taken the Remedy use their position to dominate their subordinates and force their way, yet call themselves 'doers of good.' 26 But you are not to operate on the power-over-others principle of the world. No;

greatness is not attained by seniority or title or position, but by childlike innocence of character, and the ruling power is loving service. 27 Who do you think is greater: the one at the table who is being served dinner, or the one who serves? Is it not your opinion that it is the one at the table? Well, think about it: I am here to serve, not to be served. 28 You have joined with me, so remember what you learned as you stood by, watching my trials. 29 I appoint you as distributors of the Remedy—as representatives of my kingdom of love—just as the Father appointed me to bring the Remedy and reveal his kingdom of love. 30 This is so you may be healed and restored to unity with me, eat and drink at my table in my kingdom of love, and sit on thrones, diagnosing accurately the people of God.

Lk 22:31 "Simon, Simon, Satan desires to thrash all of you and separate you from me like chaff from wheat. 32 But I am especially concerned for you, Simon—and have spoken to my Father about you—that your trust in me won't fail. So when you turn back in full surrender to me, go to those who have partaken of the Remedy and strengthen them."

Lk 22:33 But Peter protested, "Lord, I am ready now. I will go with you to prison, or even to death."

Lk 22:34 Jesus smiled sadly: "Peter, the truth is, before the rooster crows in the morning, you will deny knowing me—three times."

Lk 22:35 Then Jesus turned to the rest and asked, "When I sent you out without provisions, money, or other resources, was there anything you needed that you didn't have?"

"Not a thing, Lord," they answered.

Lk 22:36 Somberly, he said: "This time it will be different. Now you need to prepare. Take some money, pack some provisions, and get a hunting knife; and if you don't have one, sell a coat and buy one. 37 For the Scripture states:

'He was counted with the criminals;' and I am telling you, this must happen to me. Be certain that what is written about me is being fulfilled."

Lk 22:38 The disciples said, "Look, we already have two hunting knives."

"That will do," he replied.

Lk 22:39 Then Jesus went out to the Mount of Olives, and his interns followed him. 40 When they arrived, he said to them, "Ask God for wisdom and strength to recognize and resist temptation." 41 He then went about a hundred yards away, knelt down and talked with God: 42 "Father, if there is any way, in harmony with your will, for this cup to be taken from me, then please remove it; but Father, not as my emotions desire — only as your will determines is best." 43 Then an angel from heaven appeared to give Jesus the physical strength to endure what was transpiring. 44 The anguish and torment of heart and mind was overwhelming, so he prayed more intently, and his sweat, like heavy drops of blood, fell to the ground.

Lk 22:45 When he finished praying and went back to his interns, he found them sound asleep, exhausted from sadness. 46 He said to them, "Why are you asleep when you so desperately need God's strength? Wake up and ask God for wisdom and strength to recognize and resist temptation."

Lk 22:47 While he was still trying to prepare his interns, a mob came up, and Judas, one of the Twelve, was leading them. He walked right up to Jesus and kissed him in greeting, 48 but Jesus cut through the subterfuge and asked, "Judas, is it with a kiss that you betray the Son of Man?"

Lk 22:49 When Jesus' interns saw what was happening, they asked, "Lord, should we slash them with our knives?" 50 And one of them, not waiting for an answer, slashed out and cut off the right ear of the high priest's servant.

Lk 22:51 But Jesus intervened immediately: "Stop this at once!" And then he touched the man's ear and healed him.

Lk 22:52 Then Jesus turned to the senior pastors, church leaders, officers of the guard and elders who had come for him, and said: "Do you think I am some terrorist trying to evade the authorities that you come here at night with clubs and swords to capture me? 53 Every day I sat openly in the temple courts teaching, and you didn't arrest me. But this is your time, when darkness is in charge."

Lk 22:54 So they grabbed him and led him away, taking him to the home of the high priest. Peter trailed behind at a safe distance. 55 But once a fire was burning in the courtyard and everyone settled down around it, Peter slipped in and sat down with them. 56 A serving girl saw him sitting there by the fire. She paused and looked at him closely, then said, "This man is with him."

Lk 22:57 But Peter denied it: "Woman, you're mistaken. I don't know him."

Lk 22:58 Later, another person saw him and said, "I recognize you. You are one of Jesus' followers."

But Peter vehemently denied it. "Mister, I am not, and stop making false allegations!"

Lk 22:59 An hour later, another exclaimed, "This man has to be one of them; he's a Galilean!"

Lk 22:60 Peter said, "For the last time, I don't know what you are talking about!" Just as the words left his mouth, the rooster crowed. 61 The Lord turned and with sadness upon his face looked Peter in the eye. Then Peter remembered what the Lord had said to him: "Before the rooster crows, you will deny knowing me—three times." 62 He ran out, overwhelmed with grief, and cried so hard he wanted to die.

Lk 22:63 The guards watching Jesus began making fun of him and beating him. 64 They blindfolded him, and while hitting him, shouted, "Come on, use your magic powers and tell us who hit you!" 65 And they hurled many other derogatory comments at him.

Lk 22:66 At dawn, the church board, senior pastors and theologians who taught a legal religion convened a tribunal and had Jesus brought before them. 67 They demanded, "How do you plea? Do you claim to be the promised Messiah or not?"

Jesus answered, "It doesn't matter what I say; you don't want the truth and will not believe me, 68 and if I ask you to explain what you mean, you wouldn't answer me. 69 But you can be sure that you will see the Son of Man seated at the right hand of Almighty God."

Lk 22:70 They asked, "Are you the Son of God?"

He replied, "You said it."

Lk 22:71 Then they concluded, "We don't need any other testimony. We have heard his blasphemy from his own mouth."

23 All those at the tribunal got up and took him to Pilate, 2 where they made their allegations, saying: "This man is a traitor to our nation. He opposes paying taxes to Caesar and claims to be the deliverer king."

Lk 23:3 Pilate asked Jesus, "Is this true? Are you the king of the Jews?"

"Your words, not mine," Jesus replied.

Lk 23:4 Then Pilate announced to the church leaders and mob, "Your accusations against this man are unfounded. I find no reason for the charges."

Lk 23:5 But they persisted: "He's an agitator! All over Judea he stirs up the people with his teachings; he started in Galilee and has now come here."

Lk 23:6 Pilate instantly asked if Jesus was a Galilean. 7 Upon learning that he was from Herod's jurisdiction, he thought to sidestep the issue and sent him to Herod, who just happened to be in Jerusalem at that time.

Lk 23:8 Herod was most happy when they brought Jesus to him, because for a long time he had wanted to see him. After hearing about all that Jesus had done, he wished to be entertained by Jesus performing some miracles. 9 He interrogated him with question after question, but Jesus gave no answer. 10 The church leaders, senior pastors and theology professors stood there, angrily accusing him. 11 Then Herod and his soldiers began to make fun of Jesus and call him names. They dressed him up in mock royal attire, and sent him back to Pilate. 12 Herod, grateful for the respect Pilate showed him by sending Jesus to him, changed his hostile attitude toward Pilate and they became friends that day.

Lk 23:13 Pilate called in the church leaders, senior pastors, theology professors and the people, 14 and told them, "You brought this man to me accused of inciting the people to rebel. I examined him in front of you and found no basis for your charges.

15 Further, I sent him to Herod, and he also found no basis for your charges—that is why he sent him back to me. So, as you can see, he has done nothing to deserve death. 16 Therefore, I will punish him, but then release him." 17 (He was expected to set one prisoner free each Passover.)

Lk 23:18 But with a frenzy of bloodlust, the mob screamed out as one voice, "Away with him! Away with him! Set Barabbas free! Set Barabbas free!" 19 (Barabbas was an insurrectionist in prison for murder.)

Lk 23:20 Pilate wanted to release Jesus, so he tried again to reason with the crowd, 21 but they were mad with hate and just kept shouting, "Crucify him! Crucify him!"

Lk 23:22 A third time Pilate tried to speak to the mob: "Why should he be crucified? What crime has he committed? I have found no reason for the death penalty. Won't you be satisfied if I simply flog him and release him?"

Lk 23:23 But the mob went into a greater frenzy of rage—screaming, demanding that he be crucified—and their insistence worked. 24 Pilate gave in to them and granted their demand. 25 He released the insurrectionist in prison for murder (the one the mob requested by name), and gave them Jesus to crucify.

Lk 23:26 As they led him away, they forced Simon—a man who was traveling from his home in Cyrene—to carry the cross behind Jesus. 27 A large crowd trailed behind, including many women who wailed and mourned for him. 28 Jesus turned to them and said, "Women of Jerusalem, don't cry for me; cry for yourselves and your children. 29 For now, a time will come when you say, 'The women without children are the lucky ones. Those who never gave birth or nursed a child—they are the lucky ones!' 30 Then you will beg the mountains, 'Fall on us!' and the hills, 'Cover us!'"

Lk 23:31 "For if men destroy a fruitful tree, what will happen to a dead and barren tree?"

Lk 23:32 There were two other men, both criminals, who were led out to be executed with Jesus. 33 When they arrived at the place called the Skull, they crucified him and the criminals—one on his right and the other on his left. 34 Jesus, revealing his character of love, said, "Father, forgive them, for they don't know what they are doing." And the soldiers tossed dice to determine who would get his clothes.

Lk 23:35 The people stood by, watching as the church leaders ridiculed, sneered and insulted him. They said, "He saved others, so if he is the Savior from God—the Chosen One—then let him save himself!"

Lk 23:36 The soldiers also mocked him and ridiculed him. They offered him wine vinegar 37 and tempted him, "If you are the king of the Jews, then do something to save yourself!"

Lk 23:38 Above him, posted on the cross, was a written notice which read:

THIS IS THE KING OF THE JEWS

Lk 23:39 One of the criminals also ridiculed him and tempted him: "Aren't you supposed to be the Deliverer? Well then,

save yourself, and us while you're at it!"

Lk 23:40 But the other criminal confronted him, saying, "What's wrong with you? Have you no regard for God and the future afterlife? You're being executed as well. 41 And our punishment is deserved: our actions put us here. But this man has done nothing wrong."

Lk 23:42 Then he turned to Jesus and said, "Jesus, please, will you remember me when you come into your kingdom?"

Lk 23:43 Jesus smiled and said to him, "Today, I tell you truly, you will be with me in paradise."

Lk 23:44 It was noon, and suddenly a deep darkness came over the entire area and persisted until three o'clock in the afternoon. 45 It was as if the sun had stopped shining. And during that time the veil in the temple was torn into two pieces. 46 Jesus cried out in a loud voice, "Father, I trust you, and into your hands I commit my spirit." When he said this, he expired, giving up his life.

Lk 23:47 The centurion on duty saw all of this and praised God, saying, "Surely this was a holy and sinless man." 48 The crowd who had gathered to watch the execution, seeing how Jesus conducted himself, and all that transpired, were overcome with sorrow and left, beating their chests in grief. 49 But those who knew him personally, including the women who had followed him from Galilee, stood back and thoughtfully watched all that happened.

Lk 23:50 There was a man named Joseph, a member of the Jewish high court (but an honest and trustworthy man), 51 who was not party to the decision to seek the death of Jesus. He hailed from a town called Arimathea and was eagerly waiting for God's kingdom of love. 52 He went to Pilate and asked for the body of Jesus. 53 He took it down, wrapped it in linen, and gently laid it in a tomb cut into the rock, one that had never been used.

⁵⁴ It was Friday, Preparation Day; sunset was approaching and the Sabbath was about to begin.

Lk 23:55 The women who came with Jesus from Galilee followed Joseph and saw the tomb where Jesus' body was laid. ⁵⁶ Then they went home and prepared spices and perfumes to anoint the body, but they rested on the Sabbath, in harmony with the commandment.

24 Early on Sunday morning—the first day of the week — the women went to the tomb, carrying the spices they had prepared. ² When they arrived, they found the stone rolled away from the tomb, ³ and when they entered, the body of the Lord Jesus was not there. ⁴ While they were considering what this could mean, suddenly, two angels in the form of men, dressed in clothing as brilliant as lightening, stood beside them. ⁵ Frightened, the women dropped to their knees and bowed with their faces to the ground, but the angels said to them, "Why are you looking for the living where the dead are found? ⁶ He is not here; he has arisen from the dead! Don't you remember what he told you, when he was with you in Galilee, ⁷ 'The Son of Man must be delivered into the power of evil men, be crucified, and on the third day rise again'?" ⁸ Then his words came back to them.

Lk 24:9 When they returned from the tomb, they told the Eleven and the others all that happened. ¹⁰ It was Mary Magdalene, Joanna, Mary the mother of James, and the others with them who told the interns what had transpired, ¹¹ but the men didn't believe the women, because what they said was so incredible that it didn't seem real. ¹² Peter, however, went to check for himself. He ran to the tomb, and bending over, saw the strips of linen lying there that had wrapped Jesus' body. He walked away, trying to figure out what it all meant.

Lk 24:13 That very same day, two interns were walking to a town called Emmaus, which was about seven miles from Jerusalem, ¹⁴ discussing all the events that had just happened. ¹⁵ As they were talking, Jesus himself came up and began walking with them, ¹⁶ but they didn't recognize who he was.

Lk 24:17 He asked them, "What are you talking about?"

They stopped, their faces filled with sorrow. ¹⁸ One of them, named Cleopas, asked him, "Are you visiting Jerusalem? Haven't you heard the news about everything that has happened in the past few days?"

Lk 24:19 "What has happened?" Jesus asked.

So they told him: "Jesus of Nazareth was a spokesman of God, filled with the power from God. He revealed the truth about God in word and deed to all the people, ²⁰ but the church leaders, senior pastors, lawyers and theology professors plotted against him and accused him falsely, and turned him over to be sentenced to death. They crucified him. ²¹ But we had really thought he was the One who would heal and restore Israel. Oh, and today is the third day since the crucifixion. ²² And some of the women brought us the most incredible news. They told us they went to the tomb early this morning, ²³ but his body was gone. They said they were visited by angels, who told them, 'Jesus is alive.' ²⁴ Then some of our fellow interns went to the tomb and found it empty—as the women had said—but they did not see him."

Lk 24:25 Then Jesus said to them, "How much you don't understand, and how reluctant you are to believe what God's spokespersons have said! ²⁶ Didn't the Messiah have to go through all of these things in order to complete his mission, procure the Remedy, and enter his glory?" ²⁷ Then, beginning with Moses and going through all the Old Testament, he explained to them what was said about himself in all the Scriptures.

Lk 24:28 As they approached Emmaus, Jesus indicated that he was going to continue traveling farther, 29 but they passionately requested, "Please stay with us! It's almost dark; the day is over." So he went in to stay with them.

Lk 24:30 At the dinner table, he took the bread, gave thanks, then broke it and gave it to them. 31 Then they recognized him, but he simply disappeared from their presence. 32 They said to each other, "Did not our hearts burn with conviction, certainty, joy and relief when he spoke to us and explained the Scriptures to us?"

Lk 24:33 So they got up and set out immediately for Jerusalem. When they arrived, they found the Eleven and the others meeting together, 34 who said, "It's true! Jesus has risen from the dead and has appeared to Simon." 35 Then the two from Emmaus told what happened to them, and how Jesus appeared to them, explained the Scriptures to them, and broke bread with them.

Lk 24:36 While they were all discussing this, suddenly Jesus himself appeared right there among them and said, "Relax, it's me. Don't be afraid."

Lk 24:37 But they were shocked and afraid, thinking superstitiously that it might be a ghost. 38 So he said to them, "Why do you think such thoughts, and why do you let doubts into your minds? 39 Look at me: it's me! Look at my hands and feet. Come and touch me and see for yourselves. A ghost doesn't have flesh and bones; and as you can see—I have."

Lk 24:40 After saying this, he held out his hands, and also showed them his feet. 41 But they still had trouble believing, because it seemed too good to be true, so he asked them, "Do you have anything to eat?" 42 They gave him a piece of broiled fish, 43 and he took it and ate it while they watched.

Lk 24:44 He smiled and said to them, "This is exactly what I told you was going to happen, when I was still with you: All things must happen as it is written about me in the books of Moses and the rest of the Old Testament."

Lk 24:45 Then he went on explaining the Scripture, opening their understanding to what it really means. 46 He told them, "This is what is written: The Messiah will suffer and then rise from the dead on the third day, 47 and the Remedy—which transforms lives, eradicating fear and selfishness and regenerating people to live in harmony with God's kingdom of love, thus putting sinfulness into remission—will be taken in his name to the entire world, starting in Jerusalem. 48 You are the witnesses to what I have achieved.

49 I am going to send you what my Father has promised, but remain here in the city until you have been equipped with the power from heaven."

Lk 24:50 After leading them out near Bethany, he held up his hands and blessed them. 51 While he was blessing them, he left them and went home to heaven. 52 They worshipped him, and returned to Jerusalem overwhelmed with joy. 53 And they spent all their time at the temple, praising God.

John

1 In the beginning was Jesus—God's very thoughts made audible and visible—and Jesus was with God, and Jesus was God.

Jn 1:2 He was with God before anything else existed.

Jn 1:3 Through Jesus everything was created; without Jesus nothing was created that has been created.

Jn 1:4 In Jesus was life—original, unborrowed, underived—and his life enlightens the mind about God: about his character, methods, and principles.

Jn 1:5 The light of Jesus' life shines into the darkened minds of human beings—darkened by Satan's lies about God—but their darkened minds have not understood the light.

Jn 1:6 There was a man called John who was empowered and directed by the Spirit of God.

Jn 1:7 He came as a witness to testify that Jesus was the true light sent to dispel the darkness enshrouding the mind, so that everyone might believe the truth about God and be healed.

Jn 1:8 John was not the light of truth; he came only as a witness to the light.

Jn 1:9 The true Light that enlightens everyone—God's very thoughts made visible and audible—was coming into the world.

Jn 1:10 Jesus—the true Light—was in the world, and even though the world was created by him, the world was so blinded by Satan's lies that it didn't even recognize him.

Jn 1:11 Jesus came to his own people whom he had especially chosen, instructed and blessed, but many refused to accept him because they preferred Satan's version of a savior.

Jn 1:12 But all who recognized and accepted him—all who valued and accepted the character, methods and principles he revealed—he made them children of God, transforming them into like character, practicing God's methods and principles.

Jn 1:13 They were made God's children not because of genetics or biological descent, or because of human procreation, but because of the transformation of mind, heart and character brought about by God.

Jn 1:14 Jesus became a real human being, and he established his temple—the temple of his body—among us. We have seen the glory of his character—the character of the One and Only true God. He came from God, and perfectly revealed the Father who is the source of all grace and truth.

Jn 1:15 John the Baptist testified concerning Jesus. He proclaimed, "This is the One I was talking about when I said, 'He who begins his public ministry after mine is superior to me because he existed before I was even born.'"

Jn 1:16 From all that Jesus is, and all he has to give, we have received every blessing heaven has to give—one blessing after another.

Jn 1:17 The written rules, which were designed to protect us while we were still ignorant of God's methods and principles, were given through Moses; but the truth of God's gracious character and His methods for running the universe is revealed through Jesus Christ.

Jn 1:18 No human being has ever seen God, except God's One and only Son—Jesus Christ, who stands with his Father and has perfectly made the Father known—because Jesus and the Father are One: one in character, power, divinity and authority.

Jn 1:19 John was giving this testimony about Jesus when the Jewish authorities in Jerusalem sent religious leaders to ask him who he was.

Jn 1:20 John didn't hesitate for one second to freely proclaim, "I am not the Deliverer of Israel or the Savior of the world."

Jn 1:21 The religious leaders asked him, "Then who are you? Are you Elijah who went to heaven in a chariot?" John stated clearly, "I am not Elijah who went to heaven in a chariot." "Are you the Prophet Moses?" He answered, "No, I am not."

Jn 1:22 They finally asked, "Who are you then? We need to report back to those who sent us, and we must tell them something. So who do you think you are?"

Jn 1:23 John replied by quoting the prophet Isaiah's famous reference about the one who would prepare for the Messiah's coming:

"I am the voice calling in a dark and
    desolate land,
'Prepare your minds, untwist your
    hearts,
and prepare for the Lord to come
    with his healing Remedy.'"

Jn 1:24 Some of the legalistic religious lawyers who had been sent by the authorities in Jerusalem 25 asked him more questions: "Why then do you immerse people in water if you are not the Messiah, nor Elijah who went to heaven in a chariot, nor the Prophet Moses?"

Jn 1:26 "I simply immerse people in water to symbolize the washing away of the old selfish life; but among you, right now, is the Messiah, and you don't even recognize him.

Jn 1:27 "He is the One who comes after I have called people to turn their lives around, and who will bring real healing and transformation of heart. He is so awesome that I am not worthy to untie his shoes."

Jn 1:28 All this happened at Bethany on the other side of the Jordan River, where John was immersing people in water.

Jn 1:29 The next day John saw Jesus coming toward him, and said, "Look, everyone! The sacrificial Son of God, who reunites this world with God by restoring in humans God's character, and removing from people the rebellious principles of Satan!

Jn 1:30 "This is the One I was talking about when I said, 'He who begins his public ministry after mine is superior to me because he existed before I was even born.' 31 I personally didn't know him nor had I ever met him, but the reason I was immersing people in water was to prepare their hearts to recognize him when he came."

Jn 1:32 Then John gave this testimony: "I saw the Spirit of God come down from heaven in the form of a dove and settle on him. 33 Because I had never met him, I wouldn't have known him, except that God, who sent me to call people to a new life and immerse them in water, told me, 'The man on whom you see the Spirit come down on and remain, is the One who will immerse people's minds and hearts in love and truth from the Holy Spirit.' 34 I have seen and hereby testify that Jesus is the Son of God."

Jn 1:35 The next day John was there again with two of his disciples. 36 When he saw Jesus passing by, he said, "Look, the sacrificial Son of God!"

Jn 1:37 When the two disciples heard him say this, they left John and followed Jesus. 38 Turning around, Jesus saw them following him, and asked, "What do you want?" They said, "Teacher, where are you staying?"

Jn 1:39 "Come," Jesus replied, "and you will discover for yourselves." So they went and saw where he was staying, and spent that day with him. It was about four o'clock in the afternoon.

Jn 1:40 Simon Peter's brother Andrew was one of the two who heard what

John said, and followed Jesus.

Jn 1:41 The first thing Andrew did was to find his brother Simon and tell him, "We have found the Savior of the world. We have found the Christ!" 42 And he brought Simon to Jesus, who looked at him and said, "You are Simon, son of John. You will be called Pebble." (When translated, "Pebble" means "Peter.")

Jn 1:43 The next day Jesus decided to leave for Galilee. Finding Philip, he said to him, "Follow me."

Jn 1:44 Philip, like Peter and Andrew, was from Bethsaida. 45 Philip found Nathanael and told him, "We have found the One Moses wrote about in the Law, and about whom God's spokespersons also wrote—Jesus of Nazareth, the son of Joseph, but really—the Son of God."

Jn 1:46 "Nazareth! Can anything good come from Nazareth?" Nathanael asked. "Come and see for yourself," answered Philip.

Jn 1:47 When Jesus saw Nathanael approaching, he said of him, "Here is a true and faithful son of Israel, in whom there is a pure heart and nothing false."

Jn 1:48 "How do you know me?" Nathanael asked. Jesus answered, "While you were still under the fig tree— before Philip called you, and even before you were born—I saw you."

Jn 1:49 Then Nathanael declared, "Great Teacher, you are the Son of God; you are the King and Deliverer of Israel."

Jn 1:50 Jesus said, "You believe because I told you that I saw you under the fig tree. You shall see much greater things than that." 51 Then he added, "I tell you the truth, you shall see heaven open, and you shall see all the blessings of heaven flowing to the earth as the angels of God ascend and descend on the Son of Man." (He said this indicating that he is the connecting link between heaven and earth.)

2 One Tuesday, a wedding took place at Cana in Galilee. Jesus' mother was there, 2 along with Jesus and his disciples, who had also been invited.

Jn 2:3 When all the wine had been consumed, Jesus' mother said to him, "They are all out of wine."

Jn 2:4 Jesus said to her, "Dear mother, why are you trying to involve me? It is not yet time for me to begin my public ministry."

Jn 2:5 His mother didn't respond to Jesus, but said to the servants, "Do whatever he tells you."

Jn 2:6 Nearby were six stone jars—the kind used by the Jews for ceremonial washing—each holding twenty to thirty gallons (ninety to one hundred and fifteen liters).

Jn 2:7 Jesus said to the servants, "Fill the jars with water;" so they did—all the way to the brim.

Jn 2:8 Then Jesus told them, "Now draw some out and take it to the wedding coordinator." They did exactly as he said, 9 and the wedding coordinator tasted the water—but it was no longer water, for it had been turned into the freshest, sweetest wine. He did not realize where this new wine had come from, although the servants who brought it to him knew. Then the wedding coordinator called the bridegroom aside 10 and said, "Everyone else brings out the best wine at the beginning of the wedding and saves the cheaper wine for later, when the guests are full or have already had too much to drink; but you have saved the premier wine until now."

Jn 2:11 Jesus performed this—the first of his miracles—at Cana in Galilee. In doing this miracle, he revealed the glory of his compassionate character as well as his power; and his disciples' faith in him increased.

Jn 2:12 After the wedding, he went with his mother, brothers and disciples to Capernaum, where they stayed for a few days.

Jn 2:13 As the Jewish Passover was approaching, Jesus went to Jerusalem.

Jn 2:14 In the temple courts, he found

men selling cattle, sheep and doves at exorbitant prices, and others were cheating the people by exchanging money at a marked-up rate. These people, by carrying on their thievery in the temple, made it appear that such behavior was in keeping with God's will and character. ¹⁵ So Jesus made a whip out of cords, and drove all those liars, cheaters and thieves from the temple area. He drove out their sheep and cattle, and overturned their money tables, scattering the coins. ¹⁶ To those selling doves, he said, "Get out of here! How dare you turn my Father's house into a den of thieves!"

Jn 2:17 His disciples remembered that the Scriptures said: "A passionate desire to reveal and complete God's healing plan, which was all symbolically taught in the temple service, will consume me."

Jn 2:18 Then the Jewish leaders demanded of him, "What miracle can you perform to prove to us that you have the right and authority to come in here and change what we have been doing for hundreds of years?"

Jn 2:19 Jesus answered them, "If you destroy this temple, I will raise it again in three days."

Jn 2:20 The Jewish leaders replied, "This temple is one of the greatest accomplishments in the world. It has taken thousands of men forty-six years to build this temple, and you, all by yourself, are going to raise it in three days? What kind of nonsense are you talking about?"

Jn 2:21 But the temple of which Jesus spoke was the temple of the Holy Spirit—the true original temple of God—of which the building in Jerusalem was only a symbol. He was speaking of the temple of his body.

Jn 2:22 After he was raised from the dead, his disciples remembered what he had said, and their confidence and trust in the Scriptures and Christ's words increased even more.

Jn 2:23 While Jesus was in Jerusalem at the Passover Feast, many people saw the miracles he performed and were convinced that he was the Messiah. ²⁴ But Jesus would not put his plans and mission in their hands nor allow them to influence his decisions, because he knew that all people were infected with selfishness, which tainted their motives. He knew that humans did not yet understand his true mission and instead were looking for a kingdom of power rather than a kingdom of love. ²⁵ He did not need humankind to inform him of their sick state of heart and mind because he already knew that selfishness had infected the deepest wellsprings of the soul.

3 There was a Pharisee, a member of the Jewish Sanhedrin—the highest ruling council of the Jews—whose name was Nicodemus. ² Because he was afraid of what others might think if a member of the ruling council was seen talking with Jesus, he came to Jesus at night. He asked, "Teacher, we know you must have come from God, as no one could perform all these miracles you are performing if God were not with him."

Jn 3:3 Jesus ignored the attempted flattery, and cut directly to the heart of the issue which Nicodemus needed to understand. He said, "I tell you plainly, no one can see God's kingdom unless they are born again."

Jn 3:4 But Nicodemus was resistant to Christ's teaching and asked, "How can a person, once they are already born and fully grown, be born again? Surely one cannot reenter their mother's womb to be born again!"

Jn 3:5 Jesus answered, "I tell you plainly, no one can be part of God's kingdom unless they are first born into the world and then renewed by the Spirit. ⁶ The first birth—the natural, water birth—is a birth of individuals infected with sin and selfishness, but the second birth—the birth of the Spirit—is a birth of a right heart and a new mind: a new mind that is no longer controlled by sin and selfishness. ⁷You should not be so astounded by me telling you that you must be born again. ⁸The wind blows wherever it pleases: you hear its sound, you see its effects, but you cannot tell from where it comes or to where it is going. So it is with those born of the Spirit: you can see the transformation and renewal of their minds and characters, but you cannot explain how the Spirit accomplished it."

Jn 3:9 "How is this possible?" Nicodemus asked.

Jn 3:10 "Nicodemus, you're one of the teachers in Israel — one of the most educated men in the country — and you don't understand these things?" Jesus replied. ¹¹ "I tell you plainly, we are discussing the clear facts and realities of what we know and have seen, but still, you theologians and teachers of the law will not accept what I am telling you. ¹²I have told you about things happening here on earth — right in front of you — and you do not believe; how then will you believe if I tell you about heavenly things? ¹³No human now living on earth has gone into heaven except the One who lived in heaven and came to earth from heaven—which is I, the One speaking to you—the Son of Man. ¹⁴Just as Moses lifted up the snake in the desert in order to bring healing to those who would look at it and trust, so also I—the Son of Man— must be lifted up ¹⁵so that everyone who looks to me and trusts in me may be healed and live eternally.

Jn 3:16 "For God loved the world so much that he gave me, his One and only Son, that all who open their hearts and trust me will be healed and not perish, but have everlasting life. ¹⁷For God did not send me, his Son, into the world to condemn the world, but to provide healing from sin in order to restore the world to unity with God through me. ¹⁸Whoever genuinely trusts me experiences renewal of mind and re-creation of heart, and therefore is no longer out of harmony with God: such a one will not be lost. But whoever does not trust me and does not experience renewal of mind and heart is hopelessly lost because they have not trusted in God's One and only Son—the only healing solution. ¹⁹This is the reality: I have come into the world as the light to reveal the truth about God, his character, methods, and principles—the very principles upon which life is based—but all of mankind have loved the dark lies of Satan and his methods of selfishness, which lead only to death, because their habits, lifestyle—their very character—is evil. ²⁰Everyone who does evil is practicing Satan's methods of selfishness, and hates the light of truth and self-sacrificing love. They will not come into the light of love and truth for fear that the corrupt condition of their heart and mind will be exposed. ²¹But whoever opens their heart in trust to me and lives by the truth comes into the light of God's love, methods and principles, so that it is plainly seen that both their transformed character and their life of selfless love have been accomplished by God."

Jn 3:22 After this, Jesus and his disciples went out into the Judean countryside, where he spent time with them and immersed believers in water. ²³Now, John was also immersing the repentant ones in water at Aenon near Salim, as the water was plentiful there and people were constantly coming to be immersed — symbolically washed clean from sin. ²⁴(This was before John was put in prison.) ²⁵An argument developed between some of John's disciples and a certain Jew over the issue of ceremonial washing. ²⁶They came to John and said, "Teacher, that man Jesus, who was with you on the other side of the Jordan — the One you testified was the Messiah to come—well, he is also immersing people in water. Everyone is going to him for this symbolic cleansing, and soon no one will come to us."

Jn 3:27 To this, John replied: "An honest person can only receive that which is given to them by God. 28 You know it very well, and you can verify that I have said it all along that I am not the Savior but am sent ahead of him. 29 The bride belongs to the bridegroom; and Jesus is the bridegroom, and his followers—the bride. The best man, who serves the bridegroom, waits and listens to his instructions and follows his directions, and is overwhelmed with joy when he hears the bridegroom's voice. That is my joy. I have heard the voice of the bridegroom, and my joy and mission are now complete. 30 He must become the One whom all seek after and love, and I must fade into the background.

Jn 3:31 "Jesus—who comes from heaven, and who created everything—is above all that is created; I—a man who is from this earth—am simply a creature belonging to earth, and speak as one who has only an earthly perspective. 32 Jesus reveals what he has seen and heard about God and God's heavenly kingdom, but no one believes or accepts what he reveals. 33 But I have accepted what he has revealed, and I certify that God is truthful and that Jesus is a revelation of that truth. 34 Jesus—the One God has sent—speaks only the words of God, for Jesus is God's thoughts made audible and visible, as God's Spirit is upon him without limit. 35 The Father loves Jesus, his Son, and has placed all things—whether in heaven or on earth—in his hands. 36 Whoever trusts in God's Son Jesus is recreated within and has eternal life, but whoever rejects God's Son will not see life because they reject the only Remedy for their otherwise terminal condition; and God, sadly, grants them their free choice."

4 Some of the legalistic religious lawyers heard that more people were becoming followers of Jesus than of John, 2 and that these new followers were being immersed in water by Jesus' disciples. 3 When the Lord Jesus learned that the Pharisees were turning the numbers of those immersed by John and his own disciples into a competition, he left Judea and returned to Galilee.

Jn 4:4 On his way to Galilee, he had to pass through Samaria, 5 and came to a town called Sychar, near the parcel of land Jacob had given to his son Joseph. 6 This is where Jacob's well was located. Jesus was tired from his journey and sat down by the well. It was about noon.

Jn 4:7 While Jesus was resting at the well, a Samaritan woman came to draw water. Jesus asked her, "Would you be kind enough to give me a drink?" 8 (Jesus was alone because his disciples had gone to town to buy food.)

Jn 4:9 The Samaritan woman was momentarily stunned by Jesus' request because Jews were notorious for discriminating against Samaritans (women in particular), and wouldn't even talk to them. Once she recovered from her shock, she said to Jesus, "What's going on that you, a Jew, would ask me, a Samaritan woman, for a drink?"

Jn 4:10 Jesus, with courtesy and respect, said, "If you knew the gift that God has provided for all humanity, and who it is that is asking you for a drink, you would ask me and I would give you the water of eternal life."

Jn 4:11 "Sir," the woman replied, "the well is deep, and you have nothing with which to draw the water, so where do you propose to get this water of eternal life? 12 Are you greater than our father Jacob who dug this well and drank from it himself, as did all of his family and their flocks and herds?"

Jn 4:13 Jesus patiently answered, "Everyone who drinks of the water from this well, in just a short time becomes thirsty again, 14 but whoever drinks the water of life I give them will never thirst again. In fact, the water of life I give will actually become a new fountain inside them that will overflow to eternal life."

Jn 4:15 Upon hearing what Jesus said, the woman eagerly requested, "Sir, please give me this water so that I won't ever get thirsty again and have to keep coming here to draw water."

Jn 4:16 Jesus told her, "Go and get your husband and come back."

Jn 4:17 She replied, "I don't have a husband." Jesus gently said to her, "You are right when you say that you have no husband. 18 In fact, you have had five husbands, and the man you now live with is not your husband. So when you said that you don't have a husband, that was quite true."

Jn 4:19 Shocked and somewhat uncomfortable with such a personal revelation, the woman said, "Sir, to know such things you must certainly be a prophet. 20 So please help me with a problem: Our people have always worshiped God here on this mountain, but you Jews claim that the place we must worship God is in Jerusalem; so, which is it?"

Jn 4:21 Jesus declared, "Believe me, dear woman, the place where one worships God is not important; it is the condition of the heart of the worshiper that matters. Very soon, you will worship the Father neither on this mountain nor in Jerusalem.

22 You Samaritans worship a confusing tradition of rituals that doesn't enlighten the mind and has no ability to heal the worshiper; we worship the Creator God, and our minds are enlightened and healed by him because all that he asks of us is sensible and reasonable. The plan to heal humanity from the infection of selfishness and sin is provided through the Jews. 23 The time has now come that all true worshipers will worship the Father with an intelligent, reasonable understanding of who he is—loving, admiring, and respecting the truth about his nature, character, and methods. These understanding worshipers are the kind the Father seeks. 24 God is intelligent and reasonable, and his worshipers must worship him intelligently and reasonably, appreciating and valuing the truth of God's methods and principles."

Jn 4:25 The woman said thoughtfully, "I know that the Savior of the world, called Christ, is coming. When he comes, he will make plain the truth about God and untwist all the confusing ideas about the Father. He will destroy the lies of Satan that prevent us from knowing God. He will explain the real problem regarding the infection of selfishness and sin within mankind, and he will reveal God's plan to heal and restore mankind to God's original ideal."

Jn 4:26 Then Jesus proclaimed, "I, who stand before you and am speaking with you, am he."

Jn 4:27 Just as Jesus said this, his disciples returned and were shocked to find him talking with a woman—and not just any woman, but a Samaritan. They were too insecure to ask, "Why are you talking with her?" or "What do you want with her?"

Jn 4:28 After hearing what Jesus had just told her, the woman forgot all about her water jar, rushed back to town, and said to the people, 29 "Come, see a man who knew everything about me. Could this be the Savior we have been waiting for—the Christ?" 30 The townspeople were so intrigued by the woman's testimony that they made their way toward Jesus.

Jn 4:31 While the woman was witnessing to the townspeople, the disciples urged Jesus, "Teacher, eat something."

Jn 4:32 But he said to them, "I have food that nourishes me that you don't yet understand."

Jn 4:33 The disciples were puzzled and said to each other, "Did someone else bring him food?"

Jn 4:34 Jesus said to his disciples: "The food that nourishes me and gives me strength is to do the will of the Father who sent me, and to finish the work he has given me to do: to reveal the truth about him, expose the lies of Satan, and cure human sinfulness. 35 Do you not say, 'Only four months longer and the harvest will be ready'? I tell you, open your eyes, enlighten your minds, and look all around you, and you will see that the world is a vast field of souls! And they are ripe for harvest. 36 At this very moment, the reaper receives the wages of joy and thanksgiving as he harvests souls from death into life eternal. This is so that the one who sows the truth into the heart, and the one who reaps the converts that result from the growth of the truth in the mind, may rejoice together. 37 Thus the saying 'One sows and another reaps' is true. 38 I sent you to reap those individuals who have already had the truth planted in their hearts. Others have done the hard work of planting the truth, and you have reaped the benefits of their labor."

Jn 4:39 Many of the Samaritans from the town where the woman lived trusted Jesus as the Messiah because of the witness of the woman who'd said, "He knew everything about me." 40 Because of this, when the Samaritans came to see Jesus, they urged him to stay with them and share with them the truth about God and the plan to heal mankind. So Jesus stayed with them two days, 41 and because of the truth he revealed to them, many more put their trust in him.

Jn 4:42 They said to the woman, "We trust Jesus not only because of what you said; now we have heard the truth for ourselves, and we know that this man really is the Savior of the world."

Jn 4:43 After the two days in Samaria, Jesus left for Galilee. 44 (Jesus himself had already pointed out that a prophet is not respected, valued or believed in his own country.) 45 When he arrived in Galilee, the Galileans were glad to see him and made him welcome. They had seen all that he had done in Jerusalem at the Passover Feast, for they had been there, and their hearts were warmed by the truths he presented.

Jn 4:46 Once again he went to Cana in Galilee, where he had previously turned the water into sweet, fresh wine. And there was a royal official in Capernaum, whose son was sick and dying. 47 When this official heard that Jesus had arrived in Galilee from Judea, he went to him and begged him to come and heal his son who was nearly dead.

Jn 4:48 Jesus said to him, "Unless you people see miraculous signs and wonders, you will never believe. Won't you ever value the truth because it is true even if no miracle attends it?"

Jn 4:49 The royal official said, "Sir, please come down before my child dies."

Jn 4:50 Jesus replied, "You may go home. Your son will live." The man believed what Jesus said and left for home. 51 While he was on the way home, his servants met him with the news that his son was healed and well. 52 When the man inquired as to the time his son got better, they said, "The fever left him yesterday at one o'clock in the afternoon."

Jn 4:53 Then the father was overwhelmed with awe and joy as he realized that it was the exact time at which Jesus had said to him, "Your son will live." So he and his entire household believed fully that Jesus was the Savior of the world.

Jn 4:54 This was the second miracle Jesus performed after coming from Judea to Galilee.

5 Some time later, Jesus went to Jerusalem for a Jewish festival. 2 Near the Sheep Gate in Jerusalem, there is a pool which in Aramaic is called Bethesda, and which is surrounded by five covered porches. 3 It was here that a great number of people with various diseases or disabilities would gather—

the blind, the crippled, and the paralyzed. [4] They gathered about this pool because, in their desperation for a cure, they had come to believe a superstitious tale—a tale that, sadly, made God appear cruel and arbitrary. They erroneously believed that an angel would periodically come down and stir the waters, and whoever noticed that the waters were stirred, and was first to enter the water, was supposedly healed. [5] There was one particularly sad case of a man who had been paralyzed for thirty-eight years. [6] When Jesus saw him lying there, and learned that he had been in this condition for such a long time, he asked him, "Do you want to get well?"

Jn 5:7 "Sir," the paralyzed man replied, "I have no one to help me into the water when it is stirred. While I am trying to get in, those who are quicker and faster enter before me."

Jn 5:8 Then Jesus said to him, "Get up! Pick up your mat and walk."

[9] Immediately the man was completely cured: he jumped up, picked up his mat, and walked. This happened on the Sabbath, [10] and when the legalistic Jews saw the man who had been healed carrying his mat, they said, "It is the Sabbath; the law forbids you to carry your mat."

Jn 5:11 But he defiantly replied, "I was paralyzed for thirty-eight years; and today, a man completely healed me—something you priests and lawyers could never do—and this man told me, 'Pick up your mat and walk.'"

Jn 5:12 So they asked him, "Who is this man who told you to pick up your mat and walk?"

Jn 5:13 The man had no idea who it was because Jesus had quietly slipped away. Jesus was so humble and meek that he never made a show or sought personal attention, but he always wanted God to be recognized.

Jn 5:14 Later, Jesus found the man at the temple and said to him, "You are completely healthy again. Don't go back and engage in selfish behaviors, for such practices actually damage and destroy you, and you could easily damage yourself more severely next time." [15] The man was glad to find out who had healed him, and went and told the Jews that it was Jesus who had made him well.

Jn 5:16 Because Jesus was healing on the Sabbath, the Jews, who were more concerned with rules and regulations than restoring God's children to health, ridiculed and harassed him, seeking to undermine his ministry. [17] Jesus said to them, "My Father is always working—always giving of himself for the good of his creation. Today, right now, he continues to work for the healing and restoration of this world, and I too am working—working with him in all he does." [18] The Jews were outraged after hearing this, and tried even harder to kill him. In their minds, he was not only breaking the Sabbath, but he was also calling God his own Father and claiming equality with God.

Jn 5:19 Jesus knew that their minds were darkened with misunderstanding, so he gave them this answer: "I tell you the truth, I don't do anything in my own strength or by using my own power; everything I do I am only able to do because my Father in heaven directs and enables me. Everything I do is exactly what my Father would do if he were here in my place. [20] For my Father loves me and shows me all his ways. And yes, I know this is hard for you to comprehend, but he will show, through me, even greater revelations of his character and the healing methods of his kingdom. [21] For just as my Father restores the dead to life, so I — his Son — give life to all those who open their hearts and minds to receive the healing truth I bring. [22] Not only will my Father not judge you, but he has entrusted me, his Son, with revealing the truth necessary for each person to be able to judge whether to accept God's Remedy to sin, or not. Thus all judgment is simply a matter of whether a person has accepted the Remedy to sin that I bring and is healed, or rejected the Remedy and remains infected with selfishness. 23 All those who accept the Remedy to sin that I bring, and experience healing of mind and character, bring honor to me and thus to my Father whom I reveal. But those who reject the Remedy to sin that I bring, reject the only cure for their infected hearts, and their lives do not honor me or my Father who sent me.

Jn 5:24 "I tell you the truth: Those who comprehend what I am saying, and therefore trust my Father, will experience complete regeneration of heart and mind, and live forever. They are no longer sick and will not be diagnosed as terminal; they have been delivered from certain death to life eternal. 25 I tell you the truth, the time is now here when all those whose minds are infected with the lies of Satan—that lead only to death—will hear the truth that I, the Son of God, reveal; and all those who understand and accept this truth will have the lies dispelled from their minds and will be reconciled to God, and will live. 26 Just as the Father has life original, unborrowed, underived, so I—his Son—also have life original, unborrowed, underived. 27 The Father has given me the responsibility to bring to humanity the Remedy for sin and selfishness, and to diagnose the condition of all people, because I am not only God's Son, but also the Son of Man.

Jn 5:28 "Don't be so shocked by what I am telling you, because a time is coming when all those who are in their graves will hear my voice calling them back to life 29 and will arise out of their graves. Those who have accepted the truth I reveal and have had God's methods, principles and character restored in them, will arise and live forever; but those who have rejected the healing truth and preferred Satan's methods of selfishness—they will arise and sadly, have their diagnosis reveal that their condition is terminal. 30 I do nothing by myself, but everything I do is in harmony with my Father; I diagnose only as I examine the evidence, and my diagnosis is accurate because I am not seeking to make myself happy, but to bring joy to my Father who sent me.

Jn 5:31 "If the only evidence of who I am and of the truth I bring was my own proclamations about myself, such evidence would not be reliable. 32 But there is an abundance of other evidence that verifies that what I say is true, and this evidence is reliable and valid.

Jn 5:33 "You already inquired of John, and he has confirmed the truth of who I am. 34 It is not because I need his testimony that I mention this, but I hope you will accept his testimony and be healed. 35 John was a source of light—on fire to reveal the truth—and for a time you willingly rejoiced in it.

Jn 5:36 "I have evidence more compelling than John's testimony: the very work of revealing the truth of the Father's character and the fact that his principles of love, truth and freedom are the foundation of life, while exposing that Satan's principles of selfishness and survival-of-the-fittest lead only to death. This is the work I am doing, and it is the evidence of who I am and that the Father has sent me. 37 Not only this, but the Father himself has given evidence that he has sent me. But you have never understood his truth nor comprehended his character, 38 nor do you have his methods in your hearts, because your minds are so in tune with Satan that the revelation I have brought about the Father is rejected as faulty. 39 You diligently study the Scriptures because you think that in them you will find some secret that will give you possession of eternal life, but the Scriptures are simply the written revelation about me; 40 yet you refuse to come to me and accept the healing I offer, and live.

Jn 5:41 "Praise from people is not important to me nor does it matter to me, 42 but I know you. I know you do not love God's methods of self-sacrificing love. You would not be willing to lay your life down for another. No! Instead, you prefer Satan's methods of survival-of-the-fittest, and you would gladly kill to protect yourself. 43 I have come as a direct revelation of the Father—his thoughts made visible and audible—and you will not accept that the Father is like me, or that I am sent from the Father to reveal him. But if someone comes promoting their own agenda, seeking to make a name for themself, you eagerly accept and praise them because self-promotion is in harmony with your own self-centered hearts. 44 How can you claim to trust in God when you seek praise from each other, refuse to accept God's truth, and refuse to cooperate with him in the healing of your minds?

Jn 5:45 "Stop thinking that I will accuse you before the Father, or that the Father's attitude is what determines your destiny! I and the Father are One, and we do not accuse anyone. Your destiny is determined by the choices you make; and by choosing to reject the Remedy that Moses taught, you accuse yourself. 46 You claim to believe in Moses and tout him as your guiding light, but everything Moses wrote was designed to teach you about me. 47 But since you have already rejected the Remedy he wrote about, how are you going to believe the Remedy now, that I am here?"

6 Some time after this, Jesus crossed to the far side of the Sea of Galilee (also known as the Sea of Tiberias), 2 and a very large crowd of people followed him because they had seen the miraculous healing of the sick he had performed. 3 Then Jesus went part-way up the mountainside, found a level place and sat down with his disciples. 4 It was almost time for the Jewish Passover Feast.

Jn 6:5 When Jesus looked up and saw the great crowd of people coming toward him, he said to Philip, "Where can we buy food for all of these people?" 6 Jesus asked him only to provide Philip an opportunity to expand his thinking and strengthen his confidence in him, as Jesus had already decided how he was going to feed them.

Jn 6:7 But Philip was still struggling to see beyond the immediate earthly perspective, so he answered, "Even if we had eight months' wages, it would not be enough to buy food to feed everyone!"

Jn 6:8 Another of his disciples, Andrew (Simon Peter's brother) spoke up: 9 "We found a young boy with five small barley loaves and two small fish, but how far will they go among so many?"

Jn 6:10 Jesus said, "Have the people sit down." There was a large meadow there, and the people sat down. There were about five thousand men, as well as women and children. 11 Jesus took the five loaves and two fish, gave thanks to his Father, and distributed them to all those who were seated. Everyone ate as much as they wanted.

Jn 6:12 When they were all satisfied, Jesus said to his disciples, "Gather all the leftovers and don't waste anything." 13 So each disciple took a basket and filled it with pieces, so that twelve baskets of leftovers were collected.

Jn 6:14 After the people saw the miracle of feeding such a large crowd, they began to say, "Surely this is the Messiah who is to come into the world and deliver us." His own disciples were becoming caught up in such talk, as they seemed to always focus on earthly triumph rather than spiritual healing. 15 But Jesus, knowing that they were intending to come and use the methods of Satan—the methods of force to make him king—and because he would never use such methods, withdrew to a mountain retreat by himself.

Jn 6:16 When evening came, his disciples went down to the lake, 17 got into a boat, and set out for Capernaum. Darkness had fallen, and Jesus had not yet joined them. [18] A severe storm arose and the waters became very rough. [19] After they had rowed about three and a half miles, they saw Jesus approaching the boat, and he was walking on the water. They saw that it was Jesus, but their understanding of his true nature was so clouded by their lifelong misconceptions that instead of rejoicing, they became terrified. [20] But Jesus was patient and gentle with them, and said, "It is just me; there is no need to be afraid." [21] Hearing Jesus' voice calmed them, and they were willing to let him into the boat; and immediately the boat reached the shore they were heading to.

Jn 6:22 The next day, the crowd that Jesus had fed with the loaves and fish realized that the disciples had left in the only boat around, and Jesus had not been with them. [23] Then some boats from Tiberias landed nearby. [24] As soon as the crowd realized that both Jesus and his disciples had gone, they got into the boats and went to Capernaum in search of them.

Jn 6:25 When they found Jesus on the other side of the lake, they asked him, "Teacher, when did you get here and how did you come since your disciples took the only boat?"

Jn 6:26 Jesus answered, "I tell you plainly, you seek me not because you saw the miracles and understood the truth I have come to reveal, but because you were fed with loaves and fish and are no longer hungry. [27] Do not make the pursuit of food that feeds the body your main objective in life, but instead pursue as your main objective the food that heals and restores the mind and results in eternal life. I, the Son of Man, am the source of the food that heals the mind and brings life eternal. I am the source of truth that refutes the lies of Satan and reveals God's true character; because of this, God the Father has placed his seal of approval on me."

Jn 6:28 Then they asked him, "What do we have to do in order to do the work God requires, so we can receive this food that heals the mind and results in eternal life?"

Jn 6:29 Jesus answered, "God doesn't require that you perform some work or task in order to enjoy complete healing of mind, reconciliation with him, and eternal life. All he requires of you is this: Believe the truth that I have come to reveal—which will result in the lies of Satan being expelled from your minds, trust in God being restored, and you being healed by God's recreative power—so that you may live forever."

Jn 6:30 So they asked him, "What miracle will you perform so that we may see it and then trust you? What will you do to prove that you are not lying to us? [31] Our forefathers ate manna in the desert; as it is written: 'He gave them bread from heaven to eat.'"

Jn 6:32 Jesus smiled as he saw an opening through which to reach them, and responded by saying, "I tell you plainly, it was not Moses who gave you bread from heaven but my Father, who gives you the real Bread from heaven. The manna your forefathers ate in the desert was given as a symbol of the true Bread of Life to come. Just as the manna was given freely, and provided health to the body, so too the true Bread of heaven is given freely and heals the mind and heart. [33] For the true Bread of God is the One who comes down from heaven bringing the truth about God, which brings life to the world."

Jn 6:34 "Sir," they said, "please give us this bread that we may live forever."

Jn 6:35 Then Jesus told them directly, "I am the Bread of Life. I am the Truth that sets your minds free. I am the Remedy that heals your soul. Whoever comes to me and accepts the truth, principles and methods that I bring, and trusts in me, will be fully restored to God's original ideal. He will never hunger for peace of mind, or thirst for love or contentment of soul. 36 But as I have already told you, you have seen me and all the evidence I have given, and yet you still do not value my principles, or trust what I say. 37 But all those who hear the Father's voice recognize that I represent the Father, and they come to me to be healed. And whoever comes to me for healing I will never turn away. 38 For I have come down from heaven not to pursue my own agenda but to do the will of the Father who sent me. 39 And it is the will of the Father who sent me that I not lose even one of those who have heard the Father's voice and have come to me for healing. I will heal their minds, perfect their characters, and restore them to unity with the Father; and I will raise them up to everlasting life at the last day. 40 For my Father's will is that everyone who trusts in me, his Son, shall be completely healed—having the full image of God restored within them—and thus have eternal life; and I will raise them up at the last day."

Jn 6:41 When the Jews heard this, they became upset and began to grumble because he said, "I am the Bread that came down from heaven; I am the Truth that sets your minds free; I am the Remedy that heals your soul." 42 They resisted accepting the truth, saying, "Isn't this Jesus, the son of Joseph and Mary, who was born right here on earth just like the rest of us? So what's all this rubbish he's talking about when he says, 'I came down from heaven'?"

Jn 6:43 "Stop criticizing and grumbling," Jesus said. 44 "No one who hardens their heart to the Father's call and to the evidence he provides will come to me. Only those who respond to the Father's call and cherish the truth he provides will come to me; and I will raise them to everlasting life at the last day. 45 It is written in the Scriptures: 'They will be taught by God.' Everyone who listens to the Father and embraces his methods, principles and character, comes to me. 46 No one has ever seen the Father except the One who is one with him and has come from God; only I—his Son—have truly seen the Father. 47 I tell you the plain truth, whoever trusts me will be recreated within, have the very principles upon which life is based written in their heart, and they will have eternal life. 48 I am the Bread—the very source—of life. 49 Your forefathers ate the manna in the desert, yet they died and were buried there. 50 But here I am, the Bread—the food the mind and soul needs—sent from heaven, which a person may ingest and not die. 51 I am the very source of life—the heavenly Bread for the soul. If anyone partakes of and ingests this Bread, they will live forever. This Bread is my very being which I give so that the world may live."

Jn 6:52 Then the Jews became very agitated and argued severely among themselves: "How can this human give us himself to eat? Does he think we are cannibals?"

Jn 6:53 Jesus said to them, "I tell you the plain and simple facts: Unless you internalize into your minds the truth which the life of the Son of Man reveals, and incorporate into your characters the principles, methods and merits of his life, your condition is terminal and you are already as good as dead. 54 Whoever partakes of the truth my life reveals, and incorporates my character into theirs, is cured of their terminal condition, and I will raise them up to eternal life at the last day. 55 For my principles, methods and teachings are real truth to be brought into the mind, and my life is the full revelation of God's character to be incorporated into the heart. 56 Whoever internalizes my principles, methods and teachings, and brings within themself my character, is in unity with me, and I with them. 57 Just as the living Father sent me, and I draw all my sustenance from the Father, so the one who connects to me and takes me into their mind will live because I will cure them. ⁵⁸ I am the Bread—the heavenly Remedy for your diseased minds. Your forefathers ate manna and died, but whoever partakes of this Bread—this Remedy—will be cured and live forever." ⁵⁹ He said this while teaching in the synagogue in Capernaum.

Jn 6:60 On hearing this, many of his disciples said, "This is a very difficult assignment. Do you think anyone will do it?"

Jn 6:61 Jesus was aware that his disciples were complaining about this, so he said to them, "Does this offend you? ⁶² What if you see me, the Son of Man, ascend into heaven where I was before? ⁶³ The Spirit of God is the Spirit of love, truth and freedom, who brings life; humanity is currently infected with selfishness, which brings death and counts for nothing good. The words I have spoken to you are the truth; they heal and bring life. ⁶⁴ Yet there are some of you who do not believe me." For Jesus had known from the beginning which of them did not trust him and would betray him. ⁶⁵ He added, "This is why I told you that only those who respond to the Father's call and cherish the truth he provides will come to me."

Jn 6:66 It was at this time that many of his disciples turned back and no longer followed him.

Jn 6:67 Jesus looked sadly at the Twelve and said, "You don't want to leave me too, do you?"

Jn 6:68 Simon Peter responded, "Master, where would we go and whom would we follow? You are the Remedy to heal our minds and give eternal life. ⁶⁹ We trust you and know that you are the Holy One of God—the exact expression of his being."

Jn 6:70 Jesus replied, "I have chosen you, the Twelve, yet one of you is filled with the devil's principles of selfishness." ⁷¹ (He was referring to Judas, the son of Simon Iscariot, who—though one of the Twelve—would later betray him.)

7 After Jesus had said this, he stayed around Galilee, purposely avoiding Judea because the Jews there were so upset by what he said that they were waiting to kill him. ² But as the Jewish Feast of Tabernacles approached, ³ Jesus' brothers said to him, "You should leave here and go to Judea; there are much larger crowds there and you can attract many more followers with the miracles you perform. ⁴ If you want to become popular with the people, you have to stop being so quiet and unassuming, or no one will notice you. Since you are doing these things, start doing them more publicly, and your name will be known around the world." ⁵ His brothers said this because they did not understand the true nature of his mission and did not trust him to make wise decisions.

Jn 7:6 Therefore Jesus told them, "It is not time for me to draw more attention to myself or my ministry; but you can draw attention to yourselves anytime you like. ⁷ The people of the world will not hate you, because you share their values and—like them—you prefer power, pomp, might, and intimidation; but they hate me because my life exposes their ways as unhealthy and destructive. ⁸ You go on to the Feast. I am not going, because the right time for me to go has not yet come." ⁹ After saying this, Jesus stayed in Galilee.

Jn 7:10 However, after his brothers had left for the Feast, Jesus decided to go; but he went quietly, without drawing any attention to himself. ¹¹ The Jews were expecting him to come to the Feast, and were asking, "Where is this man Jesus?"

Jn 7:12 Rumors and gossip about him were spreading through the crowds. Some said, "He is a good man;" others replied, "No, he's a liar and deceiver, and only fools would believe him." ¹³ But no one would speak openly about him for fear of what the Jewish religious leaders might do.

Jn 7:14 It wasn't until the Feast was halfway over that Jesus went up to the temple courts and began to teach. 15 After hearing his eloquence and depth of scriptural knowledge, the Jewish religious leaders were bewildered and asked, "How is it possible that this man could know so much about the Scriptures without having ever gone to one of our seminaries and been properly taught by us?"

Jn 7:16 Jesus heard their questioning and answered, "What I teach is not of my own creation or devising. My teaching comes directly from my Father who sent me. 17 If anyone chooses to follow God's will, they will discover that the healing power of my teaching comes directly from God, and they will know that I don't speak to promote myself. 18 Someone who speaks about self does so only to promote self, but one who presents the beauty and truth of God's character and methods is a person of purity and honesty; there is nothing deceitful or dangerous about them. 19 Has not Moses given you the law of love — the principles of selflessness upon which life is based? Yet not one of you values or practices the principles of love. Instead, you practice the principles of selfishness. Why don't you value God's methods of love? Why are you trying to kill me?"

Jn 7:20 The crowd was stunned by his keen discernment and simple honesty, yet they continued to hide their true heart's desire and said, "You are either crazy or possessed by a demon. Who do you think is trying to kill you?"

Jn 7:21 Then Jesus said to them, "I performed one miracle to heal a man on the Sabbath, and you are all shocked as if I have done some horrible act. 22 Yet, because Moses codified circumcision (even though circumcision really did not come from Moses but from the patriarchs), you circumcise a child on the Sabbath. 23 Now if a child can be circumcised—which is only a symbol of God's plan to heal the heart —on the Sabbath, so that the ordinances Moses instituted won't be broken, why are you angry at me for healing the entire man on the Sabbath? 24 Stop valuing symbols and rituals over God's children; learn what really matters in God's kingdom."

Jn 7:25 With that, some of the people of Jerusalem had their minds aroused and began to ask, "Isn't this the man the religious leaders are trying to kill? 26 Here he is, speaking openly in the temple, and they don't say anything to him. Have the authorities really concluded that he is the Christ?" 27 But others countered, "We know where this man is from; but no one is supposed to know where the real Christ is from."

Jn 7:28 Jesus was still teaching in the temple courts, and when he heard what the crowds were saying, he proclaimed, "Yes, you know me, and you know where I am from, and because of this you close your minds and fail to realize that I am not here on my own but am the ambassador of the Father who sent me. He sent me because you do not know him; 29 but I know him because I am from him, and he sent me to reveal his true nature and character to you."

Jn 7:30 When the religious leaders and some in the crowd heard this, they became enraged and tried to seize him, but no one could touch him because his mission was not yet complete and the time of his death had not yet come. 31 But many in the crowd ignored the protests of the religious leaders and put their trust in him. They said, "When the Christ does come, will he do more miracles than this man?"

Jn 7:32 The religious leaders (known as the Pharisees, and preoccupied with rules and performance) heard the crowd whispering such things about Jesus and became fearful that they would lose power and control over the people. So, together with the chief priests, they sent the temple guard to arrest him.

Jn 7:33 Jesus was still teaching in the temple and said, "I am here with you for only a short time, and then I will return to my Father who sent me. 34 You will search for me, not because you have come to love and trust me, but in order to further interfere with my mission to restore the world, therefore you will not be able to find me; and where I am going you will not be able to come."

Jn 7:35 The Jews said to each other, "What is he talking about? Where does he think he can go that we won't be able to find him? Will he go to Greece and hide among the Jews scattered there? 36 What did he mean when he said, 'You will search for me, not because you have come to love and trust me, but in order to further interfere with my mission to restore the world, therefore you will not be able to find me,' and 'where I am going, you will not be able to come'?"

Jn 7:37 On the last and most important day of the Feast, Jesus stood up and said in a loud voice: "If anyone is thirsty for truth, love and freedom; if anyone is parched for health of mind, happiness, contentment and joy, let them come to me and drink freely of the healing Remedy. 38 Whoever trusts me, and opens their mind, and partakes of the truth I bring, they will have the healing truth and love of God —as the Scriptures say—'like streams of living water, flow from within them.'" 39 By this he meant the Spirit of love and truth—who heals the mind and heart—recreating Godlike character within, which those who trust in him would receive later. Up to this time, the Spirit had not been received because Jesus had not yet fully revealed the selfless character of God, and the people had not yet surrendered their hearts to him.

Jn 7:40 On hearing what he said, some of the people remarked, "This must certainly be Moses the Prophet."

Jn 7:41 But others countered, "No! He is the Christ." And others asked, "How can the Christ come from Galilee? 42 Doesn't the Scripture teach that the Christ will come from the line of David, and be born in Bethlehem?" 43 Thus the people were confused and divided on whether to trust Jesus or not. 44 Some even wanted to seize him and put him in jail, but no one touched him.

Jn 7:45 Finally, the temple guards who had been listening to Jesus' teaching went back to the chief priests and Pharisees, who asked them, "Why didn't you arrest him and bring him back here like we told you?"

Jn 7:46 The guards responded, "We have never heard anyone speak the way this man speaks."

Jn 7:47 The Pharisees were incensed and, with disgust in their voice, countered: "You mean you are so foolish that you have been deceived by him? 48 Have any of the rulers or religious leaders or Pharisees believed the garbage he is spreading? 49 No! But this uneducated, simple-minded mob, that has no clue about what the law teaches, thinks he is something special—well, curse them all!"

Jn 7:50 Nicodemus, who had previously gone to Jesus, and who was one of the Pharisees, asked, 51 "Does our law condemn anyone without first hearing what they have to say, and without examining the evidence to find out what they are doing?"

Jn 7:52 They replied, "Are you a Galilean also? Then why don't you go and investigate, and you will discover that prophets do not come from Galilee."

Jn 7:53 Then they each went to their own home.

8 But Jesus went to the Mount of Olives to meditate and rest. 2 At dawn, he again went to the temple courts where the people had gathered, and began to teach them. 3 The lawyers and Pharisees entrapped a woman into

adultery and then threw her down before Jesus in front of the crowd. [4] Then they slyly said to Jesus, "Wise teacher, this woman was just caught in the very act of adultery. [5] The Law that Moses gave us commands us to stone such women. Now, wise teacher, what do you say we should do with her?" [6] They brought her to Jesus and asked this question in an attempt to trap him. If he said, "Let her go," they would accuse him before the people of undermining the Law of Moses; but if he said, "Stone her," they would report him to the Romans as usurping their authority, because only the Romans could inflict the death penalty.

But Jesus was not deceived by their trickery. He calmly bent down, and using his finger, began to write in the sand the various sins that those who'd brought the woman before him had committed. He wrote just the sins—no names, no details. [7] And when they persisted in demanding that Jesus answer, he stood up and said to them, "Whichever of you is without sin, let him be the one to cast the first stone." [8] Then he bent down and wrote more of their sins in the dirt—no names, no details.

[Jn 8:9] At this point, those who heard what he said, and saw what he wrote, quietly slipped away... one person at a time: the older ones first, until only Jesus and the woman were left standing there. [10] Then Jesus said gently to her, "Dear woman, where are all those who brought you here? Has no one condemned you?"

[Jn 8:11] "No one, sir," she said. "I don't condemn you either," Jesus said. "Now go, and stop injuring yourself by deviating from God's design for life."

[Jn 8:12] When Jesus again spoke to the people, he said: "I am the true light revealing God's character, principles and methods to the world. Whoever prefers what I am revealing, and opens their mind to understand this truth, will no longer walk in the darkness of Satan's ways, or live in fear of God because of the devil's lies, but will have the truth that brings eternal life."

[Jn 8:13] But the Pharisees challenged him: "Here you are, promoting yourself! Your testimony is not reliable. You yourself already said that a person promoting themself is not reliable."

[Jn 8:14] Jesus calmly replied, "Even though I am the One telling you about my purpose here, my account is valid because I know where my mission began and where it will end. But you have no idea where my mission began, or what it entails, or where it will end. [15] You are always making judgments, using narrow and self-centered perspectives; I don't judge anyone—I heal and restore. [16] But if I do judge, my conclusions are right, because they are based on the truth, and the truth is seen not by me alone. The truth is also known by my Father who sent me and with whom I stand. [17] In your own Law, it is written that any testimony, to be valid, must be corroborated by another person. [18] I am One who bears witness about myself, my mission and purpose; my other witness is my Father who sent me."

[Jn 8:19] Then they asked him, "Are you sure you even know who your father is? Where is your father?" Jesus replied, "You don't know me nor my character, methods or principles; you don't understand my purpose or mission, nor do you know or understand my Father. If you really knew me (and who I am), you would know my Father also."

[Jn 8:20] He said this while teaching in the temple near the place where the offerings were put. Yet, even though the religious leaders were enraged by his teaching, no one laid a hand on him, because his mission was not yet complete.

[Jn 8:21] Again Jesus said to them, "I am going away, and you will look for me—not because you will have come to love and trust me, but in order to undermine me. Having rejected the Remedy for the infection of selfishness, you will die. Where I am going, you are unable to come."

Jn 8:22 The Jews were so darkened in their understanding that they asked, "Will he kill himself? Is that why he says, 'Where I am going, you are unable to come'?"

Jn 8:23 But Christ continued, "You are from this world below and practice the methods of selfishness, which lead only to death; I am from heaven above and practice the methods of selfless love—the principle upon which life is based. You are in harmony with this world's principle of survival-of-the-fittest, and you will kill in order to save yourselves. I am not in harmony with this world's principle of survival-of-the-fittest, and I will lay down my life to save others. 24 I told you that you would die, because without a Remedy, your condition is terminal: your methods of selfishness lead only to death if you do not believe that I am the One I claim to be—the Remedy for your terminal condition; and if you do not experience a change of heart and mind, you will surely die in the misery of your own selfish state."

Jn 8:25 "Who do you think you are?" they asked incredulously. "Exactly what I have been telling you all along: I am the living truth to cure your terminal condition," Jesus replied. 26 "You are so infected with selfishness and so sick in mind that I could easily spend my time pointing out the extent of your sickness, but the One who sent me is the source of all truth, and my mission is to spend my time revealing the truth about him to the world."

Jn 8:27 They did not understand that he was actually speaking about his Father, 28 so Jesus said, "When you succeed in your schemes and have lifted up the Son of Man, then you will see my true character and know that I am all that I have claimed to be—that all I do is exactly what the Father would do if he

were here, because all I have learned has come from him. 29 The One who sent me is always with me; he enlightens my mind, he has never left me alone, and everything I do pleases him, for I represent his character perfectly." 30 While he was speaking, many of the people put their trust in him.

Jn 8:31 Jesus said to those Jews who trusted him, "If you value and internalize the truths, principles and methods I am teaching, you will experience transformation of mind and regeneration of character, and will be my true followers and representatives. 32 Then you will experience the healing power of the truth, and the truth will set your entire being free."

Jn 8:33 But the Jews who rejected him answered indignantly, "We are the descendants of Abraham and are no one's slaves. Since we are not slaves, what are you talking about when you say that we shall be set free?"

Jn 8:34 Jesus replied, "I tell you the simple truth: Everyone who practices the methods of selfishness is a slave to selfishness. 35 Now, a 'slave of selfishness' has no permanent place in the family of love, but a 'son of love' belongs to the family forever. 36 So if the Son sets your hearts and minds free from selfishness, you will be free to love indeed. 37 I know you are genetic descendants of Abraham. Yet unlike Abraham, you have rejected my methods, teachings and principles and are ready to kill me. 38 I am showing you and telling you the way the Father runs his kingdom—in truth, love, and freedom; but you prefer the methods of deceit, selfishness and coercion, which you learned from your father."

Jn 8:39 "Abraham is our father!" they shouted.

"If you were more than genetic descendants—if you were children of Abraham in values and character—then you would practice the methods Abraham did, and embrace the truth. 40 But instead, you prefer lies, and you are determined to kill me, the One who has brought you the truth—the only Remedy to heal you—which God himself gave me. Abraham did not reject truth or prefer lies, ⁴¹ but you don't practice Abraham's values. No! You are doing what your own father does."

"We were not born illegitimately!" they protested; "The only Father we have is God himself."

^{Jn 8:42} With tears in his eyes, Jesus replied, "If God were really your Father, you would love me, for I came from the Father and am an exact representation of him. I have not come on my own account but as his ambassador to reveal him to the world. ⁴³ Why don't you understand what I am saying to you? It is because your minds are so darkened with your preconceived ideas and your preference for a god like yourselves that you are unwilling to open your minds and receive the truth I bring. ⁴⁴ You belong to your father, the devil: you prefer his methods, share his motives, and carry out his desires. His methods lead only to death, and from the beginning he has been murdering all who follow him. He rejects all that is true, because truth exposes him as a fraud. He speaks the language of lies, which he invented, for he is a liar and the father of all who lie. ⁴⁵ And because I tell the truth, and you prefer lies, you will not believe me! ⁴⁶ Can any of you prove me guilty of selfishness or any violation of God's methods and principles? Since I am telling the truth and reveal only God's character, why don't you believe me? ⁴⁷ A person who has been reconciled to God, and practices God's methods and principles, understands God's ways. The reason you do not understand is that you have rejected God's methods and principles, and refuse to be reconciled to him."

^{Jn 8:48} The Jews were incensed and said, "We know we are right to call you a filthy Samaritan and a crazy, demon-possessed nut."

^{Jn 8:49} Jesus calmly replied, "I am not crazy or demon-possessed. My actions and conduct bring honor to my Father, as I accurately represent him. But you dishonor me. ⁵⁰ I am not here seeking glory and honor for myself; there is One other who is concerned with my honor, and he accurately diagnoses all things. ⁵¹ I tell you the truth, if anyone incorporates into their lives the principles I am teaching, they will never die."

^{Jn 8:52} The Jews were shocked and exclaimed, "Now we know for sure that you are either crazy or demon-possessed! Abraham died and so did God's spokespersons, yet you say that if anyone practices what you teach, they will never die. ⁵³ Are you greater than our father Abraham? He died, and so did God's spokespersons. Who do you think you are?"

^{Jn 8:54} Jesus replied, "If I promote myself or seek glory for myself, it is meaningless. But my Father, whom you claim as your God, is the One who honors and glorifies me. ⁵⁵ You do not know him or value his methods, or appreciate his character, but I do. If I said I did not, I would be a liar like you; but I do know him and value his methods, appreciate his character, and practice his principles. In fact, I am his very thoughts made audible and visible. ⁵⁶ Your father Abraham was filled with joy just at the thought of seeing me; and he did see me and was glad."

^{Jn 8:57} "You are not yet fifty years old," the Jews retorted, "and you have seen Abraham?"

^{Jn 8:58} "I tell you the truth," Jesus said, "before Abraham was even born, I AM! I AM he who created all things. I AM he who has always been." ⁵⁹ The Jews could take no more, and in a rage, they picked up stones with which to stone him; but Jesus disappeared from their sight and left the temple grounds.

9 As Jesus was walking by, he saw a man who was blind from birth. ² His disciples asked him, "Teacher,

who broke God's law—this man or his parents—that God would punish him with blindness?"

Jn 9:3 Jesus answered them, "This man's blindness was not due to some act either he or his parents committed, but because the world is infected with selfishness, and defects have entered the human body. God permitted this to occur so that his work of healing and restoration can be clearly distinguished from Satan's methods that destroy. 4 As long as minds are still open to receive and understand the light of truth, we must work to reveal the truth of God's character, methods, and principles. Minds are darkening and hearts are closing, so the work of revealing the truth will one day be of no avail. 5 While I am in the world, I am the light of truth, opening the eyes of everyone in the world who is willing to see."

Jn 9:6 After saying this, Jesus spat in the dirt, made some mud, and put it on the blind man's eyes. 7 "Go" he said, "and wash in the Pool of Siloam" (which means Sent). So the man went and washed, and his vision was fully restored.

Jn 9:8 His neighbors and those who had seen him begging, asked, "Isn't this the same man who was blind and used to sit and beg?" 9 Some said he was; others said, "No, he only looks like the blind man." But the man himself insisted, "Yes! It is me. I am the man who was blind, but now I can see!"

Jn 9:10 "If you were blind, how is it that you are now able to see?" they demanded.

Jn 9:11 He joyfully proclaimed, "Jesus made some mud and put it on my eyes. He told me to wash the mud off in the Pool of Siloam, so I went and washed off the mud and immediately I could see!"

Jn 9:12 "Where is this man?" they asked. "I don't know," he replied.

Jn 9:13 The crowd that had gathered brought him to the Pharisees. 14 This was sure to cause a stir, because the day Jesus made the mud and cured the blind man was the Sabbath, and the Pharisees had all kinds of rules about what they thought was appropriate conduct on the Sabbath. 15 Therefore the Pharisees interrogated the man who had been blind. They asked him how he had received his sight. "Jesus put mud on my eyes," he replied, "and I washed, as he instructed, and now I see."

Jn 9:16 Some of the Pharisees were so biased by their own rules and false concepts of God that they said, "This man cannot be from God because he does not keep the Sabbath as we have determined it should be kept." But others, who were not so hardened, asked, "How can a person in rebellion against God do such miraculous healings?" So they were divided.

Jn 9:17 In frustration, those who believed that Jesus was not from God turned again to the man who had been blind, and asked, "What do you have to say about him? It was you he has healed." The man replied boldly, "He is an envoy of the Most High God!"

Jn 9:18 The Jewish leaders were unwilling to accept his answer, and were looking for a way to deny the truth that this man had been blind and healed by Jesus, so they sent for his parents. 19 "Is this your son?" they asked. "Was he born blind? And how is it that he is now able to see?"

Jn 9:20 The parents answered, "This is definitely our son and he was certainly born blind, and has been blind his entire life until today. 21 But how he is now able to see, or who it is that has healed him, we have no idea. But you can ask him; he is old enough to speak for himself." 22 His parents said this because they were intimidated by the Jewish leaders who were angry and had started banning Jesus' followers from the temple and its services. 23 That is why the parents said, "He is old enough to speak for himself."

Jn 9:24 So the leaders summoned the

healed man a second time and commanded him, "Give God the glory for your healing, because we know that this man, Jesus, is a rebel against God."

Jn 9:25 But the man was not intimidated (as his parents had been) and said, "Whether he is a rebel against God or not, I don't know. But one thing I know for sure: I was blind, and now I see—and Jesus is the One who healed me!"

Jn 9:26 Then they began their interrogation again in an attempt to confuse him and find some minor point with which to discredit the entire account. They said, "What did he do to you? How did he give you back your sight?"

Jn 9:27 He answered, "I have already told you, but you are so bent on denying the truth that you won't accept what I say." Then he added, hoping to put them on the defensive, "Why do you want to hear it again? Do you want to become his followers also?"

Jn 9:28 Then the religious leaders became upset and hurled insults at him: "You are one of his followers! We are loyal followers of Moses! 29 We know that God spoke to Moses, but as for this drifter, we don't even know where he's from."

Jn 9:30 The healed man answered without hesitation, "Now that's amazing! You say you don't know where he's from. I find that unbelievable. You claim to know about God and his workings, yet this man opened my eyes and you don't know anything about him. 31 We know that God does not support the requests of those in rebellion against him. He supports those who are in harmony with him and working for him. 32 No one has ever heard of someone opening the eyes of a man born blind. 33 If Jesus was not from God and blessed by God, he could do nothing like this."

Jn 9:34 When they heard this, their pompous self-importance was offended and they angrily retorted, "You are a homeless beggar who was born defective and accursed of God; how dare you lecture us on such matters!" And then they threw him out.

Jn 9:35 Jesus heard how the man had been treated by the religious leaders, and when he found him, asked, "Do you trust the Son of Man?"

Jn 9:36 "Who is he, sir?" the man asked; "Please tell me, so that I may put my trust in him."

Jn 9:37 Jesus said, "You have now seen him; in fact, I, the One speaking with you, am him."

Jn 9:38 Then the man fell down on his knees, and with praise and adoration in his heart, said, "My Lord, I give you my life and trust you completely."

Jn 9:39 Jesus said, "I have come to diagnose the true condition of the world. Those who realize they are blind and accept my Remedy—will see; but all who reject my Remedy, claiming they can see on their own—will remain blind."

Jn 9:40 Some of the Pharisees who heard what Jesus said, asked, "What are you suggesting? Are you saying we are blind too?"

Jn 9:41 Jesus said, "If you had not been enlightened with the knowledge of the true Remedy, you would not be guilty of rejecting it; but now that you claim to know the true Remedy and yet refuse to hear anything that disagrees with your own opinions—your condition remains terminal."

10 "I tell you the truth: Anyone who does not enter the sheep sanctuary through the gate but climbs in by some other way, is a rustler and a burglar. 2 But the shepherd of the sheep enters through the gate. 3 The guard opens the gate for the shepherd, and the sheep that know him listen to his voice. He calls the sheep by name, and all who know the shepherd, he leads out of the pen. 4 When he has brought out all who know him, he goes ahead of them, leading the way—never driving them from behind—and his sheep follow, because they know his

voice and love him and all his ways.

Jn 10:5 "But they will not follow a stranger or an imposter posing as the shepherd. No! They will run away from him because they don't see the shepherd's methods being practiced, or hear the shepherd's voice." 6 Jesus used this analogy, but they did not understand the point he was making.

Jn 10:7 Therefore Jesus explained further: "I tell you the truth: I am the way of escape from the prison for the sheep. 8 All others who came before me—claiming to know a way of escape—were rustlers and burglars, seeking only to destroy the sheep; but the sheep who know me and value my methods did not listen to them. 9 I am the exit door from death—the only entryway to life: whoever goes through me will be completely healed and transformed. He will no longer be captive in a fatal situation, but will come and go freely, and find health and peace. 10 The rustler comes only to steal and slaughter and destroy; I have come to give life—complete, full, and abundant—beginning here and now.

Jn 10:11 "I am the Good Shepherd who practices only the methods of love. The Good Shepherd loves his sheep and lays down his life for them. 12 Those hired to watch the sheep do not love the sheep but love themselves and the money they can make. So when the hired hands see the wolf coming, they abandon the sheep and run away to save themselves. Then the wolf attacks the flock and scatters it, 13 and the hired hands run away because their hearts are selfish and they do not love the sheep.

Jn 10:14 "I am the Good Shepherd. I know my sheep well, and they know me and value me and my methods and principles— 15 just as the Father and I know each other perfectly and are in complete unity in heart, mind, methods, and principles. I voluntarily lay down my life to free and restore my sheep. 16 I have other sheep that are not part of the flock here in Palestine; I must bring them back into unity with the Father and me also. They will hear my voice, value my methods and practice my principles, and there will be unity—only one flock under one shepherd. 17 The reason my Father loves me is that I lay my life down voluntarily, and I will take my life up again—all in order to set my sheep free and heal all their defects. 18 No one can take my life from me, but I voluntarily surrender it. I have the ability to lay it down and to take it up again; and in so doing, I will bring unity and healing to my sheep. This is the mission and purpose I received from my Father."

Jn 10:19 Upon hearing these words, the Jews were divided again. 20 Many said, "He is insane or possessed by a demon. Don't listen to him!"

Jn 10:21 But others countered, "His teachings of self-sacrificing love are not the teachings of selfish and evil demons. And can a demon open the eyes of the blind?"

Jn 10:22 Then came the time for the Feast of Dedication at Jerusalem. It was winter, 23 and Jesus was walking in the temple area in Solomon's Colonnade. 24 The Jewish leaders gathered around him and said, "How long are you going to avoid disclosing your true identity? Do you like keeping people in suspense? Why don't you just come out and tell us plainly: Are you the Messiah—the Christ—or not?"

Jn 10:25 Jesus answered, "I have already told you! My character tells you, my deeds tell you, my ministry tells you, and the miracles I perform in my Father's name all tell you that I am the One sent to heal and restore the world back into unity with my Father. 26 But you do not believe my testimony or the abundance of evidence I have given, because you do not value my ways or follow where I lead. You are not my sheep. 27 My sheep value my ways, methods and principles; I know them intimately and they follow where I lead.

²⁸ I heal them from their terminal condition and give them eternal life, and they will never perish—no thug can kidnap them away from me. ²⁹ My Father, who has placed their healing and recovery in my hands, is greater than all; no thief can kidnap them away from my Father. ³⁰ I and the Father are One. We are one in purpose, character and substance."

Jn 10:31 Again the Jews were enraged and picked up stones, intent on stoning him, ³² but Jesus, with incredible calmness, said to them, "I have revealed a number of great and miraculous signs from my Father. For which of these are you going to stone me?"

Jn 10:33 The Jews replied, "We are not stoning you for the miracles you performed but for blasphemy, because you, a mere human, claim to be God."

Jn 10:34 Jesus answered them, "Is it not written in your own Scriptures, 'I have made you like me. You are Godlike'? ³⁵ If God called 'Godlike' those whom he created, and through whom his word was given—and the Scripture is infallible— ³⁶ then what about me, the One who was not created but sent directly from God into the world and ordained as God's very own ambassador to reveal him? Why are you accusing me of blasphemy because I said, 'I am God's Son'? ³⁷ If I don't do what my Father does—if I don't accurately represent his character, reveal his methods, and practice his principles—then don't believe me. ³⁸ But if I do—even though you refuse to believe my testimony—believe the overwhelming evidence that I have provided, so that you may realize and truly understand that the Father is in me, and I in the Father. The Father and I are One!" ³⁹ Again they were enraged and attempted to seize him, but he disappeared from their midst.

Jn 10:40 Then Jesus went back across the Jordan and stayed at the place where John had previously been immersing people in water. ⁴¹ Crowds came to him there and said, "Though John never performed a miracle in an attempt to prove that what he said was true, we believe all that John said about you. You are the Messiah to come." ⁴² And many put their trust in him, experienced healing of mind, and began to practice his methods of selfless love.

11

Now Lazarus, a man from Bethany and the brother of Mary and Martha, was sick. ² (His sister Mary is the one who would pour expensive perfume on the Lord Jesus and then wipe his feet with her hair.) Jesus was their friend, ³ so the sisters sent word to him, "Lord, Lazarus—your dear friend—is sick."

Jn 11:4 When Jesus heard the news, he said, "Don't worry, this sickness will not end in death. It is permitted so that God's gracious character of healing love may be manifested through God's Son—so that all can see that God's Son is the source of life and health." ⁵ Jesus loved Mary, Martha and Lazarus dearly, ⁶ yet after he heard that Lazarus was sick, he stayed where he was for two more days.

Jn 11:7 Then he said to his disciples, "Let's go back to Judea."

Jn 11:8 But the disciples were afraid, and said, "Teacher, the Jewish authorities just recently tried to stone you. You aren't serious about going back there, are you?"

Jn 11:9 Jesus answered, "Are there not twelve hours of light each day? A person who travels during the day will not stumble because they can see where they are going. ¹⁰ It is when traveling at night that one stumbles and falls, as they can no longer see. A person must follow the truth wherever it leads, and do what is right because it is right, and then they will no longer stumble. It is by ignoring the truth, practicing deceit, and choosing selfishness over what is right that the mind is darkened and the life shipwrecked."

Jn 11:11 After saying this, he told them, "Our friend Lazarus has now fallen asleep; it is time for me to go there and wake him up."

Jn 11:12 His disciples said, "Then there is no need to worry, Lord. If he is resting, he will recover. We don't need to go and risk harassment by the Jewish authorities." 13 They did not understand that Jesus was speaking of Lazarus' death and was describing death as a sleep; they thought he meant a physiological sleep.

Jn 11:14 So Jesus told them plainly, "Lazarus is asleep in death, 15 and because I care about you, and want your confidence and trust in me to grow, I am glad I was not there. Had I been there, he could not have fallen asleep in death; but now you will see the crowning evidence that I am all that I have claimed to be. So let us go to him."

Jn 11:16 Then Thomas (also known as Didymus), failing to understand what Christ was trying to reveal to them, said to the rest of the disciples, "Well, if he's bound and determined to die, let us go with him that we can all die together."

Jn 11:17 When Jesus arrived, he was told that Lazarus had already been buried in the tomb for four days. 18 Because Bethany was less than two miles from Jerusalem, 19 many Jews had come to Mary and Martha to comfort them during their mourning. 20 When Martha heard that Jesus was near, she went out to meet him, but Mary stayed at home.

Jn 11:21 Martha said to Jesus, "Lord, if you had been here, I know my brother would not have died. 22 But I know that even now God will do whatever you ask of him."

Jn 11:23 Jesus gently said to her, "Don't be sad. Your brother will awaken from this sleep of death."

Jn 11:24 Martha answered, "I know he will awaken at the resurrection at the last day."

Jn 11:25 Jesus said to her, "I am the Resurrection from death and the source of all life. Whoever trusts in me will be healed and live, even though they fall asleep in death; 26 and whoever is alive and believes in me will never cease to live. Do you believe this?"

Jn 11:27 "Yes, Lord," she proclaimed. "I believe you are the Christ—the Son of God—who has come into the world from God to heal and restore the world."

Jn 11:28 And after Martha had professed her confidence in Christ, she went and found her sister Mary, and said to her, "The Teacher is here and is asking for you." 29 When Mary heard this, she got up quickly and went to him. 30 Jesus had not yet entered the village, but was still at the place where Martha had spoken with him. 31 When the Jews who had been comforting Mary noticed how quickly she got up and went out, they followed her, thinking that she was going to the tomb to mourn.

Jn 11:32 When Mary reached Jesus, she ran to him and fell down at his feet, weeping as she said, "Oh Lord, if you had been here, my brother would not have died."

Jn 11:33 When Jesus saw her crying, and the Jews who had come with her also crying, he realized they did not comprehend his mission, and his heart was moved in compassion and sadness for them. 34 "Where have you laid him?" he asked.

"Come and see, Lord," they replied.

Jn 11:35 Then Jesus wept, because he was here to vanquish death but no one recognized it.

Jn 11:36 The Jews didn't realize that Jesus was about to awaken Lazarus from the sleep of death, and naively thought he was mourning him, and said, "See how he loved him!"

Jn 11:37 But some of them said, "If he could heal a blind man whom he didn't even know, why couldn't he keep his close friend from dying?"

Jn 11:38 Jesus, once more deeply moved with compassion for the people whose heartache and fear were magnified by their failure to understand his true nature, came to the tomb. It was a cave with a stone laid across the entrance. 39 "Remove the stone," he said.

"But, Lord," said the dead man's sister, Martha, "it has been four days, and in this heat, there will be a terrible smell."

Jn 11:40 Then Jesus said gently yet firmly, "Did I not tell you that if you have confidence and trust in me, you would see the true life-giving power of God's loving character?"

Jn 11:41 Without further hesitation, they removed the stone. Then Jesus looked up to heaven and said, "Father, thank you for hearing me. 42 I know that you always hear me, but I say this out loud so that all the people standing here may know that you sent me, and that what I do reveals you; and that their trust may grow."

Jn 11:43 After he had said this, Jesus called in a clear and loud voice, "Lazarus, arise and come forth!" 44 Then the dead man arose from the dead and came out, with his hands and feet still wrapped in the grave clothes, and his face also covered with a cloth. Jesus instructed them, "Take off the burial clothes and set him free."

Jn 11:45 Many of the Jews who were there, visiting Mary, were stunned with awe and amazement when they saw what Jesus did, and they put their trust in him. 46 But some of them refused to change their attitude toward Jesus, and went to the Pharisees and reported what he had done. 47 Then the chief priests and Pharisees called a meeting of the Sanhedrin to strategize how to deal with him. "What good are all our words and rules, and our criticism of Jesus?" they asked. "We are having no impact. We have words, but this man is performing numerous miraculous signs, and his popularity is rising. 48 If we don't do something to stop this,

everyone will stop listening to us and follow him, and then the Romans will have no further use for us and we will lose our position and power, and possibly—our nation."

Jn 11:49 Then the high priest, named Caiaphas, spoke up: "You fools! You don't know anything. 50 Don't you realize that—for our own sake—it is better for one man to die in order to save the people, rather than the entire nation be lost?"

Jn 11:51 He did not realize the full meaning of his words, but spoke them in accordance with the Spirit of God, prophesying that Jesus would die as the Remedy for sin; 52 and not just for the Jewish nation, but as the Remedy for the entire world—for everyone who values God's methods and principles. 53 From that day on, they laid plans to kill Jesus.

Jn 11:54 Therefore Jesus withdrew from public discourse and stayed with his disciples in a village called Ephraim, near a desert.

Jn 11:55 When the time for the Jewish Passover was near, large crowds went to Jerusalem for their symbolic cleansing before the Feast. 56 They were eagerly looking for Jesus, and kept asking one another, "Do you think Jesus will come to the Feast? Where do you think he is?" 57 But the chief priests and Pharisees had given orders that anyone who found out where Jesus was should report it at once so they could arrest him.

12 Six days prior to the Passover, Jesus arrived at Bethany where Lazarus (the man Jesus raised from the dead) lived. 2 There, Simon the leper, whom Jesus had healed, gave a banquet in honor of Jesus. Martha catered the dinner, and her brother Lazarus was one of the guests reclining at the table near Jesus. 3 Then Mary, the sister of Martha and Lazarus, took a pint of pure nard worth a year's wages and poured it on Jesus' feet, and then

wiped his feet with her hair. Suddenly, the room was filled with the intensely sweet aroma of the perfume and everyone realized what Mary had done.

Jn 12:4 But Judas Iscariot, the disciple who later betrayed him, was irritated by Mary's gift to Jesus, and objected: 5 "This woman doesn't value the less fortunate, but tries to promote herself with expensive gifts. If she cared more about others than herself, she would have sold the perfume and given the money to the poor. It was worth more than a year's wages." 6 Judas said this not because he cared about the poor, but because he was selfish and motivated by greed; and as keeper of the moneybag, he would help himself to what was in it.

Jn 12:7 "Leave her alone and don't criticize this beautiful thing she has done," Jesus commanded. "She has understood my mission, and with perfume costing all that she had, has anointed me for burial. 8 The poor will always be here for you to minister unto, but you will not always have me with you."

Jn 12:9 Meanwhile, word had spread that Jesus and Lazarus were at Simon's house, and a large crowd began to gather. 10 The chief priests realized that Lazarus was a compelling witness to the healing power of Jesus, so they began to plot to kill Lazarus as well, 11 as—because of him—many Jews were no longer listening to the Jewish religious leaders but were putting their trust in Jesus.

Jn 12:12 The next day, the great crowd gathering for the Passover Feast heard that Jesus was entering Jerusalem riding on a colt—the symbol of a king. 13 They became excited and took palm branches and went out to meet him, shouting:

"Save us, O King! Deliver and heal us, O Messiah!"

"Worthy of all praise is he
who comes in the full and perfect character of the Lord!"

"Worthy of all adoration is the King of Israel!"

Jn 12:14 Jesus rode upon a young donkey —as it is written:

Jn 12:15 "Do not be afraid, O Daughter of Zion;
see, your king and deliverer is coming,
seated on a donkey's colt."

Jn 12:16 The disciples didn't understand at all what was happening. Only after Jesus arose from the dead, and his true nature and character were fully revealed, did they realize that the entire Scriptures were written about him, and that the Scriptures were fulfilled in him.

Jn 12:17 The crowd that saw Jesus call Lazarus from the tomb, and who watched Lazarus rise from the dead, told everyone about the miracle. 18 Because of their enthusiastic testimony, huge crowds went out to meet Jesus. 19 When the Pharisees saw this, they said to one another, "Look at this! Everyone in the world is following Jesus. Our plots and planning are not turning the people back to us—we are losing our influence and status; we are going nowhere!"

Jn 12:20 Now, some Greeks who had come to worship at the Feast 21 came to Philip, who was from Bethsaida in Galilee, and asked, "Sir, we would sure like to see Jesus. Would it be possible to meet him?" 22 Philip went and told Andrew, and the two together went and told Jesus.

Jn 12:23 Jesus replied, "It is now time for the Son of Man to have his character and nature fully revealed. 24 I tell you the clear truth, unless a kernel of wheat gives itself up to be buried and die, it will remain a lone and solitary seed. But if it surrenders itself and dies, it produces many seeds. 25 The person who practices the principle of survival-of-the-fittest, and loves their own life so much that they will kill in order to preserve it, will ultimately destroy themself and lose their life. But the person who loves others more than themself and is willing to give their life freely, so that others may live, is back in harmony with the principles of love upon which life is based, and will preserve their life and live eternally.

26 Whoever wants to serve with me in my healing ministry must practice my methods, value my principles, and follow my ways. All those who serve with me will be with me where I am. My Father will fully heal, restore and exalt all those who truly serve with me in this way.

Jn 12:27 "My heart is heavy, but what shall I say? 'Father, deliver me from this hour'? No; my entire purpose for being here is to come to this very hour. 28 Father, may your true character and nature be fully revealed and may Satan's lies about you be fully exposed!"

Then a voice came from heaven, "I have revealed my true character and nature, and will reveal it again." 29 The crowd, with their darkened minds, couldn't understand the voice; some thought it was thunder, but others thought that an angel had spoken to him.

Jn 12:30 Jesus said, "This voice was to strengthen your faith, not mine. 31 Now is the time for the infection of selfishness and sin in this world to be fully diagnosed and revealed as destructive; now, Satan—the prince of this selfish world—will be driven out into the open, out of the shadows, out from behind his lies and distortions about God and God's methods, out where all can see him as the murderer he truly is, and thus out of the hearts of all who love me. 32 When I am lifted up from the earth, I will draw all intelligences throughout the universe to me." 33 By saying this, he was revealing the kind of death he was going to face.

Jn 12:34 The crowd spoke up and questioned Jesus: "We have heard from the Scriptures that the Messiah will deliver us and establish a kingdom here forever, so how can you say, 'The Son of Man must be lifted up'? And who is this 'Son of Man'?"

Jn 12:35 Then Jesus told them, "You are going to have the light of my life revealing the truth of God's character, methods and principles just a little while longer. Incorporate the light of truth into your lives while you still comprehend it, before the darkness of Satan's lies so blinds you that you can no longer tell the truth from a lie. Those who make choices based on lies, distortions and feelings rather than on the truth, damage their minds and can no longer tell where they are going. 36 Put your trust in the light of truth while your faculties can still see and understand it, so that you may be healed and restored fully into God's enlightened children." When he had finished speaking, Jesus left and hid himself from the crowds.

Jn 12:37 Even though Jesus had performed so many miracles before their eyes, spoken the word of truth in their hearing, and lived a life of selfless love in their presence, they still refused to trust him. 38 This was in harmony with the prophecy of Isaiah:

"Lord, who has believed our message,
and to whom has the ambassador
of the Lord been revealed?"

Jn 12:39 Isaiah tells elsewhere the reason they would not believe:

Jn 12:40 "Their minds have been
blinded by their rejection of truth,
their hearts have been deadened
by their selfish pursuits,
therefore, they neither see the truth
with their minds,
nor understand it with their
hearts,
nor will they turn from their evil
ways;
for if they did, I would heal them."

Jn 12:41 Isaiah said this because he saw Jesus' true character, methods and principles, and spoke about him.

Jn 12:42 Yet while the crowds were rejecting him, many others, even among the leaders, trusted in him. But because of the threats and malice of the Pharisees, they would not confess their allegiance openly for fear of being denied access to the temple. ⁴³ This is because they loved the praise and admiration from men more than praise from God.

Jn 12:44 Then Jesus proclaimed: "When a person trusts in me, they do not trust in me only, but also in the Father who sent me. ⁴⁵ When they look at me, they see the Father who sent me, because the Father and I are one. ⁴⁶ I have come into the world as the Father's ambassador—to bring the light of truth about the Father into the world so that all those who trust in me will be healed and have their minds and hearts set free from the darkness of Satan's lies and the domination of Satan's methods of selfishness.

Jn 12:47 "As for the person who hears my words and sees all the truth I have revealed but does not apply it to their life, I do not speak against them. I did not come into the world to condemn it, but to bring the only Remedy to sin and selfishness in order to heal and save the world. ⁴⁸ There is an accounting—a reckoning, a final conclusion—for the one who does not value the principles and methods I have revealed; the reality of their own condition will condemn them in the last day. By rejecting me — the only Remedy — their infected selfish state is fatal, and the truth of their unhealed terminal condition will be their judge. ⁴⁹ I did not speak words to promote myself, but spoke only the truth necessary to reveal the Father who sent me. ⁵⁰ I know that his methods and principles are the basis of life, and they result in eternal life. So whatever I say is exactly what the Father would say if he were here, because he has told me the exact truth to reveal."

13 It was Thursday, the day before the Passover Feast was to begin. Jesus knew that the time for the culmination and completion of his mission had come, and he would soon be leaving this world and returning to his Father. He loved his children who were living in the world and would now show them that his love has no limits.

Jn 13:2 Supper was being served, and Simon Iscariot's son, Judas, had already decided to follow the devil's suggestion and betray Jesus. ³ Jesus knew that his Father had placed all things—whether in heaven or on earth—in his hands, and that he had come from God to reveal him and was returning to God when his mission was complete. ⁴ So in order to give his disciples a further revelation of God, he got up from his meal, took off his outer garment, wrapped a towel around his waist, ⁵ then poured water in a bowl and began to wash the dirty feet of his disciples, drying them with the towel that was tied around him.

Jn 13:6 When he came to Simon Peter, Peter objected, "Lord, are you going to wash my feet?"

Jn 13:7 Jesus replied, "You don't realize the significance of what I am doing, but later you will understand the importance of all that I have done."

Jn 13:8 Peter resisted, saying, "No, you are my Lord; I will never let you wash my feet." Jesus answered gently, "Unless I cleanse you, you will be unable to be unified in partnership with me."

Jn 13:9 "Then, Lord," Simon Peter exclaimed, "wash not only my feet but my head and hands as well!"

Jn 13:10 Jesus smiled and said, "A person who has already bathed needs only the dirt remaining on their feet washed away; the rest is already clean. A person who has had the rebellion of selfishness washed from their heart needs only the residual habits of selfishness and lingering misconceptions about God and his methods removed; the rest is already clean. You are already clean, though not every one of you." ¹¹ He said "not everyone was clean" because he knew that Judas' heart remained in rebellion, and that Judas was going to betray him.

Jn 13:12 When he had finished washing their feet, he put on his outer garment and returned to his place at the table. "Do you understand the significance of what I have done for you?" he asked them. 13 "You call me 'Teacher' and 'Lord,' and you are right in doing so, because that is what I am. 14 Now that I—your Lord and Teacher—have humbled myself and washed your feet, demonstrating selfless love in action, you also should wash each other's feet. 15 I have set an example of loving service—putting the needs of others ahead of my own—that you should lovingly serve others as I have served you. 16 I tell you truly, no servant is greater than their master, nor is a messenger greater than the one who sent them. 17 Now that you know the selfless principles of love—upon which life and health are based—you will be happy and healthy if you practice them.

Jn 13:18 "But my comments about knowing God's principles of selfless love do not refer to all of you; I know those of you who love God's methods and principles. But the Scripture foretold the choices of the one 'who shares my bread and lifts up his heel against me.'

Jn 13:19 "I am telling you now—before it happens—so that when it does happen, you will be convinced that I am the I AM. 20 I tell you truly, whoever accepts anyone I send accepts me; and whoever accepts me, accepts my Father who sent me."

Jn 13:21 After Jesus said this, his heart ached over the one disciple who refused his methods of love and truth, and he said: "I tell you the truth: One of you is going to betray me."

Jn 13:22 His disciples were disturbed by Jesus' statement and looked closely at each other, trying to figure out who he could be talking about. 23 One of them, the disciple who had grown closest to Jesus, was reclining next to him.

24 Simon Peter prodded this disciple, saying, "Ask him which of us he means."

Jn 13:25 Leaning his head against Jesus' shoulder, he asked, "Lord, who is it?"

Jn 13:26 Jesus answered sadly, "It is the one to whom I give this piece of bread after I have dipped it in the bowl." Then he dipped the bread and gave it to Judas Iscariot, son of Simon. 27 Instantly Judas was angered and surrendered his mind completely to the influence of Satan, preferring his methods of selfishness and greed. Jesus said to him, "Complete your business quickly."

28 But even though Jesus had just indicated who would betray him, none of the remaining disciples understood why Jesus had said this to Judas. 29 They thought that because Judas controlled the purse, Jesus was instructing him to buy what they needed for the feast, or to give something to the poor. 30 As soon as Judas took the bread, he left. And it was nighttime.

Jn 13:31 Once Judas had gone, Jesus said, "Now is the time for the Son of Man to fully reveal the glory of his gracious, unselfish and loving character, methods, and principles, and thus make known the truth of God's glorious character. 32 If God's glorious character of selfless love is revealed through him, then God will honor the Son by revealing the same glorious and selfless character of the Son in himself, and this mutual self-sacrifice will happen without delay. 33 My dear children, I am here with you for only a little while longer. After I am gone, you will look for me, and just as I told the Jews so I am telling you: Where I am going, you cannot now come.

Jn 13:34 "A new understanding of Moses' command I give you: Love one another as I have loved you—freely, not from a sense of obligation, but from a renewed heart of true regard and concern for one another, genuinely loving others more than yourself. 35 By this everyone will know that you are my disciples, because you will practice my methods and principles of selfless love for one another."

Jn 13:36 Simon Peter asked him, "Lord, where are you going?"

Jesus answered, "Where I am going, you cannot now follow, but you will follow me later."

Jn 13:37 Peter then asked, "Lord, why can't I follow you now? Don't you trust me? Don't you know I would die for you?"

Jn 13:38 Jesus gently answered, "Would you, Peter? Would you really die for me? I tell you truthfully, before the rooster crows in the morning, you will deny three times that you know me."

14 "Don't let fear and doubt trouble your hearts. Put your full trust in God and trust me too. ² In my Father's home, there is room for all who want to be there; if this were not true, I would have told you. I am going there to direct all my Father's resources who are not only preparing heaven for you, but also preparing you for heaven. ³ And when all things are ready, I will come back and take everyone who has been brought back into unity with the principles of heaven to be there with me, so that we may all be together. ⁴ You now know the way to the place where I am going."

Jn 14:5 Thomas was confused and said, "But Lord, we don't know where you are going, or how to get there, so how can we know the way?"

Jn 14:6 Jesus answered gently, "I am the Way back to my Father. I am the Truth revealing my Father's character and the principles upon which life is based; I am the Source of all life. I am the Bridge, and no one comes to the Father except through me—because all truth revealing the Father has been provided by me. ⁷ If you really knew me, you would know my Father as well, for the Father and I are One. From now on, you do know him and have seen him, for I am the Father's thoughts made visible and audible."

Jn 14:8 Philip then said, "Lord, then show us the Father, and that will be all we ever need."

Jn 14:9 Jesus answered patiently, "Don't you know me, Philip, even after all I have said and done among you over these years together? Anyone who has seen me has seen the Father. Don't you understand that I am an exact representation of the Father? So how can you say, 'Show us the Father'? ¹⁰ Don't you believe that I am in complete unity with the Father—in mind, heart, attitude, character, method, disposition, principle and will—and the Father is in unity with me? The words I speak are not my own ideas or methods, but are the exact thoughts of my Father whose character and principles live in me. His work is being carried out through me. ¹¹ Believe me when I tell you that I am in complete unity in every way with my Father, and he is in complete unity in every way with me; or at least believe all the evidence I have provided that reveals this truth. ¹² I tell you the truth: Anyone who genuinely trusts me will also be in unity with the Father and will reveal his character—just as I have been doing. His life will be a further revelation of the life-giving power of God and the healing power of his methods. My life reveals the truth of God's character and methods; but those who trust in me will reveal that God's methods, when applied in trust via the Spirit of God, actually heal and transform those who are deformed by sin. I am going to the Father. ¹³ And I will do whatever you ask—that is in harmony with my character, methods, and principles—so that the Son may bring honor and glory to the Father by revealing the healing and life-giving power of his methods. ¹⁴ You may ask me for anything in harmony with my character and methods, and I will do it.

Jn 14:15 "If you love me, you will practice all my methods and principles because you understand, agree, and prefer my ways. [16] And the Father and I will give you another Helper to be with you forever— [17] the Spirit of Truth, who will enlighten your minds to comprehend the truth. Those who prefer the methods of this world—the methods of deceit—cannot accept him, because, having rejected truth, they don't recognize or know him. But you know him, for you know me; and he represents all that I am. He will establish my character, methods and principles within you. [18] I will not abandon you and leave you as orphans; I will come back to you. [19] It is not long until I leave this world. Those who reject me also reject the Spirit of Truth, and therefore their minds will be so darkened that they will no longer be able to see me or comprehend my character and methods. But you will continue to see and understand me more and more, because you accept the Spirit of Truth. Because I live, you, who have accepted me, will also live. [20] On the day I leave this world, you will finally know that I am in every way in complete unity with the Father; and you are in unity with me, and I with you.

[21] Those who understand my methods and principles, and incorporate them into their lives, are the ones who love me and embrace all that I stand for. Those who love me will be transformed back into complete perfection by my Father, and I too will love them back to health, and share myself with them."

Jn 14:22 Then Judas (not Judas Iscariot) asked, "But Lord, why will you show yourself to us and not to the rest of the world?"

Jn 14:23 Jesus answered, "All are given freedom to choose their own course. Those who love me will choose to practice all my methods and principles because they understand, agree, and prefer my ways. My Father will transform such ones back into perfection, and we will be united with them, and

make our home with them. [24] But those who do not love me will reject truth and evidence, and choose not to practice my methods and principles. The words I have spoken are not mine only; they are the words of the Father who sent me.

Jn 14:25 "I have said all this while I'm still with you. [26] But the Helper—the Holy Spirit—whom the Father will send as my representative will enlighten your minds with all truth and will remind you of all the evidence I have given you. [27] Peace with God, and peace of heart and mind, I leave with you; my perfect peace I give to you. I do not give as the world gives, expecting to get something in return. No! I give freely, because I love you and want only the best for you. So don't worry or let your hearts be consumed with fear and doubt.

Jn 14:28 "You heard me say 'I am going away,' but I am coming back to be with you. If you love me, you will realize that this is for your benefit, and you will be glad that I am going to the Father, for the Father is even greater than I. [29] I have told you before it happens, so that when it does, you will be confident that I do know the beginning from the end—and none of this has taken me by surprise—and your confidence in me will then increase. [30] I will not be here to speak with you much longer, for the prince of this world of selfishness is coming. He has no right to harm me, and there is nothing I have done that warrants his malice toward me, [31] but the world must learn the truth that all I do is from love for the Father. Therefore, I will finish the work that the Father has given me to do— reveal the truth about the Father's supreme love, perfect character and faultless methods, and procure the Remedy to sin—while exposing Satan for the liar and murderer he is, and his methods as the source of all destruction and death.

"Come, it is time for us to leave."

The Remedy

149

15 As they were walking, Jesus saw a grapevine, and pointing to it, said: "I am the vine from which all truth and life originates, and my Father is the gardener who tends the vine. ² You are the branches which have life and grow—as long as you are connected to me. Any branch that does not grow and bring forth the fruit of a transformed character reveals that it is not genuinely connected to me, and therefore my Father will remove it. Any branch bringing forth fruit of a transformed character my Father prunes and disciplines in order to bring forth even more fruit. ³ Your hearts have already been cleansed from the lies of Satan as a result of the truth I have revealed to you. ⁴ Remain connected and in unity with me, and I will remain connected and in unity with you. No branch can live, grow, and bear fruit on its own; it must remain connected to the vine. Likewise, you do not have life and cannot grow and bear fruit unless you remain connected to me.

Jn 15:5 "I am the vine from which all truth and life originates, and you, who receive truth and life from me, are the branches. If one remains connected to me and in unity with me, I will never sever the connection, and they will develop a fruitful, Godlike character; but separated from me—they can do nothing good. ⁶ If anyone severs their connection to me and refuses to be reunited with me, they are like a branch that is cut off from the vine and thrown away, and then withers and dies. Such dead branches are picked up, thrown into the fire and burned. ⁷ If you remain connected and in unity with me, and my character is reproduced in you, ask whatever you wish—in harmony with my methods and principles—and it will be given you. ⁸ This healing of damaged hearts and minds, which results in the development of godly character in my followers, brings honor and glory to my Father, as it reveals that his methods are the only methods of life, health, and happiness.

Jn 15:9 "My love for you is just as free, complete and abundant as the Father's love for me. And just as the Father's love lives in me and flows through me to the world, so you must continue to let my love live in you and flow through you to others. ¹⁰ If you value my methods and practice my principles of selfless love, my love will live in you—just as I have valued my Father's methods and practiced his principles of selfless love, and his love lives in and flows through me. ¹¹ I have told you this so that you may be completely restored to the Father's original ideal for mankind—to unity with him—and you may then experience the joy I have known in my unity with the Father; and then your joy will be complete also. ¹² My prescription to heal your minds and hearts is this: Love each other as I have loved you. ¹³ There is no greater love than this—that a person lay down their life to save their friends. This is the principle of life—the central principle of the kingdom of God. This love is the Remedy for the infection that is destroying mankind, and the infection is this: Satan's wicked disease of survival-of-the-fittest, which is preferring self so much that one will kill their friends in order to save themself. ¹⁴ You are my friends if you take my prescription and love one another. ¹⁵ I do not want you to be my servants, because servants only do what they are told but do not understand what the master is doing, nor do they understand the master himself. Their hearts are not in harmony with the master, and what they do they do not do freely. I want you to be my friends—to understand what I am doing—and to freely choose to be in unity with me. That is why I have told you about everything the Father and I are working to accomplish, so your hearts and minds will be in harmony with us. ¹⁶ You did not come seeking me, but I came seeking to heal and restore you, so that you will develop character in harmony with mine — character that will not be shaken. Then the Father will give you whatever you ask as you work in harmony with us to finish our mission. ¹⁷ This is my prescription: Love one another.

^{Jn 15:18} "If the selfish, survival-of-the-fittest world hates you, remember that selfishness hates love, and it hated me first. ¹⁹ If you were also selfish and valued the methods of the world, then the world would love you as part of itself. But as it is, you do not value the selfish methods of the world or practice its principles, for I have taken you out of the world and restored my methods within you. That is why the world hates you. ²⁰ Don't forget what I have told you: 'No servant is greater than his master.' If they have tried to destroy me to prevent me from revealing the truth about the Father's methods of love, they will also try to destroy and prevent you from spreading the message about the Remedy. If they have partaken of the Remedy and helped me promote it, they will help you also. ²¹ They will oppose you because they hate my character of love revealed in you, for they are completely wrong in their understanding about the One who sent me. ²² If I had not come as the Remedy for their infected hearts and brought the truth about my Father and his methods and principles, their terminal condition would be no fault of their own. Now, however, they have no excuse for their terminal state or the fact that selfishness in their hearts has not gone into remission, for they have rejected the Remedy. ²³ He who hates me hates my Father as well, as I am an exact representation of my Father. ²⁴ If I had not revealed, in their very presence, the Remedy for man's sinfulness—a life operating perfectly on my Father's principles of selfless love — their fatal condition would not be their fault. But now they have seen the miracles of

healing that have occurred as goodness has flowed from the Father through me to the world—so that all may see that life is designed to operate on my Father's methods of selfless giving—and still they hate both me and my Father and thus reject me, the only Remedy. ²⁵ But this is in harmony with what was written in their Scriptures: 'They hated me without cause or reason.'

^{Jn 15:26} "When the Helper comes, whom I will send as my representative to you from the Father—the Spirit of Truth—he will work to reveal me. ²⁷ And you must also work to reveal me, because you have been with me from the beginning of my ministry and now understand my purpose and mission.

16 "I have told you all of this so that you will never believe things about me or my Father that are inconsistent with what I have revealed, and so that your confidence will never waver. ² They will disfellowship and excommunicate you, and call you 'evil' and 'heretic;' in fact, a time is coming when anyone who kills you will actually think they are doing what God would have them do. ³ They will practice methods of misrepresenting what you teach, using force, intimidation and coercion—just because they have accepted Satan's lies about me and my Father, and they believe we are like them. ⁴ I tell you this now so that you will remember: None of this has taken me by surprise, and since you have been warned, it will not take you by surprise either. I did not tell you earlier because I didn't want you to worry and be distracted from learning all that I had to teach you.

^{Jn 16:5} "Now the time has come for me to return to him who sent me, yet none of you are now asking me, 'Where are you going?' ⁶ Because I have told you I am leaving, you are sad and grieving. ⁷ But I tell you the truth: It is because I love you and want what is best for

you that I am leaving. Unless I go away, you will not stop coming to me to answer your questions, you will not start thinking through the issues for yourselves, nor will you seek the guidance of the Helper; but if I go, you will open your hearts and minds to the Helper, and he will come with all the truth I have revealed. 8 When he comes, he will expose clearly the sickness of selfishness infecting the human heart, dispense the Remedy necessary to experience a new and righteous heart, and reveal the inevitable outcome of rejecting the Remedy. 9 He will expose the fact that the sickness of selfishness persists because people do not value or trust me. 10 He will dispense the Remedy, as I will be with my Father and no longer here to apply it myself. 11 And he will reveal that the inevitable consequence of rejecting the Remedy leads only to death, as the prince of this world of selfishness now stands fully exposed as a liar, fraud, and failure.

Jn 16:12 "I have so much more to tell you, but you are not currently able to comprehend or understand it. 13 But when you open your minds to the Spirit of Truth, he will guide you in comprehending all truth. He will not be speaking for himself; he will speak what he hears from me, and he will reveal to you what the future holds. 14 He will honor and glorify me by taking what I have done and reproducing it in you. He will connect together in your minds all the evidence I have provided—so that you will comprehend the truth about me and the Father, our methods and principles, the nature and character of sin, the destructiveness of Satan's methods, the true character of Satan—and he will take my perfect character and reproduce it in you. 15 Everything that belongs to the Father is equally mine. That is why I said that the Spirit will not be speaking for himself but will take all I have achieved and reproduce it in you.

Jn 16:16 "In a very short time I will be gone from you, and then after a short time I will return to you."

Jn 16:17 Some of the disciples were confused by Jesus' comments and began to ask one another, "What does he mean when he says, 'In a very short time I will be gone from you, and then after a short time I will return to you,' and 'I am going to the Father'?" 18 They kept asking each other, "What does he mean by 'a short time'? We don't know what he means." But none of them asked Jesus to clarify.

Jn 16:19 Jesus, however, seeing that they were confused and wanted to ask him about this, said to them: "Are you wondering what I meant when I said, 'In a very short time I will be gone from you, and then after a short time I will return to you'? 20 I tell you the truth: Your hearts will be broken, and you will cry and grieve while the selfish world rejoices. You will grieve for a short time, but then your grief will be turned to overwhelming joy.

21 Consider a woman in labor: she has pain because the time to complete her pregnancy has come, but when her baby is born, she forgets the pain and is filled with joy. 22 So it will be with you: Now your time for grief has come, but I will come back to you, and then you will be filled with joy; and such joy no one can take away. 23 In that day, you will no longer need to present your requests through me, since you will finally be in complete unity with the Father yourselves; and anything you ask the Father in harmony with me and my methods and principles, he will give you. 24 Thus far, you have not asked the Father for anything in harmony with me or my methods and principles. Ask with your heart unified with me in purpose, principle and love, and your joy will be full and complete.

Jn 16:25 "Thus far, I have been speaking to you in figures of speech and symbolic language; but now, I will not use symbols and metaphors any more but tell you plainly about my Father. 26 You will simply ask the Father yourselves— in harmony with my character, understanding my mission, and valuing my methods. I will not ask the Father for you: 27 there will be no need, because the Father has always loved you, and now that you understand that I came to reveal the Father, you realize that your love for me is love for the Father. 28 I came from the Father and brought the truth about him into the world; now my mission here is almost complete, so I am leaving the world and returning to the Father."

Jn 16:29 Jesus' disciples said, "Finally, you are speaking clearly and without symbols or metaphors. 30 Now we understand and realize that you do know all things; you even know what we are thinking, before we ask you any questions. You are able to know our thoughts before we tell you, and this convinces us beyond any doubt that you came from God."

Jn 16:31 Jesus answered, "Praise God! You finally believe! 32 But even so, the time has come when you will all flee to your homes and abandon me—you will leave me all alone. Yet, even though you leave me, I am not alone, because my Father is with me.

Jn 16:33 "I have told you all these things so that you will not be afraid when they transpire, and that you may have peace knowing that nothing takes me by surprise. In this selfish world, you will be opposed and harassed. But be courageous! I have overcome the world."

17 After Jesus finished speaking with his disciples, he looked toward heaven and began talking with his Father:

"Father, the time for the completion of my mission has come. Now bring the attention of the entire universe to your Son, that I may reveal your true nature, character and government, and thus bring all glory and honor to you. 2 For you placed the security of the entire universe in my hands, so that all who unite with me may have eternal life. 3 Now, eternal life is this: having an intimate knowledge of you, and connection with you—the only true God, and me—Jesus Christ, your Son whom you have sent. 4 I have exalted and magnified you on earth by completing the mission you gave me. I have revealed your true character, methods and principles, exposed Satan as a liar (and his methods of selfishness as the cause of death), and procured the Remedy for sinfulness. 5 And now, Father, bring me back to you that I might occupy my rightful place at your side— the very place I had before this world was made.

Jn 17:6 "I have revealed your gracious, loving and benevolent character and methods to those you chose to be my disciples, and who receive this healing truth. Their hearts were loyal to you; you gave them to me to instruct and heal, and they have listened, understood, and freely chosen to follow your ways. 7 Now they understand that everything I did was a revelation of you. 8 For I presented the truth about you— your love and kindness, your respect for freedom of choice and truthfulness, your graciousness and constant giving of yourself for the welfare of your creation—and they wholeheartedly embraced it. They know with certainty that I am here as your ambassador, with your full approval and authority. 9 My heart yearns for them, Father—that the Remedy complete its work of healing their characters. I'm not asking that the Remedy heal those who have refused to take it, but I'm asking for those whom you gave me to instruct and heal, for they now love and trust you too. 10 Our love is pure, as all I have are yours, and all you have are mine. And their transformed hearts and minds powerfully confirm that I have faithfully discharged my mission and brought them back to you. 11 My mission here is almost complete, and I will no longer stay in this selfish world, but they will remain to carry the Remedy throughout the world. I am coming home to you. Holy Father, protect them from the lies and deceptions of Satan by reinforcing in their minds the truth of your character and principles—your character of love and your principles of truth and freedom that you revealed through me—so that they may be unified in love, truth, freedom, purpose, motive, and righteousness of character, as you and I are united. 12 While I was with them, I protected them from deception by constantly revealing the truth and showing them love. None has been lost to the infection of selfishness, except—as the Scriptures foretold—Judas, who refused the Remedy, and whose death was the inevitable result of unimpeded selfishness.

Jn 17:13 "I am coming home to you now, but I say these things while I am still here on the earth so that they may see the importance of daily heart-searching conversation with you, and experience the full joy that comes from constant unity with you. 14 I have given them the truth about you, but the selfish world hates them because they have the antidote to fear and selfishness, and are not in harmony with the principles of the world any more than I am. 15 My desire is not that you take them out of the world, but that you protect their minds from being reinfected with deceit, fear and selfishness from the evil one. 16 They are not in harmony with the world, even as I am not in harmony with it. 17 Settle their minds so fully and completely into the truth that nothing can ever move them from it— your word is truth. 18 As you sent me into the world to be your ambassador—to reveal the truth about you—so have I sent them into the world to be our ambassadors to reveal the truth about us. 19 I have committed myself completely—holding nothing back—in order to bring them the only antidote to sin through which they may be fully restored to your original ideal for mankind.

Jn 17:20 "My heart's desire is not for them alone. My heart also longs for those who will accept the Remedy they will spread — 21 that those who accept the Remedy will also be fully restored to your original ideal and will be in complete unity, Father, just as you and I are in complete unity in all things. May they also be in unity with us, so that the selfish world may see the power of the healing truth I have brought, and know that you have sent me. 22 I have given them the full truth about you, your methods, principles and character that you gave me, that they may be in complete harmony and unity as we are: 23 my character reproduced in them, and your character flowing out from me. May they be restored to complete unity—practicing only your methods—so the world will know that you sent me as the healing solution, and that you have loved them even as you have loved me.

Jn 17:24 "Father, I want those you gave me (to instruct and heal) to be with me wherever I am, and to see my unveiled glory—the glory that comes from your love—the glory of being one with you before the world was created.

Jn 17:25 "Perfect and righteous Father, though the selfish world believes all sorts of lies about you—and therefore does not know you—I know you, and they know that you have sent me. They hate me because they prefer their lies about you to the truth. 26 But I have made you known to them in order to dispel the lies about you that Satan has spread—the lies that prevent them from knowing you. I will keep making you known, for this is the only healing solution—the truth about you which dispels the lies, restores trust, and results in the love you have for me being reproduced in them. Then the infection of selfishness will be removed, and my character of selfless love will be restored within them."

18 When he had finished talking with his Father, Jesus with his disciples crossed the Kidron Valley. On the other side was an olive grove on a mount, and they went into it.

Jn 18:2 Judas, the one who betrayed Jesus, was familiar with the place in the grove, as Jesus would often retire there with his disciples. 3 So Judas led a detachment of soldiers and representatives of the chief priests and Pharisees, who came carrying weapons, torches, and lanterns.

Jn 18:4 Jesus, knowing people's decisions before they are made, was not taken by surprise and went out to meet the mob, asking, "Who are you looking for?"

Jn 18:5 "Jesus of Nazareth," they replied. "I am he," Jesus answered. (And Judas, who preferred greed and selfishness to love, was standing there with them.) 6 When Jesus said, "I am he," for a brief moment the mob caught a glimpse of the radiance of Christ's true self, and being overcome with guilt and fear, fell to the ground.

Jn 18:7 So he asked them again, "Who are you looking for?" And they answered, "Jesus of Nazareth."

Jn 18:8 Jesus said, "I have already told you that I am he. If it is me you want, then let these men go." 9 This happened just as Jesus foreknew when he said "I have not lost one of those you gave me to instruct and heal."

Jn 18:10 When Simon Peter saw the soldiers and others fall to the ground, he drew his sword and struck Malchus, the high priest's servant, cutting off his right ear.

Jn 18:11 But Jesus stepped forward and commanded Peter, "Put away your sword! Don't you realize my methods are not the methods of force and coercion? If they were, I could call my Father and he would send more than twelve legions of angels. But if I did that, how could I reveal the truth about myself and my Father? The weapons that we use are the weapons of truth, spoken in love, leaving people free to decide for themselves. Don't you want me to complete the mission my Father has sent me to accomplish?"

Jn 18:12 Then the soldiers with their commander and Jewish officials, angry at themselves for falling to the ground, shook off their conviction and arrested Jesus. They tied his hands 13 and brought him to Annas, the former high priest, who was the father-in-law of that year's high priest, Caiaphas. 14 Caiaphas was the one who advised those plotting to kill Jesus that it would be better for one man to die than for them to lose their positions, and for the entire nation to be destroyed.

Jn 18:15 Simon Peter and John were following as the soldiers took Jesus away. Because John was known to Caiaphas and his household, he was allowed into the high priest's courtyard when Jesus was taken there. 16 Peter had to wait outside at the door, but John came back and spoke to the girl at the door and got Peter admitted.

Jn 18:17 The girl at the door looked at Peter and said, "You are one of his disciples, aren't you?" Peter lied and said, "I am not."

Jn 18:18 It was a cool night, and the servants and officials warmed themselves around a fire they had made; Peter also warmed himself around the fire.

Jn 18:19 While Peter was warming himself, the high priest interrogated Jesus about his teaching, mission, and disciples.

Jn 18:20 Jesus answered by saying, "Everything I have taught, I did openly so all could hear. I always taught in the synagogues or at the temple, in front of large crowds. My teachings are well known. I have nothing to hide and I do not work in secret. 21 So why are you interrogating me like this? All you need to do is ask the thousands of people who heard me. They know what I have said."

Jn 18:22 Upon hearing Jesus' reply, one of the officials hit him in the face and said, "Is this the way you speak to the high priest?"

Jn 18:23 Jesus calmly and gently answered, "If I said something wrong, show me what is wrong. But if I spoke the truth, why did you hit me?" 24 Then Annas had Jesus sent, still bound, to Caiaphas, the high priest.

Jn 18:25 As Simon Peter stood warming himself by the fire, someone asked him, "Aren't you one of Jesus' disciples?" Peter again lied and said, "I am not."

Jn 18:26 But one of the high priest's servants, who was related to Malchus— the man whose ear Peter had cut off— confronted him: "I saw you in the grove. You cut off Malchus' ear. I know you are one of his disciples." 27 Then Peter began to curse and swear, and for the third time denied knowing Jesus. At that moment the rooster began to crow.

Jn 18:28 The Jewish leaders took Jesus from Caiaphas to the palace of Pilate, the Roman governor. By this time it was early Friday morning, and to avoid ceremonial uncleanness (so that they could eat Passover), they refused to enter the palace. 29 So Pilate came outside to meet with them and asked, "Why have you brought this man before me? What do you accuse him of doing?"

Jn 18:30 The Jews didn't want to tell him the truth, so they simply said, "If he were not a criminal, we would not have brought him before you."

Jn 18:31 Pilate said, "Don't bother me with this. Take him and judge him by your own law." The Jews objected and said, "But we are not permitted to execute anyone." 32 This happened exactly as Jesus foretold, indicating again that Jesus knows people's decisions before they make them, yet never restricts their freedom to make their own choices.

Jn 18:33 Pilate then went back into his palace and had Jesus brought to him. He asked, "Are you the King of the Jews?"

Jn 18:34 Jesus' heart longed to save Pilate, and in an attempt to open his mind to the truth, he asked, "Are you asking me this because you have some question about me, or are you simply repeating what others have told you?"

Jn 18:35 However, Pilate was too fearful and insecure to be open and honest with Jesus, so he answered, "Am I a Jew? Your own people and religious leaders have condemned you and seek your execution. I am only concerned with whether you deserve to die or not. So, what is it you have done?"

Jn 18:36 Jesus gently replied, "My kingdom is not here on this earth, nor does it use methods of force and coercion. If it did, my followers would fight to prevent my arrest and execution. But my kingdom is from another place and of completely different principles, values, and methods."

Jn 18:37 "So you are a king!" Pilate exclaimed. Jesus answered, "You are quite right to realize I am a king. In fact, I was born into the world to reveal the truth about my kingdom and my kingship, and bring back into my kingdom all those who value truth. Everyone who loves truth follows me."

Jn 18:38 "What is truth?" Pilate mumbled, and without giving Jesus time to answer, he turned and went out to meet the Jews. He said to them, "I have interrogated him and find no basis for your charge against him. 39 I know it is your custom for me to release to you one prisoner at the time of Passover. Why don't I release Jesus, 'the King of the Jews'?"

Jn 18:40 But the crowd was in a frenzy to kill Jesus and shouted back, "No! We want Barabbas!" They wanted Barabbas even though he was a murderer and part of a rebellion against Rome.

19 Even though Pilate was convinced of Jesus' innocence, in an attempt to appease the Jews he ordered that Jesus be flogged. He hoped this would satisfy them, but instead, he

only revealed to the Jews his own weakness of character and encouraged them to press harder until he would succumb to their demands. [2] The soldiers began to make fun of Jesus. They made a crown of thorns and smashed it down on his head. They put a purple robe on him [3] and began bowing down mockingly, saying, "Hail, King of the Jews!" And they punched him in the face repeatedly.

Jn 19:4 Pilate came out to the Jews one more time—this time appearing a little less confident. He said, "I find no fault in him or any basis for the charges you have brought against him." [5] Then Jesus was brought out wearing the crown of thorns and the purple robe, and he was bleeding from the wounds inflicted by his beating.

Jn 19:6 When the Jews saw that Pilate had had Jesus beaten and tortured—even though he had declared him innocent—they knew he could be pressured to their will, so they shouted in overwhelming rage, "Crucify him! Crucify him!" Pilate answered, "If you want to crucify him, take him and do so. I find nothing in him deserving of crucifixion."

Jn 19:7 But the Jews wouldn't have this Roman insinuate that he was more just than they, so they shouted, "Our law says he deserves death, because he, a mere man, claims to be the Son of God!"

Jn 19:8 Pilate was shocked and overcome with fear when he heard what the Jews had said. [9] He went back into his palace and questioned Jesus. He asked, "Where do you come from?" But Jesus kept silent. [10] "Are you refusing to answer me?" Pilate said. "I have the power to set you free or have you crucified, so you better answer my questions."

Jn 19:11 Jesus replied calmly, "You would have no power over me if it had not been granted you from God. Therefore those who have rejected the truth, plotted my death, and are now manipulating you, are much sicker in heart, darker in mind, and more evil in character than you are."

Jn 19:12 From then on, Pilate tried to get the Jews to agree to set Jesus free, but they were frothing for his blood and kept shouting, "If you let him go, you are an enemy of Caesar! Anyone who claims to be a king opposes Caesar!"

Jn 19:13 When Pilate heard this, he became fearful for his own position and authority, so he brought Jesus out, and sat down in his judgment seat. [14] It was Friday before Passover, about noon. Pilate said to the Jews, "Here is your King."

Jn 19:15 But the Jews knew they had Pilate about to capitulate and shouted all the louder, "Away with him! Away with him! Crucify him!"

"Do you want me to crucify your King?" Pilate asked.

Then the chief priests answered, "We have no king but Caesar."

Jn 19:16 Exhausted and frustrated, and not knowing how to save Jesus and appease the Jews in order to secure his own position, Pilate finally handed Jesus over to them to be crucified. So the soldiers took Jesus, [17] placed a cross on his shoulders, and led him to The Place of the Skull (which in Aramaic is called *Golgotha*). [18] Here they crucified him, with two thieves—one on either side, and Jesus in the middle.

Jn 19:19 Pilate had a sign placed on the cross, which read:

JESUS OF NAZARETH
THE KING OF THE JEWS

[20] It was written in Aramaic, Latin, and Greek; and many of the Jews read the sign because the place of the crucifixion was near the city. [21] The chief priests were upset that Pilate would put such a sign on Jesus' cross, and protested, "Don't write 'The King of the Jews,' but that this man claimed to be king of the Jews."

Jn 19:22 But Pilate was tired of the Jews and their scheming, and said, "What I have written is what I have written."

Jn 19:23 The soldiers who crucified Jesus

divided his clothes among them—one piece for each—with the undergarment remaining. The undergarment was seamless, ²⁴ so rather than tear it, they decided to roll dice to see who would get to keep it. This happened as further evidence that God knows people's decisions before they are made, yet doesn't use this knowledge in selfish or manipulative ways. For the Scriptures said:

"They divided my garments among them
and rolled dice for my clothing."

And the soldiers freely chose to do exactly what God foreknew and foretold that they would do.

Jn 19:25 The women who loved and trusted Jesus had followed him to the cross: his mother, his mother's sister, Mary the wife of Clopas, and Mary Magdalene. ²⁶ When Jesus saw his mother and his disciple John standing nearby, his heart went out in compassion and concern for them. He said to his mother, "Mother, here is your son. He will take care of you from now on." ²⁷ And to John he said, "Here is your mother." From then on, John took her to his home and cared for her.

Jn 19:28 Jesus knew that he had completed his mission. He knew that he had revealed the truth about God and himself, and the nature of sin; that he exposed Satan as a liar and murderer, and that he had lived perfectly as a human being. Knowing all this, Jesus was aware that the war was won and his mission was finished, and he whispered, "I'm thirsty." ²⁹ A jar of vinegar was there. They soaked a sponge in the vinegar, put the sponge on a hyssop stalk, and lifted it to Jesus' mouth. ³⁰ When he had moistened his lips, Jesus said in a clear voice, "It is finished." With that, he bowed his head and breathed his last. He had completed his mission—he had finished the work given him to do.

Jn 19:31 It was Friday — the day of Preparation for the Sabbath — and the next day was the special Sabbath of the Passover. The Jews did not want bodies left on the crosses during the Sabbath, so they asked Pilate to have the legs of the victims broken and the bodies taken down. ³² The soldiers came and broke the legs of the two men crucified with Jesus, ³³ but when they came to Jesus, they were shocked to discover that he was already dead, so they did not break his legs. ³⁴ Instead, one of the soldiers, just to be sure Jesus hadn't simply fainted, pierced his side with a spear, penetrating up to the heart, and a mixture of blood and water flowed from the wound. ³⁵ John, who saw this, has given testimony to what he saw, and his account is accurate and reliable. He knows exactly what he saw and he recounts it so that you may also know and have confidence in the truth. ³⁶ All of these things occurred exactly as God foretold in the Scriptures, where it says, "Not one of his bones will be broken," ³⁷ and "They will look on the one they have pierced."

Jn 19:38 Later, Joseph of Arimathea went to Pilate and asked for the body of Jesus. Joseph was a follower of Jesus, but he feared the Jews, so he had followed Jesus secretly. Once he had obtained Pilate's authorization, he came and took Jesus' body away from Golgotha. ³⁹ Nicodemus, the man who had previously visited Jesus at night, helped Joseph carry the body. Nicodemus also brought about seventy-five pounds (thirty-four kilograms) of aloe and myrrh for the burial. ⁴⁰ Taking Jesus' body, they reverently wrapped it, applying spices in the strips of linen. This was in keeping with Jewish burial customs. ⁴¹ Near where Jesus was crucified was a garden with a tomb that had never been used. ⁴² Because it was nearby, and the Sabbath was approaching, they laid Jesus in this tomb.

20 Early on Sunday, before sunrise, Mary Magdalene went to the tomb and discovered that the stone

covering the entrance had been removed. ²She immediately turned and ran to Simon Peter, John, and the other disciples, and said, "They have taken our Lord! He is not in the tomb, and we don't know where he is!"

Jn 20:3 Peter and John both ran for the tomb. ⁴But John was younger and fitter, so he reached the tomb first. ⁵He bent down and looked into the tomb, saw the strips of linen used to bury Jesus, but did not see Jesus, and did not enter the tomb. ⁶Then Simon Peter arrived and went directly into the tomb. He saw the strips of linen; ⁷he also saw the burial cloth that had been around Jesus' head, folded neatly, by the linen. ⁸Finally, John also entered the tomb and saw the linen and burial cloth, and believed that Jesus was gone. ⁹(But they still did not understand that Jesus had risen from the dead.)

Jn 20:10 The disciples, discouraged and confused, went back to their homes. ¹¹But Mary stayed by the tomb grieving and crying, longing to see Jesus again. She bent over and looked inside the tomb, ¹²and saw two angels in white, seated where Jesus' body had been: one at the head and the other at the foot.

Jn 20:13 They gently asked her, "Miss, why are you crying?"

"They have taken my Lord away and I don't know where they have put him," she cried." ¹⁴Then she turned around and saw Jesus standing there, but she did not recognize him.

Jn 20:15 "Miss," Jesus said, "why are you crying? Who are you looking for?" Mary thought Jesus was the gardener, and said, "Sir, if you know where he is or where they have put him, please show me and I will take him away."

Jn 20:16 Then Jesus spoke gently, in his familiar tone, "Mary."

Mary's heart leapt. She turned toward him, and cried with inexpressible joy, "Teacher!" as she fell at his feet, hugging him.

Jn 20:17 Jesus said, "You must let me go, Mary, for I have not yet returned to the Father. Go and tell my brothers that I am returning to my Father and your Father, to my God and your God."

Jn 20:18 Mary Magdalene eagerly ran to the disciples with great good news: "I have seen the Lord! He is alive!" And she told them what he had said.

Jn 20:19 On Sunday evening before nightfall, as Monday was approaching, the disciples were gathered together, with the doors locked for fear of the Jews, when Jesus suddenly appeared in the room in the midst of them and said, "Peace be with you!" ²⁰After he said this, he showed them his wounded hands and side. The disciples were overwhelmed with joy and thanksgiving when they saw their Lord.

Jn 20:21 Then Jesus said again, "Peace be with you! As the Father has sent me to bring the healing Remedy to the world, I am now sending you, who have partaken of this healing Remedy, to spread the good news about the Remedy throughout the world." ²²And just as he had breathed into Adam the breath of life, filling Adam with his Spirit and bringing him to life, so now he breathed on his disciples and said, "Receive into your hearts and minds the Spirit," and he invigorated them with renewed life. ²³Then he said to them, "Anyone who accepts the healing Remedy you distribute will get well; but those who reject the healing Remedy you distribute—will not get well."

Jn 20:24 Now Thomas (called Didymus), one of the Twelve, was not with the disciples when Jesus appeared in the upper room. ²⁵But the other disciples told him, "The Lord is alive! He is risen from the dead and we have seen him!"

But Thomas said, "Unless I see him for myself and feel the wounds in his hands and touch his side for myself, I won't believe it."

Jn 20:26 Eight days later, the disciples were again gathered in the upper room with the doors locked. Suddenly, Jesus appeared in the room with them and said, "Peace be with you!" 27 Then he turned to Thomas and said, "Come and feel the wounds in my hands and touch my side. Become confident in the truth and stop doubting."

Jn 20:28 Then Thomas, with great emotion, said, "You are my Lord and my God!"

Jn 20:29 Jesus said to him, "Because you have seen and touched me, you believe; blessed are those who have not seen my physical body nor touched my wounded hands—yet have seen the evidence in Scripture and nature of who I am, and have heard the testimony of witnesses about all I have done, and have thought it through—and been convinced."

Jn 20:30 Jesus performed many more miracles in the presence of his disciples that are not written down in this book. 31 But what has been written is recorded to provide evidence demonstrating that Jesus is the Christ, the Son of God—the only cure for the infection of selfishness, the only Remedy for the diseased human mind—and that by trusting him you may experience complete healing of mind, restoration of Christlike character, and life eternal.

21 Later on, Jesus again appeared to his disciples, by the Sea of Tiberias (Sea of Galilee). 2 Simon Peter, Thomas (called Didymus), Nathanael from Cana in Galilee, Zebedee's sons James and John, and two other disciples were together on the beach. 3 Simon Peter said, "I'm going fishing." And the rest said, "We'll go with you." So they went out by boat, but caught nothing all night.

Jn 21:4 Early in the morning, Jesus appeared on the shore, but the disciples didn't recognize him.

Jn 21:5 He called to them, "Friends, haven't you caught any fish?"

"No," they answered.

Jn 21:6 They had their nets cast on the side of the boat away from shore, and Jesus said, "Throw your nets on the right side of the boat, toward me, and you will find some fish." When they did, the catch was immediate and so great that they couldn't haul it into the boat.

Jn 21:7 Then John realized it was Jesus and said to Peter, "It is the Lord!" As soon as Simon Peter heard him say, "It is the Lord," he picked up his outer garment, jumped into the water, and swam to shore. 8 The other disciples followed in the boat, towing the net full of fish, and they were only about one hundred yards from shore. 9 When they landed, they saw fish grilling on the fire, and some bread.

Jn 21:10 Jesus said to them, "Bring some of the fish you have just caught."

Jn 21:11 Simon Peter climbed aboard and helped them drag the net ashore. It was full of one hundred and fifty-three large fish, yet the net was not torn. 12 Jesus, always concerned for their every need, said, "Come and have some breakfast." While they ate, none of the disciples needed to ask him "Who are you?" for they all knew it was the Lord. 13 Jesus broke the bread and gave it to them, and he did the same with the fish. 14 This was the third time Jesus had appeared to his disciples after he had risen from the dead.

Jn 21:15 After breakfast was over, Jesus said to Simon Peter, "Simon son of John, do you love me more than you love others?"

"Yes, Lord," he said, "you know that I love you."

"Then take the Remedy to my infected children," Jesus said.

Jn 21:16 Again Jesus said, "Simon son of John, do you really love me?"

He answered, "Yes, Lord, I really love you."

Jesus said, "Then nurture and care for my children."

Jn 21:17 A third time Jesus said, "Simon son of John, do you truly love me?" Peter was hurt by this third request. He began to doubt himself, and with tears in his eyes said, "Lord, as far as I know my own heart, I love you. You know all things and you know the inmost secrets of my heart, so you know the depth of my love for you."

Jesus said, "Yes, you do love me, and I want you to take the Remedy I have provided and distribute it to my children. 18 I will tell you the truth about your life: When you were a young man, you were free to choose what clothes you would wear and the places you would go; but when you are old, your freedom will be taken from you and your hands will be stretched out and you will be taken where you do not want to go." 19 Jesus said this disclosing that Peter's death would reveal how God's glorious healing power had completely transformed Peter's character to be exactly like that of Jesus. Then Jesus said, "Follow me!"

Jn 21:20 Peter looked behind him and saw John following. 21 Peter then looked to Jesus and said, "Lord, what about John? What will happen to him?"

Jn 21:22 Jesus answered, "What happens to John is between me and John. If I want him to remain alive until I return, how does that change your duty to me? You must complete the mission I have assigned to you regardless of what happens to John." 23 Because of this, the rumor spread among the believers that John would not die. But Jesus did not say that John would not die; he only said,

"If I want him to remain alive until I return, how does that change your duty to me?"

Jn 21:24 I am John, the disciple who witnessed these events and testifies to them. I have written them down myself. Everything written here is the truth.

Jn 21:25 Jesus did many other things beyond what is written here. If everything he did were written down, the entire world could not hold all the books that would be written.

Acts of the Apostles

1 Honorable Theophilus:
In my previous book, I wrote the historical facts of the life of Jesus—what he did and taught— ²right up until he left this earth and returned to heaven, just after giving directions to his ambassadors, through the Holy Spirit, for the distribution of the Remedy. ³After his ordeal, he appeared physically, in person, to these men and provided testable evidence that he was alive. He appeared to them at different times and places over a period of forty days, and taught them about God's kingdom of love. ⁴Once, when eating with them, he gave them this command: "Stay in Jerusalem until you receive the gift I told you about, the one my Father promised. ⁵For John immersed you in water, but in a few days you will be immersed in the Holy Spirit."

Ac 1:6 When they got together, they asked him, "Lord, is now the time you are going to restore Israel to power and make it the Kingdom of God?"

Ac 1:7 He answered, "The specific time and date for events, which the Father holds by his omnipotence, is not necessary nor helpful for you to know. ⁸When the Holy Spirit comes upon you, you will receive the power needed to accomplish your mission, and then you will reveal the truth about my kingdom of love, and take the Remedy to Jerusalem, Judea and Samaria, and to the entire world."

Ac 1:9 After telling them this, he went up into heaven, right in front of them. They watched with their own eyes until he was hidden by a cloud.

Ac 1:10 As they stood there staring up into the sky, suddenly two angels dressed in white, in the form of men, appeared next to them. ¹¹They said, "Men of Galilee, what are you doing standing here staring off into the sky? This same Jesus, who has gone into heaven, will come back to earth in the same way you have just watched him go into heaven."

Ac 1:12 So they left the Mount of Olives and returned to Jerusalem, about a half mile away. ¹³Upon arriving, they returned to the upstairs room where they were staying. Those present were James, Peter, John, Andrew, Philip, Thomas, Bartholomew, Matthew, James the son of Alphaeus, Simon the Patriot, and Judas, son of James. ¹⁴Along with the women and Mary the mother of Jesus, and his brothers, they united together in conversation with God, keeping their hearts and minds connected with the Father.

Ac 1:15 While they were together—about one hundred and twenty in all—Peter stood up ¹⁶and said: "Brothers and sisters, what God foreknew—and long ago revealed in Scripture through David concerning Judas—had to occur. He chose to lead to Jesus those who arrested our Lord, ¹⁷even though he was one of us and shared in distributing the Remedy."

Ac 1:18 Judas used his traitor's reward to buy a field, and it was there that his body fell, rupturing open, and his guts spilled onto the ground. ¹⁹All of Jerusalem heard about this, and the field is now called, in their language, *Akeldama*, which means Blood Field.

Ac 1:20 "For it is written in the Psalms,
'Let his field be deserted;
may no one live there.'
And it is also written,

162

'May someone else replace him in leadership.'

Ac 1:21 "So the traitor must be replaced, and we must choose one of the men who learned to distribute the Remedy directly from the Lord Jesus, and who worked with us the entire time— 22 from John's immersion of Jesus right up until Jesus went back to heaven. One of these men must join us in witnessing to his resurrection."

Ac 1:23 They narrowed it down to two men: Joseph, also called Barsabbas and nicknamed Justus, and Matthias. 24 Then they asked Jesus, "Lord, you know the true condition of every person's heart. Reveal to us who you have chosen 25 to be your ambassador, taking the position Judas abandoned to go his own way." 26 They drew straws, and Matthias was chosen and became one of the Twelve.

2 On the day of Pentecost, the believers gathered together in one place. 2 Without warning, there was the sound of a mighty wind coming from heaven, and it filled the entire house where they were. 3 They saw two separate streams of fire—the fires of truth and love—emanating from God, which flowed out and flowed into each one of them. 4 They were all infused with the Holy Spirit and began to speak different languages, as the Spirit enabled them.

Ac 2:5 Because of the Pentecost holiday, there were honest-hearted, God-seeking Jews from all over the world staying in Jerusalem. 6 The loud sound of the wind drew a curious crowd to the house, and people were initially confused, as each of them heard their own language being spoken. 7 Amazed at how clearly they heard their own language, they asked: "What's going on? Every one of them is Galilean, 8 so how is it that each of us hears them speaking perfectly well in our own native language? 9 Parthians, Medes, Elamites, people from Mesopotamia, Judea, Cappadocia, Pontus and Asia, 10 Phrygia, Pamphylia, Egypt and parts of Libya near Cyrene, travelers from Rome 11 (both genetic descendants of Abraham and converts to Judaism) as well as Cretans and Arabs—we all hear them declaring the wonderful Remedy from God's kingdom of love in our own languages!" 12 Confused and in wonder at the same time, they tried to figure out what was happening, asking each other, "What's going on? What does it mean?"

Ac 2:13 But there were some who ridiculed and criticized, saying, "They're just drunk!"

Ac 2:14 Then Peter stood up along with the other Eleven Ambassadors, and in a commanding voice spoke to the crowd: "My fellow Jews, and all people here in Jerusalem, listen to me, and I will explain this to you: 15 These men are not drunk. They haven't taken a drop of wine; it is only nine o'clock in the morning! 16 No; this is what God's spokesperson Joel said would happen:

Ac 2:17 "'God says,
In the last days I will pour my
Spirit out on all people.
Your sons and daughters will be
spokespersons for me,
telling the world of my Remedy;
your young people will have a vision
of my character of love
that will motivate them to action;
your elders will dream dreams of my
kingdom of love.
18 And in those days, I will pour out
my Spirit upon my spokespersons,
both men and women,
and they will tell the world the truth
about me
in the setting of the cosmic
conflict over my methods of love.
19 I will grant wonders to appear in
the sky, and evidences of change
in the earth
resulting in devastation, disaster,
blood and smoke.
20 The sun will not give its usual
light,

and the moonlight will be seen as the color of blood
before the day the Lord returns—
that great and glorious day.
21 And everyone who relies upon the character of the Lord,
partaking the Remedy he provided,
will be healed.'

Ac 2:22 "People of Israel, listen to me: Jesus of Nazareth was confirmed as being God's agency on earth as evidenced by miracles, power over nature, wonders and signs—as you already know. 23 And you did exactly what God foreknew and foretold: You handed him over to evil men and helped them put him to death by nailing him to the cross. 24 But God caused Jesus to return to life. Through the selfless death of Jesus, God fulfilled his purpose of destroying the infection of fear and selfishness—that causes death—and restored his law of life into the humanity that Jesus assumed; therefore it was impossible for death to keep its hold upon Jesus. 25 As David said about him:
'I saw that God is before me for all eternity.
Because he stands beside me,
guarding me,
I will not waver from my mission.
26 My heart rejoices, my mouth proclaims the glad tidings,
and my body rests in hope,
27 because you will not leave me in the grave,
nor will you allow your perfect Remedy to decompose.
28 You will make me known as the only way of life,
and the joy of your life-giving presence in me will be overflowing.'

Ac 2:29 "Brothers and sisters, I tell you with absolute certainty, our ancestor King David died and was buried, and his body remains here in his tomb to this day. 30 But he was God's spokesman and knew that God promised him, with a solemn vow, that one of his descendants would be king. 31 Seeing future events, he spoke about the resurrection of the Messiah:
'His body was not left to decompose in the grave.'

32 It was this very Jesus that God raised to life, and we — all of us! — are witnesses to the truthfulness of it, having seen him alive again. 33 He took his humanity to heaven and is exalted to God's right hand; and from the Father, he received the promised Holy Spirit whom he has poured out upon us. This is what you see and hear today. 34 For King David most certainly did not ascend into heaven, yet he said,
'The Lord said to my Lord: Sit on my right hand
35 until I place your enemies under your feet.'

Ac 2:36 "So let all God's people be certain of this: God has made this Jesus, whom you crucified, both Ruler and Remedy."

Ac 2:37 When the people heard this truth, they were convicted by it and sick over what they had done, so they asked Peter and the other ambassadors of Christ, "Oh, brothers, please tell us, what should we do now?"

Ac 2:38 Peter answered, "Turn away from fear and selfishness and be immersed in the Remedy — in the character of Jesus Christ — in order to be healed from sin and selfishness and be restored in heart and mind to love and unity with God. And you will receive the gift of the Holy Spirit. 39 This promise of healing and restoration is for you and your children, and for all humanity, no matter how far off, for God invites everyone to be healed."

Ac 2:40 With many other examples he warned them, and pleaded with them: "Take the Remedy! Experience a new heart and save yourselves from the terminal condition of selfishness which is destroying this generation." 41 Those who partook of the Remedy demonstrated the beginning of their new life of love by being symbolically immersed in water; about three thousand were added to the number of those being healed that day.

Ac 2:42 They committed themselves to studying the truth taught by Christ's ambassadors, encouraging each other, sharing meals together, and talking with God daily. 43 Everyone was filled with awe at the miracles performed and signs shown by Christ's ambassadors. 44 They were filled with love for one another and were united, sharing with each other what they had. 45 They sold what they had and pooled their resources for the benefit of all, and provided for everyone's needs. 46 They fellowshipped and studied together in the temple courts each day. They had meals together in their homes, with hearts full of gladness and affection for each other, 47 giving praise to God. They were so kind and gentle that the people enjoyed having them around. And every day the Lord brought more people to them to partake of the Remedy and be healed.

3 Peter and John went to the temple one day at prayer time, which was three o'clock in the afternoon. 2 As they approached the temple, a man who was crippled from birth was being carried to the Beautiful Gate. He was brought there every day to beg from those going to worship at the temple. 3 When he spotted Peter and John entering the temple, he asked them for money. 4 Peter and John stopped and looked at the man, and then Peter said to him, "Look at us!" 5 So the man stopped scanning the crowd for more potential donors and paid attention to them, expecting some money from them.

Ac 3:6 When he had the man's attention, Peter said, "I don't have money, but what I do have I give you: In accordance with the character of Jesus Christ of Nazareth, be healed and walk." 7 Reaching down and taking his right hand, Peter helped him up, and immediately the man's feet and legs went from being shriveled, weak and deformed to a normal size and strength. 8 He leapt to his feet, bouncing up and down, and began to walk. Then he went into the temple courts with them and was walking, skipping, jumping, and praising God. 9 When the people saw him walking and shouting praises to God, 10 they realized who it was—the cripple who begged at the Beautiful Gate—and they were amazed, and wondered how this had happened to him.

Ac 3:11 As the beggar hugged and embraced Peter and John, the people, amazed and bewildered, rushed to them at Solomon's Colonnade where they had stopped. 12 When Peter noticed the stunned and wondering crowd, he said to them: "People of Israel, why are you shocked by this? Why do you look at us as if we somehow have the power of God to restore life to dead limbs and make this man walk? 13 The God of Abraham, Isaac and Jacob—the God our fathers worshiped —sent his Son Jesus to procure the Remedy and save us. But you rejected him and demanded that Pilate execute him, even though Pilate found him innocent and wanted to set him free. 14 Don't you realize what you did? You rejected the Perfect One — the Remedy from God—and asked that a murderer be released to you. 15 You killed the Designer of life, but God raised him from the dead. We have seen him alive and witness the truth of it. 16 It is by Jesus—his victory, the Remedy he achieved—that this man, whom all of you see and recognize, was enabled to walk. It is Jesus' character of love and the trust that comes through him that has caused the complete healing of this man, as all of you can see for yourselves.

Ac 3:17 "Now, my fellow Israelites, I know you didn't realize what you were doing when you killed Jesus, and neither did your leaders. 18 But God knew exactly what you would do, and foretold through his spokespersons the suffering the Messiah would endure to fulfill God's purpose of procuring the Remedy. [19] So don't reject him again! Turn your hearts back to God so that your sinfulness may be purged and the time of renewal—the time of hearts refreshed in love from the Lord—may come, [20] so that he may send you the Messiah—the Remedy made for you; the Remedy who is Jesus. [21] He must keep his radiant physical form hidden in heaven until all who are willing are restored in love to be like him, and until the time comes for God to put creation back to his original perfection, just as he promised through his holy spokespersons. [22] For Moses told us,

'The Lord your God
  will raise up a great Spokesperson
  from among you,
  just as he raised me up
  from among you;
you must listen to him
  and follow all his instructions.
[23] Anyone who refuses
  to listen to him and follow his
  instructions
will be without Remedy
  and die of their terminal
  condition,
  disconnected and cut off
  from the family of God.'

Ac 3:24 "In truth, all God's spokespersons, from Samuel on down—all who have spoken for God—have been foretelling of these very days. [25] And you are the beneficiaries, the ones who are to receive the completed Remedy that God promised and his spokespersons foretold. God promised Abraham, 'It is through your offspring that all humanity will be blessed.' [26] But because you are part of Israel—God's helpers to spread the Remedy—once he raised his Son, he sent him to you first: to heal you and cleanse you from all fear and selfishness, so you might fulfill your calling and distribute the Remedy to the world."

4 The church leaders, pastors and priests, along with security guards and the theologians of the Sadducee sect, came to where Peter and John were speaking to the people. [2] They were very angry because Peter and John were teaching the truth about Jesus and the resurrection of the dead. [3] They arrested Peter and John, and because it was already evening, they put them in jail overnight. [4] But many of those who heard what Peter said believed it, and the number of men who accepted the Remedy grew to about five thousand.

Ac 4:5 The next day, the church leaders, administrators, board of elders, legal-teaching theologians and law professors met in Jerusalem. [6] The high priest Annas was there, as was Caiaphas, John, Alexander, and other men of the high priest's family. [7] They had Peter and John stand before them, and interrogated them: "Who authorized you to speak in the temple? By what right do you do this?"

Ac 4:8 Then Peter, with his mind filled with the Holy Spirit, said to them: "Rulers and leaders of Israel! [9] If we are here to answer for an act of kindness done to a lame man and are asked how he was healed, [10] then you and all of Israel should know: It is by the power and authority of Jesus Christ of Nazareth—the one you rejected and crucified, but whom God raised from the dead—that this man was healed and now stands on his own two feet before you. [11] It's about Jesus that the Scripture says,

'The stone that you, who are in
  charge of building up God's
  people, have rejected
has become the foundation stone of
  life itself.'

Ac 4:12 "Eternal healing is found in no one else, for there is no other Remedy in the entire universe provided for humanity by which we must be healed."

Ac 4:13 When they saw the confidence

and courage with which Peter and John spoke—and recalled that they were not seminary-trained but average church members—they were shocked, and then remembered that the two had been educated by Jesus. 14 But since the healed man was standing right before them, there was nothing they could say to refute them. 15 So they ordered them out of the courtroom and then plotted together. 16 They asked each other, "How are we going to undermine the influence of these men? Everyone in Jerusalem knows about the incredible miracle they have done, and we can't simply deny it. 17 But we must stop this message about Jesus from spreading any further. We have to threaten them to never speak or teach in Jesus' name again."

Ac 4:18 So they called them back in and commanded them, by their authority as church leaders, to never speak or teach in the name of Jesus again. 19 But Peter and John were not intimidated but boldly said, "You will have to decide for yourselves: what do you think is right for us to do—what you say or what God says? 20 But as for us, we will put God first and will not stop telling the truth of what we have seen and heard."

Ac 4:21 They threatened them some more, but then released them. They could not figure out a way to punish them that wouldn't cause more problems, because the people were praising God for what had happened, 22 as the healed man had been crippled for over forty years.

Ac 4:23 After being released, Peter and John returned to their team of believers and retold everything that the church leaders, priests and theologians had said to them. 24 When they heard the report, the believers joined together to talk to God. They said, "Designer, Creator and Sustainer of heaven, earth and the sea, and all that is in them: 25 by the Holy Spirit you spoke to us through your servant, our father David,

'Why are the nations of this selfish world angry at my character of love?

Why do their people plot in vain against my design?

26 The kings of the selfish world take their stand;

they gathered together with self-promoting rulers

to oppose the Lord of life and his chosen Remedy.'

Ac 4:27 "Yes, Herod and Pontius Pilate did meet together, along with foreigners and even the leaders of Israel, right here in this city, to plot against your holy Son Jesus, the One you designated to be our Remedy. 28 And they did exactly what you knew they would do: abuse the freedom you predetermined to give them. 29 So now, dear Lord, make note of their threats and overrule their opposition, and enable us, your agents, to speak the truth with clarity and distribute the Remedy with boldness. 30 Pour forth your life-giving power to heal and perform miracles, signs and wonders in harmony with the character of your holy Son Jesus."

Ac 4:31 As the prayer ended, the building in which they met shook, and they were filled with the Holy Spirit; and they went forth and spread the Remedy of God confidently and effectively.

Ac 4:32 All those who had partaken of the Remedy and trusted Jesus were united in love, sharing a common purpose. No one thought selfishly or claimed possessions for self, but with love for others shared everything they had. 33 With great power and effectiveness, the ambassadors of Christ continued to spread the Remedy and testify to the resurrection of the Lord Jesus; and the loveliness of Jesus emanated from them all. 34 There wasn't one person among them who was in need, for when necessary, those who owned lands or houses—sold them 35 and gave the money from the sales to the Lord's ambassadors, and it was distributed to anyone as need arose.

Ac 4:36 A Levite from Cyprus, named Joseph—whom the Lord's ambassadors called Barnabas, which means Encourager— 37 sold a strip of land and gave the money to the Lord's ambassadors.

5 A man named Ananias and his wife Sapphira agreed to sell a piece of property and give the entire amount to the Lord's cause. 2 When the Lord blessed it and the property sold for more than expected, Ananias, with the full consent of his wife, kept back the unexpected extra and turned in only what the property was thought to be worth. As he lay the offering at Peter's feet, 3 Peter said, "Ananias, why did you choose to side with Satan and fill your heart with greed? You lied to the Holy Spirit and chose to keep some of the money you received for the land. 4 Wasn't the land yours before you sold it? You didn't have to promise to give all the money from the sale. Were you not free to promise only a portion? Why would you promise it all and then hold a portion back? You haven't lied to finite humans; you have lied to God."

Ac 5:5 When Ananias was confronted with the truth, it shocked him, and he fell down and died. All who heard what happened were overcome with fear. 6 The young men came right in, wrapped up the body, carried it out, and buried it.

Ac 5:7 Three hours later, Sapphira, Ananias' wife came in, but she didn't know what had happened to her husband. 8 Peter asked her, "Is this the entire price you and Ananias received from the sale of the land?"

"Yes, that's the full price," she answered.

Ac 5:9 Peter confronted her with the truth: "What were you and your husband thinking, lying to God? A few hours ago your husband, when confronted with the truth of what you have done, died. The men who buried him are coming through the door, and they will carry you out and bury you also."

Ac 5:10 When she heard this, it shocked her, and she fell down and died. Then the young men came in, and finding she was dead, carried her out and buried her beside her husband. 11 The entire congregation and all who heard about this were gripped with fear.

Ac 5:12 Many miracles and wonderful signs were performed among the people through the Lord's ambassadors. All those who partook of the Remedy met regularly at Solomon's Colonnade. 13 Though they were highly respected by the people, no one who refused the Remedy dared to join them. 14 Yet every day, others who trusted Jesus partook of the Remedy and joined them. 15 Because of what was happening, people began lining the streets with the sick, positioning them on cots or mats so that when Peter walked by, his shadow might fall on some of them. 16 Masses of people from all over the country came to Jerusalem; they brought those who were sick or afflicted by an evil spirit, and everyone was healed.

Ac 5:17 The high priest and his leadership team, who were all members of the Sadducee theological society, were burning with jealousy, 18 so they arrested the Lord's ambassadors and put them in the community jail. 19 But the Lord's angel came during the night and opened the door of the jail and led them out. 20 The angel told them, "Go back to the temple, stand in the courts and teach the people the truth about this life—about their terminal state, the need for the Remedy provided by Christ, and the gift of eternal life."

Ac 5:21 They entered the temple courts at dawn, just as they were instructed, and began to teach the people. When the high priest and his leadership team arrived, they called an immediate meeting of the High Court, the senior pastors, priests, lawyers and theologians of Israel, and then ordered that the Lord's ambassadors be brought from the jail. ²²But when the officials arrived at the jail, they found the Lord's ambassadors were not there, so they went back and reported: ²³"We found the jail locked up tight and the guards alert, manning their posts; but when we opened the doors, no one was inside." ²⁴The senior leadership team and captain of the temple guard were confused when they heard this, and wondered what would happen next.

Ac 5:25 Suddenly, someone ran in and said, "Come and look! The men you put in jail last night are standing in the temple court teaching the people!" ²⁶Upon hearing this, the captain of the guard went with his officers and got the Lord's ambassadors. They didn't force them, because they were afraid the people would riot and stone them.

Ac 5:27 The guard stood them before the High Court where they were questioned by the high priest. ²⁸He told them, "We gave you explicit orders not to teach in the name of the man you keep proclaiming. But your teachings have spread all over Jerusalem, and you want to blame us for this man's death."

Ac 5:29 Peter and the other ambassadors boldly said, "You don't understand! Life only exists in harmony with God and his design, therefore we must harmonize with God and obey him, and not deviate from God's design by obeying the rules of men! ³⁰The God our fathers worshiped, the source of all life, raised Jesus from the dead— yes, the same Jesus you murdered by hanging him on a tree. ³¹And God exalted him to rule the universe as Prince and Remedy in order to give a transformed character, and remission of sin and selfishness, to humanity. ³²We are witnesses to the reality of these things—we and the Holy Spirit whom God has given to all those who follow his prescription."

Ac 5:33 When the members of the High

Court heard this, they were so outraged that they wanted to put them to death, ³⁴but Gamaliel, a theologian and lawyer of the Pharisee sect who was well respected by everyone, stood up and ordered that the men be taken out while he spoke. ³⁵Then he addressed the rest of the members of the High Court: "Leaders of Israel! Don't be rash, but think carefully what you will do to these men. ³⁶Remember Theudas, who some time back claimed to be on a mission for God, and about four hundred men followed him? He was killed, his followers dispersed, and nothing came of it. ³⁷And after him, the year the census was taken, Judas the Galilean showed up, claiming to be on a mission for God, and led a mob in revolt. But he too was killed and his followers dispersed. ³⁸So, I recommend we leave these men alone! Let them go! For if their ministry and mission are only of human origin, they will fail. ³⁹But if it is from God, there is nothing you can do to stop them; you will only find yourselves fighting against God."

Ac 5:40 The logic of his argument convinced them to follow his recommendations, so they had the Lord's ambassadors beaten, then ordered them to stop teaching, speaking, or promoting the name of Jesus, and let them go.

Ac 5:41 The Lord's ambassadors left the High Court overjoyed that they were worthy to exalt the character of God through their suffering. ⁴²Every day, in the temple and in homes, they continued teaching the truth of what has transpired, and proclaiming the good news that Jesus is the Remedy.

6 At that time, the number of people partaking of, and then distributing the Remedy was increasing. But tension arose between the Grecian and local Jews, because the widows of the Grecian Jews were being overlooked in the daily food distribution. ²So the Twelve gathered all the Lord's followers and said, "It would not be right for

us to stop our duties—distributing the Remedy and teaching the truth of God's kingdom of love—in order to pass out food. [3] Friends, select seven of you, who have partaken of the Remedy, are filled with the Holy Spirit, and are wise. We will entrust them with this responsibility, [4] and focus our energies on talking with God and distributing the Remedy to sin and selfishness."

Ac 6:5 Everyone was happy with this solution. They selected Stephen, a man who trusted God completely and was full of the Holy Spirit; they also selected Philip, Procorus, Nicanor, Timon, Parmenas, and Nicolas from Antioch, who had converted to Judaism. [6] They presented them to the Lord's ambassadors, who put their hands on them and asked God to bless them.

Ac 6:7 So the truth about God and his Remedy spread. The number of those who partook of the Remedy in Jerusalem increased quickly, and a large number of Jewish priests partook of the Remedy and became faithful to Jesus.

Ac 6:8 Stephen, a man whose character radiated the grace and beauty of God and who was filled with power from heaven, performed many miracles and incredible wonders among the people. [9] But Jews from Cyrene, Alexandria, Cilicia and Asia, who were members of the Synagogue of Freemen, opposed him. They tried to debate with Stephen, [10] but their arguments couldn't stand against his wisdom or the Spirit who empowered his words.

Ac 6:11 So they bribed some men to slander him. They said, "We heard Stephen teach lies about Moses and God."

Ac 6:12 By doing this, they agitated the people, church leaders, and theologians who preferred a legal theology. These people arrested Stephen and brought him before the Jewish High Court. [13] They brought in their bribed witnesses, who perjured themselves by saying, "This man is always speaking against this temple and God's written law. [14] We even heard him say that Jesus of Nazareth would destroy this building, and do away with what Moses taught us."

Ac 6:15 All those sitting in the courtroom turned and looked closely at Stephen, and they saw his face radiating light, like that of an angel.

7 The high priest asked him directly, "Are these charges true?"

Ac 7:2 Stephen answered: "My fellow Israelites and honored leaders, please listen to me! Before our father Abraham left Mesopotamia for Haran, the God of glory appeared to him and said, [3] 'Leave your homeland and family, and go to the place I will show you.'

Ac 7:4 "So he left his homeland in the east and settled in Haran. After his father died, God led him to this land where you now live, [5] but gave none of it to Abraham as his—not even one square foot of ground. But God promised the entire land to him and to his children, even though at that time Abraham had no children. [6] God said to him, 'Your descendants will live in a foreign country where they will become slaves, and be abused for four hundred years. [7] But I will intervene with the nation they serve as slaves, and after that they will leave that country and serve me in this place.' [8] Then God gave Abraham the ceremony of circumcision. Abraham had a son, Isaac, and circumcised him on the eighth day after birth. And later Isaac had his son Jacob, and Jacob was the father of the twelve patriarchs.

Ac 7:9 "Because Joseph's brothers—the men who became the patriarchs of our nation—were jealous, they sold him as a slave into Egypt. But God was with Joseph [10] and delivered him from every obstacle. He gave Joseph wisdom and caused the pharaoh to value and trust him; so he made him ruler over Egypt and his entire palace.

Ac 7:11 "Then the predicted famine hit

Egypt and Canaan, causing great suffering, and our ancestors could not find food. 12 So Jacob, after hearing there was grain in Egypt, sent our forefathers on their first trip. 13 And on their second trip to Egypt, Joseph revealed himself to his brothers, and Pharaoh learned about Joseph's family. 14 After this, Joseph invited his father, Jacob, and the rest of the family—seventy-five in all—to come to Egypt. 15 So Jacob went to Egypt, where he and our forefathers died. 16 Later, their bodies were brought back to Shechem and laid to rest in the tomb that Abraham had purchased from the sons of Hamor at Shechem.

Ac 7:17 "When the four hundred years were almost over, and the time approached for God to fulfill his promise to Abraham, the number of our people in Egypt had grown very large. 18 A new pharaoh, who didn't care about Joseph, took power in Egypt. 19 He dealt underhandedly with our people, abused our ancestors, and killed their babies.

Ac 7:20 "It was at that time that Moses was born, and he was a special child. He was nurtured for three months at home, and 21 when he was hidden outside the home, Pharaoh's daughter found him and raised him as her own son. 22 Moses was given the best education available, being taught all the wisdom of the Egyptians. He was a powerful speaker, leader and athlete.

Ac 7:23 "At forty years of age, Moses visited his fellow Israelites. 24 When he saw one of them being abused by an Egyptian, he rescued him and killed the Egyptian. 25 Moses thought his people would realize that God was using him to free them and happily rally to him, but they did not. 26 Instead, the very next day, when Moses found two Israelites fighting, he tried to end their dispute by saying, 'What are you doing? You are brothers, why are you trying to hurt each other?'

Ac 7:27 "But the one who started the fight pushed Moses back and said, 'Who made you our ruler and judge? 28 Are you going to kill me like you murdered that Egyptian yesterday?' 29 Upon hearing this, Moses fled to Midian, where he lived as a foreigner and had two sons.

Ac 7:30 "Forty years later, an angel appeared to Moses from the flames of a bush that seemed to be on fire, but didn't burn up, in the desert near Mount Sinai. 31 Such a sight amazed him, and as he approached to get a closer look, he heard the voice of the Lord say: 32 'I am the God of your forefathers, the God of Abraham, Isaac and Jacob.' At that, Moses shook with fear and was too frightened to look.

Ac 7:33 "Then the Lord instructed him, 'Remove your shoes, because where you are standing is sacred ground. 34 I have seen the pain and suffering of my people in Egypt. I have heard their cries and have come to set them free. So prepare yourself, for I am going to send you back to Egypt.'

Ac 7:35 "Now, this was the same Moses they had already rejected with the words, 'Who made you our ruler and judge?' It was God himself who, through the angel that appeared to him in the bush, sent him to be their ruler and deliverer. 36 And he led them out of bondage—with many wonders, signs, and miracles in Egypt, at the Red Sea, and during the forty years in the desert.

Ac 7:37 "This Moses, the one who led them from Egypt, is the one who told Israel, 'God will send you another spokesperson, who, like me, will be from among your own people.' 38 This Moses is the one who stood between the angel who spoke on Sinai and the assembly of people in the desert, and brought the words of life from God to our ancestors to pass on to us.

Ac 7:39 "But our ancestors rejected what he brought, and refused to listen and do what he taught. Instead, they turned their hearts and affections back to Egypt and the ways of this selfish world. ⁴⁰ They demanded of Aaron, 'Make us gods who will lead us. Moses led us out of Egypt and left us here, and we don't know where he has gone!' ⁴¹ That was when they made the idol of a golden calf. They sacrificed to it, and celebrated over what they had created. ⁴² So God set them free to their own choice, and they even worshiped the stars in the sky. This is exactly what is written in Scripture:

'Were you loyal to me when in the
    desert, children of Israel?
Were you bringing your sacrifices
    and offerings only to me?
⁴³ No! You praised Molech and adored
    your god Rephan,
    the idols of your own hands.
So I let you go into exile,
    to be with your preferred gods in
    Babylon.'

Ac 7:44 "Our ancestors had the dwelling place of God's truth with them in the wilderness. It was built according to the pattern God had shown Moses. ⁴⁵ Having built the dwelling place of God's truth, our ancestors, under the leadership of Joshua, brought it with them when they possessed the land from the nations God drove out before them. It remained in the land until David's time. ⁴⁶ David, who found favor with God, asked to build a permanent house for God, ⁴⁷ but it was Solomon who built it.

Ac 7:48 "However, the Most High God does not live in buildings made by human beings. As God's spokesperson says,

⁴⁹ 'Heaven is my throne, and the
    earth is where I rest my feet.
What kind of house could you build
    for me? says the Creator.
Where will I go to rest?
⁵⁰ Have I not created all these things?'

Ac 7:51 "You close-minded, stubborn people with hearts tied to this selfish world, and ears that prefer lies! You are exactly like your ancestors: You constantly reject God's Spirit of Truth and Love! ⁵² Was there even one of God's spokespersons your ancestors did not persecute? They even killed those who spoke about the coming of the Remedy—the Righteous One. And now it is you who have rejected, betrayed, and murdered him; ⁵³ you have received the blueprint of God's plan to heal and save humanity, given through angels, but you have not followed it."

Ac 7:54 Upon hearing this, the crowd became a rioting mob, screaming, cursing, whistling, hissing and booing him. ⁵⁵ But Stephen, filled with the Holy Ghost, looked toward heaven and saw God in glory and Jesus standing at God's right hand. ⁵⁶ Pointing upward, he said, "Look, I see heaven opened and Jesus, the Son of Man, standing at the right hand of God."

Ac 7:57 Yelling and screaming, they put their fingers in their ears and surged at him. ⁵⁸ They dragged him out of the city and stoned him. The witnesses laid their coats at the feet of a young man named Saul.

Acts⁷:⁵⁹ While being stoned, Stephen asked the Lord, "Lord Jesus, take my individuality to be with you—receive my spirit." ⁶⁰ Then, falling to his knees, he cried out, "Lord, don't count this sin against them!" After saying this, he fell asleep in death.

8 And Saul stood there, applauding Stephen's murder.

That very day, terrible persecution broke out against those in Jerusalem who had partaken of the Remedy and were part of the church—the Lord's 'spiritual health-care' team. They all scattered throughout Judea and Samaria—all, that is, except for the Twelve. ² Men who were loyal to God buried Stephen and grieved deeply for him, ³ but Saul set out on a mission to destroy the church. He went on a house-by-house search and dragged away any who had partaken of the Remedy, imprisoning both men and women.

Ac 8:4 Those who had scattered out from

Jerusalem spread the Remedy wherever they went. ⁵Philip took the truth of the Messiah to a city in Samaria. ⁶When the people heard the beauty and clarity of the Remedy he presented, and saw the miraculous healings, they were riveted to his every word. ⁷Evil spirits shouted in protest as they were driven out, and many paralyzed and crippled people were healed. ⁸So the city was filled with great joy.

Ac 8:9 Simon was a magician who had for years amazed the people of the city with his sorcery. He proudly promoted himself as a person of power and importance, ¹⁰and the people from all levels of society revered him and paid attention to him. They believed that his magic was done by power from God. ¹¹They followed him, because he had amazed them with magic for years. ¹²But when they heard Philip, they believed him and partook of the Remedy he presented. Their minds were immersed in God's kingdom of love, and they were renewed to be like Jesus Christ in character; then they were symbolically immersed in water, both men and women. ¹³Simon publicly stated that he believed, and went through the symbolic immersion in water. Stunned by the miracles and signs he saw, he followed Philip everywhere.

Ac 8:14 When the Lord's ambassadors in Jerusalem heard that Samaria had partaken of the Remedy and accepted the truth about God, they sent Peter and John to them. ¹⁵When the two arrived, they asked the Lord to empower the Samaritans for service with the mighty agency of the Holy Spirit, ¹⁶as the Holy Spirit had not yet gifted and empowered any of them for service; they only had their minds immersed in the truth and hearts renewed to be like the Lord Jesus in character. ¹⁷So Peter and John put their hands on them, and they received the indwelling of the Holy Spirit empowering them for ministry.

Ac 8:18 Simon saw that the Spirit was imparted when the Lord's ambassadors placed their hands upon the people, so he tried to buy this power from Peter and John with money. ¹⁹He said, "I will pay you whatever you want; just sell me this power, so that I can sell the Holy Spirit to those who pay me to put my hands on them."

Ac 8:20 Peter was sickened at the thought and said, "You and your money will perish, because you are out of harmony with how life is constructed to operate. Life is built on giving, but you violate that design by trying to buy with money what God gives freely! ²¹You, in your selfishness, cannot participate in this ministry of love because your heart is not harmonized with God's design. ²²Turn around now! Repent of this sick state of heart and ask God to cleanse and heal you from cherishing such selfishness in your heart. ²³I can see your heart is consumed with fear, insecurity and self-centeredness, filling you with jealousy, envy and resentment of anyone or anything that takes attention away from you."

Ac 8:24 Then Simon said, "Please ask the Lord that nothing as bad as you have described will happen to me."

Ac 8:25 After Peter and John had shared their testimony and the truth about God in Samaria, they went back to Jerusalem, distributing the Remedy in many Samaritan villages along the way.

Ac 8:26 Now, one of the Lord's angels told Philip, "Go south on the desert road that goes from Jerusalem to Gaza." ²⁷So he went, and while he was walking, he saw an Ethiopian eunuch, who was the national treasurer of the Ethiopian queen Candace. He had been to Jerusalem to worship, ²⁸and on his way home was sitting in his carriage, reading from the book written by God's spokesperson Isaiah. ²⁹The Spirit instructed Philip, "Go and walk beside that carriage, and stay close to it."

Ac 8:30 So Philip ran, and as he caught

up to the carriage, he heard the man reading from Isaiah. So Philip asked him, "Do you understand the meaning of what you are reading?"

Ac 8:31 "No, not really," he said. "I need someone to explain it to me." Then he asked Philip if he would ride with him and explain what it meant.

Ac 8:32 The eunuch was reading this portion of Isaiah:

"Like a sheep being led to the
slaughter,
or as a lamb is silent while it is
sheared, so he remained silent.
33 By his selfless death he cured our
terminal condition
and thus the condemnation was
taken away.
Who can count the number of his
children—
those who partake of the Remedy
he achieved?
For the humanity which he
assumed—
the humanity inherited from
Adam—was eradicated."

Ac 8:34 The eunuch asked Philip, "So who was he talking about? Please tell me, was it himself or someone else?"

35 Philip, starting with that very passage from Isaiah, told him the amazing good news of Jesus becoming human, taking up our terminal condition, loving perfectly and dying selflessly—all this in order to procure the Remedy, save the human species, and secure the universe unfallen.

Ac 8:36 Soon they came to a place along the road with water, and the eunuch said, "Look, here is some water. Why shouldn't I take a public stand and be symbolically immersed into the family of Jesus?" 37 "If you sincerely believe in your heart, you may," replied Philip. The eunuch answered, "I do believe! Jesus is the Christ, the Son of God." 38 So he ordered his carriage to stop, and they went into the water where Philip immersed him. 39 When they came out of the water, the Spirit of God suddenly transported Philip away.

The eunuch never saw him again, but went home rejoicing. 40 Philip appeared in Azotus and traveled through the land, preaching the truth about God and distributing the Remedy in all the towns and villages along the way, until he reached Caesarea.

9 But Saul was still fuming threats to kill any who joined the Lord's spiritual health-care team. He went to the high priest 2 and obtained arrest warrants to take to the synagogue in Damascus, so if he found any there who had partaken of the Remedy, he could take them as prisoners to Jerusalem. 3 As he approached Damascus, a light from heaven blazed around him. 4 He threw himself to the ground and heard a voice say, "Oh, Saul, why are you persecuting me?"

Ac 9:5 "Lord, who are you?" Saul asked.

"I am Jesus, and it is me that you are attacking," the voice replied. 6 "Now you need to get on your feet and go into the city where you will be told what you must do."

Ac 9:7 The men traveling with Saul froze where they were, unable to speak; they heard the voice but didn't see anyone. 8 Saul stood up, but when he opened his eyes, he was blind. They took him by the hand and led him into Damascus. 9 For the next three days, he was blind and didn't eat or drink.

Ac 9:10 Ananias, one of the members of the Lord's spiritual health-care team, lived in Damascus. The Lord called to him in a vision, "Ananias!"

"Lord, I'm listening, what would you have of me?" he answered.

Ac 9:11 The Lord instructed him, "Go to Judas' house on Straight Street and ask for Saul of Tarsus, for he has been talking to me. 12 He has seen in a vision that a man named Ananias will come and place hands on him and restore his ability to see."

Ac 9:13 "But Lord," Ananias cautioned, "the reports I've heard say this is the man who has injured your friends in

Jerusalem. ¹⁴And he has come here with arrest warrants from the chief priests to imprison all who partake of the Remedy and trust in you to reveal your character of love."

Ac 9:15 But the Lord encouraged Ananias, saying, "Go and do this, for this man is my chosen ambassador to take my Remedy and reveal my character to the Gentiles and their rulers, as well as to the people of Israel. ¹⁶I will reveal to him how much he will suffer for embracing and sharing my character of love."

Ac 9:17 So Ananias found the house and went in. He placed his hands on Saul and said, "Brother Saul, the Lord Jesus himself, who appeared to you on the road here, has sent me to you so you may see, both physically and spiritually, as you are filled with the Holy Spirit." ¹⁸Immediately, something like scales fell from Saul's eyes and he could see. He got up and publicly joined the Lord's spiritual health-care team by the ceremony of being immersed in water. ¹⁹Then he ate some food to regain his strength, and stayed there several days, visiting with members of the Lord's spiritual health-care team in Damascus.

Ac 9:20 Then he went straight to the Jewish synagogue and began preaching, admitting that he had been wrong, and that Jesus really is the Son of God. ²¹Those who heard him couldn't believe it, and wondering if it was a trick, asked, "Isn't this the same man who in Jerusalem sought to destroy those who follow Jesus? And hasn't he come here with arrest warrants to take them back to the chief priests?" ²²But Saul's presentation of the truth proving that Jesus is the Savior of the world — the Messiah — became so powerful that the Jews living in Damascus couldn't refute it.

Ac 9:23 Realizing they couldn't kill the message of truth which Saul presented, the Jews plotted to murder the messenger, ²⁴but Saul discovered their plans. The Jews placed assassins at the city gates, who watched for him in order to kill him. ²⁵But his followers foiled the assassins' plans, and one night they helped him escape by lowering Saul in a basket through a hole in the city wall.

Ac 9:26 When he arrived in Jerusalem, he tried to join with members of the Lord's spiritual health-care team, but they were afraid of him, not trusting he was really one of them. ²⁷Barnabas took him to the Twelve. He told them about Saul's journey, how he had seen Jesus and how Jesus had spoken to him, and how he had courageously and powerfully promoted the truth about Jesus in Damascus. ²⁸So Saul was invited to stay with them. As a team-member, he went about Jerusalem boldly teaching the truth about Jesus. ²⁹He powerfully confronted the distortions held by the Greek-speaking Jews, but they became agitated and tried to kill him. ³⁰When those who had partaken of the Remedy learned of this, they took Saul to Caesarea and sent him on to Tarsus.

Ac 9:31 Those who had partaken of the Remedy throughout Judea, Galilee and Samaria enjoyed a time of peace. The Holy Spirit gave them strength, courage and confidence, and the number of people who partook of the Remedy and joined them increased daily. They lived in a state of deep reverence and admiration for the Lord.

Ac 9:32 As Peter traveled throughout the country, he visited the living temples of God—those people who were renewed in holiness by the indwelling of the Holy Spirit—in Lydda. ³³He found a man there named Aeneas, who was paralyzed and had been bedridden for eight years. ³⁴Peter said to him, "Aeneas, Jesus Christ heals you, so stand up and put your mat away." Immediately Aeneas got up. ³⁵Everyone living in Lydda and Sharon saw him healed and accepted Jesus.

Ac 9:36 In the city of Joppa there was

one of the Lord's interns named Tabitha, which in Greek is *Dorcas* and means 'gazelle.' She was constantly doing good, helping the poor and homeless. [37] At that time, she became sick and died, and her body was washed and laid in an upstairs room. [38] When the interns heard that Peter was in Lydda, which was near Joppa, they sent two men who implored him to come at once!

Ac 9:39 Peter returned with them, and when he arrived, he went upstairs to the room. The room was filled with widows who stood around crying and showing him all the clothes Dorcas had made for them while she was alive.

Ac 9:40 Peter had everyone leave the room, then he knelt down and talked to Jesus. When finished, he turned toward the dead woman and said, "Tabitha, get up." She opened her eyes, looked at Peter, and sat up. [41] He took her hand and helped her stand. Then he called the believers and widows into the room and presented her to them alive. [42] News of this spread rapidly throughout Joppa, and many people believed in Jesus. [43] Peter remained there for some time, living with a tanner named Simon.

10 At Caesarea, there lived a centurion named Cornelius, a member of the Italian Regiment. [2] He and his entire family loved God and lived in harmony with the law of love, giving generously to those in need. Cornelius opened his heart to God in conversation regularly. [3] One afternoon, about three o'clock, he had a vision: He saw with absolute clarity an angel of God who came right up to him and said, "Cornelius!"

Ac 10:4 Cornelius was stunned and initially just stared at him, but finally said, "Yes sir, what can I do for you, sir?"

The angel answered, "The outpouring of your heart, and your gifts to the needy have become a memorial of love before God. [5] Send men to Joppa to bring back the man Simon Peter. [6] He is staying at the home of Simon the tanner who lives on the coast."

Ac 10:7 After the angel departed, Cornelius summoned two servants, and a devoted soldier who was his aide-de-camp. [8] He told them everything that had happened and then sent them to Joppa.

Ac 10:9 The next day around noon, as they were approaching the city, Peter went up on the roof to talk with God. [10] He was hungry, and smelling the aroma of the meal being cooked, was longing to eat. Just then, he had a vision [11] in which he saw the skies open, and an object—that appeared to be a large sheet—being lowered to the earth by its four corners. [12] It contained every known animal, reptile and bird. [13] A voice instructed him, "Peter, sacrifice any of these and eat."

Ac 10:14 But Peter protested, "Lord, there must be some mistake! I have never sacrificed nor eaten anything impure or not on the approved script."

Ac 10:15 The voice spoke to him again. "Don't reject as 'unapproved' or 'impure' what God has healed and made clean."

Ac 10:16 This vision was repeated three times, and then the sheet disappeared into the sky.

Ac 10:17 While Peter was contemplating the meaning of the vision, the men sent by Cornelius approached the gate to Simon's house and [18] called out, asking if Simon Peter was there.

Ac 10:19 Peter was still trying to figure out the meaning of the vision when the Spirit of the Lord said to him, "Simon, there are three men here looking for you. [20] Go downstairs and go with them, for I have sent them to get you."

Ac 10:21 So Peter went down and said to them, "I am Peter, the one you are looking for. What can I do for you?"

Ac 10:22 The men replied, "Cornelius the centurion sent us to find you. He is a man who loves God and lives right.

He helps those in need and even the Jewish people speak well of him. An angel from God told him to invite you to his home to hear the message you have to share." 23 Then Peter invited them in and made them welcome, giving them a place to spend the night. The next day, Peter and some of the other members of the Lord's spiritual health-care team from Joppa started out with the men.

Ac 10:24 They arrived in Caesarea the following day. Cornelius knew they were coming, and had called his entire family and close friends to join him. 25 When Peter entered his home, Cornelius knelt down in reverence before him. 26 But Peter immediately ordered him to get up, saying, "Stand up. I am only a man, born infected with sin and selfishness, just like everyone else, and in need of the same Remedy."

Ac 10:27 As they greeted each other, they walked inside, where Peter discovered a large crowd of people waiting. 28 He said to them, "As you all know, religious rules forbid Jews from visiting or socializing with non-Jews. But God has revealed to me that such rules are not from him, and that no human being is to discriminate against, shun, or treat another as inferior. 29 So when I heard that you sent for me, I came eagerly. So tell me, how can I help you?"

Ac 10:30 Cornelius answered, "Three days ago, just at this time (three o'clock in the afternoon) I was praying, when a man radiating light appeared out of nowhere and stood right in front of me. 31 He said, 'Cornelius, God has heard your request and knows you care for the poor. 32 Send men to Joppa for a man called Simon Peter. He is visiting at the home of Simon the tanner, who lives on the coast.' 33 So I sent men for you right then, and I thank you for coming. Now, all of us have gathered here, in God's presence, to hear the truth the Lord has instructed you to deliver to us."

Ac 10:34 Then Peter said, "I now understand the truth that God isn't prejudiced and doesn't play favorites, 35 but views humanity as a whole—every person as a member of the same race—and will heal all who trust him and partake of the Remedy. 36 You have heard that the Remedy from God was sent through Israel; it is the good news of healing and restoration through Jesus Christ, who is Lord of all. 37 You have heard the reports of what happened in Judea—beginning in Galilee after the call to repentance preached by John and symbolized by immersion in water—38 how God empowered Jesus of Nazareth with the indwelling of the Holy Spirit, and how he went throughout the land giving of himself for the good of others. He healed everyone who was oppressed by the devil, because he was God's very thoughts made audible and visible.

Ac 10:39 "We are eyewitnesses to it all; we saw everything he did in Israel and Jerusalem. They murdered him by nailing him to a cross, 40 but on the third day, in response to God's call, he arose from the dead and went about where he was seen. 41 Not everyone saw him— only those of us chosen to be on his spiritual health-care team; we were the ones to eat and drink with him after he arose from the dead. 42 He gave us the duty of sharing the Remedy with the world and telling people that God appointed Jesus as the One who diagnoses the hearts of the living and the dead. 43 All God's spokespersons spoke of him, and described how every person who trusts him will be delivered from their terminal condition of fear and selfishness by having his character of love reproduced in them."

Ac 10:44 While Peter was presenting these truths, the Holy Spirit filled the hearts and minds of all who embraced the message.

45 The circumcised members of the Lord's spiritual health-care team were surprised when the gift of the Holy

Spirit was given to the uncircumcised Gentiles, 46 but they knew it was so because they heard the praises of the Gentile converts in their own language.

Then Peter said, 47 "These people have already had their hearts and minds immersed in the Holy Spirit just as we did, so how could anyone object to them being immersed in water?" 48 So he instructed that they be immersed in water according to the accepted ritual, publicly declaring their unity with Jesus Christ. Then they invited Peter to stay with them for a few days.

11 The Lord's ambassadors and members of his spiritual health-care team throughout Judea got word that the Gentiles had partaken of the Remedy. 2 When Peter returned to Jerusalem, the circumcised men who had accepted Jesus criticized him, 3 saying, "You entered the home of uncircumcised men and not only ate with them, but stayed with them."

Ac 11:4 But Peter explained exactly what had happened and why: 5 "I was in Joppa, praying, when I was taken away in vision by the Spirit. I saw what appeared to be a great sheet lowered from the sky by its four corners. It came all the way down to where I was. 6 On it, I saw four-footed animals from all over the earth—wild beasts, reptiles and birds. 7 Then a voice from heaven said, 'Go and sacrifice any of these, and eat it.'

Ac 11:8 "But I protested, saying, 'Lord, there must be some mistake. I have never sacrificed nor eaten anything that is impure or not on the script.'

Ac 11:9 "The voice from heaven spoke again: 'Don't reject as unapproved or impure what God has healed and made clean.' 10 Three times this vision was presented and then it disappeared up into the sky.

Ac 11:11 "Immediately, the three men from Caesarea arrived where I was staying. 12 The Spirit told me to go with them without reservation. So I went, and these six members of the Lord's team went with me, and we entered the man's home. 13 He told us that an angel came to him and said, 'Send men to Joppa to bring Simon Peter. 14 He has the Remedy which will heal you and your entire household.'

Ac 11:15 "When I began speaking to them, the Holy Spirit filled them, as he did us in the beginning. 16 Then I recalled what our Lord had said: 'John immersed people in water, but you will immerse their minds and hearts in the Holy Spirit.' 17 So if God poured upon them the same gift as he gave to those of us who accepted the Lord Jesus Christ, what reason could I have for opposing him?"

Ac 11:18 Upon hearing this, they had no further objections and praised God, saying, "God's Remedy which provides eternal life is for all people."

Ac 11:19 Some of the Lord's team who had scattered as a result of the persecution when Stephen was killed took the good news of the Remedy to Phoenicia, Cyprus and Antioch, but shared it only with Jews. 20 Others, however, from Cyprus and Cyrene, went to Antioch and began sharing the good news of the Remedy procured by the Lord Jesus to Greeks as well. 21 The Lord's power was with them, and large numbers of people partook of the Remedy and turned to the Lord.

Ac 11:22 When the church at Jerusalem heard this, they sent Barnabas to Antioch. 23 When he arrived, he saw the evidence of God's transforming work in their lives, and rejoicing, he encouraged them to trust the Lord with all their hearts and faithfully follow his treatment plan. 24 He was a good man, genuinely caring about people, full of the Spirit and strong in his trust, and because of him, many people partook of the Remedy and accepted Jesus.

Ac 11:25 Then Barnabas went to Tarsus to find Saul, 26 and when he found him, he brought him back to Antioch.

For the entire next year, Barnabas and Saul met regularly with the Lord's team and instructed many people. The Lord's team first took the name "Christians" at Antioch.

Ac 11:27 During this time, some of the Lord's spokespersons came to Antioch from Jerusalem. 28 One of them, a man named Agabus, publicly foretold that a great famine would come upon the Roman Empire, which did occur later during the reign of Claudius. 29 The Christians in Antioch, as they were able, chose to provide financial assistance to the believers living in Judea. 30 They had Barnabas and Saul take their donations to the church leaders for distribution.

12 About this time, King Herod began persecuting those who partook of the Remedy and accepted Jesus. 2 He had John's brother James executed with a sword. 3 When he realized the political support he gained from the Jews for doing this, he had Peter arrested. This happened during the Feast of Unleavened Bread. 4 He had him imprisoned and guarded by four squads of four soldiers each. Herod planned to make a public-show trial after the Passover.

Ac 12:5 While Peter was confined in prison, the believers in Christ earnestly asked God to intervene in his behalf.

Ac 12:6 The night before Herod was going to bring him out for the show trial, Peter was asleep, chained to two guards—one on either side, and two sentries guarded the door to his cell. 7 Suddenly, one of God's angels stood beside him, and the cell was flooded with brilliant light. He tapped Peter on his side and woke him up. He said to Peter, "Quickly, get up!" and the chains just fell off his wrists.

Ac 12:8 The angel instructed him, "Get dressed, and don't forget your sandals." Peter immediately did as told. Then the angel said, "Put on your coat and follow me." 9 So Peter walked right behind the angel out of the prison, but he didn't know it was real. He thought he was dreaming. 10 They walked right past the first and second guards, and the guards didn't even see them. They came to the iron gate separating the prison from the city; it opened all by itself as they approached, and they quickly walked through it. When they had walked about another city block, the angel just disappeared.

Ac 12:11 Then Peter realized it wasn't a dream and said to himself, "Wow, it's real! The Lord sent his angel and set me free from Herod's control, and delivered me from the abuse the Jews were hoping for."

Ac 12:12 Having realized he was free, he went to the house of Mary, the mother of John Mark, where many of his friends and supporters had gathered to ask God's intervention. 13 Peter knocked at the entrance to the courtyard, and one of the house servants, named Rhoda, came to the door. 14 She recognized Peter's voice and was so excited with joy that she forgot to let him in, and ran back shouting, "Peter is here! He's at the door!"

Ac 12:15 "You're hysterical," they said, trying to calm her. But when she persisted, they said, "Well, perhaps she saw an angel and that's what has got her so excited?"

Ac 12:16 But Peter continued knocking, and when they finally opened the door and saw that it really was him, they were at first stunned, but then began rejoicing. 17 Peter motioned with his hands for them to quiet down and then told them how the Lord rescued him from prison. He told them, "Be sure and let James and the other members of the Lord's spiritual health-care team know about this," and then he left town.

Ac 12:18 The next morning, the prison guards were in a panic, frantically trying to find out what happened to Peter. 19 Herod had the prison searched from top to bottom, and after interrogating the guards, he had them executed. Then Herod left Judea and went to Caesarea where he stayed for a while. ²⁰ He had been in a long-standing dispute with the residents of Tyre and Sidon, who had joined forces, and with the support of Blastus, one of Herod's trusted advisors, sought a negotiated peace with Herod, as he controlled their food supply.

Ac 12:21 On the day of their scheduled appointment, Herod, dressed in royal garb, sat on his throne and delivered a speech to the people. ²² The people, seeking to flatter the king, shouted, "We have heard a god speak, not a man!" ²³ Herod failed to glorify God, and instead — misrepresented God, therefore an angel of the Lord touched him; the reality of his worm-eaten condition was made plain for all to see, and he died.

Ac 12:24 But the Remedy of God continued to spread throughout the land.

Ac 12:25 After Barnabas and Saul finished up their work in Jerusalem, they left and took John Mark with them.

13 Amongst those loyal to Jesus in Antioch were God's spokespersons and teachers: Barnabas, Simeon (also called the Black), Lucius of Cyrene, Manaen (who was raised with Herod the tetrarch) and Saul. ² While they were fasting and working together for the Lord, the Holy Spirit said, "Dedicate to me Barnabas and Saul for the work that I have assigned them." ³ So after fasting and talking with God, they laid their hands on them and sent them on their way.

Ac 13:4 On the mission directed by the Holy Spirit, the two of them went down to Seleucia and caught a ship to Cyprus. ⁵ Upon arriving at Salamis, they proclaimed the truth of God's Remedy in the Jewish synagogues. John accompanied them as their assistant.

Ac 13:6 They traveled across the entire island, arriving at Paphos. There they encountered a spiritual quack — a person who claimed to speak for God but who misrepresented God and confused the mind. His name was Bar-Jesus, ⁷ and he was an advisor to the proconsul, Sergius Paulus. The proconsul was a wise man, open-minded and intent on examining the evidence for himself. So he sent for Barnabas and Saul because he wanted to hear the truth about the Remedy. ⁸ But Mr. Illumination, the spiritual quack (for that is what his name means), worked against them, trying to confuse the proconsul and prevent him from partaking of the Remedy and trusting in Jesus. ⁹ Then Saul, who was also known as Paul, empowered by the Holy Spirit, looked directly at Mr. Illumination and said, ¹⁰ "You are a true son of Satan, an enemy of light and truth! Rather than illuminating others, you obstruct the truth with lies. Will you ever stop misrepresenting God? ¹¹ Now God's power will come over you and reveal the truth: You are no illuminator; you are spiritually blind, so now you will be physically blind, and for a while you won't even be able to see sunlight." Immediately, his vision became cloudy and he began groping about. Rather than leading others, he needed someone to lead him by the hand.

Ac 13:12 When the proconsul saw what had happened, he accepted the Remedy and was transformed by the truth about Jesus.

Ac 13:13 Paul and his friends left Paphos and sailed to Perga in Pamphylia. John left them there and returned to Jerusalem. ¹⁴ From Perga they traveled to Antioch in Pisidia. On the Sabbath they went to the synagogue and sat down. ¹⁵ The worship leader, after reading the Bible passage for the day, said to them, "Brothers, if you have a message that would encourage the people, please share it with us."

Ac 13:16 Paul stood up, and motioning with his hands for silence, said, "People of Israel and other friends who love and adore God, hear me! ¹⁷ The God of

Israel chose our ancestors for his purpose. During their sojourn in Egypt, he blessed them, and with great power he led them out of that country. ¹⁸ He patiently took care of them for forty years in the desert, ¹⁹ and then removed the seven nations that stood as obstacles in Canaan and gave the land to his people as their staging ground. ²⁰ All of this took about four hundred and fifty years to accomplish. Once in Canaan, God gave them judges until the time of his spokesman Samuel.

Ac 13:21 "It was then that the people demanded a king, and God chose Saul, son of Kish, from the tribe of Benjamin, who ruled for forty years. ²² God then removed the family of Saul from office and made David their king. And God testifies about David, saying, 'I have examined David, son of Jesse, and his heart is renewed to be like my own; he will fulfill my plan.'

Ac 13:23 "And it is from David's descendants that God has accomplished his plan to save the world by bringing Jesus—the Savior—just as he promised. ²⁴ Before Jesus began his public ministry, John appealed to all Israel to prepare their hearts for his arrival and demonstrate it through symbolic immersion in water. ²⁵ As John's work was nearing completion, he declared publicly: 'Do you think I am the promised One? I am not the promised One. Absolutely not! He comes after me, and I am not even worthy to untie his shoes.'

Ac 13:26 "Fellow Israelites and other friends who love and adore God, it is to us that this Remedy—the truth that heals and restores—has been given. ²⁷ The people living in Jerusalem, along with the leaders of the church and the city, did not recognize Jesus as Savior; but even in their rejection and condemnation of him, they fulfilled the words of God's spokespersons that are read each Sabbath. ²⁸ Even though they had no basis for condemning him to death, they petitioned Pilate to have him executed. ²⁹ And after they did to him all the Scripture foretold, he was taken from the cross and laid in a tomb. ³⁰ But God raised him from death, ³¹ and he was seen over and over again—on different days and in different places—by people who traveled with him from Galilee to Jerusalem and thus knew him very well. These people continue to witness to our people that he is alive.

Ac 13:32 "Now, we are here to bring you the good news: The Remedy which God promised our fathers ³³ he has now provided for us—their descendants—by raising Jesus from the dead, exactly as the second Psalm says,

'You are my Son;
today my Fatherhood to you has
become known.'

Ac 13:34 "The reality that he arose from the dead in a perfected humanity, never again to be tainted with death, is confirmed in this Scripture:

'I will give you holiness,
the Remedy promised to David.'

Ac 13:35 "And it is further confirmed in the Scripture:

'You will not allow your Remedy to
decay in the grave.'

Ac 13:36 "King David fulfilled God's mission for his life in his own generation and then fell asleep in death. He was buried with his family, and his body decayed. ³⁷ But the Remedy—the one whom God raised from the dead—did not decay.

Ac 13:38 "So, my dear friends, I want you to understand that it is through Jesus that sinfulness in our hearts remits and we are restored to God's original ideal. ³⁹ Through what he achieved, every person who trusts him is healed and set right from every defect of character that the diagnostic code, given through Moses, could not fix. ⁴⁰ So be very careful that what God's spokespersons have predicted does not happen to you:

⁴¹ 'Look, you who resist truth,
be amazed and vanish,

for I am going to work out something
in your days
that you will refuse to believe,
even when someone explains it to
you.'"

Ac 13:42 When Paul and Barnabas were leaving the worship service, the people were so moved that they invited them to speak more about these things the following Sabbath. 43 After the meeting, many of the Jews and sincere converts to Judaism followed Paul and Barnabas who instructed them and encouraged to continue partaking of God's gracious Remedy.

Ac 13:44 When the next Sabbath arrived, almost the entire city turned out to hear the truth about the Remedy of the Lord. 45 When the Jews who'd rejected the Remedy saw the size of the crowds, they became jealous and began to argue against what Paul said, and to slander him.

Ac 13:46 So Paul and Barnabas fearlessly spoke the truth to them: "It was proper to share the Remedy with you, children of God's chosen helpers, first. But since you reject it, you judge yourselves unworthy of eternal life. We leave you to your choice and take the Remedy to the Gentiles. 47 For this is God's command to us:
'I have made you a shining light of
truth to all peoples,
that you may take the Remedy to
the entire world.'"

Ac 13:48 When the non-Jewish people heard this, they rejoiced, and all who trusted God and partook of the Remedy were set to receive eternal life.

Ac 13:49 The truth about God spread throughout the entire region, 50 but the Jews who rejected the Remedy told lies to godly men and women who were leaders of the city, thus turning them against the truth. They also incited persecution against Paul and Barnabas, and had them driven from the region. 51 So, in an effort to demonstrate to the people that they were rejecting truth, Paul and Barnabas shook the dust from

their feet as they left, and went to Iconium. 52 And the Lord's spiritual health-care team was filled with joy and empowered by the Holy Spirit.

14 Upon arriving in Iconium, Paul and Barnabas followed their usual pattern of evangelism and went to the Jewish synagogue. Their presentations of the good news were so effective that a large number of Jews and non-Jews believed them and partook of the Remedy. 2 But the Jews who rejected the Remedy told lies about them, stirring up the non-Jews and poisoning their minds against God's ambassadors. 3 So Paul and Barnabas spent many hours there speaking fearlessly for the Lord who confirmed them as distributors of the Remedy by enabling them to do miracles and wonders. 4 The city became divided: some sided with the rejecters of the Remedy, others with the Lord's ambassadors. 5 Those who rejected the Remedy, both Jews and non-Jews, plotted with their leaders to strip them, shave them bald, drag them publicly through the streets and stone them. 6 But Paul and Barnabas discovered the plot and fled to the towns of Lystra and Derbe, and that region of Lycaonia, 7 and they continued proclaiming the good news there.

Ac 14:8 There was a crippled man in Lystra, who was paralyzed from birth and had never walked. 9 He embraced what Paul taught. Paul looked at him and saw that he trusted God and could be healed. 10 Paul called out to him, "Stand up on your feet and walk!" Instantly the man jumped up and began to walk.

Ac 14:11 When the crowd saw Paul heal the man, they shouted in the Lycaonian language, "The gods are here among us in human form!" 12 They called Barnabas Zeus, and Paul—Hermes, because he was the main spokesperson. 13 Just outside the city was the temple of Zeus, and the priest brought bulls and wreaths to the city gates because he, along with the crowd, wanted to offer these as sacrifices to Paul and Barnabas.

Ac 14:14 But when Paul and Barnabas realized what the people were doing, they tore their clothes in horror and ran into the crowd, shouting, 15 "Stop! What are you thinking? We are not gods! We are only human beings, just like you. We are here on behalf of the Creator God, bringing you the good news of his Remedy. He is the Designer—the One who constructed the universe, the heavens, earth, the sea, and all living things. 16 It is true that in times past he permitted all nations to go their own way, 17 but even then he did not leave them without evidence of the truth. He has revealed his character of love, the principle of giving in nature, the circle of rain, rivers and streams, the crops every season; he provides plenty of food so you never go hungry, and fills your hearts with joy." 18 But the crowd was so animated that even with these words, Paul and Barnabas had difficulty keeping them from sacrificing to them.

Ac 14:19 Then some Jews who rejected the Remedy arrived from Antioch and Iconium, and won the crowd over with lies. The mob stoned Paul and dragged him out of the city, assuming he was dead. 20 But when the members of the Lord's spiritual health-care team gathered around him, he got up and went back into the city. The next day he set out with Barnabas for Derbe.

Ac 14:21 In that city, they proclaimed the good news about God, and a large number of people partook of the Remedy and became part of God's family— members of the Lord's spiritual health-care team. Then Paul and Barnabas returned to Lystra, Iconium and Antioch, 22 where they confirmed and expanded the truth amongst the Lord's spiritual health-care team, encouraging them to continue to live in harmony with God's design of love. "We must choose the right—staying loyal to love in the face of difficulty—in order to leave selfishness behind and enter into God's kingdom of love," they said. 23 Paul and Barnabas selected leaders of spiritual maturity, who understood God's methods of love, to oversee the spiritual development of each congregation. With fasting, and asking God's blessing, they dedicated them to the Lord, in whom they trusted. 24 They traveled through Pisidia, on to Pamphylia, 25 and after preaching in Perga, went on to Attalia.

Ac 14:26 From Attalia they caught a ship back to Antioch, where they had been empowered by God's grace for the mission trip they just completed. 27 On arriving there, they gathered the Lord's spiritual health-care team together and gave them a detailed report on all that God had done through them, and how the Remedy was spreading through the non-Jewish world. 28 And they fellowshipped a long time with their coworkers in Christ.

15 Some men came to Antioch from Judea and began telling those who had partaken of the Remedy: "Unless you are circumcised and follow the script given to Moses, you cannot be saved." 2 Paul and Barnabas opposed them fiercely, knowing they were focused on ritual and legalities rather than regeneration of heart. So Paul and Barnabas were selected as delegates, along with some local members of the Lord's spiritual health-care team, to go to Jerusalem and discuss this question with the Lord's ambassadors and mission leaders. 3 After they left for Jerusalem, and as they passed through Phoenicia and Samaria, they told of how the non-Jews had partaken of the Remedy and been joined to Christ. This brought great joy to the brothers and sisters there. 4 When they arrived in Jerusalem, the members of the Lord's spiritual health-care team there, along with the Lord's ambassadors and mission leaders, welcomed

them. They gave a report of all that God had accomplished through them.

Ac 15:5 Then some of those who had partaken of the Remedy and proclaimed loyalty to Christ, but were still stuck in their Pharisaical traditions, stood up and said, "The non-Jews must be circumcised, as the script given through Moses requires."

Ac 15:6 The Lord's ambassadors and mission leaders counseled together, considering this issue. 7 After a long discussion, Peter stood up and said, "Friends and co-workers in God's cause, you know full well that some time ago God decided that the good news of his Remedy should be taken to the non-Jews by me, so that they might trust him and be healed. 8 God, who is concerned with the heart and knows their hearts well, poured the Holy Spirit upon these non-Jewish people—just as he did to us—thus confirming they were right with him. 9 God didn't make any difference between us and them, who are of different ancestry, for he cleansed their hearts through their trust—not by some legal act or ritual. 10 So why are you trying to prove you know better than God by putting legal requirements and rituals on them, which will only enslave them like a yoke around their neck, and which neither we nor our ancestors have been able to bear? 11 No way! Don't do it! We believe it is through the gracious Remedy of our Lord Jesus that we are healed, and so are they!"

Ac 15:12 The entire room remained silent. No one said a word as they listened to Paul and Barnabas tell of the miracles and wonders God had done among the non-Jews through them. 13 When they finished, James said, "Friends and co-workers for God, listen to me: 14 Simon has told us that God shows no racial preferences—but sees all humanity as one—and has healed non-Jews, bringing them back to unity with him. 15 The words of the Lord's spokespersons agree, as it is written:

16 'After this, I will come again
and rebuild the fallen family of David.
Though decayed and dying, I will be its Remedy,
17 so that the rest of humanity may come to me:
yes, all the peoples of the world who desire my character restored in them.
So says the Lord who accomplishes this
18 and has been making it known from ages past.'

Ac 15:19 "Therefore, it is my judgment that we should not put obstacles in the way of the non-Jews who are turning to God and desire to partake of the Remedy. 20 Instead, let's send them a letter advising them to live pure lives: to keep their hearts pure toward God and therefore avoid anything that leads the mind toward idols; to keep their relationships pure and therefore avoid all sexual impurity; and to keep their bodies pure by not eating blood, raw meat, or any meat from animals whose blood was not drained. 21 For these principles are the basis of what Moses taught; they have been preached in every city since his time, and read in the synagogues each Sabbath."

Ac 15:22 Then the Lord's ambassadors, along with team leaders and the entire spiritual health-care team, selected delegates of their own to accompany Paul and Barnabas back to Antioch. They chose Judas Barsabbas and Silas, who were both leaders among them. 23 They sent this letter with them:

"We, the Lord's ambassadors and team leaders, and fellow workers for God's cause, send greetings to you, fellow members of the Lord's spiritual health-care team in Antioch, Syria and Cilicia. 24 It has come to our attention that some individuals came to you from our group, without our knowledge or authorization, and presented contradictory and burdensome ideas that have undermined your peace and security in the Lord. 25 Because of this, we met together and decided to send out authorized delegates to you, accompanied by our dear friends Barnabas and Paul — 26 men who, as you know, have risked their lives to reach people with the Remedy of the Lord Jesus Christ. 27 We are sending Judas Barsabbas and Silas to tell you face to face that the letter we are sending is genuine, and to answer any questions you may have. 28 The Holy Spirit helped us realize that it is best not to burden your spiritual treatment-plan with unnecessary rituals, but you will do well to enhance your transformation with the following guidelines: 29 You are to live pure lives—keep your hearts pure toward God by avoiding anything that leads the mind toward idols; keep your relationships pure by avoiding all sexual impurity; and keep your bodies pure by not eating blood, raw meat, or any meat from animals whose blood was not drained. You will be physically, spiritually and relationally healthier if you avoid these things. May all go well with you."

Ac 15:30 The delegates went to Antioch, where, upon gathering the Lord's spiritual health-care team together, they delivered the letter. 31 The people read it and were greatly relieved and encouraged by it. 32 Judas Barsabbas and Silas, who were both spokesmen for the Lord, shared many truths that encouraged and strengthened the team members. 33 After enjoying fellowship there for a time, they returned home with the love, affection, and goodwill of their new friends in Antioch, 35 but Paul and Barnabas stayed in Antioch, where, with many others, they continued to distribute the Remedy and teach the Lord's methods for spiritual renewal.

Ac 15:36 Some time later, Paul said to Barnabas, "Let's go back and visit our team members working to distribute the Remedy in all the towns we have taken it to, and see how it is going."

37 Barnabas wanted John Mark to go with them, 38 but Paul disagreed, because he had lost confidence in John Mark's commitment to the cause, given that he'd abandoned them in Pamphylia and stopped distributing the Remedy. 39 They were both so convicted of their own positions that they couldn't reach a compromise, so they decided to separate their ministry: Barnabas took Mark and sailed for Cyprus, 40 while Paul took Silas and set out, with the blessings and encouragement of the team and empowerment of the Lord, 41 and went throughout Syria and Cilicia, building up the Lord's team.

16 Paul went to Derbe and Lystra, where one of the Lord's interns named Timothy lived. His father was Greek, but mother was Jewish, and therefore he was considered a Jew by the Jews. 2 He was well liked by the Lord's people in Lystra and Iconium. 3 Because Paul wanted him as his aide and understudy, he circumcised him in order to remove any erroneous distractions from critical Jews who knew that his father was Greek. 4 In every town they entered, they told the people of the treatment guidelines reached by the Lord's ambassadors and team leaders in Jerusalem. 5 And every day more people partook of the Remedy, and everyone who participated in the Lord's plan grew stronger in love and trust.

Ac 16:6 Paul and the rest of his team traveled throughout Phrygia and Galatia, but didn't go into Asia, as the Holy Spirit instructed them not to. 7 When they arrived at the border of Mysia, they headed for Bithynia, but the Holy Spirit brought them instructions from Jesus not to go there. 8 So they passed by Mysia and went to Troas. 9 That night, Paul had a vision of a man in Macedonia pleading with him, "Please come to Macedonia and help us."

10 After Paul's vision, we all concluded God was leading us to take the Remedy to Macedonia, so we packed up and headed that way.

Ac 16:11 We sailed from Troas to Samothrace and spent the night there. The next day we went on to Neapolis, 12 and from there we traveled to the Roman colony of Philippi—the chief city of that region of Macedonia—and spent several days there.

Ac 16:13 On the Sabbath, we sought a place of worship, but finding no synagogue, we left the city in search of a gathering place by the river. We found the place where Jewish women had gathered, and we sat down and began speaking to them. 14 One woman who listened was Lydia, the owner of an exclusive retail store that sold elegant clothing in the city of Thyatira. She worshiped God, who enlightened her mind to understand the significance of what Paul said. 15 Once she and her family and staff partook of the Remedy and publicly demonstrated the beginning of their new life of love by being symbolically immersed in water, she invited us to her home. She said, "If you accept me as a true member of the Lord's spiritual health-care team, then come and stay at my home." She was so persuasive that we couldn't say 'no.'

Ac 16:16 On one occasion, while heading to our prayer retreat, we ran into a slave girl who was a medium channeling the foretellings of a fallen angel. She earned a lot of money for her masters by fortune-telling. 17 The girl hounded us everywhere, shouting, "These men are the agents of the Most High God! They have the Remedy and are telling you how to be eternally healed." 18 She kept doing this day after day. Finally, Paul had had enough of this distraction, so he turned to her and said to the fallen angel, "In harmony with the character, methods, and principles of Jesus Christ, I command you to free her, and don't trouble her again!" Instantly, the fallen angel left, and her mind became clear.

Ac 16:19 When her slave masters realized she could no longer make them money, they dragged Paul and Silas into the city square to face the authorities. 20 They hauled them before the city officials and said, "These men are Jewish insurrectionists and are stirring up trouble 21 by promoting beliefs contrary to Roman law and custom."

Ac 16:22 The crowd that had gathered joined in jeering and shouting against Paul and Silas, so the officials ordered them stripped and beaten. 23 After being flogged, they were thrown in prison. The jailer was ordered to guard them tightly, 24 so he put them in a dungeon with no outer wall and chained their feet to blocks.

Ac 16:25 It was near midnight; Paul and Silas were praying and singing, and the other prisoners were listening when 26 an earthquake hit. It was so powerful that the foundations of the prison moved. The prison doors burst open, and all of the prisoners' chains fell off. 27 When the jailer awoke and saw the prison doors open, he thought the prisoners had escaped, so he drew his sword, intending to kill himself. 28 But Paul shouted, "Stop, don't hurt yourself! No one has escaped. We are all here!"

Ac 16:29 The jailer grabbed a light and rushed in to see for himself. He fell down in front of Paul and Silas, shaking with relief. 30 He then brought them out of their cells and asked, "Sirs, what must I do in order to be healed from sin and selfishness?"

Ac 16:31 They told him, "Trust the Lord Jesus. Open your heart to him and he will heal you from sin and selfishness. This healing is for you and your entire household." 32 Then they taught him and his entire household the truth about God, his character, methods, and principles. 33 Though it was the middle of the night, the jailer cleaned and bandaged their wounds. Then he and his family, having opened their hearts to

Jesus and partaken of the Remedy, demonstrated the beginning of their new life of love by being symbolically immersed in water. ³⁴ The jailer then took them home and prepared a meal for them. He was overwhelmed with joy because he and his entire family had come to know and trust God.

Ac 16:35 That morning, after dawn, the city officials sent officers with an order for the jailer to release Paul and Silas. ³⁶ The jailer told Paul, "The city officials have ordered you and Silas to be released. You are free to go. Godspeed."

Ac 16:37 But Paul said to the officers, "Not so fast. They had us publicly flogged without a trial and locked us in prison, even though we are Roman citizens. And now they want us to slip quietly out of town so everyone will believe their actions were appropriate. No way. If they want us to leave, they need to come down and personally escort us out, demonstrating their mistake."

Ac 16:38 When the officers reported back to the city officials that Paul and Silas were Roman citizens, they became afraid. ³⁹ They came to apologize and acknowledge that they were wrong, and personally escorted them out of prison. Then they asked them to leave the city. ⁴⁰ After leaving prison, Paul and Silas went to Lydia's house, where they encouraged the members of the Lord's spiritual health-care team. When that was done, they left the city.

17 After traveling through Amphipolis and Apollonia, they arrived in Thessalonica, where there was a Jewish synagogue. ² As Paul had done his entire life, he went to synagogue on Sabbath. And for three Sabbaths he reasoned with them, explaining to them how the Scriptures ³ absolutely teach that the only way for the Messiah to save humanity was for him to suffer, die, and rise from the dead. Then he told them, "This Jesus that I am telling you about is the Messiah!" ⁴ The truth convinced some of the Jews, who then partook of the Remedy and joined Paul and Silas, as did a large number of the Greeks who loved God, as well as many of the influential women.

Ac 17:5 But the Jews who rejected the truth were envious: they recruited some street thugs from the marketplace, formed a mob, and started a riot. They marched on Jason's home, hoping to find Paul and Silas in order to drag them before the mob. ⁶ Not finding them there, they grabbed Jason and some other members of the Lord's spiritual health-care team and dragged them before the city officials. They shouted: "Paul and Silas are infamous troublemakers who have traveled all over the world stirring up dissention! They have now come here, ⁷ and Jason put them up at his home and is in collusion with them. They are trying to undermine the authority of Caesar, teaching that there is another king we should follow, named Jesus." ⁸ These accusations caused the crowd and city officials to become very upset. ⁹ They required Jason and the others to post a bond, and then let them go.

Ac 17:10 Once it was dark outside, the team members slipped Paul and Silas out of town and sent them to Berea. When they arrived there, they went to the Jewish synagogue. ¹¹ The Jews at Berea were of a more mature character than those in Thessalonica, for rather than feeling threatened, they opened their minds to grow in truth. They received the Remedy eagerly and examined the Scripture each day to verify that what Paul said was true. ¹² Many of the Jews believed and partook of the Remedy, as did a large number of influential Greek women and many Greek men.

Ac 17:13 When the Jews in Thessalonica heard that Paul was distributing the Remedy in Berea, they marched right over and incited a mob to begin public protests. [14] The Lord's team members immediately sent Paul to the coast, but Silas and Timothy remained in Berea. [15] The men who escorted Paul to Athens returned to Berea with instructions for Silas and Timothy to join Paul as soon as possible.

Ac 17:16 While Paul was waiting for them in Athens, he became distraught because so many people's minds were being ruined by the worship of a plethora of idols. [17] So he went to the synagogue, sharing the Remedy and reasoning with the Jews and Greeks who loved God. Day after day, he went to the market and reasoned with whomever was there, sharing the Remedy wherever he went. [18] It was there that he met a group of Epicurean and Stoic philosophy professors, and they discussed these issues at length. Some of them discounted Paul as an "ignorant know-it-all," but others were intrigued and said, "He seems to know something about foreign gods." They said this because Paul was telling them about the Remedy procured by Jesus, and the resurrection to eternal life. [19] They invited him to present his ideas at a meeting at the Areopagus. They said, "Will you tell us about this new philosophy you are advocating? [20] We've never heard anything like it. Please explain it to us in detail." [21] (Listening to the newest philosophy and debating the latest ideas was a favorite pastime for the Athenians and many foreigners who lived there).

Ac 17:22 So Paul took the stage at the meeting of the Areopagus and said: "People of Athens! I see that you are very conscientious people who take your religious beliefs seriously. [23] As I walked through your city, I noted your points of worship, and I found an altar with this inscription: 'To an Unknown God.' It is this unknown God that I am here to tell you about.

Ac 17:24 "The God who built the fabric of the cosmos, including this world and everything in it, is Master of heaven and earth and does not live in shrines built by created beings. [25] Human beings do not provide for him — as if there was anything he needed. No; he is the source of all and gives of himself for our good. From him come life, health, and everything else. [26] He created the human species in one individual, and from that one man all human beings, from all the nations in the world, have descended. He provided the entire earth for us to inhabit, and created time and space for us to live within. [27] He did all of this so that human beings would experience the joy of discovering him—actually reaching out and connecting with him, for he is near to each one of us. [28] As some of your own poets have said,

'In union with him
   we live and move,
   and have existence.
We are his offspring.'

Ac 17:29 "So, since we are the offspring of God, how can God be an inanimate, lifeless object made by human beings out of gold, silver or stone? [30] God didn't expect any better when you didn't know any better, but now God has provided the evidence—so you do know better—and calls all humanity to a renewed mind and unity with him. [31] For he has set a time when all humanity will be accurately diagnosed, defects from his design will be permanently eliminated, and all creation will be set right by the Man whom he has selected to be the Remedy. He has proven it by raising this Man from the dead."

Ac 17:32 When they heard him mention the resurrection, some scoffed, but others said, "We would like to hear more about this." [33] With that, Paul left the meeting. [34] A few people, including Dionysius, who was a member of the Areopagus, a woman named Damaris, and a number of others accepted what Paul taught, partook of the Remedy, and trusted Jesus.

18

After this, Paul left Athens and went to Corinth. ²At Corinth he met Aquila, a Jew who was from Pontus but had left Italy with his wife Priscilla because Claudius ordered all Jews to leave Rome. Paul visited them, ³and when he discovered that they were tentmakers, just as he was, he stayed and worked with them. ⁴But every Sabbath he went to the synagogue and reasoned with Jews and Greeks, trying to persuade them to take the Remedy.

Ac 18:5 Once Timothy and Silas arrived from Macedonia, Paul used all his time to preach and teach, trying to persuade the Jews that Jesus was the Messiah. ⁶But when the Jews rejected the truth and began misrepresenting Paul and speaking evil of Jesus, he demonstrated his heartbreaking indignation by shaking the dust off his clothing, and said, "Your deaths are your own fault! I have fulfilled my duty by bringing you the Remedy to your terminal condition. From now on I will take the Remedy to the Gentiles."

Ac 18:7 Paul turned around and left the synagogue, and to demonstrate that he meant what he said, went straight to the home of Titius Justus, a Gentile who worshiped God and lived next to the synagogue. ⁸Crispus, the chief administrator of the synagogue, along with his entire household, partook of the Remedy and trusted in Jesus; and many others in Corinth who heard Paul also partook of the Remedy, trusted in Jesus, and demonstrated the beginning of a new life of love by being immersed in water.

Ac 18:9 The Lord came to Paul in a vision one night and said to him: "Don't be afraid to share the Remedy; keep on speaking, preaching, teaching—and don't quit. ¹⁰I am with you, and nobody is going to physically assault you or injure you; for I have many people in this city who trust me and have partaken of the Remedy." ¹¹So Paul stayed for eighteen months and spread the truth about God and the Remedy of Jesus.

Ac 18:12 During Gallio's rule as proconsul of Achaia, the Jews banded together to oppose Paul and brought him into the Roman court. ¹³They alleged, "This man is teaching a religion that is not approved by the laws of Rome."

Ac 18:14 Paul was about to speak when Gallio said to the Jews, "If your complaint was about a crime or injustice, then this court would hear your arguments, ¹⁵but since your concern is a matter of interpreting Scripture—you must settle this matter yourselves. I will not judge such issues." ¹⁶So he dismissed their case and had them thrown out of the court. ¹⁷Then the crowd attacked Sosthenes, the leader of the synagogue, and beat him severely in front of the court, but Gallio didn't show the least concern.

Ac 18:18 Paul remained in Corinth for a while, then left the Lord's team members and sailed for Syria. Priscilla and Aquila went with him. Before sailing, he cut his hair at Cenchrea, in accordance with a vow he had taken. ¹⁹Upon arriving in Ephesus, Paul left Priscilla and Aquila and went to the synagogue to engage the Jews in a reasonable examination of the evidence about Jesus. ²⁰When they invited him to stay longer, he declined. ²¹But as he was leaving, he promised, "If it is God's will, I will come back." Then he sailed from Ephesus. ²²Upon arriving at Caesarea, he greeted the members of the Lord's spiritual health-care team, and then went on to Antioch.

Ac 18:23 After staying awhile in Antioch, Paul traveled throughout the region of Galatia and Phrygia, teaching the Lord's interns.

Ac 18:24 A Jew named Apollos, who was born in Alexandria, came to Ephesus. He was a powerful speaker with an incredible knowledge of the Scriptures. ²⁵He had studied the truth of God's design, methods and principles, and presented with incredible effectiveness the truth about the Remedy of Jesus, even though he had only experienced the immersion in water of John. 26 He spoke powerfully in the synagogue. Priscilla and Aquila heard him, and then invited him to their home, where they explained to him God's healing plan in greater detail.

Ac 18:27 Apollos wanted to go to Achaia, and the Lord's team members thought that it was a great idea, so they wrote to the interns there asking them to welcome him. Once there, he was a great help to those who had partaken of the Remedy and trusted Jesus, 28 for he consistently defeated the Jews in public debates, proving from the Scriptures that Jesus was the Messiah—the Savior of the world.

19 While Apollos was in Corinth, Paul journeyed inland to Ephesus. There he found some of the Lord's interns 2 and asked them, "When you accepted Jesus as Messiah, did you receive the Holy Spirit who applies into your hearts and minds what Jesus achieved?" They replied, "No, we didn't even know there is an inner working of the Holy Spirit."

Ac 19:3 So Paul asked, "What immersion in water did you participate in?"

They answered, "The immersion by John."

Ac 19:4 Paul explained, "John immersed people in water to symbolize repentance, which is the preparation of the heart to receive the Remedy. He told people to trust the One coming after him, the One with the Remedy—that is, Jesus." 5 When they heard the truth about the Remedy of Jesus, they were immersed into the character of the Lord Jesus. 6 Paul placed his hands on their heads, and they were filled with the Holy Spirit. They began presenting the truth about God, and the Remedy of Jesus, in many languages. 7 There were about twelve people in all.

Ac 19:8 For three months Paul went to the synagogue and spoke out powerfully.

He persuasively presented the evidence revealing God's kingdom of love, 9 but some of them hardened their hearts, dug in their heels, and refused to believe the truth. They publicly ridiculed the Remedy as the only way to be healed, so Paul left them. He took the interns with him and began instructing them daily in the lecture hall of Tyrannus. 10 He continued teaching there for two years, so that all of the Jews and non-Jews living in the province of Asia heard about the Remedy of Jesus.

Ac 19:11 God's healing love flowed through Paul in amazing ways. 12 Scarfs, napkins, or other pieces of cloth that had touched Paul were taken to the sick, and when the fabric touched the sick, their illness was cured, and any evil influences departed.

Ac 19:13 Some Jewish exorcists who went around driving out evil angels thought they could use the name of Jesus like a magic incantation to free those whose minds were dominated by demons. They would say, "In the name of Jesus, whom Paul preaches, I command you to leave." 14 Sceva, a Jewish chief priest, had seven sons who were doing this. 15 One day, they were trying it when an evil angel mocked them: "I know Jesus, and I know Paul, but who are you?" 16 Then the man whose mind was possessed by an evil angel attacked them, and overpowered them all. He beat them so badly that they ran out of the house naked and bleeding.

Ac 19:17 When news of this spread throughout Ephesus, both Jews and non-Jews were overcome with fear, and the name of the Lord Jesus was given much more respect. 18 Many people who believed the truth about Jesus confessed their evil deeds publicly.

19 A large number of people who had practiced witchcraft, black magic and sorcery brought their books of magic and burned them publicly in a large bonfire. When they calculated the value of the books burned, it totaled fifty thousand silver coins (and one coin

was a day's wage). [20] With events like this, the message of the Remedy of Jesus spread widely and kept growing.

Ac 19:21 After all of this occurred, Paul decided to go to Jerusalem, via Macedonia and Achaia. He said, "After Jerusalem, I must visit Rome." [22] He sent two of his aides, Timothy and Erastus, ahead of him to Macedonia, while he remained a little longer in Asia.

Ac 19:23 But before Paul left Ephesus, a great uproar arose about the Remedy. [24] Demetrius, a silversmith who made a lot of money making silver shrines of Artemis, employed a large number of craftsmen. [25] He called them together, along with others whose income depended on their business, and said: "Friends, you know what a good income we make from this business. [26] And you have heard that this fellow Paul has come along teaching people that the gods we make with our own hands are not gods at all. He has convinced large numbers of people of this—here and all across the province of Asia. [27] This is not only an attack on our livelihoods, but more so, it threatens to destroy the temple of the great goddess Artemis; and the goddess herself, who is worshiped all over the world, will be robbed of her glorious majesty."

Ac 19:28 They became so agitated upon hearing this, that they began chanting, "Ephesus, the state of Artemis the Great! Ephesus, the state of Artemis the Great!" [29] The uproar spread throughout the entire city. A mob seized Gaius and Aristarchus, two men traveling with Paul from Macedonia, and marched as a group into the amphitheater. [30] Paul wanted to go and speak to the crowd, but the interns would not allow it. [31] Even some of the city officials, who were friends of Paul, sent messages, warning him not to go to the amphitheater.

Ac 19:32 The mob was frenzied. People were yelling many different things all at once, but most didn't even know why they were there. [33] The Jews pushed Alexander to the front, and some people in the crowd began shouting at him, telling him what to say. He held up his hands, trying to silence the crowd in order to present a defense. [34] But when the mob realized he was a Jew, they began chanting, "Ephesus, the state of Artemis the Great! Ephesus, the state of Artemis the Great!" This went on for about two hours.

Ac 19:35 Finally, the city clerk managed to quiet the mob, and said, "People of Ephesus, the entire world knows that Ephesus is the state of Artemis the Great, who came down from heaven, and that we guard her temple. [36] Since these facts are irrefutable, you should quiet down and not do anything rash. [37] Why have you brought these men here? They have done no wrong. They have not robbed temples nor spoken against our goddess. [38] If Demetrius and his trade union have a complaint against anyone, then they should file charges in court, and let the matter be settled there. [39] If you have any other issues, they too need to be settled in a legal assembly, not by mob action. [40] What you have done has put us in danger of being charged with rioting, and if we are charged, we won't have any defense, for there is no reason for this uproar you have incited." [41] After saying this, he sent them home.

20

Once the protests died down, Paul met with the interns, gave them some departing words of encouragement, and left for Macedonia. [2] As he journeyed through the region, he spoke uplifting words to the people, and finally arrived in Greece, [3] where he stayed for three months. Just as he was about to leave for Syria, he discovered that the Jews hatched a plot against him, so instead, he decided to go back through Macedonia. [4] He didn't go alone. Those who went with him were Sopater son of Pyrrhus of Berea, Aristarchus and Secundus from

Thessalonica, Gaius from Derbe, Timothy, and Tychus and Trophimus from Asia, ⁵ but they went ahead and waited for us in Troas. ⁶ We traveled by boat, sailing from Philippi after the Passover, and five days later met up with the others in Troas, where we stayed for a week.

Ac 20:7 On Saturday night (the beginning of the first day of the week), we met together for a meal. Paul spoke to the people who gathered, and because he wanted to leave on Sunday morning, he stayed up talking to them until midnight. ⁸ As there were many lamps in the upstairs room, the air was warm and smoky. ⁹ A young man named Eutychus was sitting on a window ledge, and because of the late hour, he became sleepy as Paul talked on and on. He fell asleep and then fell out of the third-story window, and died when he hit the ground. ¹⁰ Paul went down, lay on him, gave him a big hug, and said, "Don't worry. He lives!" ¹¹ Then he went back upstairs and had some more food. After talking until dawn, he left. ¹² The people took Eutychus home alive, and were themselves invigorated.

Ac 20:13 The rest of us went on ahead and took a ship to Assos, where Paul was to join us. He had arranged for this as he planned to walk there. ¹⁴ He came aboard in Assos, and we sailed to Mitylene. ¹⁵ The next day we sailed to Chios. The day after that, we went across to Samos, and the following day to Miletus. ¹⁶ Paul decided to sail past Ephesus in order to avoid Asia, hoping to make it to Jerusalem by Pentecost.

Ac 20:17 While in Miletus, Paul sent word to Ephesus for the leaders of the Lord's spiritual health-care team to come to him. ¹⁸ When they arrived, he said to them: "You know me, and you know how I lived the entire time I was with you, from the first day I arrived in Asia. ¹⁹ I promoted the Remedy of Jesus with a humble heart—and was grief stricken for those who refused it—despite being tempted otherwise by the constant plotting of the Jews. ²⁰ You know very well that I have not held back any resource that would be beneficial for your healing, but have taken the Remedy door to door. ²¹ I have made it clear that whether a Jew or non-Jew, all humans must have a change of heart toward God and come to trust our Lord Jesus.

Ac 20:22 "Now, I can't shake the deep conviction in my inmost being that I have to go to Jerusalem, but I have no idea what will happen to me there. ²³ I do know that the Holy Spirit has warned me that I will face imprisonment, abuse and hardship in every city to which I go. ²⁴ But trying to save myself is not my motive; no, what is important to me is finishing the race, and completing the mission the Lord Jesus has committed to me—the job of sharing God's gracious Remedy.

Ac 20:25 "So, this is it; as far as I know, none of you with whom I have shared the Remedy of God's kingdom of love will ever see me again. ²⁶ So let me be clear: If any of you are lost, it is not because I have failed to share God's Remedy. ²⁷ I have taught you God's entire healing plan, ²⁸ so keep your minds sharp and lead the flock in advancing truth, as the Holy Spirit has put you in position to do. ²⁹ I know that as soon as I am gone, savage wolves are going to attack; they will infect your minds with lies about God and cause the flock to be torn apart. ³⁰ Even some of your own members will rise up and present distortions about God, splitting and dividing the flock into more and more fragmented groups. ³¹ So guard your minds! Remember your three years of training with me, the warnings I taught you day after day, and how I poured my heart out to you.

Ac 20:32 "Now I entrust you to God, whose gracious truth is transformational and able to rebuild your character to be like Christ's, and give you the promised inheritance of eternal life, joining all those who are fully healed.

[33] I never sought any compensation from anyone, whether money or fine clothing. [34] As you well know, I have worked to support myself and provide for my co-workers. [35] In all my actions, I demonstrated to you how to live in harmony with God's design for life— the law of love. By hard work, we support the weak, remembering the truth the Lord Jesus taught: 'It is a greater blessing to give than to receive.'"

Acts 20:36 After saying this, they all knelt down and he spoke with God. [37] They wept as they hugged him goodbye, [38] terribly saddened by his statement that they would never see him again. Then they walked him to his ship.

21 After heart-wrenching goodbyes, we sailed straight to Cos. The following day we went to Rhodes, and then on to Patara, [2] where we found passage on a ship going to Phoenicia. [3] We sighted Cyprus, sailed south of it and on to Syria, landing at Tyre, where our ship was to unload cargo. [4] Finding the Lord's interns there, we spent a week with them. Impressed by the Holy Spirit, they warned Paul not to go on to Jerusalem. [5] But at the end of the week, we left and continued toward Jerusalem. All the interns, along with their wives and children, accompanied us out of the city. We all knelt together on the beach and spoke with the Lord. [6] After saying goodbye, we boarded the ship, and they went back to their homes.

Ac 21:7 We continued our journey from Tyre, arriving in Ptolemais, where we greeted our fellow workers and friends of God, and spent a day with them. [8] We left the next day and arrived in Caesarea, where we stayed at the home of Philip the disseminator of the Remedy, one of the seven chosen in Jerusalem to distribute food. [9] He had four unmarried daughters who were spokespersons for God.

Ac 21:10 Several days after we arrived at Philip's place, one of the Lord's spokespersons, Agabus, came down from Judea. [11] Coming right over to us, he took Paul's belt and tied his own hands and feet, and said, "The Holy Spirit sent me to warn you with this message: 'If you go to Jerusalem, the Jews will tie you up like this and turn you over to the non-Jewish authorities.'"

Ac 21:12 Upon hearing this, we, along with all our friends there, begged Paul not to go to Jerusalem. [13] But Paul said, "Why are you crying like this? Are you trying to undermine my resolve? Don't worry, I am ready not only to be imprisoned, but also to die in Jerusalem to promote the true character of the Lord Jesus." [14] Once we understood that he would not change his mind, we stopped trying and said, "It's in God's hands. May his will be done."

Ac 21:15 So we packed up and headed to Jerusalem. [16] Some of the interns from Caesarea went with us and took us to the home of Mnason, where we stayed. He was from Cyprus and had become one of the Lord's interns early on.

Ac 21:17 When we arrived in Jerusalem, the friends of God welcomed us warmly. [18] The next day, Paul and our whole team went to see James, and all the church leaders were present there. [19] They exchanged greetings, and Paul gave a detailed account of what God had accomplished amongst the non-Jews through his ministry.

Ac 21:20 This news brought joy to them, and they praised God. Then they said to Paul, "Tens of thousands of Jews have believed, yet they all remain slavishly devoted to enacting the little drama, adhering to the script. [21] They have been told that you teach the Jews living among the non-Jews that they no longer need to enact the drama and follow the script given through Moses, such as circumcising their children or adhering to other symbolic rituals. [22] What are we going to do? It's only a matter of time and they will know you are here. ²³ So follow our instructions. There are four men who have taken a vow in harmony with the script given through Moses. ²⁴ Join these four men and participate in the enactment of their purification ritual; pay their expenses so they can shave their heads, just as the script describes. Then everyone will know that what has been said about you is not true, and you continue to follow the script and act out its lessons. ²⁵ As far as the non-Jews who have partaken of the Remedy, we have sent them our decision that they should abstain from meat sacrificed to idols, from blood, from the meat of strangled animals, and from sexual immorality."

Ac 21:26 The next day, Paul went with the four men and acted out the purification ritual according to the script. Then he went to the temple to notify them of the date when the purification enactment would end, and the ritual offering for each of them would be made.

Ac 21:27 As the end of the seven-day purification period approached, some Jews from Asia spotted Paul at the temple. They started a riot and seized him, ²⁸ shouting, "People of Israel, help us! This is the man who teaches people all over the world that our ways are outdated, the law of Moses is obsolete, and the temple is unimportant. He has even brought Greeks into the temple and desecrated this holy place!" ²⁹ (They had seen Trophimus the Ephesian in the city with Paul and assumed that Paul brought him to the temple.)

Ac 21:30 The riot spread out across the entire city, and people came running from all directions. They dragged Paul out of the temple area, and the gates were immediately shut. ³¹ As the mob was attempting to kill Paul, the Roman commander got word of the riot consuming the city. ³² With his officers and soldiers, he immediately ran down to the crowd. When the rioters saw the soldiers, they stopped beating Paul.

Ac 21:33 The commander ordered Paul arrested and bound with two chains, then he asked who he was and what he had done. ³⁴ But the crowd was in a frenzy, with multiple people shouting at once. Since the commander could not get the truth of what happened, he ordered Paul taken to the barracks. ³⁵ As Paul approached the steps, the mob became so violent that the soldiers had to carry him to keep him safe from attacks. ³⁶ The mob followed, shouting, "Take him away!"

Ac 21:37 The soldiers were about to take Paul into the barracks when he asked the commander, "May I speak with you?"

"Do you speak Greek?" he replied. ³⁸ "Aren't you that Egyptian who started a rebellion here a while back and then fled to the desert with four thousand terrorists?"

Ac 21:39 Paul answered, "I am a Jew, from Tarsus in Cilicia, still a citizen of that important city. Please, will you allow me to speak to the people?"

Ac 21:40 With permission from the commander, Paul stood on the steps and motioned with his arms for silence, and when they had quieted, he spoke to them in Aramaic.

22 "My fellow Jews, let me answer the charges brought against me." Ac 22:2 When they heard him speaking in Aramaic, they became silent and listened. Paul said, ³ "I am a Jew, born in Tarsus of Cilicia, but I grew up here in Jerusalem. I was one of Gamaliel's students, and received a doctorate in theology with special emphasis on the Law of Moses, and have been just as devoted to God as anyone here today. ⁴ I was ruthless in my attack against those who followed this way of salvation, willing to kill if needed. I arrested anyone who I thought was associated with this movement, men or women, and threw them in prison ⁵ (as the high priest or anyone of the High Court can confirm). I even got written authorization to take to the Jewish authorities in

Damascus, and went there intent on arresting these people and bringing them back to Jerusalem to be punished.

Ac 22:6 "As I approached Damascus, around noon, a blazing light from heaven shone all around me. 7 As I fell to the ground, I heard a voice say to me, "Saul! Saul! Why are you attacking me?"

Ac 22:8 I asked, "Who are you, Lord?"

"The voice replied, 'I am Jesus of Nazareth, whom you are warring against.' 9 My traveling companions saw the light, but they didn't understand what the voice said to me.

Ac 22:10 "'What do you want from me, Lord?' I asked.

"The Lord said, 'Stand up and go on to Damascus. There, you will be told the assignment I have for you.' 11 But when I got up, I was blind, so instead of marching into Damascus, my friends led me, holding my hand.

Ac 22:12 "Once there, Ananias came to see me. He is a devoted man of God, faithful in his observation of all the instructions given through Moses, and highly respected by the Jews living there. 13 Standing next to me, he said, 'Brother Saul, see again!' And immediately I was able to see him.

Ac 22:14 "Then he said, 'The God of our ancestors has chosen you to understand his purpose, methods and principles, and to see the Perfect One and hear him speak. 15 You will be his ambassador to all people, testifying to what you have seen and heard. 16 So don't just sit there; get up and begin your new life of love, and be immersed in water to symbolize the washing away of selfishness and partaking of the Remedy—his perfect character of love.'

Ac 22:17 "After returning to Jerusalem, I was praying at the temple when I was taken away in a vision 18 and saw the Lord speak to me. He said, 'Get up now and leave Jerusalem. Don't delay, for they will not believe your testimony about me.'

Ac 22:19 "I said to the Lord, 'But Lord, these men will take me seriously because they know I went from synagogue to synagogue imprisoning and beating anyone who believed in you. 20 And when your martyr Stephen was killed, I stood there approving, and watching over the coats of those who murdered him.'

Ac 22:21 "But the Lord simply said to me, 'Leave this place. I am sending you far away to take the Remedy to the non-Jewish people of the world.'"

Ac 22:22 The crowd was listening up to this point, but when they heard about God sending Paul with the Remedy to non-Jews, they became enraged and began shouting, "Kill him! Wipe him from the face of the earth! He doesn't deserve to live!"

Ac 22:23 As the crowd escalated toward violence, taking off their coats, shouting and throwing rocks, 24 the commander ordered Paul be taken into the barracks. He ordered that he be flogged, and then questioned to find out why the mob was in such an uproar. 25 As they tied him to the flogging post, Paul asked the centurion, "Is it legal to flog a Roman citizen who hasn't been found guilty of a crime?"

Ac 22:26 Upon hearing this, the centurion reported to the commander, asking, "What do you want to do? This man is a citizen of Rome."

Ac 22:27 The commander questioned Paul, "Be truthful: are you a Roman citizen?" "Yes, I am," Paul replied.

Ac 22:28 The commander challenged him: "How is that? The price I paid for citizenship was quite high." Paul answered, "I was born a citizen."

Ac 22:29 Upon hearing this, the interrogators left the room immediately. The commander, realizing he had chained a Roman citizen, began to worry.

Ac 22:30 The commander wanted to find out the truth about why Paul was being accosted by the Jews, so the next day he released Paul and ordered the leading priests and Jewish High Court members to assemble. Then he had Paul brought before them.

23 Paul, looking directly at the leaders of the Jewish High Court, said, "My fellow Israelites, all I have done I have done to honor God, and have fulfilled my duties to him with a clear conscience." ²Upon hearing this, the high priest Ananias ordered his aides to strike Paul on the mouth. ³Paul blurted out, "I hope God strikes you down, you white-washed impediment to truth! You sit there pretending to follow the law in judgment of me, yet you command I be struck—in violation of the law!"

Ac 23:4 Those standing near Paul gasped: "How dare you insult God's high priest like that!"

Ac 23:5 Paul humbly said, "I'm sorry, brothers. I didn't know he was the high priest; for the Scripture says:

'Don't speak badly about the ruler of your people.'"

Ac 23:6 Paul knew that some of them were Sadducees and others Pharisees, so he called out to the High Court, "Brothers, hear me: I am a Pharisee, the son of a Pharisee, and I am on trial because of my hope in the resurrection of the dead." ⁷Instantly, upon hearing this, an argument erupted between the Pharisees and the Sadducees, and the court was split. ⁸(The Sadducees teach there is no resurrection, no angels, and no demons, but the Pharisees teach all are real.)

Ac 23:9 They began arguing loudly at each other, then some of the theologians of the Pharisee school stood up and, shouting over the others, said, "We don't find anything wrong with this man. What if an angel has spoken to him?" ¹⁰Their disagreement became so violent that the commander became afraid that Paul would be attacked and killed. He ordered his troops to remove Paul by force and secure him in the barracks.

Ac 23:11 The next night, the Lord came to Paul and said, "Don't be afraid. Just as you have told the truth about me here in Jerusalem, you must now tell the truth about me in Rome."

Ac 23:12 The next morning, some of the Jews formed an assassination team dedicated to killing Paul. They bound themselves together with an oath not to eat or drink until Paul was dead. ¹³More than forty men took part in this plot. ¹⁴They conspired with the chief priests and community leaders, instructing them, "We have committed with a solemn vow not to eat or drink until we have killed Paul. ¹⁵So get the High Court to tell the commander that there are more questions that need answering, and request that he brings Paul before you. We will have an ambush set to kill him before he gets here."

Ac 23:16 But when Paul's nephew (his sister's son) heard about this plot, he went to the barracks and told Paul.

Ac 23:17 Paul immediately called one of the centurions and said, "Please take this young man to the commander; he has important information to tell him." ¹⁸So he did. The centurion said to the commander, "The prisoner Paul asked me to bring this young man to you because he has something important to tell you."

Ac 23:19 The commander led the young man aside and asked, "What is it you want to tell me?"

Ac 23:20 He said, "The Jews have plotted to kill Paul. They are going to ask you to bring him before the High Court on the pretext of needing to answer more questions. ²¹But don't do it, because more than forty men have set an ambush to kill him. They have taken an oath not to eat or drink until he is dead. They are all set, just waiting for you to agree to their request."

Ac 23:22 The commander dismissed him with the warning, "Don't tell anyone you have told me about their plot."

Ac 23:23 Then he ordered two centurions: "Prepare a detachment of two hundred soldiers, seventy horsemen and two hundred spearmen, and march to Caesarea tonight at nine o'clock. ²⁴ Give Paul a horse, and ensure he is taken safely to Governor Felix."

Ac 23:25 He wrote this letter:

Ac 23:26 "Claudius Lysias,

to the Honorable Governor Felix:

Greetings!

Ac 23:27 This man Paul was mobbed by the Jews and they were about to kill him, but when I learned he was a Roman citizen, I ordered my troops to rescue him. ²⁸ In order to discover why they were accosting him, I brought him before their High Court. ²⁹ I found that their accusations were over their theology and religious rules and views, but there was no charge against him that warranted death or imprisonment. ³⁰ When I learned that an assassination plot had been set against him, I immediately sent him to you. I also ordered his accusers to present their case against him."

Ac 23:31 The soldiers, following their orders, took Paul out of the city during the night and made it as far as Antipatris. ³² The next day the cavalry went on with Paul, while the foot-soldiers returned to the barracks. ³³ When the cavalry arrived in Caesarea, they handed Paul over to the governor, along with the letter. ³⁴ The governor read the letter and then asked what province Paul was from. After being told he was from Cilicia, ³⁵ he said, "When your accusers arrive, I will hear your case." Then he ordered Paul be secured under guard in Herod's palace.

24

Five days later, the high priest Ananias, some of the religious leaders, and a lawyer named Tertullus went to Caesarea and put their charges against Paul before the governor. ² Once Paul was brought in, Tertullus presented his case before Felix: "Because of your vision, wisdom and the reforms instituted in our nation, we have enjoyed a long period of peace and prosperity. ³ Most Honorable Felix, we acknowledge our gratitude to you constantly, everywhere we go. ⁴ Therefore, we don't want to take too much of your time, but request your kind indulgence to listen to this brief account.

Ac 24:5 "We have determined that this man is an insurrectionist, traveling all over the world instigating riots amongst the Jews. He is one of the ringleaders of the Nazarene cult ⁶ and even tried to defile our holy temple—so we seized him, and would have judged him as our law demands, ⁷ but commander Lysias took him by force ⁸ and ordered his accusers to appear before you. If you question him yourself, you will discover that all the charges we have made against him are true."

Ac 24:9 The Jews then spoke up and said they agreed with the charges cited by Tertullus.

Ac 24:10 When the governor indicated for Paul to speak, he answered the accusations: "I know you have ruled over our nation for many years and are familiar with our customs, and therefore I'm glad you will hear my defense. ¹¹ You can easily confirm that it was only twelve days ago when I arrived in Jerusalem to worship. ¹² I argued with no one at the temple, nor did I incite any disturbance at any worship center or any other place in the city, as my accusers well know. ¹³ They cannot provide any evidence to support the charges they have brought against me. ¹⁴ But this I admit: I worship the God of our ancestors, following the Way of unfolding truth that the Jews call a cult. I believe all things that are in agreement with the books of Moses and the Prophets, ¹⁵ and I hold to the same hope in God as these people do—that there will be a resurrection of both the healed and the terminal. ¹⁶ So I am dedicated to living in harmony with God's design for life, keeping my conscience clear before God and people.

Ac 24:17 "After being away from Jerusalem for several years, I returned with gifts for the needy and offerings for God's cause. 18 I was completing a ceremony of purification when they found me in the temple courts, quietly praying. There was no crowd or commotion of any kind. 19 But there were some Jews from Asia there who instigated this entire issue, and they should be here to present their charges if they have any evidence to present. 20 Or these men here accusing me should present evidence of whatever crime they claim I committed while I stood in their High Court— 21 unless I am here for shouting in their presence: 'I am on trial today because I believe in the resurrection from the dead!'"

Ac 24:22 But Felix, who knew all about the expanding way of worshiping God, rather than giving a ruling, adjourned the proceedings. He said, "When Commander Lysias arrives, I will decide your case." 23 Then he ordered the centurion to guard Paul, but to also give him some freedom and allow his friends to provide for his needs.

Ac 24:24 Several days later, Felix and his wife Drusilla, who was Jewish, sent for Paul and listened to his presentation about the Remedy of Jesus Christ. 25 As Paul taught them about the restoration to God's righteous design for life, with recovery of self-mastery and the future diagnosis of all people, Felix became afraid and said, "That's all for now. You may leave. When I have the time, I will call for you." 26 He was hoping Paul would offer him a bribe, so he sent for him often and talked with him.

Ac 24:27 After two years of this, Felix left office, but because he wanted to remain popular with the Jews, he left Paul in prison. He was replaced by Porcius Festus.

25 Three days after his arrival in the province, Festus traveled from Caesarea to Jerusalem, 2 where the chief priests and Jewish leaders assembled before him and presented their charges against Paul. 3 They desperately wanted Festus to transfer Paul to Jerusalem because they were plotting an ambush to kill him on the way, so they requested Festus to do them a favor and transfer Paul to Jerusalem. 4 But Festus told them, "Paul is secure in Caesarea, and I will soon be heading there. 5 If he has done anything wrong, then arrange for some of your leaders to come with me and present your charges there."

Ac 25:6 About eight to ten days later, Festus returned to Caesarea. The next day he opened court and ordered that Paul be brought before him. 7 With Paul in court, the Jews who had come from Jerusalem surrounded him and began making all types of serious charges against him, none of which they could prove.

Ac 25:8 Then Paul defended himself: "I haven't done anything wrong. I haven't broken any Jewish civil law, temple law, or Roman law."

Ac 25:9 Festus, wanting to gain favor with the Jews, asked Paul, "Are you willing to go to Jerusalem and stand trial before me there?"

Ac 25:10 Paul answered, "Am I not now standing before Caesar's justice? Is it not here that my case should be tried? I have committed no crime against the Jews, as you very well know. 11 If I were guilty of a capital crime, I would not refuse to die. But I am not guilty of any of the charges brought against me by these Jews, therefore it is not right to hand me over to them. I appeal to Caesar!"

Ac 25:12 After Festus consulted with his advisors, he declared, "Since you have appealed to Caesar, then to Caesar you will go!"

Ac 25:13 Several days later, King Agrippa and Bernice arrived at Caesarea to welcome Festus. 14 After spending several days there, Festus brought up Paul's case with them. He said, "I have a man in prison whose case Felix never decided. [15] When I was in Jerusalem, the chief priests and Jewish leaders brought a variety of charges against him and asked me to condemn him.

Ac 25:16 "I told them that Romans don't condemn people without a trial and without an opportunity to face his accusers and present a defense. [17] When they returned here with me, I wanted this case determined quickly, so I convened court the very next day and ordered the man to be brought in. [18] When his accusers presented their complaint, they didn't charge him with any crime I expected. [19] Instead, they disagreed with him on some religious issues and a dead man named Jesus, who Paul claimed was alive. [20] Not being familiar with Jewish culture and religion, I was at a loss how to resolve the matter, so I asked the man if he would be willing to stand trial on these charges before me in Jerusalem. [21] Paul appealed his case to the Emperor, so I ordered that he be held until I could send him to Caesar."

Ac 25:22 Agrippa was intrigued and said to Festus, "I would like to hear for myself what this man has to say." Festus replied, "Very well, I will arrange it for tomorrow."

Ac 25:23 The next day, with a great show of wealth and rank, Agrippa and Bernice entered the courtroom along with high-ranking officials in the military and government. At Festus' command, Paul was brought in. [24] Then Festus said: "King Agrippa, and honored guests present here today, take a look at this man! The Jews have been in an uproar about him. They have petitioned me in Jerusalem and here in Caesarea, shouting that he deserves to die. [25] But my investigation found that he has committed no crimes and doesn't deserve to die. Because he appealed his case to the Emperor, I decided to send him to Rome, [26] but I don't have any specific charges or facts to write to His Majesty about him.

Therefore I have brought him before you and would like your input, especially yours, King Agrippa, so that after this inquiry I might have something specific to write. [27] For it seems unreasonable to me to send him as a prisoner without some specific charges against him."

26

Then Agrippa said to Paul, "You have permission to present your case." Paul motioned with his hands for silence and then began his defense: [2] "King Agrippa, I am thankful that you are here to hear my defense against these allegations of the Jews, [3] because you know Jewish tradition, custom, and theological controversies. So please be patient as I lay out my case.

Ac 26:4 "The Jews know very well that I was raised in my own country, and later—in Jerusalem. [5] They have known me for years and, if they are honest, they can confirm that, by the strictest standards of our people, I lived as a Pharisee and did everything according to their most severe rules. [6] I am on trial now because I believe that what God promised our ancestors has been fulfilled— [7] the promise our twelve tribes long to see fulfilled as they diligently serve God every day. O King, I am being accused because I believe that this promise has been fulfilled. [8] Why should any of you who know the history of our people find it impossible to believe that God raises the dead back to life?

Ac 26:9 "Yes, at one time I too believed it was my duty to do everything in my power to oppose Jesus of Nazareth. [10] And I did just that in Jerusalem. With the approval and backing of the chief priests, I arrested many of his followers, and when they were executed, I voted for them to die. [11] I went from synagogue to synagogue, punishing his followers and trying to force them to curse his name. In my vigilance, I even traveled to other cities to persecute them.

Ac 26:12 "I was on one of these trips, heading to Damascus with arrest warrants from the chief priests. 13 About noon, O King, I was on the road, when a bright light from heaven, brighter than the sun, blazed around me and my traveling companions. 14 We all instantly fell to the ground, and I heard a voice from heaven say to me in Aramaic, 'Oh Saul, why are you persecuting me? Isn't it difficult for you to kick against the thorns?'

Ac 26:15 "I asked, 'Who are you, Lord?' The voice replied, 'I am Jesus, whom you are persecuting. 16 Now stand up, for I have come to you to commission you, as my ambassador, to witness what you have seen of me, and what I will yet show to you. 17 Don't be afraid, for I will rescue you from your own people and from the Gentiles. I am sending you to them 18 to open their minds to the light of truth, and lead them out of the darkness of lies about me—and thus free them from Satan's power and unite them with God—so they might have sin and selfishness remit from their hearts, and be among those who are recreated in righteousness through trust in me.'

Ac 26:19 "So, King Agrippa, what was I to do? I did what I believed was right after such a vision from heaven: 20 First I went to those in Damascus, then to those in Jerusalem, and then—all over Judea, to Jews and non-Jews alike. I told everyone they should turn away from selfishness, love God with their whole heart, and demonstrate their love for God by their acts of service to help others. 21 That is why the Jews seized me in the temple courts and are trying to kill me. 22 But God has been watching over me to this very day, and has brought me here to tell the truth about him to small and great alike. I am only teaching what the prophets and Moses said would happen— 23 that the Messiah would be rejected, suffer, die, and then be the first to rise from the dead to provide the Remedy to his own people and all peoples of the world."

Ac 26:24 When Festus heard this, he interrupted Paul's defense: "Are you crazy, Paul?" he shouted. "You've studied yourself insane!"

Ac 26:25 Paul calmly replied, "I am not insane, most honorable Festus. What I am saying is not only true, it is also reasonable. 26 The king is familiar with all of this, so I am presenting this to him freely, without the need to lay the groundwork for each point. I believe he is aware of all the events that have transpired, because it all happened very publicly. 27 King Agrippa, you believe what the prophets have written, don't you? Surely, you do."

Ac 26:28 Agrippa answered, "Do you think you can convert me to be a Christian in such a short time?"

Ac 26:29 Paul smiled, "No matter how long it takes, I pray to God that not only you, but everyone here listening will become what I am, except retain your freedom, of course."

Ac 26:30 At this, the king, governor, Bernice, and those sitting with them stood up 31 and left the room. While they were talking amongst themselves, they said, "This man hasn't done anything deserving of death or imprisonment."

Ac 26:32 Agrippa said to Festus, "If he hadn't appealed to Caesar, he could have been set free."

27 Once it was decided that we would sail for Italy, Paul, along with some other prisoners, was transferred to the custody of a centurion named Julius, who was a member of the Imperial Regiment. 2 We boarded a ship from Adramyttium, bound for ports along the coast of Asia, and soon put to sea. Aristarchus, a Macedonian from Thessalonica, traveled with us.

Ac 27:3 The next day we made port at Sidon, and Julius, showing kindness to Paul, allowed him to visit his friends so they might provide for his needs. 4 We sailed from there past the lee of Cyprus because the winds were against us. [5] After sailing the open sea off the coast of Cilicia and Pamphylia, we reached Myra in Lycia. [6] There, a centurion found a ship from Alexandria heading for Italy and got us on board. [7] It was slow going for many days, and with great difficulty we finally arrived off Cnidus. When the wind would not permit us to stay on course, we sailed to the lee of Crete, opposite Salmone. [8] It was a rough ride, but we slowly moved along the coast and came to a place near Lasea, called Fair Havens.

Ac 27:9 We had lost a lot of time, and the weather had turned—as it was late in the year, and the Day of Atonement had already past—making sailing dangerous. Paul attempted to warn them: [10] "Men, I have been shown that if we continue on, we will meet disaster and experience great loss to the ship and cargo, and even to our lives." [11] But the centurion, instead of heeding Paul's warning, listened to the advice of the captain and owner of the ship. [12] Since the harbor wasn't suitable for wintering in, the majority determined that it would be best to sail on hoping to reach Phoenix—a harbor in Crete that faces southwest and northwest—and winter there.

Ac 27:13 A gentle south wind began to blow, and they thought the weather favored them, so they set sail along the shore of Crete. [14] But before long, a storm with hurricane-strength winds, called a "northeaster," blew down from the island. [15] The ship couldn't maintain course in such a strong wind, so we gave way and were driven along by it. [16] As we passed the lee of a small island called Cauda, we almost lost the lifeboat, [17] but the men finally got it on board. Next they passed ropes under the ship to hold it together. Afraid of running aground on the sandbars of Syrtis, they put out the sea anchor and let the ship be driven along. [18] The battering from the storm was so severe that the next day they began tossing cargo overboard. [19] By the third day, they were so desperate that they even threw over some of the ship's equipment and supplies. [20] After many days without seeing sun or stars, and with the storm continuing to rage, we finally gave up hope of surviving.

Ac 27:21 After everyone had gone without food for quite some days, Paul stood up before the crew and said, "Men, you would have done well to take my counsel and not sail from Crete. If you had, you would have spared yourself all this loss. [22] So listen to me now: Take courage, because not one of you will die; only the ship will be destroyed. [23] Last night, an angel of the God to whom I belong and whom I serve came to me [24] and said, 'Paul, don't be afraid. You must stand trial before Caesar, and God has protected the lives of all those who sail with you.' [25] So take heart, men, for I trust God. It will happen just as he told me. [26] But we will run aground on one of the islands."

Ac 27:27 On the fourteenth night of the storm, we were still being driven across the Adriatic Sea, when around midnight the sailors sensed we were approaching land. [28] The soundings they took found that the water was a hundred and twenty feet deep. A short time later, the water was only ninety feet deep. [29] Afraid of crashing against the rocks, they dropped four anchors from the stern and prayed for dawn. [30] Some of the sailors were planning on escaping the ship in the lifeboat and lowered it into the sea, but were pretending to lower anchors from the bow. [31] Paul told the centurion and the soldiers, "If these men leave the ship, you will all die." [32] So the soldiers cut the ropes holding the lifeboat and let it fall away.

Ac 27:33 Just before dawn Paul encouraged them to eat. He said, "For the last fourteen days you have been so stressed and worried that you haven't eaten a thing. ³⁴So take a moment and eat something. You will need your strength to survive. Not one of you will even get a scratch." ³⁵After saying this, he took some bread, thanked God for it in front of them all, then broke it and began to eat. ³⁶They all relaxed and ate some food— ³⁷counting everyone, there were two hundred seventy-six of us on board. ³⁸When everyone had had enough to eat, they lightened the ship by throwing the grain into the sea.

Ac 27:39 At dawn, they didn't recognize the place, but saw a bay with a sandy beach, where they decided to run the ship aground if they could. ⁴⁰They cut the anchors loose leaving them in the sea, untied the ropes holding the rudder, hoisted the foresail to the wind, and headed for the beach. ⁴¹But the ship grounded on a sandbar and wouldn't budge. The stern was breaking apart from the pounding surf.

Ac 27:42 The soldiers formed a plan to kill the prisoners to prevent any of them from swimming away and escaping, ⁴³but the centurion, wanting to protect Paul, ordered the soldiers not to do it. He commanded those who could swim to jump in first, and get to the shore. ⁴⁴The rest were to get there floating on planks and pieces of the ship. In this way, everyone reached the land safely.

28 After we were safe and sound on shore, we discovered that the island was called Malta. ²The residents of the island were exceptionally kind to us. They built a fire and welcomed us in from the rain and cold. ³Paul gathered some brushwood, and as he was putting it on the fire, a viper, driven out by the heat, bit him, latching on to his hand. ⁴When the islanders saw this, they said, "This man must be a killer; for even though he escaped the sea, justice has found him and will not allow him to live." ⁵But Paul just smiled and shook the snake off into the fire, and suffered no ill effects.

⁶The people watched closely, expecting his hand to swell, or turn black, or for him to suddenly drop over dead. But after waiting a long time and seeing no ill effects, they changed their minds about him and decided he was a god.

Ac 28:7 A nearby estate belonged to Publius, the mayor of the island. He welcomed us to his home and entertained us for three days. ⁸His father was sick in bed with fever, nausea, vomiting and diarrhea. Paul went to him, prayed for him, and then placed hands on him and healed him. ⁹After this happened, all the sick on the island came to Paul and were cured. ¹⁰They treated us with great respect, and when it was time for us to sail, they provided us with all the supplies we needed.

Ac 28:11 Three months later, we put out to sea in a ship that had wintered at the island. It was from Alexandria and had the figurehead of the twin gods Castor and Pollux. ¹²We made port at Syracuse and stayed there three days. ¹³From there we sailed to Rhegium, and the following day, with a south wind, we reached Puteoli. ¹⁴There we found some members of the Lord's spiritual health-care team, who invited us to spend the week with them. And then we came to Rome. ¹⁵The Lord's team members there had heard we were coming, and they traveled out to the Forum of Appius and the Three Taverns to meet us. When Paul saw these people, he thanked God and was cheered. ¹⁶In Rome, Paul was given permission to live by himself, with a soldier to guard him.

Ac 28:17 Three days later, he called a meeting with the Jewish leaders. When they assembled, Paul said: "My fellow Israelites, although I have done no wrong to our people nor violated any customs of our ancestors, I was arrested in Jerusalem and handed over to the Romans. ¹⁸They examined me and wanted to set me free, because I was not guilty of any crime worthy of imprisonment or death, [19] but the Jews protested so adamantly that I was forced to appeal my case to Caesar—not that I intended to bring any charge against my own people. [20] This is the reason I have asked to speak with you, since it is because of the hope held by all Israel that I am bound in these chains."

Ac 28:21 They answered, "We have not received any letters of warning from Judea about you, and no Jews who have come from there have reported or said anything negative about you. [22] We would like to hear what you have to say, because this cult is becoming so popular that people everywhere are talking about it."

Ac 28:23 They set a date to meet with Paul, and showed up in even larger numbers at the place where he was staying. All day long, from dawn until late at night, Paul explained the reality of God's kingdom of love to them and tried to convince them from the books of Moses and the Prophets about Jesus. [24] Some were convinced, but others refused to believe. [25] They disagreed with each other and got up to leave after Paul's final statement: "The Holy Spirit spoke the truth to our ancestors when he said through God's spokesperson Isaiah:

[26] 'Go to the people and tell them,
    "You listen but you don't
    understand;
    you look but you don't
    comprehend."
[27] For the hearts of these people
    have become selfish and hard;
they close their ears
    to avoid hearing the truth,
    and shut their eyes
    to avoid seeing the truth.
If they didn't do this,
    then they would understand
    with their hearts
    and turn to me,
    and I would heal them.'

Ac 28:28 "So understand this: God's Remedy has been sent to the rest of the non-Jewish world, and they will partake of it!"

Ac 28:29 After Paul said this, the Jews left, arguing amongst themselves.

Ac 28:30 For two entire years Paul lived in Rome in his own rented house and welcomed any who came to see him. [31] Boldly and without hesitation, he shared the Remedy of God's kingdom of love and taught the truth about the Lord Jesus Christ.

Romans

1 From Paul, a serving friend of Jesus Christ, recruited to be an ambassador for him, and assigned the duty of distributing good news about the healing Remedy achieved by Christ, to all who would receive it. ² God promised this Remedy before the world was created and before humankind became infected with distrust, fear and selfishness. This is the Remedy told about by God's spokespersons in the Holy Scriptures. ³ This good news is the Remedy of his Son—whose human nature was genetically descended from David, ⁴ yet the purity of his divine nature, as the Son of God, was powerfully revealed by his resurrection from the dead. ⁵ Jesus is the conduit through which God's healing grace has reached us. And as evidence of his healing power, our minds have been cleansed from fear and selfishness. We have been enabled, as his ambassadors, to call people from among the sin-sick, dying world to the restoration and health that come from trusting Jesus and following his methods. ⁶ And you are among those called to join the spiritual health-care team of Jesus Christ and become his ambassadors.

Rom 1:7 To all in Rome who love God and have been healed from the infection of distrust, fear and selfishness, and have been transformed into loving, kind, gentle, humble people who value and practice God's methods:

Grace and peace are poured out over you from God our Father and from the Lord Jesus Christ.

Rom 1:8 First, I give thanks to God—whom I know through Jesus Christ—for all of you, because your confidence in him and in his methods is serving to broadcast his healing truth all over the world. ⁹ God, whom I wholeheartedly serve by distributing the Remedy which was revealed and obtained by his Son, is my witness that I constantly remember you ¹⁰ when I talk with him. And it is my great desire, if it be God's will, that I will be able to come to Rome and visit with you.

Rom 1:11 I am eager to see you and share with you additional truths and insights of our great God that will enlighten your minds and strengthen your hearts. ¹² What I mean is that I hope we may share together what God has done for us, and that we may all grow in understanding, confidence and Christlikeness of character. ¹³ I want you to know that if various obstacles hadn't prevented me, I would have already come to work with you in spreading the healing truth throughout Rome in order to increase the number recovering and getting well from the infection of distrust, fear and selfishness, just as I have done in other cities.

Rom 1:14 My heart goes out to all humanity: Greeks and non-Greeks, wise and foolish. ¹⁵ That is why I am so eager to bring to you, who are in Rome, the antidote to sin and selfishness.

Rom 1:16 I am not ashamed of spreading the good news about God and his character, methods and principles, as this is God's power which heals everyone who believes and trusts in him: firstly to the Jews—those initially called to assist in spreading the Remedy, and then to the Gentiles—those most recently called to help spread the Remedy. ¹⁷ For the good news is a revelation of God's true righteousness—character, methods and principles—

that restores trust in God and results in re-creation of a righteous and Christlike character in humans, just as it is written:

"The Christlike will live by choosing what is right in governance of themselves, and by trusting God with how things turn out."

Rom 1:18 God's wrath against human selfishness, godlessness and wickedness is being revealed from heaven: God is showing what he does and how he responds to those who are infected with selfishness, yet refuse his antidote. These sick-of-heart and twisted-of-mind humans reject the Remedy and suppress the truth of God's character by their wicked and godless lives. 19 For God has clearly revealed himself and his principles of love, beneficence, and giving, in all he has created. 20 From the very moment the earth was created, God's true self has been constantly revealed: his eternal life-giving power, his loving nature, his respect for freedom, and his methods of gracious giving; his character is seen in everything he has made, so that humans are not left in darkness, and have no excuse for remaining in their terminal state.

Rom 1:21 For although they knew the truth about God and his methods, they did not appreciate his gracious, humble character nor did they honor him by trusting him and incorporating his methods into their lives. Therefore their reasoning was damaged, their consciences seared, their thoughts became illogical and irrational, and their minds were darkened with lies and falsehoods. 22 They deceived themselves and claimed to be wise, but were actually fools who lost the ability to discern the right from the wrong, the healthy from the unhealthy, the true from the false, 23 and exchanged the values, methods and principles of the immortal God for man-made figurines of mortal humans, birds, mammals and reptiles, and even developed theories that humanity evolved from such lower creatures.

Rom 1:24 Therefore, because they persistently refused the gracious Remedy freely offered, God gave them up to reap the consequences of the unremitting infection of fear and selfishness. As the sensual desires took greater control, and self-governance was lost, they degraded themselves in sexual perversions with one another. 25 They exchanged the truth of God—his loving and forgiving character, his respect for freedom, his willingness to sacrifice for his creation—for Satan's lies about God, and worshiped and served false gods (who required payment to appease their angry wrath) rather than the Creator, who alone is worthy of our praise. Amen.

Rom 1:26 Because they rejected the truth—the Remedy for their twisted and deceived minds—God gave them up to reap the results of unrestrained selfishness, and they became debased and practiced shameful lusts. Even their heterosexual women exchanged natural relations for homosexual ones. 27 Likewise, their heterosexual men rejected natural relations and became inflamed with homosexual lust. Men committed all kinds of perverse and disgusting acts with each other, and thus their characters were distorted and their minds warped.

Rom 1:28 Furthermore, since they abandoned and rejected the truth about God—the only solution capable of healing their minds—he gave them up to experience the consequence of rejecting truth, and their minds became filled with lies and were horribly depraved. They did evil and called it good, and they rejected goodness and called it foolishness. 29 They have become filled with every kind of selfishness, wickedness, evil, greed and lustful perversion. They think only about themselves and are jealous of others, they destroy anyone who gets in their way, they lie and cheat and exploit, they spread rumors and gossip, 30 they

The Remedy

destroy reputations and hate God and everything for which he stands, they deny creation and call those who trust God "fools," they are arrogant, proud and boastful, they constantly think up new ways to do evil and disregard authority by following their own impulses, they call their parents fools and reject their guidance, 31 they are unreasonable, irrational, mean-spirited, hardhearted, and they trust no one.

32 Although they know God's righteous law—to love others before oneself—and realize their lifestyle leads only to death, they not only persist in their self-destructive ways, but throw parties and give awards to others who practice them.

2 If, therefore, you make judgments about others, you have no excuse for your failure to experience transformation of heart and mind. For whenever you judge another, you are revealing your own sickness of heart—you are revealing that selfishness, unforgiveness, unkindness and hardheartedness still live in you, and unless you experience a change, your condition remains terminal. 2 Now we know that when God diagnoses someone as sick, infected with selfishness and dying, his diagnosis is based on the actual condition of the heart and mind of the individual being diagnosed. 3 So when you, a mere human, who sees only the outward appearance, pass judgment on others, condemning them to ruin and eternal loss, you only reveal the lack of love and the persistence of an infected, selfish heart within you. If you remain like this, do you think you will somehow evade God's diagnosis of your fatal state? 4 Or do you purposely disdain the abundance of God's gentle, kind, patient bedside-manner, completely oblivious to the fact that it is God's tolerant, kind and gentle character that wins us back to trust and leads us to leave our destructive ways behind?

Rom 2:5 But because of your refusal to change, and your persistence in practicing selfish and destructive methods, you are solidifying your minds in opposition to God. If you continue in this way, you will destroy the very capacity to recognize and respond to truth, and God will ultimately let you go to reap the consequences of your own self-destructive choice. This will occur when the condition of each person's heart and mind is revealed. 6 Every person will receive from God what they have chosen for themselves. 7 Those who have valued God and his methods and have persisted in doing good, and who have sought to be more like Jesus in character and to honor God with their lives will be fully healed and receive eternal life. 8 But those who reject truth and love, and seek only self-gratification and self-interest, who have allowed themselves to be controlled by evil desires—develop a character like Satan, and God gives them up to their own persistent rebellious choice. 9 All who persist in evil, will have troubled lives: their minds will be distressed, their relationships tormented, and they will not experience peace—first for the Jew whom God first called to assist in spreading the healing Remedy, then for the Gentile most recently called to assist in spreading the healing Remedy. 10 But there will be complete transformation to Christlikeness of character and honor and peace for everyone who accepts God's healing truth and practices God's methods of goodness and love—first for the Jew, and then for the Gentile. 11 For God loves all humankind, and all humankind has the exact same healing Remedy offered freely, for God does not show any favoritism.

Rom 2:12 All who practice selfish methods and behaviors without knowing about God's principles of love and freedom still experience the damage that occurs when such methods are practiced, and will perish; and all who know about God's law of love and liberty but choose to persist in selfishness will be diagnosed as incurable and shown to be out of harmony with the principles life is based upon. [13] For it is not those who hear about love, truth and freedom that are healthy and right in God's sight; but it is those who internalize in their hearts and minds the principles of love, truth and freedom—and have characters transformed to be like Jesus—that are diagnosed as righteous. [14] (Indeed, when Gentiles who have not heard the truth about God's character, methods and principles as revealed in Scripture internalize in their characters God's methods of love, truth and freedom—which they have understood from God's revelation in nature—they are in harmony with God and his great law of love, even though they have not had the benefit of Scripture, [15] since their lives reveal that the infection of selfishness has been removed and love has been written in their hearts, their consciences are cleansed and in harmony with God, and their thoughts are able to discern the right from the wrong—the healthy from the unhealthy.) [16] This revelation of the effect of God's healing plan (and the disclosure of who has accepted it and who hasn't) will occur when God compares a person's inmost, secret self with the character of Jesus—as my healing message declares.

Rom 2:17 Now, I'm writing to those of you who call themselves Jews and claim to have some special privilege as Abraham's descendants: If you rely on keeping the rules and work on behavioral conformity and brag about your special connection to God; [18] if you know God's methods and agree with his plan to heal and restore because you have studied the Scriptures; [19] if you are confident that you are enlightened with truth and able to lead those who are blind or in the darkness of Satan's lies; [20] if you believe you have been enabled to instruct the ignorant and teach the immature because you have the laws of Moses—the basic framework of knowledge and truth; [21] you, then, who set yourselves up to teach others, why don't you teach yourselves? Why don't you do what you teach? You who preach against stealing, do you steal? Why don't you practice what you preach? [22] You who criticize homosexuals and pornographers, why do you visit prostitutes? Why do you divorce your spouse without reason? You who abhor idols and criticize the infidel, why do you advocate the same methods of coercion and force? [23] You who brag about the temple and its service, why do you misrepresent God by failing to practice his methods of love and thus defile the Spirit's temple? [24] It is true what has been written about you:

"God's character is misrepresented
    and distorted among the Gentiles
    because of you."

Rom 2:25 Circumcision has value as a symbol of the transformation of heart (experienced by those who practice God's law of love and liberty), but if you violate God's law of love and practice Satan's methods of selfishness—the symbol of circumcision has no meaning or purpose. [26] Those who have not been circumcised in their body but have been changed in the heart, and as such they practice God's methods of love—have they not already experienced what circumcision represents and thus will be considered circumcised? [27] The life of those who have not been circumcised physically but have been transformed within to be like Jesus will reveal that you, who have had the benefit of the written code yet have failed to be transformed within, are without excuse.

Rom 2:28 One is not a Jew because one is descended from Abraham, or has been circumcised in his body, or dresses like one. [29] No! A real, genuine Jew is a person who is like Abraham in character, and has been changed within to value truth and practice God's methods; and so circumcision is cutting away the heart's attachments to worldly things and establishing attachments to godly things. This is accomplished by the Spirit of Truth working in the mind, and not by rules performed for outward show. Such a person's life is evidence that God's healing principles work. Such a person receives appreciation from God—not from humans.

3 If anybody can be saved—and genetics don't make a difference—then you might ask: "What advantage is there in being a Jew, and what good is circumcision?" 2 Being a Jew has tremendous advantage! The Jews have been given the truth from God himself. They have been blessed with the Scriptures, with the teaching tools of circumcision, the sanctuary and feast days—all designed to enlighten the mind with healing truth. Not only that, but they have been given instructions on healthy living, which results in better health and more efficient mental function.

Rom 3:3 But what if some have not recognized the meaning of all that God has given them and have not developed trust in God? Will their failure to trust God nullify God's trustworthiness? 4 Absolutely not! God is trustworthy even if every human being is a liar and a fraud. As it is written:

"God, may you be proved right and true
in the hearts and minds of your
intelligent creatures
when you present yourself openly for
their judgment."

Rom 3:5 But if our sickness and selfishness make God's enduring, healing love easier to see and understand, how do we interpret that? Do we say that since our wickedness makes God's goodness easier to see, since our selfishness makes God's love easier to comprehend, since our sickness makes God's

Remedy easier to understand, that we are therefore helping God win his case? Is God unjust if he doesn't give us a free pass? (I am using a human argument that fails to understand the basic principles upon which the universe operates.) 6 Absolutely not! If that were the case, how could God allow anyone to experience the consequences of the persistent refusal of his life-giving Remedy? 7 Some who see sin as a legal problem might argue, "If I were to lie in order to help God reveal what truthfulness is and thus increase his glory, I am actually on his side helping him, so why should I suffer the fate of a sinner?" 8 They might as well try claiming—as we are being falsely accused of saying—"It is by doing wrong that the right occurs. It is by doing evil that good results. It is by acting selfishly that love grows." Those who teach such things deserve the consequence of a depraved and destroyed mind, which is the only result of practicing methods at variance with God's. They fail to understand that violations of God's law of love actually damage the sinner and destroy God's image, methods and principles within them.

Rom 3:9 What conclusion shall we then draw? Are we any better than anyone else? Of course not! We have already shown that all humanity, Jews and Gentiles alike, are all infected with the same destructive element—distrust, fear and selfishness—and all are in need of the same Remedy. 10 As it is written:

"There is no one whose heart and
mind is perfectly healthy,
no one that is free from the
infection of distrust, fear and
selfishness—not even one.

Rom 3:11 "There is no one who
understands God's character,
methods and principles;
no one who seeks to know God.

3:12 "The entire human race
has accepted lies about God
and has turned away from him.

They have become completely
necrotic in character;
there is no one who does good,
who loves others, who is selfless
and kind—not even one."
Rom 3:13 "The words they speak bring
only death;
Their mouths utter only lies about
God."
"The poison of lies from the serpent
Satan is on their lips
because they have accepted
his version of God."
Rom 3:14 "Their voice is filled
with cursing and bitterness,
and they complain about life being
unfair."
Rom 3:15 "They are quick to murder;
Rom 3:16 "They are tornadoes of
destruction,
whirlwinds of misery wreaking
havoc wherever they go.
Rom 3:17 "They don't know how to bring
peace, heal wounds, be kind,
or sacrifice self for the good of
others."
Rom 3:18 "They don't admire or respect
God,
but are afraid of him
because they don't know him."
Rom 3:19 Now, we know that the Ten
Commandments are like a medical diagnostic instrument identifying infection and exposing disease. It diagnoses
accurately everyone who is infected
with distrust of God—filled with selfishness and dying of sin—so that everyone who claims to be sin-free or free
of selfishness will be silenced, and the
entire world will recognize their need
of God's healing solution. 20 Therefore
no one will be recognized as having a
healthy relationship with God and being like Christ in character by adhering
to a set of rules; rather, it is through
the Ten Commandments that we become aware of our sickly state of mind.
Rom 3:21 But now God has revealed a
healthy state of being—a character that
is right and perfect in every way—that
did not come from the written code,

but is exactly what the Scriptures and
the Ten Commandments were pointing
your minds toward. 22 This perfect
state of being comes from Christ and is
created within us by God when we
place our trust in him. Our trust in him
is established by the evidence given
through Jesus Christ of his supreme
trustworthiness. There is no difference
among any ethnic groups, 23 for all
humanity is infected with the same
disease—of distrust, fear and selfishness—and is deformed in character
and falls far short of God's glorious
ideal for humanity. 24 Yet all who are
willing are healed freely by God's gracious Remedy which has been provided
by Jesus Christ. 25 God presented Jesus
as the way and the means of restoration. Now, through the trust established by the evidence of God's character revealed when Christ died, we may
partake of the Remedy procured by
Christ. God did this to demonstrate
that he is right and good—because in
his forbearance he suspended, for a
time, the ultimate consequence of us
being out of harmony with his design
for life—yet he has been falsely accused of being unfair. 26 He did it to
demonstrate at the present time how
right and good he is, so that he would
also be seen as being right when he
heals those who trust in Jesus.
Rom 3:27 Where, then, is human bragging or accomplishment? It has no
place, for our healing has been accomplished by God, through trust made
possible by Jesus. And why is boasting
not possible? Because our efforts to
conform to a set of rules do not establish trust, or remove the infection of
selfishness from our hearts! Only trust
in God eliminates fear and opens the
heart to him. Then, in order to recreate
us to be like Jesus, God lovingly applies to our hearts and minds the Remedy Christ achieved. 28 Therefore, we
insist that a person is cleansed (set
right with God) only by trusting in God
and opening their heart to him—and

The Remedy

this is different from keeping rules. ²⁹ Is the Creator of the entire human race the God of the Jews only? Is he not God of all humanity, including Gentiles? Of course!—he is the God of all humanity, ³⁰ and he will heal the circumcised if they trust him, and the uncircumcised will also be healed if they trust him. ³¹ Do we then destroy, or make useless by our trust, the written code God gave to help us? Of course not! We show that the written code was helpful in diagnosing our sickness, revealing God's plan to heal, and leading us back to trust, so we could be healed.

4 What about our father Abraham: what did he understand about this issue? ² If Abraham was somehow healed by his own efforts at keeping a set of rules or performing certain rituals, then he would have his own healing formula to promote, and would not need trust in God. ³ But what does the Scripture say?

"Abraham trusted God, and his trust
   was recognized as righteousness
because the distrust caused through
   Satan's lies had been removed,
and through trust he was endowed
   with a new heart, right motives
   and Christlike principles."

Rom 4:4 Now, when a person works, their wages are earned and are not a gift or an endowment. ⁵ But the person who doesn't try to earn God's Remedy by working for it, but instead comes to know and trust God—that person's trust is recognized as righteousness because the distrust caused by Satan's lies has been removed, and through trust they receive from God transformation of heart and experience God's own righteous character created within. ⁶ David says the exact same thing when he describes the blessedness of the person to whom God bestows his perfect cure without them working to earn it:

Rom 4:7 "Happy are they whose wicked

minds are restored to perfect
   purity,
whose selfishness is eradicated.
Rom 4:8 "Happy is the person whose
   infected heart
the Lord transforms to
   perfection."

Rom 4:9 Is this gracious re-creation of mind only for the small number of humans who have been physically circumcised, or is this for all humanity? We have been saying all along that Abraham trusted God—and his trust was recognized as righteousness because trust in God replaced mistrust of God—and through trust he was endowed with a new heart, right motives, and Christlike principles. ¹⁰ And when did God accept his trust as righteousness? Was it before he was circumcised or after? It was before! ¹¹ Circumcision was the sign—a seal in his body—of the new heart and mind he had already received when he was still uncircumcised. Therefore Abraham is the father of all who trust in God (whether they are circumcised or not circumcised), those who are endowed with a new heart, right motives, and Christlike principles—just like Abraham was. ¹² Don't be confused; he is also the father of those who are not only circumcised physically, but who have also trusted God and have been endowed with new minds and Christlike principles, just like Abraham had before he was circumcised.

Rom 4:13 It was not because Abraham kept a certain set of rules or practiced certain rituals that he and his descendants (those who are like Abraham in character—not in genetics) were promised to inherit the earth, but because of Christlike motives and methods that are endowed to them through trust in God. ¹⁴ For if it were possible to develop perfect motives, methods and principles by performing rituals or following a certain code, then there would be no need to trust God for his healing power in our lives, and his promised inheritance would be meaningless. [15] The written law or code simply exposes the extent of our sickness of mind and heart which, if not cured, results in death. If it weren't for the written law, we wouldn't even know how sick we are, for without some standard of health to measure by, no defect could be diagnosed.

Rom 4:16 Therefore the restoration to a perfect state of being and the inheritance of eternal life on a renewed earth come by trusting the One who made the promise to do it. This transformation is accomplished by God's graciousness and is guaranteed to all the children of Abraham—not only his genetic descendants, who were given the written diagnostic code, but also to his spiritual descendants who, just like him, trust God. Abraham is the father of all who trust God. [17] As it is written:

"I have made you the father of many different ethnic groups."

The God in whom Abraham trusted—the Creator God who is the source of all life and who calls things into existence from nothingness—considers all of us who trust him to be descendants of Abraham.

Rom 4:18 In the face of human opinion and conventional wisdom, Abraham placed his hope and trust in God and thus became the father of many ethnic groups, just as God told him, "Your descendants will be numerous." [19] Without doubting God for a moment, he accepted it in the reality that he was one hundred years old and his ability to procreate was severely limited, and Sarah had gone through menopause and was beyond child bearing years. [20] Even though in human understanding the promise seemed hopeless, Abraham did not waver in his confidence in God, but praised God as he [21] realized that God was able to miraculously fulfill the promise. [22] This unwavering trust in God, in the face of scientific evidence to the contrary, was recognized as righteousness because

this trust replaced distrust and opened Abraham's mind to receive the endowment of a new heart, right motives, and Christlike principles established by God's re-creative power. [23] This record of his "trust being recognized as righteousness" is not written merely for Abraham, [24] but for everyone who trusts in God. Everyone who trusts in the God who raised Jesus from the dead is recognized as righteous because through trust they receive the endowment of a perfect heart and have new motives created within, and their distrust of God disappears. [25] Because our minds were infected by distrust of God, and our condition was terminal, Jesus was given up to experience death in order to procure the Remedy. Having achieved God's purpose, he was raised to life, and now distributes this Remedy to completely restore us into perfect harmony with him.

5 Therefore, if our minds and hearts have been set right through trust, we are at peace with God through the Remedy achieved by our Lord Jesus Christ. [2] It is through Jesus that we know the truth about God and are won back to trust, and thus open our minds to experience God's gracious healing power. Our joy is found in the hope of full restoration into beings possessing Godlike character. [3] Because of this, we rejoice in our trials and afflictions, for we know that trials bring to light our shortcomings and defects of character. [4] If we persevere, choosing God's methods, the defects are removed and character is purified, and pure character increases our hope for God's kingdom. [5] And our hope will not be disappointed, because God pours out his love into our hearts and thereby matures, ennobles, and restores us into his image by the Holy Spirit, whom he has given to us.

Rom 5:6 You see, at the exact moment it was needed—when we were infected with distrust, rebelling against God, and our condition was terminal—Christ died to restore trust and cure the terminally ill. [7]Very rarely will someone die for a healthy man; [8]but God the Father demonstrates his own love for us in this: While we were dying and in rebellion against him, Christ died to restore trust and cure sinfulness in order to heal us and bring us back to unity with God.

Rom 5:9 Now that we have been won back to trust, cleansed in mind and set right with God by all that Christ accomplished at the cross, it is ridiculous to think that God would now let us go! [10]For since—while we distrusted God and fought against him in every way—his Son died to win us back to trust and friendship with himself and to cure our rebellious hearts, how much more, having won us back to trust and friendship, will God heal all the damage caused to us while we were in rebellion against him! [11]And even better still, having experienced this healing of mind and heart, we are overjoyed because God, through Jesus, has made us his friends.

Rom 5:12 Therefore, the infection of distrust of God—which deformed humanity's heart and mind with selfishness and fear, and which results only in death—infected the human race when Adam accepted Satan's lies about God and broke trust with him. This infection of fear and selfishness is inherited by all human beings, so all are born infected.[13]This is revealed by the fact that before the written law was given, the infection of distrust, fear and selfishness was already present in the world. But this infection of distrust, fear and selfishness is not diagnosable without the law. [14]Nevertheless, even without being diagnosed as infected with this terminal condition, humans still died, all the way from the time of Adam to Moses—even those who did not break a specific command, like Adam did—revealing that the problem is the infected state of our minds and

not a legal issue with God. Adam, the first man, being the conduit through which the infection entered humanity, also represents the one man who is the conduit of the antidote that cures all those who accept it.

Rom 5:15 But the gift of the antidote is not like the infection. For if everyone is born infected with a terminal condition because of the choice of Adam, how incredibly effective must the antidote supplied by Christ be, since it cures all who take it! [16]Again, the gift of the antidote is not like the result of the breach of trust. Adam's breach of trust infected all humanity, therefore all humanity is diagnosed as sick and dying. This occurred without each individual choosing to be infected; but the antidote, which came after humanity had been severely damaged and deformed by selfishness and sin, brought cleansing, purification, health, and complete restoration. [17]If, by the choice of one man's distrust, selfishness and death permeated all humanity, how much more will those who accept the Remedy that Christ has achieved experience restored trust and complete healing to live forever with God!

Rom 5:18 Therefore, just as Adam's distrust infected humanity with the fatal condition of fear and selfishness, so too Christ's choice to sacrifice self achieved the life-giving Remedy for all humanity. [19]Just as Adam's choice infected the human race with a terminal condition, so too Christ's perfect life has brought the Remedy to heal all who accept it.

Rom 5:20 The written law was added so that the infection of distrust and selfishness could be more easily seen and diagnosed. As the exposure of sin and selfishness increased, God's willingness to heal increased all the more, [21]so that—just as distrust and selfishness brought deformity and death—even more importantly, God's gracious Remedy, brought by Jesus Christ, results in complete healing and life eternal.

6 What then should we say about this amazing healing plan? Should we spread the infection of distrust and selfishness and cause more devastation and destruction so that the power of God's healing solution may be more fully displayed? ²Absolutely not! We have taken the antidote, and the infection of distrust and selfishness has been purged from our hearts and minds. How then can we choose to be reinfected with distrust of God and practice selfish methods again? ³Or don't you realize that all of us who were immersed into union with Christ Jesus were immersed into selflessness and have died to self-centeredness? ⁴We symbolically demonstrate that we have joined him in dying to self by being buried in water, in order that—just as Jesus rose from the dead, displaying the life-giving glory of the Father—we too may live a new life, displaying God's glorious character.

Rom 6:5 If we have joined him in dying to self, we will absolutely join him in his resurrection and in new life! ⁶For we know that when our old selfish hearts and fear-ridden minds trust God and surrender to be crucified with Christ—the infection of selfishness is purged, and our hearts are no longer controlled by Satanic principles, ⁷as anyone who dies to selfishness is free from Satan's methods, principles, and control.

Rom 6:8 Now, if we join Christ in dying to self, we are confident we will live with him forever. ⁹Because Christ was raised from the dead and cannot die again, he has secured the Remedy and has revealed the truth; and death cannot touch him again. ¹⁰The death he died, he died once, destroying Satan's lies and the infection of fear and selfishness, and restoring love and trust; therefore the life he lives, he lives to glorify God.

Rom 6:11 In the same way, recognize that you are dead to the ways of Satan and alive to the ways of God as revealed in Christ Jesus. ¹²Therefore do not indulge selfish desires or participate in destructive activities. ¹³Do not use your physical body for evil (to indulge selfishness), but rather offer your entire being to God, revealing that Satan's principles of death have been replaced by God's principles of life. So offer your entire self to God, doing what is right and healthy because it is right and healthy. ¹⁴For distrust, fear and selfishness will no longer hold control over you, as you are no longer under the law's terminal diagnosis, but—having partaken of God's gracious Remedy—you are under his healing care.

Rom 6:15 What then? Shall we indulge selfish desires because God has provided a gracious Remedy for our terminal condition? Absolutely not! ¹⁶Don't you realize that when you gratify selfish desires, you are being slowly transformed and become more and more selfish, destroying the very faculties that recognize and respond to God's healing truth? Don't you realize that over time you lose your freedom to choose and become a slave to selfishness and lust, which leads only to self-destruction and death? Conversely, if you accept God's gracious Remedy and choose his methods, you are transformed and become Christlike in character. ¹⁷Thanks be to God, for even though you used to be slaves to selfishness, you wholeheartedly accepted the truth revealed by Jesus, trusted God, and now practice his methods of love, truth and freedom, which you were taught. ¹⁸Therefore you have been freed from distrust, fear and selfishness, and have been bonded to love, truth and liberty, doing what is right because it is right.

Rom 6:19 I state this as simply as possible, using human terms, because it is easier to understand and learn that way: Just as you used to choose to use your bodies in lewd, vile and debasing ways, so now you choose to use your bodies to do what is right, reasonable and healthy, which leads to purity and holiness. 20 When you slavishly indulged selfish desires, you avoided what was healthy, right, and good. 21 But what good did that do you? It only caused pain, heartache, and ultimately—death. 22 But now that you have accepted the truth about God, you have been restored to trust, and set free from fear and selfishness. You are wholeheartedly committed to God and are receiving complete re-creation of heart and mind, resulting in eternal life. 23 For the infection of selfishness leads only to death, but the gift of God is eternal life through the healing Remedy procured by Jesus Christ our Lord.

7 Since I am speaking to those who love the law, let me use a legal analogy: Don't you realize that law has authority over someone only if they are alive? 2 For instance, a married woman is legally tied to her husband as long as her husband is alive, but if her husband dies, marital law no longer binds her to him. 3 If she were to marry another man while her husband was alive, marital law would make this action illegal, and she would not be recognized as the wife of the new man, but as an adulteress to her husband. But if her husband were to die, marital law would no longer bind her to her husband—she could then marry another man in harmony with marital law.

Rom 7:4 Therefore, your selfish, fear-ridden heart died when you accepted the truth revealed by Christ's death, and you received a new heart from him who was raised from the dead, in order that you might grow in character—to be like Jesus—and live to honor God. 5 For when we were controlled by the infection of fear and selfishness—which resulted from distrust—the destructive passions revealed by the law were ravaging our bodies: we were terminally ill and spreading death wherever we went. 6 But now, as we die to the distrust, fear and selfishness that once bound us, the law no longer diagnoses us as infected and terminal. In fact, the law now confirms that we have a new heart — not by observing rules, but created within by the Spirit. We are now healthy and loving like Jesus.

Rom 7:7 What shall we say then? Is the law evil and selfish because it increases the amount of evil and selfishness we see? Absolutely not! I would not have known what evil and selfishness looked like if it wasn't for the diagnostic efficacy of the law. I would not have realized that coveting was evil and selfish if the law didn't say, "Don't covet." 8 But selfishness, taking advantage of the fact that the law is only a diagnostic instrument — and not a Remedy — magnified every covetous desire within me. For apart from the diagnostic ability of the law, sin is unrecognizable. 9 Once I thought I was healthy and free from the infection of distrust, fear and selfishness, but then the commandment examined me, exposed how utterly infected I was, and diagnosed me as terminal. 10 I discovered that the very commandment given only to diagnose my condition I had unwittingly attempted to use as a cure, and thus my condition only worsened. 11 For selfishness, taking advantage of the fact that the commandment could only diagnose and not cure, deceived me into thinking that I could be cured by working to keep the commandments, but instead my terminal state only worsened. 12 So understand this: The law diagnoses perfectly, and the commandment is the standard of what is right and good, set apart by God to reveal what is evil and destructive.

Rom 7:13 Did the law, which did good by diagnosing what was wrong with me, become the source of my terminal

214

condition? Of course not! It only exposed what was already in me, so that I could recognize how totally decayed, putrid and near death I was, and so that through the lens of the commandment I might become utterly disgusted with evil and selfishness, and long for a cure.

Rom 7:14 We know that the law is consistent, reliable and reasonable; but I am inconsistent, unreliable and unreasonable, because the infection of distrust, fear and selfishness has warped my mind and damaged my thinking. 15 I am frustrated with what I do! For having been restored to trust, I want to do what is in harmony with God and his methods and principles; but I find that even though I trust God, my old habits, conditioned responses, preconceived ideas and other remnants of the devastation caused by distrust and selfishness are not yet fully removed. 16 And if I find an old habit causing me to behave in ways that I now find detestable, I affirm that the law is a very helpful tool revealing residual damage in need of healing. 17 What is happening is this: I have come to trust God, and I desire to do his will, but old habits and conditioned responses—which present almost reflexively in certain situations—have not yet been totally eliminated and thus cause me to do things I do not want to do. 18 I know that my mind was completely infected with distrust, fear and selfishness which totally perverted all my desires and faculties, so that even when distrust has been eradicated and trust has been restored, the damage caused by years of distrustful and selfish behavior has not yet been fully healed. So I find that, at times, I have the desire to do what is right, but do not yet have the ability to carry out the desire. 19 For the old habits and conditioned responses are not the good I want to do; no, they are remnants of my selfish, unconverted mind. 20 So, if I find myself doing what I no longer desire to do, it is not myself that acts, but the vestiges of old habits and conditioned responses that have yet to be removed. And through God's grace, they will soon be removed.

Rom 7:21 So I find this reality at work: When I want to do good, my old selfish habits and residual feelings of fear are right there with me. 22 In my mind, I rejoice in God's methods and principles, 23 but I recognize that I remain damaged from years of being infected with distrust and practicing Satan's methods, so that even though the infection of distrust has been removed, the old habits of fear and self-promotion tempt me from within. 24 What a damaged and corrupt man I am! Who will deliver and heal me from a brain and body so diseased and deformed? 25 Praise be to God—for he has provided the healing solution through Jesus Christ our Lord!

So then, I find that in my mind I am now renewed with trust in God and love of his methods, but my brain and body remain damaged by years of self-indulgent behavior.

8 Therefore, those who trust in Christ Jesus are no longer destined to die, 2 because through Christ Jesus the law of love has cleansed and healed them from the law of selfishness and death. 3 The written law was powerless to restore trust, as it could merely diagnose the infection of distrust and selfishness pervading us all. God accomplished this restoration of his character of love in humans by sending his own Son in human flesh to eradicate selfishness from humanity, reveal the truth about God, expose the lies of Satan, and reveal what happens when the infection of sin is not cured. And so he condemned the infection of selfishness as the destroying element in sinful humanity 4 in order that the law of love—the principle upon which life is based—might be fully restored in us, who no longer live according to selfish

desires, but in harmony with the Spirit of love and truth.

Rom 8:5 Those who live with the selfish nature in charge have their minds bent on self-indulgence and selfish pursuits; but those who live in harmony with the Spirit of truth and love have their minds focused on living in harmony with God's principles of truth, love, and liberty. 6 The mind of the selfish person is filled with death, but the mind governed by the principles of the Spirit of truth and love is filled with life and peace. 7 The selfish mind operates on the survival-of-the-fittest principle, which says, "I love myself so much that I will kill you in order that I may live;" and such a mind is at war with the God of love, who says, "I love you so much that I will give my life in order that you might live." The mind of the selfish person does not surrender to the principle of love—which requires death to self-interest—nor can it do so; 8 those controlled by the selfish nature cannot please God, because everything they do is opposed to all that God is.

Rom 8:9 If God's Spirit has recreated within you his methods, principles and character, then you are no longer controlled by the desires of the selfish nature, but operate by the principles of love and truth. But if anyone does not have a Christlike character and attitude renewed within, they do not belong to the family of Christ. 10 But if trust in God and Christlike character has been recreated in your mind, yet your physical body remains defective and dying, don't be distressed, for your mind and character are alive, as the principles of life have been renewed in you. 11 And if the Spirit of him who raised Jesus from the dead is living within you, he who raised Christ from the dead will give you the power to live victoriously here and now in your mortal bodies. This is accomplished by living in trust and receiving the power of the Spirit.

Rom 8:12 Therefore, brothers and sisters, we have a responsibility—and it's not to our old selfish desires: We are not to live selfishly. 13 For if you live a life that indulges your selfish desires, you will destroy yourself, and the only result is death. But if by the enlightenment of the Spirit you make the choice to say "No" to selfish desires, the Spirit will provide divine power to successfully put to death the selfish desires within you, and you will be transformed and live forever. 14 You will live because those who follow the Spirit of God are the sons and daughters of God. 15 For the new heart and mind that you received is not riddled and consumed with fear and doubt; No! Trust has been restored and you received the mind, heart and attitude of Christ himself—the mind of God's very own child. And now we are not afraid to cry out to him, "Daddy, Papa, Father." 16 The Spirit himself confirms in our hearts and minds that we are God's children. 17 Now, understand this incredible good news that if we are God's children, then we are heirs — heirs of God himself and joint-heirs with Christ — to all the goodness in the universe! This is true if indeed we have died to self and share in his character of love.

Rom 8:18 The present struggles and discomforts are inconsequential when we consider the magnitude of transformation being accomplished in us. We are privileged to reveal the very power of God's healing principles in the transformation of our minds. 19 This entire planet eagerly waits for wicked, sinful, selfish humanity to be gloriously transformed back into perfect sons and daughters of God. 20 For this entire creation was infected—not by its own choice, but by the choice of Adam—with the principle of the survival-of-the-fittest. 21 It longs for the day when this destructive, selfish, fear-based, survival-of-the-fittest principle will be completely eradicated and all nature will be healed and restored into God's original ideal.

Rom 8:22 We know that the entire creation has been agonizing as in the pains of childbirth, longing for delivery from Adam's fall, right up to the present time. 23 Not only this, but we—who have been restored to trust, and have the outpouring of the Spirit renewing our minds—ache in our hearts and long for the culmination of our adoption as children of God in new bodies, free from the damage of sin. 24 Our minds have been healed, and trust in God has been restored, yet we still hope for the day we will receive new bodies, free from disease and defect. But hope that has been realized is no longer hope, for who hopes for what they already have? 25 But since we hope for what we have not yet received, we wait patiently.

Rom 8:26 This is exactly what the Spirit is doing: He is interceding in our minds, bringing the truth, convicting of right and wrong, and leading us to a higher plane of existence. Even when we don't know what to pray, the Spirit is there, leading our minds and turning our thoughts in a higher and nobler direction. 27 And he who knows how the infection of selfishness has invaded the deepest levels of our hearts, also knows the mind and desire of the Spirit, because the Spirit intercedes for us by bringing his healing power, and cleansing and restoring the saints in accordance with the will of God.

Rom 8:28 And we know that in all things, at all times, in all circumstances, God works for the good of his creation and for the good of all who love him. Those who have accepted God's call—to work with him according to his purpose—experience the good things that God has for them. 29 For God foreknew who would accept and value his methods of love, and who would reject him and his methods of love. And God predetermined that all who accept the truth about him and trust in him would be fully healed and transformed in character to be like his Son, so that Jesus would be the prototype of all who are fashioned in his likeness.

30 And he called all humanity—whom he predetermined should be healed and restored—to repentance and reconciliation. Those who accept the truth and respond to the call, he sets right with himself and trust is restored; and those whom he sets right in trust, he also transforms in character to his glorious ideal as revealed in Jesus.

Rom 8:31 What, then, can we possibly say in response to this? Don't you realize that God is on our side? And if God is for us, who can be against us? God does not need convincing to be good to us; No! It is we who need convincing that God is good to us! 32 If he did not withhold his own Son—but gave him up for us all—don't you realize that he will withhold nothing good from us? But along with his Son, he will give us all things that are for our good! 33 Who is it, then, that brings charges against those whom God has chosen? Stop believing Satan's lies about God; it is not God who brings charges against us! It is God who sets us right with himself. It is God who heals and transforms us. 34 Then who condemns? It is not Jesus, oh no! Christ Jesus, who died—and more importantly, who was raised from death to life—is sitting at God's right hand and is working hand in hand with his Father. Together they are interceding with the malignancy of sin in our minds and holding in check the power of the evil one, while providing the Remedy for our deliverance, healing, and restoration. 35 Who, then, shall ever separate us from the love of Christ? Shall problems, or hardships, or criticism, or persecution, or hunger, or disease, or homelessness, or nakedness, or imprisonment, or financial ruin, or terrorists, or war? 36 As it is written:

> "For no matter what we face, including death, we will not doubt you;
> even if we are treated as sheep led to the slaughter—our confidence in

you will not waver."

Rom 8:37 In all things—no matter what we face—we are more than conquerors through trust in him who loved us. 38 For I am absolutely convinced that God is totally on our side and nothing can separate us from his love: neither death nor life, neither angels nor demons, neither the past nor present nor future, nor any power in the universe; 39 neither things exalted nor things debased, nor anything else in all creation—nothing can separate us from the love of God that is in Christ Jesus our Lord.

9 What I am saying is true and spoken in Christlike love; I am not lying—my conscience is clear, and the Holy Spirit confirms my testimony. 2 My heart is in great agony and deep sorrow. 3 I so much want my brothers and sisters, those of my own race—the genetic descendants of Abraham—to accept this healing truth, that I would gladly sacrifice myself if it would do any good. 4 They have had such privilege: they were adopted by God as children to help him reveal the truth about himself—his character, methods and principles; they have been blessed with the written rules—the diagnostic tool of the Ten Commandments; they received the sanctuary service with its symbolic lessons, the feast days, God's spokespersons, the illumination of Scripture, and all the promises of God. 5 Their forefathers are the patriarchs, and from them is derived the human ancestry of Christ, who is God over all, forever praised! Amen.

Rom 9:6 But don't be confused: It is not as if God's word has failed just because not all genetic descendants of Abraham will be saved. For not all who are genetic descendants of Israel are part of God's Israel, 7 nor are all those who are genetic descendants of Abraham considered Abraham's true children. Oh no! Only those who are like Abraham in character are considered his children. This is obviously demonstrated by the fact that the Scripture says, "It is through Isaac that your offspring will be recognized." 8 In other words, it is not the genetic offspring who are God's children, but those who are his by a miraculous birth—the renewal of mind and heart—the rebirth. 9 For this is exactly how Isaac came to be: by a miracle birth! God promised that Sarah would have a son, and her ability to do so was brought about by God himself.

Rom 9:10 Not only this, but Rebekah's children were both sons of Isaac. 11 But before the twins were born or had done anything good or bad—in order that it might be clearly seen that it was God's plan at work and 12 not man's natural right of inheritance—she was told, "The older will serve the younger." 13 Just as it is written: "Jacob accepted my love, but Esau did not."

Rom 9:14 How shall we interpret this? Is God unfair? Is God arbitrary or unjust? Absolutely not! In no way! 15 For he says to Moses,

"I choose to be merciful to all humanity,
and I will have compassion on the entire human race."

Rom 9:16 Our healing doesn't depend on some effort, desire or work on our part, but on the fact that God is merciful and offers the Remedy freely to everyone. 17 For the Scripture says of Pharaoh, "I raised you up so that I might pour out my truth upon you and that my character might be known throughout the entire world. And even though you resisted me and fought against me, I was patient and merciful with you." 18 Therefore, God is merciful to whom he chooses, and stern to those he chooses.

Rom 9:19 One of you might protest and say, "Then why does God still blame us, if he does whatever he wants?" 20 But this complaint only shows how little you know about God and his methods and purposes. You confuse

God's desire to heal and restore everyone to his original ideal with his wise plan to assign different duties and responsibilities to different individuals. You also fail to realize that different conditions require different applications of the Remedy. 21 Doesn't the potter have the right to use some clay to make pottery for noble uses, and from the same clay to make pottery for ordinary purposes?

Rom 9:22 What if God, choosing to reveal what will happen, patiently continued to offer treatment to those who refuse his healing Remedy, and yet they refused to take his free cure anyway? What if, in this way, God revealed that such people prepare themselves for death and destruction? 23 What if he did this to make the richness of his character known to those who would accept the Remedy, and thus, by the revelation of the truth about himself, prepare them to be fully transformed into Christlike glory? 24 This is what he has done! He has called all people, both Jews and Gentiles, to healing and restoration into Christlikeness of character and into partnership with him to spread the Remedy. 25 As he says in Hosea:

"I will call them 'my representatives'
    who were not my representatives;
and I will call her 'the conduit of my
    love' who had previously rejected
    my love."

Rom 9:26 And,

"It will happen that even though they
    were told,
    'You do not represent me,'
they will be changed in character
    and called 'children of the living
    God.'"

Rom 9:27 Isaiah declares concerning Israel:

"Though the genetic descendants of
    Abraham are as numerous as the
    sand by the sea,
only a small remnant will accept
    the Remedy and be healed.
Rom 9:28 "For the Lord will carry out his
    diagnosis on the earth

with accuracy and certainty."
Rom 9:29 It is, sadly, as Isaiah has said:

"If the Lord Almighty hadn't worked
    so hard, so patiently and so
    diligently to preserve us,
we would have no descendants.
We would have ended up like Sodom;
    we would have ended up like
    Gomorrah."

Rom 9:30 How then do we understand this? It is very simple: The Gentiles—who had no idea that they were infected with selfishness and therefore dying, and certainly unaware that a Remedy to heal them was available—didn't pursue God's healing cure; but when they became aware of their condition and that a Remedy existed, they obtained it by trust in him who heals and restores. 31 But Israel—who knew their condition and that a Remedy was available, and who had been given the teaching tools designed to lead them back to trust—did not attain it. 32 Why not? Because instead of trusting God and accepting his free Remedy, they attempted to cure themselves by their own efforts. Thus they stumbled over the "stumbling stone," refusing to trust in him, 33 as it is written:

"See, I have placed in Zion a stone of
    truth that reveals the stumbling
    and shortcomings of humans,
and a rock of righteousness that
    exposes how far short they fall;
but the one who trusts in him
    will be completely healed and
    never stumble or fall again."

10 Brothers and sisters, my heart's great desire and constant request to God is that the Israelites—the genetic descendants of Abraham—will accept the truth and be healed. 2 I can assure you from my own experience that they are zealous to serve God, but their zeal is based on the wrong concept of God, as they don't really know him. 3 And because they do not know him—his goodness, mercy, forgiveness, kindness, love, and his free gift of

healing and restoration—they have sought to please him by working to create their own cure, and thus have refused God's free Remedy. ⁴In Christ, God's design (law) is complete, so that there may be perfection of character and healing of mind and heart for all who trust him.

Rom 10:5 This is how Moses describes the state of being right with God which comes from keeping the law: "Those who seek to be right with God through their performance must be perfect in everything they do." ⁶But the state of being right with God that comes from trusting him, says: "Be humble in your heart and recognize that you can do nothing to add to what Christ has done for you," and "Do not try to exalt yourself into heaven and pretend you are equal with Christ," ⁷and, "Do not think that Christ needed your help to arise from the dead." ⁸It also says this: "The truth about God is with you. You have seen the evidence and have been won back to trust. Your heart is right with God, and your mouth proclaims the truth." And the truth, which restores trust, and which we are proclaiming, is this: ⁹If you accept the truth that Jesus is God, then confess with your mouth that he represents the Father perfectly, trust God in your heart—realizing that he raised Jesus from the dead—and you will be completely healed and restored to God's original ideal. ¹⁰For it is with the deep places of the soul that one trusts, and when distrust is removed, unity with God is restored; and it is with the mouth that we reveal that the inner person has been healed. ¹¹As the Scripture says, "Anyone who trusts God will never be destroyed by guilt." ¹²For there is no difference between the Jew and Gentile: All humanity is infected and dying, and the same Lord is Lord of all and provides the rich blessing of his perfect Remedy to all who accept it. ¹³For "Everyone who opens their heart and trusts in God will be completely healed."

Rom 10:14 But how can anyone possibly seek help from the One they do not trust? And how can they trust God if they have not heard about him? And how can they hear the wonderful truth about him without someone to tell them? ¹⁵And how can the Remedy be shared with them if no one is sent? Thus, it is written, "How beautiful are those who bring the good news about God!"

Rom 10:16 But not all the genetic descendants of Abraham accepted the good news about God. For Isaiah says, "Lord, is there no one who has believed our message about you?"

¹⁷Consequently, trust comes from hearing the truth, examining the evidence, and understanding the facts; and the message of truth—the evidence of God's character and the facts about his methods—are all revealed in Christ. ¹⁸But I ask: Did Israel—the genetic descendants of Abraham—not hear the truth? Did they not have the evidence presented, or the facts revealed to them? Of course they did, as it is said:

"The voice of truth has been
  proclaimed into all the earth,
  the evidence—to the ends of the
  world."

Rom 10:19 Again I ask: Did Israel—the genetic descendants of Abraham—fail to understand the truth? Did they fail to comprehend the evidence? No; they understood, because Moses says:

"You will become envious of those
  who are not a nation,
you will be angered by a nation who
  didn't understand what you have
  understood."

Rom 10:20 And Isaiah fearlessly declares:

"Those who did not seek me, found
  me; those who did not ask for me
  have seen me."

Rom 10:21 But concerning Israel he says,

"Constantly I have reached out to
  you, but you are a rebellious and
  obstinate people
who have rejected me."

11 I ask then: Did God reject the people whom he chose as his helpers in revealing his plan of saving the world? Absolutely not! I am an Israelite myself—a genetic descendant of Abraham, from the tribe of Benjamin. ² God did not reject the people he chose as his helpers in revealing his plan, but he foreknew that only some would trust him. Don't you realize what the Scripture says about Elijah— that he thought he was the only one left in all Israel loyal to God? He said to the Lord: ³ "Lord, they have killed all your prophets and representatives, and torn down all your altars; I am the only one left loyal to you, and they are trying to kill me!" ⁴ And what did God tell him? "There are seven thousand who remain loyal to me and have not bowed the knee to Baal." ⁵ So too, at the present time—even though the officials of Israel have rejected God's healing plan, even though the majority of the people he chose as his helpers to reveal his healing plan have rejected it—there remains a remnant of Abraham's descendants who have accepted the truth about God and his gracious Remedy, and who have been restored to trust. ⁶ And if they have been restored to trust through God's grace, then it is no longer by some work or effort to earn favor with God; if it were, then God's graciousness would not be gracious at all.

Rom 11:7 What, then, does this mean? That Israel as a nation did not achieve the reunification with God they sought, except for few individuals. What Israel sought to earn by working to induce God to be gracious, actually caused them to misunderstand God, become self-sufficient and arrogant, and fail in obtaining restoration with God. But those who trusted God, based on the truth as revealed in Jesus, obtained God's gracious gift of healing and restoration. The others, instead of being healed and restored, were hardened, ⁸ as it is written:

"When they rejected truth, God gave them over to a dull mind:
eyes trained to no longer recognize truth
and ears tuned to no longer hear truth;
and this goes on to this very day."
Rom 11:9 And David says:
"May what they rely on for strength and sustenance be revealed as a snare and a trap, the actual cause of their stumbling and the source of their pain.
Rom 11:10 "May the result of their rejection of truth damage their minds so they can no longer comprehend;
may their characters be so twisted by persistent rebellion that they will not reform."

Rom 11:11 So, again I ask: Did they stumble and fall so low that they are beyond recovery? Absolutely not! Rather, because of their transgression, the privilege of joining God's spiritual health-care team has come to the Gentiles—in order to inspire the descendants of Abraham to accept God's healing and rejoin his team. ¹² But if their failure to fulfill the mission God assigned them means riches and opportunity for the rest of the world, and their lost position means that their mission was given to the Gentiles, how much greater will the richness of love and grace be if they accept the truth and fulfill their mission!

Rom 11:13 I am talking to you, Gentiles: I am the apostle to the Gentiles, and I take my responsibility to you seriously. ¹⁴ I hope that by leading you to trust God—and thus to experience the healing, love, peace and joy that reconciliation with God brings—I may somehow arouse my own people with a desire for this same experience, and maybe some of them will respond and be saved. ¹⁵ For even though they rejected the truth that brings trust, reconciliation and life eternal, this healing truth was still revealed to the world. What would have happened if they had accepted the truth? An unbelievably powerful revelation of God's character, methods and principles seen in action would have transformed the entire world! [16] If the ingredients used to make the loaf are untainted and pure, then the entire loaf will be perfect and healthy. If the roots of the tree are pure and unpolluted, then every branch and all the fruit will be perfect and healthy.

Rom 11:17 If some of the branches have broken off from the vine, and you—though not natural to the vine—have been grafted in and now share the nourishment from the root, [18] don't feel that you are somehow superior to the branches that have broken off. If you do, remember this: The root does not draw sustenance from you, but you are nourished by the root. [19] You might try to argue, "But we must be something special, because the natural branches were broken off to make room for us." [20] Don't be ridiculous. They broke away because they did not trust, and you were grafted in because you did trust. Don't be conceited, but be afraid of conceit or pride, or anything that will undermine your abiding trust in God. [21] For if God did not stop the natural branches from distrusting and breaking away, he will not restrict your freedom to break away either.

Rom 11:22 Consider how kind and gracious, and how true and consistent God is. He is true and consistent to the principles of love and freedom, and forces no one to remain connected to him, but allows those who choose to break away to do so if they insist. He is kind and gracious to you, allowing you to abide in his goodness. But if you choose to break away, you too will be permitted to sever your connection with him. [23] And if those who have broken away have a change of heart and again trust God, they will be reconnected to him, for God is able to heal them if they let him. [24] After all, if you—who were not originally attached

to the vine—were successfully grafted in, isn't it a lot easier to reattach branches that were once part of the parent plant?

Rom 11:25 I want to explain to you this mystery—this unexplainable rejection of God's plan by Israel—so that you will not become conceited and make the same mistake: A large part of the genetic descendants of Abraham have hardened their hearts to God and rejected the truth as revealed by Jesus; therefore God's plan for Abraham's descendants will not be fulfilled until those hardened and broken off are replaced by a large number of Gentiles who are grafted in. [26] And so all true children of Abraham—those like Abraham in character, not in genetics—will be saved, as it is written:

"The deliverer will come from Zion;
  he will remove all selfishness and
  sin from everyone who trust God,
  like Jacob.
Rom 11:27 "And my promise to them is
  this:
Complete healing from sin and
  perfect restoration to my original
  ideal."

Rom 11:28 As far as the good news about God and his plan to heal and restore is concerned, they are enemies of God and oppose his healing plan; but as far as God's loving attitude and desire to reach them and heal them—they remain loved just as in the times of the patriarchs, [29] for God's love and gracious, forgiving character are unchangeable. [30] Just as you, who were at one time infected with distrust of God and dominated by selfishness, have now found the mercy that could have been theirs if they would have been willing to listen and obey, [31] so they, who now distrust God and are dominated by selfishness and therefore don't listen to God, may still receive God's mercy and come to trust him again as they see what God has done for you. [32] For from God's perspective, all humanity is infected with the same illness of distrust and selfishness, and the entire human race is dying and in need of the same Remedy; and God mercifully offers full healing and restoration to all who trust him.

Rom 11:33 Oh, the magnitude of the worth and value of the wisdom and knowledge of God! How infinite is his intelligence; and his method of governing is beyond the ability of humans to reproduce!

Rom 11:34 "What created being can know what God is thinking?
Who would ever presume they could share with God wisdom or insights that he doesn't already know?
Rom 11:35 "Who has ever provided God with something that didn't come from him to begin with?
Who could ever have God indebted to them?"

Rom 11:36 For it is from God that all things exist. To him be glory forever! Amen.

12 Therefore with all my heart I urge you, brothers and sisters, to consider how merciful God is in providing his Remedy, and to surrender your entire being to God as a living sacrifice—to be healed and transformed into God's image. This is the most reasonable, logical and intelligent worship you could ever offer. 2 Do not continue to practice the destructive methods of selfishness, which infect the world, but be completely transformed into God's image by the renewing of your mind. Then you will value God's principles, practice his methods, and discern his will—his good, pleasing and perfect will.

Rom 12:3 For by God's grace poured out on me, I say to all of you: Don't get caught in the trap of thinking you are somehow better than others; rather, be honest with yourself about your own state of spiritual health. The greater your trust in God is, the more you will realize that all your strength, wisdom, and godliness of character have come from him, and you will no longer consider yourself in any way superior to others. 4 Just as each one of us has one body with many different parts, and these different parts all have different functions and abilities, 5 so it is with those of us who belong to Christ: We are one body, with each individual believer—each individual part—belonging to a larger whole, with duties and responsibilities byond the self. 6 We each have different talents, gifts, abilities, experience and perspectives, in harmony with how God's graciousness has worked in our lives. If anyone is blessed with the ability to prophesy, let them prophesy more effectively as their confidence in God grows. 7 If some are gifted with serving others, let them serve; if it is teaching, let them teach; 8 if it is encouraging, let them encourage; if it is giving financially to the needs of others, let them give generously; if it is leadership, let them govern diligently and with Christlike principles; if it is showing mercy, let them do it cheerfully. In this way, the body grows in strength as each member exercises their gifts, talents and abilities for the good of the whole.

Rom 12:9 Love must be genuine, not fleeting or based merely on feelings. Hate what is selfish and evil (not the people infected with selfishness and evil, but the principles, motives, attitudes, activities and practices that spread selfishness and evil), and cling to all that is good and healthy. 10 Be devoted to the welfare, healing, advancement and growth of one another in genuine Christlike love. Value others and their needs above yourselves. 11 Don't become apathetic, lazy or indifferent, but keep your passion for God and his ways as the motivating force in all you do. 12 Be joyful in hope, patient in trials and tribulations, consistent and diligent in talking with God. 13 Give to God's people who have genuine needs, and be hospitable and friendly.

Rom 12:14 Seek healing and restoration for those who persecute you, for the infection of selfishness and sin is destroying them; do good to them, and do not be reinfected with evil.

15 Empathize with others, share in their joy as well as their sorrows—thus grow together in Christian love 16 and you will live in harmony with one another. Don't be reinfected with pride, but remember that we are all infected with the same selfish condition and need the same Remedy freely provided by God. Don't make class distinctions, or refuse to associate with those who are considered by some to be of low position. Don't be deceived by conceit.

Rom 12:17 Don't repay evil with evil, for in so doing you only allow the infection of selfishness to be strengthened and thus damage your mind and character. Be sure to do what is right because it is right—openly for all to see. 18 Do all in your power to live at peace with others, but be aware that others may still perpetrate evil against you. 19 And when this happens, my friends, do not take revenge—there is no need for it!—for every act of sin reacts upon the sinner, damaging and slowly destroying their God-given faculties. Be patient and permit God's wrath to work—God's wise method of letting one go to reap the consequences of one's choice—and hopefully it will bring your enemy to repentance; as it is written: "It is mine to discipline; I will settle any debts," says the Lord. 20 Rather than taking revenge,

"If your enemy is hungry, feed him; if he is thirsty, give him something to drink.
In doing good to your enemy, you will bring guilt and mental anguish like burning coals down on their head."

Rom 12:21 So don't let evil and selfishness consume you, but rather expel evil and selfishness from your heart by doing good and loving others.

13 Everyone must obey—and not rebel against—the governing authorities, as they govern to bring order to society. All true authority comes from God, and the current authorities hold power in harmony with God's plan. 2 So, if you rebel against the Roman government and choose insurrection, you are not practicing God's methods but actually misrepresenting God and interfering with his plan. Those who rebel will condemn themselves, 3 for there is no reason to fear the one in authority if you do what is right; you only need to fear if you are doing what is wrong. Do you want to be free from fear of the ruler? Then do what is right, and those in authority will reward you, 4 for they are God's servants to do you good. But if you do wrong, fear the consequences, for the power to punish, which they have, is not for nothing. They are God's servants—agents of discipline—to bring consequences on the wrongdoer, and hopefully to awaken the wrongdoer to a better course. 5 Therefore, it is important to obey the authorities that are part of God's plan—not merely because of fear of punishment, but because it is the right thing to do.

Rom 13:6 This is exactly the same reason for which you pay taxes, for the authorities are God's servants to provide order, safety, security, economy, emergency services, courts of justice, utilities, and so forth. 7 Be sure to give to everyone what you owe them: If you owe taxes, pay the taxes you owe; if revenue, then the revenue you owe; if respect, then respect; if honor, then honor.

Rom 13:8 Don't remain in debt of any kind, except the debt to love one another, for the one who loves their fellow humans has fulfilled all that the law requires, for the law is simply about love. 9 The commandments are a diagnostic tool to reveal where love has broken down: for when you love, you "do not commit adultery," and you "do not murder," and you "do not steal," and you "do not covet." For all ten commandments are summed up in this one principle: "Love! Love the Lord most of all, and your neighbor as yourself." [10]Love is the principle of beneficence and does no harm, but does only what is in the best interest of another, therefore love is the law upon which life is based.

Rom 13:11 And do this (love one another), understanding the time in which we live. The time has come for you to wake up and realize that our deliverance from this world of sin is nearer now than when we first came to trust God. [12]The night of darkness and separation from God is nearly over; the day of his coming is almost here. So let us put aside the deeds of darkness, the deeds that misrepresent God and separate us from him, and put on the armor of light—the character of Christ and the truth about God. [13]Let us live righteously, as in the light of God's truth, and not in the darkness of orgies, drugs and drunkenness; not in pornography and debauchery; not in envy, rumor-mongering and jealousy. [14]Rather, clothe yourself with the Lord Jesus Christ—develop your character to be just like his in all you do, and choose to say "No" to the desires of the selfish nature.

14 The young in Christ often have weak confidence in God and limited understanding of his methods, so don't be critical of them and don't argue over trivial matters. [2]Consider foods offered to idols: A mature Christian, whose trust in God and understanding of his methods are strong, recognizes that an idol is just a piece of wood or stone that cannot affect the nutrition of the meat offered to it, so they will eat the meat without worry. But the immature Christian, whose trust in God and understanding of his methods is weak, continues to struggle with misconceptions about idols and thinks that maybe the idol has the power to contaminate the meat offered to it, and thus eats only the vegetables that were not set before the idol. [3]The mature person, who eats everything that is healthy, must not demean or make fun of the person still struggling with fear and insecurity over what they eat; and the person who is afraid to eat all healthy foods must not condemn as wicked the person who eats everything healthy, for they are at peace with God. [4]Don't you realize it is not your place to make judgments about the condition or quality of another person's servant? The master of the servant determines whether the servant is in good standing or not. And the one who is no longer bound by fear and superstition, and therefore eats everything that is healthy, is in good standing with God, because God has healed that person's mind and renewed their heart.

Rom 14:5 One person considers one day more sacred than another; another person considers all days the same. A person's opinion doesn't make a day sacred or not sacred, but each person can only benefit by what they have come to understand and believe for themself, so each person must study the evidence and be fully convinced in their own mind. [6]The person who regards one day as special is choosing to honor the Lord in accordance with their understanding of the truth. The person who eats meat is choosing to honor the Lord by demonstrating that idols are powerless, and instead gives thanks to God for the food; and the person who abstains from eating meat is also honoring God by recognizing that all they have comes from God. [7]For none of God's children live selfishly any longer, and none of us die alone and abandoned. [8]If we live, we live for the Lord—a cause greater than ourselves—and if we die, our death will also serve God's cause. So, whether we live or die, we have surrendered all to the Lord.

The Remedy

225

Rom 14:9 This is the very reason Christ died and rose to life again—his was a cause that encompassed more than himself. He died and rose from the dead to heal the universe from distrust of God, selfishness, and death; he is therefore the Lord of both the living and the dead. 10 Who are you then to judge your brother or sister? Do you think you are somehow better? Why do you belittle and look at others with disdain? Don't you realize that we are all infected with the same sickness and one day all of us will stand before God to see if we have been healed? 11 It is written:

"'As surely as I live,' says the Lord,
'everyone will kneel before me and
be examined;
every mouth will reveal what the
condition of the heart is.'"

Rom 14:12 So then, each of us will stand before God, and the true condition of our hearts will be revealed.

Rom 14:13 Therefore let us stop criticizing and being judgmental toward one another. Instead, realize that each of us is in need of healing, and do all in your power to remove barriers to compliance with God's treatment plan from your own and also your brother's or sister's way. 14 As one who is reconciled to the Lord Jesus, and who is working in union with him, I am fully convinced that no nutritional substance can contaminate the soul or sear the conscience. But if anyone thinks that a certain food is evil, wicked or somehow wrong to eat, and then eats it anyway, that person will experience guilt, fear, insecurity, confusion, worry, and a damaged mind. 15 If you know that your brother or sister is struggling with such issues and you purposely, in front of them, eat foods that upset, worry and distress them, you are not acting in love toward your brother or sister. Or if you invite your brother or sister to your home and serve them food offered to idols, knowing they are still fearful of such things, you are not acting in love toward your brother or sister. Do not, by the use of food, place in your brother's or sister's way barriers to compliance with God's healing plan. 16 Don't practice what you know is good in such a way that it lends itself to be easily misconstrued as evil. 17 For God's kingdom—his method of governing—is not about control or about a set of rules regarding what to eat and what not to eat. God's kingdom is about living in harmony with the principles on which life is based—about doing what is right simply because it is right. Such a kingdom brings peace and joy, and the indwelling of the Holy Spirit. 18 Anyone who cooperates with Christ in this way pleases God and is admired by people.

Rom 14:19 Let us therefore consider the wellbeing of others, and do whatever we can to assist in their healing and to promote peace with each other. 20 Do not destroy God's work of rebuilding his character in humanity by arguing over food. All food is clean from such things as demonic influences, or evil spells or curses (though that doesn't mean that everything people eat is healthy for the body), but even though no food is unclean in this way, it is wrong to eat anything that you know will confuse, upset or somehow undermine your brother's or sister's growth with God. 21 It is better not to eat meat or drink wine, or do anything that will cause your brother or sister to misunderstand God and fail to experience healing of heart and mind.

Rom 14:22 So whatever you believe about such inconsequential things, rather than stir up unnecessary controversy, keep such things between yourself and God. You will be happy and at peace if you don't have superstitious fears about what you eat. 23 But the person who eats food and then is afraid or guilt-ridden because of superstitious fears, damages their mind, because they are eating without trusting God; and everything that doesn't stem from trust in God is sin.

15 We, who have had our minds set free from distrust and fear and are therefore strong in our confidence in God and in understanding his methods, have a responsibility to help those still weakened by the infection of distrust and selfishness—and to not simply live to please ourselves. ⁷Each of us should do all in our power to help our neighbor recover from the devastation caused by distrust in God, fear, and selfishness. We should strive to help heal and restore our neighbor. ³Christ himself has shown how to live, for he did not live to please himself, but, as the Scriptures state, "I have accepted the abuse meant for you, in order to protect and heal you." ⁴All of the inspired writings of the past were recorded for our benefit—to teach us the truth about God and his plan to heal and restore—so that we would not become discouraged but endure, and remain confident and hopeful.

Rom 15:5 May God, who strengthens and encourages, give you an attitude of unity as you seek to be like Christ Jesus, ⁶so that with hearts and minds united in the truth you may bring glory to the true God—the Father of our Lord Jesus Christ.

Rom 15:7 Accept one another as sick in need of God's free Remedy (just as Christ has accepted and healed you) and thus bring praise to God—the source of all goodness and health. ⁸For I tell you plainly, Christ promised the patriarchs that he would bring the Remedy to heal humanity, and he came with the truth to the Jews as a humble servant and procured the Remedy, thus keeping his promise. ⁹And this same Remedy, brought by Christ to the Jews, has been made available to all humanity, and thus the Gentiles may glorify God for his mercy, as it is written:

"Therefore I will reveal the truth
   about you among the Gentiles;
I will sing the beauty of your
   character."

Rom 15:10 Again, it says,
"Be joyful, O Gentiles, with his
   people—
the Remedy is for all humanity."
Rom 15:11 And again,
"Accept the cure and be healed to be
   like Jesus, all you Gentiles,
and sing joyful thanks to him,
   all people of the earth."
Rom 15:12 And again, Isaiah says,
"A descendant of Jesse will grow up,
   one who will arise to govern the
   world;
and the Gentiles will trust in him."
Rom 15:13 As you trust in God, may your fear be expelled, and your hearts filled with joy and peace, so that by the power of the Holy Spirit you may be continually filled with hope.

Rom 15:14 I am convinced, my brothers and sisters, that you have opened your hearts and minds to God and are filled with goodness, and that you genuinely know God and are capable of teaching others about him. ¹⁵I have been quite direct on some issues in my letter to you, but only to remind you of the important matters we are all aware of. I have done this because God graciously called me ¹⁶to be his ambassador in taking the healing truth about Jesus Christ to the Gentiles. I have been privileged to carry out my duty as a faithful minister of spiritual health and to proclaim the good news about God to the Gentiles so that they, by the working of the Holy Spirit, may be fully healed and restored back into God's original ideal for humanity.

Rom 15:17 Therefore it is my glory and joy to serve God by presenting the truth as revealed in Christ Jesus. ¹⁸I will not waste my time talking about anything except what I have been privileged to accomplish by working with Christ— bringing the transforming truth to the Gentiles. ¹⁹God has revealed himself in signs and miracles, and through the power of truth and love brought by the Spirit. So from Jerusalem all the way to Illyricum, I have fully proclaimed the good news about God as revealed in Christ. 20 It has always been my heart's desire to take the healing Remedy about God to where the truth of Christ was not yet known, so that I would be working with those who are most in need. 21 As it is written:

"Those who have never heard the truth about God, which heals the mind, will see and understand."

Rom 15:22 This is what has kept me from coming to you.

Rom 15:23 But now that the truth has been taken to all these places, and since I have been longing to come to you for so many years, 24 I plan to do so on my way to Spain. I hope to be able to visit with you on my journey to Spain, and after spending some time with you, I hope you can assist me on my way. 25 But currently, I am on my way to Jerusalem to be of service the saints there, 26 for our brothers in Macedonia and Achaia were eager to make a donation for the poor among the saints in Jerusalem. 27 They were glad to help, and even felt a sense of obligation to them, as they felt a real sense of gratitude for being able to share in God's healing Remedy, which came through the Jews, and so they wanted to share their financial blessings with the Jews. 28 So once I have taken this gift to the saints in Jerusalem, I will go on to Spain and visit you on the way. 29 I know that when I come to you, I will do so with Christ's blessing.

Rom 15:30 I beg you, brothers and sisters, by your desire to be like our Lord Jesus Christ, and by the love of the Spirit who lives in you, to pray to God with me. 31 Pray that I will be protected from the unbelievers in Judea and that the believers in Jerusalem will accept my service and the gifts I bring from their fellow believers, 32 so that if it be God's will, I will come to you rejoicing, and together we will be refreshed. 33 The great God of peace be with you all. Amen.

16

I recommend to you our sister Phoebe, a friend of God and servant of the church in Cenchrea. 2 I ask you to welcome her in God's love worthy of the saints, and to provide her with any help she may need, for she has been helpful to many people, including me.

Rom 16:3 Welcome Priscilla and Aquila, my co-workers in Jesus Christ. 4 They risked their lives for me. And not only I, but all the churches of the Gentiles are grateful to them.

Rom 16:5 Welcome also the believers that meet at their house. Welcome my dear friend Epenetus, who was the first person in the province of Asia to trust in Jesus Christ.

Rom 16:6 Welcome Mary; she worked very hard for you.

Rom 16:7 Welcome Andronicus and Junias, members of my family, who have been imprisoned with me. They are outstanding apostles who had accepted the truth brought by Jesus before I did.

Rom 16:8 Welcome Ampliatus, whom I love in the Lord.

Rom 16:9 Welcome Urbanus, a faithful representative of Christ, and my dear friend Stachys.

Rom 16:10 Welcome Apelles, tried and matured in Christ.

Welcome the family of Aristobulus.

Rom 16:11 Welcome Herodion, a member of my family.

Welcome the family members of Narcissus, who have accepted the truth Jesus has brought.

Rom 16:12 Welcome Tryphena and Tryphosa—these women have worked hard to promote God's cause.

Welcome my dear friend Persis, another woman who has worked hard promoting God's cause.

Rom 16:13 Welcome Rufus, healed by the truth, and his mother, who has been a mother to me as well.

Rom 16:14 Welcome Asyncritus, Phlegon, Hermes, Patrobas, Hermas, and the brothers in Christ with them.

Rom 16:15 Welcome Philologus, Julia,

Nereus and his sisters, and Olympas. and all the saints with them.

Rom 16:16 Welcome each other with the right-hand of fellowship and the bond of Christian unity. All the churches of Christ send greetings.

Rom 16:17 I caution you, brothers and sisters: Be alert and on-guard, watching for those who spread rumors and gossip, misrepresent God, or in any other way cause division and obstruct the truth about God as revealed in Jesus. Keep away from them, 18 for no matter what they profess, such people are not serving our Lord Jesus Christ, but are actually working against him. By eloquent speeches, emotional appeals and boisterous preaching they deceive the immature and naive. 19 Everyone has heard about how willing you are to humbly listen and follow wherever the truth in Christ leads. I am so proud of you, and your Christlike lives bring joy to my heart. I want you to be wise about the power of goodness, and to avoid all that is evil.

Rom 16:20 And when we open our hearts to love others completely, totally selflessly at all costs, rejecting Satan's methods of selfishness, then the God of peace crushes Satan and all his lies under our feet. May the grace of Christ be with you.

Rom 16:21 Timothy, my co-worker in distributing God's healing Remedy, sends his warm regards to you, as does Lucius, Jason and Sosipater—members of my family.

Rom 16:22 I, Tertius, who transcribed this letter for Paul, greet you in the Lord.

Rom 16:23 Gaius, who has been so hospitable to me and to the entire church here, sends his greetings. Erastus, who is the city's director of public works, and our brother Quartus also send you their greetings. 24 May the grace of the Lord Jesus Christ be with you always.

Rom 16:25 Now to God, who is able to perfectly heal your mind and heart by the good news revealed in Jesus Christ—this good news is the revelation of God's character that was obscured by Satan's lies long ago, 26 but now has been clearly revealed and made known through Christ's life and the prophetic writings by God's direction, so that the entire world might reject Satan's lies about God, see the truth as revealed in Jesus and again trust God fully and follow his treatment plan— 27 to the only wise God be glory forever through the truth revealed by Jesus Christ!

Amen.

1 Corinthians

1 Paul, commissioned as an ambassador of the celestial government of Jesus Christ and confirmed by God, and our brother Sosthenes,

1Cor 1:2 To the residents of Corinth who love and trust God, those who have partaken of the healing Remedy procured by Christ Jesus and are called to be his representatives, along with everyone everywhere who has accepted the truth about God as revealed by Jesus, and trusts our Lord Jesus Christ:

1Cor 1:3 Grace and peace are poured out on you from God our Father and from the Lord Jesus Christ.

1Cor 1:4 Whenever I talk with God, I thank him for his gracious Remedy poured out on you in Christ Jesus. 5 For as you have partaken of the healing Remedy brought by Jesus, you have become healthier in every way: your minds are sharper, your understanding and wisdom—deeper, and your characters—more Christlike. 6 Your transformed lives testify to the healing power of the Remedy brought to us by Christ—and which we shared with you — 7 and you have received every blessing heaven has to give as you eagerly anticipate the return of our Lord Jesus Christ. 8 He will fill you with confidence and remove your fear—right up to the very end—so that your minds will be fully healed, selfishness will be removed from your characters, and you will be ready to see him on the day our Lord Jesus Christ appears. 9 God is absolutely trustworthy, and he is the one who wants you free from selfishness and restored to complete unity with his Son, Jesus Christ our Lord.

1Cor 1:10 Brothers and sisters, as an ambassador of our Lord Jesus Christ, I call on you to come into agreement with each other on the truth about God as revealed by Jesus, and be fully united in mind, heart, attitude and motive around the beautiful character and methods of God. 11 My brothers and sisters, I have heard from some of Chloe's household that disagreements and arguments have developed among you. 12 Evidently, some of you have lost the main focus of the truth about God as revealed by Jesus, for one of you says, "I am Paul's disciple;" another, "I adhere to the teachings of Apollos;" yet another, "I belong to the order of Peter;" and still others, "I follow Christ."

1Cor 1:13 What are you thinking? Is there more than one Christ? Do you think Christ has multiple personalities, or is two-faced? Were your minds immersed in the truth about Paul or in the truth about God as revealed by Christ? 14 I am thankful that—after your minds were immersed in the truth about God as revealed by Christ—I didn't assist any of you in the symbolic water immersion, except for Crispus and Gaius, 15 so none of you would get confused and think you were immersing your hearts in loyalty to me. 16 (Oh yes, I also assisted the household of Stephanas in the symbolic water immersion, but other than that, I don't remember assisting anyone else with this ritual.) 17 For God did not send me to perform rituals, but to present the good news about him, about his methods, principles and character as revealed by Christ—not some human theory of appeasement—lest the death of Christ be seen as some payment to an offended god, and therefore lose its power to free the mind from fear and mistrust of God.

1Cor 1:18 For the truth about God—his character of absolute love, as revealed by Christ at the cross—makes no sense whatsoever to those who are dying through practicing the world's method of survival-of-the-fittest; but to those of us who are being healed and restored, it is the true power of God, the secret of eternal life.

1Cor 1:19 For the Scriptures reveal that God's method of self-sacrificing love will destroy the world's wisdom of promoting self first, but the apparent logic of working for self-exaltation, fame, personal advancement or financial wealth—rather than bringing healing and restoration, will be shown to actually accelerate the damage to one's mind and character.

1Cor 1:20 So then, what value is there in the wisdom of the selfish person? Or the agnostic professor? Or the atheistic scientist? Or the psychologist of the New Age? God has shown that all "wisdom" based on the principles of this world is in reality foolishness, silliness, nonsense! 21 For after those who value the methods of the world rejected God and denied his existence, God joyfully revealed his wisdom by actually healing and transforming all those who trust him on the basis of the simple message of God's selfless love revealed by Jesus. 22 The Jews, and many like them, demand supernatural signs and wonders, which (they fail to realize) can be counterfeited; and the Greeks look only for intellectual explanations, 23 but we preach God's self-sacrificing character of love revealed by Christ crucified. It's a roadblock to the ego-centric Jews, and utter nonsense to the self-seeking Gentiles, 24 but to all those who respond to God's call—whether Jew or Gentile—Christ is the embodiment of the character, wisdom and power of God! 25 For the simple love of God is wiser than all humankind's self-centered scheming; God's love literally heals and restores. And this love of God, which appears weak to the world, is stronger than all the strength of selfish humanity.

1Cor 1:26 Brothers and sisters, remember where you were, and what you were like, before you responded to God's call. From the world's perspective, not many of you were successful or wise, or powerful, or high on the social scale. 27 But God has purposely chosen what appears to be the worst cases—the ignorant and foolish—to reveal the tremendous transforming power of his Remedy and thus expose the futility of the world's wisdom. God has purposely chosen what the selfish world considers weak to reveal how impotent the world's power really is. 28 He has chosen what the selfish world criticizes and looks down on, and mocks, ridicules, and considers as nothing, in order that his love may eradicate selfishness from the world— 29 for then no one will ever be able to take credit to themselves for the healing and transformation that comes from God alone. 30 It is because God is always on our side and working for our good that our minds have been set right, and we are in unity with Jesus Christ. We recognize Jesus as the wisdom of God in human form—the source of our healing, righteousness, and re-creation into Godlikeness. 31 Therefore, just as it has been written: "If you want to brag and promote something, then brag about the Lord and promote the truth about him."

2 Brothers and sisters, when I came to you with the truth about God, that had been hidden by years of misunderstanding and distortion, I did not add to your confusion by using theological jargon, but instead, I presented the truth in simple language, so even the children could understand. 2 It was my goal to present the simple truth about God's character of love as revealed in Jesus Christ and his self-sacrificing death on the cross. 3 When I

came to you, I was so unsure of how to present this life-saving truth in a way you would appreciate, that my hands trembled with nervousness.

⁴ While my preaching was not the preaching of a professional speaker— and I didn't impress you with eloquent dialogue—the Holy Spirit worked through me to make clear the truth about God's character of love, ⁵ so that your confidence and trust would not rest on human charisma but on God himself and his character of love.

1Cor 2:6 We speak a message of genuine wisdom, which only those whose minds are being healed and transformed can understand. It is not the so-called wisdom of worldly science or of the coercive religions of the world who are only destroying themselves. ⁷ No; we speak of God's secret wisdom—the wisdom that is the basis of life and which has been hidden by Satan's lies and distortions; the wisdom that God determined to restore in us before anything was created, in order that we may be the evidence of his glorious power of love. ⁸ None of the scientific or religious leaders who value the survival-of-the-fittest principle understood it—for if they had, they would not have killed Jesus Christ, the Lord of glory. ⁹ It is just as the Scripture has said:

"No one has ever seen this,
nor has anyone ever heard of
something like it,
neither has anyone ever imagined
anything as incredible as what
God has done
for those who love him."

1Cor 2:10 But God has revealed his secret plan to us by his Spirit, for the Spirit examines, explores, investigates and researches everything, even the heart and mind of God. ¹¹ Who knows what a person is really thinking, except the mind of the person themself? In the same way, no one knows God's thoughts except God's own Spirit. ¹² We have not received the perspectives, thoughts, values, methods or principles of the world, but we have received God's very own thoughts, attitude, methods and principles—brought to us by his Spirit—so that we may understand God and all he has done for us. ¹³ This is the message we bring: not a message based on the selfish principles of the world, but the very secret thoughts of God—his true nature and character of love taught by his Spirit— expressing the life-giving truths in ways we can comprehend. ¹⁴ The person who rejects the Spirit of God rejects the truth the Spirit reveals about God's character of selfless love; such absolute love is foolishness to them, and they cannot even comprehend it because it is understood and experienced only by the work of the Holy Spirit. ¹⁵ The person who opens their mind to the Spirit of God has their mind enlightened with God's values, principles and perspectives, and is able to discern and make accurate assessments about all things, but they themself cannot be understood by the spiritually immature:

1Cor 2:16 "For is there anyone
who knows what God is thinking
that they can counsel or instruct
him?"

But we, who have opened our minds to the Holy Spirit, have Christ's mind reproduced within us!

3 My dear brothers and sisters, I was not able to address you as grownups who have been enlightened by the truth about God's character of love, whose minds have actually been regenerated to be like Christ's. No; I had to speak to you as those still infected with the principles of the world—the survival-of-the-fittest methods; people who are just starting God's treatment plan, newborn babes in Christ. ² Therefore, I gave you baby food, the ABCs of God's treatment plan. And instead of growing beyond the basics, many of you have preferred the

elementary teachings and are still not ready to grow in Christ Jesus. ³In fact, the infection of selfishness, which the world loves, still dominates your lives. Is this not demonstrated by your persistent jealousy, arguing, bickering and infighting? Are you not acting just like the rest of the world, looking out for yourselves and promoting your own agenda rather than surrendering all you have for the cause of Christ? ⁴You even promote the spirit of division and competition, just like the world does, and turn the mind away from Christ when you say, "I'm a follower of Paul," and another says, "But I follow Apollos."

1Cor 3:5 Who, after all, is Paul? Or who is Apollos? We are merely aides of God; conduits of his, who have brought you the same healing Remedy—each doing their part in the healing process, as the Lord has assigned. ⁶I planted the truth about God, and Apollos watered this truth with the wisdom God has given him, but it is God who causes the truth to grow and bring forth fruit of a Christlike character. It is God who heals; it is God who restores. ⁷So neither he who plants the truth about God nor he who waters this truth is of any significance—God is the only one important, the only source of life, the only source of healing. ⁸So you see, the one who plants the truth and the one who waters it, both have the very same purpose—to see God's image fully restored in people—and such labor brings its own reward. ⁹For we are coworkers with God, and you are the field in which we labor; you are God's building upon which we work.

1Cor 3:10 By using the wisdom, insight and understanding that God has given me regarding his plan for rebuilding the human heart and mind, I laid a foundation in harmony with his original design, and others are now building on it. ¹¹For Jesus Christ is the only true foundation—the real source of God's character, methods and principles—and no one can replace him.

¹²One can build on this foundation using pure, holy and costly materials, or using ordinary, common and cheap materials, ¹³but ultimately, the work will reveal itself for what it is, because the day on which Christ returns will bring everything into the light of truth. On that day the quality of a person's character-building will be revealed by the fiery glory of God's presence—for only those whose characters are in harmony with God's character will be able to stand in the fiery presence of his life-giving glory. ¹⁴And if those whom the builders have worked to build up in Christ survive, the builders will be rewarded with happiness and joy. ¹⁵If, however, the builder's work is burned up, the builder will suffer great sorrow and loss; the builder will be saved, but only as one whose misunderstandings, errors, misconceptions and mistakes are consumed in the fire of God's truth and love.

1Cor 3:16 Don't you realize that you yourselves are the very temple of God—the place he dwells on earth—and that God's Spirit actually lives in you (in your heart and mind)? ¹⁷If anyone fills the heart and mind with the destructive principles of this world, then when God returns, his presence will be a consuming fire to such people and will destroy them; for you are created to be God's temple—to have your hearts and minds filled with his character, methods and principles—and God's temple is to be kept pure.

1Cor 3:18 Don't deceive yourselves! If you think you are wise because you practice the principles and standards of the world, then you must completely reverse your thinking and become a "fool" to the world, and practice God's methods in order to truly be wise. ¹⁹For the survival-of-the-fittest method that the world considers as wise—always looking out for self—is insanity in God's sight. As it is written, "He exposes the worldly wise by their own evil schemes;" ²⁰and, "The Lord knows that the reasoning of the worldly wise is misleading and destructive." ²¹ So stop all efforts to promote or follow a person—man or woman! Everything is yours, and provided for your good: ²² whether Paul, or Apollos, or Cephas, or the world, or life, or death, or the present, or the future—everything is yours, ²³ because you are Christ's, and Christ is God's.

4 You should consider us as Christ's ambassadors whose mission it is to share with you the secret things of God. ² The requirement to be trusted as an ambassador of Christ is to accurately reveal Christ in word and deed. ³ Your assessment of me is not relevant, nor do I concern myself with the conclusions of a human court; indeed, I do not even diagnose myself. ⁴ My conscience has been cleansed, but that does not mean I am totally cured. It is the Lord who diagnoses me. ⁵ Therefore don't diagnose anyone's final state before the appointed time; wait until the Lord returns. He will expose the true condition of every person and bring into the open the real character formed in each individual's heart. At that time, all who have been healed will receive affirmation from God.

1Cor 4:6 Understand, brothers and sisters, that I have applied all these truths to myself and Apollos for your good, so that you may learn from us the meaning of the saying, "Don't add human fables or selfish interpretations to the Scriptures." Then you will remain humble and not promote one human above another. ⁷ Who makes you healthier or holier than anyone else? What do you have—whether health, purity of character, riches, talents, or anything else—that was not given to you? And if God gave it to you, why do you brag as though you obtained it on your own?

1Cor 4:8 You act as though you have all that you need! You act as though you are rich, as though you are already kings in God's kingdom, even though you are not! Oh, how I wish you really were kings in God's kingdom, for that would mean God's kingdom is already here and we would be kings with you! ⁹ As I see it, God has put us ambassadors on display, at the end of a great procession of his witnesses. Just like people who die in the arena, we—who have partaken of the Remedy procured by Jesus—are now center stage. We have been made examples and evidence of the healing power of the Remedy—procured by Jesus Christ—before the entire universe, revealing the truth to angels as well as to people! ¹⁰ Our commitment to Christ and his method of love brings the accusation that we are fools, but you claim to have received superior wisdom from Christ! Our meekness is thought of as weakness, but you view yourselves as strong! While you are adored, we are degraded! ¹¹ Often we go hungry and thirsty. Our clothes are rags, we are abused and mistreated, and we are homeless. ¹² Yet we are not lazy; we work diligently to provide for ourselves. We bless those who curse us, patiently endure all persecution, ¹³ and speak kindly of those who lie about us. We are treated like waste—discarded and reviled.

1Cor 4:14 I am not writing this to shame or discourage you, but to warn you as the children I love. ¹⁵ Even though through Christ you have ten thousand caregivers, you do not have many fathers; for in union with Jesus Christ I became your spiritual father through the Remedy he brought. ¹⁶ Therefore model yourselves after me. ¹⁷ To help you do this, I am sending to you Timothy, my son whom I love, and who knows God and is true to him. He will share with you how I live victoriously in Christ Jesus, which is in harmony with what I teach in every church.

1Cor 4:18 Some of you are self-righteous and arrogant, as if I were never coming. ¹⁹ But very soon, if it is God's will,

I will come and discover not only what these arrogant people are saying, but also the impact or power their words are having. 20 For the kingdom of God is not simply a matter of words, but of power—the power to heal and transform hearts and minds! 21 When I come, which manifestation of love would you prefer me to reveal? A whip with which to discipline and correct, or a gentle spirit with which to reason and teach?

5 Unbelievably, it has been reported that there is open sexual immorality among you, even worse than what pagans practice: A man has his own father's wife! 2 And some of you are proud? What are you thinking! Shouldn't your hearts have been broken in sadness and remorse? Should you not have disciplined this man and woman, and if they persist, put them out of your fellowship? 3 Even though I am not physically there with you, I am with you in heart, and I have already—just as easily as if I were there—diagnosed the ones who did this as being out of harmony with God's methods. 4 When you assemble, with hearts and minds in harmony with our Lord Jesus, knowing that I am with you in heart and that the power of our Lord Jesus is present, 5 call this man and woman to account, and if they refuse to repent—abandon them to their own choices, so that in reaping the consequences of choosing Satan's kingdom—their flesh will suffer, and they will recognize their error and have a change of heart before it is too late, and thus be saved when the Lord returns.

1Cor 5:6 Your pride and bragging is destructive. Don't you realize that yeast is a symbol of sin, and it only takes a little to spread through the entire batch of dough? 7 Get rid of old yeast—the old selfish methods—so you, as you are, may be a new batch without pride or selfishness. For Christ, our Passover meal, has already been prepared

for us to partake of. 8 So don't celebrate the feast as bread raised up with selfishness and arrogance, but as humble flat bread, free of selfishness and pride—pure bread of truth and love.

1Cor 5:9 Previously, I wrote instructing you not to associate with sexually immoral people. 10 Obviously, I didn't mean non-church members who are immoral, greedy, cheats, or pagans. If that were the case, you would have to leave the world. 11 So let me clarify: You must not fellowship with anyone who claims to be Christian but practices sexual immorality, is dominated by greed, cheats, worships false gods, is an addict or alcoholic who refuses treatment, is a swindler or a gossip and slanderer. Don't even go to lunch with such a person.

1Cor 5:12 What business is it of mine to diagnose those outside the church? Are we not to diagnose those inside to determine who is participating in God's Remedy and is well enough to serve others? 13 God will diagnose those outside the church. "Expel from among you the one who insists in practicing Satan's methods, yet claims to represent Christ."

6 If any of you has a disagreement that you cannot resolve on your own, why would you take it before the ungodly—to those who don't understand God's methods and principles—to get their evaluation and resolution? Why not take your dispute to members of the church who have renewed minds and godly wisdom? 2 Don't you realize that the saved will discern the right and wrong of the entire world? And if you are to discern the right and wrong of the entire world, are you not competent to figure out trivial matters? 3 Do you not realize we will even look into the lives of angels and evaluate what they did? How much more should we be able to rightly discern things of this life! 4 Therefore, if you have disputes, appoint as arbiters any members of the

church who have Christlike character, even if they are not in leadership. [5] I say this to shake you out of your confused thinking. Is it really possible that there isn't one person among you wise enough to negotiate a dispute between believers and bring them back to unity and love? [6] But instead, one brother goes to court against another—and all of this fighting in front of those who don't even believe in God's unifying love!

1Cor 6:7 The very fact that you have lawsuits among you is evidence that selfishness has already defeated God's love in your hearts. Why not let love reign, and forgive the wrong? Why not, rather than fighting back and filing lawsuits, allow yourselves to be cheated and trust God with the outcome? [8] Instead, each of you selfishly retaliates and cheats and exploits—back and forth, brother against brother, sister against sister.

1Cor 6:9 Don't you know that those who stay solidified in selfishness will not be part of God's kingdom of love? Don't be deceived: Neither the pornographers, nor those who idolize false conceptions of God, nor self-centered spouses, nor those who use sex to make money, nor selfish homosexuals, [10] nor thieves, the greedy, addicts or drunkards, nor gossipers or cheats will be part of God's kingdom of other-centered love. [11] And some of you were just that. But your minds have been washed in the truth about God that Jesus brought, your hearts' motives and attitudes have been set right with God, and your characters have been cleansed to reveal the character of Jesus Christ our Lord by the working of God's Spirit.

1Cor 6:12 Some say: "I am free to do everything"—but not everything is healthy. "I am free to do everything"—but I will not do anything that destroys my autonomy and takes away my freedom. [13] Over-eating engorges the system, leading to disease and decreased autonomy.

While God created food for the stomach and the stomach to digest food, we are not to be slaves to appetite, for everything touched by sin—such as food and our mortal stomachs—God will eradicate and replace with perfection. The body is not made to gratify sensual appetites and sexual immorality, but to be a temple for God. [14] By God's power our Lord was raised from the dead, and by God's power we will also be raised. [15] Don't you realize that your bodies contain your brain, and through the electrical circuits of your brain you are connected in union with Christ himself? Should I take that which is now a living conduit for Christ and join it to a prostitute? Never! [16] Don't you understand that he who unites himself with a prostitute causes brain changes that increase lust and emotional attachment to her? For it is said, "The two will become one." This weakens the connection to Christ. [17] But the person whose mind is joined to Christ experiences unity with Christ, which purifies their heart and renews the character to be like his!

1Cor 6:18 Recoil and flee from sexual immorality! Don't you realize that sexual sin is different from every other sin? Human sexuality is sacred. It not only reveals Godlike love and creative power, but is designed to bond beings together in unity. Those who sin sexually not only misrepresent God, but damage their own brain (body) and its ability to bond, thus undermining their unity with Christ. [19] Don't you comprehend what is happening? Your brain and body are designed as a complete unit to be a sacred temple for the Holy Spirit who comes from God and lives within you, intimately—in a bond of sacred love. You are not a self-originating or self-sustaining being; you belong in intimate connection with God! [20] It cost God an infinite price to restore this connection with you, so let God and his love be revealed in the way you treat your body.

7 Now in answer to the questions you asked me in your letter: Is it good for a man not to marry? [2] Since sin has so perverted human sexuality, and sensual temptations are so strong, every man should have his own wife, and every woman her own husband. [3] The marriage bed is sacred—a place each seeks to please the other in the physical culmination of other-centered love and mutual service. [4] In the marriage bed, the wife surrenders her body to her husband, and the husband—his body to his wife. Thus they selflessly become one in love. [5] Do not refuse to share your body with your spouse, except by mutual agreement and for a short time devoted to meditation and prayer. But then join yourselves to each other again in the bonds of marital love, and thus shut the door to Satan's temptations which may arise due to your lack of self-control. [6] I am not commanding periods of abstinence, but conceding that they may be beneficial at times. [7] I wish everyone was like me and could devote all their energy into distributing the Remedy, but not everyone is cut out to be single. Some serve God more effectively when married, others are better suited to be single.

1Cor 7:8 To the unmarried and widows who are content to be single: My recommendation is to stay single and be like me in devoting your full energy toward distributing the Remedy. [9] But if single life causes restlessness, discontent and loss of self-control, then by all means marry. It is much better to marry and find contentment than to burn with discontent and passion.

1Cor 7:10 To the married, the Lord has given this instruction: A wife must not leave her faithful and loving husband. [11] But if she does, she must live as a single person, unmarried, or else be reunited with her husband. And a husband must not divorce a faithful and loving wife.

1Cor 7:12 To the rest, I give this instruction (this is my counsel, not the Lord's): If a brother in the church has a wife who doesn't believe in Christ, but she lives agreeably with him, he must not divorce her. [13] If a Christian woman has a husband who does not believe in Christ, but he lives agreeably with her, she must not divorce him. [14] For if they live agreeably, the marriage functions within the sacred blessing that God designed, and the unbelieving partner experiences the joy of this sanctified union and the Spirit's presence in the home. If it were not this way, their children would be filled with unclean ideas, attitudes and motives, but as it is—they are filled with holy thoughts, ideas, and example.

1Cor 7:15 But if the unbelieving spouse leaves, respect their freedom and let them go. A believer respects the free choices of others and would not seek to bind an unwilling spouse to themselves — it is God's design that we live in peace. [16] How you handle this will have an impact on your spouse. If you reveal God's love and grace, you never know what influence it will have— perhaps even leading your spouse to a saving relationship with God.

1Cor 7:17 Regardless of what your spouse does, recognize your role in God's plan and fulfill your responsibilities in God's cause to the best of your ability. Your value to God is not determined by whether your spouse stays or leaves. This is the counsel I give all the churches. [18] If a man was a circumcised Jew when he accepted the Remedy to sin and was called to be a member of God's treatment team, he should not deny who he is and try to become uncircumcised. If a man was an uncircumcised Gentile when he accepted the Remedy to sin and was called to be a member of God's treatment team, he should not deny who he is and become circumcised. [19] Nationality means nothing! What matters is whether one has partaken of the Remedy to selfishness and sin, has God's law of love written on the heart, and lives in harmony with

God and his methods. [20] God needs members of his treatment team in all walks of life, so minister the truth about God, and his Remedy to sin, in whatever station you are. [21] If you accepted God's Remedy while a slave, don't be discouraged by your situation. Of course, gain your freedom if you can, but if you can't, then represent God's truth where you are. [22] For even though a slave to a human master, once you have partaken of God's Remedy to sin—your mind, heart and character were set free to love as Jesus loves! And the one who was free when he partook of God's Remedy became bound by love to Christ's service. [23] It cost God infinitely to procure your freedom from the domination of selfishness and sin, so don't let your hearts become bound to any master other than Christ. [24] Church family, every one of you should remain loyal to God and fulfill their call to reveal God's kingdom of love in whatever situation you find yourselves.

1Cor 7:25 Regarding those who are single, I have not been given any direction from the Lord, but will share my personal opinion as one who, by the Lord's mercy, has your best interest at heart and is therefore trustworthy: [26] Because of the present crisis the church is facing, it is my opinion that it would be best for you to remain as you are. [27] If you are married, do not seek a divorce; and if you are single—don't look for a spouse. [28] If you do marry, you have not sinned, but marriage brings many new stressors and responsibilities (such as children); and given the current crisis the church is facing, I want to spare you as many problems as possible.

1Cor 7:29 What I want you to understand is that we have a mission, and the time to complete it is limited, so don't let your spouse distract you from fulfilling God's purpose for your life— [30] don't get stuck in grief, but realize that when we have fulfilled our mission, Christ will return and grief will turn to joy; if you are happy in this world, then open your eyes to God's reality and become unhappy with the world; use your resources to fulfill God's mission—not indulge self— [31] and don't get engrossed or preoccupied with the world's entertainment, politics or agendas, because the world as we know it will soon be gone.

1Cor 7:32 I want you to be free from the worries, stresses and anxieties of this world, so that you can be most effective in God's cause. A single man can focus all his energies on fulfilling the Lord's work, [33] but a married man has responsibilities to his wife and family, [34] and his energies are divided. An unmarried woman can focus all her energies on fulfilling the Lord's work and devote her entire self to God's cause, but a married woman has responsibilities to her husband and family. [35] I am not placing any restrictions upon you, but sharing this wisdom for your good, so that you may decide how to live your lives completely devoted to the Lord.

1Cor 7:36 If anyone is engaged to a woman who is past her prime, but worries that his actions toward her have been indecent and is convinced that he should marry her, then by all means he should do so. He is not sinning, and they should marry. [37] But the man who is convinced that the marriage would be a mistake, and, under no external pressure, freely decides—with a clear conscience and self-governance—not to marry the woman, this man also does the right thing. [38] So then, he who marries the woman does right, but he who does not marry her does even better.

1Cor 7:39 A married woman is not free to be with another man as long as her husband is alive, but if her husband dies, she is free to marry any man she chooses. Of course, as a believer, she can only experience the unity God designed for marriage if the man she marries is a believer. [40] But in my opinion, she would be happier if she stayed single. And this counsel, which leaves each person free to decide for themself, is in harmony with the Spirit of God.

8 Now in regard to your question about whether to eat food offered to idols: There are many who have some knowledge about this subject, but possessing knowledge doesn't mean one actually understands the issues or discerns the right answer. Knowledge alone leads to pride and arrogance. It is love that enlightens the mind, brings unity, and strengthens the church. 2 Those who think they know the "right" answer for all situations, and especially for what others should do, reveal how little they actually comprehend or understand. 3 But God knows those who love him—those who filter their answers through the lens of love.

1Cor 8:4 So what about foods sacrificed to idols? What about it? –An idol is nothing but wood, metal, stone—just inanimate material. There is no other God but the one who created all things. 5 For even though there are many false gods worshiped by the ignorant, 6 there is but one reality and one true God, the Father, who is the source of all creation and from whom we derive life; and there is but one Lord, Jesus Christ, who is the source of all creation and from whom we derive life.

1Cor 8:7 But not everyone knows the truth about God. Many people have held distorted ideas about God for so long that they think if they eat the meat offered to idols, either the idols will have power over them, or God will be angry with them. Their spiritual comprehension is very weak, and believing such lies corrupts their minds even further. 8 The problem is not with the food, for it's obvious that the nutritional value of the food doesn't change by being offered to an idol, and food does not bring us closer to God. We are no better off for eating or not eating food offered to idols. The problem occurs from the belief one holds about idols, and the conclusion one draws when eating food sacrificed to an idol.

1Cor 8:9 But be careful with the freedom you have in Christ. Do not act in ways that would easily confuse a weaker believer or introduce false ideas into their mind. 10 For if someone whose spiritual comprehension is weak sees you—who understand the reality that an idol is nothing—eating food from the idol (maybe even at the temple of the idol), they might also go ahead and eat such food. But having not first removed the distorted ideas about idols from their mind, they will become insecure, superstitious, and fear-ridden. 11 So this believer, for whom Christ died to save, may be damaged by how you live out what you know. 12 When you fail to love your weaker brother or sister by considering how your actions will impact them—and therefore solidify distortions and unhealthy practices into their mind and thus wounding them—you betray Christ because you are not living in harmony with his character of love. 13 Therefore, if my eating cau-ses confusion and distorted thinking in the mind of my fellow believer, leading them into doubt, superstition and selfishness, I will never eat meat again so that I will not confuse them and lead them astray.

9 Yet I am still free—free to love as Christ loves. Am I not an ambassador for Christ? Have I not seen our Lord Jesus and been instructed by Him? Is not the healing occurring in your very own lives a result of my ministering God's love and truth to you? 2 Even though I may not be Christ's ambassador to others, I certainly am to you! Your changed lives and commitment to Christ are the evidence that I am an ambassador for the Lord.

1Cor 9:3 To those who criticize me, I say:

4 Isn't it in harmony with God's methods to receive food and drink? 5 Isn't it right to travel with one's Christian spouse, just like some other ambassadors and brothers of the Lord do, including Peter? 6 Or should Barnabas and I be cut off from the loving support of church members and be required to earn our own way?

1Cor 9:7 Doesn't a soldier give of themself to protect their country and receive the support of their government? Doesn't a gardener give their time and energy in planting and tending the garden, and then eat of the fruit of that garden? Doesn't the shepherd give of themself to watch over the flock and then drink of the milk? 8 This is not merely a human point of view or idea, but an expression of God's law of love. Everything—as God designed it—gives freely to another. 9 It is even written in the Law of Moses: "Do not stop the ox from eating while it treads the grain." Is God concerned only with oxen? 10 Of course not! This was written for us. When the farmer gives of themself to plant and harvest their fields, they do so understanding God's law of love, that when we give of ourselves, we receive a blessing in return. Thus the farmer receives back a share of the harvest. 11 If we have planted seeds of truth and love into your hearts, it is completely natural—and in keeping with God's law of love—that we receive your loving sustenance. 12 Others have received your support; shouldn't love motivate you to support us even more? Yet we have never sought to get anything from you, as we would much rather give of ourselves and tolerate injury in order to bless you with the good news about God as revealed in Jesus.

1Cor 9:13 Don't you realize that the temple service symbolically reveals God's kingdom of love? Those who give of themselves to serve there receive from the temple their food, and those who serve at the altar receive nourishment from what is offered on the altar. 14 This is how the Lord has constructed his universe to run—on the law of giving, on the principle of love—so that those who spread the Remedy for sin and selfishness receive their support from those who are healed by receiving that Remedy.

1Cor 9:15 But I have not received my sustenance from those who have received the Remedy of Christ. And I am not writing now in order to get you to give me anything, for I would rather die than do anything that could possibly suggest a selfish motive and thus misrepresent God and his kingdom of love. 16 When I am spreading the Remedy to sin and selfishness, I cannot brag or take credit, for having partaken of the Remedy myself, I can do nothing other than spread the good news of this cure to others. How horrible if I didn't spread the good news of God's Remedy to sin! 17 If I became a preacher as a vocation, then I could expect to get paid, but what I do is not simply a job, but a sacred trust that my heart passionately burns to carry out. 18 What do I get out of it? The joy of not being a burden to anyone, and knowing that I present God's Remedy to sin freely, without charge, without any strings attached.

1Cor 9:19 Although I am free and not required to live by the rules of others, I freely choose to identify with everyone's plight and become a servant to all in order to inoculate as many as possible with the Remedy to sin and selfishness. 20 When I am with Jews, I respect their customs and traditions in order not to offend, so their hearts may open to be inoculated with the Remedy of Christ. When I am with legalists, who adhere to many rules, I respect their rules (even though I know they provide no remedy to sin), in order not to offend, so that their hearts may be opened and inoculated with the Remedy of Christ. 21 When I am with those who don't know about God's law of love or his methods that heal, I respect their customs and don't act in ways that will make them feel inferior or condemned (but I continue to live in harmony with God's law of love as revealed in Christ), in order not to offend so their hearts may be opened and inoculated with the Remedy from God as revealed in Christ. [22] As to the weak in faith—I empathize with their weakness in order to win them to the truth about God as revealed in Christ. I meet all people where they are in order to open their hearts to the Remedy Christ has procured, and thereby save as many as possible. [23] I do this for God and his kingdom of love as one who is renewed and empowered by that love.

[1Cor 9:24] Don't you realize that in a race, even though all the athletes run, only one wins the race and gets the prize? Not so in God's kingdom—all who run may win the prize! So run the race in harmony with God's methods of love in order to receive the prize of reunion with God. [25] Olympic athletes spend years in rigorous training. They work hard for a crown that will not last; but we do it to be crowned with the mind of Christ, which will last forever. [26] Therefore I run hard, with the purpose to win. I don't shadowbox. [27] No; I fight against self, surrendering my will to Christ, and establish reason in governance of my selfish desires, so that after having shared the Remedy with others, I will not be overcome by a resurgence of selfishness and lose the prized unity with God.

10

I want you to understand clearly that all humanity suffers from the same sin sickness and is in need of the exact same Remedy. In fact, when our forefathers were protected by the cloud of God's presence and passed through the sea, [2] their journey through the sea was a symbolic immersion in water by Moses—like our symbolic water immersion called baptism—which symbolizes leaving the life of sin and death behind for the new life in Christ. [3] They all partook of the same spiritual food [4] and drank the same spiritual drink as you and I do—the truth about God as revealed by Christ; for they received the spiritual truth (the Water of Life) from the Rock who went with them, and that Rock was Jesus Christ. [5] But God was disappointed with most of them because even though Christ provided all that was necessary to save them, they rejected what he offered, and died, scattered throughout the desert.

[1Cor 10:6] All of this history is a lesson for us, teaching us not to act as they did, and not to reject God's Remedy to sin in exchange for the counterfeits the world offers. [7] Do not worship false gods or believe lies about God, as some of them did. The Old Testament Scripture tells us: "They ate and drank, and gave thanks to idols, indulging in lewd behavior." [8] We must not engage in sexual immorality, as some of them did — and in one day, twenty-three thousand died. [9] We should not test whether the Lord will leave us free to reap the consequences of our own choices if we persist in rebellion. This is what many of them did, and when, at their insistence, God stepped back, poisonous snakes came into the camp, and many of the people died. [10] And do not harden your hearts against God and his methods of love by grumbling and complaining as some of them did, for such a course results in death.

[1Cor 10:11] Since we suffer with the same sickness of heart and mind as they did, all of this history is recorded for our benefit—to warn and protect us—so we won't refuse the Remedy as they did, but will fulfill God's purpose of victorious living at this present time. [12] So, if you are in God's treatment program and believe you are doing well, be careful that you don't fall behind in your appointments with God, or in the partaking of his Remedy. [13] For there is no temptation to discontinue God's treatment that has come upon you except for the fear and selfishness that infects all mankind. God is reliable and trustworthy; he will not allow temptation beyond your ability to resist, but when you are tempted, he will always provide resources, options, opportunities, supports, and alternate ways out so that you can stand your ground and overcome the temptation, thereby growing stronger with each victory.

1Cor 10:14 Therefore, my cherished friends, flee from false gods and all false God-concepts. 15 You can think for yourselves, so examine the evidence and draw your own conclusion regarding the value and reasonableness of what I am saying. 16 Isn't the communion cup, of which we thankfully partake, a symbolic ingestion of the life of Christ? And is not the communion bread a symbolic internalization of the character, methods and principles of Christ? 17 Even though we are many individuals, when we partake of Christ, we partake of the only genuine Bread that gives life, and therefore become united into one body, for we all assimilate the same character of love.

1Cor 10:18 Consider the theatrical lesson Israel enacted for us: Didn't those who ingested the sacrificial meat also faithfully fulfill their duties at the altar? When we ingest Christ, we become like him and faithfully live out his principles in fulfilling all our duties. 19 But don't get confused about sacrifices to idols: The sacrifice is nothing, and the idol is nothing, for neither have any power; 20 but the sacrifices of pagans are done with hearts in harmony with demons—not in harmony with God— and I do not want you to align yourselves with demons. 21 You cannot drink the cup of the Lord and partake of the life of Christ, and also drink the cup of demons and partake of Satan's principles; you cannot internalize both the character of Christ and the character of demons. 22 Besides, the Lord won't allow partial healing; he wants

complete eradication of selfishness from the heart! Do you think you can heal yourselves, that you have a more powerful remedy than his?

1Cor 10:23 In God's universe, we have the freedom to do anything we want, but not everything is healthy or in harmony with God's design. 24 So live in harmony with God's design and do not seek to promote self, but promote the eternal good of others.

1Cor 10:25 You are free to eat anything sold in the market without being concerned about spiritual contamination from the food being offered to an idol, 26 because the entire earth was created by God, and physical matter cannot soil the conscience.

1Cor 10:27 If an unbeliever invites you to a meal and you want to go, eat whatever is served—without worrying about whether it was offered to an idol, or whether you are sinning by eating it— for food is food, and the only thing that matters is its nutritional value. 28 But if the unbeliever makes it a point to tell you that it was offered in sacrifice to their idol, then don't eat it—not because there is actually anything wrong with the food, but to avoid confusion: 29 not confusion to you, but to the other person, who believes their idol actually has some power, and you don't want them to think you believe in their god. 30 In general, I eat my meals with thankfulness to God and will not be held hostage by the opinions of others; and I let others think what they want.

1Cor 10:31 So, whether you are eating or drinking, or whatever you are doing— do it to reveal the truth about God's character of selfless love. 32 Do not knowingly act in ways that confuse others about God, or lead them astray—whether believers or unbelievers. 33 Remember to be winsome in dealing with others, just as I strive to do, for I am not promoting my own agenda, but spreading the Remedy of Jesus Christ so that many may be eternally healed.

11 Follow my example in reaching others in love, just as I follow the example of Christ.

1Cor 11:2 I'm so pleased with you for remembering all I have taught you and for holding firmly to the truth I shared with you.

1Cor 11:3 Now I want you to realize that every man is to follow the loving leadership of Christ; and within a marriage—the wife is to follow the loving leadership of her husband, just as Christ follows the loving leadership of his Father. 4 In our culture, any man who prays or prophesies with his head covered, symbolically hides himself from God, which makes it appear that he is going his own way and is no longer following the loving leadership of Christ. Such behavior is dishonorable and destructive. 5 And every woman who prays or prophesies with her head uncovered, symbolically breaks the circle of God's love, which makes it appear that she is selfishly seeking to sever herself from her husband and wants to take his place in God's plan. This is dishonorable and destructive, and is as repulsive as the shaving of the heads by the cult prostitutes who do it to let everyone know how lewd they are.

1Cor 11:6 If a woman insists on presenting herself in ways that break God's circle of love, she should at least advertise the fact that she is selfish and not on God's team, and shave her head just like the cult prostitutes do. 7 In our culture, a man should not cover his head, because he was created first and is to lead in revealing God's character of self-sacrificing love by humble service to his wife, who is to glory in her husband's love and return that love freely to him. 8 For man did not originate from a woman, but woman was created from man; 9 and woman was created to help man enter into the fullness of Godlike love by being the selfless recipient of man's humble, loving, service. 10 It was for this purpose—so that man could experience greater depths of God's love through the giving of himself to uplift his wife, which reveals the truth about God's nature of love to angels—that woman is to be led by the loving leadership of her husband.

1Cor 11:11 In God's design, and in unity with him, husband and wife are not independent of each other but are united in an intimate bond of love and trust. 12 God reveals this intimate connection by creating woman from man, and then designing it so that all future men are born from women; with everything, of course, coming from God. We are all connected, united, bonded together, and have our own place in God's design! 13 Consider the evidence for yourselves: Is it healthy for a woman to try to deny her own identity and instead live like a man? 14 Doesn't nature itself teach that each individual has their own place, role and responsibilities, and if a man denies his identity and tries to live like a woman, it is unnatural and unhealthy; 15 but it is beautiful and healthy for a woman to embrace her femininity and let her hair grow long. 16 Please don't waste time arguing about this; this is the only healthy way to live, and that's how all the churches of God understand it.

1Cor 11:17 Because your meetings create a toxic environment which causes damage and does not heal injuries, I am not going to sugarcoat the following prescription. 18 I have heard that when you assemble to worship, you divide into factions, gossiping and working against each other—and I suspect this is true. 19 There is no doubt that there are differences in spiritual maturity among you, as some of you are cooperating more fully with the Holy Spirit than others. 20 But remember that when you come together, it is from the Lord's table that you are eating—so emulate him! 21 He served his disciples; yet when you eat, it's everyone for themselves, one rushing ahead of another, no one serves another—it's all about gratifying self. Some remain hungry while others get drunk.

22 Church is an opportunity to love and serve each other; if you are only interested in gorging yourselves, don't you have a home where you can do that? Or are you intentionally trying to make God's church appear heartless and cruel by mistreating those less fortunate? What do you expect me to say of such behavior? Should I commend you? Absolutely not!

1Cor 11:23 Everything the Lord taught me I am teaching you. The Lord Jesus —while at dinner on the night he was betrayed—took the bread, 24 and after thanking his Father, broke it and said, "This bread symbolizes my body, which is broken for your healing. When you eat together, break the bread and remember me and the Remedy to sin I have procured." 25 Then, after they had eaten the bread, he took the cup and said, "This cup symbolizes the true Remedy of internalizing my character into your hearts. The wine symbolizes my blood, which in turn symbolizes my perfect life. As you drink, you symbolically ingest into your hearts my perfect character of love. Whenever you drink it, remember me and what I have done for you." 26 So whenever you eat this broken bread and drink of this symbolic cup, you proclaim the Remedy to sin the Lord's death procured—until he comes again.

1Cor 11:27 Therefore whoever eats or drinks of the symbolic bread or cup of our Lord in a manner that misrepresents the Remedy our Lord achieved, fails to partake of the cure Christ has provided, and instead is guilty of promoting a false remedy. 28 Each person should take a moment and reflect upon the motives of their heart before eating the bread or drinking from the cup. 29 For any who partake of the Lord's table without a heart open to internalize Christ—which we symbolize by eating and drinking the bread and

wine—diagnoses themself as terminal. 30 That is why so many of you remain weak in character and sick of heart, worn down by worry and fear, some even falling asleep in death. 31 If we would admit the reality of our own terminal condition and accept God's Remedy, we would not be subjected to diagnostic scrutiny. 32 But when our condition is diagnosed by the Lord, it is so we may be treated and cured and not be condemned with the rest of the unremedied world.

1Cor 11:33 So then, my brothers and sisters, when you come together to eat of the Lord's table, serve each other in love. 34 Those simply looking for a meal and not the internalization of Christ into the heart should eat at home, so when you gather together in Christ's love it will not result in misunderstanding and misdiagnosis. When I come, I will give further insights and instructions.

12 Also, I want you to understand about spiritual gifts—gifts given by God in order to mature, develop and equip believers to be successful members of God's spiritual health-care team. 2 You remember quite well that when you were pagans, your minds were confused and you superstitiously revered mute idols. 3 Therefore, understand this clearly: No one who is led by God's Spirit will misrepresent Christ or distort his character by word or deed, and no one whose words and deeds accurately reveal the Lordship of Christ can do so except by the Holy Spirit.

1Cor 12:4 While there is a variety of gifts, there is only one Spirit. 5 And though there are many ways to help people, there is only one Lord. 6 While there are many methods to bring God's healing truth to people, it is the same God who orchestrates his team and whose power works to heal the heart from sin.

1Cor 12:7 So, the Holy Spirit works in each person to bring out the abilities and gifts best suited for that individual to use for the common good of all. 8 One is blessed with wisdom, another with knowledge, 9 another with unwavering trust, another with great skill in healing; 10 another has the ability to perform miracles, another has the gift of prophecy, another—keen discernment in distinguishing truth from error and the difference between the true and false spirits; to another is given the gift of speaking many languages, to another—the ability to translate many languages. 11 But all of these abilities and gifts are the result of the same Spirit, and it is the Spirit who determines which gift is given to which person.

1Cor 12:12 Consider your physical body: It is a single body, but it's constructed of many individual parts; and though there are many parts, it is still one body. So it is with Christ. 13 For all of us had our hearts and minds immersed into Christ by the same Spirit and thus are part of the same body. It doesn't matter whether Jew or Greek, slave or free—we have all internalized the same Remedy to sin from the same Spirit of God!

1Cor 12:14 The body is a cohesive unit constructed of many parts, and all the parts play a vital role. 15 What if the foot said, "I am not a hand and never get to wave, touch things or write, therefore I don't even belong to the body;" would that make it so? 16 What if the ear said, "I am not the eye and I never get to look at things or read, therefore I'm not part of the body;" would the ear suddenly disappear from the head? 17 Or what if the entire body were just an eye? It would be grotesque, and where would hearing be? And for that matter, how would the eye move, or even survive, without a heart and lungs to give it blood and oxygen? And if the entire body were an ear, where would the sense of smell be? 18 God has built the body with all its parts right where he wanted them, all perfectly complementing each other and fulfilling their purposes for the good of the entire body. 19 If they were all the same part, it would cease to be a body. 20 But as it is, there are many parts perfectly united in one magnificent body.

1Cor 12:21 The eye cannot say to the hand, "I don't need you!" for the hand wipes the tears from the eye. And the head cannot say to the feet, "I don't need you!" for the feet take the head where it wants to go. 22 Every part is indispensable. The parts that seem to be weaker are essential, 23 and the parts we consider less honorable, like the feet, we treat with special honor by providing shoes specialized for all occasions. And the parts that are unpresentable are treated with special care and attention, 24 while the parts we present publicly don't need any special treatment. God has designed the body, creating a perfect organism where all the various parts are united in serving each other, where each part is honored to fulfill its appointed purpose for the good of all. 25 No disunity or competition exists in the body, but all the parts are equally concerned for the health of the others. 26 If one part of the body is in pain, the other parts suffer with it; if one part is healthy and honored, the others rejoice with it and are blessed by it.

1Cor 12:27 Now understand the point of this illustration: You all are parts of the body of Christ; each one of you is a part of it. 28 And just as in the body different parts have different roles, so God has appointed in the church different people for different roles in distributing the Remedy. First, there are ambassadors, second—God's spokespersons, third—teachers, then workers of miracles, also healthcare practitioners, helpers, administrators, and translators. 29 All are necessary to accomplish God's purpose of healing the world—but are all ambassadors? Are all God's spokespersons? Is everyone a teacher? Can all do miracles? 30 Are all suited for healthcare? Can everyone translate languages? 31 So don't get sidetracked by trying to do someone else's job, but instead fulfill your purpose in the church, eagerly striving for the greater gift. And now I will show you the only true and most excellent way.

13 If I am gifted to speak the language of people and angels but do not have God's love in my heart, I am only making meaningless noise, because I remain terminal and dying. [2] If I am gifted with prophetic insight and understand all mysteries and knowledge, and if I am trusted to move mountains but do not have God's love in my heart, I am a fraud because I am still dying in sin and am nothing at all. [3] If I give away all my possessions to the poor and die as a martyr tied to a burning stake but don't have God's love in my heart, I am still unhealed and have gained nothing.

1Cor 13:4 Love is the principle upon which life and health are built to operate, and when active in intelligent beings, love is patient and kind. Love gives in order to bless others and does not envy, boast, or promote self. [5] Love is not intrusive, rude, selfish, irritable, or hot-tempered. And love doesn't hold grudges or keep a record of wrongs. [6] Love takes no pleasure in evil but rejoices with the truth. [7] Love always protects, heals, restores, builds up, trusts, hopes, and perseveres.

1Cor 13:8 Love originates in God and therefore will never stop and never fail. But one day, prophecies will cease, talking will be paused, and human knowledge will fade. [9] We are finite—knowing just a part of all truth, and prophecy is just a piece of a greater whole. [10] But when God restores the universe to His perfect design of love, all imperfection will disappear. [11] When I was a child, I talked like a child, bragging about myself; I thought like a child, focusing on the dos and don'ts, and I reasoned like a child. But when I grew up, I embraced God's kingdom of love and put the childish ways behind me. [12] Our minds are so darkened by selfishness that we see God's kingdom poorly, like a reflection in a cloudy mirror; but when he returns, we shall see perfectly—face to face! Right now I know only part of God's reality; then— I will have all questions answered and fully know the truth, just as God fully knows me.

1Cor 13:13 So these three endure: trust, hope and love; but the greatest of these is love.

14 Live in harmony with other-centered love and eagerly pursue gifts that develop your character and enable you to spread the Remedy of Christ—especially the gift of speaking clearly the truth about God. [2] For anyone who speaks unclearly, or in a foreign language, does not communicate healing truth to others but is speaking to God the secrets of the heart. [3] But those who speak clearly the truth about God communicate to others the healing Remedy to sin—for their strengthening, encouraging, and comfort. [4] Those who speak in a foreign language benefit only themselves, but those who speak the truth about God clearly—for others to hear and understand—benefit the entire church. [5] I would like all of you to speak multiple languages, but even more, I want you to be able to effectively present the truth about God. Those who present the truth about God effectively and accurately are more essential in spreading the healing Remedy to sin than those who speak multiple languages, unless they are the translators for those who speak the healing truth so the church can hear and understand.

1Cor 14:6 For instance, if I come to you and speak in a foreign language, and only God understands, what good will I be to you? Unless I communicate truths in ways you can comprehend, how can you benefit? [7] Even for musical instruments, such as a flute or

246

harp, the notes must be distinct and harmonious for a tune to be heard, otherwise it is meaningless noise.

8 Likewise, if a trumpet doesn't make its call clear and distinct, who would understand the message and get ready for battle? 9 It is the same for you. If you don't speak clear, intelligible words in a known language, how will anyone understand what you are saying? You will just be a noisemaker, cluttering the air with your meaningless words. 10 Of course, there are many languages in the world, and all have a meaning to their people. 11 If I don't understand someone else's language, then we are foreigners to each other and our words have no benefit to the other. 12 This is exactly how it is with you—too many people talking with very little understanding. Since you are eager for gifts that develop your character, then develop those gifts that effectively communicate the Remedy to the church.

1Cor 14:13 This is why those who speak a foreign language should pray that they may interpret what they say, so all may be benefited by their words. 14 For if I pray with my heart, baring my inmost feelings in a language that expresses my emotional state, my understanding and insight are not developed. 15 So what is the healthy option? I will pray with my heart and mind united in appreciation and understanding of God's character of love; I will sing with my heart and mind united in devotion to God's kingdom of love. 16 If you are praising God by expressing your inmost feelings in unintelligent utterances, how can those who don't understand say, "That makes sense and I agree" to your praise, since they have no idea what you are saying? 17 You may be giving thanks, but others are not benefited by your expression.

1Cor 14:18 I thank God that I speak in more languages than all of you. 19 But when I am in church, I would rather speak five words that people can understand—in order to enlighten others—than ten thousand words in an unknown language.

1Cor 14:20 Brothers and sisters, stop thinking like children! When it comes to evil, be innocent in thought—like infants who don't see the worst in people—but in your reasoning be mature, understanding God's methods and principles. 21 In the Scriptures it is written:

"Through men of unknown languages
    and through the mouths of
    foreigners
I will speak truth to these people,
but even that will not impress them,
    and they will not listen to me,"
says the Lord.

1Cor 14:22 The gift of languages, then, is a sign—not for those who already know and trust God, but for those who don't know or trust him. Clearly speaking the truth about God, however, is for those who do know and trust God, not for those who don't know him. 23 Think about it: If the church comes together and everyone is speaking a different language, won't those who don't understand, and visitors, think you are incoherent and deranged? 24 But if those who don't know God, or who don't understand the truth, come in while people are speaking clearly the truth about God, they will recognize the truth and be convinced of their own terminal condition. They will be diagnosed accurately by all, 25 and the hidden symptoms in their hearts and minds will be exposed. So they will humble themselves in adoration to God, acknowledging, "God's presence and truth are really among you!"

1Cor 14:26 Brothers and sisters, what then is a reasonable and healthy course of action? When you fellowship together, everyone has a song that touches their heart, or an idea which has helped in their growth, or an insight, or an instruction, or they speak a language that they understand best, or have an interpretation that makes most sense to them; but all of this sharing must be done for the building up and strengthening of the entire group. [27] As for those sharing in their language, allow only two or three at most and then one at a time and, of course, have someone interpret for the rest of the church. [28] If there is no interpreter, then the speakers should keep quiet in church and speak only to themselves and God.

1Cor 14:29 Two or three who can speak clearly the truth about God should speak, and the others should think for themselves and consider carefully what is said. [30] And if an insight, revelation or inspiration comes to someone in the audience, the speaker should pause and allow the other to speak. [31] For all of you can speak the truth about God clearly, in an orderly fashion, so that everyone can be instructed and encouraged. [32] The hearts of those who speak the truth about God are subject to their own self-governance, [33] for God is not a God of chaos and disorder but of order and peace. All the congregations of God's people worship in an orderly fashion, [34] so don't act like pagans and allow the women to shout, scream, roll on the floor or carry on hysterically. Your women should be respectful and quiet. They should not interrupt the speaker with questions, but wait and listen to what is being presented from God's word. [35] And if they are still confused, then each one should ask her own husband for clarification when the meeting is over, for it is shameful for women to misrepresent God by acting like pagans and shouting in the church.

1Cor 14:36 Did you write God's word—the Bible? Are you the only people who have heard the truth about God? [37] If any one of you thinks they are a spokesperson for God, or that they have gifts or talents from God, let them embrace and endorse the truths I have written, which are from the Lord. [38] If they ignore this, they also will be ignored.

1Cor 14:39 Therefore, my brothers and sisters, be eager to speak the truth about God, and don't forbid foreign languages with translation, [40] but do everything in a loving, peaceful and orderly manner.

15 Now, my brothers and sisters, let me remind you of the good news about God that I taught you, which you embraced and to which you have committed your lives. [2] It is by the Remedy procured by Jesus that you have been healed—so long as you remain connected to Christ, holding firmly to the truth about God that I preached to you. For if you let go of this truth, you will relapse into selfishness and fear.

1Cor 15:3 The Remedy to selfishness—that I received and passed on to you as the single most important truth to share—is that Christ died in order to cure our selfish hearts and minds, just as the Scripture foretold. [4] He died and was buried, but because—by his death—he destroyed the infection of selfishness and restored perfectly God's law of love within his humanity, he rose again on the third day in a perfected humanity, according to the Scriptures. [5] Then he physically appeared to Peter, and then to the other twelve ambassadors. [6] After that, he physically appeared to more than five hundred of the brothers at one time, most of whom are still alive and can confirm this fact, though some have fallen asleep and rest in Christ. [7] Then he physically appeared to James, then to all the ambassadors, [8] and last of all, he physically appeared and spoke to me—a man who, like a premature baby, needed extra care and attention.

1Cor 15:9 For I am the least deserving of all Christ's ambassadors and not even worthy to be called an "ambassador of Christ" because I attacked and persecuted God's people. [10] But because God is so gracious, I am his representative, and his work in and for me has positively transformed me. I have worked harder than all of the other ambassadors—or rather God's grace had much more work of healing, restoring and re-educating of me to do. ¹¹ So regardless of whether it was one of God's other ambassadors or it was I, the truth about God as revealed by Jesus is what we preach and what you have believed.

1Cor 15:12 Since we preach that Christ has risen from the dead, how is it that some of you are saying that the dead will never live again? ¹³ If it is impossible for the dead to come back to life, then not even Christ has risen from the dead. ¹⁴ And if Christ is still dead, then our preaching is worthless and so is all in what you have believed. ¹⁵ Even worse, we would be charlatans, con-men, and liars who misrepresent God, for we have testified that God raised Christ from the dead. But if in fact the dead are not raised to life, then he did not raise Christ. ¹⁶ So then, if the dead do not live again, Christ does not live either. ¹⁷ And if Christ does not live, then everything you have believed is pointless because you are still terminal, dying in selfishness without hope, ¹⁸ and those who have fallen asleep trusting in Christ are eternally lost. ¹⁹ If our hope in Christ is only for this earthly life, we are more pitiful than all, for we would have lived a hopeless lie.

1Cor 15:20 But Christ has risen from the dead as the living Remedy for those who have fallen asleep. ²¹ For since our terminal condition and subsequent death came through a human being, the Remedy to death and our terminal condition must also come through a human being. ²² We are all terminal and will die because of the infection of self-ishness passed down from Adam, but all who unite with Christ will be cured and made alive! ²³ But each in their proper time: Christ, the Remedy—first; then, when he returns, all those who have opened their hearts in trust to him will rise again. ²⁴ Then the end of the earth as we know it will happen: Having destroyed all earthly and self-ish dominance, authority and power, he will hand over the kingdom to God the Father. ²⁵ For Christ's healing reign must continue until he has destroyed completely the infection of sin and selfishness, and all enemies of love are eradicated. ²⁶ The last enemy to be destroyed is death, ²⁷ for God has put everything under Christ's authority. Of course, when we say everything has been made subordinate to him, it obviously doesn't include God himself, who put everything under Christ's healing power. ²⁸ When he has completed his mission—eradicating sin from God's universe, healing all those who let him, destroying death, and restoring God's creation back to its original design—then the Son himself will resume his place as God's humble envoy to creation so that God will be utterly supreme and all will be fully reunited with him.

1Cor 15:29 Think of it another way: If there is no resurrection from the dead, why do some people get immersed in water for those who have already died? Isn't it that they expect to see them alive again? ³⁰ And what about us? Why do we put ourselves in danger constantly? ³¹ It is because we glory in bringing the Remedy of Christ to people like you, so each day I accept the inevitability of my earthly death, knowing there will be a resurrection, and I don't let fear of death stop me from promoting Christ. ³² If my battles with wild beasts in Ephesus were merely for human reasons, what is the point? If the dead are not raised, then we are wasting our time and we might as well eat, drink, and party like the rest of the world, for tomorrow we die.

1Cor 15:33 But don't be deceived by what the world promotes! The reality is that unhealthy friends and associates corrupt good character. ³⁴ Be sensible, do what's right and healthy because it is right and healthy, and stop acting like there is no life after this one; for there are still some among you who don't know God, and their fear of death, and living for self, is infecting your thinking. I say this to wake you up to what is happening.

1Cor 15:35 But some people, who doubt God's healing power and want to undermine your confidence in the resurrection, may ask, "How are the dead raised? What is the mechanism? What kind of body will they have?" 36 Such questions show their foolishness! What is planted in the ground doesn't sprout into new life unless it dies to what it was. 37 When you sow, you do not bury the mature plant that you harvest, but a seed—like a grain of wheat or something else. 38 Then God gives it its form and body, and it grows from the ground. To each plant, he gives its own unique body. 39 All bodies are not the same: humankind has one kind of body, animals have different body types, birds and fish—still other types of bodies. 40 The heavenly beings have their real physical bodies, just as we on earth have our earthly bodies; and each body, heavenly and earthly, is splendid in its own way. 41 Just look in the sky: The sun is splendid, but so is the moon, and the stars—and all in their unique way.

1Cor 15:42 This is how it will be when the dead are raised to life: The diseased body that was buried in its terminal state is raised brand new, 43 and though buried defective, it is raised perfected; though buried fragile, it is raised powerful; 44 and though it is buried mortal, it is raised immortal.

If there is a mortal body, there is also an immortal body. 45 The first man, Adam, was formed out of the soil of earth, and God breathed into him, and he became a living being; Christ, the second Adam, is the source of life itself—eternal, immortal, everlasting. 46 Be clear on the sequence of events: 47 Humanity first received a mortal body, which became diseased through Adam, and then, through Christ, came the immortal, perfected body. The first

Adam was formed out of the dirt of the earth, but Christ came from heaven. 48 As the earthly man was mortal and became terminal in sin, so all born on earth are mortal and born terminal in sin; and as Christ—the man from heaven—cured the terminal condition and is sinless and immortal, all who accept his Remedy are cured and reunited with heaven. 49 And just as we have been formed in the likeness of fallen Adam—with our selfish natures and diseased bodies—so we shall bear the likeness of Christ with perfect bodies and natures of selfless love.

1Cor 15:50 Let me make this plain and simple: Sinful, selfish, fear-ridden humanity cannot enter into God's kingdom of perfect other-centered love, nor can malignancy produce eternal life. 51 Listen carefully and I will tell you a secret: Not all of us will sleep in death waiting to be resurrected; some of us will be changed—52 in an instant, as quick as blinking an eye—when the last trumpet blows. For the trumpet of God will sound, and the dead in Christ will arise in perfect health, with perfect bodies, and we who are alive will be transformed. These diseased bodies will disappear, and we will be clothed with our perfect, heavenly bodies.

53 For this sick, terminally ill body must be replaced with the eternal, heavenly one; this mortal body must be replaced with an immortal one. 54 Then, when sickness has been replaced with eternal health, and mortality with immortality, the Scripture that says, "Death has been eradicated by life victorious," will be fulfilled.

1Cor 15:55 "Ha! Death, where is your victory now?

Ha! Death, now, where is your bite?"

1Cor 15:56 Death's bite is sin—deviating from the law of love—and sin's power to destroy comes from the fact that life is built to operate only in harmony with the law of love. Therefore all deviations from the law result in pain, suffering and death unless the law is perfectly restored in the being. [57] So give thanks to God, for he has given us victory and Remedy through our Lord Jesus Christ who perfectly restored the law of love into humanity.

1Cor 15:58 Therefore, my dear brothers and sisters, don't waver. Be rock-solid and let nothing move you away from the truth about God as Jesus revealed. Always live in harmony with the law of love, and give yourselves freely to the Lord's work, because you know that loving others as the Lord does is never a waste of time.

16 In regard to donations to help God's people, I recommend that you do what I told the Galatian churches: [2] On the first day of the week, each person should assess their finances and set aside the appropriate sum in keeping with their income. Save it, so that when I come, there will be no need to take up a collection, as you will have your donations ready. [3] When I arrive, I will give letters of introduction for the persons you have selected to deliver your gift to the church leadership in Jerusalem. [4] If it seems best for me to go to Jerusalem at that time, then they will go with me.

1Cor 16:5 My plan is to come to you after going through Macedonia. [6] It is possible that I may be able to spend the winter with you, and you can help me prepare for the journey to my next destination. [7] When I come, I don't want to just pass through; I want to spend time with you if it is in the Lord's plan. [8] But I will stay at Ephesus until Pentecost [9] because, even though an incredible opportunity for me to spread the truth about God has opened, there are many who are opposing me.

1Cor 16:10 If Timothy visits you, make him welcome and secure in your love, for he is spreading the Lord's Remedy to sin and selfishness, just as I am. [11] No one who wants the Remedy to sin should refuse to accept him, but rather support him and send him back to me

in peace. I am looking forward to seeing him and his Christian friends.

1Cor 16:12 Also, I have strongly encouraged Apollos and his Christian friends to visit you. He didn't think it was necessary, but will come when his schedule permits.

1Cor 16:13 Watch out for ideas that distort the truth about God as Christ revealed. Stand firm in your trust in God, be courageous for the truth, and be strong; [14] and do everything in other-centered love.

1Cor 16:15 You know that Stephanas and his family and staff were the first in Achaia to accept the Remedy to sin and selfishness procured by Christ. They have joined God's spiritual health-care team and are devoted to spreading the Remedy to sin, and to serving others wherever they go. I urge you, brothers and sisters, [16] to also embrace the Remedy of Christ, to follow their example, serve others, and work to spread God's Remedy to sin. [17] I was so happy when Stephanas, Fortunatus and Achaicus arrived, because having them near brings my heart closer to you. [18] They have rejuvenated and encouraged me, as they have you. Such men deserve our support, encouragement, and appreciation.

1Cor 16:19 The churches in Asia send their love and affection. Aquila and Priscilla, and the church that meets in their home, also send their love. [20] All the Christians here likewise say "hello" and send their love. Be sure to always greet each other with love and a big hug.

1Cor 16:21 I, Paul, write this greeting in my own hand.

1Cor 16:22 Those who do not love the Lord refuse the only Remedy to their terminal state and will inevitably experience the curse of unremedied sin. Oh, come quickly and heal us all, Lord Jesus!

1Cor 16:23 The gracious presence of the Lord Jesus be with you.

1Cor 16:24 I love you all in Christ Jesus, Amen!

2 Corinthians

1 From Paul, an ambassador of Jesus Christ, appointed by God himself, along with our brother Timothy,

To all those in Corinth who have partaken of the healing Remedy to fear and selfishness—provided by God through Christ—together with all those participating in God's healing program throughout Achaia: ²May God and our Lord Jesus Christ pour out their grace and peace upon you.

2Cor 1:3 All thanks, acclaim and recognition be to God, the Father of our Lord Jesus Christ—for he is the Father of mercy, compassion and healing—⁴who provides Remedy for everything that troubles our minds and warps our characters, so that we can share this Remedy, which has brought peace to our minds, with everyone in any distress. ⁵As we emulate Christ—suffering as he did—we, through Christ, experience healing and restoration of godly character. ⁶If we suffer, it is to comfort you by our example and to encourage you with evidence that in God's plan, suffering results in healing. It is our comfort to then comfort you with the assurance that endurance in God's treatment plan, though at times uncomfortable, results in healing and wellness. ⁷Our hope for you is strong because we know that if you participate in God's treatment plan and suffer as we have, you will, like us, experience the comfort of a transformed character and peace with God.

2Cor 1:8 Brothers and sisters, we want you to know exactly what we have experienced in Asia. We have been under extreme pressure, far beyond our human ability to endure, and our despair has been so great that we have even considered death to be preferable to life. ⁹Truly, our hearts felt like we were going to die. Why did this happen? So that we might stop relying on our own strength and trust our entire selves into God's hands, as he is able to breathe life into the dead. ¹⁰And sure enough, he has delivered us from many deadly threats, and he will continue to deliver us. We have placed all our hope in him, and he will continue to provide for our needs and deliver us from danger. ¹¹Your prayers have been a great help to us, and many will praise God on our behalf for his gracious favor granted in answer to so many prayers.

2Cor 1:12 Now this is what we are truly proud of: That in all our actions in the world, and in our relationship with you, we have done what is right, reasonable and healthy, in harmony with God's methods, and with a clear conscience. We have not practiced the worldly methods of self-first, but God's gracious methods of love, truth, and freedom. ¹³We do not write complex theories, but the simple realities of God's kingdom, which are easy to understand. And I hope that ¹⁴what you have understood thus far will lead you to greater understanding and experience in God's methods, so that we can rejoice together in the day of the Lord Jesus.

2Cor 1:15 Because of my confidence in your growth, my original plan was to visit you twice: first ¹⁶on my way to Macedonia, and then on my return from Macedonia, so that you may send me to Judea. ¹⁷Do I make my plans impulsively? Or do I make plans like the world, with fear and uncertainty, trying to be a people-pleaser and cover all the bases by saying "Yes" to some and "No" to others?

2Cor 1:18 But as certain as God is true, reliable and faithful, our message is not "Maybe" or "Perhaps." 19 To God's Son — Jesus Christ — who you were taught about by myself, Timothy and Silas, it has never been "maybe" or "perhaps," but it has always been "yes" and "absolutely certain!" 20 All of God's promises are realized through unity with Christ, and through him we are healed and restored in his image to be the final piece of evidence that brings glory to our God of love. 21 For it is God who recreates both us and you into the full stature of Christ, enabling us to stand firm in love and truth. He has cleansed our minds, 22 restored his character in us—and thus sealed us as his—and has put his Spirit in our hearts as a guarantee of our complete restoration that is to come.

2Cor 1:23 As God can confirm, the reason I did not return to Corinth was to spare you discomfort. 24 We are not trying to control you or dictate your relationship with Christ, but are working on your behalf to see you completely restored to God's ideal, because it is through abiding trust that you will overcome.

2 Therefore, I decided not to make another emotionally stressful visit to you; 2 for if I come and cause you discomfort, how will you be able to cheer me up? 3 My letter was written in order to avoid conflict when I came, so that we could instead enjoy each other's company. I had confidence that you would prefer to share joyful fellowship rather than deal with problems, 4 so I wrote to you with a heavy heart, anguishing over you—not to cause pain, but for your eternal wellbeing—so you would know the depth of my love for you.

2Cor 2:5 As for the one whose struggles caused these problems, he has not injured me but has injured himself and perhaps some of you, but the injury to you was not as severe as to himself. 6 The therapeutic intervention chosen by the majority is appropriate for him. 7 Now be sure he knows your forgiveness and experiences your encouragement and comfort so that he will not despair or give up. 8 I urge you to show him your love! 9 My letter was to teach you how to intervene therapeutically so that you would follow God's healing principles in everything. 10 When you forgive someone, know that I also have forgiven him. And what I have forgiven, if there actually was anything to forgive, I have forgiven as Christ forgives—freely, as a witness to you— 11 in order that Satan might not trick us into holding grudges and thereby infect our hearts with bitterness, for we are well aware of his malicious schemes.

2Cor 2:12 When I went to Troas to preach the good news about God as revealed in Christ, and I discovered that the Lord had opened a door for me, 13 I was not at peace, because my dear brother Titus was not there with news about you; so I said my goodbyes and went to Macedonia.

2Cor 2:14 But thanks be to God, who always leads us like a victorious parade to reveal the beauty of being in union with Christ and thus spread the loving fragrance of his character, methods and principles everywhere we go. 15 For in God's plan, we are like the incense from the sanctuary—the aroma of Christ—to those who are being healed as well as to those who are dying. 16 Those who refuse the Remedy and are dying find the scent of Christ offensive, while to those who have partaken of the Remedy, it is the smell of victory, the aroma of transformation, and the balm of life. And who is capable of such a task? 17 Only those who accept the Remedy freely and share it freely, not seeking to peddle God's word for selfish profit. The Remedy Christ procured we have received straight from God, and share it freely, in all sincerity, as messengers sent from God.

3 Don't think that we are starting to market ourselves or that we need, like some people, letters to promote our ministry. ²The letter that promotes our message is you! The healing of your hearts and characters, known and read by everybody you encounter, ³reveals that you are a message from Christ—the result of our bringing you the truth about God—not tattooed upon your skin, but written in your characters by the Spirit of the living God; not on stone but upon human hearts and minds!

²Cor 3:4 We say this because we have absolute confidence in God to perfectly heal through the Remedy procured by Christ. ⁵We do not claim that we created the Remedy or possess the ability to heal, but our effectiveness comes from Christ and what he accomplished. ⁶He has made us competent members of His spiritual health-care team to distribute his Remedy—not merely the diagnostic tool of the law but the healing power of the Spirit; for the law diagnoses us as terminal, but the Spirit restores us to life.

²Cor 3:7 Now if the agency that diagnosed mankind as terminal (the one written on stone) was inaugurated with the brilliance of divine fire radiating from Moses' face so intensely that the Israelites couldn't gaze upon him because of the terrible agony in their unconverted hearts caused by the already fading splendor of fire of God's presence, ⁸will not the mighty agency of the Holy Spirit be even more brilliant? ⁹If the agency that diagnoses people as terminal is glorious, how much more glorious is God-the-Spirit who brings the Remedy that Christ achieved and restores us to righteousness! ¹⁰A candle is brilliant in a dark room, but it has no brilliance in comparison to the brightness of the sun. ¹¹And if what was written on stone (like a fading candle) came with glory, how much more glorious is it when the living law of love is eternally restored into the heart!

²Cor 3:12 Therefore, since we have such a certain outcome, we are very bold! ¹³We are not like Moses, who covered his face with a veil to hide the fading glory from the Israelites. ¹⁴Sadly, their minds were dull; even to this day a veil of misunderstanding obscures their minds whenever the symbolic teaching system and diagnostic code is read. The veil of confusion has not been removed because they misunderstand or reject Christ; and it is Christ who reveals the true meaning of it all. ¹⁵Yes, even today, when the first five books of the Old Testament are read, a veil of confusion and misunderstanding covers their hearts. ¹⁶But whenever anyone accepts Jesus and the truth he has revealed, the veil of confusion is taken away. ¹⁷We experience Jesus through the Spirit, and where the Spirit of the Lord is, there is freedom from confusion, fear, and selfishness. ¹⁸And we, whose minds are not veiled by confusion, and who reveal the truth about the Lord's glorious character, are being transformed into his likeness with ever-increasing glory which comes from the Lord and is applied in us by the Spirit.

4 Therefore, since God, in his great mercy, has called us to be part of his spiritual health-care team, we don't get discouraged or give up. ²Rather, unlike so many religious leaders, we reject secrecy, politicking, back-door deals, conniving, manipulating, deception, and we don't make the word of God difficult to understand. On the contrary, we present the truth simply, plainly and openly so that everyone can understand and, in God's sight, decide for themselves if this is not so. ³But if the good news that we present about God's healing Remedy is veiled by confusion, it is only veiled in the

confused minds of those who reject the truth and are dying. ⁴Satan, the god of this pagan age, has blinded the minds of unbelievers, so they don't see or comprehend the truth about God—his methods and principles as revealed in Christ, who is God's very thoughts made audible and visible. ⁵We do not promote ourselves, but we promote Jesus Christ as Lord; we are here to serve you for Jesus' cause. ⁶For God, who said, "Let light illuminate the darkness," made the light of his being shine into our hearts to enlighten us with the intimate knowledge of his glorious character as revealed perfectly in Christ.

2Cor 4:7 We carry this precious Remedy within these frail human bodies made of dirt to show that the supreme power to heal our characters is from God and does not originate in us. ⁸We are under constant pressure but are not crushed by it. While we often don't understand the immediate reason for the stress, we don't get discouraged, because we know the ultimate outcome. ⁹We are attacked by the enemies of love and truth but are never left without friends. We may suffer injury, but we are not destroyed. ¹⁰In this defective body, which tempts to selfishness, we surrender to die to self—as Jesus did—so that the perfect life of Jesus may be fully revealed in us. ¹¹For we who are alive are only alive because we surrender to die to selfishness—for Jesus' cause—so that his perfect life may be reproduced in our decaying bodies. ¹²Therefore we die to self in order to bring you the Remedy of Jesus—that his life may work its healing power in you.

2Cor 4:13 It is written, "I am confident in it; therefore I share what I know." With that same attitude, we are confident in what Jesus has done, and we tell what we know. ¹⁴We know that the one who raised the Lord Jesus from the dead will also raise all of us together in his presence. ¹⁵All of this is for your healing and restoration so that the Remedy

that is reaching more and more people will transform hearts and cause a greater overflow of thanksgiving to glorify God.

2Cor 4:16 That is why we don't get discouraged. Though our bodies are aging and wasting away, our hearts and minds are growing more like Jesus' every day. ¹⁷Therefore the momentary pain and discomfort that come during the healing process is insignificant when compared to the results of eternal perfection. ¹⁸We keep our minds focused—not on the day-to-day immediate struggles, but on the eternal outcome of reunion with God. For what is seen today is temporary, but the unseen future with God is eternal.

5 Now, we know that this earthly body is like a tent or hospital gown that wears out easily and leaves us exposed. And if this earthly body—which our individuality currently occupies—is destroyed, we have an eternal body that will never wear out; a heavenly dwelling place for our individuality, but not built by human hands. ²Meanwhile, the older we get, the more we groan, longing to be free of this deteriorating body and to be clothed in our perfect heavenly body, ³because when we have exchanged this mortal body for our heavenly one, we will not be found sick, dying, and exposed. ⁴For while we are in this collapsing tent, we groan with the burden of aging and slow decay. We don't want to die to be rid of this worn-out body, but we want to be translated directly into our heavenly body so that what is mortal may be swallowed up by eternal life. ⁵God's intention for us has never changed: He created us to live eternally and—as the first phase of our restoration—has given us the Spirit to heal our minds, guaranteeing our future complete re-creation.

2Cor 5:6 We certainly know that as long as this frail body is our home, we remain away from the Lord; ⁷but we live by trusting God with how things will turn out—not by waiting to see the future restoration. [8] Therefore we are confident while in the mortal body, even though we prefer to be translated into our heavenly body and be at home with the Lord. [9] Our goal is to be pleasing to him by living in harmony with his design for life—whether we are in this mortal body or our heavenly one—[10] for we will all appear in Christ's examining room so that each one may be accurately diagnosed and receive what their condition warrants, whether from compliance or non-compliance with God's treatment plan.

2Cor 5:11 Because we are completely in awe of the Lord, we try to persuade everyone of his goodness and trustworthiness. God knows the condition of our hearts perfectly, and I hope our motives are also clear to you. [12] We are not trying to promote ourselves, but reveal ourselves, so you can be confident that God is healing us, and so that you can effectively deal with those who value external appearances rather than what really matters—character development. [13] If we are in a frenzy, it is for God's cause; if we are calm and coherent, it is for your need, [14] as Christ's love—the design protocol upon which all life is built—is what rules our lives. We realize that one Man died to provide Remedy for every human being, as all are terminal. [15] He died to provide Remedy to all humanity so that those who live will not live dominated by selfishness, but in love for him who died to heal them and was raised again!

2Cor 5:16 We no longer view people through the lens of self-promotion, like the world does. Sadly, we had once regarded Christ as foolish for not promoting himself, but gladly, we no longer do. [17] For anyone who has joined their heart in unity with Christ receives regeneration of character and is created anew to be like Christ. The old selfish character is replaced with the new Christlike character. [18] All of this healing and transformation is from God, who—in the person of Christ—fixed the damage sin did to humanity and restored humanity into unity with himself, and now gives us the privilege of sharing with others the healing Remedy that Christ achieved. [19] God has not been counting men's defects and sins against them as something to be punished, but has been working through Christ to heal mankind and restore humanity back into perfect unity with himself. And he has given to us the mission of sharing this healing Remedy with everyone! [20] We are therefore Christ's ambassadors, reaching out to you as though God himself were pleading with you to come home and be healed. We beg you, on behalf of Christ: Let God heal you from certain death to eternal life! [21] He can do this because he ordained that Christ, who had no selfishness of his own, take our selfish condition upon himself in order to cleanse and recreate humanity back to God's original ideal, so that by uniting with Christ we might be restored to the perfect righteousness of God.

6 As members of God's spiritual health-care team, we implore you not to waste God's gracious Remedy. [2] For God says,

"When the time came that you
   needed my assistance, I heard you;
and when the day arrived for me to
   provide you Remedy, I helped you."

I state this plainly, God is assisting us right now, and now is the time to partake of his Remedy.

2Cor 6:3 We don't put obstacles to healing in anyone's way, so our ministry is not the reason some fail to get well. [4] Rather, as God's representatives, we do all we can to make ourselves useful in spreading the Remedy. We endure opposition, misrepresentation, shortage of helpers, lack of supplies, [5] attacks, imprisonment, riots. Some nights we work all night or skip meals in order to administer the Remedy. [6] We work with pure hearts, understanding the problem and God's solution for it, reaching out patiently, gently, kindly. Empowered by the Holy Spirit, we are filled with love [7] and speak the truth to bring the power of God to bear. With all our beings, we wield the weapons of right —doing what is right, healthy and reasonable because it is right, healthy and reasonable— [8] regardless of whether we receive honor or dishonor, praise or criticism, whether we are seen as legitimate or regarded as frauds. [9] Even if people pretend they don't know us when they really do, we still will do what is right. Though regarded as being terminal, we have taken the Remedy, so we live on; though beaten, we are not killed. [10] We are saddened by such opposition, but our hearts always rejoice in sharing the Remedy; though poor, we make others rich; though we have nothing the world values, we possess everything, for we possess the Remedy of Jesus Christ.

2Cor 6:11 Dear friends in Corinth, we have spoken freely to you from the love that is in our hearts. [12] We have not closed our hearts to you, but you have closed your hearts to us. [13] I reach out to you as a parent to their child: Open your hearts and love!

2Cor 6:14 Do not become partners with those who reject the Remedy. For what do wellness and sickness have in common? Or how can light and darkness fellowship together? [15] Are Christ and Satan allies, working together? What does one who shares God's Remedy have in common with those who spread Satan's terminal illness? [16] Would you put a pagan idol in God's temple? Well, remember that you are the living temple of God where he dwells by his Spirit, so don't put pagan ideas about God into your hearts. As God has said,

> "I will live among them and share life with them.
> I will be their God, and they will be my people."

2Cor 6:17 The Lord says,

> "Come out from the sick
> and be separate from the dying.
> Don't touch that which will poison your body,
> contaminate your soul, or soil your character.
> [18] I will be your Father,
> and you will be transformed to be like me,
> to be my sons and daughters,"
> says the Lord Almighty.

7 My good friends, since all of these guarantees are for us, let us choose to follow God's treatment plan and detach ourselves from everything that poisons the body or damages the mind, and let us develop Christlike character out of admiration for God.

2Cor 7:2 Won't you open your hearts to us? We have harmed no one, we have misled no one, nor have we taken advantage of anyone. [3] I don't say this to make you feel bad; as I have told you before, you are so special to us that whether we live or die we hold you close within our hearts. [4] I am confident in your healing and so proud of your participation in God's Remedy! Your continued growth brings me great happiness. Regardless of trials, my joy in you never stops.

2Cor 7:5 When we arrived in Macedonia, we were so strained that we couldn't rest well at all. We were harassed constantly, which created external conflicts and internal fears, [6] but God— who aids the discouraged—aided and encouraged us by sending Titus. [7] Seeing Titus was a great joy, but we were also greatly comforted by your thoughtfulness. He told us about your concern for me, your deep sorrow, and your longing for my good. Your concern has brought me the greatest joy.

2Cor 7:8 Even if my letter was uncomfortable to read and brought you grief, I do not regret it. I initially feared its impact, but now I see that though my letter did cause you pain, its therapeutic

2 CORINTHIANS 7:9

purpose was realized and thus the pain was only brief. ⁹ So now I am very happy! Not because you suffered discomfort, but because your discomfort occurred from the application of the truth and resulted in healing and transformation. Your pain was the godly pain of accurate diagnosis of your true condition, so our actions were therapeutic and did not harm you in any way. ¹⁰ Godly sorrow—which is due to disgust with the selfish state of the heart, and which brings repentance resulting in healing and wellness—leaves no regrets. But worldly sorrow is the sorrow for not getting one's own way; it leaves one terminally ill, culminating in death. ¹¹ Do you see how this godly sorrow has left you dissatisfied with the way things were? Do you see how eager you are to be healthy, how afraid you are to remain unhealed? You're longing for everything to be set right. Your passion to properly diagnose the spiritually sick and to see God's Remedy applied has demonstrated that you are not at fault in this recent problem.

2Cor 7:12 Please understand that my purpose in writing to you was not primarily for the one who did wrong, nor for the one injured, but that you would be stirred enough by your love and devotion to us to see the importance of using God's methods in dealing with such matters, and act as if you are always before God. ¹³ All of this has encouraged us. Not only were we encouraged by the manner in which you handled this problem, but we were especially pleased by the way you poured your love upon Titus. He is happy and refreshed because of you. ¹⁴ I told him how proud I am of you and that you have not disappointed me. Just as all that we told you is true, so our bragging about you to Titus has proved to be true. ¹⁵ Titus is so exuberant; he tells us over and over how quick you were to open yourselves to him, and how you received him with humble

hearts, being willing to listen and apply what you learned. ¹⁶ I am so glad that I can have complete confidence in you.

8 Brothers and sisters, we are excited to tell you how God's Remedy has infused the Macedonian churches. ² Even though they have suffered terrible hardship, and despite their extreme poverty, they have given an incredible offering. ³ They gave beyond what I thought they could possibly afford, and we didn't even pass a collection plate. ⁴ They begged us to take this offering, counting it a privilege to help those working to spread God's Remedy throughout Judea. ⁵ This spontaneous gift was completely unexpected, but they had already given their hearts to the Lord, and when we arrived—in keeping with God's kingdom of love—gave their hearts to us also. ⁶ So we asked Titus, who had already been working with you, to make you aware of this opportunity to share in the blessing of giving to support the work in Judea. ⁷ Just as you already do so many things well—trust God, speak effectively, know God's word and methods—then with sincere hearts and love for us, excel at being a conduit of God's grace as you give to others.

2Cor 8:8 This is not a command, for love cannot be commanded. I want to stretch and expand your love in response to the witness of the Macedonians, ⁹ for you know the absolute generosity of our Lord Jesus Christ: Even though he was rich in all things, yet for your need he gave up everything and became empty—nothing!—so that you, through what he achieved when he emptied himself, may be restored to eternal riches.

2Cor 8:10 Last year you were not only the first to give, but the first to have hearts transformed from selfishness to love, so my advice is simple: ¹¹ Continue applying to your lives God's method of selfless giving, and finish what you started last year—giving what you are able. ¹²God knows your hearts, and it is the willingness of heart that matters. Every gift from a willing heart is pleasing to God, no matter the size; so don't be discouraged if you don't have more to give than you do.

2Cor 8:13 We are not trying to enrich others while impoverishing you, but trying to put God's design law of love into action and thus bring equilibrium and healthiness to all. ¹⁴Presently you have plenty and can relieve the suffering of those who are in need, but later, when you are in need, their abundance will provide for you. Then none will suffer. ¹⁵As it is written, "Those who had the most did not hoard it, and those who had the least did not go without."

2Cor 8:16 I am so thankful to God who filled the heart of Titus with the same love I have for you. ¹⁷Titus was so happy with our request that he can hardly wait to see you, and has planned the trip himself. ¹⁸We are sending with Titus a friend who all the churches cherish because he is so effective in spreading the Remedy. ¹⁹Additionally, the churches chose him to go with us as we spread the Remedy and use the gifts given to honor the Lord by eagerly helping those in need. ²⁰We are being transparent with the use of these donated funds to avoid any false allegation or criticism. ²¹We are very careful to do what is right—not just before God, but so that others will know the principles by which we live.

2Cor 8:22 We are also sending a friend who is highly energized for God's cause, and who is even more excited because of his certainty about your healing. ²³Titus works with me and represents my ministry; the others are coming on behalf of the churches in honor to Christ, ²⁴so be sure to demonstrate to them God's love in action and show them why we are so proud of you—then the churches will know it for themselves.

9 I know I really don't need to request that you help those working to spread the Remedy in Judea, ²because you are already eager to help. I also know how enthusiastically you have been recruiting those in Macedonia to join in this giving, and telling them of the blessings you have received from all that you have already given. And your witness has stirred most of them to also give. ³Therefore, I am sending the representatives from the churches to see how your lives have been transformed, so that our praise may not be just empty words, but you will actually be ready and waiting to help. ⁴If any of the Macedonians come with us and find that you have not prepared your gift, then not only would you be embarrassed, but we would be ashamed for having bragged so strongly about you; ⁵so I thought it best to send some friends ahead to help get ready the generous gift you had promised. Then your gift will be seen for what it is—given from the heart—and not misunderstood as given under the pressure of an offering call.

2Cor 9:6 Remember that those who put little into any endeavor get small results, but those who invest much—experience much in return. ⁷Every person should decide in their own heart what to give, and give it freely—without pressure or fear—because God loves it when hearts are healed to give gladly. ⁸And God can heal and transform you so that in all situations, at every moment, you will have all that you need to represent him and his kingdom of love accurately. ⁹As it is written:

"He has spread his Remedy to those who have nothing;

his righteousness will last eternally."
2Cor 9:10 Now he who provides seed for the farmer, and bread for eating, will also provide you with Remedy, increase your stockpile of truth and love, and cause your character to grow in righteousness. ¹¹You will be healed—

enriched in every aspect of God's kingdom—so that you will be generous all the time, and as we share your generosity around, many others will give thanks to God.

2Cor 9:12 Your actions not only meet the real needs of God's helpers but inspire many hearts to give thanks to God. 13 Because your actions are in harmony with God's methods of love—and by sharing with others you have shown that your acceptance of Christ's Remedy is more than lip service, but actual change in character and lifestyle—people praise God that his Remedy to sin and selfishness really works. 14 As they pray for you, their hearts are transformed into the unity of love by the incredible effectiveness of God's Remedy already given to you. 15 Thank you, God, for your incredible Remedy!

10 With the gentleness of Jesus, I humbly implore you to stay faithful. I understand that some are misrepresenting me as two-faced: "soft, uncertain, and insecure" when in your presence, and "confident, assertive and direct" when not around you. 2 I am begging you not to be fooled by gossip about us, so that I won't have to spend time speaking out against the distortions (as I expect to do with those who believe the rumors that we live by the selfish standards of the world). 3 Remember that even though we live in the world, the war in which we are engaged is not like wars the world fights. 4 We don't use worldly weapons designed to kill the body or destroy physical structures, nor do we use the world's weapons of lies, distortion, manipulation, deceit, flattery, coercion, sanctions, or trickery. On the contrary, our weapons are from God and have divine power to free the mind, heal the heart, and demolish Satan's stronghold of fear, lies and selfishness. 5 We demolish every idea, argument, doctrine, teaching or concept that infects the mind and distorts or obstructs the truth about God, and we reclaim the thoughts, feelings and attitudes into the truth about God as revealed by Jesus Christ. 6 We stand ready to bring discipline to bear to help break destructive habits so that maturity and health will be fully realized.

2Cor 10:7 Look at the evidence right in front of you: If anyone is confident that they have taken the Remedy and been united with Christ, then examine the evidence of the methods you live by and remember that we have taken the Remedy and are united with Christ. 8 For I am not ashamed to boast about the responsibility the Lord has given me to bring you the Remedy in order to heal you; not to damage you further. 9 So understand this clearly: I am not trying to frighten you with my letters! 10 I know some people try to undercut my ministry by saying, "He writes well and his letters are dynamic and inspiring, but his speaking skills are weak and his presentations are boring." 11 These people need to remember that the truth we present in our letters is revealed in the way we live, and is the same message taught in our lectures.

2Cor 10:12 But we would never try to compete with others who are merely promoting themselves. Those who spend their lives in competition with others for the best reviews, highest ratings and greatest popularity on the speaking circuit are foolish. 13 We won't waste our time boasting about ourselves, but will boast about God's kingdom—the power of his Remedy and how it has changed your lives. 14 We are not making empty boasts or claims without evidence, because we have presented the Remedy to you, and your lives have been changed by it. 15 Nor do we misrepresent the work of others. We hope that as you continue to heal, more opportunities to work among you will open 16 so that we may spread the Remedy into new communities beyond you. We never want to rest feeling satisfied by the work done by others. 17 No; let our pleasure and delight come from what the Lord has achieved, 18 for it is not the one who claims to be healthy who is recognized as healed, but it is those whom the Lord has healed who are recognized as actually being healthy.

11 If what I say next seems absurd, please appreciate my heart's motive in saying it, 2 because I am watching out for you with a godly watchfulness: I determined to present you to Christ—with hearts and minds cleansed—as a pure woman to her husband. 3 But I am concerned that just as Eve was deceived by the lies of Satan, so your minds may be tricked into turning away from the pure love and devotion to Christ. 4 For when a great speaker comes and thrills you with moving sermons but distorts Jesus' character—suggesting his spirit is something other than love, or his Remedy is something different than what you have already partaken of—you embrace it eagerly. 5 But don't think I am somehow less qualified than these so-called "experts." 6 I may not be a professional speaker, but I know what your actual diagnosis is, I and have God's Remedy for it; we have made this explicitly clear to you in every way possible.

2 Cor 11:7 Was it a mistake for me to bring you the Remedy for free, or would you have valued it more had I charged you for it? 8 The cost of bringing you the Remedy was paid by the other churches. 9 Even when I was with you, I didn't present my expenses to you for reimbursement, but I had my needs supplied by members of Christ's health-care team from Macedonia. I made sure not to place any obstacles that would interfere with your healing, and I will continue to do so. 10 As surely as I brought you the Remedy Christ achieved, I will not be quiet about this point. 11 Why? Not because I don't love you, but — as God well knows — I do love you and I want you to know it! 12 And I will keep making this point in order to expose the difference between those who claim to be like us in promoting Christ but are actually promoting themselves.

2 Cor 11:13 These people are conmen, charlatans, peddling a false remedy, pretending to be ambassadors of Christ. 14 This shouldn't surprise anyone, for Satan himself claims to be interested in the betterment of humanity, masquerading as an angel of light and truth; 15 so it is no shock to realize that Satan's agents also masquerade as members of God's spiritual health-care team. But their end will be what comes to all who take a false remedy for their terminal condition.

2 Cor 11:16 Don't think I am just playing around or being silly, but if it does sound ridiculous, then hear it like it was coming from someone who is willing to go to extremes—even boasting— to protect you. 17 In this example, I am not presenting things as the Lord does, but as a child does. 18 Because many who have come to you spend their time touting their accomplishments and boasting about their credentials, I will too. 19 It seems that you think it wise to listen to such childlike talk. 20 In fact, you even enjoy childlike behavior and put up with those who manipulate you, exploit you, take advantage of you, push their ideas onto you, and even slap you. 21 If that is what you needed, then I regret that we just couldn't stomach acting that way with you. So speaking like a child — whatever qualifications others brag about, I can brag about even more.

2 Cor 11:22 Are they Hebrews, genetic descendants of Israel and Abraham? Well, so what? I am also. 23 Are they ambassadors of Christ? This is so immature to say, but I am a better ambassador for Christ! I've done more, worked harder, been imprisoned more often, been beaten more frequently and

more severely, received many more death threats, and experienced more life-threatening encounters. 24 The Jews beat me with thirty-nine lashes on five different occasions. 25 I was beaten on three different occasions with rods, stoned once, shipwrecked three times, and spent thirty-six hours stranded in the open sea. 26 I have to move constantly. My life has been in danger on rivers, in danger from pirates, from my own countrymen, and from Gentiles. My life has been threatened in cities, in the country, at sea, and by those pretending to be on Christ's team. 27 I have worked long hours and often gone without sleep. I know real hunger and thirst, and I have gone without food more than once. I have even been with nothing, out in the cold, and naked. 28 On top of all this, I am constantly pressured because of my desire to help the churches. 29 When someone feels too weak to go on—I've been there; I feel their pain. When someone is overcome with fear and selfishness, my heart burns with desire to help.

2Cor 11:30 If, like a child, I must focus on myself, I will focus on how deficient—in and of myself—I am. 31 God—the Father of our Lord Jesus—who is forever to be praised, knows that I am not lying. 32 The governor under King Aretas in Damascus had the city locked down and ordered the guards to arrest me, 33 but I was lowered in a basket from one of the windows in the city wall and got away.

12 I have started bragging like a child, so I must continue, although I doubt it will accomplish much. I will now tell you about visions from the Lord: 2 I know a Christian who, fourteen years ago, was taken to the third heaven where God is. I am not certain whether it was an actual physical transportation to heaven or only a vision of heaven occurring in the mind —only God knows that— 3 but even though only God knows whether this man was physically transported to heaven or experienced heaven as a vision in his mind, 4 I know he was taken to paradise where God is. While there, he heard wonderful truths—truths beyond earthly comprehension; truths human beings are currently unable to explain. 5 As a man, to talk about such a thing makes me proud, but I will not focus attention on myself, except for my deficiencies. 6 But if I did choose to talk about what I have done, I wouldn't look ridiculous, because I would only be recounting facts of what has transpired. But I will not speak about myself, because I want people to form their conclusions about me from the way I live, not by what I say about myself.

2Cor 12:7 To keep me humble and to protect me from arrogance in the aftermath of seeing the incredible beauties of heaven and hearing heavenly truth, I was afflicted with a physical ailment. It was really an attack from Satan, designed to discourage me and divert me from fulfilling God's purpose for my life. 8 Three times I talked with Jesus and asked him to heal me, 9 but he said to me, "My Remedy is more than enough for you, for my power is most clearly seen by transforming the weak." Therefore I will make my infirmities even more plain so that Christ's power may be more fully revealed in me. 10 Do you understand? It is so that Christ's Remedy—his power to transform lives and deliver hearts and minds from fear and selfishness—can be more easily seen that I delight in weakness, insults, mistreatment, difficulties, persecution, and hardships. The weaker I get, the more of Christ's power is manifest in me, and the stronger I become.

2Cor 12:11 I have spoken like a child, but it was because you needed me to talk to you this way. I should already have your endorsement, trust and support, for my qualifications are certainly not less than those professional speakers —those so-called "experts" you listen to—even though of myself I am nothing. [12] Signs and wonders accompanied my ministry and were done with humility, gentleness and patience, which marks me as one of Christ's ambassadors. [13] In what way did I treat you worse than the other churches, other than that I never burdened you with my expenses, so I took less money from you than from them? If this troubles you, please forgive me.

2Cor 12:14 I am coming to you for my third visit, and I will not burden you with my expenses, because I want it clearly understood: I do not want your property—I want your love! Little children should not have to earn money to support their parents, but parents should provide for their children, [15] so I am eager to spend everything I have for your good. I will even give my life if necessary. Will you really love me less if I love you more? [16] So the facts are clear: I have not burdened you in any way, yet some still whisper that I am a conman and somehow try to scam you by not asking for your money. [17] Well, think for yourselves! Did anyone whom I sent try to cheat you? [18] I encouraged Titus to visit you, and I sent a close friend with him. Did Titus try to cheat you? Or did he act in the same patient, humble, loving attitude, and did he practice the same honest methods as I did?

2Cor 12:19 Don't think we are writing in order to defend ourselves to you. Our lives are open before God as the lives of people united with Christ. My dear friends, everything we do is for your eternal healing, development, and growth. [20] I am quite concerned that when I arrive I will not find you in the healthy condition I would like to, and you may not find me as pleased with your condition as you hope. I am afraid you have been reinfected with selfishness, which is causing arguments, envy, temper tantrums, internal sects, slander, gossip, arrogance, and a general breakdown in decency and good order. [21] I am afraid that when I visit

again, God will permit me to be embarrassed and have my heart broken over those who have previously engaged in destructive sexual behavior and still have not experienced Christ's Remedy or had their hearts transformed.

13 This is my third visit to you, and—as the Scriptures say— every accusation must be confirmed by the testimony of two or three witnesses. [2] When I was with you the second time, I warned you of the dangers of selfishness. Now, while I am away, I repeat this warning. Understand this: When I return, I will not ignore those who live in selfishness and are not partaking of the Remedy. [3] I will intervene aggressively—since you insist on evidence that Christ is speaking through me—for Christ is not weak in his ability to heal the heart from selfishness. He shows his healing power among you! [4] While he surrendered all his strength when crucified, he now lives in the fullness of God's life-giving power. As Christ was "weak" in his ability to save himself at the cross, we are weak in our ability to save ourselves. It is by God's life-giving power that we are made alive with Christ in order to serve you.

2Cor 13:5 Look inward and examine your heart motives to see whether you have been renewed and genuinely trust God. Test yourselves to see if you really do love others more than self. Don't you realize that the perfect character of Christ Jesus is being reproduced in you by the Spirit—unless of course you fail the test and discover that selfishness still rules your heart? [6] I truly hope you will see that we have not failed to love others more than self. [7] We ask God to protect you from yourselves so that you will not live selfishly—not so that people will think well of us, who brought you the Remedy, but that you will get well even if we seem to get worse. [8] For we cannot change the truth; we can only effectively deal with it. [9] In our weakness, we rejoice to see you strong, and we pray continually for your complete restoration to Christlike perfection. ¹⁰ It is for your good that I write this: The authority the Lord has given me is for your healing, not for your destruction. I certainly hope you will apply Christ's Remedy now, so that I won't have to apply painful treatments when I arrive.

2Cor 13:11 Finally, my friends, I say goodbye. Strive to experience the perfect character of Christ, think carefully about what I have said, be united in heart, live in peace, and the God of love and peace will be with you.

2Cor 13:12 Greet each other with Christlike love. ¹³ All Christ's spiritual healthcare team members send their love and encouragement.

2Cor 13:14 May the Remedy achieved by the Lord Jesus Christ, and God's love, and the presence of the Holy Spirit, be yours!

Galatians

1 Paul, an ambassador of the celestial government of God—not appointed or sent by men or women but called by Jesus Christ and confirmed by God the Father who raised him from the dead— ² and all the brothers and sisters with me,

To those who have partaken of God's healing Remedy in Galatia:

Gal 1:3 God our Father sends his goodwill and peace to you, as does the Lord Jesus Christ ⁴who voluntarily sacrificed himself to restore trust and heal us from the infection of fear and selfishness and thus deliver us out of this present self-indulgent, self-destructive evil age, according to the eternal purpose of our God and Father ⁵to whom be all honor and praise and glory for ever and ever. Amen.

Gal 1:6 I am shocked and amazed that you are so quick to reject the truth about God and turn away from his gracious character and methods of love as revealed by Christ, and instead are turning to a different message of "good news"— ⁷which really isn't good news at all but a grand deception that will only destroy. Evidently, there are some people who are twisting and perverting the good news about God that Christ has brought, and thus throwing you into all kinds of confusion. ⁸ But even if we, or an angel from heaven, should come and present a different message of "good news" from what we have already presented — a message that, in effect, misrepresents God and changes the meaning of what Christ accomplished — then they will be eternally lost, because they are presenting a message without truth and with no power to heal and restore. ⁹ As we have said once before, I now say again, so that no one will misunderstand: If anyone, from anywhere, regardless of accompanying signs or miracles, presents a so-called message of "good news" that is different from what you already accepted, that person will be eternally lost, because they are presenting a false message with no power to heal or restore!

Gal 1:10 What do you think I am doing with my life: do you think I am trying to win the approval of people or the favor of God? Or do you think I am trying to please men and women, or make human beings happy with me? If I were still worried about what people thought of me, or trying to get the approval of humankind, I would not be a serving friend of Christ.

Gal 1:11 Brothers and sisters, I want you to be perfectly clear on this: The good news that I proclaim—the message of healing and restoration, the truth about the character of God as revealed by Jesus—is not something fabricated or concocted by human beings. ¹²I did not receive this healing message from any human, and neither did I learn it in school; rather, Jesus Christ revealed it to me directly.

Gal 1:13 For you have heard of my previous life in Judaism: I practiced the methods of force and coercion and persecuted the people of God, and I tried to destroy them or pressure them back into the empty rituals of Judaism. ¹⁴I was promoting the forms and ceremonies of the old symbolic system more intensely than most of my fellow Jews, and I was unreasonably zealous for the powerless traditions of my fathers. ¹⁵But when God—who guided my life and development from birth, and graciously called me to his service— [16] decided to reveal his Son to me and recreate the character of his Son within me so that I might be enabled to present the truth about God among the Gentiles, I did not seek the approval or validation of any human, [17] and neither did I go to Jerusalem to be taught by those who were ambassadors of Christ before I was, but I immediately went into Arabia, and later—to Damascus.

Gal 1:18 Then, after three years of being taught by the Lord, I went up to Jerusalem to get to know Peter, and I stayed with him for fifteen days. [19] The only other ambassador of Christ I saw was James, the Lord's brother. [20] As God is my witness, what I am writing to you is no lie. [21] Later I went to Syria and Cilicia. [22] In the churches of Judea, I was not known by anyone who loved and accepted Christ. [23] They had only heard the report: "The man who used to persecute us is now proclaiming the good news that he once tried to destroy—the good news about God as revealed in Christ." [24] And they rejoiced and praised God because of me.

2 It wasn't until fourteen years later that I returned to Jerusalem, and this time I took Barnabas and Titus along. [2] I went because of what had been revealed to me, and I presented to them the good news that I teach among the Gentiles—God's plan to heal and restore all humanity. I presented this good news privately to those who were looked upon as leaders, because I was concerned that my efforts to promote the freedom all humankind experiences in Christ might have been in vain. [3] But such was not the case, as evidenced by the fact that Titus, who was with me (and Greek by birth), was not required to be circumcised. [4] This issue came up because some individuals, pretending to be our brothers in Christ, had snuck in to spy on us and criticize the freedom we have in Christ,

and attempted to enslave our minds again with meaningless rules and rituals. [5] But we were not swayed by them for one second, so don't waver, but cling to the truth of the good news we have presented to you.

Gal 2:6 As for those men and women in leadership, whom some consider important (their position doesn't matter to me because God does not judge by earthly, external appearances), they contributed nothing to my message. [7] On the contrary, they recognized the truth and power of my message and realized that I had been entrusted with the responsibility of taking this healing message to the Gentiles, just as Peter had been sent to the Jews. [8] For there is only one healing truth and one God— the source of this Remedy. God was working both in Peter's ministry as an ambassador of God to the Jews, and in mine as his ambassador to the Gentiles. [9] James, Peter, and John, who are considered pillars in the church, recognized God's graciousness at work in me and accepted me and Barnabas as co-workers with them in distributing God's healing Remedy. They agreed that we should take this message to the Gentiles, while they focus their energies on enlightening the Jews. [10] The only requirement they asked of us was that we remember the needs of the poor—something I was already eagerly doing.

Gal 2:11 But when Peter came to Antioch, I opposed him openly and publicly, because he was clearly wrong, and, if not corrected, would cause serious confusion. [12] You see, prior to the arrival of certain church leaders from church headquarters—who valued the Jewish traditions—he would socialize and eat with the Gentiles. But when these leaders arrived, he suddenly distanced himself and wouldn't socialize with the Gentiles for fear of what these leaders—who promoted circumcision— would think. [13] The other Jewish believers followed his lead and joined him in this hypocrisy, and there was danger of an artificial class distinction being established; and because of their inconsistent and hypocritical behavior, even Barnabas was led astray.

Gal 2:14 When I realized that they were not acting in accordance with the truth or the good news about God and his desire to freely heal all humankind, it became necessary to take a public stand, and I said to Peter in front of them all, "You are a Jew, yet you have experienced the freedom that Jesus brought and no longer live under the restrictions of all the Jewish traditions and rituals. Why, then, are you forcing the Gentiles into the bondage of Jewish customs and traditions?

Gal 2:15 "We, who were born Jewish— part of God's specially chosen educational team, blessed with the symbolic teaching tools, and not part of the ignorant Gentile world— 16 clearly know that a person is set right with God not by rituals, symbols, or keeping to a certain educational script, but simply by trusting Jesus Christ. We, too, have been won back to trust by the evidence of God's true character and methods revealed by Christ and thus our minds are set right with God by trust in Christ, and not by rituals or adhering to a certain set of rules, because it is not possible to heal the mind and set the heart right with God by behaviorally following a set of rules.

Gal 2:17 "If, while we seek to be healed and set right with God through the truth that Christ has revealed, it becomes obvious that the infection of selfishness has not been eradicated from our hearts, does that mean that Christ promotes selfishness? Absolutely not! 18 If I stop taking the Remedy and re-infect myself with selfishness, I only prove that I am sick and out of harmony with God's law of love and life. 19 For through the written law I was diagnosed as terminal so that I might give up trying to cure myself and instead trust God and live for him.

20 The old 'me' who lived for self—who sought to 'get' instead of 'give,' the 'me' who lived on the survival-of-the-fittest principle—died when I recognized the true significance of all that Christ has done. That old 'me' no longer lives, but Christ—with his character of self-sacrificing love now lives in me. The life I now live in this body I live by trust in the Son of God, who loved me and freely gave himself to win me back to trust and to purge humanity from selfishness and death. 21 I do not discard God's graciousness, for if healing and restoration could have been achieved from human observance of a set of rules, or if the diagnostic instrument of the law could have healed us, then Christ's death was pointless!"

3 You foolish Galatians! Who has clouded your minds and confused your thinking such that you would prefer lies to the truth? Before your very eyes Jesus Christ was clearly portrayed as crucified, and as the only Remedy for our sin-infected minds! 2 I would like to know just one thing from you: Did you receive the Spirit of love and truth, and experience his healing power, by practicing rituals and observing rules, or was it by understanding and believing the truth that you heard? 3 Are you really so foolish that you think that after experiencing the healing power of the Spirit, which came by trust alone, you can now complete the healing process by your own effort— without the Spirit? 4 Have you really gone so far in the treatment course for nothing? And it will be for nothing if you persist in trying to heal yourselves! 5 Is it because you observe a set of rules that God enlightens your minds with his Spirit and miraculously transforms your characters, or is it because you have been won to trust by the evidence Jesus revealed?

Gal 3:6 Consider Abraham: "He trusted God, and his trust was recognized as

The Remedy

righteousness: The distrust caused through Satan's lies had been removed, and through trust he was endowed with a new heart, right motives, and Christlike principles." 7 Be clear on this: All those who trust God, as he did, experience the same transformation of character and are considered children of Abraham. 8 The Scriptures foretold that God would set the Gentiles right with himself by trust — just like Abraham — and announced this incredible good news to Abraham: "All nations, peoples and ethnic groups will be blessed through you." 9 So those who trust God experience healing of heart and mind — just like Abraham, who trusted God.

Gal 3:10 All who try to get well and experience unity with God by observing certain rituals or following a written script, or obeying a set of rules, are abandoned to their own fate, for it is written: "Abandoned to your own choice is everyone who fails in the slightest to do everything written in the Book of the Law." 11 Clearly, no one is healed and set right with God by working to follow a set of rules, because "Those set right with God live by trust." 12 The written law, as applied by the Jews, is not based on trust; on the contrary, it is based on individual performance—on attempts to heal oneself—as it is written: "The one who works to save self will live in fear and only get worse." 13 Christ saved us from where the law leaves us—diagnosed as terminal and abandoned to die—by being himself abandoned on the cross in order to restore us to trust and to purge humanity from the infection of selfishness and death; for it is written: "Abandoned to die is everyone who is hung on a tree." 14 He saved us from a futile, self-focused works system in order that the blessings of love, life, and freedom — given to Abraham — might come to the Gentiles through Jesus Christ, so that by trust we might receive the full enlightenment, renewal,

and regeneration of heart and mind that comes by the Spirit.

Gal 3:15 Brothers and sisters, consider the example of a legal contract: Just as no one can simply make void or change a legal contract that has been properly established, so it is in this case. 16 God gave the promises to Abraham and his seed. The Scripture does not say "seeds," meaning many people or all his descendants, but "your seed," meaning one single person, who is Jesus Christ. 17 What I am trying to make clear is this: The law—the diagnostic instrument designed to reveal our illness, and the symbolic script designed to teach God's true Remedy—introduced 430 years later, does not make void the agreement previously established by God and thus does not replace the promise, but it was designed to help us see and appreciate the promise. 18 For if our healing and restoration could be accomplished by keeping the law or performing rituals, then God did not need to promise to heal us, because we could have healed ourselves; but God did graciously promise Abraham to provide the only Remedy to cure our sin-sick hearts and minds.

Gal 3:19 If God promised to heal us, then what was the purpose of the law? It was added because of our sin-sick state—our darkened minds and the rapid rate at which we were destroying ourselves—in order to diagnose our condition and teach us a healthier way to live until the only true cure, Jesus (the promised One) had come. God communicated this law through angels, and then through Moses as an intermediary to the people. 20 But when there is only one party involved—and God and his Son Jesus are One—an intermediary is not needed.

Gal 3:21 Is the written law, then, somehow in opposition to the promises of God? Of course not! The written law was simply a tool to diagnose our sickness and lead us to God for healing. If the written law could somehow cure the infection of selfishness and promote life, then healing would certainly have followed the giving of the law. 22 But Scripture is clear: All humanity is infected with selfishness and is imprisoned by this terminal condition. It is by trust that we experience the only cure, the One promised Jesus Christ who was given to humankind as the Remedy to this terminal condition.

Gal 3:23 Before Christ came, we were quarantined by the written law—restrained from continual self-destruction—until Christ procured the only true cure. 24 The written law was provided as a safeguard to protect us and lead us to Christ—the Great Physician—so that we might be restored to unity with God by trust in, and partaking of, Christ. 25 Now that trust in God has been restored—and we are set right in heart, mind, and character, and again practice God's methods—we no longer need the law to diagnose our condition or lead us back to God.

Gal 3:26 Through the Remedy established by Jesus Christ you are all loyal children of God, 27 for all of you who have immersed your minds and hearts into the truth of God as revealed by Christ have had your characters changed, and—like a new set of clothing—replaced with the character of Christ. 28 Your station on earth is irrelevant: it doesn't matter whether you are Jew or Greek, slave or free, male or female—for you are all one in character, method, principle and motive through all that Christ has done. 29 If you are Christlike in heart and mind, then you are one of Abraham's descendants and an heir to all the promises of God.

4 What I am trying to explain to you is that as long as the heir remains immature, they are really no different from a slave, because they need someone to supervise their behavior, make their decisions, and guide their actions—even though they own the entire estate.

2 They don't have self-governance, so they need the guardians and trustees to protect them from their immature self until such time as they can handle their own affairs. 3 Likewise, when we were childlike in character and immature in our thinking, we had no self-control and were slaves to selfish impulses. 4 But when the time was right, God intervened and sent his Son—born of a sin-infected human mother, as real human baby, with a humanity weakened by the law of sin and death— 5 in order to purify, cleanse, and purge humanity from the infection of selfishness and fear. He did this in order to heal and restore those diagnosed as "terminal" by the written law, so that we might receive all the blessings of sons and daughters of God. 6 Because we are children of God, God sent the Spirit of his Son into our hearts to restore Christlikeness of character so that we genuinely call out to God, "Daddy, Father!" 7 Rejoice! You are no longer childlike, needing the supervision of a slave, but are adult children, wise and mature; and as mature children—heirs with Christ of all that is promised!

Gal 4:8 In the past, before you knew God as revealed by Jesus, your minds were held in the bondage of fear and superstition by gods of your own darkened imaginations. 9 But now that you have come to know God as revealed by Jesus (or, more importantly, now that Christlike character has been developing within you, and you are known as God's children), how could you possibly return to the dark, powerless, destructive beliefs and practices of your former lives? Do you wish to have your minds destroyed and be enslaved by superstition and ignorance all over again? 10 You are actually observing ceremonial holidays as if somehow such observances could heal the mind, remove selfishness and guilt, or restore the character to Christlikeness. 11 I can hardly believe it! I am beginning to wonder whether all my time with you has been wasted.

Gal 4:12 I beg you, seek to understand my concerns and try to see things from my perspective, as I have sought to understand your concerns and see things from your perspective. You have not offended me, nor do I hold a grudge against you. 13 You know that when I shared the Remedy with you for the first time, I was in poor health. 14 I remember how sick I was when I visited you and how kind and tender you were to me—as if I were an angel from God! You couldn't have treated me better if I were Christ Jesus himself. 15 What has happened to all your love and graciousness and willing self-sacrifice? I can personally testify that you used to be so generous and caring that—if it were possible—you would have plucked out your own eyes and given them to me. 16 Will you now treat me as an enemy because I am bringing you the truth?

Gal 4:17 Those other people who have been talking to you are passionately motivated to win you over to their way of thinking—but not because they care about you or want what is best for you. No! They want to turn you away from us and re-infect your minds with lies, distortions, and self-promoting methods, so that you will use your energies promoting their destructive principles. 18 It is good to have passion and be strongly motivated, as long as the motivation is to do good and promote God's methods (which should be done all the time, whether I am there or not). 19 Don't you understand that you are like my own children? With all my might I have struggled to help free you from the infection of selfishness, and I long to see Christlike character formed within you. 20 Oh! I wish I could be there with you now to look you in the eye, and maybe then discover another way to communicate my anguish, fear, and heartache over you!

Gal 4:21 So tell me, those of you who are trying to heal yourself by observing the written law or by performing certain rituals: Don't you realize the real purpose of that entire symbolic system? Let me tell you: 22 As it is written, Abraham had two sons: one from a slave woman, and the other—from his wife (a free woman). 23 His son from the slave woman was born by Abraham's effort (through natural conception), but the son by his wife (the free woman) was conceived and born by miraculous intervention—as the result of a promise.

Gal 4:24 This is more than a literal story; it is also a metaphor of God's plan to heal and restore humankind. The women are symbolic of two contracts (or two different treatment plans). One contract (or treatment plan) was given at Mount Sinai, and it produces children who are slaves to a system full of works (one that fails to heal and transform the mind). This contract (or treatment plan) is represented by Hagar, the slave woman. 25 Hagar represents a system in which selfish humans work, trying to heal and free themselves, just as the people chose to do at Mount Sinai and continue to do in present-day Jerusalem. Hagar was a slave along with her children, and she could never free herself, regardless of how much work she did. So too, slaves to selfishness can never free themselves, regardless of how much work they do. 26 But Sarah (the free woman) represents the New Jerusalem, the heavenly city, home to those who are healed and set free by God—healed and set free from sin and selfishness as a result of receiving the promised Remedy. She is our mother. 27 For it is written:

"Be glad, O heavenly city, barren of
   people, empty of children;
lift up your gates and sing with joy,
   O city who doesn't know pain;
because more are your free and
   healthy children than the slave
   children in the earthly Jerusalem."

Gal 4:28 Understand clearly then that you, like Isaac, are children born of God's promise—his promise to heal and restore you to his original ideal. 29 But the son born by human effort (through normal conception) persecuted the son born by the life-giving power of the Spirit. It is the same now, that those who pursue a system of human works (a self-motivated system) will persecute those who have been reborn within by the life-giving power of the Spirit. 30 But what does the Scripture say will be the ultimate outcome? "Away with the slave woman and her enslaved son, for a slave woman's son can never share in the inheritance of the free woman's son." 31 Therefore, friends, all of us who have stopped trying to create our own cure for selfishness but instead have accepted the free Remedy provided by Christ are not children of the slave woman, but of the free woman.

5 Christ has set us free from selfishness, free from fear, free from ignorance about God, free to be his friends. So stand firm in the truth about God as revealed in Jesus, and don't let yourselves be duped back into a system of rituals and works motivated by fear and selfishness.

Gal 5:2 Now listen carefully. I, Paul, want to make this extremely clear: If you include circumcision as a necessary element in the Remedy to sin and selfishness, then you dispel Christ and nullify the true Remedy he brought. 3 I say it again: Any person who is circumcised as a means of healing from sin and selfishness is choosing a course without Christ's free Remedy and thus is required to heal and cure themself. 4 Those of you who are trying to be healed and set right with God by observing a set of rules or rituals have rejected Christ and his methods that heal; they have rejected God's graciousness and accepted a false remedy. 5 But we, who accept Christ's Remedy,

trust that God will finish his work of healing and transforming us back into righteous, Christlike friends of his. 6 For Christ Jesus revealed that no ritual—such as circumcision—has any value with God. The only thing that counts is trust in God, established by the evidence of God's supreme trustworthiness revealed by Christ, which expels fear and selfishness and results in loving, Christlike character developed within.

Gal 5:7 You were doing fine and were getting well. Who tricked you into abandoning God's Remedy for a lie? 8 Persuasion based on deceit and flattery does not come from God. 9 You well know that only a little yeast will transform the entire batch of dough. Likewise, even a small lie, cherished and believed, infects and deforms the entire person. 10 But I am confident in the Lord that — after reasoning it through — you will reject the lies and hold earnestly to the truth. But the one who has rejected the truth and is presenting these lies to you is already reaping the consequences of a darkened mind and damaged heart— whoever they are. 11 Isn't it clear, brothers and sisters, that if I were still promoting circumcision or any ritual as a remedy for the heart and mind, I would not be persecuted? If I were promoting ritualistic remedies, then the self-denying, self-sacrificing message of the cross would lose its power and the legalists would no longer be offended. 12 If those who are confusing you by promoting circumcision believe that cutting themselves somehow brings healing, maybe it would be better if they kept on cutting and just castrated themselves—at least then they might stop producing more people to follow their lies!

Gal 5:13 You, my brothers and sisters, were called to be free—free from selfishness, free from fear, free from death. So do not use your freedom to gratify the selfish desires, which only destroys your freedom and makes you slaves all over again, but rather minister to each other in love. [14] The entire written code and Ten Commandments law are all designed to reveal the one true Law of the universe, the one true principle on which life is based — the great Law of love. So love your neighbor as yourself. [15] But if you instead practice the principle of survival-of-the-fittest and attack and destroy others in order to promote yourselves, you will only experience ruin and death.

Gal 5:16 So I tell you plainly: Live by the principles and power of the Spirit, and you will not practice the selfish methods of survival-of-the-fittest. [17] For the selfish nature desires to promote self at the expense of everyone and everything else, and this is exactly the opposite of the Spirit of love, as the Spirit of love desires to promote the good of everyone else at any expense to self. The selfish nature and the Spirit of love are diametrically opposed to each other, so if you follow the Spirit of love, you will no longer do what your selfish nature wants. [18] Therefore if you practice the methods of the Spirit, you no longer need to be quarantined and supervised by the written law.

Gal 5:19 When the selfish nature is in charge, it is obvious, because the life reflects the destructive behaviors of the selfish nature, which include lewdness, sexual perversion, immorality, all kinds of self-promoting, [20] self-worship, Wicca, voodoo, mysticism, all forms of idolatry, gossip, envy, jealousy, loss of control, all types of acting-out, rage, hatred, grudge holding, self-exaltation, racial and caste discrimination, [21] drunkenness, getting high on drugs, orgies, and the like. Let me warn you again: All such behaviors destroy the image of God in humankind, dethrone reason, sear the conscience, inflame the debasing desires, and result in individuals—although created in God's image—digressing into nonthinking, animalistic brutes incapable of entering the kingdom of God.

Gal 5:22 But the outgrowth of the Spirit of love is a character like God's—manifesting character traits of love, joy, peace, patience, kindness, goodness, trustworthiness, [23] gentleness, and self-control—complete self-governance. With character like this, there is no need for a written law to diagnose defects, or quarantine, or provide external supervision, [24] because those who have been unified with Christ Jesus have had the selfish nature with all its motives and desires eradicated from their characters. [25] Since we are being healed by the working of the Spirit of love and truth, let us choose to cooperate with him in every way. [26] So don't show off or try to make a name for yourself; this only tempts others to become jealous and envious, and leads their minds away from Jesus.

6 Dear brothers and sisters, if it is discovered that someone among you is engaged in some self-destructive activity, those of you who are mature and understand how indulging the selfish nature destroys God's image within, and how God longs to heal and restore us, should gently lead them back to the path of health while doing all in your power to protect their reputation. And remember to be humble, lest you open yourself up to temptation. [2] Do what is in the best interest of each other, including sharing each other's burdens: this is the true meaning of the law of love that emanates from the character of God. [3] If anyone thinks that they are (in and of themselves) great—the model to which others should seek to attain—when in reality they are (like everyone else) infected with selfishness, fear, and character deformity, they only deceive themselves and get worse because they don't partake of God's free Remedy. [4] Each one should honestly evaluate their own character, motives and actions, and rejoice in the healing,

272

growth and maturity experienced as they cooperate with God, without comparing self to others, [5] for each one is responsible for their own health and engagement with God in their own healing therapy.

Gal 6:6 Anyone who receives instruction and applies to their life the good news about God and his methods and principles will—along with their instructor—share in all good things.

Gal 6:7 But don't delude yourself: God cannot be tricked or fooled, and his methods cannot be evaded. A person actually reaps what they sow; a person actually receives the results of their own choices. [8] The one who indulges the selfish nature will experience the natural consequences of a damaged mind—increased fear, broken relationships, separation from God, and eventual death; but the one who chooses to follow the Spirit, from the Spirit they will experience a healed mind, internal peace, unity with God, and eternal life. [9] So let us never become tired of living in harmony with God's methods of goodness, for if we don't turn back to self-destructive behaviors, we will—in time—experience a bountiful harvest. [10] Therefore, at every opportunity, do good; and especially do good to other Christians so that God's principles may shine brightly in the church.

Gal 6:11 Notice the change in handwriting, how the letters are now larger. This is because I close this letter in my own handwriting!

Gal 6:12 Those people who are only interested in external appearances—and not in genuine heart change—are trying to pressure you into being circumcised. They do this because they value the opinion of people more than the truth, and are afraid of criticism and persecution if they actually accept the truth Jesus revealed at the cross. [13] But even those who are circumcised don't actually live their lives in harmony with the written law; they want you to be circumcised not because they care about you, but so they can brag that they have won you over and that you now follow their teaching. In other words, they want others to think they are important because they were able to convert you to their way of thinking. [14] May I never boast about, or take pride in, anything except the truth about God as revealed by Christ at the cross. Ever since I have realized the truth that Christ revealed at the cross, I have lost all interest in promoting myself and don't care what the world thinks of me. [15] It doesn't matter one whit whether someone is physically circumcised or not; the only thing that matters is whether the heart and mind have been recreated into Christlikeness of character. [16] And all those who follow God's methods in their lives— those who comprise the true house of God—will experience God's mercy and peace.

Gal 6:17 In closing, don't trouble me again with ridiculous concerns about rituals and ceremonies that have no power to heal the mind and only scar the body, for my body has been scarred repeatedly by beatings for teaching the Remedy of Christ.

Gal 6:18 Brothers and sisters, may your minds be filled with the graciousness of our Lord Jesus Christ. Amen.

Ephesians

1 Paul, an ambassador of Christ Jesus, appointed by the will of God, to those who have partaken of God's healing Remedy—those set right in heart and mind with God through Jesus Christ:

Eph 1:2 God our Father and the Lord Jesus Christ pour out their graciousness and peace to you.

Eph 1:3 All praise and honor be to God—the Father of our Lord Jesus Christ—who, through Christ, has poured out all heaven for our good. 4 For before the creation of this world, he determined that he would send Jesus to heal and restore humankind deceived by Satan's lies back to unity with himself. In love, 5 he predetermined that—through Christ—he would provide the Remedy to remove the breach of distrust in our minds and hearts and restore us to full sonship with him, all in perfect keeping with his character, pleasure, and will. 6 How amazing is God's glorious character of grace that he has freely given us all heaven in the One he loves. 7 It is through the truth of God revealed in the life and death of Christ that we are won back from enemies of God into friendship and unity with him, and now experience the forgiveness and healing that God has so freely given. All of this is in accordance with the richness of God's character of grace, 8 as he constantly provides everything for our good so that we may grow in true wisdom and understanding. 9 Because Satan's lies obscured the truth about God—making confusing and mysterious what was once plain— God sent Christ to reveal the truth and thereby remove the confusion and mystery by making plain the truth about himself and his will. 10 This truth about God will — in time, under the leadership of Christ—reunite the entire universe in perfect harmony with God.

Eph 1:11 In the person of Jesus Christ, we experience restored unity with God —the culmination of the Father's plan, the result of what God predetermined to do—as he always works for the healing and restoration of his creation. 12 This is in order that we—who were the first to recognize the significance of all that Christ is, and all he has done—might bring praise and glory to God by experiencing re-creation of Christlike character within. 13 And you also were reunited with Christ when you accepted the Remedy that Christ has achieved. Having trusted God on the basis of the truth Christ revealed, you have been marked with God's seal —you have been so settled into the truth that you cannot be moved! This transformation of heart and mind is brought about by the Holy Spirit 14 who is the first installment of our rich inheritance, and evidence guaranteeing that our inheritance is secure until we take possession of it—so that God may be praised.

Eph 1:15 Because of this, ever since I heard about your trust in Jesus and your love for all our fellow believers, 16 I have not stopped giving thanks for you, or remembering you in my prayers. 17 I keep asking the God of our Lord Jesus Christ—the glorious Father —to pour out his Spirit of wisdom and revelation upon you so that you may know him and all he is trying to accomplish. 18 I also pray that your reasoning abilities and conscience may be healed so that you can discern and understand God's purpose for all humanity — the incredible, rich inheritance in store for his children — 19 and God's incomparable power to heal and restore all who trust him. That life-giving power was seen as the outworking of his true strength, 20 which he exerted when he raised Christ from the dead and seated him at his right hand in heaven, 21 above all power, rulers and authority, above all other kingdoms, empires or governments, and above every title that can be given—now and forever. 22 And God placed everything under Christ's governance and appointed him the Supreme Head over all creation, including the church— 23 his body, the showcase of his character—which he fills with every blessing and ability.

2 As for you, you were terminal and dying in the distrust, fear and self-ishness 2 in which you used to live when you followed the survival-of-the-fittest principle of the world instituted by the ruler of the kingdom of the air—the intelligent being whose principles are now at work in all those who reject truth, love, and freedom. 3 All of us also were born infected with this destructive survival-of-the-fittest principle and at one time gratified its selfish and unhealthy desires and thoughts. Like the rest of humanity, we were born infected with this principle which—if not removed—would result in our self-destruction. 4 But because God is love, because he is merciful, gracious, forgiving, patient and kind, and because he truly loves us, 5 he removes the infection of distrust and selfishness and heals us through Christ. It is because God is gracious, loving and kind that you have been healed and set right with him. 6 God raised the human race from its degraded and detestable state through Jesus Christ's victorious life, and humanity again occupies its seat in God's heavenly counsel—in the person of Jesus Christ our Lord — 7 in order

that the amazing truth of God's gracious character may be showcased for all eternity through the love expressed to us in Jesus Christ. 8 It is only because of God's grace that you have been healed through trust—and you did not create this trust yourself, but it was established through the evidence of God's character revealed in the gift of Jesus Christ. 9 This is not by some human work—No way!—so there is no room for anyone to boast. 10 We are God's special creation brought to existence by Christ Jesus to showcase his character—his living law of love—which was always God's design for us.

Eph 2:11 Therefore remember that you, who were born into the dark superstitions of the world, were considered "uncircumcised" by those who call themselves "the circumcised" (as they experienced bodily circumcision by human hands). 12 That was before your minds were enlightened about Christ—and therefore you were separate from him—and you were not members of Israel (who was God's spiritual health-care team), and therefore were unacquainted with God's plan to heal and restore. Your condition was terminal because you were without God—and therefore without hope—and in the darkness of the world. 13 But now, you—whose minds were once far away, and who were practicing the principles of selfishness and survival-of-the-fittest—have been enlightened and brought near to God, and are in unity with Christ through the truth revealed when he died.

Eph 2:14 For Christ himself is the Remedy that heals the species and brings peace. He has removed fear and self-ishness that cause division, mistrust, prejudice, and hostility. 15 He did this by partaking of our human condition, and—via the exercise of his human brain—he loved perfectly, thereby destroying in his flesh (in the humanity he partook) the selfish survival-of-the-fittest drive along with the lies of Satan. In this way, he destroyed the need for the law (with all its regulations) to expose Satan's lies and methods. His purpose was to be the template of a new humanity born out of the unification of the two—our selfish, infected condition merged with his sinless state —thereby purging selfishness from the human heart, and transforming, healing, renewing, regenerating and recreating humanity back to God's original ideal; 16 and in this new being, to reconcile the human race—regardless of ethnic background—into loving unity with God and each other through the revelation of truth at the cross, by which he destroyed the lies of Satan, reestablished trust, and removed fear, selfishness, and hostility. 17 He came and demonstrated the truth of God's character and the offer of peace available to all humanity—to those far away in darkness and those blessed with the truth of God's word. 18 For Jesus reveals the truth about God to all, and— through what Jesus has done—all have access to the Father by one Spirit.

Eph 2:19 Therefore your minds are no longer confused, and you are no longer in darkness and are no longer foreigners, aliens or outcasts, but members of God's house and citizens with God's people — living components of God's heavenly sanctuary 20 built on the foundation of the apostles and prophets, with Christ Jesus himself as the chief cornerstone — the source of all truth. 21 In Christ, the entire structure is unified, and grows to become a holy temple filled with God's Spirit, revealing God's character. 22 And with your minds in harmony with Christ, you too are being healed and transformed— rebuilt to become a dwelling in whom God lives by his Spirit.

3 It is because I have brought the healing truth about Christ Jesus to you, Gentiles, that I, Paul, am now a prisoner.

Eph 3:2 Surely you have heard how God graciously gave me the healing message of truth for you— 3 that is, the truth previously not understood but made known to me by revelation, as I have already written to you. 4 In reading this, you will be able to understand the insight I have into the truth about God and Christ, that was previously hidden by Satan's lies and distortions. 5 These insights were not understood by previous generations because the lies of Satan were so effective that only Christ himself could refute them and provide the truth sufficient to make plain what God's Spirit had previously revealed to his holy apostles and prophets. 6 This is the truth previously hidden and not understood: God loves all humanity, and all humanity is included in God's plan to heal and restore, and—through the incredible good news of God as revealed in Christ—all humans are included in the promises given to Abraham, and are therefore heirs of the blessings of salvation which come through Christ Jesus.

Eph 3:7 I became an ambassador of this incredible truth by receiving the gift of God's healing Remedy graciously given to me through the working of his power—the power of truth and love. 8 Although I am the least deserving of all God's people, this gracious privilege was given me to take to the Gentiles the incredible truth of Christ, 9 and to explain to everyone God's methods and principles which had been misunderstood because of Satan's lies and distortions, and for ages past were hidden in God, but are now revealed by Christ, who created all things. 10 His intent was that now, through the church, God's wisdom, methods, principles and character should be revealed to all intelligent beings throughout the entire universe as we experience God's methods and character recreated within us, 11 according to his eternal purpose which he accomplished in Christ Jesus our Lord. 12 In Christlikeness of character experienced by trust in him, we may approach God freely and with confidence. [13] Therefore please don't be discouraged because of my sufferings for you—they are for your healing, and beneficial for your character development.

Eph 3:14 It is for your healing and transformation that I kneel before the Father, [15] from whom his entire family in heaven and on earth derives its character, methods and principles. [16] I pray that out of the glorious riches that emanate from his being, and through the working of his Spirit in your minds, you will be fully transformed into Christlikeness and so settled into God's methods and principles that you cannot be shaken, [17] so that Christ will dwell in your hearts through trust. And I pray that you, rooted and transformed by love, [18] will have your minds enabled (together with all the saints) to grasp how immense, and wide, and long, and deep, and high is the love of Christ, [19] and to know in every fiber of your beings this love that surpasses intellectual knowledge, that you may become living showcases of God's loving character.

Eph 3:20 Now to him who is able to do immeasurably more than all we ask or could ever imagine—according to his life-giving power at work within us— [21] be all honor, and praise, and glory in the church and in Christ Jesus throughout all time, forever and ever! Amen.

4 As one in prison for preaching the message of Jesus, I urge you to live a life that reveals the incredible benefits of God's way of living. [2] Think first of others and be gentle; be loving, patiently working with each other, helping each other to grow and mature. [3] Do all in your power to stay united with the Spirit in promoting the principles of truth and peace. [4] There is only one way of life and health, one body, and one Spirit of truth—just as you were called to the one hope of recovery and restoration when you were called; [5] there is one Lord, one principle of life (the principle of love), one immersion for the mind, [6] and one God and Father of all, who is over all, and through all, and in all.

Eph 4:7 But Christ gives each one of us just what we need in each circumstance for our good and our development. [8] This is why it is said:

"When he ascended to heaven,
he took with him those who were
once captive in the grave,
and gave gifts to men."

Eph 4:9 The phrase "he ascended" is meaningful only because he had first descended from heaven to this lowly earth. [10] And he who descended to earth is the very One who ascended higher than all the heavens in order to fill the entire universe. [11] It was he who selected some as his ambassadors, some to be spokespersons, some to be preachers of the healing message, some to care for and minister to his children, and some to educate and instruct— [12] all in order to heal God's people, enabling them to help each other—so that the body of believers may grow in number and strength [13] until we all reach true unity of heart, methods, motives and principles in harmony with the knowledge of God as revealed in Jesus, and become mature, developing Christlike character.

Eph 4:14 Then we will no longer be children—unable to think for ourselves and easily confused, tossed back and forth by every new and emotional teaching brought by the scheming trickery of charismatic speakers. [15] Instead, we will grow up and be like Christ — presenting the truth in love, and leaving others free to come to their own conclusions based on the evidence. [16] The entire body of believers is joined together with Christ; each member draws their strength from him and then ministers in love to the needs of the rest of the body as each part does its assigned task.

Eph 4:17 So I tell you this plainly, and I insist on it in the Lord: If you are to grow and mature, you must think for yourselves and not live like the Gentiles, who believe all kinds of things that don't make sense. [18] Their minds are darkened and their thinking is confused because they have rejected the truth of God and his methods, and have preferred lies that harden their hearts and separate them from God. [19] They have lost all compassion, morality and tenderness, and have immersed themselves in sensuality (practicing every kind of impurity) and are constantly lusting for more.

Eph 4:20 You, however, did not come to know Christ by practicing such impure behavior. [21] Instead, you heard of him and studied the truth of God's methods and character as revealed by Jesus. [22] You were taught that the former ways of life—the survival-of-the-fittest ways, the selfish me-first ways—only lead to self-destruction and death, and that health and life consist of putting off such motives and desires. [23] You were taught the importance of being recreated in heart and mind and displacing the principles of selfishness with those of love, [24] and experiencing a complete transformation of character such that you are an entirely new being recreated in heart-attitude to be like God—truly righteous and holy.

Eph 4:25 Therefore each of you must choose to stop being deceitful in every way, and instead be truthful and honest in all your conduct, for we are members of one body, and such behavior injures both you and the body. [26] "In your anger do not sin"—Do not let your anger or any strong emotion take control of your minds and determine your choices; don't retain anger in your hearts. [27] The devil tempts us through our emotions, so don't give him any opportunity to confuse you or lead you astray. [28] The person who has been stealing has been practicing the methods of selfishness, and if they desire to get well, they must have selfishness replaced by love.

When selfishness is replaced with love, they will stop stealing, and instead get a job in order to be able to give to others in need. Eph 4:29 Don't speak unwholesome words, for your words react on the mind, and unwholesome words damage and destroy; instead, speak what is helpful and uplifting, encouraging others and benefiting those who listen. [30] And do not close your minds to seeking more truth and thus grieve the Spirit of truth who set your minds free from Satan's lies and settled you into the truth of God's character and methods for the day of our deliverance. [31] Purge your hearts from all bitterness, rage and anger, desire for vengeance, conflict and rumor-mongering, along with every other form of malice and ill will. [32] Be kind, gentle, compassionate and forgiving with each other as God is forgiving to you; remember that all humanity suffers with the same infection of selfishness, and God provides the same Remedy for all.

5 Model yourselves after God, as children after their father, [2] and live your life in love—practicing the principle of beneficence, the principle of giving, upon which life was created to operate—just as Christ loved us and gave himself for us, beautifully revealing God's character to all.

Eph 5:3 But within you, there must not be even a trace of sexual immorality or any kind of impurity, because these arise out of selfishness and destroy the higher faculties of the mind, and are inconsistent with growth into God's holy people. [4] Nor should there be cursing, foul language, vulgarity, ugly comments, coarse joking, or rumor spreading—these are all evidence of a heart filled with selfishness and evil. Instead, speak words of praise and thanksgiving, and reveal that God's love is in your heart. [5] For you can be sure of this: No immoral, impure or greedy person (such a person is an idolater because their character is selfish, and they worship themself) will be in the kingdom of Christ or God, because God's kingdom is the kingdom of self-sacrificing love. ⁶Don't be deceived by flattery, or proclamations, or declaration without evidence, for those who believe claims without evidence are easily deceived, and God ultimately lets them follow the self-destructive course of their choosing. ⁷Therefore do not join forces with them.

Eph 5:8 In the past, you promulgated the dark lies and methods of Satan, but now you are conduits of the light of truth and the life-giving methods of the Lord. Live as children of this light ⁹(for those who live by the light practice the principles of goodness—doing right in all situations) ¹⁰and understand God and his purposes, and what he is pleased with. ¹¹Don't have anything to do with the destructive practices of those whose minds are darkened, but rather present the light of truth, which exposes them. ¹²For it is damaging and degrading to dwell upon what the disobedient do in secret. ¹³But everything exposed by the light of truth becomes understandable, ¹⁴for it is the truth that reveals all things. This is why it is said:

"Wake up your brain and start thinking.
Stop zoning out like you're dead, and Christ will shine the light of truth into your mind."

Eph 5:15 Be vigilant in your lifestyle—make choices that are healthy and wise, not unhealthy and foolish—¹⁶and make the most of every opportunity for growth, because the days in which we live are filled with temptations that lead to self-destruction. ¹⁷Don't be foolish, but understand God's methods and what he is trying to accomplish, so that you can cooperate intelligently with him. ¹⁸Do not get drunk on wine or get high on drugs, as it leads to wild living and destroys the brain. Instead, be filled with the Spirit of truth and love. ¹⁹When talking with each other, talk of God's love and character, and sing songs of praise together. Keep your hearts in tune with the Lord, ²⁰and be thankful to God the Father for everything revealed in the character of our Lord Jesus Christ.

Eph 5:21 Humbly serve one another out of appreciation for Christ.

Eph 5:22 Wives, follow the Christlike leadership of your husbands. ²³For the husband is the spiritual leader of the wife, as Christ is the leader of the church—his body—of whom he is the Savior. ²⁴As the church follows the leadership of Christ, so also wives should follow the Christlike leadership of their husbands in everything.

Eph 5:25 Husbands, love your wives as Christ loved the church and gave everything he had (including his life) for her, ²⁶to purify her—by the application of the truth, cleansing her from everything that destroys and defiles— ²⁷to perfectly heal her, enabling her to meet him face to face, without any defect or deformity, but perfect and pure. ²⁸In the same way, husbands should love their wives as part of themselves, doing everything in their power for the good of their wives. He who loves his wife loves also himself. ²⁹Think about it: Does a healthy person hate their own body? No! They care for it, eat nutritiously and exercise regularly, just as Christ constantly nurtures the church — ³⁰for we are members of his body. ³¹"For this reason, a man will leave his parents and join himself together with his wife; and the two separate individuals will become one joint partnership united in heart, love, mind, devotion, confidence, purpose, and motive." ³²This is a wonderful mystery—I am talking about Christ and the church— ³³but remember that each husband must love his wife, sacrificing himself for her good, and each wife must respect the Christlike leadership of her husband.

6 Children, obey the Christlike leadership of your parents, for this is healthy and right. ² "Honor your father and mother"—which is the first commandment to reveal some of the benefits of developing healthy relationships— ³ "that life may go well and you may live long on the earth."

Eph 6:4 Fathers, do not mistreat your children; instead, raise them with God's principles of love and teach them to think for themselves, always searching for truth.

Eph 6:5 Slaves, be respectful, honest and faithful to your earthly masters, just as you would to Christ. ⁶ Follow their leadership—not just to get their praise, but to reveal the high standard of character possessed by those who are Christlike—always doing God's will from a sincere heart. ⁷ Serve lovingly and wholeheartedly, as if you were serving Jesus himself, ⁸ because you know that character development and our rewards in Christ are the same, whether we are slaves or free.

Eph 6:9 And you, masters, treat your slaves in the same way: look out for their health and good, and do not abuse or mistreat them, since you understand that all humanity is infected with the same sickness of heart and mind, and he who is both their Master and yours is in heaven and distributes his healing Remedy equally to everyone, and without favoritism.

Eph 6:10 Finally, stay strong in your connection and devotion to the Lord and his mighty power. ¹¹ Arm your minds with God's complete set of armor so that you can join the ranks of Christ's soldiers and stand successfully in the face of the devil's schemes. ¹² For our struggle is not against flesh and blood, with man-made weapons, but against all individuals, entities and powers that misrepresent God and darken minds, and against Satan—the originator of lies about God—and his cohorts who also misrepresent God in the heavenly realms. ¹³ Therefore arm your minds with God's full set of armor so that when Satan's grand deception comes and it seems the heavens are about to fall, you are able to stand; and when you have done everything to present the truth and expose Satan's lies don't falter; stand! ¹⁴ Stand firm, with the truth of God wrapped around you like a belt, with a righteous, Christlike character developed within— like a breastplate, ¹⁵ and the peace that comes from accepting the good news about God—like track shoes providing good traction and a solid foundation. ¹⁶ Also, hold fast the shield of trust, which extinguishes all the burning fear and insecurity brought by the devil's temptations. ¹⁷ Take with you the helmet of a healed mind—a mind protected from the assaults of Satan; and attack the lies about God with the sword of the Spirit, which is the word of God—the truth.

¹⁸ And talk with God with an enlightened mind, intelligently, on all occasions, about all of your concerns, requests, plans, and issues. With all of this in mind, be alert and always keep praying for the God's people.

Eph 6:19 When you talk with God, remember me also — that whenever I speak, God will give me wisdom and courage to speak clearly the truth of his character, methods and principles, ²⁰ of which I am an ambassador in chains; request divine assistance that I may declare this truth fearlessly.

Eph 6:21 Tychicus, our dear brother and faithful servant of God, will tell you everything so that you may know all that I am doing, and how I am. ²² I am sending him to you especially for this purpose so that you may know how we are, and that he may encourage you.

Eph 6:23 Peace to the brothers and sisters, and love with trust from God the Father and the Lord Jesus Christ. ²⁴ God's blessing to all who love our Lord Jesus Christ with an undying love.

Philippians

1 Greetings from Paul and Timothy, ambassadors of Christ Jesus, to all those at Philippi (including the ones in leadership) who trust Jesus and have partaken of his healing Remedy to sin.

Phl 1:2 May God our Father and our Lord Jesus Christ pour out their transforming power and peace upon you.

Phl 1:3 I am so thankful for you, that every time I speak to God I tell him how thankful I am. 4 In all my conversations with God about you, I always talk with joy, 5 because you have been effective partners in promoting the good news about God—from the first day you heard it until now. 6 I am completely confident of this: God, who began his good work of healing and restoring you to his original ideal, will continue healing you right up to the day Jesus Christ returns to take us home.

Phl 1:7 It is only natural that I am filled with joy, because you are so dear to me; for no matter what I have been doing, whether in prison or freely proclaiming the good news about God, you have been partakers with me of God's gracious Remedy. 8 God can testify how I share with Christ Jesus the deep desire to be with you.

Phl 1:9 And when I talk with God, it is my desire for you that your love may grow—with ever-increasing knowledge and understanding of God's character, methods and principles, with ever-increasing depth of insight— 10 so that you may be able to distinguish with cutting efficiency the difference between the healthy and unhealthy, the true and false, the right and wrong— right up to the day when Jesus comes and takes us home. 11 I want you to become true friends of God, who have recovered the ability to think clearly, choose wisely, live completely in harmony with God's methods and principles, and who reveal Christlike love in everything you do.

Phl 1:12 Brothers and sisters, please understand that my imprisonment, while appearing to be something bad, in actuality has enabled the truth about God to spread much faster and farther than if I had not been imprisoned. 13 The entire palace guard and everyone else in Rome has heard that I am imprisoned because of the truth of Jesus Christ. 14 Not only that, but many of our brothers and sisters in Christ have been emboldened to present more clearly and forcefully the truth about God as revealed by Christ.

Phl 1:15 It is true that some have begun to preach Christ in order to make themselves popular and draw attention and affection to themselves, but others promote Christ in humility, truly desiring to see Christ exalted. 16 The latter work in self-sacrificing love, with empathy and compassion in their hearts, knowing that I am here to promote and defend the truth about God as revealed in Christ Jesus; 17 but the former preach Christ only as a way to promote themselves, without love or concern for others. Such selfishness misrepresents the truth about God's self-sacrificing character and brings grief to my heart—even more so while I am locked away and unable to actively counter their distortions. 18 But in this pagan world with so many minds in the grossest darkness about God, what does it matter? The most important thing is that the truth about God as revealed by Christ is being preached; whether the motive is true or false—Christ is still being preached. And knowing this brings me joy. Yes, it most certainly does! And I will go on rejoicing, [19] knowing that because of your prayers and the working of Jesus in my life, what has happened to me will eventually, one way or another, result in my deliverance. [20] For it is my great expectation and hope that I do nothing to misrepresent the truth about God but that I will have sufficient courage, wisdom and grace so that now, as always, the truth about Christ will be exalted in everything I do—whether I am released or whether I am put to death. [21] For me, the only purpose in living is to promote the truth about God as revealed in Christ, but I know that when I die, my earthly struggles will be over and I will gain all that I have sought in Christ. [22] But if I am to go on living in this sin-infected and weak body, it will mean more productive work in spreading the good news about God. So what should I choose? –I don't know! [23] Part of me wants to be with Christ as soon as possible, which, of course, is the ultimate goal; [24] but unscrupulous people are attacking you, and you still need my guidance. [25] Knowing that you are being attacked, I feel certain that I will soon be released so that I may return to you and assist in your continued growth and development in Christ. [26] And in our fellowship together, we will rejoice in all that Christ Jesus has done for us.

[Phl 1:27] But whatever happens to me, always continue to live in harmony with God's methods and principles, revealing Christlike character in all you do. Then, whether I am able to come and join you or not, I will know that you are united as one body in understanding about God, in appreciation for his methods and in Christlikeness of character, [28] without being intimidated by those who threaten and oppose you. Their use of coercion, threat, intimidation, manipulation, deceit and the like reveals that the infection of selfishness is ravaging their minds and they will eventually be destroyed, but your selfless love and patient endurance reveals that you have been healed by God and will receive eternal life. [29] For you have been privileged to not only trust Christ, but to agonize with him in promoting this healing message, [30] just as I have been struggling to do.

2 If you have experienced the courage that comes from unity with Christ, if you have experienced the peace and life-giving warmth of his love in your heart, if you have experienced the enlightening and transforming power of the Spirit, if you are now tender and compassionate in heart, mind and character, [2] then—if you want to make me happy beyond words—be united in love, purpose, motive, method, and constant care and concern for each other. [3] Don't do anything for selfish reasons or seek to promote yourself ahead of others, but in humbleness and love be more concerned for the welfare and good of others than for your own. [4] Each one of you should not only be concerned with your own health and growth, but also work to help others become the healthiest Christians they can be.

[Phl 2:5] Your attitude, motives and mindset should be that of Christ Jesus,

[Phl 2:6] who, though by his very nature
has always been God,
did not use his divine power, might,
knowledge or other prerogatives
to promote himself.

[Phl 2:7] But in order to save his creation,
he willingly laid all those abilities
aside
and voluntarily made himself,
by comparison, powerless.
He made himself as powerless as a
slave—a real human being.

[Phl 2:8] And after becoming human,

he voluntarily humbled himself
to perfectly reveal God's character of
    love, choosing to love at all costs.
He wouldn't even use his power to
    prevent his own death on the cross
and thus he overcame selfishness
    with love!

Phl 2:9 This is why
    (because his love is without limit)
    God has exalted him to the highest
    place in all the universe
    and has given him a name of
    recognition and respect
    above any other,

Phl 2:10 so that at the name of Jesus,
    every intelligent being—
    whether in heaven or on earth—
    will bow in acknowledgement of
    his true character and worthiness,

Phl 2:11 and every intelligent being will
    confess that Jesus Christ is truly
    Lord—
    the eternal visible expression
    of God's glory and character.

Phl 2:12 Therefore, my friends, as you
have always followed my instructions
in applying God's Remedy to your lives
when I was with you, it is even more
important now, that I am gone, that
you continue to apply God's methods
to your lives with reverent admiration
and humility, 13 because it is God himself working in you to heal, restore and
recreate you perfectly in his image,
enabling you to understand the truth
and empowering you to do what is
right—all in perfect harmony with his
will.

Phl 2:14 Carry out your duties cheerfully, without conflict, argument or
complaint: 15 in so doing, you cooperate with God for transformation of
character and re-creation of a pure
heart within, and become radiant children of God—shining brightly for good
in this perverse and wicked world—for
all the universe to see. 16 With such
conduct, your very lives broadcast the
principles of life, sending an open invitation for all to come to Christ and
live; and when Christ takes us home

with him, I will be so proud of you, and
be content knowing that my labor was
not in vain. 17 And even if it becomes
necessary that my life is sacrificed as
the price for bringing you this healing
message—I am glad to do it, and I rejoice that you have received the good
news about God and are being healed.
18 So whatever happens to me, you
should be glad and rejoice with me, for
I have achieved my heart's desire in
bringing you this message of life.

Phl 2:19 I hope that it is God's will that I
can send Timothy to you soon so that
he may bring me news of your growth
in Christ, and I may be cheered.
20 Timothy shares my love for you like
no one else. 21 Most people look out for
their own selfish interests, and not for
the interests of Christ Jesus, 22 but
Timothy has been like a son to me and
has proved his loyalty to Christ over
and over again. 23 I genuinely hope to
send him as soon as I know what is
going to happen with me. 24 But I am
confident that if it is God's will, I will
be coming to join you soon myself.

Phl 2:25 I think I am going to have to
send Epaphroditus back to you (even
though you sent him to help me and he
has been a faithful soldier for Christ)
26 because he is very homesick and
knows that you have worried about
him since you heard he was ill. 27 And
he was very sick and almost died, but
God graciously intervened and not only
saved his life, but spared me much
grief and sadness. 28 I am very eager to
send him back to you now that he is
well so that you too can rejoice in
God's graciousness when you see him,
and I will have one less thing to worry
about. 29 Welcome him with the joy and
enthusiasm you would show the Lord,
and honor ones like him—those who
are willing to lay their lives on the line
for God's cause. 30 He almost died
promoting the message of Jesus, and
most certainly risked his life in order
to provide me the help that distance
kept you from providing.

3 Finally, my brothers and sisters, always rejoice in God and in all he is doing and has done. I don't mind repeating myself to you, because repetition will help you grow more quickly.

Phl 3:2 Keep your minds sharp and be on guard, watching out for those who have stopped thinking and have become like non-thinking animals, creatures of instinct driven by passion and lust, just like dogs. Some of these non-thinking individuals insist on circumcising the body rather than healing the mind. 3 But we, who have been healed in mind, who have had the old motives of selfishness—the old survival-of-the-fittest methods—cut out of our hearts, who worship God intelligently, enlightened by his Spirit, whose characters reflect that of Christ Jesus, are the ones who are truly circumcised. We know that cutting the body is irrelevant. 4 If there was anyone who could have been healed by cutting of the body, it would have been me! If any of you think you are being healed by circumcision or any other ritual, then I am way ahead of you: 5 I was circumcised on the eighth day, a genetic member of Israel, of the tribe of Benjamin, a paragon of Hebrew virtue; in regard to the rituals and rules of Judaism—I kept to the script exactly, always knowing my role, always doing precisely what the script said had to be done. 6 I was so zealous to promote the rituals that I persecuted those who were taking God's true Remedy! As far as the rules and rituals were concerned, I was perfect—there was nothing more I could do for myself.

Phl 3:7 But how did it benefit me? I was still just as sick of heart, just as diseased of mind, and my condition was just as terminal. I gladly give up all that work (all that ritualistic, legal role-playing) for the only true Remedy, the only true cure—Jesus Christ. 8 I will say even more: The fanciest delicacies, the richest treasures, the highest honors this world has to offer — they are all nothing but garbage compared to the greatest gift of all that comes from knowing Christ Jesus my Lord. I give up everything this world has to offer so that I might be with Christ 9 and be recreated in Christlike character—not from my own efforts or attempts to cure myself, not by observing some code, but by true re-creation of mind, heart and character that God accomplishes when we trust him. And this trust is established by the evidence of God's supreme trustworthiness provided by Christ. 10 My one and only goal is to be intimately connected with Christ in heart, mind, motive, character and sympathy, to genuinely know him and be known as his friend, to experience the eradication of selfishness and the growth of the life-giving power of his love within me, to die completely to self— 11 and to one day experience resurrection from the dead, and life everlasting.

Phl 3:12 I am not saying that I am currently perfect in every way, but I strive with all my strength to experience this fullness, this healing, this ideal state of perfect existence that Christ longs to recreate within me. 13 Brothers and sisters, I have not yet experienced this perfect, total, and complete restoration, but there is one thing I can do to assist God in his plan to heal and restore: I don't lament past mistakes nor grow content with past victories; rather, I constantly push for the perfection that still lies ahead. 14 I press forward, constantly toward the goal of Christlike perfection—one day to experience the ultimate prize for which God has called me heavenward—the joy of seeing him face to face.

Phl 3:15 All of us who have grown up into the truth of God's character and methods should understand things this way. But if someone sees things differently, keep your mind open to truth, and God will make this clear to you. 16 The most important thing is not that we know all things, but that we honestly live up to what we do know.

Phl 3:17 Brothers and sisters, if you are unsure of what I am trying to describe to you, then model yourselves after me and practice in your lives the principles you have seen in my life. Observe those whose lives accurately reflect the character of Christ which we described to you, and learn from us. 18 It saddens me to have to say this, but as I have warned you before, I warn you again: Not all who claim to be Christians are Christlike. In fact, many are Christ's worst enemies, taking his name while revealing in their characters the attributes of the evil one. 19 They have refused Christ's true Remedy, and therefore their condition remains terminal; their god is self, and self-gratification is all they pursue. They are actually proud of the lewd, disgusting and shameful things they do. Their minds are focused only on things of this selfish, self-indulgent world. 20 But our minds and hearts—our very citizenship is in heaven. And we eagerly await the return from heaven of our Lord and Savior Jesus Christ, 21 who, by the power with which he governs the universe, will replace our diseased, defective and dying bodies with perfect, healthy, eternal bodies, just like his.

4 Therefore, my dear brothers and sisters—you whom I love and have worked so hard for, and whom my heart yearns over—your healing has brought me joy, and your salvation is the crown of my life. So stand firm in your confidence in the Lord, my dear friends!

Phl 4:2 Euodia and Syntyche, in light of all that God has done for you, please put aside your differences and be reconciled to each other in love! 3 Syzygus, my faithful co-worker, will you please help these women work out their differences? They have worked closely with me in promoting the good news about God as revealed in Christ, as did Clement and the others working with me, whose characters, identities and individualities are saved in God's book of life.

Phl 4:4 Revel in the Lord and in all that he has freely given you. Yes, rejoice in the Lord and in all he is and provides! 5 Live reasonably, revealing goodness and gentleness in everything you do, for the Lord is very near. 6 You don't need to worry or fret about anything: with a thankful heart, just talk to God about all your concerns, troubles and stresses, 7 and God's peace—that is beyond words and human explanation—will fill your minds and strengthen your hearts as you trust totally in Christ Jesus.

Phl 4:8 Finally, my dear brothers and sisters, if you want to cooperate most effectively with God for the healing of your mind, then always choose the truth, hold on to what is honorable, pursue everything that is right and reasonable, practice whatever is healthy, love everything that is pure, embrace whatever is lovely and beautiful, promote whatever is good, and—if there is anything that is truly excellent or worthy of praise—fill your minds with such things. 9 Put into practice all that I have taught you or whatever you have learned from watching me, and God will never let you go.

Phl 4:10 I am filled with such joy as I see how your concern for me has increased, because I know that the power of God's love is transforming you. I know how concerned you have been for me, even though in the past you had no opportunity to show it. 11 I am telling you this not because I need something from you—not at all! I have learned the peace and contentment that comes from being united with Christ, regardless of current circumstances. 12 You see, I have had times of extreme deprivation of the most basic earthly comforts as well as times of great richness. I have learned the secret—the secret to real peace and contentment in every situation, regardless of circumstance, regardless of whether I'm hungry or well fed, regardless of whether I am rich or poor. ¹³ The secret to real peace and contentment is an abiding trust in Christ—realizing that my strength comes from him; and through the peace, strength, wisdom and perspective that Christ gives me, I can handle whatever happens.

Phl 4:14 Having said all this, it is still true that I have appreciated your willingness to share in my troubles. ¹⁵ Even more—as you Philippians well remember, back when you were just learning the good news about God—when I had just left Macedonia, you were the only church that actually kept in touch with me regarding what was needed to promote the spreading of this healing message. ¹⁶ I remember well that when I was in Thessalonica and resources were low, you sent aid again and again, whenever I needed it. ¹⁷ I am telling you this not because I want another gift, but I am acknowledging how much I appreciate what you have already done, and want you to experience joy and

reward for your Christlike sacrifices. ¹⁸ Indeed, I already have all I need, and even more, thanks to the generous gifts you have sent with Epaphroditus. Such selfless giving reveals hearts healed to be like Jesus and is exactly what God is working to accomplish in each of us. Therefore your gifts are like sweet perfume, imbuing the atmosphere with Christlike love. ¹⁹ And my God will continue to provide—from the abundant riches poured out in Jesus Christ—everything you will ever need for complete healing and transformation.

Phl 4:20 All glory and praise and honor to our God and Father forever and ever. Amen.

Phl 4:21 Greet all believers with Christlike love. The brothers and sisters here in Rome send their greetings. ²² And all the believers here send you their warm regards; especially those living and working in the emperor's palace.

Phl 4:23 May the graciousness of the Lord Jesus Christ fill your hearts and minds and permeate your entire being. Amen.

Colossians

1 Paul, an ambassador of the celestial government of Jesus Christ by the will and confirmation of God, and our brother Timothy,

Col 1:2 To those at Colossae who have partaken of the healing Remedy procured by Christ Jesus and have been renewed in heart and mind, and are trustworthy friends of God: God our Father pours out his healing power and peace upon you.

Col 1:3 Whenever we talk about you to God—the Father of our Lord Jesus Christ—we always thank him, 4 because we have heard that you truly trust Jesus and live the lives of self-sacrificing love, sharing God's healing Remedy with everyone. 5 Your trust and love, which fill your hearts with hope of the good things awaiting you in heaven, reveal that you have truly internalized the healing Remedy, and this results from embracing the truth about God as revealed in Christ Jesus. 6 Throughout the entire world, this good news about God is changing hearts and minds, freeing people from fear and selfishness, and resulting in healing and transformation into Christlikeness, just as it has been doing among you since you heard it and understood the incredible goodness and graciousness of God. 7 You learned this truth from Epaphras, our beloved co-worker, who has been Christ's ambassador to you 8 and who told us of your growth in love through the healing power of the Spirit.

Col 1:9 Because of this, ever since we heard about you, we have not stopped talking to God about you and asking him to enlighten your minds with truth and with a greater knowledge of his character, methods, principles and will, thus increasing your wisdom and understanding of eternal realities. 10 We ask God to do this for you so that you might experience true re-creation of Christlike character within—here and now—and live lives revealing his healing power for all to see: practicing his methods of selfless love in everything you do, growing daily in your knowledge and experience of God, 11 being transformed by the power of his indwelling Spirit so that you might have unlimited patience and perseverance, and joyfully 12 give thanks to the Father who has healed you so that you are able to—along with all who have been healed—live in his kingdom of light. 13 For he has rescued us from the dominance of selfishness and survival-of-the-fittest methods that darken the mind and lead only to death, and has brought us into the kingdom of truth, righteousness, and self-sacrificing love —the kingdom of the Son he loves 14 and through whom we have been healed and experienced complete forgiveness.

Col 1:15 Jesus is the physical manifestation of the invisible God—the first being to leave infinity and manifest in physical form, and the conduit from which all creation flowed. 16 For he created everything: the entire universe, the heavens and all galaxies, angels and all intelligent life, things visible and invisible. All authority and power stem from him, and everything that exists was created by him. 17 He existed before anything, and it is he who holds all things together. 18 And among the body of believers—the church—Christ is supreme: He is the model of true perfection, the only rightful leader who by love voluntarily sacrificed himself, destroying selfishness and death in his body on the cross, and thus is the very source of life—God's rightful heir arisen from the dead—so that he is supreme in all things. ¹⁹For it was God's pleasure to have his entire identity, character—the fullness of his essence—live in Christ ²⁰and through Christ to destroy the infection of selfishness in his body, to obliterate the lies of Satan, to close the breach of distrust, and to reconcile the entire universe back into unity with God by revealing God's true character and the nature of sin through Christ's voluntary self-sacrifice on the cross.

Col 1:21 At one time, you were totally clueless about God's true character. Your minds were filled with lies about him, and you practiced the methods of selfishness that are at war with God's methods of love. ²²But now you are God's friends, his allies, having been won over to his side by the evidence of God's true character—revealed when Christ died—so that you may be completely healed and restored into Christian perfection, without any remaining defects of character. ²³This is the inevitable outcome if you continue to trust God and faithfully practice his methods in your lives, never losing hope in the good news of God as revealed by Christ. This good news about God is the truth of his character and methods, of which you have heard, and which have been revealed to all intelligent creatures throughout the universe. This is the good news to which I, Paul, have dedicated my life to proclaim.

Col 1:24 I am glad and rejoice in bringing you this healing truth about God despite all the unavoidable sacrifices, and eagerly follow in Christ's footsteps; and, if necessary, I willingly suffer physical torment for the good of the body of believers—the church. ²⁵God has given me the responsibility of working for the full healing and restoration of the church by presenting the truth about God and his plan in its fullness— ²⁶the responsibility of making clear the mystery of God's true nature, character, and government; the mystery that was hidden for generations by Satan's lies about God but is now fully revealed by Christ—and all those who love Jesus see it. ²⁷God has chosen to enlighten our minds with his secret plan: By revealing the truth of his character of love, he wins human beings back to trust in himself, restores in them perfect Christlike character, and through them, he wins more back to trust in himself (by also restoring them back into perfect Christlikeness), continuing on until our hope is fulfilled in the fullness of his glory.

Col 1:28 We eagerly proclaim the truth about God as revealed in Jesus, warning everyone of the consequences of accepting lies about God, and teaching everyone the wisdom of accepting God's true character. We do this so that everyone might accept the truth about God and be restored into Christlike perfection. ²⁹This is the goal for which I work so hard, relying upon his strength, which is the mighty source of power that enables all my success.

2 Please understand how much my heart agonizes over you, and over those at Laodicea, and over all who have not met me in person. ²My goal is for their fear and insecurity to be replaced with confidence, and for them to be united in love and thus experience the overwhelming joy of truly understanding God's character. This understanding is the result of knowing—intimately knowing!—God's secret, Jesus Christ, ³who is the very thoughts of God made audible and visible, the true source of all wisdom and knowledge, the perfect revelation of God. ⁴I warn you: Don't be deceived by sophisticated arguments that diminish the

full divinity of Christ, or by attempts to generate contradictions between the character of Christ and God. [5]For even though I am separated from you by distance, you are very near to me in my heart, and I rejoice knowing that you are standing firm in the truth about God as revealed by Christ.

Col 2:6 Now that you have accepted Jesus Christ as Lord—the true revelation of God—continue to live in union and harmony with him: [7]your minds rooted deep in the truth he has revealed, your character built up by his indwelling Spirit, your resolve to do right strengthened by trust, and your hearts overflowing with thanksgiving.

Col 2:8 Be sure your minds are not enslaved with lies about God—stemming from the empty traditions of paganism which require the appeasement of God, or from the world's principle of survival-of-the-fittest which teaches that one must do something to save themself—but instead, continue to trust in God as revealed in Christ.

Col 2:9 For Jesus Christ is God in human flesh. Jesus is the very nature and substance of Divinity manifested in humanity; he is the channel through which God's character, methods and principles flow into mankind, [10]and through him you have been given the character of Christ who is the supreme Lord over all other powers and authorities. [11]By trust in him, your hearts have been cut away from everything that destroys, so the selfish motives no longer control you. This cutting out of selfishness did not come about by human effort or by works, but by the cutting power of the truth brought by Christ. [12]Having been immersed into the truth of Christ Jesus, you have been immersed into selflessness and have died to selfishness, and through trusting in the power of God who called Christ back from the dead, you are renewed with his character and principles.

Col 2:13 When your condition was terminal, when selfishness reigned unchecked in your minds, and when your hearts were tied to the destructive cravings and practices of the world, God intervened and brought you the life-giving Remedy—Jesus Christ. He reclaimed you from your terminal condition, [14]nullifying the pathology report that certified you as dead in sin; he made it clear that the written code, with its regulations, was only a diagnostic instrument designed to expose our terminal state and teach us the need for a true cure, and he nailed it to the cross. [15]Through his death, he revealed the truth about God and—in his humanity—eradicated selfishness, thus he completely destroyed Satan's weapons of lies and selfishness, and triumphed over Satan at the cross.

Col 2:16 Therefore, don't worry about the opinions of those who promote certain rituals, foods, drinks, holy days or religious festivals as a means of being healed and being reunited with God. [17]We know these are merely symbols or metaphors designed to teach the truth of God's healing plan; but the actual Remedy is found only in Christ. [18]So don't be seduced by the pretentiously pious, or allow those who claim to be guided by angels to trick you into giving up the healing found only in Christ. Such people write detailed manuscripts supposedly revealed by angels, but their only inspiration has been their own self-inflated imagination filled with all types of fantasies and nonsense. [19]Such individuals are not connected to Christ—the true head of the church—from whom the entire body of believers experiences healing, unity and nourishment, and grows as God has planned for it to grow.

Col 2:20 So, if through trust in Christ you have died to the world's principle of survival-of-the-fittest, why act like you are still part of this world's work-to-save-yourself system? Do you think such things as [21]what you touch, handle or taste can actually heal your mind or transform your heart? [22] All such activities will inevitably perish, for they are completely useless in their ability to heal the mind; they are merely man-made rules (focused on human effort) and not renewal of heart that comes by trust. [23] Such codes of conduct appear wise—with their required rituals and worship ceremonies, with their pompous and grand displays of supposed humility, and with their self-flagellation and other mortifications of the body—but they are completely void of any ability to free the heart and mind from the domination of selfishness and lust.

3 Since your minds have been renewed by Christ in selfless love, set your hearts' desire on the things of heaven, where Christ reigns enthroned at God's right hand. [2] Focus your minds on the principles, values and methods of God as revealed in Christ, and not on the selfish activities and practices of the world, [3] because your old life—based on selfishness and motivated by survival-of-the-fittest—died, and your new life of love is submerged in God through Christ. [4] And when Christ, who is the source of your new life in God, comes again, then you will be united with him in glory.

Col 3:5 Therefore put to death your selfish nature by choosing to say "No" to all its desires. Say "No" to sexual promiscuity, perversions, pornography, lust, any impure thoughts, selfish desires and greed—all of which are forms of self-worship. [6] Persistence in such behaviors destroys the capacity and desire to be healed, and because of this, the day is coming when God finally lets all reap the full consequences of their destructive choices. [7] You used to live your lives driven by selfishness, and you gratified the desires of your selfish nature, [8] but now—to be fully healed—you must rid yourselves of selfishness in all its forms, including hatred, rage, vengeance, jealousy, envy, gossip, slander, prejudice, hostility,

and all coarse and vulgar language. [9] And, of course, don't lie or deceive each other, for—having rejected selfishness with all its practices—you have had a change of mind (a change of operating system), [10] and have a new identity, with new methods and motives being created within you. You are being transformed back into the image of the Creator through ever-increasing knowledge and experience of God as revealed by Christ. [11] In such a place—a place where everyone is restored to God's image—there is no division or preference based on ethnic background, religious affiliation, education, physical abilities or financial status, but Christ is all that matters, and Christlikeness is restored in all.

Col 3:12 As God's chosen messengers, who have responded to his love and partaken of his healing Remedy, represent God's character and methods faithfully by being compassionate, kind, humble, gentle, and patient. [13] Empathize and be understanding with one another, recognizing that we are all infected with the same ailment and all need the same cure. Forgive whatever wrongs or injustices you may have with one another; forgive as freely as the Lord forgave you. [14] And above all else, love each other completely, and love will meld your hearts together in perfect unity.

Col 3:15 Let the serenity that comes from reconciliation with Christ be a compass guiding your decision making, for as members of God's family you were called to join the one harmonious pulse of love that emanates from the heart of God. And let thanksgiving overflow from your hearts of love. [16] Fill your minds with the truth of God's character, methods and principles as revealed by Christ and as recorded in Scripture, and teach each other how to apply God's methods to your lives here and now; and sing praises, hymns, and spiritual melodies with your hearts filled with appreciation and thankfulness to God. [17] And in all your endeavors, no matter what the activity—whether speech, song, actions, or writings—do everything in keeping with the character of the Lord Jesus, practicing his methods and giving your thanks to God the Father.

Col 3:18 Wives, submit to the Christlike leadership of your husbands.

Col 3:19 Husbands, love your wives and don't be rough, cruel, unpleasant or unkind with them.

Col 3:20 Children, have a humble willingness to listen and follow the Christlike guidance of your parents in everything, for such a healthy mindset pleases God.

Col 3:21 Fathers, don't ridicule, antagonize, or harshly criticize your children, or they will be turned off from the truth about God.

Col 3:22 Slaves, carry out all duties given you by your earthly masters with respect, faithfulness and diligence; do this not simply to get their praise, but with genuine Christlike character seek to honor God. [23] So whatever you do, do it with integrity and full devotion, as if you were working for Jesus and not for people, [24] because you know that you receive the true reward of a healed mind, a pure heart and eternal life from God. You are actually serving Christ by revealing his methods, character and principles to those who do not yet know him. [25] All those who persist in selfish or evil living will reap the pain, destruction and death that such living inevitably brings. Everyone reaps the consequences of their choices.

4 Masters, treat your slaves with love and kindness, providing for their health and wellness, because you want to model yourselves after your Master in heaven.

Col 4:2 Steadfastly maintain your relationship with God by talking with him often; be alert, keeping watch over your hearts, and preserve thankfulness. [3] And remember us also in your conversations with God: ask that he will open a way for us to proclaim more broadly the truth about him—hidden by Satan's lies, but revealed in Christ Jesus—this truth for which I am imprisoned. [4] Ask God to enable me to speak this message with cutting clarity, for this is the mission he has given me. [5] Be wise when you interact with non-Christians—those who don't know the truth about God as revealed by Jesus; seek every opportunity to reveal this healing truth to them in gentleness and love. [6] Talk with them graciously, gently sprinkling new truth in appropriate amounts — like salt: enough to whet their appetites for more, but not so much that it makes it too hard to comprehend or handle all at once. Practice this so that you may become efficient and know how to share God's healing truth with everyone.

Col 4:7 When Tychicus gets there, he will tell you everything that is going on with me. He is a real brother in the Lord—a fellow worker for God—who faithfully ministers God's healing truth to all who will accept it. [8] I am sending him specifically to share with you all that is happening with us, in order to strengthen your confidence in God as you understand more clearly how he is working in our lives. [9] Onesimus, our good and trustworthy friend and brother in Christ, who is from your congregation at Colossae, will be coming with Tychicus. Together they will fill you in on everything happening here.

Col 4:10 Aristarchus, who is imprisoned with me, sends you his respects and best wishes, as does Mark, the cousin of Barnabas. (I've told you before about him; if he comes, welcome him warmly.) [11] Jesus Justus is also here and sends his blessings and best wishes. These are the only Jews here, working to spread the truth about God's true character as revealed in Christ Jesus, and they have been a real encouragement to me. [12] Epaphras, another member of your congregation at Colossae and a hard worker for Christ Jesus, sends greetings. He constantly presses God to enlighten and strengthen you to stand firm and grow into full stature as confident sons and daughters of God. [13] I can tell you from my own observations that he works tirelessly for you and those at Laodicea and Hierapolis. [14] And our good friends, doctor Luke and Demas, send their best wishes and blessings. [15] Please extend my personal greetings to our brothers and sisters at Laodicea; greet Nympha and the believers meeting in her home.

Col 4:16 And be sure that after this letter is read to you, it is also read in the church at Laodicea, and that you read the letter I sent to them.

Col 4:17 And tell Archippus to stay on task and complete the work the Lord has given him to do.

Col 4:18 I, Paul, write this greeting myself, in my own handwriting. Remember my imprisonment. May God's graciousness abound with you.

1 Thessalonians

1 From God's Ambassadors—Paul, Silas and Timothy,

To the people in Thessalonica who have taken the Remedy and have hearts united with God the Father and the Lord Jesus Christ: Grace and peace to you!

1Ths 1:2 We are so thankful for each of you, that every time we speak with God we tell him of our gratitude. ³We continually recount to our Father God your application of the Remedy: because you trust him, your ministry is motivated by love, and your perseverance is inspired by hope in our Lord Jesus Christ.

1Ths 1:4 We know that God loves you and has chosen you as his children—our siblings—in his rebuilt family. ⁵We know this, because when you partook of the Remedy we brought, your acceptance of it was accompanied by the life-transforming power of the Holy Spirit who renewed your hearts. You remember how we modeled Christ-like living when we were with you. ⁶You changed to be like us: living in harmony with God's methods—living like the Lord lived. You embraced this message, and—despite the pain that comes with transformation—rejoiced in the healing brought by the Holy Spirit. ⁷And you became an example to all those who partake of the Remedy in Macedonia and Achaia. ⁸For the effectiveness of the Lord's Remedy and your confidence in it became known not only in Macedonia and Achaia, but everywhere we have gone, people talk about how you have been renewed. We haven't even had to tell people! ⁹Instead, they tell us how loving you are, how graciously you treat others,

how you rejected pagan gods and embraced the God of love, ¹⁰and how you long to meet his Son Jesus (who rose from the dead) when he returns from heaven and rescues us from an otherwise inevitable doom.

2 Brothers and sisters, you know that we did not fail in our mission to you. ²You know how we were mocked and mistreated in Philippi, yet with God's help, we brought you the Remedy despite intense opposition from those peddling a false remedy. ³Unlike the opposition's, our Remedy is not based on lies, greed, or a desire to promote ourselves; and we are not trying to trick you. ⁴What we do is just the opposite: as messengers commissioned by God and entrusted with the Remedy, we do not pursue the approval of people, but we seek to please God who examines our hearts and knows our motives. ⁵But you should know this because of the manner we dealt with you: we never tried to influence you by flattery or hide what we were doing, as the greedy ones do; and God certainly knows this is true. ⁶We don't want fame or praise, or fan-worship—not from you or anyone else. As ambassadors of Christ, we had authority over you, ⁷but we did not order you about. We were tender and compassionate, caring for you like a mother who seeks the best for her children. ⁸We love you! So much so, that we not only brought you the Remedy, but we also gave you our hearts! ⁹Don't you remember that while distributing God's Remedy among you, we worked hard in order to avoid placing any extra burdens upon you?

1Ths 2:10 Both you and God can testify that while we were with you, we did what was right, healthy, reasonable, and in harmony with God's law of love. 11 You know that we treated you as a loving father treats his own children, 12 intervening to build you up, strengthen, and keep you on the road to full recovery—restoration to God's ideal—heeding his call to live in his eternal kingdom.

1Ths 2:13 We also thank God that when you heard the truth we brought about God, you did not regard it as something made up by human imagination, but accepted it for what it actually is: the truth about God, which transforms those who believe it. 14 For you have been changed and now live like God's friends from Judea, who, having taken the Remedy, are in unity with Jesus Christ. You have been mistreated, maligned and abused by your countrymen—just as those in Judea who have partaken of the Remedy have been persecuted by the Jews 15 who murdered the Lord Jesus as well as God's spokespersons, and then drove us away also. They wage war against God, and their actions are destructive to all humanity, 16 because they try to obstruct the distribution of the Remedy to the world. In so doing, their own terminal state worsens, their characters are damaged beyond repair, and God will eventually surrender them to receive what they have chosen.

1Ths 2:17 My Thessalonian family, though we had to leave for a short time, we have missed you terribly and can hardly stand to be away from you. We have done all in our power to return to you, 18 because we really want to see you. I, Paul, especially wanted us to come, but Satan obstructed us. 19 Don't you realize the joy we have in you and how eager we are to present you to the Lord Jesus? We are beaming with happiness over you, for you are the fulfillment of our work! 20 Truly, you are our pride and joy!

3 When we couldn't stand to be away from you any longer, we decided to wait in Athens and 2 send to you Timothy, our partner in spreading God's Remedy achieved by Christ. We sent him to strengthen your minds and increase your confidence, 3 so no one will become confused or give up because of criticism, abuse, loss of job, sanction, arrest, or other affliction. You know that from the very moment we chose to accept healing, we were destined for mistreatment by those who refuse the Remedy. 4 We told you many times when we were with you that we were going to be attacked, harassed and tormented, and—as you know—we have been. 5 So I have been worried about you, and when I couldn't take any longer not knowing how you were, I sent Timothy to find out how you are holding up. I wanted to be sure that Satan didn't trick you into giving up on the Remedy.

1Ths 3:6 Thankfully, Timothy has just returned and told us the good news that you are well and continue to live in love. He told us of the fond memories you have of us and how you are eager to see us, just as we can't wait to see you! 7 I want you to know that it is your healing, your confidence in God, and your spiritual development that have kept us from getting discouraged through all the trials we have endured. 8 Knowing that you are steadfastly growing in the Lord keeps us going. 9 Words cannot express the gratitude we have to God as we rejoice in his presence over you. 10 Every day and every night we ask God with all our hearts to see you again so that we can assist in your growth and add what is missing to bring you to complete maturity.

1Ths 3:11 We pray that the Father himself and our Lord Jesus will open the way for us to come to you. 12 May the tidal wave of God's love overflow your hearts, flooding your lives with love for each other and everyone else, just as our hearts overflow with love for you. [13] May he solidify your character in purity and love so that you will be found Christlike in God's presence when our Lord Jesus comes back with all those in unity with him.

4 In closing, my dear Thessalonian family: We taught you how to live in harmony with God's design for life— the law of love—just as you are now doing, so now we implore you on behalf of our Lord Jesus to do so more and more every day. [2] Remember the treatment guidelines we laid out for you, exactly as the Lord Jesus prescribed. [3] These are to help you experience God's will—the healing of your mind, the restoration of Christlike character in you—that you will no longer be controlled by lustful impulses, and [4] that each of you will experience governance over your own body in harmony with God's design: healthy and honorable, [5] and not in hedonistic self-gratification like those who don't know God. [6] It is damaging to wrong another person sexually: don't do it! For we have already told you that such acts of selfishness violate God's design and thus result in self-destruction; and God diagnoses the state of each heart accurately. [7] For God called us not to be defective, selfish and deformed in character, but to live pure, selfless, and loving lives. [8] So understand this: The one who rejects these instructions rejects not human rules, but rejects God and his design for life—the law of love, the principle of giving, and the Holy Spirit whom God gives.

[1Ths 4:9] We don't have to describe the amazing love, unity and affection that occur among those who have taken the Remedy, because you have already experienced this from God himself. [10] And you have lived your love in action toward all those who have taken the Remedy in Macedonia. We urge you to continue to do so more and more.

[1Ths 4:11] Stay focused on your own responsibilities, fulfilling your duties, leading a tranquil, peaceful life, supporting yourself—just as we have taught you. [12] Living like this will enhance your autonomy and demonstrate the transforming power of the Remedy, which will attract the unhealed to God and his Remedy.

[1Ths 4:13] My Thessalonian family, we want you to understand the truth about those who sleep in death, so that you won't grieve like those who haven't taken the Remedy and therefore have no hope of seeing their loved ones again. [14] We know that Jesus died, destroying the infection of selfishness and restoring God's law of love into humanity, and thus he rose from the dead in a humanity he cured. We also know that the individualities of those who have partaken of the Remedy Christ achieved are secure with God in heaven, and when Jesus returns, God will bring with Jesus the individualities of those who currently are asleep in him. [15] So don't worry: according to God's own word, we who are alive when Christ returns will be taken to heaven, but not without those who are asleep. [16] For the Lord will come down from heaven in humanity, as commander of the angelic host, and his voice will resound over the entire earth; and the trumpet of God will sound, and the dead who have partaken of Christ will have their individualities downloaded into perfect bodies—and they will rise first. [17] And then, after they have arisen, those of us who have partaken of the Remedy and are still alive on earth will join them in the air, and together, all of us will meet Christ in the clouds. And then we will live forever with the Lord. [18] So please, encourage each other with this truth.

5 My Thessalonian family, we don't need to write to you about the time and date for the Lord's return, [2] because you already know that the date and

time of his return are unknown, and will come like a thief—when not expected. 3 When people are saying, "Everything is finally calm; we are safe," then events will unravel, and destruction will come: it will come like labor pains to a pregnant woman, and there will be no escape.

1Ths 5:4 But your minds are not darkened by the lies of the world, so Christ's return should not surprise you like a thief. 5 You are children of enlightenment—children who live in daylight. We don't operate in secret, cloaked with the night, and we are not part of the dark lies about God. 6 So don't be like those who sleep—hypnotized by the routines of this world, unaware of the eternal realities of God's kingdom of love—but be alert, clear-minded, and self-controlled. 7 For those who sleep, sleep in the dark—whether it is physical sleep in the darkness of night or mental sleep in the dark distortions of this world—and likewise those who get drunk, are drunk in darkness. 8 We belong to the kingdom of light; so maintain self-control, let love and trust shield your hearts, and let the expectation of complete healing be a helmet to protect your minds. 9 For God did not make us to let us go and be separated from him, but to be his—united to him in love through our Lord Jesus Christ 10 who died to heal and restore us, so that those who are currently alive, and those asleep in death, will live together with him. 11 Build each other up and continue encouraging each other with this truth, as you are already doing.

1Ths 5:12 Also, be sure to respect those who give their time and energy ministering to you—those who are like the Lord in character. They are in the position to lead and teach you. 13 Love and honor them, because they sacrifice themselves for you. And always live in peace with each other. 14 And please, set healthy boundaries with the unruly (warn them of the consequences of allowing their feelings to overrule good judgment), buttress the overly sensitive, spend extra time helping the weak-willed, and be patient: healing doesn't happen overnight. 15 Follow the treatment plan, and be sure not to respond with selfishness or evil to those who act selfishly or evil. Instead, always choose to live in harmony with God's design—the law of love—and be kind to everyone.

1Ths 5:16 Always be joyful; 17 keep an open conversation with God and talk with him about everything, 18 and no matter what your situation—be thankful, because God is for you in Christ Jesus.

1Ths 5:19 Don't suppress or quench the work of the Spirit in your hearts and minds; 20 don't ignore the instructions from God's messengers. 21 But also be sure not to believe without thinking for yourself: whatever is said, test it against the evidence God has provided, and hold to that which is good—which is in harmony with God's law of love. 22 Avoid every kind of evil, selfishness, and deviation from God's design.

1Ths 5:23 May God himself—the God who restores peace—heal you, so that your character, mind and body will be kept pure until the Lord Jesus Christ comes again. 24 God—who calls you to be healed—always keeps his word, so you can be sure he will heal you.

1Ths 5:25 My Thessalonian family, please remember us when you talk with God. 26 Greet with a big, loving hug all those who have taken the Remedy. 27 By the authority the Lord has given me, I instruct you to have this letter read to all those who have partaken of the Remedy.

28 May the grace of the Lord Jesus Christ be with you.

2 Thessalonians

1 Greetings from Paul, Silas and Timothy,

To those in Thessalonica who, having partaken of the Remedy, are united with God our Father and the Lord Jesus Christ:

2Ths 1:2 God the Father and the Lord Jesus Christ send their goodwill and peace to you.

2Ths 1:3 We owe our thanks to God for healing your hearts and minds. We see that your trust and confidence in him is growing stronger every day, and your love for each other is constantly increasing. 4 We are so proud of you! Everywhere we go we tell God's people that you don't give up but trust God and keep advancing despite trials and persecution.

2Ths 1:5 All this proves that God's diagnosis is right and that his treatment plan works. As a result, you will be found fit for God's kingdom of love despite your current sufferings. 6 God always does what is merciful, loving and right: those who refuse the Remedy and cause harm, he will give up to reap the torment they have chosen— the destruction that comes from unremedied selfishness— 7 but he will free us from our afflictions. This will happen when the Lord Jesus appears in the sky in the full brilliance of his unveiled fiery glory, surrounded by his powerful angels. 8 Truth and love will burn free, and those who have rejected the Remedy procured by Jesus will experience the punishment that unremedied selfishness and sin bring: they will be unfit to tolerate the intensity of absolute truth and pure love of God's presence; the anguish of facing the reality of their true selves and of all they have done will overwhelm them; 9 they will be punished with eternal separation from the glorious presence of God— separation from their source of life that unremedied sin and selfishness bring—and sink into everlasting non-existence. 10 This will happen on the day Christ returns to be glorified in his people when he restores to his original ideal those who have taken the Remedy. This includes you, because you have believed us and have taken the Remedy.

2Ths 1:11 Understanding this reality, we keep your case before God: that he will restore you fully—making you fit to live in his presence—and that he will fill all your ideas and efforts in spreading the Remedy with his power so that his kingdom will be promoted successfully. 12 We ask God to do this so that his character may be radiant through you, and you will be radiant in him—all in exact accordance with the healing work of our God and the Lord Jesus Christ.

2 Now, my Thessalonian family, in regard to the second coming of our Lord Jesus Christ—the time when we will be together with him— 2 don't get upset, excited, alarmed or concerned about some prediction, prophecy or letter, supposedly from us, claiming that the Lord has already come back. 3 Don't be fooled by any idea like this, because, before the Lord returns, Satan will counter everything Christ taught, and a rebellion against God's law of love will occur: a man-made theological system of imposed law will form, and this system—which promotes god-concepts outside God's law of love—

will be exposed. This man-made system is destined for destruction, [4] because it opposes God's design for life and instead exalts a human concept of law and punishment over the way God built things to operate. This distorted view of God will become so accepted and orthodox that it will set itself up in God's spirit temple—the minds of people—and it will be proclaimed that God is like Satan in character.

2Ths 2:5 Surely you remember how I taught you these things when I was with you? [6] As you know, Satan's power is being held back, but will be loosened when the time is right. [7] But even now, the covert operation to develop a theological system contrary to God's design for life, and promoting Satan's distorted view of God, is already happening; but this perverse system will not arise until the restraining power lets go. [8] And then, the one operating outside of God's design template for life will be revealed. But he will be overthrown by the truth from the mouth of the Lord Jesus and destroyed by the brightness of his coming. [9] The rise of the deviant one will be accompanied by manifestation of Satan's methods and power, counterfeit miracles, signs and wonders, [10] and anything else that deceives and darkens the minds of those who are dying—those who did not develop minds that love the truth, and thereby did not partake of the Remedy. [11] Because they reject the truth, God leaves them to their delusional world built on lies. [12] All who reject truth and love, and prefer lies and selfishness, will be diagnosed as terminal and die from their unhealed condition.

2Ths 2:13 We always owe our thanks to God for you. My dear ones, the Lord loves you and determined from the very beginning to heal you through the truth, winning your trust so you would open your hearts to experience the transforming work of the Spirit. [14] Through the Remedy we brought, God called you to share the perfect character of our Lord Jesus Christ. [15] So, my dear friends, don't get discouraged but be confident in the truth we have taught you both in person and by letter.

2Ths 2:16 May Jesus Christ himself and God our Father, who loves us and graciously works to give us never-ending support and confidence, [17] heal your hearts and rebuild your characters in every good trait.

3 In closing, my family, remember us when you talk with the Lord—that the Remedy may spread rapidly and be well received, just as it was with you. [2] And ask the Lord to protect us from selfish and evil people, for not everyone has taken the Remedy. [3] But the Lord is trustworthy, and he will solidify your character growth and protect you from Satan. [4] We are confident in what the Lord is doing in you, and that you are doing everything we taught you. [5] May the Lord lead your hearts and minds into the ever-increasing experience of God's love and Christ's unwavering reliability.

2Ths 3:6 In harmony with the character, principles and methods of our Lord Jesus Christ, we instruct you to cut loose those who try to attach themselves to you but refuse to contribute to their own upkeep, and therefore don't apply to their lives the treatment plan you received from us. [7] You know very well how healthy it is to follow our example: we were not negligent, nor did we shirk our responsibilities when we were with you, [8] or take advantage of your hospitality by accepting your food without paying for it. Oh no! We worked hard, providing for ourselves in order to be givers not takers, so we would not burden any of you. [9] We did this, not because it wouldn't be acceptable as heralds of the Remedy to receive such help, but in order to demonstrate a model of living for you to follow. [10] We made it clear that in order to get well, you must apply the

Remedy and live lives of love; so we gave you this rule: "If a person won't work, they shall not eat."

2Ths 3:11 We hear that some of you are not contributing to your own upkeep, and instead of fulfilling your own responsibilities, you are meddling in others' lives and derailing them from their duties. 12 All such people we instruct—as the Lord Jesus Christ himself would instruct—to stop these practices and do your duty, provide for yourselves, and earn your own way.

2Ths 3:13 As for the rest of you, continue doing what is right: minister to others, but pace yourselves, and don't burn yourselves out. 14 If anyone refuses to apply this written prescription—note it, and then set therapeutic boundaries so that such a person will not feel that their misconduct is acceptable, but will be convicted, ashamed, and hopefully will reform. 15 So don't treat them as enemies, but as friends in need of your loving discipline, and warn them appropriately.

2Ths 3:16 May the Lord of tranquility give you abiding peace, rest, and serenity in every aspect of your life and being. May the Lord be with each one of you.

2Ths 3:17 This greeting, I Paul, write in my own handwriting, which is my signature and authentication in all my letters. This is how I write. 18 May the loving interventions and healing presence of the Lord Jesus Christ be with you all.

1 Timothy

1 Paul, an ambassador of Jesus Christ, appointed by God our Savior and Jesus Christ our hope,

1Tim 1:2 To Timothy, my faithful partner in distributing God's healing Remedy: God the Father and Jesus Christ our Lord send their grace, mercy and peace to you.

1Tim 1:3 When I was in Macedonia, I urged you to stay in Ephesus; well, I still want you to stay there so you can instruct those who are peddling a false remedy to stop doing it. 4 Tell them to stop confusing people with fables and wasting time with never-ending genealogies. Such activities only cause conflict and interfere with God's healing work which is experienced by trust. 5 The purpose of this instruction is the restoration of love—which flows from a heart purified from lies about God, from a conscience clear of selfishness, and from a genuine trust in God.

6 Some have turned away from God's healing plan and are engaged in childish discussions. 7 They want to teach a legal remedy, but they don't have a clue what they are talking about. They don't understand the problem or the false remedy they so confidently promote.

1Tim 1:8 We know that the written law is a diagnostic instrument for the soul, and it is good if used properly. 9 We also know that this diagnostic tool was not made for the spiritually healthy, but for those who are selfish in character, those who are spiritually diseased, who don't know God, who don't love others but kill their fathers and mothers, the ill at heart, murderers, 10 sexual perverts and adulterers, human traffickers, liars, deceivers, and for every-one and everything else that is out of harmony with God's design for life or 11 doesn't harmonize with the incredible truth about God's character of love that he has entrusted me to share.

1Tim 1:12 I give my thanks to the Lord Jesus Christ who has healed my character and now finds me trustworthy enough to choose me as a member of his rescue team. 13 Yes, I once misrepresented God, persecuted Christ's followers, and was a cruel man who opposed what Christ is doing. But because I didn't know God or his character and methods of love, mercifully, I was still healable. 14 I was infused with God's healing power: truth dispelled lies from my mind, trust replaced distrust, and I partook of the Remedy that is from Jesus Christ.

1Tim 1:15 This is the absolute truth, so embrace it: Christ came into the world to heal and restore selfish mankind back into God's original ideal, and I am the one who needs the healing and restoration most, as I was the most selfish of all. 16 It was because I was one of the worst cases that I was chosen for God's merciful healing, so that Jesus Christ might showcase his never-ending desire to heal those who will yet trust him, and thereby experience regeneration and eternal life. 17 Let all the credit, honor, recognition and praise go to the eternal King—the immortal, invisible, and only true God—for all time. Let it always be so!

1Tim 1:18 Timothy, you are like a son to me, and—in keeping with the work of the Spirit in your life—I give you this assignment so that you will fight successfully the battle against the lies about God: 19 With a clear conscience, stand confident in the truth about God's character of love. Some have not listened to their conscience and accepted lies about God, and thus have destroyed themselves. 20 Among them are Hymenaeus and Alexander, who—as they preferred Satan as a master—have been given up to their choice and will experience the terrible results of teaching lies about God.

2 You must first of all remember that your effectiveness starts with unity with God, so talk with him constantly about everything, big or small; make your requests, praise and intercessions known to him. 2 Talk with God about rulers and politicians—that they might govern well and that our land may be at peace, giving us freedom of conscience—so that we can live gracious and loving lives. 3 Such goodness makes God happy, 4 as he wants every human being to receive his Remedy, be healed, and come to know the truth about him and his methods of love. 5 For there is only one God and one reconnecting bridge—one emissary from God to the human race—the man Jesus Christ, 6 who gave himself to free us from the bondage of lies about God and from our own selfish natures. His sacrifice proves that God wants everyone to be healed. 7 It was for the purpose of spreading the Remedy Christ achieved that I have been appointed a teacher and ambassador of Christ. I'm not making this up—it is the truth! I am Christ's representative to take his true Remedy to the Gentiles.

1Tim 2:8 In public meetings, I want men whose hands are free from doing harm to humble their hearts in conversation with God, and not promote self with angry confrontations. 9 And I want the women to also have humble hearts before God, and dress accordingly, spending their resources to uplift God and not promote themselves. 10 I want to see them adorned with Christlike character—loving others with actions—

behaving like women who are devoted to God, and not like women who visit fertility cults.

1Tim 2:11 A woman learns quickly when her heart is humble and her mind quiet. 12 I do not authorize the female pupil to teach or have authority over the male teacher; she must not talk but listen to what is being taught. 13 Adam was created first; then Eve was created as his perfect partner. 14 Eve was deceived, and the first to break the law of love, while Adam broke the law of love without being deceived. 15 Women, who bring babies into the world, will—if they are faithful, loving, and spiritually mature mothers—experience healing of character as they allow God's love to flow through them in loving actions to their families.

3 Of this you can be sure: Anyone who has a heart for ministering to others as a spiritual leader in the church desires a responsibility worth having. 2 However, spiritual leaders must have taken the Remedy and possess a Christlike character. If married, they must not be polygamists. They must live in harmony with God's laws of health, have governance of their own impulses, be honorable, make people feel welcome, and be effective teachers. 3 They must not be drunkards or have rage problems but be gentle and not argumentative or antagonistic. They must not be greedy. 4 They must lead their own family effectively, setting healthy boundaries with their children and teaching them intelligent obedience, thereby earning their respect. 5 (If anyone does not know how to apply God's principles in leading their own family, how can they be an effective spiritual leader in the church?) 6 They must not have just recently taken the Remedy—as they need time for the Remedy to heal and transform them—lest the admiration received in leadership cause self-glorification, and as a result they experience the same

fate as the devil. [7] Their reputation with those who have not taken the Remedy must be as kind, compassionate, trustworthy and approachable people, so that they will not fall into the devil's trap of spiritual arrogance, or misrepresent God and disgrace God's cause.

1Tim 3:8 Church stewards must also be honorable, dedicated, responsible, with mature character, not drunkards, and not seeking selfish gain. [9] With a clear conscience, they must operate upon the foundational principles of God's government—truth, love and freedom. [10] Examine those being considered for the position, and if they meet the qualifications, let them serve as stewards.

1Tim 3:11 Their spouses must also be honorable and respectable: not gossips, but mature and self-controlled, living in harmony with God's principles, completely trustworthy individuals. [12] Stewards, if married, must not be polygamists, and must set healthy boundaries with their children and govern their home in harmony with God's design. [13] Those who consistently minister in love will develop mature character and draw closer in unity and friendship with Christ Jesus.

1Tim 3:14 I hope to be with you soon, but I am writing these instructions just in case [15] I am delayed, so that you will know how people need to conduct themselves in God's household—which is the temple of the living God—the earthly depository of his Remedy. [16] And this Remedy, which restores mankind to God's ideal, in many ways is a mystery. But we know that

Christ left heaven and partook of our fallen humanity,

was empowered by the Spirit to set humankind right,

revealed the truth about God to the unfallen beings,

was proclaimed as the Remedy to all peoples on earth,

was trusted and received by many in the world, and

was taken to heaven in perfected humanity.

4 The Spirit plainly says that in the last days, some will reject the Remedy and promote a deadly false concoction originating in the minds of demons. [2] These toxic constructs are peddled by deceptive charlatans whose characters have been forged in the Satanic mold. [3] They oppose God's design for life, which brings blessings to those who know and love God—like marriage and eating the foods God created to be eaten. [4] For everything God created is good, and nothing good for you is to be rejected, but received thankfully [5] because it was blessed by God's creative word and our thankful prayers.

1Tim 4:6 Teach truth to those on Christ's spiritual health-care team and you will be a competent spiritual physician, effectively applying the Remedy that you yourself have taken. [7] Reject pagan appeasement myths and other superstitious tales that turn off thinking; rather, train yourself to be a godly evidence-based thinker. [8] Just as physical training strengthens the body, in the same way, mental training—exercising self-control, reasoning, thinking and weighing evidence for one's self—develops mature character, which makes one fit for today as well as for eternity.

1Tim 4:9 This is the truth, so embrace it fully [10] (because this is what we live and work for): Our only hope is in God, who is the Healer of the human race, and specifically of those who take the Remedy.

1Tim 4:11 Proclaim and teach these truths. [12] Don't get discouraged if some don't take you seriously because you are young. Instead, demonstrate the transforming power of God's Remedy in your life by the way you speak, how you love others, by your unwavering trust in God, and by the purity of your heart. [13] While you are waiting for me to arrive, focus on making the Remedy known by public teaching, preaching, and reading of God's word. 14 Don't forget your endowment which was given to you when the church leaders laid hands on you and the Spirit of prophecy came upon you.

1 Tim 4:15 Partake of the Remedy daily, and train yourself in the practice of God's methods, so that everyone may see your continual character development. 16 Maintain a healthy lifestyle and habits, and keep your beliefs consistent with truth and evidence, so that you and those who hear and apply what you teach will be eternally healed.

5 When dealing with an older man who is in error, don't treat him like a child, but reason gently with him, as if he were your father. Treat the younger men like brothers, 2 and older women like mothers. Treat the younger women like sisters—with constant concern for their purity, protecting their reputation.

1 Tim 5:3 Help the widows who need help. 4 But if a widow has children and grandchildren, they need to live in harmony with the law of love and care for their own family members so that the circle of love may be complete in returning the love they received from their parents and grandparents back to their parents and grandparents, for this is how God designed life to operate: a never-ending circle of giving. 5 The widow who can be benefited by assistance is the one without family and who, keeping her heart in communion with God, trusts him with her future. The help given will be a blessing to her. 6 But the widow who seeks merely to gratify self is in the process of dying, and any aid given will only assist in her self-destruction. 7 Educate the people in these matters, so no one will misrepresent God. 8 If people don't use their resources to bless and uplift their family, then they misrepresent the Remedy and basically deny that it transforms the character, which makes

them worse than those who never claim to have taken the Remedy.

1 Tim 5:9 A widow over sixty may be enrolled into the church's subsistence program if she was faithful to her husband, 10 and if she represents God accurately by loving others with her actions: helping with orphans, welcoming and assisting others, humbly ministering to Christ's friends, working to rescue those in trouble, and seeking the good of others.

1 Tim 5:11 Younger widows don't need to be on permanent subsistence, because their God-given desire for a family will lead them to remarry (rather than continuing their full-time commitment to Christian ministry), 12 and if they break their pledge, they will suffer from a guilty conscience. 13 Not only that, but idleness is destructive and we want to protect them from boredom which leads to gossip, meddling in others' affairs, and instigating conflict in the church. 14 So I recommend that younger widows use their abilities successfully: remarry if well matched, have children if they so desire, but certainly take over management of the household and don't give enemies any basis for criticism. 15 Sadly, some have already turned away from loving others and instead followed Satan into selfishness.

1 Tim 5:16 Anyone who has taken the Remedy, and has widows in the family, needs to exercise their new heart of love and help those women rather than turning to the church for assistance: the church can then minister in love to other widows who have no other means of support.

1 Tim 5:17 Spiritual leaders who are especially effective at organizing and promoting the health and growth of the church should be considered for bonuses, especially if they are—in addition to their administrative and organizational duties—also preaching and teaching, 18 for the inspired record says, "Don't prevent the ox from eating while it grinds the grain," and "The

employee deserves to be paid." ¹⁹ And please don't listen to allegations against a spiritual leader unless it is brought by at least two or three witnesses. ²⁰ Those who choose to live by persistently breaking God's design protocols for life—commonly called sinning—need to be publicly confronted and educated, so that others may also see how destructive it is to violate the law which life is built upon.

1Tim 5:21 With the support and approval of God and Jesus Christ and the loyal angels, I charge you to carry out these instructions in loving equality for all people: show no prejudice or discrimination.

1Tim 5:22 Don't place new converts in positions of leadership too quickly; don't collude with others' self-destructive choices, and keep yourself pure and healthy.

1Tim 5:23 As you travel, don't be so insistent on drinking water only—impure water may be causing many of your digestive problems. Drink a little wine, as it will often kill the contaminants and reduce your risk of sickness.

1Tim 5:24 The violations of God's law— the protocols he constructed life to operate upon—are so obvious in some people that they are easily diagnosed; in others, the breaches in God's design for life are hidden, and it may take years before the damage manifests itself. ²⁵ Likewise, living in harmony with God's design brings obvious health benefits to one's body, mind and relationships, even if the healthy practices are not publicized but done in private.

6 The selfish actions of those enslaving other people don't excuse the slaves who have taken the Remedy from continuing in selfishness. Slaves therefore need to show proper respect and loving service for their masters, so that God's methods, character and principles may be uplifted and not misrepresented. ² Slaves, don't be hostile toward masters who have partaken of the Remedy. Remember that they suffer from the same character sickness as all of us, so serve them with even greater devotion because you love them; and they are actually recovering and getting well. These are the principles of love you are to teach and encourage your masters to practice.

1Tim 6:3 Those who teach lies about God—representing him as a being other than love—do not agree with the truth revealed by our Lord Jesus Christ and don't value evidence-based instruction. ⁴ They are self-centered, they understand nothing about God's kingdom, and their unhealthy minds enjoy causing problems. They instigate arguments and controversies that stir up envy, rumormongering and misrepresentation of others—all of which cause fear of God and suspicion of those who represent him rightly. ⁵ Such behavior invariably puts self at the center: their minds are so selfish, and they are so bereft of the truth that they think the Remedy—provided freely by Christ—is their means of getting rich.

1Tim 6:6 But taking the Remedy— experiencing transformation of character to be like Christ—is wealth beyond words. ⁷ We entered the world with nothing, and we won't take any earthly belongings with us when we die. ⁸ All we need is the basics to provide us enough physical and mental health to be able to appreciate and partake of the Remedy. ⁹ People who pursue earthly wealth fall into the trap of self-advancement, fail to appreciate and partake of the Remedy, and their selfish desires lead to foolish choices and ultimate self-destruction. ¹⁰ The love of money is rooted in selfishness, which is the source of all evil. Some greedy people have rejected the Remedy, injured others to get ahead, and have ultimately damaged their own character.

1Tim 6:11 But you, Timothy, who are a man representing God, must reject all this selfishness and develop a Christlike character: Be godly, abide in trust, love freely, be courageous and gentle. [12] Stay focused and purposely apply God's methods to your life every day. Embrace the full healing and restoration to eternal life that have been freely offered you, and which you wisely accepted in the presence of many witnesses. [13] Under the authority of God—who is the source of all life—and Jesus Christ, who spoke the truth about his kingdom of love before Pontius Pilate, I charge you [14] to keep fulfilling this assignment faithfully until our Lord Jesus Christ returns, [15] which will happen when God—the exalted and true Ruler, the King over all kings and Lord above all lords—has determined is best. [16] God is the only one with life original, unborrowed, underived, and who can never die. He lives in infinity—the unapproachable light of infinite truth and love that no one can fully absorb or assimilate. All honor and power is his alone forever. So let it ever be.

[1Tim 6:17] Instruct those who are wealthy in worldly goods not to be so self-absorbed, nor to put their confidence in riches which can evaporate so quickly, but instead, to put their trust in God, who abundantly provides us with everything we need for health and eternal happiness. [18] Instruct them to do what is right because it is right, to be rich in love for others, and generously give of themselves for the good of others.

[19] This is how they should live to be in harmony with God's design, develop character that will last eternally, and be rich with love and friends in heaven; this is living as God designed life to truly operate.

[1Tim 6:20] Timothy, guard the truth about God and his Remedy that has been entrusted to you. Reject the path of talking about God but not living his love, and reject the false "knowledge" of God that represents him as something other than love. [21] Some promote distorted views of God, and as they do, they walk away from the truth and reject the Remedy. God's love and power be with you.

2 Timothy

1 From Paul, an ambassador of Jesus Christ appointed by God, to promote the Remedy procured by Jesus Christ, which brings eternal life.

2Tim 1:2 Dear Timothy, whom I love like a son: May you receive strength, love and peace from God the Father and Jesus Christ our Lord.

2Tim 1:3 I am so thankful to God who has cleansed my conscience and who enabled me to represent him, as my forefathers were called to do. You are on my mind and in my prayers all day, every day. 4 I miss you and long to be with you so that my heart may rejoice in your company. 5 I remember your deep love for the truth about God, and your passion for sharing the Remedy. That unwavering confidence and trust in God's kingdom of love was first known by your grandmother Lois, and then by your mother Eunice, and I am certain is now known by you. 6 So continue to exercise, develop and expand the enabling and gifts God gave you when I laid hands on you. 7 For God did not give you a character of insecurity, doubt and fear, but a mind and character of confidence, power in the truth, love, and self-control.

2Tim 1:8 Don't ever be embarrassed to speak boldly about our Lord, and certainly don't be ashamed of me being in and out of prison for spreading the Remedy. Instead, join me, by God's power, in enduring the hardship that comes with distributing the Remedy. 9 For God has healed us and invited us to an eternal life of love—not because we somehow cured ourselves, but because he is gracious and it is his intention, will and purpose to heal all who will let him. Before time began, Jesus was his means of healing humanity, 10 but how he would do it wasn't seen until the coming of our Savior Jesus Christ who, in his human brain, loved perfectly. He destroyed death by destroying the infection of selfishness, and perfectly restored God's law of love into humanity, healing the species and revealing life and immortality through the Remedy he achieved.

11 And I was commissioned as a distributor, emissary, and teacher of this great Remedy. 12 That is why I have been harassed and persecuted. But I don't regret it for a minute, because I know and trust Jesus, and I am certain that he will oversee the distribution of the Remedy he entrusted to me, until the day he returns.

2Tim 1:13 Keep what you learned from me as a model of how to—with confidence and love in Jesus—promote and distribute the Remedy. 14 Protect the healing truth that has been entrusted to you by cooperating with the Holy Spirit who applies the Remedy within us.

2Tim 1:15 You already know that everyone in Asia has abandoned me, including Phygelus and Hermogenes.

2Tim 1:16 But may God watch over and protect Onesiphorus and his family, for his home was always open to me and he was never afraid to be seen with me, even though I was in and out of prison. 17 Just the opposite, when I was imprisoned in Rome, he searched everywhere, letting everyone know he was looking for me, until he found me. 18 It is my prayer that when Christ returns, the Lord will treat him with even greater kindness than Onesiphorus has treated me; and you know how much he did for me at Ephesus.

2 So, my son, grow stronger through the healing power that we receive when we live in unity with Christ Jesus. ²Take the healing truths you have learned from me and teach them to people who are responsible and capable of effectively teaching others.

³Remember that we are on the same team, so, as a dedicated soldier of Jesus Christ, endure with us the hardship of advancing the Remedy. ⁴No active duty soldier spends their energy on civilian matters, but carries out their orders to please the commander. ⁵Similarly, an athlete will never win a competition if they fail to exercise, work out, or operate in harmony with the laws of health. ⁶And it is the diligent farmer that plants, waters, fertilizes, and operates in harmony with laws of nature who receives the best crop. ⁷Meditate on the principles of God's kingdom I am describing, for the Lord will help you understand all of this.

2Tim 2:8 Remember it is Jesus, descended from David, who died, yet rose from the dead. It is for this incredible truth—this Remedy that cures death— ⁹that I am persecuted and imprisoned like a criminal. But the truth—the Remedy Jesus achieved—is not restrained. ¹⁰Therefore, I endure all this pain for the benefit of those who will partake of the Remedy, so they may obtain the healing of mind and character that comes from Jesus Christ and results in eternal righteousness.

2Tim 2:11 This is the simple truth:
If we unite with him and die to
  selfishness,
we will be healed and live eternally
  with him.
¹²If we don't give up, he will
  transform us and we will also
  reign with him.
If we reject him, he will respect our
  choice and let us go.
¹³If we are not trustworthy,
he will always be trustworthy
  because he cannot deny himself.

2Tim 2:14 Keep reminding the people of these truths. Invite God's presence into your meeting and then warn the people against arguing over specific words, for there is no magic or power in specific words; but focus instead on the principles of God's kingdom, for arguing over semantics confuses those who are listening. ¹⁵Do your best to follow the treatment plan approved by God; work hard, applying his methods without fear or insecurity, and present the Remedy effectively. ¹⁶Don't engage in conversations that misrepresent God, as our speech reacts upon our thoughts and reinforces them, and those who say such things will become more selfish and ungodly. ¹⁷Their deadly concepts will infect minds and spread like the plague. Among the infected are Hymenaeus and Philetus. ¹⁸They have exchanged the truth for lies, and by claiming that the resurrection of the dead has already happened, are causing some to quit God's treatment program. ¹⁹But the Remedy Christ has achieved cannot be destroyed. It is more solid than stone, and is dispensed with these words: "God knows who has been transformed into unity with him," and "Everyone who takes the Remedy will be cleansed from all selfishness and wickedness."

2Tim 2:20 In a large house, there are not only expensive items made of crystal, silver and gold, but also inexpensive items made of wood, plastic and steel. Some items are used in healthy activities; other items are used in destructive activities. ²¹If a person stops engaging in destructive activities, the Master will cleanse and heal them, and they will be useful in spreading the Remedy and other healthy activities.

2Tim 2:22 Turn away from the self-indulgent cravings of adolescence, and seek a mature Christlike character, confidence in God, love and peace, uniting together with those who have partaken of the Remedy and follow the Lord with pure hearts. ²³Don't participate in arguments that foolishly misrepresent God or ignorantly distort his character, because they only produce conflict and confusion. 24 And remember that as an ambassador of the Lord you represent the Lord, so you must not be combative; instead, the Lord's ambassador must be kind to everyone, be a teacher who—like the Master—can make complex ideas simple enough that children can understand, and must never hold grudges. 25 Educate gently those who don't comprehend and are standing in opposition to advancing truth. God's influence may yet get through to them, and they may yet understand the truth 26 and realize their error, and escape the trap of the devil who has captured their minds with lies so they do his will.

3 But mark this, and mark it well: In the last days, there will be especially horrible times. 2 Society will become entitled. The people will be malignant narcissists, completely self-absorbed, greedy, arrogant, proud, exploitive and abusive, rebellious toward their parents, ungrateful, impure, 3 without compassion, resentful, liars, speaking evil of others, unable to control their own behavior, cruel and brutal, deriding that which is healthy and good, 4 conniving and untrustworthy, impulsive and thoughtless, conceited, addicted to pleasure rather than devoted to God— 5 yet they will be religious and have a pretense of godliness, but they will deny the Remedy and God's methods of love. Don't ever let these people into your life.

2Tim 3:6 Such people scam their way into the homes of weak-willed women, and manipulate them by evoking guilt from past mistakes. These women are vulnerable because they are emotionally unstable and swayed by all kinds of selfish desires. 7 They constantly seek help but reject the Remedy and all truth that would actually heal them. 8 Just as Jannes and Jambres counterfeited Moses, so these people present a counterfeit remedy, and, since they rejected the true Remedy, their minds are damaged and degraded. 9 But these people won't get into too many homes because the result of their foolish rejection of the Remedy will be plain to all who can think for themselves.

2Tim 3:10 And I am sure you recognize this clearly because you know me, and you know what I teach. You know the way I live, my mission, beliefs, patience, love, steadfastness; 11 you know the persecutions and mistreatment I suffered in Antioch, Iconium and Lystra, and how the Lord brought me through it all. 12 The reality is that everyone who lives in harmony with God's methods, trusting in Jesus, will be persecuted by the selfish world. 13 But the selfish counterfeiters will deteriorate; their thinking will become increasingly warped by their lying to others and to themselves. 14 But you simply need to continue in the truth you have learned and are confident of, because you have seen the healed characters of those from whom you have learned it, 15 and because it is in harmony with the Scriptures you have known from childhood. And you know the Scriptures teach the Remedy that is able to heal you and make you wise through your trust in Jesus Christ. 16 For all Scripture, inspired by God, is beneficial for teaching, redirecting, correcting and training—to promote character transformation— 17 so that God's ambassadors may be exceptionally competent in application of the Remedy and every other good work.

4 In the presence of God and Jesus Christ who will diagnose accurately both the living and the dead, and with the expectation of his return and the establishment of his kingdom of love, I give you this charge: 2 Spread the Remedy; be ready at any time, day or night, to—with great patience and skillful direction—correct those who are out of

harmony with God's design; redirect those injuring themselves or others, and encourage those applying the Remedy. ³ For there will come a time when people will no longer listen to reason, truth or evidence. Instead, in harmony with their selfishness, they will amass professors, teachers and theologians to delight them with what they want to hear. ⁴ They will refuse to listen to reason and truth, and instead embrace fantasies. ⁵ But you be sure to think for yourself in all situations, and endure the inevitable difficulties while you do everything in your power to spread the Remedy and carry out all the responsibilities of your ministry.

2Tim 4:6 My time here is ebbing away like a drink flowing from a cup; the time has come for me to be executed. ⁷ I have stayed focused and fulfilled my mission; I have completed my assignment and have been true to my calling. ⁸ Now there is waiting for me the reward of being restored to complete rightness with God, which the Lord— the righteous Ruler—will award me when he returns, and not only to me but to all who have desired his appearing.

2Tim 4:9 If you can, come to me quickly, ¹⁰ for Demas loved the pleasures of this world and ran away to Thessalonica. Crescens has left for Galatia, and Titus—to Dalmatia. ¹¹ Only doctor Luke is still with me. When you come, bring Mark, because he is always so helpful in my ministry. ¹² I sent Tychicus to Ephesus. ¹³ Don't forget to bring the coat I left with Carpus at Troas, and my books—especially my notebooks.

2Tim 1:11 The metalworker Alexander harmed my efforts greatly, but the Lord will allow him to reap the results of what he has done. ¹⁵ Be careful if he shows up, because he strongly opposes the Remedy.

2Tim 4:16 At my first hearing, no one stood with me. They all ran and hid, but I don't hold it against them, ¹⁷ for the Lord stood with me and strengthened me, so that I was able to present the Remedy fully, and all the Gentiles heard it. And I was rescued from certain death. ¹⁸ I know the Lord will rescue me from all evil and take me safely to his heavenly kingdom. To him be the glory for ever and ever. So let it ever be!

2Tim 4:19 Give my greetings to Priscilla and Aquila, and Onesiphorus and his family. ²⁰ Erastus stayed in Corinth, and Trophimus was sick in Miletus when I left. ²¹ Please try to get here before winter. Eubulus says "hello," as do Pudens, Linus, Claudia and all the others. ²² The Lord be with you. God's grace be upon you.

Titus

1 Paul, a serving friend of God and an ambassador of Jesus Christ, sent to inspire God's friends with ever-increasing confidence and trust in him and his methods, and to promote the Remedy which results in cleaning the mind and the development of godly character: [2] My mission is to reveal the truth about God and his kingdom, and thereby inspire hope in our future eternal life which God has promised before time began—and God always keeps his promises. [3] At just the right time, God stepped into human history and procured the Remedy, and I have been entrusted with spreading this Remedy by the command of God our Savior.

Ts 1:4 To Titus, my faithful partner in our common goal to spread the Remedy: Strength, love and peace from God the Father and Jesus Christ our Savior.

Ts 1:5 I left you in Crete so you could finish getting the spiritual health-care teams set up, appointing spiritual leaders in each town, just as I instructed. [6] Spiritual leaders, in order to be effective, must be respected in the community, not be polygamists, and their children must have partaken of the Remedy. They should demonstrate their healing of character by their co-operative and self-controlled lifestyles. [7] It is essential that leaders represent God correctly—this means that they must have mature characters, worthy of admiration. They must not be dictators, nor be angry or gruff with those who disagree with them; not be drunkards or aggressive, and never pursue dishonesty or self-advancement. [8] Instead, leaders must reveal Christ in all their actions. They must make strangers and the hurting ones feel welcome. They must love what is good, be self-governed, be ethical and moral, lovingly help those in need, and exercise good judgment.

[9] They must be solidly grounded in the truth—understanding humankind's proper diagnosis and the only true Remedy, so that they can effectively administer it and refute those who peddle false treatments.

Ts 1:10 You must stay vigilant, because there are many people who rebel against the true Remedy and use eloquent speech to deceive — especially those who promote legal salvation schemes. [11] Their arguments must be met with the truth and shown to be false, because they are enslaving entire families into fear and distorted views of God by teaching concepts that should never be taught. And often, they do this just to advance themselves. [12] This practice of lying is well known: even a famous Cretan prophet has said, "Cretans are accomplished liars, barbaric savages, and shiftless hedonists." [13] Sadly, this description has proved to be true, therefore you must oppose them sharply: don't leave the distinctions blurry or ambiguous but make it clear, so that the people can reject the distortions, partake of the true Remedy, become mature in character, [14] stop listening to Jewish and legal myths, and stop following the instructions of those who reject the Remedy.

Ts 1:15 No ceremony or ritual can defile those who have taken the Remedy and are healed in heart and mind, but those who have rejected the Remedy remain terminal despite all their ceremonies and rituals. In fact, their minds and consciences are necrotic with selfishness. [16] They claim to know God, but their selfish and fear-based lives deny him and his kingdom of love. Their rejection of the Remedy and their claims that selfishness is actually healthy are disgusting! They are in violation of God's design for life and thereby unfit and incapable of doing anything good.

2 Teach what is in harmony with God's design for life—built upon solid evidence, not upon superstition. [2] For instance, teach the older men how to live in harmony with the laws God built life to operate upon: to be respectable, self-governed, strong in the understanding of the Remedy, and filled with love and courage.

[Ts 2:3] Likewise, teach the older women to live in harmony with the law of love—not to misrepresent God by gossiping, and not to be drunkards. [4] Then they can be competent role models and teachers to the younger ladies, teaching them how to love their families [5] by effective self-mastery, healthy boundaries, pure actions, diligence in duties, gentleness, and humble appreciation of their husbands' Christlike leadership, so that no one will devalue the Remedy provided by God.

[Ts 2:6] Also, lead the young men to obtain self-governance. [7] Show them by all you do what Christlike character looks like in action. Teach with simplicity and candor so that even the children can understand. Make the lessons real [8] and practical, built on solid evidence that cannot be refuted, so that those who oppose the Remedy may be silenced because they have nothing to say that can disprove what you are teaching.

[Ts 2:9] Teach slaves to see beyond this present reality to the principles of God's kingdom and serve their masters with love, seeking to honor them, without rebelliousness, [10] with honesty and complete trustworthiness, so that in everything they do they may reveal the beauty and attractiveness of God's kingdom of love.

[Ts 2:11] God's Remedy for the healing and restoration of all human beings has been achieved and is available to everyone. [12] It transforms us and replaces the desire for selfishness, worldliness and lust with selfless love, self-governance, and the ability to live Christlike lives right now [13] while we await the joyful Day when our great God and Savior—Jesus Christ—appears to take us to be with him. [14] He surrendered himself in order to heal us from all selfishness and to cleanse and restore for himself human beings who are healed back into God's original design, in complete unity with his character and methods of love, eager to do what is right and good.

[Ts 2:15] These are the life-changing truths you must teach. Be confident as you apply the truth to encourage and correct, and don't be intimidated by anyone.

3 Remind the people that since the church is founded upon God's kingdom and is not to spend its energy on politics, they should be law-abiding citizens, [2] not badmouth government officials, be polite and live in peace, and demonstrate genuine appreciation for all human beings.

[Ts 3:3] At one time, we were consumed by the infection of selfishness and our thinking was fear-based and irrational; we were rebellious, our minds were filled with lies and distortions, and we were in bondage to our emotions, passions, and lusts. We lived in constant threat assessment and in conflict with others; we were envious, hating, and being hated. [4] But when our God and Savior appeared with the kindness and love of God, [5] he healed us—he procured the Remedy. We could not do it ourselves, neither have we contributed anything to the cure. He did it because of his compassion. He heals us through the work of the Holy Spirit who cleanses our hearts and minds [6] by taking what Christ achieved and generously reproducing it into us, [7] so that—having been regenerated to be right in heart by the Remedy Christ achieved—we actually receive eternal life. [8] This is the truth. I want you to make this truth clear, so that those who have partaken of the Remedy and trust God will focus their resources on doing good; for living in harmony with the law of love is healthy for everyone!

[Ts 3:9] But don't get caught up in ludicrous theological debates over salvation by having the right family tree or legal salvation models, because these cannot heal the mind and are actually damaging. [10] If someone tries to promote these distortions, warn them about the futility of these false remedies, and then warn them again. If they refuse to listen, don't keep spending your energy on them, as they won't benefit by it. [11] You can be sure that such a person is damaged and selfish beyond healing; they remain terminal by their own choice.

[Ts 3:12] I will be spending the winter in Nicopolis, so please come to me there as soon as Artemas or Tychicus arrives. [13] To help Zenas the attorney and Apollos on their journey, please supply whatever provisions they need.

[14] Those who have partaken of the Remedy must learn to live in harmony with the law of love—to be productive in order to have something to give, and not find themselves as takers.

[Ts 3:15] Everyone here sends their hugs. Give all our friends there a big hug from us.

Our love to you all!

Philemon

1 From Paul — a prisoner because of my love and loyalty to Christ — and our brother Timothy,

To Philemon, my good friend and co-worker; ²also to our sister in Christ—Apphia; to Archippus—our fellow warrior for Christ; and to those partaking in the Remedy who are meeting in your home:

Phe 1:3 God our Father and the Lord Jesus Christ pour out their grace and peace to you.

Phe 1:4 My heart overflows with thanks to God for you, and every time I talk with God, I bring you up in our discussion ⁵because I hear how faithful you have been to the Lord Jesus and how consistently you reveal his love in your treatment of others. ⁶It is my desire and prayer that we may be more effective in revealing the truth about God, his methods and principles, and that we may come to full unity and oneness with him so that in all we do, Christ will be glorified. ⁷Your selfless giving, love and beneficence have brought me great joy and encouragement because you have shared the Remedy which has strengthened and helped heal the minds and hearts of the saints.

Phe 1:8 Knowing how much you love Christ and how you are willing to serve others, I could make a bold move and command you to do what is right; but that would be useless, because ⁹you already love God and willingly practice his methods. Therefore, as one who is a prisoner because of my love and loyalty to Christ, I appeal to your love for God and others: I ask you to accept Onesimus as my adopted son (while I was here in prison, he became a son to me, and I — his spiritual father).

¹¹I know that in the past he was of no benefit to you, but now he loves God as we do and is therefore useful to us both.

Phe 1:12 I am sending him back to you, and it feels like I am ripping my heart out by doing so. ¹³I so badly wanted to keep him here as a way of your helping me while I am in prison for teaching the good news about God, ¹⁴but I didn't want to take such an action without your consent: any gift you give, I want it to be freely offered and not coerced. ¹⁵Maybe his running away from you for this short time has helped change his heart, so now he comes back to you freely and thus will be with you forever: ¹⁶no longer as a slave who serves against his will, but much better than a slave—as a friend and brother who serves in love. He is very precious to me and even more so to you, both as a human being and as a brother in Christ.

Phe 1:17 So, if I am your friend and co-worker, then welcome him just as you would welcome me. ¹⁸If he has wronged you in any way or owes you any debt, charge it to me. ¹⁹As verification, I, Paul, am writing this myself, in my own handwriting. You have my pledge that I will reimburse you whatever debt he owes—even though you are indebted to me for your very life. ²⁰So, my brother, please do me this great favor and bring Christlike joy to my heart. ²¹Knowing you as I do, I am confident you will do all I ask and even more.

Phe 1:22 By the way, prepare a guest room for me, for I hope—in answer to your prayers—to be restored to you soon.

Phe 1:23 Epaphras, who is also imprisoned

here for preaching the truth about God as revealed by Christ Jesus, sends you greetings. 24 And so do Mark, Aristarchus, Demas and doctor Luke—my co-workers in Christ.

Phe 1:25 May the gracious healing power of our Lord Jesus Christ imbue your heart and mind.

Hebrews

1 God has been speaking to us throughout all human history. In the past, he worked through his inspired spokespersons (and in other ways) to send his message of truth, love and hope. ² But in these more recent times, God's very thoughts have been made audible and visible to us in the person of his Son, who is the rightful heir of all things, and through whom the entire universe was created. ³ Jesus Christ is the radiant glory of God's methods and principles lived out in human flesh. He is the exact manifestation of God's character—the complete revelation of his being—sustaining all things by his powerful word. After he provided the Remedy necessary to heal mankind from the infection of sin and selfishness, he took his seat at the right hand of the Majesty in heaven, ⁴ thus his superiority to the angels became known throughout the entire universe, just as the name he inherited is superior to theirs.

Heb 1:5 For to which angel did God ever say,

"You are my Son;
today my Fatherhood to you
has become known"?
Or again,
"I am his Father,
and he is my Son"?

Heb 1:6 And again, when God brought his Son into the world, he said,

"Let all God's angelic host realize the
truth of who he is,
and worship him."

Heb1:7 In speaking of angels, he says,

"He makes his angels intelligent
beings;
his servants—fiery channels of

heavenly light."

Heb 1:8 But about his Son, he says,

"The foundation of your
government—the throne of your
authority—O God, will last forever,
and righteousness will be
the governing principle.

Heb 1:9 "You have loved (and revealed)
the methods of righteousness—
the methods of love, truth and
freedom—
and hated the way of wickedness
with its principles of selfishness,
deceit, and coercion;
therefore God, your Father,
has set you above all beings
by anointing you with the oil of joy."

Heb 1:10 God also says,

"In the beginning, O Son,
you created the earth;
the sun, moon and planets of this
solar system
are a work of your hands.

Heb 1:11 "They will be destroyed,
but you will live forever;
they will all wear out like old clothes.

Heb 1:12 "You will roll them up
like a coat;
like old clothes,
they will be changed for new.
But you never change:
you remain the same forever,
and your years will never end."

Heb 1:13 To which of the angels did God ever say,

"Sit at my right hand
until I make your enemies
a footstool for your feet"?

Heb 1:14 Are not all angels intelligent beings sent to minister the blessings of God to those who are being healed from the infection of fear and selfishness?

2 We must keep our minds focused more consistently on the truth we have heard, so that we do not become preoccupied with trivial matters and drift away. ²For if the message brought by angels was true and real, and—as they warned—every violation of the principles of love and freedom resulted in damage and destruction, ³how shall we ever get well if we ignore God's plan to heal us? This plan of healing—of transformation and re-creation—was initially announced by the Lord and later confirmed to us when we heard him personally. ⁴God also provided signs, wonders and a variety of miracles as well as gifts of the Holy Spirit—all designed to reveal and promote his plan to heal and restore.

Heb 2:5 God did not choose angels to rule over the future kingdom about which we are speaking, ⁶for it is written somewhere:

"Why are humans so important to you,

or the Son of Man, that you care about him?

Heb 2:7 "You positioned him a little lower than the angels,

but crowned him with the glory of your character and the honor of revealing your principles:

⁸you made everything subject to his rule."

In putting all things under his authority, God left nothing on earth that is not governed by humanity. Yet presently we do not see all creation restored to human rule. ⁹But we see Jesus—who was positioned a little lower than the angels—now crowned with glory for perfectly revealing God's character, and honored for vindicating God's methods and principles of selfless love, because he voluntarily chose to die rather than use his power to save self so that by the graciousness of God, he might consume death in order to heal everyone.

Heb 2:10 In healing the minds and characters of many sons and daughters, it was necessary that God—from whom and through whom everything exists—should make the Source of the healing Remedy perfect through suffering, for only through self-sacrificial love could humanity be perfected; thus when Christ chose to love rather than act to save self, he eradicated the death-causing survival-of-the-fittest principle. ¹¹Both the one who heals the minds and characters of human beings, and those whose minds and characters are healed, are of the same family, so Jesus is not ashamed to call them brothers and sisters. ¹²He says,

"I will reveal your character to my brothers and sisters;

in the presence of humanity I will sing your praises."

Heb 2:13 And again,

"I will put my trust in him."

And again he says,

"Here I stand with the children God has given me."

Heb 2:14 And since the children are human (with flesh and blood), he too became human (with flesh and blood) so that by his death he might reveal the truth about God, consume selfishness with love, destroy him who through his lies about God holds the power of death—that is, the devil— ¹⁵and free the minds of those who have lived all their lives enslaved by their misunderstanding of God and their fear of death. ¹⁶For surely it is not to angels that he provides the Remedy to sin, but to the children of Abraham. ¹⁷For this reason, he had to become one of them—completely human in every way—in order to purge humanity of selfishness, enlighten the darkened minds of people with truth about God so they would trust him as the mediator of God's Remedy, and thus bring mankind back into unity with God in heart, mind, and character. ¹⁸Because he himself suffered when he was tempted, humanity will trust that he truly knows how to help those who are being tempted.

3 Therefore, holy brothers and sisters who share in the heavenly Remedy and in the privilege of spreading the Remedy to others: Study the life of Jesus and keep your thoughts fixed on him—the ambassador of God and minister of the truth that sets us free, ²and who faithfully completed the mission God appointed him, just as Moses faithfully carried out his duties in God's symbolic house. ³Jesus has demonstrated that he is worthy of greater honor than Moses, just as the builder of a house has greater honor than the house itself, ⁴for while every house is built by someone, God is the builder of everything. ⁵Moses was faithful in building the symbolic house, providing lessons regarding what would happen in the future; ⁶but Christ is faithful as a Son over God's true house. And we are his house — his dwelling place — if we hold on to our confidence in the truth and the hope of which we boast.

Heb 3:7 As the Holy Spirit says:
"Today, if you hear his voice offering
   healing and restoration,
Heb 3:8 do not reject the true Remedy
   and darken your minds
   as you did in the rebellion in the
   desert, during the opportunity
   to partake of God's cure,
Heb 3:9 where your fathers broke my
   heart by trying their own remedies
   and rejecting the truth which I
   brought and for forty years
   patiently tried to heal them.
Heb 3:10 That is why I was so angry with
   what happened to that generation,
   and said,
   'Their minds continually reject the
   healing truth,
   and they refuse to practice my
   ways of health and live.'
Heb 3:11 So I granted them their
   persistent choice and said,
   'Since they refuse the truth—the
   Remedy I freely offer—
   they will never be able to enter my
   rest and get well.'"

Heb 3:12 See to it, brothers and sisters, that none of you cling to lies about God and retain a selfish, distrusting mind that turns you away from the living God. ¹³But daily build each other up in the truth, as long as there is still time, so that none of you may be blinded, confused and hardened by the lies about God. ¹⁴We have become partakers of Christ's character if we hold firmly till the end to the confidence we initially had in the truth about God, revealed by Christ. ¹⁵As has just been said:
"Today, if you hear his voice offering
   healing and restoration,
do not reject the true Remedy and
   darken your minds
   as you did in the rebellion."
Heb 3:16 Who were they who heard the message of healing truth but instead rebelled and preferred lies? Were they not all those whom Moses led out of Egypt? ¹⁷And with what was God angry for forty years? Was it not with having to watch his children persistently reject his healing ways and slowly die and fall in the desert? ¹⁸And whom did God tell that they could never get well and find rest as long as they rebelled against the only Remedy if not those who died in the desert? ¹⁹So we see that they were not able to get well and enter into God's rest because they didn't trust him or accept the truth he revealed.

4 Therefore, since the Remedy is still available and the promise of complete healing and perfect rest still stands, let us be careful that none of us be found to have rejected it. ²For we also have had the good news of God's healing truth presented to us just as they did, but the message of truth had no value to them because they did not believe it nor did they trust the one who gave it. ³But we, who have trusted God on the basis of the truth Christ provided, experience healing and enter that rest, and our minds are at peace.

As God has said,
> "So I granted them their persistent
>   choice and said,
> 'Since they refuse the truth—
>   the Remedy I freely offer—
>   they will never be able to enter my
>   rest and get well.'"

It was not because God's perfect rest was not available—for it had been ready since his work of creation was complete— ⁴as the Scriptures say elsewhere regarding the seventh day: "And on the seventh day, God rested his case. He had finished all his work of providing the evidence needed to refute the lies of Satan." ⁵And yet in another passage he says, "If they refuse the truth, if they reject the evidence I have provided, their minds will never find rest and they will not get well."

Heb 4:6 The opportunity to find God's healing and rest still remains, even though those who formerly had the good news of God's healing truth presented to them did not get well or find rest because they refused to believe the truth and trust God. ⁷Therefore God again and again presents his healing Remedy, and he set a certain day which he called "today," when much later he spoke through David in the same Scripture as before:
> "Today, if you hear his voice offering
>   healing and restoration,
> do not reject the true Remedy and
>   darken your minds."

Heb 4:8 For if Joshua had already given them healing of character and rest for their minds, God would not have spoken later about another day of rest still to come. ⁹There remains then a Sabbath-rest—a rest in the evidence and truth of the character of God—which heals and transforms the people of God; ¹⁰for anyone who rests in the achievements of Christ rests from working to save themself, just as God rested from his work. ¹¹Let us therefore make every effort to rest in the truth about God as revealed by Christ, so that no one will fall by following the example of distrust and refusal to accept the truth.

Heb 4:12 For the word of God is the living and active revelation of the truth about God, his methods and principles, and the real basis of life in the universe. It is sharper than any two-edged sword: it penetrates the deepest recesses of the mind and separates thoughts and feelings, habits and motives; it also diagnoses the true intentions, attitudes, and principles of the heart. ¹³Nothing in all creation is hidden from God's sight, as he knows the true condition of our minds. Everything is open and clearly seen by him who will one day examine and accurately diagnose us all.

Heb 4:14 Therefore, since we have a great high priest (a great physician) who has gone through the heavens—Jesus, the Son of God—let us hold confidently to the truth about God and his plan to heal and restore us. ¹⁵For we do not have a heavenly physician (a great high priest) who is unable to appreciate our weakness, suffering and struggles, but we have one who in his humanity was tempted in every way—exactly as we are—yet without sin, without ever giving in to selfish temptations. ¹⁶Therefore let us approach the throne of God's grace without fear, but confidently, realizing that he longs to dispense all the resources of heaven to heal us so that we may receive mercy, grace, and every benefit to give us victory in our time of need.

5 Every earthly high priest is selected from among people and is appointed to minister to them the healing truth about God and to lead them to understand the true meaning of what the gifts and sacrifices symbolize. ²He is able to deal patiently and gently with those who are ignorant of the Remedy—and therefore are getting sicker—since he himself is infected with the same infection of selfishness and sin. ³This is why he has to offer sacrifices

for his own selfish heart—to reveal that he needs the same Remedy to bring healing and restoration for himself—as well as for the infected minds of the people.

Heb 5:4 No one takes this honor upon himself; he must be called by God, just as Aaron was. 5 So Christ also did not take upon himself the glory of becoming the great heavenly high priest—the conduit of God's healing Remedy—but it was God who said to him,

"You are my Son;
today my fatherhood to you has become known."

Heb 5:6 And he says elsewhere,

"You are a priest—a conduit of my healing Remedy—forever, in the order of Melchizedek."

Heb 5:7 During the days of his life on earth, Jesus suffered the anguish of human pain and emotions, and prayed to his Father (who could deliver him from death) and was heard because his heart and mind were pure. 8 Although he was God's son, in his humanity he suffered, yet remained obedient through trusting his Father, 9 and—once he completed his mission—lived out in humanity a perfect character of love, which conquered selfishness, and thus he became the source of eternal healing and life for all who trust and obey him, 10 and was designated by God to be high priest (the heavenly physician who is the conduit of the healing Remedy) in the order of Melchizedek.

Heb 5:11 We have so much to explain to you about this, and about God's healing plan as symbolized in the sanctuary service, but it is hard to explain because you think like children—in concrete terms—and you are slow to learn. 12 In fact, though by this time you ought to be able to clearly explain the true meaning of all the symbolism used, instead, you need someone to teach you the basic truths of God's character all over again! You need to be spoon-fed baby food because you can't handle solid food! 13 Anyone who still lives on the baby food of symbols and metaphors is an infant in their thinking and doesn't have a clue about God's true character and his Remedy for sin. 14 But the solid food of truth is for the mature, who, by constant use, have trained their faculties to distinguish true from false, good from evil, healthy from unhealthy.

6 Therefore, let's leave behind the child's understanding about Christ and move on to real comprehension and maturity—not starting from scratch with relearning to avoid self-destructive behaviors and to trust God, 2 the basics of how to baptize, how to lay on hands, the truth of the resurrection, and the final conclusion to sin— 3 and with God's help, we will succeed.

Heb 6:4 It is impossible for those whose minds have been enlightened with the truth about God—those who have tasted the goodness of heaven, who have participated in the Spirit of truth and love, 5 who have experienced how good are God's ways and the revitalizing power of the future age— 6 to be restored to health and God's original ideal if they reject all this, for they reject the only Remedy, and no other cure exists.
Their loss pierces the heart of God all over again as they spurn his never-ending love.

Heb 6:7 Land that receives the rain and produces a bountiful harvest which nurtures those who farmed it receives the blessing of God. 8 But land that receives the rain and produces thorns and thistles is useless and is in danger of being abandoned: in the end, it will be burned.

Heb 6:9 Dear friends, even though we speak of the pain of loss, in your case, we are confident of all the benefits that are part of God's healing plan. 10 God is not arbitrary or unjust: he knows full well how much you love him by the work you have done in helping his people. 11 We want each of you to continue to diligently practice love and beneficence to the very end, and your healing will be sure. 12 Don't let your guard down and become lazy, but be like those who, through constant trust and patience, experience healing of the mind and the promises of God.

Heb 6:13 When God made his promise to Abraham, there was no one greater than himself to guarantee the promise, so he guaranteed it himself, 14 saying "I will absolutely bless you and give you a multitude of descendants." 15 And Abraham trusted God and patiently waited until he received what was promised.

Heb 6:16 People will swear by someone greater than themselves that what they say is true, and the oath is supposed to guarantee that what they said was true, and put an end to any further dispute. 17 Because God didn't want any doubts —because God wanted those who are heirs of his promised redemption to be certain about the unchanging nature of his methods, principles and character of love—he confirmed it with his own word. 18 He did this so that by two utterly unchangeable things—the word of God and the character of God—we, homeless runaways, might take heart and grasp the hope that is in Jesus. 19 We have this hope in God, based on the truth revealed by Jesus, as a firm and secure anchor for our entire being. Our minds enter into the reality of God, hidden behind the veil of Satan's lies, 20 where Jesus, who went ahead, has entered to show us the way. He has become a heavenly guide—a high priest forever—in the order of Melchizedek.

7 This Melchizedek was king and ministering priest — king of Salem and priest of God Most High. He met Abraham returning from his conquest of the kings, and blessed him; 2 and Abraham paid one-tenth of his plunder to him. His name, Melchizedek, means "king of righteousness," and "king of Salem" means "king of peace." 3 With no father or mother, without lineage or proof of nobility, without a beginning or ending, he remains a ministering priest just like the Son of God—a representative of God forever.

Heb 7:4 Think how truly great he was: even the patriarch Abraham paid him one-tenth of all his wealth! 5 Now the law requires that Levi's descendants who become priests collect a tenth from their brothers, even though their brothers are also descended from Abraham. 6 This man was not descended from Levi, yet Abraham paid his tithe to him, and Abraham was blessed by him even though it was Abraham who had the promises. 7 And without question, the lesser person is blessed by the greater. 8 In the one case, a tenth is collected by those who will die; but in the other case—by him who remains alive. 9 In reality, Levi and all his descendants who collected a tenth actually paid a tenth through Abraham, 10 because when Melchizedek met Abraham, Levi was still in the body of his ancestor.

Heb 7:11 If perfect healing and restoration of mind and character could have been attained through the laws, rituals and symbols of the Levitical priesthood (remember, the Levitical priesthood is the basis for the laws given to the people), why did mankind need another priest to come—one in the order of Melchizedek, not in the order of Aaron? 12 For if the priesthood changes, then the law governing priestly selection must also change. 13 He, to whom all these things pointed, belonged to a different tribe, and no one from that tribe ever served in God's little theater we call "The Sanctuary." 14 For it is indisputable that our Lord descended from Judah, and the law governing priestly selection, given by Moses, says nothing about priests coming from the tribe of Judah. 15 And this fact is even more clear if one like Melchizedek appears— 16 one who becomes a priest not on the basis of the Levitical regulations regarding his ancestry but on the qualification of his character. His life revealed the power of the indestructible truth about God, [17] for it is declared:

"You are a priest forever—a minister
    of God's healing Remedy—
    in the order of Melchizedek."

Heb 7:18 The former Levitical regulation is discarded because it was only a symbolic teaching tool and therefore was powerless to heal [19] (for no rule, or law, or ritual, or symbol can actually heal the mind and create perfect Christlike character), but the real Remedy—the true cure, the genuine hope for health and happiness by which we are reunited with God—is now revealed.

Heb 7:20 And it was not revealed without confirmation and guarantee! Others became priests with no guarantee, [21] but he became a priest, ministering God's Remedy, with the guarantee from God himself, when he said:

"The Lord has promised
    and will not change his mind:
'You will minister the healing truth
    forever.'"

Heb 7:22 Because of this promise, Jesus has become the guarantee that the infection of selfishness will be eradicated from all who accept the true Remedy that he reveals.

Heb 7:23 Now there have been many Levitical priests, as death ended their time in office; [24] but because Jesus lives forever, he will be a priest ministering the healing truth forever. [25] Therefore, he is able to heal completely those who come to God through the truth he has revealed, because he always lives to intercede in their hearts and minds to remove selfishness and restore love.

Heb 7:26 This is the high priest who meets our need—our need to be healed and restored. He is a ministering priest who is holy, perfect, pure, and free from sin; and being the source of all health, truth, and life—he is higher than all the heavens. [27] Unlike other high priests, he does not need to offer symbolic sacrifices day after day—first for his own selfish heart, and then for the selfishness of the people. No! His heart was selfless, and he sacrificed himself to bring to mankind the truth about God, to heal the human condition, and to restore humanity into unity with God. [28] For the Levitical law appoints as high priests men who are infected with selfishness; but it was after the law was given that God's promise was fulfilled in his Son who—in his humanity—consumed selfishness with love, lies with truth, and made the perfect Remedy available forever.

8 The point of all we are saying is this: We do have such a perfect ministering high priest who sat down at the right hand of the throne of Majesty in heaven [2] and who works in the true tabernacle—the genuine temple of the Holy Spirit, the heavenly-designed dwelling place of God—built by God, not by human beings, and composed of every loyal intelligent being throughout immensity.

Heb 8:3 Every earthly high priest is appointed to act out the larger reality by offering symbolic gifts and sacrifices, and so reality requires this high priest to have what the symbols point toward. [4] If he were on earth, he would not be a theatrical priest in the little sanctuary theater, for there are already men on earth enacting the theatrical offering of symbolic sacrifices indicated by the script (which is the ceremonial law). [5] They serve in the little theater sanctuary—which is a teaching tool, a mere representation of the heavenly realities—to reveal God's plan for healing the human mind and restoring unity in the universe. This is why Moses was told when he was about to build the tabernacle: "Be sure that you make everything according to the blueprint shown you on the mountain." [6] And so the ministry of Jesus is far superior to the earthly priests' because he actually works in the human mind to heal and restore God's image within his Spirit temple—and thus perfects his heavenly sanctuary—while they only ministered symbols in a building made of stone.

Heb 8:7 For if the symbolic teaching tool could actually heal the mind and transform the heart, then it would not have been replaced with the actual Remedy. 8 But God found the people infected with selfishness and said:

"The time is coming, declares the Lord,
when I will offer anew my healing plan to the house of Israel and to the house of Judah.
Heb 8:9 It will not be in symbols—
as I gave to their forefathers when I took them by the hand to lead them, like children, out of Egypt—because they did not understand the symbolic plan
or apply its meaning,
and therefore I let them have their choice and follow their own way, declares the Lord.
Heb 8:10 This is the healing plan I will renew with the house of Israel after that time,
declares the Lord:
I will recreate and cleanse them, and restore my law of love in their minds, and write my principles of benevolence on their hearts.
I will be the God they love, admire and adore,
and they will be a people who reveal my true character.
Heb 8:11 No longer will a person need to teach their neighbor,
or tell their brother to 'know the Lord,' because everyone will know me—from the least of them to the greatest.
Heb 8:12 For I will remove wickedness from their characters, and I will never need to think about their sin-sickness again."
Heb 8:13 By calling the healing plan "new," God was simply making it clear that the symbolic plan was no longer needed to help enlighten the mind about him;

and what is no longer needed will soon disappear.

9 The symbolic system had a precise script that all the actors were to follow in revealing the plan to heal and restore, and it also had its own mini-theater—an earthly sanctuary. 2 A tabernacle—a place to act out the healing lesson—was set up. In its first (outer) room were the lampstand, the table, and the consecrated bread; this part of the set was called the Holy Place.
3 Behind the curtain was the second (inner) part of the set—called the Most Holy Place— 4 in which wafted the incense from the golden altar, and which contained the gold-covered ark of the symbolic healing plan. This ark contained the gold jar of manna, the stone tablets of the Ten Commandments, and Aaron's rod that budded. 5 Above the ark, on the lid, were the cherubim of the Glory, overshadowing the cover of reconciliation; but we cannot take time now to explain how each symbol represents some aspect of God's plan to heal our minds and restore unity to the universe.

Heb 9:6 Once the mini-theater tabernacle had all the symbols arranged according to the script, the priests acted their part by regularly entering into the outer room to carry out their symbolic tasks. 7 But only the high priest entered the inner room, and then only once a year—at the end of the year—symbolic of the completion of the healing plan. And he always entered with blood—symbolic of the healing Remedy of God's true character—which was needed to heal him as well as the selfishness of the people. 8 The Holy Spirit was revealing that the true Remedy, which heals the mind and brings us back into unity with God, had not been fully disclosed as long as the symbolic system was still in operation. 9 This is a lesson for us, revealing that the symbolic system was incapable of healing the mind, cleansing the conscience, or recreating the character of the worshiper. [10] The symbolic system was only a variety of rituals carried out by actors to prepare the mind for the true Remedy.

Heb 9:11 When Christ came as the high priest ministering God's goodness (which was already here but to which we were blind), he went through and cleansed the greater and true tabernacle—the sanctuary of the Holy Spirit that is not man-made—that is to say, not the building of stone, but the living temple built of intelligent beings. [12] He entered this temple not by means of animal blood, but he entered into the Most Holy Place permanently by his self-sacrificing death, having obtained the complete victory over the infection of selfishness and having procured the perfect Remedy! [13] In the symbolic stage play—acted out in the earthly stone sanctuary—the blood of goats and bulls and the ashes of a heifer, sprinkled on those who were cast in the role of the diseased and dying, symbolically cleansed them and symbolically made them well. [14] How much more, then, will the perfect character of Christ—wrought out by Jesus' great and perfect self-sacrifice according to God's will and through the working of the eternal Spirit—heal the mind, cleanse the conscience and recreate the character, so we no longer practice methods that lead to death but instead abide in constant love with the living God!

Heb 9:15 For this reason—because he is the source of all truth and love—Christ is the administrator of the true healing plan so that all those who desire may receive the promised re-creation, healing, and eternal life. He died to provide the ransom of the truth, necessary to free our minds from the lies about God, and the perfect Remedy to heal our characters from fear and selfishness which continued unabated during the little theater enactment of God's healing plan.

Heb 9:16 Consider the example of a will: In order for the true contents of the will to be known, the one who made it must have died, [17] because the will of a person is revealed only when they have died. It is never made known while the one who made it is alive. [18] This is why even the symbolic stage-play was not started without blood. [19] When Moses had read the entire script to the people, he took the blood of calves, together with water, scarlet wool and branches of hyssop, and sprinkled the script and all the people. [20] He said, "This is the blood of the symbolic healing plan which God has given you to act out." [21] In the same way, he sprinkled with the blood both the tabernacle and all the props used in the play. [22] In fact, the script requires that nearly everything be symbolically cleansed with blood, because without the shedding of blood, there could be no restoration to God's original ideal; without the death of Christ, we would not know the true, loving character of God and could not be restored to God's original ideal for mankind.

Heb 9:23 For the script to be accurate, it was necessary that the earthly model of God's heavenly temple be purified with the blood of these animal sacrifices; but the heavenly-designed Spirit temple itself needed purifying with the truth and righteousness only Christ's self-sacrifice could provide.

[24] For Christ did not enter a man-made, stone-and-mortar sanctuary that was only a copy of the true heavenly temple designed and built by God; he entered heaven itself, and now appears as the representative from earth in God's great heavenly counsel — in the living sanctuary built by God from the billions of intelligent loyal beings surrounding his throne. [25] And he entered heaven not in order to be sacrificed over and over again — the way the earthly high priest enters the Most Holy Place every year with animal blood; [26] absolutely not! For that would mean he would have to die repeatedly since the creation of the world. But he

appeared at the proper time, and only needed to sacrifice himself once: to reveal the truth about God, expose the lies of Satan, develop the Remedy, and bring all things into unity with God. 27 Just as everyone is destined to die once and reap the eternal destiny they have chosen, 28 so Christ sacrificed himself once to restore trust in God and purge selfishness from the hearts and minds of as many people as are willing; and he will come a second time—not to remove selfishness from the hearts and minds, but to remove the last residual traces of death, disease and the scars of sin, and to restore to complete perfection those who are waiting for him.

10 The script (also known as "the Law of Moses") was only a shadow—a stage play, a symbolic acting out—of the wonderful joys, blessings, health and happiness that are coming; it was not reality itself. This is why the law—the symbolic system—can never, by the repeated rituals year after year, perfectly heal and restore those who practice its rites. 2 If animal sacrifices could somehow actually heal and restore the worshiper to Godlikeness of character, then would not the sacrifices ceased to be offered, for everyone would have been healed, and there would have been no more sickness of heart or mind to remove? 3 Instead, the animal sacrifices were annual reminders of our sick and dying condition, 4 as it is impossible for the death of bulls and goats to heal our hearts and minds and restore us to Christlikeness.

Heb 10:5 Therefore, when Christ himself came into the world, he said:

"You never desired sacrifices and offerings,
    but you prepared a body for me;
Heb 10:6 burnt offerings and sin
    offerings are not what your heart longed for.
Heb 10:7 Then I said, 'Here I am—

I am the one written about in the Scriptures—
I have come to fulfill your will of love, to reveal your true character, and to expose the lies of Satan, O God.'"

Heb 10:8 First he said, "You did not desire sacrifices and offerings; burnt offerings and sin offerings were not what your heart longed for" (although they were exactly what the script directed to be done). 9 Then he said, "Here I am; I have come to fulfill your will of love, to reveal the truth about your character, and to expose the lies of Satan." He set aside the stage play, the symbolism, the shadowy drama, and revealed the reality—the truth. 10 And by that truth, we have been won back to trust and subsequently healed in hearts and minds, and made Christlike in character; all this was made possible by one single event—the loving self-sacrifice of Jesus Christ whereby he overcame selfishness with love.

Heb 10:11 Day after day earthly priests stand and act out their part in the religious drama; again and again they reenact the same lesson, offering the same sacrifices which can never actually transform the heart or heal the mind. 12 But Jesus Christ voluntarily sacrificed himself once, and that one sacrifice was sufficient to achieve Remedy for sin. And having achieved the Remedy, he resumed his place at God's right hand. 13 Now he waits for the Day when even his enemies will bow before him, 14 because by his one self-sacrifice he actually transforms and perfectly heals those who are being made holy.

Heb 10:15 The Holy Spirit also confirms that his sacrifice was for the purpose of healing and transforming us. First he says:

Heb 10:16 "This is the healing plan I will
    make anew with mankind
    after that time, declares the Lord:
I will recreate and cleanse them, and
    restore my law of love in their

minds, and write my principles of benevolence on their hearts."

Heb 10:17 Then he adds:

"I will never need to think about their sin-sickness again."

Heb 10:18 And when the mind and heart have been healed, there is no longer need for further treatment to cure the illness.

Heb 10:19 Therefore, brothers and sisters, since Jesus died to bring us the truth about God and to eradicate selfishness from humanity, we no longer need to be afraid but can confidently enter the Most Holy Place—God's very presence — 20 because Christ's death revealed the truth about God and ripped open the veil of lies told by Satan that blinded our minds, and destroyed the infection of selfishness that separated us from him. 21 And since we have this great ministering priest who ministers the truth to all, 22 let the truth permeate us, cleansing, transforming and changing us as we draw near to God in heart, mind, purpose, method, principle and character, 23 so that we may have ultimate confidence and trust in him who has revealed himself to be completely trustworthy. 24 And think constantly how we can work with God to help each other to grow in character to be like Jesus. 25 Don't stop meeting together, as some have done, but continue to encourage each other, and do so even more as you see the Day of our ultimate deliverance approaching.

Heb 10:26 If we deliberately reject the truth about God and his loving, life-promoting methods, and instead—after God sacrificed everything to bring us this healing truth—continue to practice self-destructive methods, no further remedy remains: 27 only the inevitable consequences of unrestrained selfishness—the total destruction of character, perversion of mind, and abject panic and fear when God unveils his life-giving glory which transforms the righteous but consumes the wicked.

28 In the symbolic stage play—which was designed to reveal the truth about God and his plan to heal—anyone who rejected the script of Moses was terminated from the group on the testimony of two or three witnesses. 29 How much more certain will the agonizing death be for those who reject the Son of God (the only Remedy for our terminal condition), who treat as poisonous the healing truth that his death revealed, and who reject God's Spirit that enlightens the mind with this life-saving Remedy? 30 For we know him who said, "It is up to me to determine when someone is beyond healing—when someone has rejected the only healing cure; I will decide when to let them go;" and again, "The Lord will accurately diagnose his people." 31 It will be horrible for those who remain God's enemies to experience his unveiled goodness and realize all they have rejected, and experience the full weight of their own guilt.

Heb 10:32 Remember those first days of recovery when you had just begun to internalize the healing truth: you stood firm for what is right and healthy in the great battle against the tormenting forces of selfishness, both internal and external. 33 Sometimes you were attacked publicly with name-calling or even physical assault; at other times you stood up and supported fellow believers who were being mistreated. 34 Your hearts went out to those imprisoned for this cause, and when your properties were seized, you remained joyful because you knew they couldn't take your possessions of real worth—God's love, a new heart, a healthy mind, and life eternal.

Heb 10:35 So don't become discouraged and lose confidence; your trust will be richly rewarded. 36 Maintain your focus and continue to implement God's methods in your lives, and you will receive all that he has promised; 37 for in the grand history of the cosmos, it is just a very short time until

The Remedy

"He who is coming to get us
   will come and will not delay.
Heb 10:38 And those who are set right
   with me will live their lives
   trusting me;
but if any stop trusting and turn
   away,
   my heart will break over them."
Heb 10:39 But we are not those who stop
trusting and turn away into the path of
self-destruction and death; we are
those who trust God and are healed.

11 Now, trust comes from our understanding with God, because
he has demonstrated that he is trustworthy to fulfill what he has promised.
And by trusting in him—the one who
made the promises—we are confident
of what we hope for, and are sure of
what we do not yet see. 2 This is what
the patriarchs were commended for.

Heb 11:3 By trust, which has been established on the evidence of God's trustworthiness, we understand that the
universe was created by God's command and that what is seen was not
made out of pre-existing materials.

Heb 11:4 By trust, Abel cooperated with
God to offer a sacrifice designed to
reveal the consequences of unrestrained selfishness; but Cain did not.
By trust, Abel was set right in heart
and mind with God and was commended when God spoke well of his
cooperation in revealing the truth. And
by trust he still reveals the truth, even
though he is dead.

Heb 11:5 By trusting God, Enoch was
completely healed and transformed,
and was taken right into heaven without experiencing death; he could not
be found on earth because God had
taken him away. Before he was taken,
he was commended as one who pleased
God. 6 But without trust in God, it is
impossible to please him. Those who
come to God must do more than believe that he exists: they must recognize the truth of his absolute trustworthiness of character as revealed in

Christ, and understand that he desires
to heal and restore all those who trust
him. Otherwise, fear will never be removed.

Heb 11:7 It was trust in God that caused
Noah to heed God's warning about rain
and flooding that had never been seen.
So he did what God said—he built an
ark to save his family. His trust condemned the untrusting world, and he
became the recipient and conduit of
the healing truth that comes by trust.

Heb 11:8 Because he trusted God, Abraham, when called to go to a far land
that would be his inheritance, listened
and went, even though he didn't actually know anything about the land or
where he was going. 9 Based on his confidence in God, he made his home in
the land promised to him, even though
he was like a stranger in a foreign
country; he lived in tents, as did his
son Isaac and grandson Jacob, who
were also heirs of God's promise. 10 He
wasn't concerned with earthly palaces,
because he was looking forward to living in the city whose foundation, archi-
tect and builder is God.

Heb 11:11 By trust, Abraham and Sarah
—even though their bodies were old
and well past childbearing—were enabled to generate a pregnancy and give
birth to a son, because they knew that
the one who had promised is absolutely
trustworthy. 12 And so, from these two
people (old and nearly dead), came descendants as numerous as the stars in
the sky or the sand by the seashore.

Heb 11:13 All of these people were living
in trust, confident in God when they
died. They did not receive all the
things promised, but they understood
them in their minds and rejoiced in
their reality. And they openly acknowledged that they were strangers and
aliens, and not part of this selfish
earth. 14 They were making it plainly
known that they wanted a different
land—a land of their own. 15 And they
didn't want the land they had left, for
they could have easily returned from

where they had come. [16]No; they were longing for a better country—a land free from selfishness, disease, death, crime and exploitation, where guards, police and security are no longer needed—they were longing for heaven. Therefore God is honored to be known as their God (for they value his methods of love, truth, and freedom) and he has prepared an eternal home for them.

Heb 11:17 By trust, Abraham—when God provided him with an opportunity for victory over fear and self-promotion—chose to trust God and offered Isaac as a sacrifice. He who had received the promises was ready to offer his only son, [18]even though he clearly knew that God had said, "It is through Isaac that your offspring will be recognized and the promises fulfilled." [19]But Abraham reasoned that if God could provide Isaac to two barren people, then he could also raise him from the dead (and symbolically, he did receive Isaac back from the dead).

Heb 11:20 By trust in God, Isaac blessed Jacob and Esau, confident in their future and in the fulfillment of God's promises.

Heb 11:21 By trust, Jacob—even though he was dying—didn't lose confidence for a moment, but blessed each of Joseph's sons, and praised God while leaning on his staff.

Heb 11:22 By trust in God, Joseph, when his life was almost over, did not waver but spoke confidently about the deliverance of Israel from Egypt and gave instructions regarding the burial of his bones.

Heb 11:23 Because of their trust in God, Moses' parents were not afraid of the king's edict, and realizing that Moses was a special child, they hid him for three months after his birth.

Heb 11:24 It was by trust that Moses, when he became an adult, refused to be known as Pharaoh's grandson. [25]Instead, he chose to be mistreated as a slave with God's people rather than enjoy the transient pleasures of selfishness. [26]He regarded personal disgrace for the glory of Christ of far greater importance and value than all the earthly treasures of Egypt, because he was looking beyond this selfish world—to the world of perfect health and happiness to come. [27]By trust, he left Egypt, not afraid of the angry king; he endured because he saw the absolute goodness and perfection of him who is invisible. [28]By understanding trust, he cooperated with God in initiating the symbolic teaching script: he kept the Passover and sprinkled blood on the doorposts so that the destroyer of the firstborn would pass by the firstborn of Israel.

Heb 11:29 By trust, the people walked through the Red Sea on dry ground, but when the Egyptian army tried to follow—they were drowned.

Heb 11:30 By trust in God, the people marched around Jericho for seven days, and the walls fell.

Heb 11:31 By trust in God, the prostitute Rahab forsook all she knew and aligned herself with God's people. She chose to hide the Israelite spies, and was not killed with those who opposed God.

Heb 11:32 And how much more do I have to say? How many more lives do I have to recount? I don't need to remind you about Gideon, Barak, Samson, Jephthah, David, Samuel, and the prophets [33]who through their trust in God conquered kingdoms, administered God's healing methods, received the promised blessings, shut the lions' mouths, [34]cooled the heat of the flames, escaped being killed by the sword, and had their weakness turned into strength and became unstoppable in battle, annihilating God's enemies.

[35]Women had their dead loved ones resurrected and brought back to them; others were tortured but refused to compromise the truth to gain their freedom, so they will gain the resurrection of life. [36]Some were mocked, others

beaten, while still others were put in shackles or imprisoned. [37] Some were stoned, others sawed in two, and still others put to death by the sword. They lived in poverty, wearing animal skins, and were constantly ridiculed and mistreated: [38] this selfish, sick world was not worthy of them. They lived in desolate places, wandering in deserts and mountains and hiding in caves.

Heb 11:39 All these people were commended for their trust in God, yet none of them received the fulfillment of all that was promised. [40] But don't get discouraged, for God has planned something much better for us: They and we together will be perfectly healed, and will rejoice together in the earth made new.

12 Therefore, since we are surrounded with so much evidence of God's goodness and with so many people who have experienced God's healing power that comes through trust, let us rid ourselves of everything that obscures our view of God (and of selfishness with its desires that so easily distract and damage) and let us diligently finish the treatment course laid out for us. [2] Let us fix our minds on Jesus—the perfect revelation of God—who establishes and fully matures our trust in God. For the joy of healing and restoring God's creation, Jesus endured the cross, nullifying its shame, and sat down at the right hand of the throne of God. [3] Consider the significance of all that Christ has done: The all-powerful Creator permitted his creatures to torture and kill him rather than use his power against them! So don't get tired, or give up, or lose heart.

Heb 12:4 In your struggle against selfishness, you have not yet had to lay down your life so that others might live. [5] And you have forgotten that God loves you as his children, for the Scripture says:

"My child, don't make fun of the
    Lord's treatment

and don't get discouraged when
    he sets you straight,
Heb 12:6 because the Lord disciplines
    those he loves,
and he works to heal everyone who
    becomes his child."

Heb 12:7 Endure difficulties as opportunities for growth: God is treating you as his children. For what father doesn't want his children to be healthy, and grow, and mature—and what child is not disciplined by their father? [8] If you do not experience God working to heal, mature, and improve you (and God works to heal everyone), then you are illegitimate children and not his true sons and daughters—you have rejected his offer of kinship. [9] Think about it: We have all had human fathers who instructed and corrected us, and we love and respect them for it. How much more should we willingly participate in the healing plan with the Father of all intelligent beings, and live! [10] Our fathers worked with us and taught us for just a few years, to the best of their ability; but God works to heal us for eternity, that we may partake of his perfect goodness and love. [11] No discipline or therapy is enjoyable at the time—it's painful! But if intelligently cooperated with, it results in healing of mind, development of Christlike character, and peace of heart.

Heb 12:12 Therefore, stiffen your upper lip and straighten your spine, and redouble your determination to stay the healing course. [13] "Remove the obstacles to your recovery" so that the infection of selfishness may not permanently deform your character, but rather that you may be healed.

Heb 12:14 Do all in your power to live peacefully with all people and to be Christlike, for without a loving, gentle, humble, Christlike character, no one will see God. [15] Be sure that no one squanders God's graciousness and instead permits bitterness, resentment, vengeance, malice, anger and the like to grow within and damage many. [16] Be sure that no one permits lust or sexual immorality to grow within, or be completely self-indulgent and godless like Esau, who had such little self-control that for a single meal he sold his inheritance. [17] Afterward, as you well know, even though he sought the blessing and his inheritance with tears, it was too late: it had already been given to his brother.

Heb 12:18 You have not come to a mountain, like Sinai—that you can touch, or that is burning with fire, or is covered in darkness or gloomy storm clouds — [19] or to the sounds of trumpets, or to a voice that spoke words so pure that those who heard it, while still preferring selfishness, became so distraught that they begged not to hear the voice again. [20] And because they were so infected with selfishness and guilt that they couldn't survive in God's presence, God, in order to protect them, put up a barrier and commanded: "If even an animal touches the mountain, it must be stoned." [21] And Moses, seeing the rebelliousness and hardness of the people, was so terrified that they would ignore God's warning, that he said, "I tremble with fear."

Heb 12:22 But you have come into the reality (of which the symbols only pointed to), to Mount Zion, the New Jerusalem—the heavenly city of the living God—and you are part of that city. You have come to join millions upon millions of angels rejoicing in God's presence, [23] into the heavenly sanctuary—the true church of Christ— whose identities are stored in heaven. You have come to God—the source and standard of righteousness for all people; to the archived individualities of righteous human beings perfectly restored into Christlikeness of character; [24] to Jesus—the conduit and administrator of God's healing plan; and to the reality of God's true nature and character, which was much more potently revealed and disseminated when Christ died than in the symbols offered by Abel.

Heb 12:25 Be certain that you do not reject him when he speaks. If those at Sinai could find no other healing solution after they rejected him when he revealed himself in symbols, how much less will we find it if we turn away from the truth about God, revealed when he came personally from heaven? [26] At Sinai, his presence shook the earth and the mountain, but he has promised, "Once more I will shake not only the earth but the entire universe." [27] The words "once more" indicate that God will finally and fully reveal himself and remove the lies that have misrepresented him, thus purifying all things so that all things in harmony with him will remain.

Heb 12:28 Therefore, since we are receiving a kingdom built on God's methods and principles that can never be shaken, let us rejoice and worship God in harmony with his ways, in reverence and awe, [29] for our "God is a consuming fire"—a consuming fire of love, holiness, purity, righteousness, goodness, and truth.

13 Continue to always be conduits of God's love and keep on loving each other as brothers and sisters. [2] Don't forget to be generous and hospitable, even to strangers; for at times, you will be entertaining angels without even realizing it. [3] Be compassionate to those in prison, just as if you were in prison with them; and also be compassionate to those who are abused and mistreated, just as if you were abused and mistreated with them.

Heb 13:4 Marriage is a sacred union, the joining of two separate individuals in love, in heart, in mind, in devotion, and ultimately—bodily, to bring forth new life in their image from the outflow of their joined love. All of this is designed in order for created beings to experience, as far as they possibly can, the joy the Godhead experiences from their unity and loving creation of new life. Thus love in the marriage is not to

The Remedy

be betrayed, for God will not prevent the damage and self-inflicted consequences that occur from betrayal and sexual deviance. [5] Don't get entrapped with greed, but be content with what you have, for God has said,

"I will never abandon you, nor will I turn my back on you."

[Heb 13:6] Therefore, we can confidently say,

"I will not be afraid, because the Lord watches over me.

What can people do to me?"

[Heb 13:7] Remember those who brought you the good news about God as revealed in Jesus Christ. Think about what they have said and also their healthy lifestyles, and follow their example, [8] but the best example to follow is Jesus himself, who is the same yesterday, today, and forever.

[Heb 13:9] Be thinkers: Examine the evidence and don't get caught up in all kinds of strange teachings that misrepresent God and are not supported by evidence and truth. It is good to open our minds to the truth about God's graciousness which brings transformation of character, but ceremonial foods cannot heal the mind or transform the heart of those who eat them. [10] We have a source of healing truth that those who persist in promoting the symbolic system refuse to accept.

[Heb 13:11] The earthly high priest carries the blood of animals into the Most Holy Place of the earthly temple to symbolize the truth of God's character—as revealed in the life and death of Jesus—being taken into the heart and mind, but the bodies of the animals are burned outside the city. [12] And so Jesus was crucified and died (outside the city) in order that the people might internalize the truth about God into their hearts and minds and thus be fully healed and restored to unity with God. [13] Let us then go to him, and follow him and be loyal to him regardless of all human opinion, bearing stigma, or shame, or disgrace, just as he did

for us. [14] Here on this earth, there is nothing that will last, so become part of that everlasting heavenly city that is to come.

[Heb 13:15] Through Jesus—through the truth he has brought that won us back to trust and through his continual work in our hearts and minds to heal and transform—let us continually offer to God the praise of transformed lives, the fruit of Christlike character. [16] And remember always to practice God's methods of love—beneficence, sharing, and giving to others—for such service reveals God's methods and is pleasing to him.

[Heb 13:17] Humbly follow the Christlike leadership of those in authority. They work to protect you from danger and assist you in growth, and they take their responsibilities seriously. Listen to them and cooperate with them eagerly, so their work will be filled with success and joy; and don't burden them, for burdening them will only undermine their ability to help you.

[Heb 13:18] Remember us when you talk with God. We are confident that our consciences are clear and our lives honor God in every way, [19] but I would appreciate you asking God to open the way for me to come to you as soon as possible.

[Heb 13:20] May the God of peace, who, through the truth of his character of love and his eternal plan to heal and restore, overcame the power of selfishness and death and brought back from the dead our Lord Jesus—the great Shepherd of the sheep— [21] recreate in you every faculty, ability and capability necessary for doing his will, and may he accomplish in us and with us what is pleasing to him, through Jesus Christ, to whom be praise and honor for ever and ever. Amen.

[Heb 13:22] Brothers and sisters, take it to heart and think seriously about my words of exhortation, for I have written only a short letter, and there is so much more to say.

Heb 13:23 Our brother Timothy has been released and if he arrives soon, I will accompany him to see you.

Heb 13:24 Greetings to all your leaders and all God's people from all those in Italy. 25 May God's graciousness be with you all.

James

1 James, a humble servant of God and the Lord Jesus Christ, to the heirs of the promise made to Abraham, scattered around the world: Greetings.

Jm 1:2 My brothers and sisters in God's family, I want you to rejoice and keep a positive attitude whenever you face troubles of various kinds, ³ because every trial exercises your trust in God —which overcomes fear and selfishness—and builds a confident, steadfast application of the Remedy. ⁴ And this steadfast engagement in God's treatment must be completed so that you may be fully healed, mature, and like Christ in character—not lacking anything. ⁵ If any of you don't understand God's methods, if any are confused in your thinking or lack wisdom, ask God—who doesn't cast blame, but enthusiastically gives wisdom to all who ask—and it will be given to you. ⁶ But when you ask, ask with the sure and confident knowledge that he longs to give you what you ask: do not waver back and forth in fear and uncertainty like a fishing bobber tossed about on ocean waves, for your fear will obstruct your ability to receive what he longs to give you. ⁷ Those consumed by fear will not think they can receive anything from the Lord: ⁸ they are unstable, controlled by emotions, and can't make up their minds about anything.

Jm 1:9 The member of God's family who is poor by worldly standards should rejoice in their high position in God's kingdom, ¹⁰ and anyone rich in the world's eye should not celebrate earthly wealth but cherish their spiritual humility, because those relying on earthly wealth will wither and die like wildflowers. ¹¹ Think how the hot sun scorches, and the plant withers: its beauty fails, and it slowly dies. In the same way, those who rely on earthly riches will age, wither, and fade away while striving to get ahead.

Jm 1:12 But the person who steadfastly continues in God's treatment despite trials, difficulties or discomfort, will be healed and receive eternal life—as promised by God to those who love and trust him.

Jm 1:13 When tempted to deviate from God's design for life, no one should ever say, "God is tempting me," for God is the source of life and cannot be tempted by deviations from His design, nor does he tempt anyone. ¹⁴ Each person is tempted when they are deceived, pulled and enticed by their own fear-based, self-centered feelings and desires. ¹⁵ Then, when the selfish desire is accepted by the will, it results in choices that deviate from God's design for life; and choices that deviate from God's design for life result in death.

Jm 1:16 So please, my dear family, don't be fooled! ¹⁷ Everything good, healthy and beneficial originates in heaven and comes down from the Father who created the universe. He is always good and will never alter his methods of love. He does not waver, and he is certainly not the source of darkness and death! ¹⁸ He is the source of life, and he chose to give us new life through Jesus—the true expression of God—that we might be the masterpieces of all his creation.

Jm 1:19 Remember this, my dear Christian family: Seek to understand before seeking to be understood, and don't be quick to take offense, ²⁰ for person's outrage is based on selfishness and does not promote restoration of Christlike character as God desires. [21] So rid yourselves of the numerous influences that debase, defile and damage the character, and humbly nurture the Remedy placed in you, which can heal you.

Jm 1:22 Don't play games with yourselves by merely listening to God's prescription—apply it and do what it says! [23] Anyone who simply listens to God's prescription and doesn't apply it to their life is like a person who looks at their face in a mirror, [24] sees the dirt, then walks away without washing it off, and eventually forgets about it. [25] But those who examine themselves honestly in the light of God's law of love—the law that heals and frees from fear and selfishness—and continue to do this daily, not ignoring what is learned but applying it diligently, experience happiness as they are healed and transformed.

Jm 1:26 Those who feel good about themselves—believing they are well but have no control over what they say—are in denial of their own worsening condition, and the treatment program they are in doesn't work. [27] The treatment program that God our Father recognizes as effective is this: actively loving others, caring for orphans and widows, and avoiding defiling self with the selfishness of the world.

2 My family of God: As people who have taken the Remedy of our Lord Jesus Christ, and as you seek to emulate him in all you do—don't discriminate. [2] Imagine that a famous person dressed in expensive attire and a poor stranger wearing dirty, torn clothes come to your meeting. [3] If you fawn all over the important person, paying them special attention and giving them the best seat, but ignore the poor person, leaving them to stand in the back or to sit on the floor, [4] haven't you failed to love all people equally? Haven't you selfishly sought to ingratiate yourself with the person you judged to be more desirable?

Jm 2:5 Listen carefully, my brothers and sisters: God has chosen to take the people whom the world scorns—those who are poor in the eyes of the world but rich in spiritual health—and restore them to his original design, making them heirs of the kingdom of love which he promised to those who love him; [6] yet you look down on and belittle the poor. But is it not the wealthy and politically connected who manipulate, exploit and harass you? Aren't they the ones who sue you and bring allegations against you in the courts? [7] Isn't it the rich and famous who mock and make fun of the humble character of Christ which you have accepted?

Jm 2:8 To genuinely live in harmony with God's majestic law—the design he constructed life to operate upon, and which is taught in Scripture: "Love your neighbor as yourself"—is doing what is right. [9] But if you display favoritism the rich and powerful while ignoring and degrading the poor and weak, you violate God's principles of love and are diagnosed as being out of harmony with his design for life. [10] For whoever loves in one area but lives selfishly in another is still out of harmony with God's design. [11] For he who gave us the prescription "Don't commit adultery," also prescribed "Do not murder." If you don't engage in adultery but do commit murder, you are still operating outside of God's design for life and his recovery plan.

Jm 2:12 Live like people who understand how God built life to operate: act like those who are going to be diagnosed by the standard that health and freedom are founded upon, [13] because one's true condition will be diagnosed accurately, without any covering-over of the actual terminal state of the one who has not been restored to selfless love. But selfless love heals our terminal condition!

Jm 2:14 My brothers and sisters, what

good does it do for a person to claim they trust God and follow his treatment if they don't actually do what is right? Does confidence in God's ability to heal, and the effectiveness of the Remedy, do any good if the Remedy isn't taken and applied? [15] Suppose a brother or sister is hungry, homeless, or without clothing: [16] If one of you says, "I am praying for you and hope you keep warm and find something to eat," but doesn't do anything to help, your prayer does nothing to help either you or them, but instead misrepresents God and hardens your heart. [17] Similarly, claiming trust in God without choosing to apply his treatment plan to your life has no healing effect, and your condition remains terminal.

Jm 2:18 But some will argue, "Gentiles simply trust God, while Jews work to be saved." Show me how a person gets well by trusting but not applying God's treatment to their lives, and I will show that real healing only happens when we do both—trust God and follow his treatment plan. [19] How does it help you to believe there is only one God? Satan and his cohort of demons also believe that and still live in terror.

Jm 2:20 You ineffectual people! Must you be shown that trust in a remedy without applying it is useless? [21] Don't you understand that our forefather Abraham was put right with God when his trust was applied in offering Isaac on the altar? [22] Can't you see that it is his trust that caused him to act as he did? His trust became effectual by what he did. [23] This is the meaning of the Scripture that says, "Abraham trusted God and was restored to harmony with God," and he was therefore God's friend. [24] Do you understand that a person is restored to harmony with God by the application of God's methods through trust, and not simply by trust without application?

Jm 2:25 This is exactly how Rahab the prostitute was put right with God: her trust in God led her to act—to risk her life by protecting the spies rather than protecting herself—and she sent them off a different way. [26] Just as the body without the breath of life is lifeless and does nothing, so trust without application is useless and does nothing.

3 My brothers and sisters, few of you are ready to become teachers, because those who teach must function at the highest standards. [2] All of us make mistakes, but it is the ones who always speak the truth and never speak evil who are healed, mature, and able to maintain governance over their entire being.

Jm 3:3 A bit in the mouth of a horse can turn the entire animal. [4] A ship, though large and fighting powerful winds, is steered by a small rudder wherever the pilot wants it to go. [5] So too the tongue, though a small part of the body, can brag, exaggerate, and even make up stories. It only takes a small spark to start a forest burning. [6] The wrong words can start an inferno: lies have infected the cosmos with evil. They damage the entire being, searing the conscience and burning the heart, but lies will be consumed by eternal fire.

Jm 3:7 Humans have tamed all kinds of animals, birds, reptiles and creatures of the sea, [8] but no one can make their words harmless. The mouth speaks venomous words, expressing the chaos and evil within the heart.

Jm 3:9 One moment we praise God our Father, and the very next moment we curse the very men and women created in his image. [10] Think about it: Out of the same mouth come both praises and curses. My brothers and sisters, this is wrong, and it must stop. [11] Does a spring bring forth fresh water one moment and sewage the next? [12] Can a fig tree produce olives, or a grapevine bear figs? Neither can a sewer produce fresh water.

Jm 3:13 Who of you is wise enough to

understand God's methods and principles? Then show it by living in harmony with God's design for life—a life of love in action, giving in humility to bless and uplift others. [14] But to cherish self-centered, arrogant, mean-spirited, jealous motives in the heart misrepresents God and defames the truth. [15] Such principles do not originate in God nor do they come from heaven, but are profane and destructive, and originate in Satan. [16] For selfishness, envy, and all violations of God's law of love break his design for life and cause chaos, disease, suffering, and everything evil.

Jm 3:17 [17] Real wisdom originates in heaven and is always pure, healing, restorative, kind, compassionate, selfless, merciful, peaceful, transformational, unbiased, and sincere. [18] Healers who share the Remedy in peace produce a gathering of the righteous.

4 Why is there so much hostility, fighting and arguments among you? Because the survival-of-the-fittest instinct controls you: [2] if you want something but don't get it, you are willing to kill. You are selfish, coveting what you cannot have, constantly fighting, trying to get for yourselves. You do not obtain because you do not seek God. [3] And when you finally do ask God—because your motives are selfish, and because you focus only on self-gratification—you don't get what you're asking for because God doesn't use his power to supply you with means to further damage yourselves.

Jm 4:4 [4] You disloyal and unfaithful people! Don't you realize that embracing the me-first, survival-of-the-fittest principle of this world is warring against God? Anyone who allies themself with this selfish world chooses to be an enemy of our God of love. [5] Don't you get it? The Scripture is clear: God longs intensely for you and gives his Spirit to live in you [6] to graciously heal you. That is why the Scripture says: "God opposes selfishness, arrogance and pride, but heals the selfless."

Jm 4:7 [7] Surrender yourselves to God and his treatment. Tell the devil "No," and you will escape him. [8] Move close to God, and God will come close to you. You selfish people! Stop choosing to indulge your desires. Stop going back and forth between love and selfishness, and purify your hearts with love. [9] Stop playing around and get real! Let your hearts break: Cry over your terminal condition, admit that you are sick, and stop pretending that all is well. [10] Then go humbly to the Lord, and he will heal and restore you.

Jm 4:11 [11] Brothers and sisters, don't disparage each other. When you demean one another, you distort God's law of love and make God's methods appear questionable. When you misrepresent God's law of love, you are no longer living in harmony with it but acting as if you have a better design for life than God. [12] There is only one Designer of life and one Diagnostician who is able to heal our terminal condition. So who do you think you are to diagnose your neighbor as "beyond healing"?

Jm 4:13 [13] Pay close attention—especially those who say, "In the next few days, we are moving to a new city and will live there a year, open a business and make huge profits." [14] You don't know what the future holds. Your life is like a vapor trail: here one minute and gone the next. You might not even be alive in a year, so stop being so rigid with your preplanning—it only increases your stress. [15] Instead, trust God with your future and how things turn out. Learn to say, "If it is in harmony with God's plan for my life, then that is what I will do," and you will worry so much less. [16] As it is, you focus on yourselves: you brag, boast, and try to control everything in order to advance your own agenda. All selfishness is destructive. [17] Anyone who knows God's methods of love but chooses selfishness deviates from God's design for life.

5 Now, those of you who have strayed from the path of love and have pursued self-advancement through riches can start crying and grieving because a terrible pain is coming. ²Your riches will erode, and your fine clothes will become rags. ³Your hoarded gold and silver are toxic: their poison corrupts—eating away your character like fire consumes flesh. Right up to the end, you selfishly take to increase your net worth. ⁴The reality of what you have done—cheating your workers out of their wages—has warped your character and speaks out against you. The Lord Almighty has heard the cries of those you have injured. ⁵Selfishly, you indulged your every pleasure, but all you accomplished was to feed and worsen your terminal condition, ⁶and then you blamed the innocent and healthy for it. You murdered people who did nothing to you.

Jm 5:7 Brothers and sisters, be patient. Wait for the Lord to come back. Consider the farmer, how he patiently waits for autumn and spring rains, and then for the crops to grow. ⁸Don't get discouraged, but stay compliant with God's plan, because the Lord's return draws closer every day. ⁹And don't harbor hostility toward others; to do so reveals how sick your own heart is. The One who diagnoses correctly is just outside the door.

Jm 5:10 Brothers and sisters, if you need an example of endurance when times are tough, remember the God's spokespersons who presented the truth about God. ¹¹We all know that those who persevere get well and are happy. You know about Job's perseverance and what the Lord finally did. That's because God genuinely cares and compassionately seeks to heal and restore.

Jm 5:12 Most importantly, be honest and truthful. Don't attempt to trick people or manipulate others by invoking various oaths, or calling on heaven, or earth, or anything else. Be so honorable that your "Yes" always means "Yes," and your "No" always means "No;" otherwise your mind will be warped, and your character debased.

Jm 5:13 Is anyone in trouble? Talk to God about it. Is anyone happy? Sing songs of praise. ¹⁴If anyone is sick, be sure to call the spiritual leaders to ask God to intervene, and to treat you with appropriate medicinals such as applying soothing oil, working in harmony with God's design, methods and principles. ¹⁵After asking God to intervene, trust him enough to follow his methods and principles. This will heal the character, and if it is in harmony with the Lord's plan, result in making the sick physically well; and the Lord will raise them up. If the illness is due to willful deviation from God's design, it won't matter once trust in God is restored and the ill are well again. ¹⁶So be sure to admit to one another where you have deviated from God's design, and request God's intervention and treatment plan for each other, so that you may be healed. The request of a person who lives in unity with God is powerful and effective.

Jm 5:17 Elijah was a man who lived in union with God. He understood God's methods and what God was trying to accomplish, so he earnestly asked God to hold back the rain, and it didn't rain for three and a half years. ¹⁸Later, when the time was right to accomplish God's plan, he asked God to send rain, and the sky poured down rain; and the earth produced its crops.

Jm 5:19 My brothers and sisters, if a person walks away from God's treatment plan, you should do all you can to bring them back.

²⁰For whoever turns a selfish person from the terminal path of self-indulgence will deliver them from death and make irrelevant a multitude of self-destructive acts.

1 Peter

1 Peter, an ambassador of Jesus Christ, to fellow citizens of God's kingdom of love and truth who are currently living throughout this world —in Pontus, Galatia, Cappadocia, Asia and Bithynia—as representatives of God's government:

²Before you were born, God determined to heal and purify you—transforming you to love others more than self—by the indwelling Spirit applying the Remedy of Jesus' victorious life.

May God's healing and transforming presence and peace be upon you without limit.

1Pet 1:3 Let the name and character of God, the Father of our Lord Jesus Christ, receive all glory, honor, and praise! In his great mercy, he has given us new life—healing, re-creation, and the cure for our terminal condition—through Jesus Christ's victorious resurrection from the dead. ⁴Not only that, but through Jesus we have a future without decay or death, a future that will endure forever and is kept safe in heaven, for we, ⁵by trust, have our minds shielded by God's power of love and truth until the Day of full healing and restoration, which will occur at the end of time. ⁶Rejoice greatly in this reality even though now, for a little while, you may suffer pain, grief, and trials of all kinds. ⁷These transient difficulties are allowed to come so that your confidence and trust in God— which is infinitely more valuable than gold, for even gold purified by fire will be destroyed—may be permanently established in your character, and result in praise, glory and honor to God when Jesus Christ comes again. ⁸Even though you have not laid eyes on him,

you love him; and even though you currently don't see him, you put your trust in him, and your hearts are overflowing with indescribable and perfect joy, ⁹for you are experiencing the inevitable result of your trust in God— the healing, restoration and re-creation of your hearts, minds and characters into God's perfect ideal.

1Pet 1:10 Regarding this healing and restoration: God's spokespersons, who taught God's gracious Remedy that would come to you, diligently and carefully searched for the truth ¹¹that would indicate the time and circumstances when Christ, through great suffering, would achieve victory over the infection that brings death, and restore God's glory in mankind, as the Spirit of Christ told them he would do. ¹²God revealed to them that their work in writing the Scripture was not for themselves but to benefit you, for they wrote about things that have now come to pass and have been told to you by those who have shared the good news about God with you by the Holy Spirit sent from heaven. Even the angels are studying these things and long for deeper understanding.

1Pet 1:13 Therefore, prepare your minds to think, to reason, to weigh out the issues, and actively apply the truth to your lives, attaining self-governance— control over your own selves. Keep your vision, goals and hopes fixed on the full healing and restoration that will occur when Jesus Christ comes again. ¹⁴As children who have thought through the issues and now understand God's principles and agree with his methods, no longer allow fear and selfish desires to control your actions as you did before you knew the truth about God. [15] But just as God is pure, undefiled and holy, accept his healing and live pure, undefiled and holy lives; [16] for God has said, "You will be pure and holy—just like me—for I am pure and holy."

[1Pet 1:17] Now that you are partaking of God's Remedy, are part of his family and are called by the Father's name, live your lives here on earth as visitors—with humble respect for others—for God freely allows every person to determine whether to accept his Remedy or not. [18] And you know very well that money, land or fame have not and can not free your minds from the infection of fear and selfishness you inherited from your parents; [19] but your minds were won back to love and trust in God when you understood and internalized the truth about God, revealed by Jesus—the perfect, sinless One. [20] He chose to reveal the truth about God—to be the Remedy—before the world was even created, but it was in these last days, for your sake, that he accomplished what he had previously chosen to do. [21] It is because of Jesus' life and death that the lies of Satan are exposed, fear is removed, trust in God is restored, and the human species is restored back to perfection; and it is God who called Jesus to arise from the dead, and who glorified him—as he was fulfilling God's purposes—therefore your trust and hope are in God.

[1Pet 1:22] Now that your hearts and minds have been cleansed and purified by your choice to accept, internalize and apply the truth—and as a result, your selfishness has been replaced with genuine love for others—you love one another deeply, completely, totally, from the heart. [23] For you have been recreated in mind, heart, and character: not from a defective self-centered template but from the perfect, eternal, immortal original—the living and everlasting character of God Himself!

[1Pet 1:24] "People are as fleeting as grass—all their glory and achievements are as transitory as the flowers of the field;
the grass withers and the flowers fade,
[25] but the character of the Lord stands forever."
And it was the truth about God's character, methods and principles as revealed by Christ that was preached to you.

2 Therefore rid yourselves of all manifestations of the infection of fear and selfishness such as malice, deceit, hypocrisy, envy, and slander of every kind, and notice how each of these harm others and promote self. [2] Instead of acting to promote self, become like newborn babies: not only craving the pure spiritual milk of love and truth, but trusting your Father to provide your needs, so that your minds and characters may be fully healed and you may grow to become mature friends of God. [3] Do this in confidence, as you have now experienced for yourselves that the Lord is truly good.

[1Pet 2:4] And as you come to Christ, who was rejected by people but was chosen by God and is precious to God because he is the living Foundation Stone of God's true temple, [5] realize that you also are living stones—the conscious, breathing, sentient building blocks—whom God is using to construct his eternal temple. You are a holy priesthood bringing intelligent, reasonable and loving self-sacrifice—that is in harmony with God's character of love—through your union with Jesus Christ. [6] This is exactly what the Scripture is talking about:
"See, I will put a Stone in the Land of Promise:
an especially chosen, perfect foundation Stone;
and whoever trusts in him and is set in harmony with him
will never be put to shame."

1Pet 2:7 For you, who know and trust God, this Stone is life's one true treasure; but to those who don't know or trust God,

"This Stone was thought to be
worthless, and rejected;
but it is actually the one upon whom
all life is built."
1Pet 2:8 "A Stone of pure love that trips
up selfish human beings,
and a Rock of holiness, humility
and truth, over whom the sinful,
proud and deceitful fall."

They trip and fall because they prefer selfishness to love, and unhealed selfishness is a terminal condition—exactly as God diagnosed.

1Pet 2:9 But you, who trust God and build upon the Stone, are a select and special people—royal ministers of God's healing Remedy, a clean and purified nation, a people whose hearts and minds are in unity and oneness with God—who with words and lives may commend him who called you out of the darkness of fear and selfishness into his wonderful light of truth and love. 10 Prior to the healing of your minds and hearts, you were not a family—but now you are the unified children of God; for you had previously not accepted God's merciful Remedy—but now you have received it.

1Pet 2:11 My dear friends, since you are now part of God's kingdom, you are his ambassadors and representatives; therefore do not choose to indulge selfish and sinful desires, as such indulgence damages the mind and warps the character. 12 Instead, live such selfless, loving and godly lives among the godless that though they may slander you, they may see your beneficent care for others and acknowledge God as righteous on the day he returns.

1Pet 2:13 Commit yourselves fully to the Lord's cause and glorify him by promoting the good news about God, and don't get diverted into politics: whether seeking to change rulers, 14 or governors, or judges who have been appointed to punish the guilty and reward those who do good. 15 For it is by God's design that you will reveal his character of love by doing good and thereby silence foolish people from saying stupid things, like accusing you of pursuing earthly power in order to control others. 16 Live as the free people you are in Christ, serving God and others in love and not indulging in evil. 17 Treat everyone with dignity: love and cherish your spiritual family, be in admiration and awe of God, and be respectful of earthly governments.

1Pet 2:18 If you are a slave, be respectful to your master and submit to their authority—not just to those who are kind and good, but also to those who are cruel and severe. 19 For God is pleased when we freely choose to honor him by graciously bearing unjust treatment and thereby revealing his character of selfless love. 20 How is God's healing of your character revealed if you endure a beating for doing wrong? But if you are beaten for doing good, and graciously endure it, this reveals the character of God and brings him honor. 21 This is what you were called to do: reveal God's character in your life, because Christ suffered for your healing and restoration—giving a perfect revelation of God—and you should model your life after his.

1Pet 2:22 "Christ never sinned, not even
in thought.
He never spoke a lie or practiced
deceit."

1Pet 2:23 When they called him every foul name imaginable, he was compassionate and did not seek revenge; when he was tortured, he forgave and made no threats. He understood the greater reality and entrusted himself to his Father who accurately assesses everyone's true condition. 24 He took upon himself our sinfulness (our terminal condition) and in his own person carried it upon the cross so that we could be freed from sin and live the right way—loving God and others more than ourselves. You have been healed by the Remedy procured by his painful ordeal. ²⁵ For you were like lost sheep wandering aimlessly in the world, but now you have come home to the Shepherd and Defender of your entire being.

3 In the same way, wives, by your conduct, actively seek to reveal God's true character to your husbands, so that even if they don't believe the Scriptures, they may be won over by your humble, loving service ²when they see genuine, selfless love in action. ³ The beauty that emanates from God cannot be revealed in outward trappings such as hairstyle, jewelry or designer clothes, so don't get tricked into making your external appearance your main concern. ⁴ Instead, real, godly beauty is found in a heart, mind and character that has been healed to be like Christ's—gentle and loving— and is of the highest worth in God's sight. ⁵ This is how the holy women of the past, who trusted God, made themselves beautiful: they lovingly sought the godly best for their husbands, ⁶ like Sarah, who graciously supported Abraham and called him 'my hero and leader.' You are truly heirs of Sarah if you give of yourself in love to build up your husband, and not give into fear and selfishness.

1Pet 3:7 If you are a husband, then be sure to always consider the needs of your wife and treat her with love, sacrificing yourselves for her good. Respect her as the weaker partner, but remember her equality to you as an heir of God's gracious gift of life. Do this so that you may experience the unity of love, and nothing will then interfere with your conversations with God.

1Pet 3:8 Finally, all of you are to be united in love, motive and principle, sharing a common vision and purpose, and harmoniously working together for the restoration of God's character in mankind. ⁹ Do not practice the principles of the world—repaying evil with

evil or insult with insult—but seek to bless, uplift and heal everyone, even your enemies. It is for this purpose—to be co-workers with God in healing humanity—that you were called, and that you may be healed in the process. ¹⁰ For the Scriptures say,

"Those who obtain eternal life and
happiness choose to love others
and refuse to gossip, speak evil,
or tell any lie or falsehood.
¹¹ They willfully reject evil and
selfishness and instead choose to
do good, sacrificing themselves
for others;
they always seek to heal and bring
peace.
¹² For God watches over those who
live rightly—in accordance with
his character of love—
and he hears all they have to say;
and the Lord works to eradicate evil
and selfishness,
and to heal all infected by it."

1Pet 3:13 Don't you see that if you are genuinely committed to God and eagerly practice his methods of love you cannot be stopped? ¹⁴ Even if you are attacked or persecuted for doing what is right, by forgiving and loving others you reveal God's true character and simultaneously are advancing to be more like him. So "do not fear for this mortal life as the world fears; and don't be frightened for a minute," ¹⁵ but make Christ the center of your heart, mind and character. Always be prepared to talk about God's character of love, as revealed in Jesus, to anyone who asks why you are hopeful in the face of persecution, trial, and difficulty. But be sure to do it with gentleness, kindness and respect, ¹⁶ with a pure heart and clear conscience, so that those who lie, gossip, and spread rumors about your ministry for Christ may be ashamed of their malicious ways.

1Pet 3:17 It is better, if God permits, to be persecuted for doing good than to suffer the results of doing evil, ¹⁸ for that is exactly what Christ did. He suffered terribly and died once in order to cure sinfulness—to provide a Remedy for all humanity and restore us to unity with God. In Christ, love vanquished selfishness, and righteousness overcame unrighteousness. He allowed the sin-sick to kill him, and in giving himself freely, he triumphed over the infection of selfishness and fear, and was renewed to life by the Spirit of love and truth. [19] It was through this same Spirit of love and truth that he preached to all humans, who were held in the bondage of sin. [20] Yes, it was Christ, working through the Spirit, who preached to those bound by sin in Noah's day. He was so patient with them, working constantly to reach them as Noah built the ark, yet only eight people responded and had a new life on the other side of that great flood. [21] The flood is symbolic of baptism: Just as those who responded to the Spirit in Noah's day and went through the water—safely in the ark—to a new life, those who follow the Spirit go through baptism to a new life in Christ today. This doesn't wash away dirt from the body, but it symbolizes the Spirit's cleansing of the conscience from fear and selfishness. You are healed by the life of Jesus Christ who rose from the dead [22] and is in heaven at God's right hand, directing the Spirit to take his perfect character and reproduce it in you. All heavenly intelligences recognize him as worthy and sovereign, and he is directing all the agencies of heaven for your healing.

4 Therefore model yourselves after Christ, who, when tempted to save himself, chose instead to sacrifice himself and thus suffered in his human nature. So, be like Jesus: love others first, and say "No" to temptations to act selfishly. Your selfish nature will suffer, but you will be done with sin. [2] As a result, right now on earth, you will no longer live your life controlled by feelings, passions and desires, but rather you will live intelligently—choosing to follow God's will—in harmony with the law of love. [3] You have surely spent enough time living like pagans and the ungodly who allow their impulses, desires and lusts to control them as they engage in orgies, debauchery, drunkenness, betrayal, and disgusting idolatry. [4] They think you are weird because you won't join them in debasing themselves, so they criticize and make fun of you. [5] But they will be speechless when they stand before God and have to explain to him why they rejected the Remedy—that he freely provided, and that cures all who accept it—whether they are currently living or dead. [6] This is the reason the good news about God has been proclaimed throughout all history—even to those who are now dead, but who were diagnosed while alive, as everyone is diagnosed—so that everyone could partake of the Remedy and have their character restored to perfect love, as God's character is perfect love.

1Pet 4:7 The end of life as we know it on planet earth is near. Therefore, keep your minds clear and sharp, and maintain governance of yourselves so that you can always talk clearly with God. [8] Above everything, love each other completely, because love destroys sinfulness. [9] Be hospitable and cheerful when doing so; don't serve others sullenly or out of obligation merely. [10] All of God's children should be conduits of his love, distributing the resources they have received to uplift, nourish and bless others in the knowledge of God's love. [11] If you have a message to give, remember that you are God's representative, so speak words that faithfully represent him. When you serve others, don't rely on your own strength, but let God's love flow through you to them so that it will be obvious that God is the one to whom praise is owed through Jesus Christ. To him be all glory, honor, power and praise forever and ever. Amen.

The Remedy

1Pet 4:12 Dear friends, don't be surprised by the painful trials you suffer. Don't think, "Why is this happening?" 13 but rejoice, recognizing that even though walking the healing path with Jesus is painful, it leads to joy as his glorious character is revealed in you. 14 If you are abused for being Christlike, be glad; it means that God's Spirit is restoring Christ's character in you. 15 Don't bring suffering upon yourself by breaking the law like a murderer, thief, common criminal, or even a meddler in other people's business, 16 but if you suffer because you live like Jesus—don't be ashamed or disheartened. Be confident and praise God that you bring honor to Christ's name, 17 because it is time for right judgment to begin with God's house; and if it has begun with us, what will happen to those who close their minds to the good news about God? 18 And

"If the healing process is agonizing
    for those who know God,
    what will happen to the ungodly—
    the sinners who reject God's
    healing Remedy?"

19 Therefore, those who suffer while complying with God's treatment program should commit themselves fully to their faithful Creator and continue to follow his good plan.

5 To the pastors and teachers among you, I call on you as a fellow pastor and teacher who witnessed Christ's sufferings, and one who also will share in the glorious re-creation to be revealed: 2 Protect God's flock selflessly, like loving shepherds, serving as guides and guardians—not out of obligation or requirement, but freely—as God designed for you to do. Watch over it willingly, not seeking reward or payment, but eager to serve others; 3 not like dictators exercising power and authority over those entrusted to their care, but modeling servant-leadership to your flock. 4 Then, when the Chief Shepherd returns, you will be crowned with the glory of Christ's perfection that will never fade away.

1Pet 5:5 Young people, respectfully listen to the counsel of those who are older, and follow their wise leadership. But all of you—old and young alike—treat each other with humble and loving service, because

"God is the opposite of self-exaltation,
    and his very nature opposes
    pridefulness;
he pours his healing power into the
    humble."

1Pet 5:6 Therefore, surrender yourselves under God's almighty healing hand that he might restore you, uplifting you to his ideal in due time. 7 Pour out all your worries, frustrations and burdens upon him, because he cares for you.

1Pet 5:8 Stay calm and keep a clear head: do not allow your emotions to take charge, because Satan, your enemy, is stalking around, roaring like a lion, seeking to consume you with fear and doubt. 9 But resist him and don't be afraid; keep your trust in God strong, because you know that your fellow believers throughout the world are also being attacked in the same way.

1Pet 5:10 Our loving God—full of all goodness and grace, who has called you to an everlasting future of perfection in Christ—will, after this brief suffering, completely recreate you, restoring you to free, self-governed beings who are strong in love. 11 Let his kingdom and dominion reign forever and ever. Amen.

1Pet 5:12 With the help of Silas, whom I love as a brother, I have written to you to encourage, uplift, and confirm that this is the truth about God. Embrace it and hold firm to it.

1Pet 5:13 Your sister church in Babylon sends you greetings, as does my son Mark.

14 Greet each other with an open heart of love. Peace to all of you who are in union with Christ.

2 Peter

1 Simon Peter, a serving friend and ambassador of Jesus Christ,

To all those who through the Remedy provided by our God and Savior Jesus Christ have experienced an abiding trust as pure and precious as ours:

2Pet 1:2 Grace and peace in ever-increasing abundance will be yours as you grow in your intimacy with God and Jesus our Lord.

2Pet 1:3 For God has poured out his divine energy to provide us the Remedy that brings life and heals our minds. He invites us into friendship and unity with himself through our knowledge of Jesus, who revealed the glory of God's true goodness.

4 Through these achievements, he has provided us with the Remedy to our terminal condition, free of charge. Incredibly, we are promised the greatest gift of all: We may partake of God's divine nature, be fully healed, and escape the corrosive and destructive ways of the selfish world.

2Pet 1:5 Because it is your desire to become more like God in character, then—in addition to trusting God—choose to do good; and in addition to doing good, study to know God's methods. 6 And in addition to knowing God and his methods, exercise self-discipline; and use your self-discipline to persevere in God's plan for you to grow in godliness. 7 And in godliness, be kind and affectionate to one another, and—above all—love! 8 For if your hearts are being healed, then you will develop these traits of character and you will not fail to reveal the truth about our Lord Jesus Christ. 9 But without these traits, people cannot comprehend God and his methods.

They fail to realize that God cleanses, heals, and renews the mind from fear and selfishness.

2Pet 1:10 So, my brothers and sisters, say "Yes" to God's invitation, and partake of the Remedy he has chosen to provide. Don't wait—do it right now! If you continue in his treatment plan, you will never turn back to selfishness: 11 rather, you will receive complete healing of mind, and restoration into the kingdom of love of our Lord and Savior Jesus Christ.

2Pet 1:12 Therefore, I will always remind you of the reality of God's kingdom of love, even though you have partaken of the Remedy and your characters are firmly established upon the truth you now possess. 13 It is right—as long as I live in this decaying old tent of a body—to use every opportunity to remind you of God's kingdom of love. 14 The Lord has let me know that I will pass away soon, 15 and I will use every tool at my disposal to ensure that after I am gone, you will always remember the truth of God's healing methods and principles of love.

2Pet 1:16 What we told you about the power of God and the coming of Christ—God's Son—to heal and restore humanity, was not some fairy tale made up by clever novelists; no way! We were eyewitnesses and saw for ourselves the beauty of his character and the glory of his majesty. 17 We saw Jesus honored and glorified by God the Father when he was clothed in heavenly light and God spoke from heaven saying, "This is my beloved Son; he is the one who fulfills my pleasure and in whom my heart rejoices." 18 Yes, we heard audibly the voice from heaven when we stood with Christ on the holy mountain.

2Pet 1:19 Do you realize the significance of what I am saying? The writings of God's spokespersons have been confirmed, and we can be certain of their ultimate fulfillment. So if you want wellness, then take seriously the written word, allowing its light and truth to shine forth and dispel the darkness of misunderstanding and the distortions about God. Do this until the day Christ returns and the Brilliant One is fully reproduced in your hearts. 20 And the first thing to remember when studying the Scripture is that no true prophecy is from the prophet's own opinion or interpretation. 21 Prophecy doesn't originate in the imagination of individual people, but people speak for God as the Holy Spirit illuminates their minds with truth.

2 In the past, among God's people were those who claimed to speak for God and bring his Remedy, but they did not speak for God at all, and they brought a false remedy. Likewise, there will be people among you who claim to teach God's truth and have God's Remedy but will teach lies. They will subtly introduce false remedies— destructive doctrines purported to heal but that will actually incite fear, shut down thinking, and damage the mind. They will even deny the Sovereign Lord who procured the Remedy, thus bringing rapid deterioration and destruction upon themselves. 2 There will be large numbers of people who embrace their corrupt ways while calling themselves Christians, thus causing the Remedy to be considered worthless. 3 In their eagerness for power, fame and wealth, these false teachers will mislead you with theories and doctrines they have made up on their own. Because of this, their terminal condition only worsens, and their ultimate destruction is unavoidable.

2Pet 2:4 For God did not suspend reality to let the angels avoid the consequences of their deviation from his design for life, but he expelled them from his presence, suspending them in utter darkness for the day they reap the full result of unremedied sin. 5 God did not allow the gangrenous ancient world to completely cut itself off from him but brought the flood to excise the necrosis and save Noah—a teacher of the Remedy—and seven others. 6 He diagnosed the cities of Sodom and Gomorrah as beyond healing, and in mercy, he cauterized those festering lesions to ash, making it clear that the unhealed will not be made to suffer eternally, but the torment of sin will mercifully be ended; 7 and God delivered Lot—a man who partook of the Remedy and was tormented by the disgusting lives of those living in violation of God's design— 8 for it was torture for that man with a healed mind and sensitive heart to live day after day among such vileness and see and hear such vulgarity. 9 If God can do all of this, he also knows how to rescue from affliction the godly—those who have partaken of the Remedy—while preserving, until the day everyone is accurately diagnosed, the ungodly—those who by refusing the Remedy suffer in persistent sin, 10 and especially those whose minds are controlled by selfishness and who are so self-centered that they despise any authority, oversight, or redirection. They are presumptuous, pompous and arrogant; they are so self-absorbed that they have no respect for heavenly beings, but instead, they denigrate them. 11 Yet even angels, who are mightier and stronger than these false teachers, do not slander such beings in the presence of God—the source of all truth. 12 These people speak foolishly about things they don't even comprehend; they are like unthinking animals, driven by fear, rage, and lust. They are caught up in their own destructive choices, and—like the unthinking beasts—they will also perish.

2Pet 2:13 They will reap what they have sown, receiving as their wages the harmful results of living outside God's design. Their idea of health and happiness is to violate trust, stay faithful to no one, and openly indulge the basest passions. They are festering lesions of decay, reveling in their orgies. 14 They constantly backstab, betray and exploit; they never stop violating God's design for life—the law of love—and instead, constantly promote selfishness. They seduce the immature and unstable; they are experts in taking for themselves, regardless of how it hurts others. They are unhealed, dying under the curse of sin; 15 they have chosen to leave the design protocols for life and have embraced the methods of Balaam, son of Beor, who loved the rewards procured by exploiting others. 16 But a donkey had more sense than Balaam and told him he was wrong. With the voice of a man, the donkey spoke and stopped the prophet's insane action.

2Pet 2:17 These people have nothing to offer; they are like dried-up springs, having no more substance than a vapor trail in the sky. Eternal darkness is what awaits them. 18 They proclaim a false message, empty of any healing power, but appealing to the selfish human desire to advance self. They entice people who are only just escaping the dog-eat-dog world. 19 They promise freedom from fear and selfishness but are themselves slaves to their own insecurities, lusts and depraved natures—for a person is a slave to whatever controls them. 20 If they have broken free from the corruption of the world by experiencing a genuine intimacy with our Lord and Savior Jesus Christ but choose to entangle themselves again in the web of selfishness, lust and deceit, they are worse than they were before they knew the freedom in Christ. 21 They would suffer less if they had never experienced the joy and freedom of righteousness than to have known it and turned back into slavery and pain,

ignoring God's design —the sacred protocols that were passed on to them. 22 Their characters prove true the proverbs: "A dog swallows its own vomit," and "You can clean a pig, but it will return to wallowing in the mud."

3 My dear friends, this is the second letter I have written to you. These letters are to motivate you to take control of your minds and engage in healthy thinking. 2 I want you to remember the truths recorded in the past by God's spokespersons and the instructions given you by our Lord and Savior through his ambassadors.

2Pet 3:3 First of all, understand and don't be surprised that in the last days, scoffers and doubters will arise; they will prefer the sickness of selfishness while ridiculing the cure, labeling the infection of selfishness as "normal." 4 They will say, "Survival-of-the-fittest is the way the universe runs, this is why we are here—not because of divine creation. Where is this so-called God? Where is the coming he promised? Ever since human history has been recorded, the principles of evolution have governed life, and all things continue just as they always have." 5 But these scoffers deliberately deny the truth and ignore the fact that long ago, by God's word, the world was created out of water and with water. 6 They reject the fact that it was by these same waters that a flood destroyed the world, 7 and they refuse to believe that the same word has testified that the present world, which is kept for the day of final diagnosis and the elimination of everyone and everything deviant from God's design, will be destroyed by fire.

2Pet 3:8 But don't forget the true nature of God's kingdom of love. Understand that the Lord lives outside the constraints of time, and with him, a day is like a thousand years, and a thousand years is like a day. 9 There is no delay on his part in keeping his promise to return; he is simply waiting for what he has always been waiting for—the Remedy to be taken to the entire world so that none who remain curable will be lost.

2Pet 3:10 But the Lord's return—coming suddenly like a thief—will surprise many people: There will be a loud roar and the sky will disappear; the very elements will melt in the intense heat, and the entire planet will be laid bare.

2Pet 3:11 Since everything the world values will end in this way, what kind of people are you to be? Each person must partake of the Remedy and be healed, live a life that loves others and honors God [12] as you anticipate our Lord's return, and work to speed his coming. On that day, the atmosphere of selfishness will be consumed by fire, and the very elements contaminated by sin will melt in the intense heat. [13] But just as promised, Jesus will make a new atmosphere and an entirely new earth—free from disease and defect, free from the infection of selfishness— the eternal home of the healed.

2Pet 3:14 So please, my dear friends: Since you long for the day our Lord returns, cooperate in every way with God's healing plan so that you will be found without any defect—totally cured and restored to complete unity with him. [15] Remember that our Lord's patience gives time for the Remedy to spread and healing to occur, just as our dear brother Paul explained in his letters—as God revealed it to him. [16] Paul writes about God's Remedy and healing plan in all his letters, but his letters contain some technical details and intricate illustrations and thus can be difficult to understand. And those who don't understand God's healing plan distort Paul's writings—as they do the other Scriptures—to misrepresent God; sadly, without the Remedy, it results in their own destruction.

2Pet 3:17 Therefore, my dear friends, since you know all of this, stay sharp and think for yourselves so that you won't be seduced into false theologies by people who deviate from God's law of love and have your minds re-infected with distortions about God. [18] Instead, grow stronger every day in the grace and truth of our Lord and Savior Jesus Christ. Let him be glorified now and forever! Amen.

1 John

1 He from whom all things began, who is the very source of all life, is he whom we have heard with our own ears, seen with our own eyes, and touched with our own hands. And he is the Word of life that we proclaim. ²This original, unborrowed, underived Life appeared on earth and we have seen him and testify to him. It is this pre-existent, eternal Life which was with the Father—and is the source of all life—that has appeared to us, and it is this Life that we are sharing with you. ³We are telling you the truth we have seen and heard, so that you may join us in the unity of friendship and love. And our unity is our companionship and oneness with the Father and with his Son, Jesus Christ. ⁴We write this to share the truth and bring more people into this fellowship and thus make our joy complete.

1Jn 1:5 This is the message we have heard him teach and seen him reveal, and which we declare to you: God is the source of all truth, love, purity and enlightenment; in him there is no deceit, selfishness, depravity, or ignorance. ⁶If we claim to be God's friends yet live selfishly, dishonestly, wickedly and ignorantly—we lie and misrepresent God and do not live by his methods of truth and love. ⁷But if we live our lives in the light of truth and love (as he is truth and love), we have unity, harmony and oneness with one another; and the life of Jesus, his Son, purges us of all selfishness.

1Jn 1:8 If we claim that we are not infected with selfishness, we deceive ourselves and the truth is not in us. ⁹If we humbly confess and acknowledge our terminal selfish condition, he faithfully and rightly forgives us for all the mistakes we made while living in selfishness; but more importantly—he heals us from all corruption, decay, and sickness of heart and mind. ¹⁰If we claim that we have not been selfish, then we call God a liar; and his truth, his methods, and his principles are not in us.

2 My precious children, I am writing to you so that you will realize the power of God's love to free you from selfishness—and therefore experience God's healing—and will no longer live selfishly. But if relapses into selfishness occur during the healing process, don't be discouraged: Jesus Christ stands at the helm of all power, right next to God, and is pouring his love into our hearts to complete his restoring and healing work. ²He is the reconciling Remedy to the infection of selfishness and fear, and not just for our terminal condition: he is also the Remedy—freely available—to heal the entire world.

1Jn 2:3 We can be confident that we have come into unity with him when we practice his methods, live his principles, and obey his teachings. ⁴The person who says, "I am a Christian," but does not love others and does not put Christ's commands into practice misrepresents God, and that person's entire life is a lie: there is no truth in such a person. ⁵But those who comprehend the truth about God, and intelligently put his methods and principles into practice, experience God's love and character renewed within them. This is how we can know if we are truly in unity with God: ⁶Whoever claims to be a Christian or a friend of God must love like Jesus loved.

1Jn 2:7 My dear friends, don't be confused, for I am not bringing a new teaching, remedy or treatment plan, but I am making it clear that from the very beginning, there has always been only one principle upon which life is founded—to love one another; and this reality you have heard many times before. 8 However, this love may seem brand new to you because it is now fully revealed in Christ, and its regenerating power is transforming you into his likeness, dispelling the darkness of this selfish world and shining forth the true light of God's character.

1Jn 2:9 Those who claim to be healed and living in the light of God's love but hate others reveal that they are not healed; and the infection of selfishness still darkens their minds. 10 All those who love others more than self are healed, live in the light of God's love, and reveal that the infection which brings death has been eradicated. 11 But whoever hates others lives in the darkness of selfishness. Such people are on the path that leads to death, but they don't even realize it; instead, they deny their terminal condition and blame others for their problems.

1Jn 2:12 Dear children, I write to you
so you will realize that you were
never in legal trouble with God:
Because of God's gracious, loving
character, he has freely forgiven
you all your sins
and longs to heal you to perfection
and unity with him.
1Jn 2:13 I write to you, elders and
leaders,
because you have come to
personally know Christ who is
eternal and is the source of all life.
I write to you who are new to Christ,
because you now know the power
of God's truth and love,
which has freed you from bondage
to Satan's lies and selfishness.
Dear children, I write to you all,

because through Christ
you have come to truly know the
Father.
1Jn 2:14 I write to you, elders and
leaders,
because you have come to
personally know Christ who is
eternal and is the source of all life.
I write to you who are new to Christ,
because you are energetic,
motivated, and on fire for the
Lord,
and you have internalized God's
methods and principles into your
character.
You have experienced the power of
God's truth and love to free you
from Satan's methods of
selfishness.
1Jn 2:15 Therefore, do not cherish this selfish world or anything of this world. Those who cherish this selfish world do not have the selfless love of the Father restored within them. 16 For everything in the world (including sinful people) is infected with selfishness, and this selfishness is expressed in three primary avenues: sensualism, materialism and egotism. And this terminal infection does not come from the Father but is part of this sick world. 17 This sick world and its selfish desires will pass away, but those who willingly experience God's healing and re-creation of hearts and minds will live forever.

1Jn 2:18 My dear children, the end is approaching. You have heard that before the end comes, the one who opposes Christ will come—and even now, many who oppose Christ have already come. From this we know the end is approaching. 19 Some, who claimed to be followers of Christ but never took God's Remedy and thus never experienced renewal of heart, have left our fellowship. If they had actually come to value God's methods of love and relinquished the methods of selfishness, they would not have left us; but their leaving reveals that they had never come into unity with us.

1Jn 2:20 But your hearts and minds have been renewed by the Holy One, and all of you know the truth of God's character of love. 21 I am writing to you not because you do not know the truth, but because you do know it; and no lie originates in the truth. 22 Who are the liars? Anyone who denies that Jesus is the Messiah, the Remedy, the Conduit of God's healing solution. Such people are opposed to Christ—they deny both the Father and the Son. 23 No one who denies Jesus the Son has the Father, as Jesus is the exact representation of the Father; but whoever acknowledges and accepts the Son has accepted the Father as well, because Jesus and the Father are One.

1Jn 2:24 Be sure that the truth you have heard from the beginning remains in your hearts, minds, and characters. If it does, you also will remain in unity with Jesus and his Father. 25 And this is what he promised us: Complete healing and restoration, and life eternal.

1Jn 2:26 I am writing to you in order to warn you about those who would lead you astray. 27 As for you, the regenerating and healing Spirit of Christ you received remains in you, and you do not need those unrenewed by the Spirit to teach you. But as the healing and renewing power of Christ's Spirit enlightens your minds and teaches you all things—and as the Spirit is the Spirit of truth and not falsehood—follow the truth and remain loyal to Christ.

1Jn 2:28 And now, my dear children, continue to practice his methods, value his principles and live his love, so that when he appears, we may rejoice in his presence.

1Jn 2:29 If you know that he is the standard and source of all that is right and good, then you realize that all who do what is right do so only because their minds have been healed and they have been restored to unity with him.

3 How amazing and awesome is the love the Father has poured out on us, that we have been transformed to be children of God! And that is exactly what we are—his offspring, born of his love! The reason the world does not know who we are is that it does not know him. 2 Dear friends, we are already children of God, but our full restoration (and what we will become) has not yet been made known. But we know that when Christ comes again, we shall be just like him in character, for we will be able to see him, face to face, just as he is. 3 All those who long for this reunion with God choose to become conduits of God's love and thus purify themselves—just as God is pure.

1Jn 3:4 Everyone who sins breaks the law of love—the law upon which life was created to operate; in fact, sin is selfishness, which means acting without love—choosing to deviate from the law upon which life is based. 5 But you know that Christ came to heal our hearts and minds and remove the infection of selfishness in order to restore love into our hearts. And in him, there is no selfishness or defilement— no sin. 6 No one who lives in unity with Christ keeps on living for self; no one who continues in selfishness has either seen or known him.

1Jn 3:7 Dear children, do not let anyone deceive you. Those who are righteous do what is right because it is right— just as Christ is righteous and always does what is right. 8 He who does what is selfish is practicing the devil's methods and principles, as the devil is the originator of selfishness. The reason the Son of God came to earth was to destroy the devil's work of selfishness and bring the universe back into unity with God and his law of love! 9 No one whose mind and heart have been recreated in Godlike love will continue to live selfishly, for God's character is reproduced in them; they cannot go on living self-centeredly, because they have been renewed in God's very likeness. [10] This is how we can know who the children of God are and who the children of the devil are: Anyone who does not love others more than self is not a child of God, nor is anyone who does not do what is right because it is right.

1Jn 3:11 The message you have heard from the beginning is this: We must be healed in hearts and minds so that we love one another. [12] Do not be like Cain, who belonged to the selfish, me-first family of the evil one, and murdered his brother. And why did he murder him? Because his own actions were self-centered and his brother's were selfless, loving, and godly. [13] So do not be surprised, my brothers and sisters, if this selfish world hates you. [14] We know that our condition is no longer terminal and that we have been restored to health and life because we have had the infection of selfishness purged from our hearts and God's love restored within. Anyone who does not love others more than self remains infected with selfishness and their condition remains terminal. [15] Anyone who hates another is a murderer, as murder happens in the mind and heart before it is carried out in action. You know that murder is the end result of the survival-of-the-fittest principle, and no one who remains infected with this self-first principle has God's eternal life recreated within them.

1Jn 3:16 This is how we know what love is: Jesus Christ voluntarily laid his life down for us. And we, who have been restored to Godlike love, will also give all we have, including laying down our lives for our brothers and sisters. [17] If one has food, clothes, or other material possessions, and rather than give what they have to help their brother or sister in need retain their possessions for themselves, how can the selfless love of God be in them? [18] Dear children, let us not simply talk about love, but let us live our lives in love, actually putting into action God's methods of truth and love. [19] Such a transformed life is evidence that God's character of love is truly rewritten within us, and with this knowledge we can have peace in his presence, [20] even when we feel inadequate and sinful. The truth is more reliable than our feelings, and God's ability to heal and restore is greater than our sickness, so be courageous, for there is nothing God doesn't already know.

1Jn 3:21 Therefore, my friends, if our hearts and minds have been healed and no longer condemn us, we are no longer afraid of God [22] and will follow his prescription and do the things that please him. [23] And this is his prescription: To value, cherish and trust in his Son, Jesus Christ, and to be like him—loving one another—just as he has prescribed. [24] Those who apply his prescription live in oneness with him and his character of love, and he—in unity with them. And this is how we know that he lives in us: His Spirit dwells in us and heals us to be like him.

4 My dear friends, do not trust every spirit-being but test all intelligent beings to see whether or not they are from God, and practice his methods and principles because false prophets, misrepresenting God, have gone out into the world. [2] Here is one way you can recognize the Spirit of God: Every intelligent being who comes from God will proclaim that Jesus Christ has come to earth in our humanity and perfectly revealed the Father, [3] but every intelligent being that does not proclaim that Jesus is the perfect revelation of the Father is not from God. This is the argument and mindset that comes from the enemy of Christ, who has been lying about God from the beginning. You have heard that false pictures of God and false purposes of the cross would come—in fact, they have already started to spread around the world.

1Jn 4:4 But you, dear children, are in union with God and have rejected the lies about God told by these false prophets, because the one who is healing and recreating you in love is greater than the power of selfishness in the world. 5 These false prophets originate from the world and therefore present a fallen human view of God, portraying him as a being who imposes law, inflicts punishment, and requires appeasement. The worldly people love this false picture of God. 6 We, however, are from God and present the truth: God was in the Son, restoring this creation to unity with himself; and all those who truly know God listen to us and realize that the Father is exactly as the Son revealed him to be. But whoever is not from God distorts the truth about God and creates a disparity between the Father and the Son. This is how we recognize the Spirit of truth and the spirit of falsehood: The Spirit of truth affirms that Christ is an exact representation of the Father, while the spirit of falsehood proclaims that the Father needed the Son to turn away his anger and wrath.

1Jn 4:7 So, my dear friends, let us live in love—giving all we have for the health and welfare of one another—for genuine, selfless love comes from God. Everyone who loves as Christ loves has been healed and recreated in heart and mind and restored to intimate oneness with God. 8 But whoever does not love others more than self has not been healed and doesn't even know God, as God is love. 9 God showed his love to us in this: He sent his one and only Son as a real human being into this selfish world that we might be healed and restored into unity with God through him. 10 This is what real love is: It is not that we have loved God, or that we have done something to get him to love us, but that he loved us so much that he sent his Son to become the Remedy and cure for the infection of sin and selfishness so that through

him we might be restored into perfect unity with God. 11 Therefore, my dear friends, since God is love—and since he loves us so much—we also should accept his cure and be transformed, and love one another. 12 No mortal has truly seen God; but if we love one another as God has loved us, then God lives in us and we see his perfect character of love lived out in us.

1Jn 4:13 We know that we have been restored to oneness with God, and have his character reproduced within us, because his Spirit lives in us. 14 We have seen with our own eyes and do testify that the Father has sent his Son to be the divine Remedy to heal and restore the world into loving unity with him. 15 Anyone who reveals God's character in their life, and who attributes all honor to Jesus as the Son of God, is living in unity, harmony, and loving fellowship with God. 16 And thus we have been genuinely transformed from beings motivated and driven by selfishness to fully healed children of God, motivated and energized by the love God has for us. God is love, and those who live a life of love live in unity and oneness with God—and God with them. 17 It is in this way—through the fellowship of a community of love—that God's true character of love is made complete among us. And because we have been restored to full unity with him and are like him in heart, mind and character, we are confident to stand before him. 18 In love, there is no fear. Fear is part of the infection of selfishness, but is purged by love, as fear has to do with concern for oneself. The one who remains self-focused and afraid has not been healed by God's love.

1Jn 4:19 We are able to love only because he first loved us. 20 If we claim to love God, sacrificing self for him, but go right on exploiting others—we are liars. For those who exploit the person near them—whom they have seen—cannot sacrifice self for God whom they have not seen. ²¹ God's prescription is this: Internalize God's love—which transforms the entire being—so that you love both God and people, for whoever loves God will also love others.

5 Everyone who trusts Jesus—God's healing Remedy—is recreated in heart and mind and is a child of God. And everyone who loves the Creator loves those he created. ² This is how we know that we love the beings God created—by loving God and living in harmony with his methods and principles of self-sacrificing love. ³ Those who genuinely love God will live lives that reveal him—lives in harmony with his commandments. And his commandments are not a burden placed upon us which we must perform, ⁴ but the natural outgrowth of love—the victory over this selfish world that everyone healed by God experiences; and this victory over fear and selfishness is achieved when we trust God. ⁵ Who is it that overcomes the survival-of-the-fittest principle of this world? Only those who recognize and accept that Jesus is God's Son.

1Jn 5:6 Jesus is the one who, by water and blood, became our Remedy. He became our Remedy not by being born into the world only, but also by shedding his blood. And the Spirit of God bears witness to it, because the Spirit reveals all truth. ⁷ For there are three that confirm this truth: ⁸ the Spirit, the evidence at Christ's baptism with water, and the evidence of his bloody death; and all three are in agreement that Jesus is the Messiah! ⁹ We readily accept the testimony or word of people; but God's testimony is more reliable because God testifies about his Son with evidence and truth. ¹⁰ Those who trust in God's Son have accepted the truth, had the lies expelled from their hearts, and are therefore won back to trust. Anyone who doesn't trust God is claiming that God is a liar, because such a one has rejected as false the truth and evidence God has given about his Son. ¹¹ And this is the truth and evidence: God has poured his eternal life into humanity, and this eternal, original, unborrowed life is in his Son. ¹² One who has come into unity of heart, mind and character with the Son has been healed and is a partaker of this eternal life; one who has not come into unity of heart, mind and character with the Son of God remains terminal and does not partake of this eternal life.

1Jn 5:13 I write these things to you who trust in Jesus and value his character, methods and principles so that you will know you have been healed and have eternal life. ¹⁴ We can therefore be confident in approaching God because we know he is eager to hear whatever we ask in harmony with his will. ¹⁵ And since we know he gladly hears us, we know that we have what we have asked of him.

1Jn 5:16 If you see a fellow Christian who desires to be Christlike commit an act of sin, you should talk with God about them, knowing that God will completely heal them and give them life if they open their heart in trust to God. Such sin does not result in eternal death, as it is merely a residual symptom of a heart in the process of being healed. However, there is no use in asking God to heal and give eternal life to the sinners who close their hearts to God and stubbornly refuse to allow God to heal them. Love cannot be forced and God cannot force people to love and trust him, so there is no use in praying for God to force people to accept him. ¹⁷ All violations of love are sin, but violations of love which occur in someone who opens their heart to God do not lead to eternal death.

1Jn 5:18 We know that anyone who is recreated in heart and mind by God does not continue to live selfishly; Jesus—God's Son—fills their mind with truth and their heart with love, and Satan's lies and selfish motives can no longer harm such a person. [19] We know that we are in unity of heart, mind and character with God, but the world is in unity with Satan. [20] We also know that Jesus, God's Son, has come and enlightened our minds with the truth—the truth about God, the nature of sin, the character of Satan, and the issues in this conflict between good and evil— so that we may come into full union and intimacy of heart and mind with God who is true; and we are in oneness with the Father of truth, and with his Son Jesus Christ. He is the true God and the source of all life.

[1Jn 5:21] Therefore, my dear children, always reject lies about God and any false concept about the character of God.

2 John

1 From your pastor and teacher, to the pure lady and her children whom I love in the truth—and not only I, but all those who love the truth about God— ²because it is this truth about God that has become a permanent part of our character:

2Jn 1:3 God the Father and Jesus—the Father's Son—freely pour out all the resources of heaven upon us for our good: grace, mercy, and peace may be ours in truth and love.

2Jn 1:4 I have been overjoyed to find some of your children walking in the truth of God's methods and principles, just as the Father prescribed for us. ⁵And now, precious lady, I am not writing a new prescription but one that is eternal and emanates from the heart of God, and is the base code upon which all life is created to operate—that we love one another. ⁶And this is love, that we freely live our lives in harmony with his methods and principles, just as he instructed. And his methods are the same now as when he created the universe—the same now as when you first heard them—that we love others completely, freely, and constantly.

2Jn 1:7 There are many liars and deceivers in the world who deny that Jesus Christ, the Son of God, actually came to earth as a real human being—with real flesh and blood—just like us. Recognize them for what they are—deceivers and enemies of Christ. ⁸Be careful that you are not duped by them and lose what you have achieved, for I want you to receive your full reward. ⁹Anyone who loses contact with Christ and begins preaching his own theories instead of the truth Christ brought is not in unity with God; whoever continues to teach the truth that Jesus is an exact expression of the Father—who became a real human being like us—is in unity and friendship with both the Father and the Son. ¹⁰If you meet anyone determined to present a false gospel—who desires to deceive—do not associate with or support them or their ministry in any way. ¹¹By giving them a platform to speak, or supporting them or their ministry, you make it appear like you share their views, and thus you will share in their wicked work of spreading lies about God.

2Jn 1:12 I have so much to tell you, but I don't want to write it on paper with ink; Oh, no! I long to see you and talk with you in person, so that we may rejoice together in God's love.

2Jn 1:13 Your sister's children send their warm regards.

3 John

1 From your pastor and teacher to my dear friend Gaius, whom I love in the truth:

3Jn 1:2 Dear friend, I pray that all things are well with you, that your health is good, and your mind is sharp, clear and at peace. 3 My heart was filled with joy when some brothers told me of your fidelity, loyalty, and unwavering constancy to the truth. 4 There is nothing that brings me greater happiness than to hear that my children are walking in the truth.

3Jn 1:5 Dear friend, your consistent ministry and service to others—even to strangers—demonstrates how faithfully you reveal the truth of God's character of love. 6 Those you have ministered to have told the church how loving you have been—in keeping with God's methods and principles—by providing whatever assistance they needed to continue their journey. 7 Their mission was to proclaim and make known God's true character, and that is why they accepted no help from those who did not know God. 8 Therefore, we should render assistance and be hospitable to such people, for we are all on the same team—God's team—working together to reveal the truth about him.

3Jn 1:9 Earlier, I wrote similar counsel to the church, but Diotrephes likes to be in charge and devalues my teachings. 10 This is terribly destructive and must be corrected, so when I come, I will expose with the truth his lies, gossip, and slander. But he doesn't just lie and slander—he also refuses to aid fellow-workers for Christ. Not only that, but he also tries to stop others, who want to render assistance, from doing so, even threatening to disfellowship them.

3Jn 1:11 Dear friend, don't get duped into imitating evil, but always do what is good. Anyone who does what is good is able to do so only because he has received goodness from God. Anyone who does evil has not been reunited with God. 12 Everyone speaks well of Demetrius: the truth itself verifies that he is in unity of heart and mind with God, and we also confirm how well he represents God in all he does—and you know we only speak the truth.

3Jn 1:13 I have so much more I want to write, but I don't want to use pen and ink. 14 I hope to be with you soon and talk face to face.

Jude

1 Jude, an ambassador and representative of Jesus Christ and a brother of James,

To those who have responded to God's call—who are being transformed by God's healing love and nurtured by Jesus Christ:

Jud 1:2 May you continue to grow in the abundance of God's mercy, peace, and love.

Jud 1:3 My dear friends, I have longed to write to you about God's healing plan (his Remedy in which we share), but instead, I must write to warn you to defend the truth about God as revealed by Jesus—this precious truth that is the foundation of our faith and the secret with which we have been entrusted. 4 Scripture from long ago tells that those who reject this truth remain terminal and cannot be healed. Such people have slipped in among you and are attempting to twist the truth about God. These people, even though they purport to be believers in God, are actually godless because they have rejected the truth about God's true character and principles, and instead, teach a powerless gospel that misrepresents God, fails to transform lives, and denies that Jesus Christ is our Lord and the source of our healing and restoration.

Jud 1:5 So let me remind you—even though you are well aware of these facts—that the Lord brought Israel out of Egypt to be his partner in teaching the truth about God and distributing his healing Remedy throughout the world. Unfortunately, God found it necessary to put into the grave those who rejected him and worked to stop his plan. 6 And the angels who rejected the truth about God chose to leave heaven and have become so settled into lies about God that no amount of truth and love can reach them; their minds are bound in darkness, and they are awaiting the final Day when the diagnosis of all will be revealed. 7 In a similar manner, the inhabitants of Sodom and Gomorrah rejected the truth about God, and their minds became so settled into lies about him that they were beyond healing; they gave themselves over to sensual indulgence and perversion. They stand as evidence of what will happen to all those who reject the truth about God and are exposed to eternal fire.

Jud 1:8 In the very same way, these infiltrators create imaginary fantasies about God and the universe. They abuse their bodies, reject divine authority, and make fun of holy beings. 9 But even the archangel Michael, when he raised Moses from the dead, did not slander the devil who tried to stop him and claim Moses for himself. Michael merely said, "Stand aside; you have no right or authority here." 10 Yet these infiltrators make fun of truths they don't even comprehend; they reject reason, and instead, like animals, do whatever they feel by instinct, thereby destroying the capacity for knowing truth, and causing their own destruction.

Jud 1:11 Oh, how sad—how terribly sad and horrible it will be for them! They have chosen, just like Cain, to reject truth and go with passion; they have sought, like Balaam, to reject beneficence and seek riches for self; they, like Korah, have rejected humility and sought to promote themselves in power and authority.

Jud 1:12 These people are festering cankers at your fellowship meals, claiming to be Christian but seeking only to get the best for themselves, trying to get attention and recognition, or gorging themselves without regard for anyone else. They are like clouds without rain —useless and blown around by the wind; they are like leafless, fruitless trees, uprooted and completely dead. 13 They are like the waves of the sea— tossed in any direction their feelings are surging; their lives are turbulent whirlpools of shame. They are like the lost stars of heaven on their way to eternal nothingness and darkness.

Jud 1:14 It was Enoch, the seventh descendant of Adam, who prophesied about people like this: "Be aware, the Lord is coming to earth with millions of his holy angels 15 in order to bring about the accurate diagnosis of all things—to bring all selfish beings face to face with their own terminal condition, with the pain and suffering they have caused, and with all the lies about God they have told." 16 These people are complainers, faultfinders, criticizers, always making excuses for themselves and blaming others; they only care about themselves and constantly follow their own selfish desires; they brag about themselves and use flattery to manipulate and exploit whomever they can.

Jud 1:17 But, my dear friends, remember what the ambassadors of our Lord Jesus Christ warned us would happen. 18 They said, "In the last days, there will be people who laugh at truth, make fun of godliness, and prefer to follow their own passions, lusts, and desires." 19 It is people like these who cause factions to form, who split families in two, who break congregations apart—and they have come in among you. They follow their own base instincts and feelings, for they have rejected God's Spirit.

Jud 1:20 But you, dear friends, as you talk to God with your minds enlightened by the Holy Spirit, continue to build your characters and relationships upon the holy truth about God and on his methods and principles. 21 Continue to be conduits of God's love as you allow the mercy and grace of our Lord Jesus Christ to heal you and bring you back into full unity with him and give you life everlasting.

Jud 1:22 Be merciful to those who don't understand and who live in doubt; 23 don't stand idly by when you see others destroying themselves in ignorance and selfishness, but proclaim God's healing Remedy and rescue them from burning up their lives in sin; be kind and patient with sinners, but hate the selfishness that covers them like putrid, germ-saturated clothing.

Jud 1:24 To him who is able to heal you completely so that you can stand in his glorious presence with perfect character, rejoicing when we meet him face to face, 25 to the only God — our Savior through Jesus Christ — be all glory, majesty, power and authority from before time began, and now, and forevermore! Amen.

Preface to Revelation

In the book of Revelation, I did a little more than paraphrase. I also added some decoding of the symbolism, some of which will be without controversy, such as "Jesus the Lamb" rather than just "the Lamb," but other places might challenge various traditional views. The reason I decided to do this is not that I want to suggest I have been gifted with some special insight beyond any believer's prayerful study guided by the Holy Spirit, but to stimulate the reader to think. Throughout the rest of this paraphrase, I have used new words to get at the real meaning and move past cliché, such as "Remedy" for "gospel."

In Revelation, I want the reader to move past the symbolism to consider a cosmic reality beyond the symbol—a reality in which God is love all the time, and Satan is a real being of complete selfishness, seeking to contaminate our minds with his lies about God. I have no doubt that as the future unfolds, events will require modification and reinterpretation of some of the conclusions I have suggested in this book. The point is not that we need to know with total certainty every detail of every symbol, but that we need to know God and Jesus Christ whom he has sent. You will therefore notice that all of the suggested interpretations always reveal God's character of love—working against Satan for the good of his creation. I hope you will enjoy reading Revelation, and that it will stimulate you with a new appreciation and love for our amazing God.

Some rules of interpretation used in the book of Revelation:

- If one part of a passage is symbolic or metaphor, then the rest is symbolic or metaphor unless clear reasons to be literal are expressed in the text.
- The Bible will be used to interpret itself (i.e. symbol interpretations will use Bible definitions before other definitions).
- The general theme is that of the conflict between Christ and Satan.
- God's character of love never changes, therefore interpretations will never result in God being represented in a character other than love.
- God's law of love never changes, therefore interpretations will always be in harmony with God's law of love.

The Author

Revelation

1 This message is from Jesus Christ, and it reveals what will soon take place, according to God's desire to show it to his ambassadors, assistants, and spokespersons. Jesus sent his angel to his ambassador John to share this future knowledge with him, 2 and John bears witness to the veracity of everything he was shown, including the message from God and the testimony Jesus gave. 3 Blessed is the person who reads this revelation of future events, and blessed are those who hear it and incorporate it into their hearts and lives, because the time is near.

Rev 1:4 From John, to the seven churches in Asia:

Grace and peace from God the Father—who is alive today, who has always been alive from eternity past, and who is coming to earth—and from the seven intelligent beings who serve before the throne of God, 5 and from Jesus Christ, who is the trustworthy representative of humanity in God's kingdom, the victor over death, and the true head of humanity and ruler of earth.

To Christ, who loves us and has healed us from our sinfulness by providing the Remedy of his perfection (achieved through his sacrificial death), 6 and who has restored us to be members of his kingdom and ministers of his Remedy in order to reveal the truth about God the Father—to him be all glory and power for all eternity! Amen.

Rev 1:7 Open your minds to understand
that he is coming back—literally,
in the clouds—
and every eye will see him, including
those who crucified him;
and all those who have not been

healed will wail in agony
because when they see him
they will know what they have
lost.
This is how it will really be! Amen.

Rev 1:8 The Lord God says, "I am the Beginning and the End—he who has always been, he who is, who was, and who is to come—the Almighty."

Rev 1:9 I, John, am your brother in Christ, friend in suffering, and fellow in the kingdom of love and enduring patience that is ours when we are united in Jesus. I was exiled to the island of Patmos because of teaching the truth about God and the message of Jesus. 10 On the Lord's holy Sabbath day, I was filled with the Spirit, and I heard a voice behind me, clear and sharp like the report of a trumpet, 11 that said: "Write down what you see and send it to the seven churches located in Ephesus, Smyrna, Pergamum, Thyatira, Sardis, Philadelphia, and Laodicea."

Rev 1:12 When I turned to see the source of the voice that was speaking to me, I first saw seven golden lampstands, 13 and among the lampstands was one who appeared to be human, just like a Son of Man. He was wearing a robe flowing down to his feet and had a golden breastplate on his chest; 14 his hair was brilliant white, like snow, and his eyes shone brightly like a fire. 15 His feet glowed like metal in a furnace, and his voice resounded with energy like a roaring river. 16 He held seven stars in his right hand, and the words coming from his mouth were the sharp double-edged sword of truth. His face radiated energy like the sun shining at midday.

Rev 1:17 When I saw him, I fell down at

his feet, afraid that I couldn't tolerate the intensity of the experience, but he gently placed his right hand on me and said, "Don't be afraid. I am the Beginning and the End. 18 I am the One with unborrowed life; yes, I died, but look: I am alive forever! And I have the Remedy for death, and the power to open the grave.

Rev 1:19 "So write what you have seen—what is happening now and what will take place in the future. 20 The meaning of the seven stars you saw in my right hand and the seven golden lampstands is this: The seven stars represent seven messengers responsible for ministering to the seven churches, and the seven lampstands represent the seven churches which are to be lights of truth to the world.

2 "Write to the messenger to my recovering children in the church in Ephesus:

This message comes from Jesus, who holds the seven stars in his right hand and walks among the seven lampstands: 2 I know you — your choices, actions, works, determination and commitment. I know that your hearts are repulsed by wickedness in humanity, and that you have examined those who claim to be my ambassadors but are not; and you rightly determined them to be false. 3 I know that you have stayed true, revealing my character of love despite persecution, and have not given up.

Rev 2:4 Yet I have diagnosed you with one serious problem: You have let go of your first love. 5 I implore you, remember the pinnacle of purity from which you have fallen! Turn back to your first love and practice again the methods you practiced before. If you do not turn back, the light of truth will be lost to you and your minds will be darkened. 6 To your advantage, you have hated the hedonistic practices of the Nicolaitans that so damage the mind—which I also hate.

Rev 2:7 Those whose minds are open to truth will understand what the Spirit reveals to the churches. Those who overcome — complete the treatment and are renewed in love—will eat from the tree of life, which is in the paradise of God.

Rev 2:8 "To the messenger to my recovering children in the church in Smyrna, write:

This message comes from Jesus, who is the Beginning and the Ending, the Origin and Completion; who died, but in so doing destroyed death and now lives again: 9 I know about your suffering and poverty, but in reality, you are incredibly rich in what heaven values! I know that you have been misrepresented by those who claim to be loyal to God but really are not; they have enthroned Satan in their hearts — their spirit temples. 10 Don't fear the coming trials. Satan will put some of you in prison, and your faith will be tried; and some will be persecuted for ten days. Trust me—even if threatened with death—and I will give you eternal life.

Rev 2:11 Those whose minds are open to truth will understand what the Spirit reveals to the churches. Those who prevail by completing the treatment and by being renewed in love cannot be harmed by the second, eternal death.

Rev 2:12 "To the messenger to my recovering children in the church in Pergamum, write:

This message comes from Jesus—the source of truth as sharp as a double-edged sword: 13 I know you live where Satan has enthroned himself, yet you have continued to live in harmony with my character, methods, and principles. You did not reject me, even when Antipas, my trustworthy witness, was executed in the place where Satan lives.

Rev 2:14 Yet I have diagnosed a few serious problems: Some of you are like Balaam, seeking to empower and enrich yourselves. You have infected the Remedy with appeasement theology, and you promote sexual practices deviant from my design in Eden. 15 And as if this isn't bad enough, you have those who advocate the hedonistic practices of the Nicolaitans, which destroy the mind. 16 Reject these falsehoods and return to my methods! Otherwise, I will come and fight against these distortions with the sword of truth spoken from my mouth.

Rev 2:17 Those whose minds are open to truth will understand what the Spirit reveals to the churches. To everyone who prevails by completing the treatment and being renewed in love, I will give some of the hidden manna—my nature and character of love. I will recreate them in my likeness, with their own unique individuality purified by my character. They will be like pure-white stones, each stamped with their own unique self, signed by me.

Rev 2:18 "To the messenger to my recovering children in the church in **Thyatira**, write:

This message is from Jesus—the Son of God—whose eyes shine brightly like a fire, and whose feet glow like metal in a furnace: 19 I know the choices you have made, your love and devotion, your service and dedication, and how your healing progresses as you are achieving more now than when you first took the Remedy.

Rev 2:20 Yet I have diagnosed this problem: You have accepted the teachings of Jezebel, which make me look like Baal—a being who imposes law, inflicts torture, and must be appeased. Her teachings mislead people

into internalizing pagan ideas about God—including God being like Baal and requiring bloody payments—and thus committing spiritual adultery by giving their hearts to a false god. 21 I have given her time to turn away from the lies about God, but she refuses; 22 so I will let her reap the suffering that comes from operating outside my design for life. And all those who accept her view of God commit adultery with her and will suffer terribly unless they reject the lies and return to the truth about God and his methods of love. 23 I will destroy her offshoots—then all my children will know that I diagnose perfectly the condition of hearts and minds—and I will provide to each person what is in accord with their own choice. 24 Now for the rest of you in Thyatira: Those who have rejected the lies about me and refused to believe that I am like Satan alleges—no other burden will come upon you; 25 just hold true to what you currently know until I return.

Rev 2:26 Everyone who prevails by completing the treatment and lives in harmony with my methods of love until the end, I will free from the power and authority of the nations.

Rev 2:27 'He will intervene
with an unbreakable shepherd's rod;
he will destroy the nations' ability to coerce and deceive
like iron crushes pottery.'
I will give them the same power to break free as I received from my Father. 28 I will give them the morning star—I will give them all of myself.

Rev 2:29 Those whose minds are open to truth will understand what the Spirit reveals to the churches.

3 "To the messenger to my children in the church in **Sardis**, write:
This message is from Jesus, who directs the seven intelligent beings

standing before the throne of God, and the seven messengers who are — like bright stars — shining forth the truth: I know your choices. You appear to be alive—living in harmony with the law of love—but you are dead in fear and self-centeredness. ²Wake up before it is too late! Heal what remains viable but is about to die if you don't take action soon, for despite all your rituals and religious acts, you are devoid of love in the sight of my Father. ³Remember the Remedy you have received: accept it, apply it to your lives, and turn away from the ways of the world. But if you refuse to wake up to your condition and embrace the truth, you will be unaware of what is happening, and my coming will be like a thief's— you will not know the time I will come to you.

Rev 3:4 Yet you still have a few faithful people in Sardis whose characters have not been stained with selfishness. They will walk by my side, dressed in the perfection of my character of love—pure and white—for they are healed. ⁵Everyone who prevails by completing the treatment and lives in harmony with my methods of love until the end will also have character perfect and pure. I will never remove them from the book of life, but proclaim to my Father and his angels that they have been completely healed. ⁶Those whose minds are open to truth will understand what the Spirit reveals to the churches.

Rev 3:7 "To the messenger to my children in the church in **Philadelphia**, write:

This message is from Jesus, who is holy and true, and who is the Key from David's line — the door to restoration, which he opens, no one can shut; and the doors he shuts no one can open: ⁸I know your choices. Recognize that I have opened before you a door for your healing, which no one can shut. I know you are exhausted, but you have not given up. You have lived in harmony with my methods and have not rejected my character of love. ⁹But those whose minds have become a sanctuary for Satan—who claim to be my children but are liars, as their characters are like Satan's—I will make them see the truth, and they will fall down at your feet and acknowledge that what I love is my children being healed, like you. ¹⁰Since you have unwaveringly followed my instructions and lived in harmony with my methods, I will heal your characters, and you will have nothing to fear during the difficult time to come upon the world, which will differentiate the true nature of those who live on the earth.

Rev 3:11 I am returning soon. Hold on to the Remedy you have received, and no one will trick you out of eternal life. ¹²Everyone who prevails by completing the treatment and lives in harmony with my methods of love until the end, I will make a pillar, a living stone, in the heavenly temple of my God—a community of holy beings. Their connection with God will never be severed, and I will write in their beings the character of my God; and they will be marked by me as citizens of the New Jerusalem which is coming down out of heaven from my God. I will also write my name upon their hearts and minds. ¹³Those whose minds are open to truth will understand what the Spirit reveals to the churches.

Rev 3:14 "To the messenger to my children in the church in **Laodicea**, write:

This message is from Jesus—the consistent, reliable, faithful and true Witness—who is the origin of God's creation: ¹⁵I know your choices. I know that you are neither on fire with love, nor do you appear cold with selfishness. I wish you were either on fire for my kingdom, or clearly opposed to it! ¹⁶But because you are a lukewarm mix of cold hearts practicing selfish methods while appearing to be on fire for my kingdom, you misrepresent me and make me sick to my stomach. I am about to vomit you out. ¹⁷You claim to be spiritually rich and full of heavenly treasure, thinking you have the truth and are in need of nothing, but you are so self-deceived that you don't realize you are devoid of my character of love. You are decrepit, pathetic, bereft of true godliness, with minds so closed that you can't even comprehend truth. You stand naked and exposed. ¹⁸My prescription for you is to exchange your corrupt motives for the gold of godly love, purified through fiery trials, so that you can be rich in what heaven values. Exchange your filthy, selfish characters for the perfect character of Christ—pure and white—so that you can cover the shame of your imperfection. And apply the salve of the Holy Spirit to your minds so that you can see and understand the reality of your own condition, and that of God's kingdom of love.

Rev 3:19 It is those whom I love that I diagnose and provide these therapeutic interventions, so take ownership of yourselves: turn away from destruction and apply the Remedy. ²⁰I am here now! I am standing at the door to your hearts, knocking with truth and love. If any hear my voice and open their hearts, I will come in and commune with them, and they with me.

Rev 3:21 Everyone who prevails by completing the treatment, and lives in harmony with my methods of love until the end, will sit enthroned with me—just as I overcame and sit enthroned with my Father. ²²Those whose minds are open to truth will understand what the Spirit reveals to the churches."

4 The next thing I saw was a door standing open in heaven, and I heard the same voice I had heard previously, speaking to me as clear as a trumpet, saying, "Come here and I will show you what will happen in the future." ²Immediately the Spirit filled me, and my mind was opened; and before me was a throne in heaven with a person sitting on it. ³The one who sat on the throne shimmered with dazzling brilliance, like polished stones in the sun: fiery reds at the base and resplendent hues of green surrounding the throne. ⁴Circling the throne were twenty-four elders sitting upon twenty-four thrones. Their characters were perfectly healed to be like Jesus, therefore they appeared dressed in white clothing, and their minds were perfect—free from all fear and selfishness—symbolized by crowns of pure gold on their heads. ⁵The one on the throne was the source of immeasurable power, greater than lightning and rolling thunder. And the Spirit of God was present before the throne, represented by seven blazing lights. ⁶The throne was set upon a vast plain that had the appearance of pure crystal, clear and smooth, reflecting the reds and greens coming from the throne. In the center of the circle, near the throne, were four living beings—brilliant, alert, intelligent, with clear understanding of the past and the unfolding future—all symbolized by eyes covering their front and back. ⁷The first was regal like a lion, the second—strong like an ox, the third—intelligent like a human, and the fourth was sharp and vigilant like an eagle. ⁸These beings could act unbelievably fast—both physically and mentally—which was symbolized by each having six wings, and eyes all over, even under their wings. And they lived constantly—day and night—in a continual state of appreciation and love for God, saying:

"God is holy, holy, holy—
Lord Almighty,

who has always been, who is,
and who is to come."

Rev 4:9 Whenever these four living beings honor God's character of love and thank him who governs the universe from the throne—the one who is the source of life and lives forever— ¹⁰ the twenty-four elders are filled with awe and humbled in hearts, and demonstrate their devotion by falling down in love before him who sits on the throne, and they worship him who is the source of life and who lives forever. They cast their gold crowns before him — demonstrating that their lives, their perfect characters and their healed minds come from him — and proclaim:

¹¹ "You are worthy, our Lord God
Almighty,
to receive all honor, praise, glory and
power
because you created all things,
and all things have their origin in
you and are sustained by you."

5 Then I looked, and I saw that he who sits on the throne had written out the history of the world before the world began, and sealed it up. It was symbolized by a book in his right hand, with writing within, and sealed with seven seals. ² And I watched as a mighty angel asked in a loud voice, "Who is worthy to break the seals and open the book of God's foreknowledge, and intervene in human history?" ³ But there was no created being in heaven, or living on earth, or amongst the dead, who could open the scroll or even look at its contents. ⁴ My heart broke with sadness because there was no one found who could open the book or look inside. ⁵ Then one of the elders said to me, "Don't be sad! See, Jesus— the Lion from Judah, the descendant of David—has overcome and is now able to open the book of God's foreknowledge, sealed by seven seals."

Rev 5:6 Then I saw a Lamb, appearing as if it had been slain—symbolizing Jesus who sacrificed himself to eradicate sin

—standing at the command center of the universe, surrounded by his staff and agents symbolized by the four living creatures and the elders. He had all heavenly power and all wisdom at his disposal—symbolized by seven horns and seven eyes, which represented God's Spirit — and he was directing every heavenly agency to rescue, heal and restore his children living on earth. ⁷ He came and took the book from God's right hand. ⁸ When he took the book, his staff—symbolized by the four living creatures and twenty-four elders—were so relieved that they fell down in joy and awe before him. They were processing requests from God's children on earth—symbolized by the golden bowls of incense they each held. They also had renewed hearts that were like musical instruments making a beautiful melody, ⁹ and they sang a new song stemming from their admiration for Jesus:

"You are able to take the book and
reveal the sealed contents
because you were killed,
and by your death you revealed the
truth and achieved the Remedy
to free humans from sin
and restore people from every
race, language, tribe and nation
to God.
¹⁰ You have healed their minds,
making them a kingdom of priests
ministering the Remedy of our
God,
and they will administer
God's methods on earth."

Rev 5:11 Then I heard many voices, so I looked, and I saw millions of angels— so many that it was beyond my ability to count. They surrounded the throne and the living creatures, and the elders. ¹² In rich, booming voices, they sang:

"Worthy is Jesus the Lamb to possess
all power, resources and ability
and receive all honor, glory and
praise, because he was slain,
proving that he will never abuse

such mighty power!"

Rev 5:13 Then I heard every living being in the universe singing in unison:

"To him who sits on the throne
and to Jesus the Lamb
be praise and honor, glory and
power,
for ever and ever, without end!"

Rev 5:14 The four living creatures said, "Absolutely right!"
and the elders fell down in adoration and awe.

6 Excitedly, I watched as Jesus the Lamb opened the first section of God's book of foreknowledge and began to reveal the warfare between God and Satan. I heard one of the living creatures say in a powerful voice that rumbled like thunder, "Come and see!" 2 So I looked, and I saw that the war began with a rider on a white horse, holding a bow and wearing a crown—symbolizing Lucifer beginning his war in heaven under the guise of righteousness, yet intent on inciting rebellion and war, and achieving conquest.

Rev 6:3 When Jesus the Lamb opened the second section of God's book of foreknowledge, I heard another living creature say, "Come and see!" 4 Then I saw a rider on a fiery red horse, holding a large sword—symbolic of Satan's lies about God—severing the bonds of love and trust, and inciting fear and selfishness resulting in people killing each other.

Rev 6:5 When Jesus the Lamb opened the third section of God's book of foreknowledge, I heard a third living creature say, "Come and see!" I looked and saw a black horse, symbolic of humanity necrotic with lies about God. Its rider was holding a yoke in his hand, symbolic of the spiritual enslavement that occurs when the mind is bound by lies about God. 6 Then I heard a voice coming from the four living creatures, saying, "A handful of wheat or three handfuls of barley will cost an entire day's pay, but the oil and

wine won't be destroyed" — which means that the lies about God will be so pervasive that a famine of spiritual truth will occur, and humanity will be near spiritual starvation; but the oil of truth and the wine of God's Remedy will not be destroyed.

Rev 6:7 When Jesus the Lamb opened the fourth section of God's book of foreknowledge, I heard the fourth living creature say, "Come and see!" 8 Then I saw a pale horse, and its rider was named Death—symbolic of a church fighting against the truth and promoting a false remedy—and the grave was filling up behind him. It had power over one-fourth of the world's population and could destroy by warring against the truth with lies about God; by restricting access to the written word of God and thereby inciting spiritual famine; by indulging selfishness—the pestilence of the soul; and by introducing wild, beastly, pagan traditions.

Rev 6:9 When Jesus the Lamb opened the fifth section of God's book of foreknowledge, I saw an altar, and beneath it I saw the individual identities of those who were killed because they embraced the truth about God's character of love and faithfully revealed his methods, rejecting the lies about God. 10 Their lives called out, "Almighty Lord who always does what is right, how long until your diagnosis of the inhabitants of earth is made known and you set right the wrong done to us?" 11 Then they were each given white clothes to symbolize that they were healed to be like Jesus in character. They were told to be patient a little longer, until the rest of their co-workers and friends completed their witness and were martyred for the truth.

Rev 6:12 I watched as Jesus the Lamb opened the sixth section of God's book of foreknowledge. There was a great shaking of ideas in the minds of people on earth: their unshakable confidence in religion was broken, as evolutionary theory—like a black cloth obscuring the sun—covered over their minds. The moon bled dry for believers, [13] and the stars fell from their high places of esteem, shaken by the mighty wind of changing ideas. [14] The mystery of the cosmos was rolled back like a scroll as science and astronomy advanced; every high place of worship was removed from its place of esteem, and every island of belief was thrown aside. [15] But the leaders on earth— presidents, kings, princes, generals, rich and poor—hid from the truth in the caves of their own lies and amongst the rocks of the mountain of false ideas. [16] They begged for their ideas to be true: they cried out, "Hide us from the truth! Hide us from him who sits on the throne of truth, and protect us from what happens when Jesus the Lamb lets us go! [17] For the day when he lets us go has come, and who can stand on their own?"

7 After the events of the first six seals, I saw four angels standing at key positions around the earth, holding back the four winds of strife to prevent them from blowing on the land, or sea, or any tree. [2] Then I saw another one of God's messengers coming from the east, with the truth about God's character of love and the Remedy of the living God, to seal the characters of God's children. He called in a loud voice to the four angels who had the power to harm the land and sea by releasing the winds: [3] "Hold! And do not harm the land or sea until we seal the minds of God's helpers and spokespersons, settling them into the truth about God's character and methods of love, so that nothing can shake them from it." [4] Then I heard the symbolic representation of those who were sealed—144,000 from all peoples of the earth, symbolized by the tribes of Israel:

Rev 7:5		
From Judah	12,000	
from Reuben	12,000	
from Gad	12,000	
[6] from Asher	12,000	
from Naphtali	12,000	
from Manasseh	12,000	
[7] from Simeon	12,000	
from Levi	12,000	
from Issachar	12,000	
[8] from Zebulun	12,000	
from Joseph	12,000	
from Benjamin	12,000	

Rev 7:9 After the spokespersons for God were sealed, the four winds were loosed, and I saw before me a great multitude won to God from the witness of God's spokespersons: They were more than anyone could count—from every nation, tribe, people, and language—standing before the throne and in front of Jesus the Lamb. Their characters had been purified to be like Jesus'—symbolized by the wearing of white clothing—and they were holding palm branches in their hands, indicating their praise and acknowledgment of Jesus as King. [10] They cried out in a loud voice:

"Healing and restoration come from
    our God who sits on the throne
    and from Jesus the Lamb!"

Rev 7:11 And all the angels who were standing around the throne, and the elders, and the four living beings—they all fell down in love and awe and worshiped God, [12] singing,

"Absolutely right!
    God is worthy of all praise,
    and glory, and honor, and thanks,
    and wisdom, and power,
    and strength—
forever and ever without end!
    So let it always be!"

Rev 7:13 Then one of the elders looked at me and asked, "These people in white clothes—who are they and how did they get here?"

Rev 7:14 I answered, "Sir, surely you know."

And he did know: He said, "These are they who — after the four winds are loosed—hear the testimony of God's spokespersons and during the great tribulation respond to the truth, accept the Remedy, and have their minds and hearts renewed to be like Jesus'—symbolized by their clothes being washed in the blood of the Lamb.

15 Therefore they are united to the
throne of God,
and—as living stones in his
temple—
reveal his character continually;
and he who sits on the throne
will cover them with his constant
love and care.
16 They will never again hunger for
truth or thirst for love.
No sun or scorching heat will ever
harm them—
symbolizing that they will never
again be burned by trial or
tribulation.
17 For Jesus the Lamb, who stands at
the command center of the
universe,
will be their protector;
he will provide them with springs of
living water.
And God will comfort them
and wipe away all their tears."

8 Jesus the Lamb opened the seventh section of God's book of foreknowledge, and there was stunned silence in heaven for about half an hour as the intelligent beings were overwhelmed with awe when they realized how God resolved the war started by Satan.

Rev 8:2 I saw seven angels standing before God, holding seven trumpets.

Rev 8:3 But a different angel, holding a golden censer and standing in front of the golden altar, was burning a large amount of incense mixed with the prayers of the saints. 4 This symbolized the character of Christ, burning within the hearts of God's representatives on earth as they prayed for the revelation of God's character of love and the re-demption of humankind. 5 Then the angel took the censer, filled it with fire from the altar, and hurled it on the earth. This symbolized the Holy Spirit empowering God's spokespersons to reveal the truth with stunning clarity. There was an incredible shaking of the minds of the people, accompanied by flashes of brilliance that battled rumblings of confusion and the thundering of opposition.

Rev 8:6 Then the seven angels holding the seven trumpets prepared to sound them, which represents seven warning messages of truth trumpeting the approaching end and exposing Satan's counterfeits to God's Remedy. [1]

Rev 8:7 The first angel sounded his trumpet, and a hailstorm of fiery truth revealing the Remedy achieved by Christ's shed blood was poured upon the earth. One-third of the earth was consumed in fiery turmoil, and the hearts of one-third of earth's leaders and people burned within them as the truth shone forth. [2][3][4][5]

Rev 8:8 The second angel sounded his trumpet, and a huge mountain of truth revealing God's kingdom, ablaze with love, was made known to the sea of earth's inhabitants. 9 One-third of the people accepted the Remedy and partook of the life of Christ, symbolized by the blood—they died to self and gave up their selfish trade.

Rev 8:10 The third angel sounded his trumpet to make it known that an angel, like a brilliant star blazing through the sky, had fallen from heaven, and one-third of the people had their minds filled with his lies about God. 11 This attack was called Bitterness, and many people died from drinking in his bitter lies. [6][7]

---

[1] Ezek 33:3
[2] Isa 28:16–18
[3] Isa 40:7
[4] Ps 1:3, 37:35
[5] Zech 13:8,9
[6] Prov 5:4
[7] Jer 19:4

Rev 8:12 The fourth angel sounded his trumpet with the warning that one-third of people would believe the lie of evolution and no longer recognize the light from the sun, moon and stars as evidence of God's creatorship. The minds of one-third of the people would be darkened and their hearts hardened by this lie, both night and day, as they no longer searched for God.

Rev 8:13 As I watched this vision unfold, I saw a messenger—represented by an eagle flying high in the sky—give a worldwide warning by calling out in a loud voice: "Woe, woe, woe to the people on earth because of the events that occur during the trumpet blasts of the other three angels!"

9 The fifth angel trumpeted his warning, and I saw a fallen angel — symbolized by a star falling from the sky to the earth—who had the key to accessing the abyss, symbolizing spiritualism and mysticism being the key to accessing the pit of demonic influences. 2 The fallen angel opened the abyss, and smoke rose from it like that from a huge furnace, symbolizing the immense rise in popularity and acceptance of spiritualism and mysticism. The sun and sky were darkened by the smoke, symbolizing the minds of people having become dark and no longer looking to God for enlightenment. 3 Out of the smoke came locusts that had the power of scorpions. As locusts consume the fruit of the land, so too the sting of sin consumes the fruit of the Spirit. 4 The locusts were unable to harm the people whose minds were so settled into the truth about God that they could not be moved—symbolized by the healthy grass, plants, and trees —but could harm those whose minds were not sealed into the truth about God. 5 They were not able to inflict direct physical harm, but caused tortured thinking and mental anguish for five months. And the agony suffered

was from the sting of living outside God's design for life — the scorpion-sting of sin. 6 Dying to self and being renewed in righteousness is preferable to living in the anguish of sin, therefore many will seek to die to self and be renewed, but they will not find it, because they seek their own mystical method of renewal.

Rev 9:7 The forces of evil, swarming like locusts, were prepared like battle horses for their assault. On their heads, they had what looked like crowns of gold, and they had human faces, which meant they claimed that their ways would ennoble the mind and cleanse the character. 8 They came subtly, pretending to be gentle helpers, like women, but in reality they were ravenous lions, devouring and destroying. 9 Rather than a breastplate of righteousness, they had breastplates of iron, symbolic of their corrupt characters and the power to enslave the mind. Their wings sounded like thunder or the rumble of horses galloping into battle, which symbolized the rapid spread of their distorted mystical ways through the minds of people on earth. 10 Their tails were like those of scorpions, symbolic of the lies that deceive, and their sting is the sting of sin that results from believing lies about God. They had the power to torment people for five months. 11 They followed their king who ruled them — the fallen angel from the abyss, also known as *Abaddon* in Hebrew and *Apollyon* in Greek, but we call him Satan.

Rev 9:12 The first woe has happened, two more are to come.

Rev 9:13 The sixth angel trumpeted his warning, and I heard a voice—coming from the horns of the golden altar before God—which is Christ speaking while he works to cleanse the minds of his people. 14 The voice said to the sixth angel, who held the warning trumpet: "It is time to release the four angels bound to the great river Euphrates, who have stood as a barrier protecting the people." [15] Then the four angels who had been waiting for that hour, day, month and year were released, and they let go of what they held back; and one-third of people on earth died. [16] The number of the enemy forces was more than two times ten thousand times ten thousand—the number was beyond counting, symbolizing the number composed of peoples from the entire world.

Rev 9:17 The horses and riders were a conglomerate of diverse forces uniting together to oppose God. They were assembled in three main divisions: Those who believed the lies about God and promoted them through churches had breastplates of fiery red; those who practiced mysticism and spiritualism had breastplates of metallic blue; and those who merely pursued political power and coerced with the power of the state had breastplates of sulfur yellow. They were all bent on destroying truth, love and freedom, as symbolized by their horses with heads like the heads of lions. They destroyed with fiery lies, smoky mysticism, and coercive pressure. [18] One-third of humanity had their characters destroyed by the combined effect of the fiery lies, smoky mysticism, and coercive pressure. [19] The power of these enemy forces came from the lies and falsehoods they promoted—symbolized by the smoke coming from their mouths, and by their tails being like heads of snakes, which were able to inflict injury. [8] [20] The rest of humanity whose consciences were not completely seared by these assaults still refused to turn away from their own self-promotion; they continued to trust demons and the idols of their own hearts' desire that are not even alive. [21] They did not turn away from destroying others, nor from mystical and magical practices, nor from sexual immorality or theft.

---

[8] Isa 9:15

The Remedy

10 Before the seventh angel sounded his trumpet, I saw another powerful being coming down from heaven. He was surrounded by clouds and had a rainbow over his head. His face shone bright like the sun, and his legs were like pillars of light. [2] He held an open book in his hand. He stood with his right foot among a sea of people and his left foot on the unpopulated part of the world, symbolizing that his influence is worldwide. [3] He shouted so loudly that it sounded like a lion roaring. When he shouted, the seven voices that sounded like thunder joined him. [4] I was about to write down what the seven thundering voices announced when I heard another voice from heaven say, "Keep sealed what the seven thundering voices said, and don't write it down."

Rev 10:5 Then the mighty messenger I had seen—standing with one foot amongst the sea of people and the other on the unpopulated earth—raised his right hand to heaven [6] and swore by the God who is immortal and who created heaven and earth and all that fills them, saying, "The time is fulfilled. No more time is to be given! [7] Just before the seventh angel sounds his trumpet, the mystery of God—the complete restoration of Christlikeness in all those who trust him—will be accomplished, just as it was foretold by God's spokespersons of old."

Rev 10:8 Then the voice that had previously spoken to me from heaven spoke to me again, saying, "Take the book lying open in the hand of the messenger who is standing with one foot amongst the sea of people and the other on an unpopulated part of the earth."

Rev 10:9 So I went to the messenger and asked for the book. He gave it to me and said, "Take it and consume it; devour its contents. Your first comprehension will be sweet as honey, but later, when further clarification comes, it will turn out to be a bitter pill."

¹⁰ So I took the book and consumed its contents, and I was initially filled with the sweetest joy, but as it settled on my mind, and further understanding came, it was a bitter disappointment that made my stomach sick. ¹¹ Then I was told, "You must tell the prophetic story again to the entire world—to all peoples, nations, races, and rulers—to all who are living on earth just before the seventh angel sounds his trumpet."

11 Next I was given a measuring device and was told, "Go and examine God's temple: Count the number of living stones, and examine the altar of their hearts, ² but exclude those outside—those who are not living stones in God's temple. Don't count them as part of God's temple, because they are taking a false remedy of pagan god constructs. For forty-two months, they will attempt to crush God's saints who are the living stones that comprise the Holy City of God. ³ But I will empower my two witnesses—the true Church and the written Word—to proclaim the truth about me, though covered with a shroud of human traditions, for 1260 days." ⁴ These two are like lamps—standing firm for the Lord, proclaiming my word on earth; like two olive trees—filled with the oil of the Holy Spirit. ⁵ If anyone tries to obstruct their work with lies and distortions, the fire of truth will be spoken and it will consume all such enemies—this is how all who want to destroy truth will die. ⁶ These witnesses have the power that exposes false ideas about God— the same power that Elijah had when it would not rain, thus exposing Baal as false; the same power that Moses had when water turned to blood and plagues covered the land, exposing the Egyptian gods as false.

Rev 11:7 When they have finished telling the world the truth about God in the setting of the great controversy, the conglomerate beast of humanism, mysticism and paganism, arising out of the abyss of Satanic deception, will overpower them and destroy their influence. ⁸ Their remnants will lie discarded and ignored along the thoroughfares of the world, symbolized by Sodom (the great city of selfishness), and Egypt (the land of pagan god constructs), exactly like the city where their Lord was crucified. ⁹ For three and a half days, people all over the world — in every country, from every ethnic group and language — will disrespect and dishonor them. ¹⁰ The people of the selfish world will mock them, and congratulate themselves by sending each other kudos for rejecting God and his ambassadors, because these two witnesses called people back to love, which tormented those who live selfishly on the earth.

Rev 11:11 But after three and a half days, the Spirit of God revived the two witnesses, and they arose and stood on their own feet; and the unhealed were terrified. ¹² Then God's people heard a loud voice from heaven, saying, "It's time to come home. Come and be with me!" And they went into heaven in a cloud while the enemies of God looked on.

Rev 11:13 At that moment, there was a trembling and shaking of the minds of people on earth, and one-tenth of the wicked world collapsed from fear; seven thousand died from the shock. The terrified survivors fell on their knees and acknowledged the righteousness of God.

Rev 11:14 The second woe has passed; the third woe will come soon.

Rev 11:15 The seventh angel sounded his trumpet, and loud voices proclaimed in heaven:

"The kingdom of selfishness, based
    on earth, has been eradicated,
and the earth has become
    the kingdom of our Lord and his
    Christ;
and he will reign forever and ever."

Rev 11:16 And the twenty-four elders who were seated on thrones before God humbled themselves in awe and admiration ¹⁷ and said,

"We are thankful to you, Lord God
Almighty—
who lives today and who has always
existed—
because you have unveiled your great
power and begun to reign in truth
and love.
¹⁸ The nations of the selfish world
lived in anger,
and you have let them reap what
they have chosen.
The time has come
for accurately diagnosing those who
sleep in the grave,
for rewarding your spokespersons—
the prophets and your saints,
and all those who revere your
character of love,
both small and great, and
for the destruction of those who
destroy the earth."

Rev 11:19 Then God's Healing Plan — represented by the Sanctuary — was disclosed, and at its heart was Jesus the Lamb, who unites the universe into one, represented by the Ark. And there came flashes of insight, rumblings of understanding, peals of thunderous adoration, a foundational collapse of earth-based thinking, and a great hailstorm of truth.

12 In my vision, I saw an incredible panoramic display across the sky: A woman clothed with the sun— symbolizing the true church clothed in God's character of love — stood upon the moon, which symbolizes the dim light of the ceremonial teachings of the Old Testament. She had a crown of twelve stars on her head — symbolic of both the twelve patriarchs that gave rise to the twelve tribes, and the twelve Apostles upon which the church was founded. ² She was pregnant and cried out as she was about to give birth — which symbolized the imminent birth of Jesus, the Savior. ³ Then I saw another panoramic display across the sky: A massive red dragon with seven heads, ten horns, and seven crowns on his heads—symbolic of Satan and the conglomerate of earthly political powers and false religions through which he works. ⁴ His tail dragged one-third of the stars out of heaven and threw them to the earth—symbolizing Satan's lies that deceived one-third of God's angels and dragged them into selfishness and sin. The dragon opposed the pregnant woman who was about to give birth, and stood ready to destroy the child the moment he was born — which symbolizes Satan's attempt to destroy the avenue through which Christ would come, and then destroy Christ when he was born on earth. ⁵ But the dragon failed, and the woman gave birth to a son—a male child Jesus, who would rule the world with a shepherd's rod of love that cannot be broken—and her child returned to God and stood at the command center of the universe. ⁶ The woman ran into the desert, symbolic of desolate retreats on earth prepared for her by God as hiding places where she would be sheltered for 1260 days.

Rev 12:7 There was war in heaven: Michael and his angels fought using truth and love against the lies and deceptions of the dragon, but the dragon and his angels fought back against the truth, spreading more lies about God and Jesus, his Son. ⁸ But his lies were not strong enough, and they lost their place of esteem and respect in heaven: ⁹ The great dragon — the ancient serpent called the devil or Satan that leads the entire world away from God and his methods of love—was cast out of the hearts, minds and affections of the loyal beings in heaven. He and his angels were cast to the earth—the only place in the universe where beings still believe his lies about God.

Rev 12:10 Then I heard a powerful voice in heaven announce:

"Now the Remedy that heals—
and the power to apply it in order

to advance God's kingdom of love and exercise the authority of his Christ—has come,

for the accuser of our brothers and sisters,
who accuses them constantly before God,
has been cast out of their hearts and minds.

11 They overcame him by partaking of the Remedy—
the perfect character of Christ the Lamb, symbolized by his blood—
and by the evidence of their self-sacrificing lives,

as they no longer loved their own selves so much as to shrink from death:

they were healed to love just like Jesus.

12 Therefore rejoice you who live in heaven,

for the sacrifice of Jesus has exposed Satan as a liar and fraud,
and confirmed God's trustworthiness!

But woe to the earth and to the sea of its inhabitants,

as the devil—who has no beings left in the rest of the universe
who will listen to him, and
therefore is furious—

has turned his entire focus on destroying you,

because he knows his time is short!"

Rev 12:13 When the dragon saw that he had been cast out of the affections of the heavenly beings, and that his lies were believed only on earth, he went after the woman—who had given birth to the male child—with a vengeance. 14 But the woman had been given wings with which to flee to the desert where she would be provided for — out of the serpent's reach—during the time, times, and half a time, which symbolized the true church fleeing to desolate places during the 1260 symbolic days of persecution. 15 But the serpent sprayed water from his mouth, like a flood, to drown the woman—symbolic of masses of people hunting down the faithful to destroy them. 16 But the earth helped the woman by opening its mouth and swallowing the flood of people sent by the dragon — which symbolized the discovery of new, unpopulated lands in which the populous could disperse. 17 Then the dragon was frantic with hate and rage at the woman and went off to make war against the remnant of her children — the end-time people who still embrace and practice God's methods of love and hold true to Jesus' testimony about his Father.

13 The dragon stood beside the massive sea of his followers, and while I watched, out of that sea of people arose a beastly power: It had ten horns and seven heads, with ten crowns on its horns (symbolizing political powers), and a blasphemous name on each head (symbolizing religious powers). It represented a conglomerate religiopolitical world power comprised of multiple governments and false religions of the world. 2 This beastly power arose from the vestiges of Greece, Persia and Babylon — symbolized by a leopard with the feet of a bear and the mouth of a lion—and it received its power and authority from the dragon, which means it will use Satan's methods of deceit, coercion and imposition of law to distort God's character with pagan concepts. 3 One of the seven heads received what appeared to be a fatal wound, but then the wound was healed—which symbolized a blow to its power, and then recovery and a resurgence in power. The entire world was in awe and followed the methods, principles and teachings of this beastly power. 4 By accepting the pagan imposed law constructs as representative of God's kingdom, people actually worshiped the dragon, as these distortions about God originated from him; and since the beast used the dragon's lies as the basis for its

authority, they also worshiped the beast. They marveled, "Who can compare to the beast? Who can fight against it?"

Rev 13:5 The beast had a mouth that boasted and blasphemed—and it exerts its power for forty-two months—which symbolizes the manner in which this beastly system would misrepresent God's character and methods while claiming to have God's authority to speak for him on earth. 6 It blasphemes God and misrepresents his character, and distorts the reality of God's dwelling place and those who live in heaven. 7 It wars against the saints with lies and distortions about God's methods and principles, teaching that God uses power—like an earthly emperor—to impose law, lord over the people, and inflict punishment for disobedience. It conquers the saints and infects the world—every tribe, nation, language, and people—with its lies about God. 8 All the inhabitants of the earth accept its distortions about God and thus give homage to the beast—all except those whose names have been recorded in the book of life that belongs to Jesus the Lamb who committed himself to be the Remedy to sin before the world was created.

Rev 13:9 Those whose minds are open to truth will understand.

Rev 13:10 Anyone determined to be
     captive to sin will into bondage go.
And anyone whose character
     develops upon the kill-or-be-killed
     principle will in the end be killed.
Overcoming the selfish drive to survive requires patient endurance and trust by those who are healed.

Rev 13:11 Next, I saw a different beast arising out of the earth. It had two horns like lamb's horns but spoke like a dragon—which symbolized a new power, arising in a different part of the earth, that initially promotes lamblike principles of freedom but eventually practices dragonlike methods of coercion. 12 As the first beast watched, the second beast exercised all the tactics of the first beast and led the world to practice its methods, thus giving honor to the first beast whose fatal wound was healed. 13 The beast required everyone to choose whom they would worship—symbolized by the miracle of calling fire down from heaven.

14 Because of the astonishing act of restricting religious freedoms and the economic coercion that it was given power to wield, it duped the entire world. It commanded them to form a coalition of religious and political power to enforce its way, which was modeled after the first beast's ways. 15 It had the resources and ability to bring this coalition into a living reality—a fitting model honoring the first beast. It even imposed a death penalty for all who refused to practice its methods. 16 It forced everyone—weak or powerful, rich or poor, free or slave—to make a choice. Some chose to believe that the methods of the beast were godly, and these were marked in their minds to be like the beast. Others chose to go along with the beast for convenience and gain, and they were marked by the work of their hands. 17 No one could buy or sell except for those who chose the methods of the beast and thus marked themselves as "loyal" by embracing its character and being numbered as its followers. 18 This calls for wisdom. Anyone with spiritual discernment—let them count the number of the beast: it is a human's number. The number is 666.

14 Then I looked and saw Jesus the Lamb standing on Mount Zion, which represented the place of victory over sin. He was with the 144,000 who had been healed and had the character of Jesus and the Father completely restored in their minds, which was symbolized by the name of the Father and Son written on their foreheads.

2 I heard the sound of God's presence—like the ocean roar or deep thunder—

and with it, what sounded like many harps being played together, symbolizing the beautiful melody that comes from the lives of the healed. ³ As God and the four living beings and the elders were watching, the healed lived Christlike lives that were like the sound of beautiful music—a song which only the 144,000 who had been redeemed from earth could sing. ⁴ These are the ones who did not corrupt themselves by filling their hearts with false views of God or practicing Satan's methods—they kept their characters pure. They follow Jesus the Lamb wherever he goes, always revealing the truth about him. They were redeemed from fallen humanity and are the first fruits—the first ones so settled into the truth about God and the Lamb that nothing could move them. ⁵ No lie about God was found in their testimony; they are without blame.

Rev 14:6 Then I saw another messenger flying in midair, and he had the eternal good news about God's character of love to proclaim to everyone living on earth—to every nation, tribe, language, and people—which represents a movement of people who arise to proclaim the truth about God's character of love throughout the world. ⁷ He said in a clear, resounding voice, "Be in awe of God, and glorify him by living his methods of love, because the hour has come for everyone to make a judgment about God, and worship the Designer, Creator and Builder who made the heavens, the earth, the sea and springs of water—all of which operate upon his law of love."

Rev 14:8 A second messenger followed the first, proclaiming throughout the world: "Don't trust Babylon the Great—a symbolic description of religions that misrepresent God—as it is fallen into the lies about God and intoxicates the world with its pagan views of God, maddening the people with its adulterous idea that God coerces and must inflict punishment if not properly appeased."

Rev 14:9 And a third messenger followed the first two and proclaimed in a voice that was heard throughout the world: "If anyone gives worth and honor to the beastly system of coercion by choosing the methods of the beast and thus marking themselves as 'loyal in heart' by embracing the character of the beast, or marking themselves as 'loyal in deed' by practicing his methods, ¹⁰ they will reap the full fury of unremedied sin when God no longer shields them from their destructive choice. They will experience immeasurable torment of mind and burning anguish of heart when they stand in God's fiery presence and are bathed in unquenchable fire of truth and love—all in the very presence of Jesus and the holy angels. ¹¹ The memory of their suffering and the lesson of their self-destructive choice will never be forgotten throughout all eternity. There will be no peace of mind—day or night—for those who prefer the methods of the beast and model after him, or for any who choose to mark themselves as followers of the beast." ¹² This requires patient endurance on the part of the healed, who live God's methods of love and remain true to Jesus.

Rev 14:13 Then I heard another voice from heaven say, "Write this: Happy are those who die to sin and self, trusting the Lord from now on." "Yes," says the Spirit, "they will rest from working to save self, and their loving deeds will follow them."

Rev 14:14 I looked, and I saw Jesus, the Son of Man, surrounded by a cloud of brilliant angels, wearing a crown of gold on his head—symbolic of his perfect character and rule of love. He had a sharp sickle in his hand, symbolizing his intent to bring his followers home. ¹⁵ Then another messenger came out of the heavenly temple and called in a clear voice to Jesus, who was in the cloud of angels: "Take your sickle and cut your followers free from all earthly ties and bring them home! The time to reap has come, because your people have matured and are ready to be cut free." ¹⁶So Jesus, seated amongst the cloud of angels, swung his sickle and all throughout the earth his people were cut free and brought to heaven.

Rev 14:17 Then another angel came out from the temple in heaven, and he had his own sharp sickle. ¹⁸Yet another angel came, from the altar, with the authority of the fire of truth, and called in a loud voice to the angel with the sharp sickle: "Take your sharp sickle and gather the cluster of those who—like grapes—have ripened, but ripened on the vine of earth's principles; for they are fully hardened in their selfish ways." ¹⁹The angel swung his sickle and gathered those who—like grape clusters—were ripened into complete rebellion against God, and he threw them into the 'winepress' where they were pressed down under the destructive force of unremedied sin when God no longer shielded them from their destructive choice. ²⁰When God finally let go, they were crushed—outside the city of God—under the weight of guilt, shame, despair and fear that unremedied sin brings. Their lives ebbed away, and the dead were piled up six feet (1.8 meters) high for nearly 200 miles (320 kilometers) around the city.

15 In my vision, I saw another amazing panoramic scene in the sky: Seven angels holding the seven last plagues—'last' because when these are released, God will have ceased all intercession on earth. ²But the healed need not worry; for I saw what appeared to be a great crystal plane reflecting the fiery presence of God, and standing beside the crystal plane were those who had been healed. They were victorious over the beastly methods of coercion and deceit, and had rejected the distorted image of God—the image of a punishing god. They were not numbered among those who were marked with the beast's character and methods permanently seared into their hearts. They held harps—symbolic of their Christlike characters—given them by God, ³and their lives were living songs of loving transformation. They sang the song of Moses—the spokesperson of God—and the song of Jesus the Lamb:

"Overwhelming and incredible are
your achievements, Lord God
Almighty!
Right and true are your methods,
King of eternity!
⁴Who will not be in awe of you,
O Lord,
and not glorify your character and
methods of love?
For you alone are holy.
All nations will come and
acknowledge you as worthy,
for your righteousness, perfection and
character have been revealed."

Rev 15:5 After I saw this, I looked and saw the temple in heaven—the tabernacle constructed of living stones whose lives give testimony to the truth about God. It was open. ⁶Out of the assembled temple came seven angels with the seven last plagues. They were wearing clean, shining linen, symbolic of their perfect unity with Christ, and had golden sashes around their chests, symbolic of God's character and methods of love filling their hearts. ⁷Then one of the four living beings gave the seven angels seven gold bowls filled with the heartbreaking disengagement of God who is the source of all life. The gold bowls are symbolic of God's stepwise release of those who choose to be separate from him. ⁸And the temple was filled with the truth about God and his methods of love, truth, and freedom; and no other idea, concern or issue could enter the minds of God's intelligent beings (the living stones of God's temple) until the final seven-step release of God's restraint—which allows Satan increasing freedom to act on earth, symbolized by the seven plagues from the seven angels— was complete.

16 Then I heard a mighty voice coming from the temple, instructing the seven angels: "Go now and pour out the seven bowls of God's heartbreaking disengagement upon the earth."

Rev 16:2 The first angel poured out his bowl on the land—symbolizing God's love granting people their final choice of rejecting him, and allowing them to reap the consequences of their choice by no longer shielding them with his protective hand—and ugly and painful sores broke out on those who had marked themselves as loyal to the beast by closing their hearts to God and modeling themselves in the image of the beast by practicing his methods of coercion and force.

Rev 16:3 The second angel poured out his bowl on the sea—symbolizing the withdrawing of God's protective and life-sustaining presence from the earth—and the oceans became like the blood of a dead person, no longer circulating properly and therefore no longer sustaining life; and every type of creature in the seas began to die.

Rev 16:4 The third angel poured out his bowl on the rivers and fresh water springs—symbolizing the withdrawing of God's protective and life-sustaining presence from the earth—and the waters became poisoned and no longer sustained life. 5 Then I heard the angel in charge of the waters of truth say:

"You are so right in your actions—
you who are the source of life, the Holy One—
because your diagnosis is right:
They are unhealable,
6 for they have rejected your Remedy
and killed your friends and
spokespersons who brought it;
so you have granted them the death
they have chosen."

Rev 16:7 And I heard the heart-response of God's healed friends:
"Yes, Lord God Almighty,
true and right are your diagnoses
and actions."

Rev 16:8 The fourth angel poured out his bowl on the sun—symbolic of the withdrawing of God's protective and life-sustaining presence from the earth—and solar radiation increased on the earth, scorching people with its rays: 9 they were burned by the intense heat and blamed God for causing it, because, as they closed their hearts, he had withdrawn his protective presence and control over nature; but they refused to turn away from selfishness and open their hearts to God and glorify him by partaking of the Remedy.

Rev 16:10 The fifth angel poured out his bowl on the beast's seat of power— symbolizing God's restraining and sustaining presence being withdrawn— and the kingdom of the beast was plunged into the most horrendous moral darkness the world has ever known: people wailed in agony, chewed their tongues in misery, 11 and blamed the God of heaven, claiming—as the beast always does—that God was inflicting the pain and sores upon them; but they refused to turn away from selfishness and from what they had done.

Rev 16:12 The sixth angel poured out his bowl on the great river Euphrates— symbolizing the withdrawing of God's forces of righteousness as a shield against the kings from the East symbolic of the corrupting powers of mysticism. 13 I saw three spirits whose minds had not been cleansed of the lies about God. They looked like frogs catching their prey with their lying tongues. They came telling the lies of mysticism and spiritualism from the dragon, the lies of coercion and force from the beast, and the lies of pagan appeasement theology from the false prophet. 14 They are the spiritual movements of fallen angels—demons who perform miracles and go to the rulers of the world to unite them in war against the truth about God and his methods of love, on the great day of God Almighty.

Rev 16:15 "Understand this:
To the unhealed, my coming will
be unexpected—like that of a thief.
But the healed, who have guarded
their hearts and kept their
characters pure,
will be happy at my coming
and will not be shamed by the
exposure of an unhealed
character."

Rev 16:16 Then the demonic forces united the nations together in their opposition to God and his methods of love, bringing them to what is known in Hebrew as *Harmageddōn,* or The Mount of Assembly—the mountain where God rules.

Rev 16:17 The seventh angel poured out his bowl into the air—symbolizing God's restraining and protective presence being completely removed from the earth. And out of the temple, from God's throne, came a mighty voice, saying, "It is done!" [18] followed by flashes of insight, rumblings of change, thundering of opposition, and a severe shaking of the peoples' minds. No breaking of humanity has ever been so great—so tremendous was the fracturing of society. [19] The great city—symbolic of the nations united against God—split back into its three parts: mysticism, humanism, and paganism. The cities of the world collapsed into anarchy and chaos. God remembered Babylon the Great and set her free to reap the fury and wrath that separation from God causes. [20] Every island of cooperation vanished; every mountain of worship was lost. [21] From heaven came a great hailstorm of crushing truth falling upon the minds of the people. They cursed God, blaming him for the suffering that the hailstorm of truth caused upon their unhealed minds, because the weight of truth was so terribly painful.

17 One of the seven angels, who had one of the seven bowls, came to me and said, "Come with me and I will show you the damning end of the great prostitute who sits upon the many waters—symbolic of false religion that misrepresents God. [2] The leaders of the world took their governments into bed with her, sharing in her plans, plots and methods, and the people of earth had their minds so filled with her lies about God and his methods that they were like drunks—stuporous and unable to be reasoned with or embrace the truth."

Rev 17:3 Then the angel led me in vision into a desert—symbolic of spiritual desolation with lack of love and truth—where I saw the woman riding upon a scarlet beast that had seven heads and ten horns and was covered with blasphemous names. This symbolized that false religion would be supported by the power of the state. [4] The woman was dressed in purple and scarlet, and was heavily adorned with gold, pearls, and jewels—symbolic of her vanity and self-promotion. In her hand, she held a golden cup filled with her intoxicating brew of lies, distortions, and false presentations about God. [5] The title written on her forehead, descriptive of her character and methods, was:

MYSTERIOUS BABYLON THE GREAT
—the confusing system of religious tradition, fable and falsehood that obscures the truth about God;
THE MOTHER OF PROSTITUTES
—the many diverse religious sects who sell their virtue for earthly advantage and seduce others into their bed of lies about God;
THE ABOMINATION OF THE EARTH

Rev 17:6 I saw that the disgusting woman was intoxicated with destroying the lives of the healed—those whose lives bear the testimony of Jesus. Seeing her, and what she was doing, shocked me. [7] The angel asked, "Why does this shock you? Let me explain to you the mysterious woman and the beast with seven heads and ten horns upon which she rides. ⁸ The beastly power is the unification of religion and state, which persecutes and coerces. It has power on earth for a period, then doesn't have power for a period, and then arises out of the abyss to menace the world one more time before going to its destruction. The people on earth whose names have not been recorded in the book of life from the creation of the world will be amazed by this beastly coalition of religion and state, as it had power for a time, then lost power, and yet it gains power again.

Rev 17:9 "To understand this, it requires a wise and discerning mind: The seven heads represent seven false theories, or theological systems, that fill the minds of human beings, and are represented as seven mountains, or high places of worship, on which the woman sits. ¹⁰ They are also represented as seven false kings who try to usurp the place of Jesus, the true King. Five of them have fallen, one is, the other has not yet come; but when he does, he will remain for only a short time. ¹¹ The beastly power of coercion, which was on earth for a period but then lost power, is going to arise as an eighth king. The first seven were the set-up for him—preparing the world for the arrival of the eighth—but he is going to his destruction.

Rev 17:12 "The ten horns you saw represent the kingdoms of the world that exist when the eighth king finally appears, and will be in power with the beastly system for only a short time. ¹³ Their one purpose is to give their political and national power and authority to the beastly system of coercion. ¹⁴ They will war against the Lamb by misrepresenting him and coercing people to accept lies about God, but the Lamb — along with his called, healed and faithful friends — will overcome them, because he is Lord of lords and King of kings."

Rev 17:15 Then the angel explained to me: "The waters you saw the prostitute sitting upon represent peoples, multitudes, races, and cultures. ¹⁶ The beast and ten horns, which represent political powers, will end up hating the prostitute — the false religions of the world. They turn on her, exposing her as false, then confiscate her properties and holdings, and burn down her lies with fiery truth. ¹⁷ For God accomplished his purpose of revealing the results of that beastly system when the ten horns chose to give the beast their power to rule. ¹⁸ The woman you saw is that great city — the distorted imposed law construct of force, intimidation and coercion that govern all the kingdoms of earth."

18 After this, I saw another messenger coming down from heaven—symbolizing the Godly origin of his message. He had the great authority and power of truth, and the earth was illuminated by his splendor. ² With a voice reverberating throughout the earth, he shouted:

"Babylon the Great is a fallen system
of religious tradition,
fable, and falsehood distorting the
truth about God!
Every demonic distortion about God,
every evil attitude toward God,
and all filthy and destructive
heart-motives find their home with
her,
³ for she intoxicates the world with
her pagan views of God,
maddening them with her
adulterous idea that God coerces
and must inflict punishment if not
properly appeased.
Earth's leaders corrupt themselves
with her by practicing her
methods,
and people not anchored in God's
kingdom of love,
and those who wander from
philosophy to philosophy,
fill their minds with her

smorgasbord of lies."

Rev 18:4 Then I heard another voice calling from heaven, saying:

"Come out of her, my people!
Leave that confusing mess of evil
thinking
so that you will not share in her
spiritual sickness and rebellion,
and so that you will not receive
the suffering she has chosen;
5 for her violations of God's design
for life have piled up to heaven,
and God diagnoses her condition
accurately.
6 She will reap what she has sown:
all that she has done will come
back on her—
with double intensity—
from her own evil condition.
7 Her suffering and torment will be
every bit as great
as the self-flattery, indulgence,
and reward she gave herself.
She deceives herself and flatters
herself in her heart, saying to
herself,
'I am a virtuous and righteous queen.
I am not dead in sin.
I have nothing for which to grieve or
repent.'
8 But in one day, the reality of her
diseased condition will overcome
her:
necrosis, overwhelming grief and
disintegration will be her end.
She will be consumed by the fire of
God's presence—the fire of truth
and love—and all her lies and
selfishness will be eradicated,
for mighty is the Lord who diagnoses
her as terminal."

Rev 18:9 When the leaders of earth—who took her in their embrace, practiced her methods, and fed on her smorgasbord of lies—see the results of the truth burning through her and rising before them like smoke, they will cry and mourn. 10 Terrified at the agony of mind and the suffering she experiences when the fires of truth burn free, they will try to distance themselves from

her, hoping to avoid the truth themselves. They will watch and cry,

"Poor Babylon the Great!
Despite all your coercive power,
in one hour your doom has come!"

Rev 18:11 The peddlers of her lies and those marketing her distorted views will cry and mourn over her because no longer does anyone buy what they are selling— 12 whether presented with gold, or the silvery tongue of deceit, or served as a string of pearly white stones, or dressed up in fine clothing, or hidden beneath fine wood carvings, or bronze, or iron or marble sculpting—their lies will not sell. 13 Whether sweetened with sugary words, or made fragrant with flowery acts, or attempted to be made digestible like olive oil, flour or wheat, or domesticated like cattle, sheep or horses, or made to appear useful like a carriage, or even if presented as healing the body or giving life to the soul—no one will buy their lies.

Rev 18:14 They will say, "The time when you would retire, enjoying the fruit of your work, is gone. All you worked to accomplish is gone, all you value is vanished, and your lies will never work again." 15 The peddlers of her lies and methods—those who enriched themselves from her—will be terrified as they see her torment and will try to get as far from her as possible. They will wail and mourn 16 and cry out:

"No! Oh no! O great city,
you appeared rich, well dressed,
organized, powerful, and in
control;
17 but in one hour all your strength
and all your power is ruined!"

All her spiritual advisors, pastors, church leaders, those who navigate the seas of life, and all who earn their living by leading people, will try to get as far away from her as they can. 18 When they see her suffering from the burning truth, they will cry out: "Was there any other organization, method or system we could have followed? No city was like her!" [19] They will be covered in shame and wail in grief as they anticipate their fate. They will cry out:

"No! Oh no! O great city—
   great system of worldly ways—
in which all who had a scheme
advanced themselves by plying her
   ways!
But in one hour she has been
   exposed and ruined!
Rev 18:20 "Rejoice, O heaven,
   for she has been exposed as false!
Rejoice, healed children of God,
   ambassadors, and spokespersons
   of God!
For God was right when he
   diagnosed her as 'terminal'
   for the way she treated you."

Rev 18:21 Then a mighty angel picked up a massive boulder and threw it into the sea—symbolic of the kingdom of Jesus the Rock being established upon earth. The angel said,

"With such overwhelming shock and
   awe will the truth overthrow the
   great city of Babylon,
   and it will never rise again.
[22] People will never sing songs
   or live lives to honor you again.
No person will work to promote you
   again.
No further lies, deceit
   or poisonous tale
   will be produced in you again.
[23] No enlightenment
   will seek to shine in you again.
The voice of love
   will never be heard in you again.
Your sales team and marketers were
   the leaders of the world.
It was by your trickery, deceit and
   mystical ways
   that all the nations were led
   astray.
[24] You killed God's spokespersons
   and friends,
   and your methods caused the
   death of all who have been killed
   on earth."

19 After watching this, I heard the thundering roar of a great multitude of people in heaven, shouting:

"Hallelujah! Healing and restoration,
   honor and power belong to our
   God,
[2] for accurate and right are his
   diagnoses!
He has diagnosed the great
   prostitute as terminal—
   the one who infected the world
   with her false beliefs
   about God and his methods.
He has brought her to face
   the results of killing his
   spokespersons."

Rev 19:3 And again the people shouted:
"Hallelujah!
   The lessons of her actions
   and her destructive ways
   will be remembered forever and
   ever."

Rev 19:4 The twenty-four elders and four living beings were overwhelmed with awe and admiration for God and fell down and worshiped him who was seated upon the throne. They cried:
"Absolutely right, Hallelujah!"

Rev 19:5 Then from the throne came a voice, saying:

"Give praise to God, all you who
   spoke the truth about him,
   and all you who love and admire
   his character of love—
   whether small or great."

Rev 19:6 Then I heard an even louder response from the multitude of people— louder than the roaring ocean or rumbling thunder. They shouted:

"Hallelujah!
   For our Lord God Almighty—
   Mighty in goodness,
   Mighty in truth,
   Mighty in love,
   Mighty in righteousness and
   Mighty in freedom—reigns!
[7] Let our joy and gladness be in him,
   and let our lives glorify him!
For the wedding of the Lamb has come
   and his bride—the church—is ready,
[8] cleansed in mind and heart from all

deviation from God's design.

She has been given fine clothes to wear—bright, clean and without blemish—

representing her perfect character of love she now possesses."

Rev 19:9 Then the angel said to me, "Write this down: 'Happy are those who are invited to the wedding celebration of the Lamb!'" And then he added, "These words of God are true."

Rev 19:10 I was so overwhelmed with awe that I fell down to honor him, but he said, "Don't honor me! I am a fellow worker on God's team with you and with your brothers and sisters who hold to the testimony Jesus revealed about his Father. Give honor to God and worship him! For the testimony Jesus gave about his Father is the same as that which inspired the prophets."

Rev 19:11 I looked and saw the heavens open, and before me was a white horse whose rider is called Faithful and True —which symbolizes that Christ makes war using the weapons of truth and righteousness, and diagnoses all things perfectly. 12 His eyes are like blazing fire, symbolic of the penetrating power of truth and love that burns within his heart and with which he sees all things. On his head are many crowns, symbolizing his rightful rule over all domains, spheres, orders, and territories. Upon him is a name that only he knows, for it represents the fullness of his infinite true self. 13 His clothes are dipped in blood, symbolic of self-sacrificing death by which he procured the Remedy. His name is the Word of God, for he is God's very thoughts made audible and visible. 14 The host of heaven followed him, also riding on white horses and dressed in pure linen — spotless white and clean—symbolic of the methods of truth, love and freedom with which they wage war. 15 He struck down the nations with a sharp sword that came out of his mouth, which symbolized the spoken words of truth that destroy everything built on the lies about God. "He will rule them with an unbreakable shepherd's rod." He crushes out all lies and selfishness in the winepress of the unrestrained burning rivers of truth and love flowing from God Almighty. 16 On his robe and on his thigh, this name is written:

KING OF KINGS AND LORD OF LORDS

Rev 19:17 And I saw an angel standing in the sun—symbolic of a messenger coming from the brightness of the presence of Jesus. He called in a loud voice to all the carrion birds flying through the air, "Come! Gather together for the great supper of God, 18 and eat the corpses of the world leaders, generals, power brokers, warriors, people—whether rich or poor, slave or free—who rejected the Remedy." He said this as a warning to all who have rejected the Remedy—but they didn't listen.

Rev 19:19 I saw the beastly power and the leaders of earth gather their armies together to make war against the rider on the horse and his army of light. 20 But the beastly power was caught in its own lies and in a web of intrigue, along with the false prophet who had performed miraculous signs on its behalf. It was with these signs that it had duped those who chose to mark themselves as loyal to the beastly power and model themselves after it. The two were thrown into the lake of unquenchable fire of truth and love emanating from the unveiled presence of God, which consumes all sin. 21 And all the followers of the beast were destroyed by the truth which cut like a sword and came from the mouth of the rider on the white horse; and all the birds filled themselves with their corpses.

20 Then I saw an angel coming down from heaven. He had the key to the abyss and a great chain in his hand. 2 He grabbed the dragon— that ancient serpent who is the devil, or Satan, also known as the fallen angel

Lucifer of past—and bound him for a thousand years. This symbolizes Satan being bound by the chain of circumstances upon a desolate and abysmal earth with no living creatures, for a thousand years. ³ The angel threw Satan into the abyss, locking and sealing him there—upon the desolate and void earth with no one to deceive—until the end of the thousand years, after which he will again have the wicked to deceive for a short time.

Rev 20:4 I looked into heaven and saw thrones, and seated on the thrones were those who had been given the ability to make correct judgments. And I saw those who—having judged God and his methods rightly—had been beheaded for giving the same testimony about God that Jesus gave, and for staying true to God's word. They did not join with the beastly power or lie about God, nor model themselves after the coercive methods of the beastly power or choose to mark themselves as loyal to the beastly power either by agreeing in heart or merely giving their support. They were resurrected at the beginning of the thousand years and reigned with Christ during the thousand years. ⁵ This is the first resurrection. (The unhealed dead were not resurrected until after the thousand years were ended.) ⁶ Happy and holy are those who arise in the first resurrection. The second, eternal death has no power over them. They will be ministers of God and of Christ and will reign with him for a thousand years.

Rev 20:7 When the thousand years are over, the wicked dead from all human history will be resurrected, and thus Satan will be released from his prison ⁸ and will again go about deceiving the nations from all over the world. All those who oppose God — symbolically referred to as Gog and Magog — he will gather together for battle. The number of those who gather to war against God is beyond counting — like sand on the seashore. ⁹ Once gathered, they march across the earth and surround the camp of God's people—the city he loves. It is then that God unveils himself fully, and rivers of fire come out from him; and the fires of truth and love consume all evil and sin. ¹⁰ And Satan—who deceived all those outside the city—along with the beastly power and false prophet, is drowned in the lake of consuming fire coming from the presence of God. They will suffer torment of mind and agony of soul as the fires of truth and love burn through every lie, distortion and self-deception—consuming all deviations from God's design—and the painful reality of their corrupt condition sears through them day and night for the conclusion of their existence.

Rev 20:11 While this was happening, I saw a great white throne and the One sitting on it. The sin-infected earth and sky faded from his presence. ¹² And I saw the unhealed dead—great and small—standing before the throne, and the books were opened. Another book was opened, which is the book of life. The dead were diagnosed according to the reality of their condition developed throughout their lives by the choices they had made, exactly as recorded in the books. ¹³ The sea, death and the grave gave up their dead, and all the unhealed were raised to life; and each person was accurately diagnosed by the characters they formed from the choices they had made. ¹⁴ Then death and the grave were thrown into the lake of fire—the lake of God's fiery presence—which is the second (or eternal) death, when all deviations from God's design for life are permanently consumed. ¹⁵ If anyone did not partake of the Remedy and have their character restored to Christlikeness and thus have their name written in the book of life, they were thrown into the lake of God's fiery presence, where truth and love consumed all lies, deceit, and selfishness.

21 Then, after all sin and sinners had been consumed, I saw a new heaven and a new earth, for the first heaven and first earth—that had been marred by Satan's rebellion—were no more, and the vast oceans were gone. ² I saw the Holy City, the New Jerusalem, coming down from God out of heaven. It was prepared as a bride beautifully dressed for her husband— symbolic of the city filled with the beautiful, healed people of God. ³ And I heard a voice from the throne say, "Now God will live with people and govern from planet earth. They are his people, and God himself will be with them and be their God. ⁴ He will tenderly wipe every tear from their eyes; and there will be no more death, or sorrow, or heartache, or sickness, or suffering or pain, for the old, sinful order of things, in which good and evil operated together, is gone forever."

Rev 21:5 He who sat on the throne said, "I am restoring everything to perfection: I am making all things new!" Then he said, "Write this down, for these words are accurate and true."

Rev 21:6 He said to me, "It is finished. I am the Origin and Summation, the Beginning and the End of all things. To anyone who is thirsty, I will freely give the water of life to drink. ⁷ Whoever partakes of the Remedy and overcomes sin and selfishness will inherit all of this, and I will be their God and they will be my children. ⁸ But those who are controlled by fear, and fight to protect self, those who don't believe in my methods of love, those who pervert the truth, the murderers, the hedonists, those who practice mysticism and magic, those who worship gods that must punish or be appeased, and all liars—they will find themselves consumed in the lake of eternal fire. This is the second, eternal, death."

Rev 21:9 One of the seven angels who had the seven bowls holding the seven last plagues came to me and said, "Come, I will show you the bride, the wife of the Lamb." ¹⁰ And he carried me away in vision to a huge mountain and showed me the Holy City, the New Jerusalem, coming down from God out of heaven. ¹¹ It shone with the glory of God, because it was inhabited by all the healed from earth who now possessed God's glorious character. Its radiance was more brilliant than a precious jewel, like jasper—without blemish, clear as crystal—because God's character radiated through the people. ¹² It had a high wall with twelve gates, and twelve angels at the gates. On the gates were written the names of the twelve tribes of Israel—symbolizing that the city will be composed of the saved from all peoples of the earth. ¹³ There were three gates on the east, three on the north, three on the south, and three on the west—further symbolizing that the city will be composed of peoples from all corners of the earth. ¹⁴ The wall of the city had twelve foundations, and on them were the names of the twelve ambassadors of Jesus the Lamb—symbolizing that the city is founded upon the truth about God which Jesus revealed and the twelve ambassadors championed.

Rev 21:15 The angel who talked with me had a gold rod with which to measure the city, its gates, and its walls. ¹⁶ The footprint of the city was a perfect square, as long as it was wide: 12,000 stadia (about 1461 miles or 2352 kilometers) on each side. Amazingly, it was also the same 12,000 stadia in height, making it a perfect cube — the same shape as the Most Holy Place of God's temple. ¹⁷ The angel measured its wall and it was 144 cubits (about 216 feet or 65 meters) thick by human measurement, which the angel was using. ¹⁸ The wall was made of a brilliant, shining stone-like material which looked like jasper, and the city was of pure gold, just like the Most Holy Place of God's temple. It was pure—almost translucent—like glass. ¹⁹ The foundations of the city walls were beautiful—

a full array of precious stones. The first foundation looked like jasper, the second like sapphire, the third like chalcedony, the fourth like emerald, [20] the fifth like sardonyx, the sixth like carnelian, the seventh like chrysolite, the eighth like beryl, the ninth like topaz, the tenth like chrysoprase, the eleventh like jacinth, and the twelfth like amethyst. [21] The twelve gates were twelve pearls: each gate was made of a single pearl of great price—symbolic of Jesus, the way into the city. The streets of the city were of pure gold, translucent like glass.

Rev 21:22 I did not see a "holy place" in the city, because the presence of the Lord God Almighty and the Lamb make the entire city a holy place. [23] The city does not need the sun or moon to provide it with light, for the fiery presence of God illuminates it, and the Lamb is its guiding light. [24] The nations will live in accord with the light of truth and love emanating from the city, and the leaders of the earth will give all their splendor to it. [25] There will never be a day when its gates will shut, and there will be no night there. [26] The glory and honor of all the nations will be attributed to it. [27] Nothing that deviates from God's design—his character of love—will enter it: none who holds to the shameful pagan views of God, or any liar, but only those whose characters are like that of Jesus' and whose names are written in the Lamb's book of life.

22

Then the angel showed me the river—full of the water of life—as clear as crystal, flowing from the throne of God and the Lamb, [2] running down the middle of the great street of the city. The tree of life was rooted on both banks of the river, and it bore twelve different fruits — a different fruit each month; and the leaves of the tree are for the healing of the nations. [3] The deviations from God's design—which cursed creation—will no longer exist. God and the Lamb will govern the entire universe from the city; and God's spokespersons will work with him. [4] They will see him face to face, and his character will be written in their hearts—symbolized by his name displayed on their foreheads. [5] There will be no more night, and they will not need any artificial light from lamps—or even natural light from the sun—for the Lord God will be their light. And they will reign with him for all eternity.

Rev 22:6 The angel said to me, "These words are accurate and reliable. The Lord—the God who inspired his human assistants—sent his angel to show his spokespersons the things that must soon occur."

Rev 22:7 "Understand this: I am coming back soon! Those who follow the prophetic truths of this book will find happiness."

Rev 22:8 I, John, am the one who heard and saw all these things. And when I had seen and heard them, I was so overwhelmed with awe that I fell down to give honor to the angel who had shown them to me. [9] But he stopped me, saying, "Don't honor me! I am a fellow worker of God's, along with you and your brothers and sisters—the prophetic spokespersons—and all who follow the prophetic truths of this book. Give honor to God and worship him!"

Rev 22:10 Then he instructed me, "Do not keep the message of this prophetic book a secret, for the time when these events will begin to happen is near: [11] let those who harden their hearts in selfishness continue to be selfish; let those who form their characters on lies continue to be liars; let those who have been healed to righteous and loving characters continue to be righteous and loving; and let those who are truthful continue to be truthful."

Rev 22:12 "Understand this: I am coming back soon! My reward is with me, and I will give to everyone exactly what they have chosen. ¹³ I am the Origin and Summation, the Beginning and the End.

Rev 22:14 "Happy are those who have their characters cleansed and minds healed, for they will have access to the tree of life and will enter through the gates into the city. ¹⁵ Outside are the scavengers—those who practice mysticism and magic that confuse the mind, the hedonists, those who use power to hurt and destroy others, those who worship gods who punish and must be appeased, and everyone who loves and practices falsehood.

Rev 22:16 "I, Jesus, have sent my angel to give this testimony for the churches. I am the Creator, the Root from which life originates, but also the descendant of David, and the true Light Bearer — the bright Morning Star of truth."

Rev 22:17 The Spirit and the bride call, "Come home!" So please, let all who hear the truth call, "Come home!" Whoever is thirsty, let them come home; and whoever wishes, let them drink freely of the water of life.

Rev 22:18 All who hear the words of this prophecy, be warned: If you change the meaning and distort the truth, be assured by God that you will be found amongst the plagues described in this book. ¹⁹ And if anyone deletes ideas and truths from this book of prophecy, be assured by God that you will lose your share of the tree of life and your place in the Holy City.

Rev 22:20 Jesus, who gives this testimony, says, "It is absolutely certain— I am coming soon."

Amen. Come soon, Lord Jesus.

Rev 22:21 The grace of the Lord Jesus be with all of God's people. Amen.